Provence
& the Côte d'Azur

Nicola Williams

LONELY PLANET PUBLICATIONS
Melbourne • Oakland • London • Paris

RHÔNE - ALPES

HAUTES - ALPES

Grignan

Valréas

Visan

D94

Nyons

Eyguians

Vaucluse
From Romans to popes – Avignon's
Palais des Papes, olives and truffles in the
Enclave des Papes, Mont Ventoux, and
truimphant arches and amphitheatres in
Carpentras, Orange and elsewhere

Sisteron

L-ANGUEDOC-
ROUSSILLON

N7

Bagnols

ORANGE

A7

Malaucène

Mont
Ventoux

The Lubéron
Hill-top villages – Bonnieux,
Ménerbes, Lacoste, Buoux,
Gordes and ochre-tinted Roussillon

Les Mées

Ganagobie

Uzès

Châteauneuf
du Pape

Monteux

D938

VAUCLUSE

Sault

Plateau d'Albion

St-Christol   Banon

Forcalquier

Oraison

Manosque

A51

D8

D942

Carpentras

D4

Pernes-les-
Fontaines

Lagarde
d'Apt

Châteauneuf du Pape
Wine fit for a pope

N100

Villeneuve-
lès-Avignon

Sorgue

GR91

Plateau de
Vaucluse

St-Saturnin-
lès-Apt

D2

D943

AVIGNON

Gard

Durance

Noves

Gordes

D22

D2

Coustellet

Apt

Céreste

GR9-97

D113

Montagne du Lubéron

PARC NATUREL
RÉGIONAL DU
LUBÉRON

N96

Marguerittes

NÎMES

D999

Tarascon

D571

St-Rémy de
Provence

Cavaillon

GR97

Caissargues

D38

Chaîne des Alpilles

Orgon

Cadenet

D956

BOUCHES - DU - RHÔNE

Fontvieille

Eyguières

D543

Vauvert

A54

Rhône

St-Gilles

ARLES

N113

Salon de
Provence

Rognes

Meyrargues

Rians

A572

St-Cannat

A51

Aigues-Mortes

Grand Rhône

Étang de Vaccarès

Réserve National
de Camargue

N568

Miramas

A7

AIX-EN-PROVENCE

Montagne
Ste-Victoire

St-Chamas

Istres

D570

PARC NATUREL RÉGIONAL DE CAMARGUE

Petite Camargue

Étang de
Berre

Vitrolles

Gabies

Gardanne

A8

Trets

St-Maximin-
la-Ste-Baume

Golfe
de Beauduc

Port St-
Louis

D5

L'Estaque

Rougiers

Rade de
Marseille

MARSEILLES

Roquevaire

Golfe de Fos

A50

Aubagne

The Camargue
Flamingo-pink wetlands and silver salt
pans – just made for walking, cycling,
horse-riding and bird-watching

GR98

D559

GR98

Cassis

D26

Sormiou

La Ciotat

Le Beausset

Marseilles
City of sights, sounds and smells – shop
for fish at the old port market or for garlic on
cours Belsunce, eat bouillabaisse and take
a boat trip to Château d'If and around
Les Calanques

Bandol

Sanary-
sur-Mer

La Brusc

M E D I T E R R A N E A N   S E A

0   10   20km

0   6   12mi

PROVENCE & THE CÔTE D'AZUR

Gorges du Verdon
Europe's largest canyon – walk, cycle or dip into white-water river sports

Alpes d'Azur
An orgy of outdoor activities – ride the narrow-gauge mountain railway, stargaze at the observatories or Via Ferrata your way to new heights

Monaco
Take a flutter – in Monte Carlo casino, along Plage du Larvotto or with the stars of motor racing at the Monaco Grand Prix

Nice
Côte d'Azur capital – belle epoque architecture, beaches to pose on, contemporary art museums and panoramic views from the Grande Corniche

Massif des Maures
A feast of local chestnuts, thick forests to get lost in, remote walking trails around La Chartreuse de la Verne monastery and a goat farm to lunch at

Îles d'Hyères
Islands of Gold – beautiful princesses chased by pirates, so folklore says

Elevation

2700m
2100m
1200m
600m
300m
0

MEDITERRANEAN SEA

Provence & the Côte d'Azur
2nd edition – March 2001
First published – June 1999

Published by
Lonely Planet Publications Pty Ltd ABN 36 005 607 983
90 Maribyrnong St, Footscray, Victoria 3011, Australia

Lonely Planet Offices
Australia Locked Bag 1, Footscray, Victoria 3011
USA 150 Linden St, Oakland, CA 94607
UK 10a Spring Place, London NW5 3BH
France 1 rue du Dahomey, 75011 Paris

Photographs
All of the images in this guide are available for licensing from
Lonely Planet Images.
email: lpi@lonelyplanet.com.au
Web site: www.lonelyplanetimages.com

Front cover photograph
Colourful murals along Cours Julien, Marseilles (Jean-Bernard Carillet)

ISBN 1 86450 196 0

Contents – Text

Contents – Maps

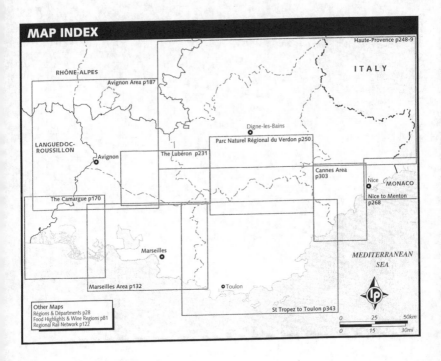

MAP INDEX

RHÔNE-ALPES

Avignon Area p187

Haute-Provence p248-9

ITALY

LANGUEDOC-
ROUSSILLON

Avignon

The Lubéron p231

Digne-les-Bains

Parc Naturel Régional du Verdon p250

Cannes Area
p303

Nice   MONACO

Nice to Menton
p268

The Camargue p170

Marseilles

MEDITERRANEAN
SEA

Marseilles Area p132

Toulon

St Tropez to Toulon p343

Other Maps
Régions & Départments p28
Food Highlights & Wine Regions p81
Regional Rail Network p122

0   25   50km
0   15   30mi

The Authors

Nicola Williams

Nicola lives in Lyons, at the crossroads of the Alps and France's hot south. A journalist by training, she first hit the road in 1990 when she bussed and boated it from Jakarta to East Timor and back again. Following a two-year stint at the *North Wales Weekly*, she moved to Latvia to bus it round the Baltics as Features Editor of the English-language *Baltic Times* newspaper. Following a happy 12 months exploring the Baltic region as editor-in-chief of the *In Your Pocket* city-guide series, she traded in Lithuanian *cepelinai* for Lyonnaise *andouillette*.

Nicola graduated from Kent and completed an MA in Islamic Societies & Cultures at London's School of Oriental & African Studies. She is also the author of Lonely Planet's *The Loire*, another French regional title. Other titles Nicola has worked on include *France, Romania & Moldova, Russia, Ukraine & Belarus* and *Estonia, Latvia & Lithuania*.

FROM THE AUTHOR

Un grand merci to French chefs Alain Ducasse and Roger Vergé for kindly contributing recipes to this book, and to their right-hand women, Madame Sylvie Charbit from Le Moulin de Mougins, and Madame Emmanuelle Perrier from the Bureau Alain Ducasse in Monaco, for organising the paperwork and illustrative slides. Equally sincere thanks to Patricia Wells for insider tips on Provence's truffle trade and divulging what makes a true tapenade.

Out of the kitchen, thank you to Mauricette Hintzy from Monaco's Musée Océanigraphique; Marc from Hôtel Les Orangers in Nice; The Cat's Whiskers bookshop, also in Nice; Frédéric from the Parc Ornithologique de Pont de Gau in the Camargue; Anne Van der Linden from St-Tropez and Reine Ortiz; and to Neil Williams, Darren Staggs & Rick Hewland for partying hard in Nice and still managing to recall the bars and clubs they hit.

Sweet *bisous* to my father Paul Williams who has always had an answer to anything I ask; to my entire family who descended on the Lubéron while I was working, and to my darling husband Matthias, without whom the world would not be nearly as much fun to discover.

This Book

The first edition of *Provence & the Côte d'Azur* was written by Nicola Williams, who updated this edition.

From the Publisher

This second edition of *Provence & the Côte d'Azur* was produced in Lonely Planet's London office. Editing and proofing was handled by Heather Dickson, with help from Abigail Hole and Imogen Franks. James Timmins coordinated the mapping, with assistance from Paul Edmunds and Sara Yorke, who also drew the climate charts. Jane Smith, Mick Weldon and Martin Harris drew the illustrations and the photographs were supplied by Lonely Planet Images. Adam McCrow designed the cover and helped with layout checks. Angie Watts and Ian Stokes also chipped in at the final stage.

Thanks to Quentin Frayne for his help with the Language chapter and Rachel Suddart for providing essential Getting There and Away information. Thanks also to Amanda Canning and Tim Fitzgerald for advice and last-minute checks.

Thanks

Many thanks to the following travellers who used the last edition and wrote to us with helpful hints, useful advice and interesting anecdotes:

Anders Jacobsen, Andrew Berger, Antonella Rosati, Betty Mekeel, Bonnie Temple, Catherine Branfield, Chrlotte Larson, Claudine Altmann, Daniel Walfish, Dave Hall, Dave Swan, David Morgan, David Smith, Dr Yitschak Copperman, Elodie Boisson Kheng, Fiona Hamilton, Gill Maddox, Gordon & Suzanne Lee, Helen & Robert Leydier, Jan Engmann, John Bannon, Josephine Hsieh, Judith & Richard Stallard, Judy & Terry Shircore, Kara Bowen, Karen Pearce, Karen Sliwinski, Koen van Dooren, Lee Kelsey, Linda Butler, Loreen Brehaut, Louis Venter, Lulu Skye, Lynn McDonald, Malgosia Dera, Marge Gruzen, Mark Pennington, Martin Lerner, Michael Haywood, Miles Coiner, Nicola & Bob Grove, Peter Sluijter, Peter Torley, Philip Atkins, Ray Hartwell, Robin Ellis, Ron Lamothe, Ron Roley, Sarah de Mas, Simone Poirier-Bures, Steve Batty, Sylvia Van Etten, Tamara Somers, Victor & Hallie Dolcourt, Yan Zhang

Foreword

ABOUT LONELY PLANET GUIDEBOOKS

The story begins with a classic travel adventure: Tony and Maureen Wheeler's 1972 journey across Europe and Asia to Australia. Useful information about the overland trail did not exist at that time, so Tony and Maureen published the first Lonely Planet guidebook to meet a growing need.

From a kitchen table, then from a tiny office in Melbourne (Australia), Lonely Planet has become the largest independent travel publisher in the world, an international company with offices in Melbourne, Oakland (USA), London (UK) and Paris (France).

Today Lonely Planet guidebooks cover the globe. There is an ever-growing list of books and there's information in a variety of forms and media. Some things haven't changed. The main aim is still to help make it possible for adventurous travellers to get out there – to explore and better understand the world.

At Lonely Planet we believe travellers can make a positive contribution to the countries they visit – if they respect their host communities and spend their money wisely. Since 1986 a percentage of the income from each book has been donated to aid projects and human rights campaigns.

Updates Lonely Planet thoroughly updates each guidebook as often as possible. This usually means there are around two years between editions, although for more unusual or more stable destinations the gap can be longer. Check the imprint page (following the colour map at the beginning of the book) for publication dates.

Between editions up-to-date information is available in two free newsletters – the paper *Planet Talk* and email *Comet* (to subscribe, contact any Lonely Planet office) – and on our Web site at www.lonelyplanet.com. The *Upgrades* section of the Web site covers a number of important and volatile destinations and is regularly updated by Lonely Planet authors. *Scoop* covers news and current affairs relevant to travellers. And, lastly, the *Thorn Tree* bulletin board and *Postcards* section of the site carry unverified, but fascinating, reports from travellers.

Correspondence The process of creating new editions begins with the letters, postcards and emails received from travellers. This correspondence often includes suggestions, criticisms and comments about the current editions. Interesting excerpts are immediately passed on via newsletters and the Web site, and everything goes to our authors to be verified when they're researching on the road. We're keen to get more feedback from organisations or individuals who represent communities visited by travellers.

Lonely Planet gathers information for everyone who's curious about the planet – and especially for those who explore it first-hand. Through guidebooks, phrasebooks, activity guides, maps, literature, newsletters, image library, TV series and Web site we act as an information exchange for a worldwide community of travellers.

Research Authors aim to gather sufficient practical information to enable travellers to make informed choices and to make the mechanics of a journey run smoothly. They also research historical and cultural background to help enrich the travel experience and allow travellers to understand and respond appropriately to cultural and environmental issues.

Authors don't stay in every hotel because that would mean spending a couple of months in each medium-sized city and, no, they don't eat at every restaurant because that would mean stretching belts beyond capacity. They do visit hotels and restaurants to check standards and prices, but feedback based on readers' direct experiences can be very helpful.

Many of our authors work undercover, others aren't so secretive. None of them accept freebies in exchange for positive write-ups. And none of our guidebooks contain any advertising.

Production Authors submit their raw manuscripts and maps to offices in Australia, USA, UK or France. Editors and cartographers – all experienced travellers themselves – then begin the process of assembling the pieces. When the book finally hits the shops, some things are already out of date, we start getting feedback from readers and the process begins again ...

WARNING & REQUEST

Things change – prices go up, schedules change, good places go bad and bad places go bankrupt – nothing stays the same. So, if you find things better or worse, recently opened or long since closed, please tell us and help make the next edition even more accurate and useful. We genuinely value all the feedback we receive. A well-travelled team reads and acknowledges every letter, postcard and email and ensures that every morsel of information finds its way to the appropriate authors, editors and cartographers for verification.

Everyone who writes to us will find their name in the next edition of the appropriate guidebook. They will also receive the latest issue of *Planet Talk*, our quarterly printed newsletter, or *Comet*, our monthly email newsletter. Subscriptions to both newsletters are free. The very best contributions will be rewarded with a free guidebook.

Excerpts from your correspondence may appear in new editions of Lonely Planet guidebooks, the Lonely Planet Web site, *Planet Talk* or *Comet*, so please let us know if you *don't* want your letter published or your name acknowledged.

Send all correspondence to the Lonely Planet office closest to you:

Australia: Locked Bag 1, Footscray, Victoria 3011
USA: 150 Linden St, Oakland, CA 94607
UK: 10A Spring Place, London NW5 3BH
France: 1 rue du Dahomey, 75011 Paris

Or email us at: talk2us@lonelyplanet.com.au

For news, views and updates see our Web site: www.lonelyplanet.com

HOW TO USE A LONELY PLANET GUIDEBOOK

The best way to use a Lonely Planet guidebook is any way you choose. At Lonely Planet we believe the most memorable travel experiences are often those that are unexpected, and the finest discoveries are those you make yourself. Guidebooks are not intended to be used as if they provide a detailed set of infallible instructions!

Contents All Lonely Planet guidebooks follow roughly the same format. The Facts about the Destination chapters or sections give background information ranging from history to weather. Facts for the Visitor gives practical information on issues like visas and health. Getting There & Away gives a brief starting point for researching travel to and from the destination. Getting Around gives an overview of the transport options when you arrive.

The peculiar demands of each destination determine how subsequent chapters are broken up, but some things remain constant. We always start with background, then proceed to sights, places to stay, places to eat, entertainment, getting there and away, and getting around information – in that order.

Heading Hierarchy Lonely Planet headings are used in a strict hierarchical structure that can be visualised as a set of Russian dolls. Each heading (and its following text) is encompassed by any preceding heading that is higher on the hierarchical ladder.

Entry Points We do not assume guidebooks will be read from beginning to end, but that people will dip into them. The traditional entry points are the list of contents and the index. In addition, however, some books have a complete list of maps and an index map illustrating map coverage.

There may also be a colour map that shows highlights. These highlights are dealt with in greater detail in the Facts for the Visitor chapter, along with planning questions and suggested itineraries. Each chapter covering a geographical region usually begins with a locator map and another list of highlights. Once you find something of interest in a list of highlights, turn to the index.

Maps Maps play a crucial role in Lonely Planet guidebooks and include a huge amount of information. A legend is printed on the back page. We seek to have complete consistency between maps and text, and to have every important place in the text captured on a map. Map key numbers usually start in the top left corner.

Although inclusion in a guidebook usually implies a recommendation we cannot list every good place. Exclusion does not necessarily imply criticism. In fact there are a number of reasons why we might exclude a place – sometimes it is simply inappropriate to encourage an influx of travellers.

Introduction

There's much more to Provence than *pétanque*, pastis and medieval villages perched on hills.

Roughly sandwiched between rough-cut Marseilles with its raucous fish markets and streetwise rap scene, and megalomaniacal Monte Carlo with its Hong Kong skyline and highest number of sports cars per capita in Europe, this sunny southern spot screams action, glamour – and just a hint of the ridiculous.

The lively port city of Marseilles, settled by the Greeks on the shores of the Mediterranean Sea, is the capital of Provence. The region is named after Provincia Gallia Transalpina, a province created by the Romans around 125 BC following their defeat of the Celto-Ligurians in Greek Massilia (Marseilles). Travellers with a fascination for the ancient will be rewarded with more triumphal arches, aqueducts and amphitheatres – used by the bloodthirsty Romans to pit gladiator against wild animal – than anywhere else in France.

The mighty River Rhône ends its 813km-long course west of Marseilles in the Camargue delta, a dramatic landscape – as untamed as the Romans – where cowboys herd cattle and Roma people flock from across Europe to honour their patron saint and blaze a fiesta of flamenco and *Bamboleo* music in the streets. Action-lovers visiting this wild waterland can ride bareback with cowboys, cycle across salt pans and sea dikes, or simply take to the skies with a pair of binoculars to watch Europe's largest colony of pink flamingos at work and play.

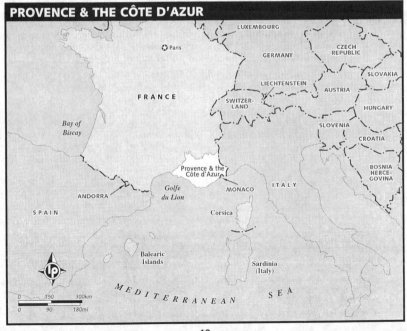

13

East of Marseilles is the famously alluring Côte d'Azur or French Riviera. Immortalised on the silver screen by Grace Kelly, Brigitte Bardot *et al* and on canvas by legions of celebrated artists, this strip of coast is a legend in its own time. Works by Renoir, Matisse and Picasso, displayed in museums in and around Nice, Cannes and St-Tropez, attract millions of tourists each year – as do the nearby Massif des Maures, Estérel, and Alpine foothills that plummet precipitously into the Mediterranean east of Nice. Cats on leads, dogs in handbags and prima donnas dusting sand from their toes with shaving brushes are among the madcap sights that await travellers to its numerous coastal resorts. Offshore is a cluster of islands that offer a rare peace and tranquillity, almost impossible to find elsewhere along this crowded coastal strip.

Inland Provence is a far cry from all this pandemonium. Avignon, the largest town in this neck of the woods, is where Rome's popes were exiled in the 14th century, leaving behind them a resplendent palace and a wealth of vineyards that today produce one of France's most sought-after (and strongest) red wines, Châteauneuf du Pape. Eating, drinking and savouring the sensual orgy of hues and scents that this papal city and Vaucluse region offers – springtime almond blossoms, asparagus, red cherries and strawberries, summer melons and pumpkins, fields of lavender in July and August, truffles all winter – are as good reasons as any to visit this pretty part of Provence.

Paragliding, walking, white-water sports and mountain biking are among the unexpected thrills and spills to be found in Haute-Provence, the region's 'great outdoors'. Dubbed the Alpes d'Azur, this is where you take your foot off the speed pedal and cruise for days without passing another tourist. Natural treasures awaiting motorists, cyclists and walkers include clear Alpine lakes, a national park with a rich archaeological heritage and Europe's largest canyon.

Then there is the great hulk of Mont Ventoux, the king of Provence who – with the sun and the mistral – commands his action-packed kingdom from the top of barren, sunbaked slopes in north-western Provence. The mistral winds add a bitter bite to the air, while the sun bathes Provence in the most glorious southern sunshine, with a warmth and intensity of light absolutely unknown in any other part of Europe.

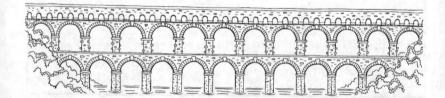

Facts about Provence

HISTORY
Early Inhabitants
Provence (Prouvènço in Provençal) was in-habited from an exceptionally early age. Prehistoric rock scratchings in the Grottes de l'Observatoire in Monaco, carved one million years ago, are among the world's oldest. Traces of fire discovered in the Grotte de l'Escale at St-Estève Janson show prehistoric people to have used fire from 600,000 BC. The Terra Amata site in Nice was inhabited as early as 400,000 BC.

During the Middle Palaeolithic period (about 90,000 to 40,000 BC), Neanderthal hunters occupied the coast. Modern man followed in 30,000 BC. The ornate wall paintings of bison, seals, ibex and other animals inside the decorated Grotte Cosquer (named after the Cassis diver who discovered it in 1991) in the Calanque de Sormiou, near Marseilles, date from 20,000 BC. Many more undiscovered examples of prehistoric art are believed to exist in the region in cave dwellings like this.

The Neolithic period (about 6000 to 4500 years ago), also known as the New Stone Age, witnessed the earliest domestication of sheep in Châteauneuf-lès-Martigues, followed by the cultivation of lands by the Ligurians. The first dwellings to be built (around 3500 BC) were *bories*, evident in Gordes. These one- or two-storey beehive-shaped huts, constructed without mortar using thin wedges of limestone, were inhabited until as late as the 18th century. The collection of 30,000 Bronze Age petroglyphs – drawings or carvings on rock – (between 1800 and 1500 BC), at the foot of Mont Bégo in the Vallée des Merveilles, remain among the world's most spectacular.

Ancient Provence
The eastern part of the Mediterranean coast was colonised around 600 BC by Greeks, from Phocaea in Asia Minor, who settled in Massilia (Marseilles). The Greeks were the first to develop the region, establishing trading posts at other coastal points from the 4th century BC: at Antipolis (Antibes), Olbia (Hyères), Athenopolis (St-Tropez), Nikaia (Nice), Monoïkos (Monaco) and Glanum (near St-Rémy de Provence). The Greeks brought olives and grape vines with them.

At the same time as Hellenic civilisation was developing on the coast, the Celts were penetrating the northern part of the region. They mingled with ancient Ligurians to create a Celto-Ligurian stronghold around Entremont. Its influence extended as far south as Draguignan.

In 125 BC the Romans were called in by the Greeks to help defend Massilia against the threat of invasion by Celto-Ligurians from Entremont. The Romans were victorious, and this marked the start of the Gallo-Roman era and the creation of Provincia Gallia Transalpina, the first Roman province (province), from which the name Provence is derived.

The Gallo-Roman Era
Provincia Gallia Transalpina, which quickly became Provincia Narbonensis, was much larger than modern-day Provence. It embraced all of southern France, from the Alps to the Mediterranean Sea and as far west as the Pyrenees. Narbonne was its capital. In 122 BC the Romans destroyed the Ligurian capital of Entremont and established the Roman stronghold of Aquae Sextiae Salluviorum (Aix-en-Provence) at its foot.

During this period the Romans started building roads to secure the route between Italy and Spain. The Via Aurelia linked Rome to Fréjus, Aix-en-Provence, Arles and Nîmes; the northbound Via Agrippa followed the River Rhône (Rose in Provençal) from Arles to Avignon, Orange and Lyons; and the Via Domitia linked the Alps with the Pyrenees by way of Sisteron, the Lubéron (Céreste, Apt and Cavaillon), Beaucaire and Nîmes. Vestiges of these roads, such as the Pont Julien (dating from

3 BC) near Bonnieux and an arch in Cavaillon, still remain.

The Roman influence on Provence was tremendous, though it was only after Julius Caesar's conquest of Gaul (58–51 BC) and its consequent integration into the Roman Empire that the region really began to flourish. Massilia, which had retained its independence following the creation of Provincia, was incorporated by Caesar in 49 BC. In 14 BC, the still-rebellious Ligurians were defeated by Augustus, who built a trophy monument at La Turbie (6 BC) to celebrate his victory. Arelate (Arles) became the chosen regional capital.

Under the emperor Augustus, grandiose amphitheatres seating 10,000 spectators were built to host gladiator combats at Arelate, Nemausus (Nîmes), Forum Julii (Fréjus) and Vasio Vocontiorum (Vaison-la-Romaine). Triumphal arches were raised at Arausio (Orange), Cabelio (Cavaillon), Carpentorate (Carpentras) and Glanum, and a series of aqueducts were constructed. The mammoth Pont du Gard – 275m in length – was part of a 50km-long system of canals built around 19 BC by Agrippa, Augustus' deputy, to bring water from Uzès to Nîmes. Most of these ancient public buildings remain exceptionally well preserved.

The end of the third century saw the reorganisation of the Roman empire. Provincia Narbonensis was split into two provinces in AD 284. The land on the right bank of the Rhône (Languedoc-Roussillon today) remained Narbonensis and the land on the left bank (today's Provence) became Provincia Viennoise. Christianity penetrated the region and was adopted by the Romans. Provençal legend says it was brought to the region by Mary Magdalene, Mary Jacob and Mary Salome who sailed into Stes-Maries de la Mer in AD 40. St Honorat founded the Lérins monastical order on the Îles de Lérins at this time.

Medieval Provence

After the collapse of the Roman empire in 476, Provence suffered successive invasions by a clutch of Germanic tribes: the Visigoths (West Goths, from the Danube delta region in Transylvania), the Ostrogoths (East Goths, from the Black Sea region) and the Burgundians of Scandinavian origin. Provence was ceded to the Franks (also a Germanic tribe, from whom the word 'France' comes) at the start of the 6th century. Rebellions in Marseilles, Arles and Avignon (732–9) against the Frankish rule were brutally squashed.

In the early 9th century the Saracens (an umbrella term adopted locally to describe Muslim invaders such as Turks, Moors and Arabs) emerged as a warrior force to be reckoned with. Attacks along the Maures coast, Niçois hinterland and more northern Alps, persuaded villagers to take refuge in the hills. Many of Provence's perched, hilltop villages date from this chaotic period. But the Saracens did teach the local population what could be done with the bark of cork oak – that is, to use it to make cork bottle stoppers. In 974 the Saracen fortress at La Garde Freinet was defeated by Guillaume Le Libérateur (William the Liberator), count of Arles, who consequently extended his feudal control over the entire region, marking a return of peace and unity to Provence, which became a marquisat. In 1032 it joined the Holy Roman Empire.

At the start of the 12th century, the marquisat of Provence was split in two: the north fell into the hands of the counts of Toulouse from 1125 and retained the title of marquisat while the Catalan counts of Barcelona gained control of the southern part, which stretched from the Rhône to the Durance and from the Alps to the sea. This was called the Comté de Provence (County of Provence). Raymond Bérenger V (1209–45) was the first Catalan count to reside permanently in Aix (the capital since 1186). In 1229 he conquered Nice to gain better control of eastern Provence and the southern Alps and, in 1232, he founded Barcelonnette. In 1246, after Bérenger's death, the Comté de Provence passed to the House of Anjou, under which it enjoyed great prosperity.

Troubadour literature composed in *langue d'oc* (Occitan, of which Provençal is a dialect) and Romanesque architecture – the grandiose 12th-century abbeys at Sénanque, Silvacane and Le Thoronet – blossomed in medieval Provence.

The Popes

In 1274 Comtat Venaissin, situated in Provence's northern realm (namely Carpentras and its Vaucluse hinterland), was ceded to Pope Gregory X in Rome. In 1309, French-born Clement V (1305–14) moved the papal headquarters from feud-riven Rome to Avignon, thus beginning the most resplendent period in that city's history.

Between 1309 and 1376, nine pontiffs headed the Roman Catholic church from Avignon. Under the reign of Avignon's third pope, Benoît XII (1334–42), work started on the resplendent Palais des Papes (Papal Palace), enlarged to monumental status during the reign of his successor Clement VI (1342–52) and admired at the time as the 'most handsome of houses and greatest of strongholds in the world'. In 1348 Pope Clement VI purchased the city of Avignon (not within the boundaries of Comtat Venaissin) from the reigning countess of Provence, Queen Jeanne of Naples (1343–82). Accused of murdering her husband, she fled to Avignon where she sold the city for 80,000 florins – in exchange for a papal pardon. Clement VI had Avignon bridge built in 1350.

In 1376 the city was given a break when Pope Gregory XI left Avignon. But his death two years later led to the Great Schism (1378–1417), during which rival popes – up to three at one time, each with his own College of Cardinals – resided at Rome and Avignon and spent most of their energies denouncing and excommunicating one another. They also went to great effort to gain control of church revenues, including the sale of indulgences. Even after the schism was settled and a pope, Martin V – acceptable to all factions – established himself in Rome, Avignon and the Comtat Venaissin remained under papal rule until 1792.

Cultural life in Provence flourished inside and outside the papal sphere during the 14th century. A university was established in Avignon as early as 1303, followed by a university in Aix, Provence's capital, a century later. In 1327, the Italian poet Petrarch (1304–74), exiled in Avignon, first encountered his muse, Laura. In 1336 he became the first person to climb to the top of Mont Ventoux. The reign of good King René, king of Naples (1434–80), further enhanced this period of peace and prosperity. French became the courtly language and a castle was built at Tarascon.

French Provence

In 1481, René's successor, his nephew Charles III, died heirless and Provence was ceded to Louis XI of France. In 1486 the state of Aix ratified Provence's union with France and the centralist policies of the French kings saw the region's autonomy greatly reduced. Aix Parliament, a French administrative body, was created in 1501.

This new addition to the French kingdom did not include Nice, Barcelonnette, Puget-Théniers and the hinterlands of these towns which, in 1388, had become incorporated into the lands of the House of Savoy. The Comté de Nice (County of Nice; essentially today's Alpes-Maritimes department), with Nice as its capital, did not become part of French Provence until 1860.

A period of instability ensued. Jews living in Provençal France fled to ghettoes in Carpentras, Pernes-les-Fontaines, L'Isle-sur-Sorgue, Cavaillon or Avignon – all part of the pontifical enclave of Comtat Venaissin, where papal protection remained assured until 1570. Following the French conquest of Milan during the Italian wars in the 1520s, Charles V invaded Provence. This was followed by another attack and further bloodshed in 1536. The Villers-Cotterêts statute approved in 1539 made French, rather than Provençal, the official administrative language in Provence.

An early victim of the Reformation sweeping Europe in the 1530s and the consequent Wars of Religion (1562–98) was the Lubéron. In April 1545, the population of 11 Vaudois villages in the Lubéron was massacred in six days. Numerous clashes followed between the staunchly Catholic stronghold of Comtat Venaissin and its Huguenot (Protestant) neighbours to the north around Orange. In 1580 the plague temporarily immobilised the otherwise volatile region. Treatments first used by the prophetic Nostradamus (1503–66) in St-Rémy de Provence were administered to plague victims. The Edict of Nantes in 1598, which recognised Protestant control of certain areas, including Lourmarin in the Lubéron, brought an uneasy peace to the region – until its revocation by Louis XIV in 1685. A full-scale persecution of Protestants in Provence ensued. Leading Huguenots were killed or imprisoned, many in the Tour de Constance in Aigues-Mortes and Château d'If near Marseilles.

The plague of 1720 killed half of Marseilles' population. The close of the century was marked by the French Revolution in 1789: as the National Guard from Marseilles marched northwards to defend the Revolution, a merry little tune composed in Strasbourg several months earlier for the war against Prussia – *Chant de Guerre de l'Armée du Rhin* (War Song of the Rhine Army) – sprung from their lips. France's stirring national anthem, *La Marseillaise*, was born.

La Route Napoléon

Provence was divided into three *départements* (departments) in 1790: Var, Bouches du Rhône and the Basse-Alpes (Lower Alps). Two years later papal Avignon and Comtat Venaissin were annexed by France, making way for the creation of a fourth department, Vaucluse.

In 1793 the Armée du Midi marched into Nice, captured the town, and declared it French territory on 31 January. France also captured Monaco, which until now had been a recognised independent state ruled by the Grimaldi family. When Toulon was besieged by the English, it was thanks to the efforts of a dashing young Corsican general named Napoleon Bonaparte (Napoleon I) that France recaptured it.

The Reign of Terror that swept through France between September 1793 and July 1794 saw religious freedoms revoked, churches desecrated and cathedrals turned into 'Temples of Reason'. In the secrecy of their homes, people hand-crafted thumbnail-sized, biblical figurines, hence the rather inglorious creation of the Provençal *santon* (see the boxed text 'Little Saints' in the Marseilles Area chapter).

In 1814 France lost the territories it had seized in 1793. The Comté de Nice was ceded to Victor Emmanuel I, king of Sardinia. It remained under Sardinian protectorship until 1860 when an agreement between Napoleon III and the House of Savoy helped drive the Austrians from northern Italy, prompting France to repossess Savoy and the area around Nice. In Monaco, meanwhile, the Treaty of Paris restored the rights of the Grimaldi royal family; from 1817 until 1860 the principality also fell under the protection of the Sardinian king.

Meanwhile, the Allied restoration of the House of Bourbon to the French throne at the Congress of Vienna (1814–15), following Napoleon I's abdication and exile to Elba, was rudely interrupted by the return of the emperor. Following his escape from Elba in 1815, Napoleon landed at Golfe-Juan on 1 March with a 1200-strong army. He proceeded northwards, passing through Cannes, Grasse, Castellane, Digne-les-Bains and Sisteron en route to his triumphal return to Paris on 20 May. Unfortunately, Napoleon's glorious 'Hundred Days' back in power ended with the Battle of Waterloo and his return to exile. He died in 1821.

During the revolutions of 1848, French revolutionaries adopted as their own the red, white and blue tricolour of Martigues, a small town near Marseilles. This became France's national flag.

The Belle Epoque

The Second Empire (1852–70) brought to the region a revival in all things Provençal, a movement spearheaded by poet Frédéric Mistral (see Literature later in this chapter). Rapid economic growth was the era's other hallmark: Nice, which had finally become part of France in 1860, was among Europe's first cities to have a purely tourist-based economy. Between 1860 and 1911 it was also Europe's fastest-growing city. The city became particularly popular with the English aristocracy in the Victorian period. They followed their queen's example of wintering in Nice to indulge in its mild winter. European royalty followed soon after. The rail line reached Toulon in 1856, followed by Nice and Draguignan, and in 1864 work started on a coastal road from Nice to Monaco. The same year, exotic palm trees, mimosas and eucalyptus plants were imported from Australia. In fine Second Empire architectural style, Nice Opera House and the neoclassical Justice Palace were built.

In neighbouring Monaco, the Grimaldi family had given up its claim over its former territories of Menton and Roquebrune in 1861 (under Monégasque rule until 1848) in exchange for France's recognition of its status as an independent principality. When Monte Carlo casino opened four years later, Monaco leapt from being Europe's poorest state to one of its richest.

The Third Republic ushered in the glittering *belle epoque* (literally 'beautiful age'), with Art Nouveau architecture, a whole field of artistic 'isms' such as impressionism, and advances in science and engineering. Wealthy French, English, American and Russian tourists and tuberculosis sufferers (for whom the only 'cure' was sunlight and sea air) discovered the coast, attracted by its beauty and temperate climate in winter. The intensity and clarity of the region's colours and light appealed to many painters including Cézanne, Van Gogh and Matisse. Writers and other celebrities were also attracted to the region and contributed to its fame. Little fishing ports such as St-Tropez became exclusive resorts with lavish, castle-like villas hugged by manicured gardens, tennis courts and golf courses. In 1887 the first guidebook to the French coast was published, following which the coast finally had a name it could call its own – the Côte d'Azur.

WWI & the Interwar Period

No blood was spilled on southern French soil during WWI although large areas of

The Sky-Blue Coast

The Côte d'Azur (literally 'Azure Coast') gained its name from an early, 19th-century guidebook.

La Côte d'Azur, published in 1887, was the work of Stéphane Liégeard (1830–1925), a lawyer-cum-aspiring poet from Burgundy who lived in Cannes. The guide covered the coast from Menton to Hyères and was an instant hit.

Its title, a reflection of the coast's clear blue cloudless skies, became the hottest buzz word to hit town. And it never tired. The Côte d'Azur is today also known as the French Riviera.

north-eastern France were devastated by trench warfare. Soldiers were conscripted from the region, however, and the human losses included two out of every 10 Frenchmen between 20 and 45 years of age. With its primarily tourist-based economy, the Côte d'Azur recovered quickly from the postwar financial crisis that lingered in the more industrial north.

The Côte d'Azur sparkled as an avant-garde centre in the 1920s and '30s, with artists pushing into the new fields of cubism and surrealism, Le Corbusier rewriting the architectural textbook and foreign writers attracted by the coast's liberal atmosphere: Ernest Hemingway, F Scott Fitzgerald, Aldous Huxley, Katherine Mansfield, DH Lawrence and Thomas Mann were among the scores to seek solace in the sun. Guests at Somerset Maugham's villa on Cap Ferrat included innumerable literary names, from TS Eliot and Arnold Bennett to Noël Coward, Evelyn Waugh and Ian Fleming. Nightlife gained a reputation for being at the cutting edge, with everything from jazz clubs to striptease. Rail and road access to the south improved: the railway line between Digne-les-Bains and Nice was completed and in 1922 the luxurious *Train Bleu* (Blue Train) made its first run from Calais, via Paris, to the coast. The train only had 1st-class carriages and was quickly dubbed the 'train to paradise'.

The glorious 1920s hailed the start of the summer season on the Côte d'Azur. Outdoor swimming pools were built, seashores were cleared of seaweed to uncover lovely sandy beaches, and sunbathing sprang into fashion after Coco Chanel made her first appearance on the coast in 1923, draped over the arm of the duke of Westminster. France lifted its ban on gambling, prompting the first casino to open on the coast in the Palais de la Méditerranée on Nice's promenade des Anglais in 1927. The first Formula One Grand Prix took to the streets of Monaco in 1929, while the early 1930s saw wide pyjama-style beach trousers and the opening of a nudist colony on Île du Levant. With the advent of paid holidays for all French workers in 1936, even more tourists flocked to the region. Second- and 3rd-class seating was added to the Train Bleu that, since 1929, had been running daily, year round.

WWII

With the onset of war, the Côte d'Azur's glory days turned grey. Depression set in and on 3 September 1939 France and Britain declared war on Germany. But again, Provence and the Côte d'Azur remained relatively unscathed. Following the armistice treaty agreed with Hitler on 22 June 1940, southern France fell into the 'free' Vichy France zone, although Menton and its northern Vallée de Roya (around Sospel) were occupied by the Italians. The Côte d'Azur – particularly Nice – immediately became a safe haven from war-torn occupied France; by 1942 some 43,000 Jews had descended on the coast to seek refuge. Monaco was neutral for the duration of the war.

On 11 November 1942 Nazi Germany invaded Vichy France. Provence was at war. At Toulon port, 73 ships, cruisers, destroyers and submarines – the major part of the French fleet and under the command of Admiral Jean-Baptiste Laborde – were scuttled by their crews to prevent the Germans seizing them. Almost immediately, Toulon was overcome by the Germans and Nice was occupied by the Italians. In January 1943 the Marseilles quarter of Le Panier was completely razed, its 40,000 inhabitants being given less than a day's notice to pack up and leave. Those who didn't were sent to Nazi concentration camps. The Resistance movement was particularly strong in Provence, where it became known as *maquis* after the Provençal scrub in which it hid.

Two months after D-Day, on 15 August 1944, Allied forces landed on the southern coast. They arrived at various beaches along the Côte d'Azur, including Le Dramont near St-Raphaël, Cavalaire, Pampelonne and the St-Tropez peninsula. St-Tropez and Provence's hinterland were almost immediately liberated, but it was not until after five days of heavy fighting that Allied troops, led by the French Général de Montsabert, freed Marseilles on 28 August (three days after the liberation of Paris). Toulon was liberated on 26 August, one week after French troops under Général de Lattre de Tassigny first attacked the port.

The Italian-occupied areas in the Vallée de Roya were not returned to France until 1947.

Modern Provence

The first international film festival at Cannes in 1946 heralded the return to 'normal life' on the Côte d'Azur: party madness resumed. Noël Coward, Somerset Maugham and the rest of the coast's intellectual set returned to their abandoned seaside villas, while Picasso set up a studio in Golfe-Juan. The 1950s and '60s saw a staccato succession of glamorous society 'events': the fairytale marriage of a Grimaldi prince to Hollywood film legend Grace Kelly in 1956; Vadim's filming of *Et Dieu Créa la Femme* (And God Created Woman) with Brigitte Bardot in St-Tropez the same year; the emergence of the bikini and the Nice new realists in the late 1950s; the advent of topless sunbathing (and consequent nipple-covering with bottle tops to prevent arrest for indecent exposure); and Miles Davis, Ella Fitzgerald and Ray Charles appearing at the 1961 Juan-les-Pins jazz festival.

In 1962 the troubled French colony of Algeria negotiated its independence with

President Charles de Gaulle. During this time some 750,000 *pieds noirs* (literally 'black feet', as Algerian-born French people are known in France) flooded into France. A substantial number settled in Provence (particularly in the large urban centres of Marseilles, Nice and Toulon), as did immigrants from other French colonies and protectorates in North Africa.

Rapid industrialisation marked the 1960s. Five hydroelectric plants were constructed in 1962 on the banks of the River Durance and in 1964 the Electricité de France (EDF, the French electricity company) started digging a canal from north of Manosque all the way south to the Étang de Berre, west of Marseilles. The following year construction work began on a 10,000-hectare petrochemical zone and industrial port at Fos-sur-Mer, the most important in southern Europe. Eyesore tanker terminals and oil refineries were raised at the site soon after. 1969 saw the inauguration of a technological park – to become Europe's largest – at Sophia-Antipolis, just north of Antibes (dubbed the California of Europe by many). The first metro line opened in Marseilles in 1977 and TGV high-speed trains reached the city in 1981.

From the 1970s onwards, mainstream tourism, which had been almost exclusively limited to the Côte d'Azur until then, started making inroads into Provence's rural heart. While a concrete marina was being constructed at Villeneuve-Lourbet-Plage on the coast west of Nice, the region's first purpose-built ski resort popped up inland at ugly Isola 2000 (1972). The small flow of foreigners that trickled to Provence to buy up crumbling old *mas* (Provençal farmhouses) at dirt-cheap prices in the late 1970s had become an uncontrollable torrent a decade on – as had the coachloads of tourists who flooded to Provence to follow in the footsteps of British novelist Peter Mayle, whose book *A Year in Provence* (1989) captured the imagination of millions with its vivid description of life in Provence and quirky characters.

Corruption cast a shady cloud over France's hot south in the 1980s and early '90s. Nice's mayor, the corrupt right-wing

Jacques Médecin (son of another former mayor, Jean Médecin, who ruled Nice for 38 years) was twice found guilty of income tax evasion during his 24-year mayorship (1966–90). In 1990, King Jacques – as the flamboyant mayor was dubbed – fled to Uruguay, following which he was convicted *in absentia* of the misuse of public funds (including accepting four million francs in bribes and stealing two million francs from the Nice opera). Médecin was extradited in 1994 and imprisoned in Grenoble where he served two years of a 3½-year sentence. Upon being released the ex-mayor, who died in 1998 aged 70, returned to Uruguay to sell hand-painted T-shirts.

In 1994 Yann Piat became the only member of France's National Assembly (parliament) since WWII to be assassinated while in office. Following her public denunciation of the Riviera Mafia, the French *député* (member of parliament) was shot in her Hyères constituency. Her assassins, dubbed the 'baby killers' by the press after their conviction in 1998, were local Mafia kingpins barely in their 20s.

Politics & Popular Culture

This blatant corruption, coupled with economic recession and growing unemployment, fuelled the rise of the extreme-right Front National (FN; National Front) in the mid-1990s. Nowhere else in France did the xenophobic party gain such a fierce stronghold as in Provence, where the FN stormed to victory in municipal elections in Toulon, Orange and Marignane in 1995, and in Vitrolles in 1997.

Despite such victories in local politics, the FN led by Jean Marie Le Pen failed to make any real headway in the national arena. Party support for the FN rose from 1% in 1981 to 15% in the 1995 presidential elections, yet the FN did not hold any seats in the National Assembly. And, despite gaining 15.5% of the nationwide vote in the last regional elections (1998), Le Pen failed in his bid to become chairman of the Provence-Alpes-Côte d'Azur *région* (administrative region).

The final blow was dealt in December

1998 when second-in-command, Bruno Mégret, split from Le Pen to create his own breakaway faction, marking the end of the FN as a mighty force to be reckoned with. In the June 1999 European parliamentary elections, Le Pen and the FN won just 5.7% of the national vote (enough to secure just five of the 87 French parliamentary seats), while Mégret's newly formed Mouvement National (MN) party trailed with a paltry 3.28% (and no seats). This was in contrast to the Socialists, Rassemblement pour la République (RPR), communists and extreme-left who won the backing of 21.95%, 12.7%, 6.8% and 5.2% of the French electorate respectively.

The next municipal elections, to take place in March 2001, are not expected to throw up any wild cards. All four extreme-right mayors – Jean-Marie Le Chevallier in Toulon (ex-FN) and Jacques Bompard in Orange (FN) and the two Mégretistes, Catherine Mégret (Vitrolles) and Daniel Simonpiéri (Marignane) – will all stand for re-election. In Vaucluse, the spotlight will be on Avignon where two women – current mayor and Vaucluse *député* (member of parliament), Marie-Josée Roig, of the right-wing RPR and left-wing heavyweight Elisabeth Guigou, justice minister in Jospin's socialist government – will battle it out for the mayorship. This is seen as a big step forwards in a region where female politicians are few and far between. Of the 122 members in the Provence-Alpes-Côte d'Azur *conseil régional* (regional council) just 29 are women. Women are equally scant in the local *conseils généraux*; until 1998 a woman had never sat on Vaucluse's 23-strong general council.

The turn of the century saw newly found optimism sweep across France. Nowhere was this upbeat turn more pronounced than in multicultural Marseilles, France's third-largest city which – since the French team's victory in the 1998 football World Cup and Euro 2000 – has been at the cutting edge of hip-hop, rap and football. In both 1998 and again in 2000 *'on est champions'* ('we are the champions') became the catch phrase of the moment thanks, in no small part, to champion-of-both-tournaments Zinedine Zidane. One of the world's greatest players, the midfielder from Marseilles has become one of France's biggest popular heroes. His humble grin has been used across the country to sell everything from Adidas sports gear (1998) to Volvic mineral water (2000). In Christian Dior's summer 1999 collection, Zidane was marketed as the 'symbol of the modern man'.

GEOGRAPHY

Provence and the Côte d'Azur cover an area of 25,851 sq km in the extreme south-eastern corner of France. The area is shaped like an elongated oval, bordered by the southern Alps to the north-east – which form a natural frontier with neighbouring Italy. Its western border – just north of Orange down to Arles and the Camargue west of Marseilles – is delineated by the River Rhône, which separates Provence from the Gard department in Languedoc-Roussillon.

The Camargue – a wetland of salt marshes – is actually the delta of the Rhône, a triangular alluvial plain (1400 sq km) formed by the Grand Rhône to the east and the Petit Rhône to the west. The three points of the triangle are marked by the town of Arles (north), Aigues-Mortes (west) and the Fos petrochemical terminal (east). The barren Crau plain, straddling the north-eastern side of the triangle, is the ancient delta of the River Durance, an affluent of the Rhône which it meets just south of Avignon.

The Mediterranean's sky-blue waters wash the entire length of Provence's southern boundary. The 70km-long stretch of coastline from Marseilles to Menton on the French-Italian border, is called the Côte d'Azur in French and the French Riviera by Anglophones. Beaches are predominantly pebbly and several groups of islands dot the shores: the Îles du Frioul (Marseilles), the Îles des Embiez (Toulon) and the Îles de Lérins (Cannes). The Îles d'Hyères, offshore from Hyères, are the region's southernmost point.

Heading inland, the coastal strip is cut off from the region's vast interior by three mountain ranges: the Massif de l'Estérel formed from red volcanic rock, the limestone Massif des Maures, and the foothills of the Alps that kiss the Arrière-Pays Niçois (Niçois hinterland) immediately north of Nice. The coastline around Marseilles is formed from a chain of calcareous rocks, known as Les Calanques. France's highest cliff (406m) crowns Cap Canaille.

The interior of Provence, east of the Rhône, is dominated by hills and mountains that become higher the farther north you climb, peaking with Mont Ventoux (1912m) in the north-west and the southern Alps – part of which form the Parc National du Mercantour – in the north-east. Lower-lying ranges from west to east include the little Alpilles, Montagne Ste-Victoire, the Ste-Baume and Vaucluse hills, and the rugged Lubéron range.

Farther east are the Gorges du Verdon, with Europe's largest most spectacular canyon. North-west, on the right bank of the Durance is the Plateau de Valensole, Provence's lavender kingdom. On the left bank of the river is the Plateau d'Albion, a vast *causse* (limestone plateau).

Provence's largest city is Marseilles (pop 807,100), followed by Nice (pop 345,900), Toulon (pop 166,500), Aix-en-Provence (pop 137,100) and Avignon (pop 88,300).

CLIMATE

If you like hot summers and mild winters, the Mediterranean climate is for you: frost is rare, spring and autumn downpours are sudden but brief and summer has virtually no rain. The region is blessed with 2500 to 2800 hours of sunshine per year – accounting for the extraordinary light, which was such a vital inspiration for painters such as Van Gogh, Cézanne and Picasso.

The Côte d'Azur enjoys an annual average temperature of 15°C, dropping to 5°C in the higher-altitude north-east. Temperatures can reach 40°C on the coast in July and August. The sea water temperature (surface) is 20°C to 25°C in summer, dropping to a toe-numbing 12°C to 13°C in winter. Annual precipitation is low: 250mm in the Marseilles region, 1100mm in the Alpes-Maritimes department and 1500mm in the southern Alps, which are usually snow-covered from December to March at least. The Camargue delta is one of Europe's most humid zones.

Storms are frequent in the mountains from as early as August onwards. See the boxed text 'Rain, Hail or Shine' for information on weather forecasts. In early spring, winter and late autumn, Provence can experience sudden bouts of extreme cold. The much-cursed, menacing mistral is usually the reason for these dramatic, unexpected and utterly miserable weather changes.

Rain, Hail or Shine

To find out the latest weather report (in French), ring any of the numbers listed below; telephone calls cost 8.91FF to connect, then 2.23FF per minute. Alternatively, surf the Web at www.meteo.fr (French only).

Alpes de Haute-Provence	☎ 08 36 68 02 04
Alpes-Maritimes	☎ 08 36 68 02 06
Bouches du Rhône	☎ 08 36 68 02 13
Var	☎ 08 36 68 02 83
Vaucluse	☎ 08 36 68 02 84

National marine forecasts are available on ☎ 08 36 68 08 08; to find out the local forecast for your area call ☎ 08 36 68 08 xx, replacing 'xx' with the two-digit departmental code (listed under Government & Politics later in this chapter). For example, call ☎ 08 36 68 08 06 for Alpes-Maritimes, which broadcasts air and sea-water temperatures for most beach resorts between 1 June and 30 September.

Riviera Radio airs weather reports in English on 106.5MHz FM (106.3MHz FM in Monaco).

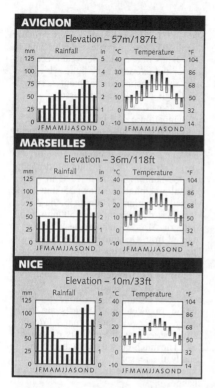

ECOLOGY & ENVIRONMENT
Ecology
The battle is far from over for some 200 environmental pressure groups who have fought tooth and nail since 1997 to prevent a proposed high-voltage line (400,000V) blighting countryside in the protected Parc Naturel du Verdon. High voltage lines electrocute at least 1000 birds of prey each year. Despite initially giving the EDF permission to build the line in the park, the Ministry of Environment subsequently withdrew the authorisation it had granted, opened a public inquiry (costing 10 million FF) into the matter and, in mid-1999, announced that the EDF should reroute the line elsewhere in Provence. The 225,000V line currently linking Nice with power plants in the Rhône Valley is insufficient to meet the city's power demands in emergency situations.

Energy Since the late 1980s, the state-owned electricity company, Electricité de France (EDF), has produced about three-quarters of France's electricity using nuclear power. EDF also controls France's hydroelectric programme. By damming rivers to produce electricity it has created huge recreational lakes such as Lac de Ste-Croix, south-west of the Gorges du Verdon, Lac de Castillon and the adjoining Lac de Chaudanne north-east of the gorges. This has destroyed the habitats of many animals.

Environment
Forest Fires Provence's 1.2 million hectares of forest, just 8.5% of which are protected, are managed by the Office National des Forêts (ONF), with a regional office in Aix-en-Provence and a Web site at www.onf.fr (French only).

Summer forest fires pose the greatest annual hazard to these forests, with great tracts of land being burned each year. These fires are often caused by careless day-trippers, although some are deliberately lit in the Maures and Estérel ranges to get licences to build on the damaged lands. In 1997 fire raged across 6663 hectares in the Provence-Alpes-Côte d'Azur region – compared with just 759 hectares in 1996 and 2500 hectares annually between 1993 and 1995. Almost 85% of the 1997 fires affected forests in the Bouches du Rhône department (mainly around Marseilles and Les Calanques) and in Alpes-Maritimes (inland from Nice). In July 1999 alone, flames whipped across hills near St-Rémy de Provence, destroying 2400 hectares in one fell swoop. By the end of August 2000, 187 recorded forest fires had burnt through 1282 hectares in Bouches du Rhône (compared with 134 fires and 2719 hectares during the same period in 1999).

Reforestation, costing a hefty 40,000FF (US$6500) per hectare, is handled by the Fondation pour La Protection de la Forêt Méditerranéenne, which has replanted more than 200,000 trees in the past decade.

Visit online at www.fondation-pour-la-foret
.enprovence.com (French only).

Preventive fire measures include replanting burnt areas with less inflammable flora such as olive trees, vineyards or plants with a naturally high water content. In summer, forests are patrolled by wardens on horseback.

Tourism The 8.3 million tourists that descend on the region are an annual environmental hazard. The Côte d'Azur – already a concrete minefield – continues to be developed to cater for the increasing number of tourists. Port-Cros' fragile ecosystem is threatened not only by fire but by marine pollution, caused mainly by the boats that bring 120,000 tourists annually to the island.

Bathing Water The quality of *eau de baignade* (bathing water) along the Côte d'Azur is surprisingly good. Of the 359 beaches in the region monitored during 1996, just 14 beaches (3.9%) did not conform to European standards. Of the rest, 228 beaches – 10% more than in 1995 – were of good quality.

Beaches awarded the European blue flag in 2000 included beaches in and around Cannes, Antibes, Cap d'Ail, Menton, Golfe-Juan, Mandelieu-La Napoule, Ste-Maxime, Port Gardian beach at Stes-Maries de la Mer and most beaches at Hyères, Le Lavandou, Grimaud and Fréjus. Of the 92 beaches in Bouches du Rhône, just 12 – in La Ciotat, Martigues and Port de Bouc – scored a blue flag. Beaches in Marseilles, Nice and St-Tropez have not been flagged for several years.

Industrial Development The menace of industrial development threatens the region. North-west of Marseilles, a large area of the Crau plain – France's last remaining steppe – has been devoured by the eyesore industrial complex and port at Fos, on the southwestern shores of the Étang de Berre. Numerous oil refineries dominate the southern and eastern shores of the lagoon. Fishing in its heavily polluted waters has been banned since 1957. As part of a huge Elf- and

Metaleurop-sponsored effort to clean up the area around L'Estaque, off the lake's southeastern tip, some 350,000 cubic metres of polluted soil will be excavated to create a rejuvenated 80-hectare zone. The 120 million FF project should be completed by 2001.

In 1993 the French and Italian governments gave their blessing to the construction of a highway tunnel that will cut beneath the Parc National du Mercantour, linking the southern Alps with Italy, to create a direct route from Barcelona to Milan. The project is estimated to cost 10 billion FF and will be completed around 2013.

Plans to construct a second inland road (55km) from Mandelieu-La Napoule, just south of Cannes, to La Turbie, just north of Monaco, were still being fought over in September 2000. The A58 project – fiercely opposed by the local residents – skims St-Paul de Vence by 500m. Steps have to be taken, however, to relieve the intense traffic load between Nice and Italy. Other options being battled include widening the existing autoroute (A8). The A58, if approved, would open in 2015. A final decision is not expected to be taken until after municipal elections in March 2001.

FLORA & FAUNA

Provence is blessed with a rich variety of flora and fauna: 2000 of the 4200 flora species known to France are found in the Parc National du Mercantour alone. Urbanisation, the encroachment of industries and an ever-expanding tourism infrastructure threaten the future of many fragile species outside protected areas.

Flora

About 1.2 million hectares of forest – 101,000 hectares of which is protected – covers 38% of the Provence-Alpes-Côte d'Azur region. The most heavily forested areas – mainly oak and pine – are in northeastern Provence and the Var (57% of which is forested).

Cork oak and chestnut trees are dominant in the Massif des Maures. Its coastal counterpart is sprinkled with the tall, upright *pin maritime* and, on its less sandy capes, the distinctive umbrella-shaped *pin parasol* and *pin Aleppo*. The *platane* (plane tree), which can be found on most village squares, is Provence's best-known tree, closely followed by the age-old *olivier* (olive tree), which the Greeks brought in the 4th century BC. The *palmier* (palm tree) arrived with the English in the 19th century, as did the sweet-smelling mimosa, eucalyptus and other succulents that were imported from Australia. Lemon and orange trees, typical only to the hot coast, have been grown since the Middle Ages.

Maquis is a form of vegetation whose low, dense shrubs provide many of the spices used in Provençal cooking. Rosemary, cistus (rock rose), laurel, thyme, myrtle, heather and strawberry bushes are among its floral patchwork. *Garrigue* grows on predominantly chalky soil and is also typified by aromatic Mediterranean plants such as juniper, broom and fern.

Fauna

The Camargue is home to over 400 land and water birds, including the kingfisher, bee-eater, stork, shelduck, white egret, purple heron and more than 160 migratory species. The Camargue's most spectacular resident is the greater or pink flamingo *(flamant rose)*. The low-lying delta is the only flamingo breeding site in France and is home to an estimated 10% of the world's greater flamingo population. Its native white horses and large bull population are the Camargue's other famed fauna.

Some 150 pairs of the pin-tailed sand grouse, typically a desert bird, have been recorded in neighbouring Crau. In Les Calanques, the endangered Bonnelli eagle can be occasionally seen – 14 couples have been recorded in Provence. Southern Port-Cros is home to 114 bird species and is an important stopover for migratory birds in autumn; seabirds include the puffin, ash-grey shearwater and yelkouan shearwater. The Parc National du Mercantour is likewise home to a dazzling array of bird species, including the golden and short-toed eagles and the buzzard. Its more northern, higher-altitude plains in the southern Alps

shelter marmot, mouflon and chamois (a mountain antelope), as well as the *bouquetin* (Alpine ibex), reintroduced into the region between 1987 and 1994. In lower-altitude wooded areas, the red and roe deer are common. Wild boar roam the entire park.

In all, France's 113 species of mammals (more than any other country in Europe), 30 kinds of amphibians, 36 varieties of reptiles and 72 kinds of fish are well represented in the region.

Endangered Species

Forest fires pose a great threat. The Hermann tortoise, once indigenous to the whole of Mediterranean Europe, is now found only in the maquis of the Massif des Maures (and Corsica). Its population in Les Calanques has already been wiped out by fires.

Fears that the flamingo was no longer breeding in the Camargue prompted ornithologists, with the assistance of the World Wildlife Fund (WWF) and a local salt producer, to construct an artificial island in 1970 – Étang du Fangassier – as a breeding safe haven for its flamingos.

Many birds, including vultures and storks, have all but disappeared from the skies and the number of Bonnelli eagles is down to about two dozen pairs (in the whole of France) from 670 only 20 years ago. Numerous animals still live in the wild thanks to a reintroduction programme based in certain national and regional parks. As part of an international programme instigated by the WWF, the vulture, extinct in the Alps in the 19th century, was reintro-

The endangered Hermann tortoise can be seen at Le Village des Tortues in Gonfaron.

duced into the Parc National du Mercantour in 1993. The vulture's wing span extends to 2.90m. It is expected to reproduce for the first time in 2003. Alpine creatures, such as the chamois and the larger bouquetin, were widely hunted until national parks such as Mercantour were established. The wolf, which disappeared from France in 1930, has recently been spotted in the Parc National du Mercantour. At least one pair were spotted in 1999 near Utelle.

National & Regional Parks

There are two national parks. The largest is the Parc National du Mercantour, created in 1979 to protect 68,500 hectares in northeastern Provence. Part of its eastern boundary adjoins Italy's Parco Naturale delle Alpi Marittime. The uninhabited park embraces seven valleys in the Alpes-Maritimes and Alpes de Haute-Provence departments: the Roya, Tinée, Verdon and Ubaye Valleys are the most spectacular. At its heart lies the Vallée des Merveilles (Valley of Marvels), an archaeological zone (12 sq km) at the foot of Mont Bégo (2873m), which protects Europe's most important collection of Bronze Age stone carvings. A 146,500 hectare peripheral zone – inhabited – surrounds the park. Mont Gélas (3143m) is the highest peak in the park. At 2802m, the Col de Restefond la Bonette is the highest *col* (mountain pass) in Europe.

The Parc National de Port-Cros – France's smallest national park and Europe's first marine park when created in 1963 – protects Provence's southernmost territory: Île de Port-Cros (650 hectares) and its surrounding waters (1800 hectares). Since 1979, neighbouring Île de Porquerolles has also been protected, following the park's creation of the Conservatoire Botanique National Méditerranéen (1254 hectares). The Port-Cros National Park also manages a 300-hectare slither of land on Cap Lardier, on the southern tip of the St-Tropez peninsula.

Large areas of the Lubéron (164,200 hectares) and the Camargue (85,000 hectares) have embraced *parcs naturel régionaux* (régional nature parks) since the 1970s. The Parc Naturel du Verdon (146,000 hectares) around the Gorges du Verdon was set up in 1997. In addition, Provence has two marine reserves – the Parc Marin de la Ciotat (60 hectares), near Marseilles; and the Parc Régional Marin de la Côte Bleue (70 hectares) around Cap Couronne, west of Carry-le-Rouet. The latter is managed by the Conservatoire du Littoral, with a Web site at www.conservatoire-du-littoral.fr, which also manages some 60 sites in the region and, as recently as October 1999, extended new pockets of adopted land around Cannes and L'Estaque. Numerous other areas, both inland (such as the Crau plain) and coastal (such as Les Calanques on the Marseilles coast) are preserved areas.

The Réserve Géologique de Haute-Provence (Haute-Provence Geological Reserve) covers an area of 190,000 hectares around Digne-les-Bains and is the largest protected area of its type in Europe. Its geological wonders include the fossilised skeleton of an ichthyosaurus dating from 185 million years ago and fossils from the tropical forests of 300 million years ago.

The region's highest mountain, Mont Ventoux, has been protected by the Réserve de Biosphère du Mont Ventoux since 1994.

GOVERNMENT & POLITICS

Provence-Alpes-Côte d'Azur is one of 22 *régions* (administrative regions) in France. It has an elected *conseil régional* (regional council) based in Marseilles, but its powers are limited.

The region is split into six *départements* (departments). This book covers five of them: Alpes de Haute-Provence (04), Alpes-Maritimes (06), Bouches du Rhône (13), Var (83) and Vaucluse (84). The town of Nîmes on the western banks of the River Rhône falls into the Gard department in the neighbouring Languedoc-Roussillon region. Departments are known by their two-digit code (listed above), included in postcodes and on the number plates of cars registered there. France (including Corsica) has 96 departments.

Each department has a *préfet* (prefect) – based in a *préfecture* (prefecture) – who represents the national government, and an

RÉGIONS & DÉPARTEMENTS

DÉPARTEMENTS
04 Alpes de Haute Provence
05 Hautes-Alpes
06 Alpes-Maritimes
07 Ardèche
13 Bouches du Rhône
26 Drôme
30 Gard
83 Var
84 Vaucluse

International Boundary
Régional Boundary
Départemental Boundary

MEDITERRANEAN SEA

elected *conseil général* (general council). There is a préfecture in Digne-les-Bains (04), Nice (06), Marseilles (13), Toulon (83) and Avignon (84).

ECONOMY

Provence is among France's wealthiest regions, thanks to its Mediterranean coastline and mild climate, which generate its primary income – tourism. An estimated nine million tourists (out of France's 68 million) visit the region each year. Almost 50% of visitors to the region are foreign, mainly from Italy, the UK, Germany, Eastern Europe, the USA or Scandinavia. Not surprisingly, 78.7% of the region's workforce is employed in the service industry.

The region's secondary income is generated by its booming technology sector, the stronghold of which is the Sophia Antipolis Science & Technology Park (technopole). Visit the Web site at www.saem-sophia-antipolis.fr. The technopole was established in 1969 by France Télécom as a launch pad for pilot testing advanced technology. In 2000 the 1164 companies at the park (510 of which were information technology companies, employing 13,350 people) employed over 20,000 people: 40% of those at managerial level are foreigners, which partly explains why the park is sometimes dubbed 'Europe's California'.

The annual revenue in 1999 of high-tech industries on the Côte d'Azur was US$3.2 billion. Despite the region's relatively high unemployment rate (15.9% in 1997, compared with 12.4% for the whole of France), continuing expansion at Sophia Antipolis ensures the region stays at the cutting edge of job creation and business growth – second only to Paris. For the first quarter of 2000 unemployment within the region was highest in Marseilles at 17.1% (compared with 10.1% for France).

The Grasse perfume industry employs 3000 people and has an annual turnover that represents 50% of country turnover and 7% of world turnover in the industry. Exports (mainly to Germany, the USA, the UK and Switzerland) account for 70% of trade.

Exports overall for the Provence-Côte d'Azur region rose, for the fourth consecutive year, to a record 76.9 billion FF in 1997 – 9% higher than in 1996. Annual imports in 1997 totalled 80.1 billion FF. Exports/ imports to/from Italy account for 16.3% and 13.3%, respectively, making Italy France's most important trading partner.

Among the region's largest employers, mainly in industrial Bouches du Rhône, are Eurocopter France at Marignane; the Sollac metallurgic works at Fos-sur-Mer; SGS Thomson microelectronic company in Rousset; and Elf, BP and the Naphtachimie chemical plant in Martigues. The Arsenal (military shipyard) at Toulon employs over 5000 workers.

Despite Provence's abundance of fresh fruit and vegetables, only 2.9% of its workforce is employed in agriculture. Almost 70% of France's rice production comes from Bouches du Rhône alone, while the region produces 30.6% of all France's tomatoes and 47.2% of its grapes. The region only grows 56% of France's olives but produces almost 75% of its olive oil.

The general economic trend in traditional, age-old industries such as bottle-stop making bodes less well. In the 1960s around 5000 tonnes of bark was stripped annually from cork oaks in the Massif des Maures, assuring a livelihood for local *bouchonniers* (cork makers). By the mid-1990s the annual yield had dropped to 500 tonnes and the bouchonnier had all but disappeared.

POPULATION & PEOPLE

The Provence-Alpes-Côte d'Azur region has a population of 4,507,706, 40.3% of whom live in crowded Bouches du Rhône, which has Marseilles at the helm. Over 60% of the population is packed in the two coastal departments of Bouches du Rhône (5087.5 sq km) and Alpes-Maritimes (4298.6 sq km).

Just 16% of the region's population inhabits the three interior departments, the most

rural, mountainous and largest being Alpes de Haute-Provence (6925.5 sq km) where 3.2% of people live. The rural population has increased by 25% since the 1970s, however, although its population density remains low – 20.6 people per sq km (compared to 356.9 per sq km in Bouches du Rhône).

Approximately 6% of the region's population is foreign (ie, not a French national), the exception being in Alpes-Maritimes where foreigners account for 8%. Of Provence's foreign population, 35% are European, 24.5% are Algerian, 16.2% are Moroccan, 14.8% are Tunisian and 1% are Turkish. Unlike in the late 1980s, which saw some 55,000 foreigners settle in Provence-Côte d'Azur, the foreign population remained static in the 1990s.

The south's Algerian community originates from the 1950s and early '60s when, as the French colonial empire collapsed, over one million French settlers returned to metropolitan France from Algeria, other parts of Africa and Indochina. At the same time, millions of non-French immigrants from these places were welcomed as much needed manpower during France's '30 glorious years' of fast economic growth. Such large-scale immigration was stopped by a 1974 law banning all new foreign workers.

ARTS
Dance

The *farandole* is a Provençal dance, particularly popular in and around Arles today. Dating from the Middle Ages, it is traditionally danced at the close of a village *fête* (festival). Young men and women take their partner by the hand or remain linked with a cord or handkerchief. The brisk jig is accompanied by a tambourine and a *galoubet* (small, shrill flute with three holes).

In the realm of classical ballet, France was in the forefront until the 19th century when the Russian Imperial Ballet became the centre for innovation. France's leading talent, Marius Petipa (1818–1910), a native of Marseilles, moved to St Petersburg in 1847 where he created masterpieces such as *La Bayadère* (1877) and *Le Lac des Cygnes* (Swan Lake, 1895). Petipa mixed French dance tradition with Slavic sensibilities. He choreographed more than 50 full-length ballets.

Literature

Middle Ages Lyric poems of courtly love composed by troubadours dominated medieval Provençal literature. This troubadour literature was written solely in *langue d'oc* (Occitan), from which Provençal evolved. Occitan was the language spoken in the court of the popes in Avignon and legend has it that Dante (1265–1321) almost wrote his *Divine Comedy* in Occitan.

Provençal life featured in the works of Italian poet Petrarch (1304–74), who was exiled to Avignon in 1327. Here he met the beautiful and elusive Laura to whom he dedicated his entire life's works. Petrarch lived in Fontaine de Vaucluse between 1337 and 1353 where he composed his song book *canzoniere* and wrote numerous poems and letters about local shepherds, fishermen he met on the banks of the River Sorgue and his pioneering ascent up Mont Ventoux.

Renaissance The great landmark in Provençal literature is the work of Bellaud de la Bellaudière (1533–88), a native of Grasse who wrote *Œuvres et Rîmes* in Occitan, a book of 160 sonnets drawing on influences by Petrarch and the French epic writer, Rabelais. In 1555, the philosopher and visionary writer Nostradamus (1503–66), a native of St-Rémy de Provence, published (in Latin) his prophetic *Centuries* in Salon de Provence where he lived until his death (from gout, as he had predicted). The papal authorities immediately banned the blasphemous work.

Classicism The 17th *grand siècle* (grand century) was the century of French classical writers. In Provence it yielded the *Noëls Provençaux*, a series of poems encapsulating a nativity scene, by Nicolas Saboly. Their pious tone, very occasionally humorous, was representative of the strait-laced fervour that dominated Baroque Provençal literature.

19th-Century Revival The 19th century witnessed a massive revival in Provençal literature, largely due to one man, Frédéric Mistral (1830–1914), the only minority-language writer to be awarded a Nobel Prize for Literature (1904). A native of Maillane, Mistral's passion for Provence, its culture, history and language, was first awakened by the Avignon tutor Joseph Roumanille (1818–91), who published *Li Margarideto* in 1847. In 1851 Mistral started work on what would become his most momentous work, *Mirèio*. Three years later Le Félibrige was founded by seven young Provençal poets who pledged to revive the Provençal language and codify its orthography. They published *L'Armana Prouvençau* (1859), the first journal to appear in Provençal.

Mistral's epic poem *Mirèio* – which tells the story of a beautiful girl who flees to Stes-Maries de la Mer in the Camargue when her parents forbid her to marry her true love, only to die of a broken heart on the beach – was published in 1859. A succession of poems followed, all written in Provençal and depicting a facet of Provence: *Les Îles d'Or* (1875), *Nerte* (1884), *La Reine Jeanne* (1890) and *Le Poème du Rhône* (1896). Between 1878 and 1886, Mistral's most influential work on Provençal culture was published, the monumental *Trésor du Félibrige*. This encyclopaedia-style work utilised parts of the first Provençal-French dictionary, published as early as 1840 in Digne-les-Bains. The 1890s saw Le Félibrige popularise his work with the opening of a museum in Arles (Musée Arletan) devoted to all things Provençal, and the publication of the less academic *L'Aïoli* journal.

Another outstanding Provençal writer was Nîmes-born Alphonse Daudet (1840–97), who spent a considerable amount of time with Mistral in Maillane. In Fontvieille, near Arles, he wrote *Lettres de Mon Moulin* (Letters from My Windmill, 1869). Daudet is best remembered for his comic novels that evoke the small Provençal town of Tarascon through the eyes of his anti-hero Tartarin. The *Tartarin de Tarascon* trilogy was published between 1872 and 1890.

Although not born in Provence, Parisian novelist Émile Zola (1840–1902) lived in

Aix-en-Provence, where he befriended Cézanne, from the age of three to 18. The aim of Zola, who claimed literary peer Flaubert as a precursor of his school of naturalism, was to convert novel writing from an art to a science by the application of experimentation. His theory may seem naive but his work (especially his *Les Rougon-Macquart* series) was powerful and innovative. He evokes Aix in *La Conquête de Plassans* (1874).

Edmond Rostand (1868–1918), author of the novel *Cyrano de Bergerac* (1897), was a native of Marseilles.

20th Century Early 20th-century Provençal literature is dominated by Provence's best-known writers who dedicated their life's work to depicting Provence, scarcely setting foot outside their homeland. Jean Giono (1895–1970), a native of Manosque, blended myth with reality in his novels, which remain a celebration of the Provençal Alps and the people who survive in this harsh landscape. Writer/film-maker Marcel Pagnol (1895–1974) spent his life in Aubagne, where he wrote numerous novels and screen adaptations (including Giono's *La Femme du Boulanger* in 1938). His realistic portraits of characters in rural Provence won him international acclaim. *L'Eau des Collines* (The Water of the Hills, 1963), a novel set in the interwar period and comprising *Jean de Florette* and *Manon des Sources*, is the best known.

The surrealism that played a vital force in French literature until WWII is evident in the works of Jean Cocteau (1889–1963), French poet, dramatist and film maker, for whom the Côte d'Azur proved to be extremely influential. Cocteau ran away from home to the coast at the age of 15, returned there again to settle from 1924 and was buried in Menton. His work, in his prose, on the cinematic set (including the allegorical *Orphée*, 1950) and in the chapels and other buildings he decorated (see Architecture later in this section), capture the spirit of the surrealist movement: the fascination with dreams, divination and all manifestations of 'the marvellous'. His best-known novel *Les Enfants Terribles* (1955) portrays the intellectual rebellion of the postwar era.

During WWII Roussillon in the Vaucluse served as a refuge to playwright Samuel Beckett, who arrived in the village in 1942 after fleeing Paris. He stayed until April 1945 and wrote *Watt* (not published until after *Waiting for Godot* in 1953) while he was here. Colette (1873–1954), who thoroughly enjoyed tweaking the nose of conventional readers with titillating novels that detailed the amorous exploits of such heroines as the schoolgirl Claudine, lived in St-Tropez from 1927 until 1938. *La Naissance du Jour* evokes an unspoilt St-Tropez before tourism took over.

After WWII existentialism, a significant literary movement, developed around Jean-Paul Sartre (1905–80), Simone de Beauvoir (1908–86) and Albert Camus (1913–60). The latter moved to Lourmarin in the Lubéron (where he is buried) in 1957, and started his unfinished autobiographical novel *Le Premier Homme* (The First Man). The same year, British novelist and travel writer Lawrence Durrell (1912–90) settled in Somières, near Nîmes, and dedicated the last 33 years of his literary career to writing about Provençal life. Other notable figures who settled in the region in the latter part of their careers include James Baldwin, Dirk Bogarde and Anthony Burgess.

Architecture

Prehistoric The earliest monuments in France were stone megaliths (huge standing stones) erected during the Neolithic period from about 4000 to 2400 BC. Although these prehistoric monuments are mainly found in northern France, dismantled remnants can be seen at Musée d'Archéologie Méditerranée in Marseilles; Monaco's Musée d'Anthropologie Préhistorique, from where it is possible to visit the Grottes de l'Observatoire; and the Musée de Digne at Digne-les-Bains. Numerous menhirs are evident in the Vallée des Merveilles and examples of the region's earliest habitats known as *bories* – beehive-shaped huts built from dry limestone – can be visited in the Villages des Bories near Gordes.

Gallo-Roman Southern France – particularly Provence – is *the* place to go in search of France's Gallo-Roman legacy. The Romans constructed an incredible number of public works throughout Roman Provincia from the 1st century BC, including aqueducts, fortifications, marketplaces, temples, amphitheatres, triumphal arches and bathhouses. They also established regular street grids at many settlements.

Testimony to Roman architectural brilliance includes the Pont du Gard (an aqueduct) between Nîmes and Avignon; the colossal amphitheatres at Nîmes and Arles; the theatres at Orange and Fréjus; the Maison Carrée (literally 'square house') in Nîmes; the public buildings in Vaison-la-Romaine; the excavated temples at Glanum; and the triumphal arches at Orange and Carpentras. See the regional chapters for details.

Dark Ages Although quite a few churches were built during the Merovingian and Carolingian periods (5th to 10th century), very little remains of them. However, fine traces of churches from this period are reflected in the octagonal, 5th-century baptistry at Fréjus. The earliest Christian relics, dating from the 2nd to 4th centuries, can be seen at the Musée du Pays Brignolais in Brignoles, Fréjus' Musée Archéologique and the Musée d'Archéologique d'Arles.

The region has numerous examples of *villages perchés* (hill-top villages) that took root in Provence from the 10th century. Villagers from the plains built new villages on top of rocky crags as a defence against Saracen attacks. Economics forced many to move back to the plains in the 19th and 20th centuries.

Romanesque A religious revival in the 11th century led to the construction of a large number of Romanesque churches, so-called because their architects adopted many architectural elements (eg, vaulting) from Gallo-Roman buildings. Romanesque buildings typically have round arches, heavy walls whose few windows let in very little light, and a lack of ornamentation bordering on the austere. The most famous examples of this era, considered typical of the high Romanesque period, are the trio of abbeys built by the Cistercian order at Sénanque (1148), Le Thoronet (1160) and Silvacane (1175).

The majestic but sober Chartreuse de la Verne (1170), the older monastery (1073) on Île St-Honorat, and the church at Stes-Maries de la Mer are examples of the fortress-like sacred buildings that also characterised this era. Chateaux – such as Château Grimaldi in Antibes – likewise tended to be sturdy, heavily fortified structures that afforded few luxuries to their inhabitants. The Romanesque style remained popular until as late as the 14th century in Provence: the exceptional dimensions of the cathedral at Digne-les-Bains (1200–1330) are typical of this late Provençal-Romanesque style.

Gothic Typical Gothic structures are characterised by ribbed vaults carved with great precision, pointed arches, slender verticals, chapels (often built by rich people or guilds) along the nave and chancel, refined decoration and large stained-glass windows. The Gothic style, which emerged in the mid-12th century in northern France, only made its mark on Provençal architecture in the 14th and 15th centuries. The most important examples of Gothic architecture in Provence are the Palais des Papes (Papal Palace) in Avignon, the Val de Bénédiction Charterhouse in Villeneuve-lès-Avignon and the Cathédrale St-Siffrein in Carpentras.

Frescoes emerged at the end of the Gothic era as an important means of rich interior decoration. Although frescoes are evident in churches such as Nice's Église St-Martin-St-Augustin and the Musée Franciscain in Cimiez, it was the small churches, tucked in the Niçois hinterland and as far north as the southern Alps, that benefited most from these treasured adornments. The interior of the Chapelle Notre Dame des Fontaines in the Vallée de la Roya is a classic example (see Painting later in this chapter).

Provence was scarcely touched by the French Renaissance period – an architectural style that began in France in the late 15th century and set out to realise a 'rebirth' of classical Greek and Roman culture. The 16th century saw the emergence of citadel architect, Sébastien Le Prestre de Vauban (1633–1707), as a force to be reckoned with. His works in Provence included the enlargement of the Fort Carré in Antibes with his signature star-shaped walls, the fortification of the hill-top village of Entrevaux, and constructions at Toulon port and Sisteron.

Baroque During the Baroque period, which lasted from the end of the 16th century to the late 18th century, painting, sculpture and classical architecture were integrated to create structures and interiors of great subtlety, refinement and elegance. The Chapelle de la Miséricorde in Nice and Menton's Italianate Église St-Michel are considered southern France's grandest Baroque churches. Marseilles' Centre de la Vieille Charité (1671–1749) is built around a beautiful Baroque-domed chapel designed by Pierre Puget (see Sculpture later in this section).

Neoclassical This architectural style emerged around 1740 and remained popular until well into the 19th century. Neoclassicism grew out of a renewed interest in classical forms; more profoundly, a search for order, reason and serenity through the adoption of the forms and conventions of Graeco-Roman antiquity: columns, simple geometric forms and traditional ornamentation.

Neoclassicism came into its own under Napoleon III, who used it extensively for monumental architecture intended to embody the grandeur of imperial France. Nice's imposing Justice Palace and Palais Masséna, and Toulon's Église St-Louis are examples. The true showcase of this era, however, is Monaco's Monte Carlo Casino (1878) and adjoining opera house (1879), both designed by French architect Charles Garnier (1825–98) and ranked among the Second Empire's finest achievements. Garnier, together with Gustave Eiffel (1832–1923), who lived in Beaulieu-sur-Mer, designed the Observatoire de Nice (1887).

Aix-en-Provence's public fountains and *hôtels particuliers* (large and elegant private residences) also date from this period; as do Provence's ornate wrought-iron *campaniles* – originally a feature of rural Provençal architecture – that top most church bell towers in cities and towns.

Eclecticism Alongside neoclassicism, the *belle epoque* heralded a more fantastical eclecticism that would last into the early 20th century. Trademarks included anything and everything from decorative stucco friezes, trompe l'œil paintings and glittering wall mosaics, to brightly coloured domed roofs, Moorish minarets and Turkish towers. In short, anything went. Nice is exceptionally well endowed with these chocolate-box creations: the Hôtel Négresco (1906), the Crédit Lyonnais Bank (1882) and the very pink Château de l'Anglais (1859) are all buoyant reflections of this beautiful age. In Barcelonnette, the Château des Magnans is Mexican-inspired.

The stark, concrete and glass Villa Noailles (1923) in Hyères is an expression of the cubist movement that gained momentum in the interwar period. Examples of surrealist interiors designed by Jean Cocteau (see Literature earlier), who lived in Menton at this time, include the Salles des Mariages (1957) inside Menton town hall, Chapelle de St-Pierre (1959) in Villefranche-sur-Mer and the magnificent amphitheatre on Cap d'Ail.

Post-WWII Architecture France's most celebrated 20th-century architect, Le Corbusier (1887–1965), had a villa and studio on Cap Martin where, in 1965, he suffered a fatal heart attack while swimming in the sea. He is buried in the Roquebrune-Cap Martin cemetery. A radical modernist, Le Corbusier tried to adapt buildings to their functions in industrialised society without ignoring the human element. His most influential achievement was his creation of the Cité Radieuse development – a low-cost housing project for 1600 inhabitants – in Marseilles, built between 1946 and 1952. Le Corbusier arranged buildings with related functions in a circular formation and constructed them in standard sizes based on the proportions of the human form. The resultant

Unité d'Habitation was considered a coup by architects worldwide, who flocked to Marseilles to see the apartment block on stilts.

The Fondation Vasarely in Aix-en-Provence, designed by Victor Vasarely (1908–97), was also considered an architectural coup when unveiled in 1976. Its 14 giant monumental hexagons reflected what he had already achieved in art: the creation of optical illusion and changing perspective through the juxtaposition of geometrical shapes and colours. Vasarely also designed the town hall in La Seyne-sur-Mer, near Toulon. The single most influential period in Vasarely's career was spent in Gordes. He was dubbed 'the father of Op Art'.

Steel meets glass at the modern Carrée d'Art (1993) in Nîmes. The reflective 'Square of Art' was designed by British architect Sir Norman Foster (born 1935), responsible for the seminal Hong Kong and Shanghai Bank building in Hong Kong. Nîmes, which prides itself as the pioneer of modern design in southern France, also sports a marble *abribus* (bus stop) on ave Carnot designed by Philippe Starck (born 1949), a contemporary French designer best known for his furniture. Starck also redesigned Nîmes' coat of arms and, more recently, worked with French chef Alain Ducasse to design the interior of the upmarket Monaco restaurant, Bar & Bœuf.

Other bold examples of modern architecture include Monaco's monumental glass-and-steel Grimaldi Forum (2000), two-thirds of which is built beneath sea level; Nice's Musée d'Art Moderne et d'Art Contemporain (1990), marketed as the Louvre of the south; and Matisse's Chapelle du Rosaire (1943–51) in Vence whose exterior reflects a traditional Provençal cottage. Port Grimaud (1969), a holiday village, was the conception of Francis Spoerry who went on to design Port Liberty in New York. The truly outstanding Fondation Maeght (1964) in St-Paul de Vence is considered the epitome of contemporary Provençal architecture.

Painting
To the 16th Century Sculpture and stained glass, rather than paintings, were the main adornments of the medieval Gothic churches, in part because the many windows left little wall space. The Sienese, French and Spanish artists working at the papal court in Avignon in the 14th century, however, created an influential style of mural painting, examples of which can be seen in the city's Palais des Papes.

While the rest of France found itself preoccupied with the Hundred Years' War, art flourished in the Comté de Nice (County of Nice), where the School of Nice emerged, led by Louis Bréa. Bréa, exalted as the 'Fra Angelico Provençal', created the burgundy colour known as *rouge bréa*. His works can be seen in Cimiez (Nice) and Menton's Palais Carnolès. This school of primitive painters worked notably for the Penitent Brotherhoods, which explains why their works are in rural chapels once used as a place of pilgrimage.

17th & 18th Centuries Blindman's bluff, stolen kisses and other such courtly frivolities were the subject matter of the French school of artists that emerged in the late 17th and early 18th centuries during the Enlightenment. Avignon-born Joseph Vernet (1714–89) was among the most influential, leaving behind him a series of 15 landscapes depicting French ports. The series, commissioned by Louis XV, included *La Ville et la Rade de Toulon* (1756). Rococo influences played on the landscapes of Jean-Honoré Fragonard (1732–1806), whose playful scenes immortalised his native Grasse and captured the frivolity of the rococo spirit. The elevated works of Nice-born Carle van Loo (1705–65) represented rococo's more serious 'grand style'. Works by these artists are displayed in the Musée des Beaux-Arts Jules Chéret in Nice; the Musée des Beaux-Arts, Marseilles; Avignon's Musée Calvet; Grasse's Musée Fragonard; and the Musée Granet, Aix-en-Provence.

19th Century François Marius Granet (1775–1849), who was born and died in Aix-en-Provence, was a pupil of the influential artist Jacques Louis David. Although less celebrated than his teacher, Granet displayed a strong empathy with nature in his watercolours, which would become the trademark of Provençal painters at this time. Works by both are in the Musée Granet, Aix-en-Provence.

Landscape painting evolved further under the Barbizon School. Jean-François Millet took many of his subjects from peasant life and had a strong influence on Van Gogh. Millet anticipated the realist programme of Gustave Courbet (1819–77), a prominent member of the Paris Commune, who made frequent trips to southern France. Among his most fervent pupils was Provençal realist Paul Guigou (1834–71), a native of Villars in the Vaucluse, who painted numerous canvases of the Durance plains over-drenched in bright sunlight. *Deux Lavandières devant la Ste-Victoire* (Two Washing Women in front of Mont Ste-Victoire) painted by Guigou near Aix-en-Provence in 1986, is in the Musée Grobet-Labadié, Marseilles.

It was Provence's astonishing clarity and intensity of light that drew the impressionists to the region. Impressionism, initially a term of derision, was taken from the title of an experimental painting by Claude Monet in 1874, *Impression: Soleil Levant* (Impression: Sunrise). Monet was the leading figure of the school, which counted among its members Alfred Sisley, Camille Pissarro, Berthe Morisot and Pierre-Auguste Renoir (1841–1919). Renoir lived in Cagnes-sur-Mer on the French Riviera from 1903 until his death. Although he broke with the movement in his later career, as an impressionist his main aim was to capture fleeting light effects, and light came to dominate the content of his paintings. Many are displayed in the Musée Renoir (his former home and studio) in Cagnes-sur-Mer. Monet painted the same

Art Portfolio

With its designer chapels, cutting-edge architecture and avant-garde art museums, the region is practically a living art museum. Its portfolio in a nutshell looks like this:

18th- to 20th-Century Art Collections

Musée Granet (Aix-en-Provence); Musée Réattu (Arles); Musée Calvet (Avignon); Centre de la Vieille Charité (Marseilles); Musée des Arts Asiatiques, Musée International d'Art Naïf Anatole Jakovsky & Musée Masséna (Nice); Musée des Beaux-Arts (Nice, Menton & Marseilles); Musée de l'Annonciade (St-Tropez)

One-Man Shows

Musée National Message Biblique **Marc Chagall** (Nice); Musée **Jean Cocteau** (Menton); Musée **Matisse** (Nice); Musée National **Fernand Léger** (Biot); Musée **Renoir** (Cagnes-sur-Mer); Musée **Picasso** (Antibes); Musée National **Picasso** (Vallauris); Fondation **Vasarely** (Aix-en-Provence)

Designer Chapels

Chapelle de la Congrégation by **Carzou** (Manosque); Chapelle Notre Dame de Jérusalem (Fréjus) & Chapelle de St-Pierre (Menton) by **Cocteau**; Chapelle du Rosaire by **Matisse** (Vence); Chapelle La Guerre et La Paix by **Picasso** (Vallauris)

Contemporary Art & Installations

Musée d'Art Méditerranéen Moderne (Cagnes-sur-Mer); Crestet Centre d'Art (Crestet); Villa Noailles (Hyères); Musée d'Art Contemporain (Marseilles); Espace de l'Art Concret (Mouans-Sartoux); Fondation d'Art de la Napoule (Mandelieu-La Napoule); Grimaldi Forum (Monaco); Musée d'Art Moderne et d'Art Contemporain (Nice); Carré d'Art (Nîmes); Fondation Maeght & Galerie Guy Pieters (St-Paul de Vence) subjects – cathedrals, haystacks, trees, water lilies – many times to show the transient effect of light at different times of day.

Paul Cézanne (1839–1906) is Provence's best-known artist. He was born (and also died) in Aix-en-Provence, and is celebrated for his still-life and landscape works that depict his native land. Cézanne painted numerous canvases in and around Aix, particularly of Mont St-Victoire. *Les Baigneuses* (The Bathers) is in Aix's Musée Granet. Southern France was also immortalised on canvas by Paul Gauguin (1848–1904), who spent much time during the late 19th century in Arles. Both he and Cézanne are usually referred to as post-impressionists, something of a catch-all word for the diverse styles that flowed from impressionism.

When in Arles, Gauguin worked for a time with the Dutch artist Vincent van Gogh (1854–90), who spent most of his painting life in Paris and Arles. A brilliant and innovative artist, Van Gogh produced haunting self-portraits and landscapes, in which colour assumes an expressive and emotive quality. Unfortunately, Van Gogh's talent was largely unrecognised during his lifetime. He was confined to an asylum in St-Rémy de Provence and eventually committed suicide. He painted his most famous works – *Sunflowers* and *Van Gogh's Chair* (1888) – in Arles. Van Gogh's later technique, exhibited in works dating from his St-Rémy period such as *Starry Night* and *Olive Trees* (1889), foreshadowed pointillism.

Pointillism was developed by Georges Seurat (1859–91), who applied paint in small dots or with uniform brush strokes of unmixed colour, producing fine mosaics of warm and cool tones. His most devout pupil was Paul Signac (1863–1935), who settled in St-Tropez from 1892 onwards. Among his many guests to the small fishing village was Pierre Bonnard (1867–1947), who lived in neighbouring Le Cannet. Part of the Musée de l'Annonciade in St-Tropez is devoted to pointillist works and includes *Étude pour le Chenal de Gravelines* (Study for the Channel at Gravelines) painted by Seurat in 1890 as well as numerous works by Signac, most of which depict the coastal towns of St-Tropez or Marseilles.

20th Century French painting in the 20th century has a bewildering diversity of styles, two of which are particularly significant: Fauvism and cubism. Two of their leading exponents, Matisse (Fauvism) and Picasso (cubism), spent their most creative years in Provence, where they contributed enormously to the development of the two movements.

Fauvism took its name from the slur of a critic who compared the exhibitors at the 1905 Salon d'Automne in Paris with *fauves* (wildcats) because of their radical use of intensely bright colours. Among these 'wild' painters was Henri Matisse who spent a considerable amount of time in the region, lapping up the sunlight and vivacity of the coast around in and Nice. While in St-Tropez with Signac, he started preliminary sketches that would produce *Luxe, Calme et Volupté* (Luxury, Calm and Tranquillity). The signature uniform brush strokes of pointillism were still evident, but were intermingled with irregular splashes of violent colour. Matisse's consequent painting, *La Gitane* (1906) is considered the embodiment of Fauvist principles. It is displayed in St-Tropez's Musée de l'Annonciade. Works such as *Hôtel-Hôtel* by Provençal Fauvist Auguste Chabaud (1882–1955), from Nîmes, can likewise be viewed here.

Cubism was effectively launched in 1907 by the Spanish prodigy Pablo Picasso (1881–1973), for whom Provence had a tremendous importance; he spent most of his creative life there. As demonstrated in his pioneering *Les Demoiselles d'Avignon*, cubism deconstructed the subject into a system of intersecting planes and presented various aspects of it simultaneously. The collage, incorporating bits of cloth, wood, string, newspaper and anything lying around, was a cubist speciality. Picasso went on to experiment (and succeed) with other mediums and concepts, but his cubist works remain highly popular.

Provence continued to inspire the leading artists of various movements. After WWI,

MICK WELDON

Picasso, famed for his cubist works of art, spent many productive years in Provence.

the School of Paris was formed by a group of expressionists, mostly foreign, such as Marc Chagall (1887–1985), who was born in Vitebsk (in present-day Belarus) and moved to France in 1922. His pictures combine fantasy and folklore, many of these from the Old Testament. Chagall spent the last few years of his life in St-Paul de Vence where he is buried. The largest collection of his works is in Nice. Many of Chagall's later works were influenced by the surrealists, most active in the interwar period. Surrealism attempted to reunite the conscious and unconscious realms, to permeate everyday life with fantasies and dreams. Naive art, common to the 1930s and sometimes known as primitive art, offered a simple but precise presentation of ordinary scenes that very occasionally veered towards surrealism.

With the onset of WWII many artists left France's sunny south, and although some returned after the war, the region never regained its old magnetism. Picasso moved permanently to the Côte d'Azur, settling first in Golfe-Juan, then Vallauris and finally Mougins, where he died. In 1946 he set up his studio in Antibes' Château Grimaldi, the works which he completed here being exhibited in the Musée Picasso inside the chateau. Among his other accomplishments was the interior decoration of the chapel in Vallauris (also a museum today).

The other great artist of this period was undoubtedly Matisse (1869–1954), who resided in Nice from 1917 until his death – with the exception of the WWII period when he took refuge in nearby Vence. He also decorated a chapel after WWII. His bold and colourful works culminated in his familiar blue and white cut-out montages, which he completed in the early 1950s prior to his death. Works representing his whole career can be seen at the Musée Matisse, Nice.

In the wake of Matisse came the French new realism movement (all represented in the Musée d'Art Moderne et d'Art Contemporain, Nice). The 1960s new realists – led by Provençal artists such as Arman, Yves Klein and César (see Sculpture later in this section) – rejected the abstraction of the postwar years and turned their attentions instead to 'modern nature'. Art was generated from recycled trash, used crockery, crushed cars and scrap metal. In 1960, Nice-born Klein (1928–1962) produced *Anthropométrie de l'Époque Bleue*, a series of blue imprints made by sweetly persuading two naked women (covered from head to toe in blue paint) to roll around on a white canvas – in front of an orchestra of violins and a sombre-faced audience in evening dress. Arman, also born in Nice in 1928, became known for his trash-can portraits, made by framing the litter found in the subject's trash bin. Another influential realist from the School of Nice was Martial Rayasse, born in Golfe-Juan in 1936, and renowned for pioneering the use of neon in contemporary art. Most notable is his 1964 portrait of *Nissa Bella* (Beautiful Nice), which incorporates a flashing blue heart on a human face.

Another artist to make his mark on a region which profoundly influenced his work was Hungarian-born Victor Vasarely (1908–97). In Gordes from 1948, the avant-gardist turned his attention to geometrical forms, juxtaposed in contrasting colours to create shifting perspectives. Forty-two works by Vasarely are displayed in the Fondation Vasarely – designed and funded by the artist himself (see Architecture earlier in this section) – in Aix-en-Provence.

The supports-surfaces movement that took root in the 1970s focused on deconstructing the traditional concept of a painting and transforming one of its structural components – such as the frame or canvas – into a work of art instead. The Groupe 70, specific to Nice, expressed an intellectual agitation, typical to Vivien Isnard's 1987 *Sans Titre* (Without Title) and Louis Chacallis' *Tension* (1978). Urban culture was the energising force behind free figuration in the 1980s.

Sculpture

At the end of the 11th century, sculptors decorated the portals, capitals, altars and fonts of Romanesque churches, illustrating Bible stories and the lives of the saints for the illiterate. Two centuries later, when the cathedral became the centre of monumental building, sculpture spread from the central portal to the whole facade, whose brightly painted and carved surface offered a symbolic summary of Christian doctrine. In the 17th century, Marseilles-born sculptor, Pierre Puget (1620–94), made his mark in France. He introduced the idea of adorning ship sterns with elaborate ornamentation, and was among the first to experiment with atlantes – the use of figures of men instead of columns to support an entablature. The anguished figures that support the balcony of honour at the old city hall on quai Constradt in Toulon is a celebrated example. The Musée des Beaux-Arts in Marseilles has a large collection of his works.

Marseilles also produced César Baldaccini (known as César), one of the most important French sculptors of the 20th century. César (1921–98) was greatly inspired by Michelangelo (a replica of his David stands in Marseilles today) and Picasso (one of the first to use scrap metal as a medium). His work after WWII used wrought-iron and scrap metal to create a series of imaginary insects and animals. Later he graduated to pliable plastics. In 1960 he became the first artist to use motorised vehicles (notably, crushed cars) as an artistic medium. Between 1960 and 1989 he compressed 23 cars, some of which are displayed in the Musée d'Art Moderne et d'Art Contemporain, Nice. His work can be also seen in Marseilles. Arguably his best-known work is the little statue handed to actors at the Césars (named after him), the French cinema awards that date from 1976 and are equivalent to Hollywood's Oscars.

Cinema

Beginnings to WWII With its spectacular light and subtle shadows, it is not surprising that Provence was as inspirational to cinema as it was to art. Cinematographic pioneers, the Lumière brothers – who invented 'moving pictures' – made their earliest films on the Côte d'Azur. The world's first motion picture – a series of two-minute reels – was shown for the first time in the Château Lumière, a property owned by their father in La Ciotat, in September 1895. The film, entitled *L'Arrivée d'un Train en Gare de La Ciotat* (The Arrival of a Train at La Ciotat Station), made the audience jump out of their seats as the steam train rocketed towards them. It only made its debut in Paris three months later. Théâtre Eden in La Ciotat is the world's oldest movie house. Auguste and Louis Lumière went on to discover colour photography.

Nice was catapulted to stardom in the 1920s. The Victorine film studios, which Serge Sandberg had established in 1920, were sold for US$5 million to Hollywood director Rex Ingram in 1925. He transformed the studios almost overnight into the hub of European film making, welcoming avant-garde directors such as the intensely productive Jean Renoir, son of the famous artist, to his studios. These were innovative times for film in France.

A big name at this time was the Aubagne-born, Provençal writer Marcel Pagnol, whose film career kicked off in 1931 with *Marius*, the first part of his legendary *Fanny* trilogy starring Raimu (see Silver-Screen Heroes later in this section) and portraying prewar Marseilles. Pagnol filmed *La Femme du*

Boulanger (The Baker's Wife, 1938) in the hill-top village of Castellet. Throughout his career, he stuck to depicting what he knew best – Provence and its ordinary people.

New Wave Nice's film industry stagnated after WWII until the 1950s, when a large group of new directors burst onto the scene with a new genre: *nouvelle vague* (new wave). With small budgets, sometimes self-financed, no extravagant sets or big-name stars, they made films such as *Et Dieu Créa la Femme* (And God Created Woman, 1956), which brought sudden stardom to Brigitte Bardot, the little fishing village of St-Tropez and the young director Roger Vadim. The film, which examined the amorality of modern youth, received international acclaim. For a list of films shot in the region by foreign directors at this time, see Film in the Facts for the Visitor chapter.

The new wave lost its experimental edge in the mid-1970s: just two films were made at the Victorine studios in 1976, followed by a paltry three in 1977. The studios have since produced television commercials.

Silver-Screen Heroes Film stars congregate on the Côte d'Azur once a year for an orgy of glitz and glamour at the Cannes International Film Festival *(Festival International du Film)*, the French film industry's main annual event (see the boxed text 'Starring at Cannes' in the Cannes Area chapter).

Provence produced one of France's earliest screen heroes – Raimu. The great comic actor was born in Toulon as Jules Auguste César Muraire (1883–1946). He is best remembered for his colourful portrayal of Provençal characters, most notably in Pagnol's early *Fanny* trilogy, *La Femme du Boulanger* and later *La Fille du Puisatier* (1940). In the latter, Raimu starred with Fernandel (1903–71), France's other legendary comic, known as 'Horseface' because of his inimitable grin. Horseface was an honorary citizen of Carry-le-Rouet, where he spent most summers.

The indisputable star of the 1950s and '60s was sexy Brigitte Bardot, who made her first appearance at Cannes in 1953, aged 18 and already married to film director Roger Vadim who would later make her a star on screen. Bardot set up home in St-Tropez. She was the first in a long long line of cinema celebrities to grace the southern French coast with their presence.

Stars galore gathered in Vallauris in October 1998 to mourn the death of French silver-screen hero Jean Marais (1914–98), who lived near Cannes most of his life. The beautiful, blonde-haired actor was best known for his lead role in Jean Cocteau's *La Belle et la Bête* (Beauty and the Beast, 1946), *Orphée* (Orpheus, 1950) and more recently as Prospero in the 1990s adaptation of Shakespeare's *The Tempest*. Marais and Cocteau (see Literature – 20th century earlier in this section) met in 1937 and were lovers until Cocteau's death in 1963.

SOCIETY & CONDUCT

While Parisians systematically slam every city other than their own, so people in Provence perceive the rest of France – cold northern capital included – as far less attractive than their own sun-lit Provence. Provence, through their rose-coloured spectacles, is bathed in a golden glow year round. Come the big chill of the mistral in autumn and winter, true Provençaux are barely bitten by the unbearable cold, unlike their foreign neighbours who shut the shutters tight, curl up by the fire – and still shiver in their sleep. Unless you're born and bred in Provence, you have little hope of ever adjusting to the mistral's menacing climes, as any true Provençaux will very proudly point out.

Provençaux are staunchly proud of their natural treasures and rich cultural heritage. Most have an equally staunch loyalty to the hamlet, village, town or city where they live. The rough and tumble Marseillais are famed throughout France for their blatant exaggerations and imaginative fancies – such as the tale about the sardine that blocked Marseilles port. The Niçois by contrast are more Latin in outlook and temperament, sharing a common zest for the good life with their Italian neighbours. Flash Monagésques in Monaco tend to drip

What a Menace

Folklore claims it drives people crazy. Its namesake, Provençal poet Frédéric Mistral, cursed it; while peasants in their dried-out fields dubbed the damaging wind *mange fange* (*manjo fango* in Provençal), meaning 'mud eater'.

The mistral (*mistrau* in Provençal) is a cold, dry north-westerly wind that whips across Provence for several days at a time. Its furious gusts, reaching over 100km/h, destroy crops, rip off roofs, dry the land and drive tempers round the bend. It chills the bones for 100 days a year and is at its fiercest in winter and spring.

The mistral's intense and relentless rage is caused by high atmospheric pressure over central France, between the Alps and the Pyrénées, which is then blown southwards through the funnel of the narrow Rhône Valley to an area of low-pressure over the Mediterranean Sea. On the upside, skies are blue and clear of clouds when the mistral is in town. A soaking of rain in July followed by a healthy dose of sun and mistral in August, followed by more showers and more mistral in early September works wonders for the grape harvest. The mistral has 31 siblings.

with gold and hair cream, while St-Tropez's colourful community is clearly split between bronzed-year-round glamour queens and reborn hippies – both ageless. Wild gesticulations, passionate cheek kissing and fervent hand-shaking are an integral part of Provençal daily life, regardless of geographical location.

Food is an extremely serious matter. Many people live, dream and sleep food – a topic that miraculously wangles its way in to the most unrelated of conversations. Offences warranting social ostracism include expressing even a mild dislike for a traditional culinary dish such as *pieds et paquets* (sheep tripe) or *testicules de mouton* (sheep testicles); declining a *dégustation* (wine-tasting) session, regardless of time, day or circumstance; or failing to show as enthusiastic an interest in food as your next-door neighbour.

Definite dining dos and don'ts include never *ever* asking for ice cubes to drop into warm wine, or ketchup/mayonnaise to douse over food. When tasting wine, don't just sniff, sip, swallow or spit (common to a true dégustation), but mimic the series of facial contortions required. If invited to lunch, don't make plans for the afternoon; lunch will last at least three hours and leave you feeling so blissfully full that it is doubtful you will be able to move. Skipping lunch (or indeed any meal) is seen as the ultimate sin, while a quick snack standing up is severely frowned upon.

Handy little tricks to make friends quickly include always saying 'Bonjour, monsieur/madame/mademoiselle' with a smile when you sail into a shop/cafe/restaurant – or saying it with flowers when visiting someone's home. Never buy/offer chrysanthemums unless you intend laying them on a gravestone. Money, time and politics are all taboo subjects.

When travelling in Monaco, don't mention the revolution – and don't refer to Monaco as part of France. Most Monagésques will explain that their principality is a distinctly separate country to France with its own strong history, culture and traditions. Listen to what they have to say and respect their patch of land.

Nude bathing on some beaches is forbidden; for more information see Legal Matters in the Facts for the Visitor chapter.

Rules of the forest include sticking to marked tracks and paths, not littering, not camping, not smoking, and not lighting camp fires.

RELIGION

Countrywide, 80% of people identify themselves as Catholic, although few ever attend church. Catholicism is the official state religion in neighbouring Monaco, which marks a number of religious feasts with public holidays (see Public Holidays & Special Events in the Facts for the Visitor chapter). Protestants account for less than 2% of today's population.

Many of France's four to five million nominally Muslim residents live in the south of France, comprising the second-largest religious group. France's Jewish community numbers 650,000, Europe's largest. There are synagogues in Avignon, Marseilles, Cavaillon and Carpentras, a traditional Jewish stronghold with just 100 Jewish families today.

LANGUAGE

French, the mother tongue of 75 million people worldwide, is one of the great languages of the world, a language of society, culture and diplomacy. Being able to speak some French will broaden your travel experience, ensure you are treated with appreciation and – in rural Haute-Provence, where tourism has not yet developed enough to persuade local people in service industries to speak English – ensure a smooth ride around the region. On the coast, practically everyone you are likely to need to speak to speaks basic English (and, in many cases, a rash of other European languages too).

For more information on the French language, some useful words and phrases and a food glossary, see the Language chapter at the back of the book.

Provençal

Despite the bilingual town signs that greet tourists when they enter most towns and villages, the region's traditional mother tongue – Provençal – is scarcely heard on the street or in the home. Just a handful of older people in rural Provence (Prouvènço) keep alive the rich lyrics and poetic language of their ancestors. In this book, we list Provençal names of towns in parenthesis after the first mention of its French counterpart.

Provençal (*prouvençau* in Provençal) is a dialect of *langue d'oc* (Occitan), the traditional language of southern France. Its grammar is closer to Catalan and Spanish than to French. In the grand age of courtly love between the 12th and 14th centuries, Provençal was the literary language of France and northern Spain and even used as far afield as Italy. Medieval troubadours and poets created melodies and poems motivated by the ideal of courtly love, and Provençal blossomed.

The 19th century witnessed a revival of Provençal after its rapid displacement by *langue d'oïl*, the language of northern France, which originated from the vernacular Latin spoken by the Gallo-Romans and gave birth to modern French (*francés* in Provençal). The revival was spearheaded by Vaucluse poet Frédéric Mistral (see Literature earlier), whose works in Provençal landed him the Nobel Prize for Literature in 1904.

Le Félibrige – a literary society created by Mistral in 1854 to safeguard Provençal literature, culture and identity – remains active today from its contemporary base at Aix-Marseilles University (☎ 04 42 26 23 41, ℮ info@felibrige.com), 8 bis ave Jules Ferry, 13100 Aix-en-Provence. It has a Web site at www.felibrige.com.

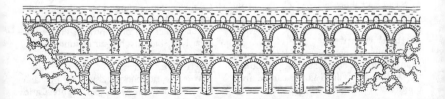

Facts for the Visitor

HIGHLIGHTS

There is a wealth of wonderful places to go to and things to see in Provence and the Côte d'Azur. See the boxed text 'Kidding Around' later in this chapter for handy hints on how to win the heart of a howling child.

Art & Architecture

Precious architectural treasures include the **Roman relics** at Pont du Gard, Orange, Arles, Nîmes and St-Rémy de Provence; the 12th-century **Romanesque abbeys** of Sénanque, Silvacane and Thoronet; the walled city of **Aigues-Mortes**; Avignon's Gothic **Palais des Papes**; Aix-en-Provence's **fountains** and hôtels particuliers; Nice's *belle epoque* **follies** and **fantasies**; the world-renowned **Musée Océanographique** in Monaco (also the region's most visited museum); the **Matisse chapel** in Vence; **Villa Grecque Kérylos** in Beaulieu-sur-Mer; Le Corbusier's **Cité Radieuse** in Marseilles; and Nîmes' **Carrée d'Art**.

Outstanding art museums include **Musée de l'Annonciade** (St-Tropez), the **Picasso** museums (Antibes and Vallauris), **Fondation Vasarely** (Aix-en-Provence), **Fondation Maeght** (St-Paul de Vence) and the Museums of Modern & Contemporary Art in Nice and Marseilles.

Villages

Hill-top villages *(villages perchés)* firmly placed on the tourist trail include Les Baux de Provence, Gordes, Bonnieux, Ménerbes, Lacoste, Èze and St-Paul de Vence. Calm, tranquil and comparatively bare of commercialism (so far) are the lovely little villages tucked in the Niçois hinterland, north of Nice; and those west of Grasse in the northern Var.

Natural Wonders

Awe-inspiring natural wonders include **Mont Ventoux's** barren summit; the **Gorges de Dalius**, a fabulous gorge carved from burgundy coloured rock in the Haute Vallée du Var; the **Pénitents des Mées**, a line-up of larger-than-life stone figurines in the Vallée de la Durance; and the dramatic breathtaking rock formations carved by the elements from vivid ochre at **Rustrel's Colerado Provençal** in the Lubéron.

The chestnut-forested **Massif des Maures**, the red-rocked **Massif de l'Estérel** and the flamingo-pink wetlands of the **Camargue** are among the region's most dramatic landscapes. The fragile beauty and isolation of the protected **Parc National du Mercantour** in north-eastern Provence remains unrivalled. The pinprick island of **Port-Cros** and its snorkelling shores – Europe's first marine national park – ranks second.

Food & Wine

Culinary thrill-seekers should shop at a Provençal market – the best of Provence's markets are listed under Self-Catering later in the chapter; watch a harvest (lavender in July, rice in August, grapes in September, olives from November to January); sniff out some truffles (November to March); sip red wine in Châteauneuf du Pape; sample bouillabaisse in Marseilles; dine a la Ducasse/Vergé in Monaco, La Celle, Moustiers Ste-Marie and Mougins; and devote plenty of time to sampling regional dishes over long and lazy lunches in less formal bistros, farmhouses and *fermes auberges*.

Activities

Activities to set the heart racing include **canyoning** through the Gorges du Verdon, exploring Les Calanques by boat or foot, **climbing** France's highest cliff on Cap Canaille near Cassis, **scaling rock faces** in La Colmiane, **paragliding** in St-André and **diving** around the Calanques. The more sedate action-seeker can drift through Provence's clear blue skies in a **hot-air balloon**.

High Life

Savour the ritz and glitz and the rich and not-so-famous in Monaco's **Monte Carlo**

Casino; in Marseilles' **Musée de la Mode** (Fashion Design Museum); on **La Croisette** in star-struck Cannes; or at St-Tropez's yacht-filled **Vieux Port**. Legendary places to eat, sleep, party (and spend a small fortune) include Hôtel de Paris, Louis XV and Bar & Bœuf (Monaco); La Colombe d'Or (St-Paul de Vence); Hôtel du Cap Eden Roc (Cap d'Antibes); the Carlton-Intercontinental (Cannes); Moulin de Mougins (Mougins); Hôtel Byblos, La Voile Rouge, Le Club 55 and La Bodega du Papagayo (St-Tropez).

Lowlights

Body-packed beaches, traffic-jammed roads and booked-up hotels in July and August.

SUGGESTED ITINERARIES

One Week

Three days in Avignon, with half-day trips to Châteauneuf du Pape and Pont du Gard, followed by two days in the Camargue or around Mont Ventoux in the Vaucluse, and two days in Marseilles and/or Aix-en-Provence. Alternatively, spend a week in Nice, with day trips along the three Corniches to Monaco, Menton, Cannes and Antibes.

Two Weeks

Combine the one-week itineraries listed above, or spend a fortnight exploring one region in more depth: From the Camargue, add side trips to Arles and Nîmes; and plan in a couple of days touring the Lubéron by car, bike or foot after visiting the Mont Ventoux area; or head north to the Gorges du Verdon. From Nice, either enjoy a week of 'the great outdoors' in Haute-Provence or continue west along the coast to St-Tropez.

Three Weeks

Combine any of the above itineraries, or linger longer in one place to enjoy the fine walking, bike rides and river activities on offer (Lubéron, Mont Ventoux and Gorges du Verdon) or immerse yourself in the glitz and glamour of Riviera high life.

One Month

The region's your oyster.

PLANNING
When to Go

In short, not in July and August.

May and June are by far the best times to visit, followed by September and October. Spring in Provence is a cocktail of flower-ing poppy fields, blossoming almond trees and colourful wild flowers. Age-old vines sag with plump red grapes in early September, pumpkin fields turn deliciously orange and the first olives turn black in Van Gogh's silver-branched olive groves. The *vendange* (grape harvest) starts around 15 September, followed by the *cueillette des olives* (olive harvest) from 15 November through to early January.

Stone-capped Mont Ventoux – Provence's highest elevation – stays snow-capped until as late as mid-May. The southern Alps in mountainous Haute-Provence are snow-covered most years from late November until early April; the ski season starts just before Christmas and lasts until March. Elsewhere, the legendary mistral chills the bones all winter long.

On the coast, sunworshippers bare their bodies from April to early October. Easter to September sees the beach resorts on the Côte d'Azur buzz with activity around the clock. July and August are notoriously hot and generally unbearable for those unfortunate enough not to be within dipping distance of a pool (or the sea). Discomfort brought on by the sweltering heat is further exacerbated by the hordes of tourists and French holiday-makers who descend on the region, clogging up the roads, hotels and camp sites and generally making life hell for anyone visiting the region to 'get away from it all'. Dream on.

Inland, sweet-smelling lavender fields carpet the region with a purple blaze for just a few weeks from late June to late July when the little lilac flower is harvested. In August and September the days shorten and sudden storms and rain showers are frequent, both on the coast and inland.

The region's rich pageant of festivals can also be a deciding factor when you are considering when to go (or not go). For details on what festival falls when, see Public Holidays & Special Events later in this chapter.

Maps

Michelin and IGN have Internet boutiques at www.michelin-travel.com and www.ign.fr (French only), where you can purchase maps.

A good selection of maps are sold in the Magellan travel bookshop in Nice and the FNAC stores in Marseilles, Nice and Nîmes.

Quality regional maps are widely available outside France. Michelin's yellow-jacketed map *Provence and the Côte d'Azur* No 245 (32FF) covers the area included this guide at a scale of 1:200,000. IGN's 1:1,000,000-scale, grey-jacketed Map No 903 (29FF), called *France – Grande Randonnée* (literally 'big walk'), shows the region's long-distance GR trails and is useful for strategic planning of a cross-country trek through Provence and the Côte d'Azur. Map No 906 (29FF) in the same series is entitled *France – VTT & Randonnées Cyclos* and indicates dozens of suggested cycling tours around rural France.

City Maps You can find city maps within France at newsagencies *(maisons de la presse)* in most towns and cities, stationery shops *(papeteries)*, tourist offices, travel bookshops and many mainstream bookshops. The free street maps *(plans)* distributed by tourist offices range from the superb to the almost useless.

Michelin's *Guide Rouge* includes maps for the south's larger cities, towns and resorts that show one-way streets and have numbered town entry points that are coordinated with Michelin's yellow-jacketed 1:200,000 scale road maps.

Kümmerly & Frey's Blay-Foldex Plans-Guides series covers Marseilles, Toulon, Hyères, Cannes–Antibes, Grasse, Cagnes-sur-Mer, Nice, Monaco, Menton, Aix-en-Provence, Arles, Avignon and Nîmes. The orange-jacketed street maps cost between 19FF and 31FF. Éditions Grafocarte publishes city maps in its blue-jacketed Plan Guide Bleu & Or series. It covers Aix-en-Provence, Antibes, Avignon, Cagnes-sur-Mer, Cannes, Grasse, Hyères, Marseilles, Menton, Monaco, Nice, Nîmes, St-Raphaël and Toulon. Maps typically cost 23.50FF to 29FF.

What to Bring
As little as possible: forgotten items can be picked up practically anywhere in the region. If you intend travelling around or doing any walking with your gear – even from the train station to your hotel – a backpack is the way to go. The type that has an exterior pouch that zips off to become a daypack is the most useful.

Hostellers have to provide their own towel and soap. Bedding is almost always provided or available for hire; sheets cost around 17FF a night. Bring a padlock to secure your backpack by day and your storage locker (provided by most hostels) at night.

Other handy little numbers include a torch (flashlight), a Swiss army knife, an adapter plug for electrical appliances, a universal bath/sink plug (a plastic film canister sometimes works) and several clothes pegs. Essential items for surviving the heat in July and August include a water bottle, premoistened towelettes or a large cotton handkerchief (to soak in fountains and mop your face with), sunglasses, a sun hat, plenty of sunscreen (including sunblock) and after-sun lotion.

A warm sweater can be useful on early and late summer evenings. If you intend venturing into the mountains in August, bring a light, waterproof garment with you. Those heading into the Camargue need to pack a pair of binoculars and an excess of mosquito repellent.

RESPONSIBLE TOURISM

The summertime tourist invasion of southern France brings environmental and social stress: coastal and narrow inland roads become clogged with horn-honking cars and coaches, overflowing car parks built at the foot of pretty villages fail to cope with the crowds, and locals go into hibernation as tourists overrun markets and festivals.

Reduce your own impact on the region by travelling by train, bike or even on foot, instead of in a car. You can do even better – and keep your own stress level down in the process – by lingering longer in a smaller number of places, and visiting during the low or mid-season. Camping on farms or staying in *chambres d'hôtes* (B&Bs) rather than mainstream hotels gives locals a bigger share of the money you spend, as does buying *produits du terroir* (local, home-made produce) straight from the farm or market stall rather than the supermarket or tourist shop.

Respect signs telling you not to walk on the grass *(pelouse interdite)*, picnic *(pique nique interdit)* or enter private property *(propriété privée)*. Likewise, adhere to the rules of the forest: don't smoke, don't light fires or barbecues (forbidden on beaches too) and don't block cleared forest tracks, be it with your bike, car, hammock or picnic rug.

TOURIST OFFICES
Local Tourist Offices
Every city, town, village and hamlet seems to have an *office du tourisme* (tourist office run by some unit of local government) or a *syndicat d'initiative* (tourist office run by an organisation of local merchants). Both are an excellent resource and can almost always provide a local map and information on accommodation possibilities. Some change foreign currency. Many make local hotel reservations.

Tourist information for the region is handled by five *comités départementaux du tourisme* (departmental tourist offices):

Alpes de Haute-Provence (☎ 04 92 31 57 29, fax 04 92 32 24 94) Maison des Alpes de Haute-Provence, 19 rue du Docteur Honnorat, 04000 Digne-les-Bains
Web site: www.alpes-haute-provence.com
Alpes-Maritimes (☎ 04 93 37 78 78, fax 04 93 86 01 06, Ⓔ crt06@crt-riviera.fr) 55 promenade des Anglais, 06011 Nice
Web site: www.crt-riviera.fr
Bouches du Rhône (☎ 04 91 13 84 13, fax 04 91 33 01 82, Ⓔ promotion@visitprovence .com) Le Montesquieu, 13 rue Roux de Brignoles, 13006 Marseilles
Web site: www.visitprovence.com
Var (☎ 04 94 50 55 50, fax 04 94 50 55 51) 1 blvd Maréchal Foch, BP 99, 83003 Draguignan; 1 blvd de Strasbourg, BP 5147, 83000 Toulon
Vaucluse (☎ 04 90 80 47 00, fax 04 90 86 86 08, Ⓔ info@provenceguide.com) 12 rue Collège de la Croix, BP 147, 84008 Avignon
Web site: www.provenceguide.com

For tourist information on the principality of Monaco, contact its national tourist office in Monte Carlo (see the Monaco chapter).

French Tourist Offices Abroad
Information on Provence and the Côte d'Azur is available from French government tourist offices abroad:

Australia (☎ 02-9231 5244, fax 9221 8682, Ⓔ ifrance@internetezy.com.au) 25 Bligh St, 22nd floor, Sydney, NSW 2000
Belgium (☎ 02-513 07 62, fax 543 375, Ⓔ maisondelafrance@pophost.eunet.be) 21 ave de la Toison d'Or, 1050 Brussels
Canada (☎ 514-288 4264, fax 845 4868, Ⓔ mfrance@mtl.net) 1981 Ave McGill College, Suite 490, Montreal, Quebec H3A 2W9
Germany (☎ 069-758 021, fax 745 556, Ⓔ maison_de_la_France@t-online.de) Westendstrasse 47, 60325 Frankfurt
Ireland (☎ 01-679 0813, fax 679 0814, Ⓔ frenchtouristoffice@eircom.net) 10 Suffolk Street, Dublin 2
Italy (☎ 02 584 8657, fax 02 584 862 22, Ⓔ info@turismofrancese.it) Via Larga 7, 20122 Milan
Netherlands (☎ 0900 112 2332, fax 020-620 3339, Ⓔ informatie@fransverkeersbureau.nl) Prinsengracht 670, 1017 KX Amsterdam
Web site: www.fransverkeersbureau.nl
Spain (☎ 91 548 9740, fax 91 541 2412, Ⓔ info.francia@mdlfr.com) Plaza de España 18, Torre de Madrid 8, 28008 Madrid
Web site: www.maisondelafrance.es
Switzerland (☎ 01-211 3085, fax 212 1644, Ⓔ tourismefrance@bluewin.ch) Löwenstrasse 59, 8023 Zürich
UK (☎ 0891 244 123, fax 020-7493 6594, Ⓔ info@mdlf.co.uk) 178 Piccadilly, London W1V 0AL
Web site: www.franceguide.com
USA (☎ 212-838 7800, fax 838 7855, Ⓔ info@francetourism.com) 444 Madison Ave, 16th floor, New York, NY 10022–6903
Web site: www.francetourism.com

Monégasque Tourist Offices Abroad
Monaco has its own string of tourist offices abroad:

France (☎ 01 42 96 12 23, fax 01 42 61 31 52) 9 rue de la Paix, 75002 Paris
Germany (☎ 211-323 7843/4/5, fax 323 7846) WZ Center, Königsallee 27–31, 40212 Düsseldorf
Italy (☎ 02 8645 8480, fax 02 8645 8469), Via Dante 12, 20121 Milano

UK (☎ 0500 006 114, 020-7352 9962, fax 7352 2103, e monaco@monaco.co.uk) The Chambers, Chelsea Harbour, London SW10 0XF
USA (☎ 800-753 9696, 212-286 3330, fax 286 9890, e mgto@monaco1.org) 565 5th Avenue, New York, NY 10017
Web site: www.monaco-tourism.com

VISAS & DOCUMENTS

A visa for France is good for Monaco too. Despite having its own diplomatic missions abroad, the principality of Monaco does not issue a visa of its own; rather it directs visa applicants to the nearest French consulate.

Passport

By law, everyone in France and Monaco, including tourists, must carry ID on them at all times. For foreign visitors, this means a passport or national ID card.

Visas

Tourist France is one of the 15 countries that have signed the Schengen Convention, an agreement whereby all European Union (EU) member countries (except the UK and Ireland) plus Iceland and Norway have agreed to abolish checks at common borders by the end of 2000. The other EU countries involved are Austria, Belgium, Denmark, Finland, Germany, Greece, Italy, Luxembourg, the Netherlands, Portugal, Spain and Sweden. Legal residents of one Schengen country do not require a visa for another Schengen country. Citizens of the UK and Ireland are also exempt from visa requirements for Schengen countries. In addition, nationals of a number of other countries, including Canada, Japan, New Zealand and Switzerland, do not require visas for tourist visits of up to 90 days to any Schengen country.

In practice, however, it is not recommended to travel without a passport, as signatories reserve the right to implement both temporary and more permanent border controls (your passport is also necessary as a form of ID in France; see under Passport earlier in this section). The French government has chosen to exercise this right and passport controls at its borders with Belgium

and Luxembourg are still in place (the differing drug laws made France nervous about removing border controls). Individual Schengen countries may also impose additional restrictions on certain nationalities. It is, therefore, worth checking visa regulations with the consulate of each country you plan to visit. For up-to-the-minute information, call the EU information office in Brussels on ☎ 02-295 1780. The standard tourist visa issued by French consulates is the Schengen visa.

To obtain a visa you must present your passport, air or other tickets in and out of France, proof of finances and possibly accommodation, two passport-size photos and the visa fee in cash. A 30-day tourist visa generally costs around US$31, while a three-month single-/multiple-entry visa costs US$37/44. Visas are usually issued on the spot. It's mandatory to apply for Schengen visas in your country of residence. You can apply for no more than two Schengen visas in any 12-month period and they are not renewable inside France. If you are going to visit more than one Schengen country you are supposed to apply for the visa at a consulate of your main destination country or, if you have no main destination, the first country you intend to visit. It's worth applying early for your visa, especially in the busy summer months.

Tourist visas cannot be extended except in emergencies (such as medical problems). If you have an urgent problem, consult your nearest consulate (probably Nice or Marseilles, depending on your country of origin) for guidance or call the nearest prefecture (see Carte de Séjour later in the chapter).

Long-Stay, Student & Au Pair If you'd like to work or study in France or stay for over three months, apply to the French embassy or consulate for the appropriate sort of long-stay (séjour) visa. Unless you are an EU citizen, it is hard to get a visa allowing you to work in France. People with student visas can apply for permission to work part time (inquire at your place of study). Au pair visas must be arranged before you leave home (unless you're an EU citizen).

Carte de Séjour If you are issued a long-stay visa valid for six or more months you'll probably have to apply for a *carte de séjour* (residence permit) within eight days of arrival in France. For details, inquire at your place of study or the local prefecture, city hall *(hôtel de ville)*, town hall *(mairie)* or police station *(commissariat)*.

The prefecture in Nice (☎ 04 93 72 20 00), cours Saleya; and in Marseilles (☎ 04 91 15 60 00, metro Estrangin-Préfecture), place Félix Baret, both have special visa sections which tackle cartes de séjour.

Travel Insurance

Travel insurance usually covers you for medical expenses (EU citizens holding an E111 form do not need to pay for medical insurance; see Health Insurance later in this chapter for details) and luggage theft or loss, as well as for cancellation or delays in your travel arrangements. Cover depends on your insurance and sometimes on your type of airline ticket, so be sure to ask your insurer and ticket-issuing agency where you stand.

Driving Licence & Permits

A driving licence from an EU country is valid in France. Most non-EU driving licences are likewise valid, although it's still a good idea to bring along an International Driving Permit (IDP; a multilingual translation of the vehicle class and personal details noted on your local driving licence). Note that the latter is not valid unless accompanied by your original. An IDP can be obtained for a small fee from your local motoring association – bring along a passport photo and a valid licence.

Hostel Card

A Hostelling International (HI) card is only necessary at official youth hostels *(auberges de jeunesse)*. You can become a member by joining your own national Youth Hostelling Association (YHA); see the HI Web site at www.iyhf.org for details. Alternatively, at many HI-affiliated hostels, you can buy a card for 70/100FF for those aged under/over 26. One-night membership

(where available) costs between 10FF and 19FF; a family card costs 100FF.

Student, Youth, Teacher & Press Cards

An International Student Identity Card (ISIC) can pay for itself through half-price admissions, discounted air and ferry tickets, and cheap meals in student cafeterias. Many places stipulate a maximum age, usually 24 or 25. ISIC cards are issued by student travel agencies such as Accueil des Jeunes en France (AJF) for 60FF. Information is on the Web at www.istc.org.

If you're under 26 but not a student you can apply for a GO25 card (60FF) issued by the Federation of International Youth Travel Organisations (FIYTO), which entitles you to much the same discounts as an ISIC. It is also issued by student unions or student travel agencies.

A Carte Jeunes (120FF) is available to anyone under 26 who has been in France for six months. It gets you discount air tickets, car rental, sports events, concerts, movies and so on. Discount details are available online at www.cartejeunes.fr (French only). In France call ☎ 08 03 00 12 26.

Teachers, professional artists, museum conservators, journalists and certain categories of students are admitted to some museums free. Bring along proof of affiliation, for example, an International Teacher Identity Card (ITIC) or official press card.

Seniors Card

Reductions are often available for people over 60 or 65, see under Senior Travellers later for more details. SNCF sells an annual Carte Senior (285FF) to those aged 60 and over, which gives reductions of 25 to 50% on train tickets.

Camping Card International

Camping Card International (CCI) is a form of ID that can be used instead of a passport when checking into a camp site and includes third-party insurance for damage you may cause. As a result, many camp sites offer a small discount if you sign in with one. CCIs are issued by automobile associations, camping federations and, sometimes, on the spot at camp sites. In the UK, the AA (☎ 0870 5500 600) issues them to its members for UK£4.

Carte Musées Côte d'Azur

The Carte Musées Côte d'Azur (French Riviera Museum Pass) gives card-holders unlimited admission to 62 museums along the coast. A three-day pass, valid for three consecutive days, costs 85FF; and a seven-day pass, valid for seven days within a 15-day period, costs 150FF. Passes are sold at participating museums, tourist offices, FNAC stores and Thomas Cook bureaux de change. There is no reduced rate for students or senior travellers. In Nice, details are available from Le Consul (☎ 04 93 13 17 52, fax 04 93 13 17 52, e cmca.nice@wanadoo.fr), 37–41 blvd Dubouchage, 06000 Nice. Online, visit www.cmca.net.

To complement the Carte Musées Côte d'Azur, the regional bus company Rapides Côte d'Azur sells cut-price bus passes to museum card-holders (see under Bus Passes in the Getting Around chapter).

Copies

Make a copy of all important documents (passport data and visa pages, credit cards, travel insurance policy, air/bus/train tickets, driving licence etc) before leaving home. Leave one copy with someone at home and keep another with you, separate from the originals.

Alternatively, store details of your vital travel documents in Lonely Planet's online Travel Vault. Keeping copies here is safer than carrying photocopies and it can easily be accessed from any one of France's numerous Internet cafes while on the road. You can create your own Travel Vault for free at www.ekno.lonelyplanet.com.

EMBASSIES & CONSULATES
French Embassies & Consulates

Diplomatic representation abroad includes:

Australia
Embassy: (☎ 02-6216 0100, fax 6273 3193) 6 Perth Ave, Yarralumla, ACT 2600
Consulates: (☎ 03-9820 0944/0921, fax 9820 9363) 492 St Kilda Rd, Level 4, Melbourne, Vic 3004; (☎ 02-9262 5779, fax 9283 1210) St Martin's Tower, 31 Market St, Sydney, NSW 2000

Belgium
Embassy: (☎ 02-548 8711, fax 513 6871) 65 rue Ducale, 1000 Brussels
Web site: www.ambafrance.be
Consulate: (☎ 02-229 8500, fax 229 8510, e consulat.france.bruxelles@skynet.be) 12a place de Louvain, 1000 Brussels
Web site: www.consulfrance-bruxelles.be

Canada
Embassy: (☎ 613-789 1795, fax 562 3704) 42 Sussex Drive, Ottawa, Ont K1M 2C9
Consulates: (☎ 514-878 4385, fax 878 3981, e fsltmral@cam.org) 1 Place Ville Marie, Bureau 2601, Montreal, Quebec H3B 4S3; (☎ 416-925 8041, e fsltto@idirect.com) 130 Bloor St West, Suite 400, Toronto, Ontario M5S 1N5
Links to Web sites at www.ambafrance-ca.org

Germany
Embassy: (☎ 030-206 39000, fax 206 39010, e presse.berlin@diplomacie.fr) Kochstrasse 6–7, D-10969 Berlin
Web site: www.botschaft-frankreich.de
Consulates: (☎ 030-885 90243, fax 885 5295) Kurfürstendamm 211, 10719 Berlin; (☎ 089-419 4110, fax 419 41141, e info@consulfrance-munich.de) Möhlstrasse 5, D-81675 München
Web site: www.consulfrance-munich.de
Other consulates are in Düsseldorf, Frankfurt, Hamburg and Stuttgart.

Ireland
Embassy: (☎ 01-260 1666, fax 283 0178) 36 Ailesbury Rd, Ballsbridge, Dublin 4
Web site: www.ambafrance.ie

Italy
Embassy: (☎ 06 68 60 11, fax 06 68 60 13 60, e france-italia@france-italia.it) Piazza Farnese 67, 00186 Rome
Consulate: (☎ 06 68 80 64 37, fax 06 68 60 12 60) Via Giulia 251, 00186 Rome
Web site: www.france-italia.it
Other consulates are in Milan, Naples and Turin.

Netherlands
Embassy: (☎ 070-312 5800, fax 312 5824) Smidsplein 1, 2514 BT Den Haag
Web site: www.ambafrance.nl
Consulate: (☎ 020-530 6969, fax 530 6988) Eerste Weteringdwarsstraat 107, 1000 HA Amsterdam
Web site: www.consulfrance.nl

New Zealand
Embassy: (☎ 04-384 2555, fax 384 2577)
34–42 Manners St, Wellington
Spain
Embassy: (☎ 91 423 8900, fax 91 423 8901)
Calle de Salustiano Olozaga 9, 28001
Madrid
Consulates: (☎ 91 7000 7800, fax 91 7000
7801) Calle Marqués de la Enseñada 10–3,
28004 Madrid
Web site: www.ambafrance.es
Switzerland
Embassy: (☎ 031-359 2111, e ambassade.fr@
iprolink.ch) Schosshaldenstrasse 46, 3006
Bern
Consulate: (☎ 022-311 0000, e consulat
.france@ties.itu.int) 11 rue Imbert Galloix,
1205 Geneva
Other consulates are in Bale, Lausanne and
Zürich.
UK
Embassy: (☎ 020-7201 1000, fax 7201 1004,
e tourisme@ambafrance.co.uk) 58 Knights-
bridge, London SW1X 7JT
Consulate: (☎ 020-7838 2000, fax 7838 2001)
21 Cromwell Rd, London SW7 2EN
Visa Section: (☎ 020-7838 2050, fax 0900
166 9932) 6a Cromwell Place, London
SW7 2EW
Web site: www.ambafrance.org.uk
USA
Embassy & Consulate: (☎ 202-944 6200,
fax 944 6212, e visas-washington@amb-
wash.fr) 4101 Reservoir Rd NW, Washington,
DC 20007
Consulate: (☎ 212-606 3600, fax 606 3620,
e info@franceconsulatny.org) 934 Fifth Ave,
New York, NY 10021
Visa Section: (☎ 606 3680, e visa@
franceconsulatny.org) 10 East 74th Street,
New York, NY 10021
Web site: www.franceconsulatny.org
Consulate: (☎ 415-397 4330, fax 433 8357)
540 Bush St, San Francisco, CA 94108
Other consulates are in Atlanta, Boston,
Chicago, Houston, Los Angeles, Miami and
New Orleans.

Monégasque Embassies

Monaco has the following diplomatic missions abroad:

Belgium (☎ 02-347 4987, fax 343 4920)
17 place Guy d'Arezzo, 1080 Brussels
France (☎ 01 45 04 74 54, fax 01 45 04 45 16)
22 blvd Suchet, 75016 Paris

Germany (☎ 0228-23 20 07/08, fax 23 62 82)
Zitelmannstrasse 16, 53113 Bonn
Italy (☎ 06 808 33 61, fax 06 807 76 92) Via
Bertolom 36, 00197 Rome
Spain (☎ 91 578 2048, fax 91 435 7132) Calle
Villanueva 12, 28001 Madrid
Switzerland (☎ 031-356 2858, fax 356 2855)
34 Hallwylstrasse, 3005 Bern

Consulates in Provence & Monaco

Foreign embassies are in Paris but most
countries have a consulate in Nice, Marseilles and/or Monaco:

Belgium (☎ 04 93 87 79 56) Bureaux du
Ruhl, 5 rue Gabriel Fauré, 06406 Nice;
(☎ 377-93 50 59 89) 13 ave des Castelans,
Monaco
Canada (☎ 04 93 92 93 22) 64 ave Jean
Médecin, 06000 Nice; (☎ 377-97 70 62 42)
1 ave Henri Dunant, Monaco
France (☎ 377-92 16 54 60) 1 chemin du
Ténao, Monaco
Germany (☎ 04 91 16 75 20) 338 ave du Prado,
13125 Marseilles; (☎ 04 93 83 55 25)
Le Minotaure, 34 ave Henri Matisse, 06200
Nice
Italy (☎ 04 91 18 49 18) 56 rue d'Alger, 13005
Marseilles; (☎ 04 93 88 79 86) 72 blvd
Gambetta, 06048 Nice; (☎ 377-93 50 22 71)
17 ave de l'Annonciade, Monaco
Monaco (☎ 04 91 33 30 21) 3 place aux Huiles,
13001 Marseilles; (☎ 04 93 80 00 22) Villa
Printemps, 12 montée Désambrois, 06000
Nice
Netherlands (☎ 04 91 25 66 64) 137 ave de
Toulon, 13005 Marseilles; (☎ 04 93 87 52 94)
14 rue Rossini, 06000 Nice; (☎ 377-92 05 15
02) 24 ave de Fontvieille, Monaco
Switzerland (☎ 04 91 53 36 65) 7 rue d'Arcole,
13006 Marseilles; (☎ 04 93 88 85 09) Le
Louvre, 13 rue Alphonse Karr, BP 1279,
06005 Nice; (☎ 377-933 15 58 15) 2 ave de
Grande-Bretagne, Monaco
UK (☎ 04 91 15 72 10) 24 ave du Prado, 13006
Marseilles; (☎ 04 93 82 32 04) 8 rue Alphonse
Kerr, 06000 Nice; (☎ 377-93 50 99 66,
e insure@monaco.mc) 33 blvd Princesse
Charlotte, Monaco
USA (☎ 04 91 54 92 00, fax 04 91 55 09 47)
12 blvd Paul Peytral, 13006 Marseilles;
(☎ 04 93 88 89 55, fax 04 93 87 07 38) 7 ave
Gustave V, 06000 Nice
Web site: www.amb-usa.fr

CUSTOMS

The usual allowances apply to duty-free goods purchased at airports or on ferries outside the EU: tobacco (200 cigarettes, 50 cigars or 250g of loose tobacco), alcohol (1L of strong spirits or 2L of less than 22% alcohol by volume; and 2L of wine), coffee (500g or 200g of extracts) and perfume (50g of perfume and 0.25L of toilet water).

Do not confuse these with duty-paid items (including alcohol and tobacco) bought at normal shops and supermarkets in another EU country and brought into France, where certain goods might be more expensive. In that case, the allowances are more than generous: 800 cigarettes, 200 cigars or 1kg of loose tobacco; and 10L of spirits (more than 22% alcohol by volume), 20L of fortified wine or aperitif, 90L of wine or 110L of beer.

MONEY
Currency

The French franc (FF) remains the national currency in France and Monaco until January 2002 when it will be exchanged for the euro (€). See the boxed text 'Euroland' on the next page for more details.

One franc is divided into 100 centimes. French coins come in denominations of 5, 10, 20 and 50 centimes (0.5FF) and 1, 2, 5, 10 and 20FF; the two highest denominations have silvery centres and brass edges. French-franc banknotes are issued in denominations of 20FF, 50FF, 100FF, 200FF and 500FF.

Exchange Rates

The Universal Currency Converter posts the currency exchange rate of the day online at www.xe.net/ucc. At the time of going to press, some exchange rates were:

country	unit	€	FF
Australia	A$1	0.62	4.05
Canada	C$1	0.75	4.91
EU	€1		6.56
Germany	DM1	0.51	3.35
Japan	¥100	1.03	6.75
New Zealand	NZ$1	0.48	3.16
UK	UK£1	1.66	10.90
USA	US$1	1.14	7.48

Exchanging Money

France's central bank, the Banque de France, can offer the best exchange rates. It does not accept Eurocheques or US$100 banknotes (due to the preponderance of counterfeit ones) or provide credit-card cash advances. Most branches only exchange foreign currency for two or three hours on weekday mornings.

Commercial banks charge between 25FF and 50FF per foreign currency transaction. Rates offered vary, so it pays to compare. Many post offices perform exchange transactions for a middling rate and charge 2% commission (minimum charge 20FF). The commission for travellers cheques is 1.5% (minimum 25FF). Most accept cheques issued by American Express (Amex; in US dollars or French francs) or Visa (in French francs).

In cities such as Nice and Marseilles, bureaux de change are faster, easier, open longer hours and give better rates than the banks. When using bureaux de change, shop around. Familiarise yourself with the rates offered by banks and compare them with those offered at bureaux de changes (generally not allowed to charge commissions). On relatively small transactions, even exchange places with less than optimal rates may leave you with more francs in your pocket.

Cash Hard currency is not a safe way to carry money. Banque de France pays about 2.5% more for travellers cheques, easily compensating for the 1% commission usually involved in buying them. Bring the equivalent of about US$100 in low-denomination notes for when you need small sums of money. Counterfeiting can make it difficult to change US$100 notes; most Banque de France branches don't accept them.

Travellers Cheques & Eurocheques

Except at some bureaux de change and at Banque de France, you have to pay to cash travellers cheques; at banks, expect a charge of 25FF to 35FF per transaction. A percentage fee may apply for large sums. Amex offices do not charge a commission on their own travellers cheques but holders of other

Euroland

Since 1 January 1999, the franc and the euro – the new currency for 11 European Union (EU) countries – have both been legal tender in France. Euro coins and banknotes have not been issued yet, but you can already get billed in euros and opt to pay in euros by credit card. Essentially, if there's no hard cash involved, you can deal in euros. Travellers should check bills carefully to make sure that any conversion has been calculated correctly. Luckily, the euro should make life easier. One of the main benefits will be that prices in the 11 countries will be immediately comparable.

The whole idea behind this paperless currency is to give euro-fearing punters a chance to limber up arithmetically before euro coins and banknotes are issued on 1 January 2002. The same euro coins (one to 50 cents, €1 and €2) and bridge-adorned notes (€5 to €500) can be happily used in Euroland's 11 countries (Austria, Belgium, Finland, France, Germany, Ireland, Italy, Luxembourg, the Netherlands, Portugal and Spain). The French and Monégasque franc will remain legal tender alongside the euro until 1 July 2002, when the franc will be hurled on the scrapheap of history.

Until then, one euro is equal to AS13.77, BF40.3, 5.95 mk, 6.56FF, DM1.96, IR£0.788, L1963, flux37.5, f2.2, 200$48 and 166.4ptas. Banque de France exchanges these currencies into francs at the official rate without charging any commission. You can log into Euroland on the Net at europa.eu.int/euro/html/entry.html. The Lonely Planet Web site at www.lonelyplanet.com has a link to a currency converter and up-to-date news on the integration process.

brands must pay a minimum charge of 40FF for non-Amex cheques up to 1500FF (3% commission for amounts over 1500FF). Travellers cheques issued by Amex and Visa offer the greatest flexibility.

Eurocheques, available if you have a European bank account, are guaranteed up to a certain limit. When cashing them (at post offices or banks), you will be asked to show your Eurocheque card bearing your signature and registration number, and perhaps a passport or ID card. Many hotels and merchants refuse to accept Eurocheques because of the relatively large commissions.

If travellers cheques issued by Amex (www.americanexpress.com) are lost or stolen in France, call ☎ 08 00 90 86 00. For reimbursements, go to the Amex office in Aix-en-Provence (04 42 26 84 77, 15 cours Mirabeau), Cannes (☎ 04 93 38 15 87, 8 rue des Belges), Marseilles (☎ 04 91 13 71 26, 39 La Canebière), Nice (☎ 04 93 16 53 53, 11 promenade des Anglais) or Monaco (☎ 377-97 70 77 59, 35 blvd Princesse Charlotte). Opening hours are listed in the Money section of the relevant chapters.

If you lose your Thomas Cook cheques, contact any Thomas Cook bureau (such as in Nice, Cannes or St-Tropez) for replace-ments. Their customer-service bureau can be contacted toll-free on ☎ 08 00 90 83 30 or visit online at (www.thomascook.com)

ATMs In French, ATMs are called *distributeurs automatiques de billets* or *points d'argent*. ATM cards give you direct access to your cash reserves back home at a superior exchange rate. Most spit out cash through Visa or MasterCard and there are plenty of ATMs in the region linked to the international Cirrus and Maestro networks. If you remember your PIN code as a string of letters, translate it back into numbers; French keyboards do not show letters.

Credit Cards This is the cheapest way to pay for things and to get cash advances. Visa (Carte Bleue) is the most widely accepted, followed by MasterCard (Access or Eurocard). Amex cards are not very useful except at upmarket establishments but they do allow you to get cash at certain ATMs and at Amex offices (see Travellers Cheques & Eurocheques earlier in this section). Taking along two different credit cards (stashed in different wallets) is safer than taking one.

If your Visa card is lost or stolen, call Carte Bleue on ☎ 02 54 42 12 12. To replace a lost card you have to deal with the issuer. Report a lost MasterCard, Access or Eurocard to Eurocard France (☎ 01 45 67 53 53) and, if you can, to your credit-card issuer back home. For cards from the USA, call ☎ 001-314-275 6690.

If your Amex card is lost or stolen, call ☎ 01 47 77 70 00 or 01 47 77 72 00. In an emergency, Amex card-holders from the USA can call collect ☎ 202-783 7474 or 202-677 2442. Replacements can be arranged at any Amex office. Report a lost Diners Club card on ☎ 01 47 62 75 75.

International Transfers Telegraphic transfers are not very expensive but can be quite slow. It's quicker and easier to have money wired via Amex. Western Union's Money Transfer system (☎ 01 43 54 46 12) is available at most post offices.

Costs

Provence and the Côte d'Azur are considered France's most expensive spots, and never more so than in July or August when prices soar sky high. There are ways to save the odd centime, however.

If you stay in a camp site, a hostel or showerless/toiletless room in a budget hotel and have picnics rather than dine out, it's possible to travel around Provence and the Côte d'Azur for about US$35 per person per day (US$45 in July/August).

Travelling with someone else immediately cuts costs: few hotels in the region offer single rooms. Those that do charge the same price for singles and doubles (or only marginally less for singles). Triples and quads (often with only two beds) are the cheapest per person and can offer an amazing price:comfort ratio. If visiting the Côte d'Azur, consider staying in Nice where accommodation is cheaper, and from where day trips can easily be made along the coast.

As far as dining is concerned, hearty picnics of baguette and cheese on the beach will cut costs dramatically. Carrying a water bottle instead of forking out an outrageous 15FF to 30FF for a poxy canned drink is another massive money-saver. In restaurants, sod the calorie count and opt for the *menu* – guaranteed to leave you stuffed and offering far better value than dining a la carte. Ask for *une carafe d'eau* instead of bottled water, and order the house wine instead of beer.

Discounts Museums, cinemas, the SNCF, ferry companies and other institutions offer all sorts of price breaks to people aged under 25 or 26, students with ISIC cards, and the *troisième age* (people over 60 or 65). Look for the words *demi-tarif* or *tarif réduit* (half-price tariff or reduced rate) on rate charts and ask if you qualify. Many museums offer special tariffs to multichildren families *(familles nombreuses)*.

Those aged under 18 get an even wider range of discounts, including free or reduced admission to most museums. For details on the Carte Musées Côte d'Azur (a card that offers a cheaper way to visit sights) see Visas & Documents earlier in this chapter.

Look out for freebies too – admission to Nice museums is free on the first Sunday of the month, for example. Throughout the region, numerous galleries, museums, palaces, gardens and other historic or cultural places that usually demand an admission fee are free for two days in mid-September during France's *Journées du Patrimoine* (Days of Patrimony).

Tipping & Bargaining

French law requires that restaurant, cafe and hotel bills include the service charge (usually 10 to 15%), so a tip *(pourboire)* is neither necessary nor expected. However, most people – dire service apart – usually leave a few francs in restaurants.

Little bargaining goes on at Provençal markets.

Taxes & Refunds

France's Value Added Tax (VAT; TVA in French) is 20.6% on most goods except food, medicine and books, for which it's 5.5%; it goes as high as 33% on such items as watches, cameras and video cassettes. Prices are rarely given without VAT.

If you are not an EU resident, you can get a refund of most of the VAT provided that you're aged over 15, you'll be spending less than six months in France, you purchase goods (not more than 10 of the same item) worth at least 1200FF (tax included) at a single shop and that the shop offers duty-free sales *(vente en détaxe)*.

Present your passport at the time of purchase and ask for an export sales invoice *(bordereau de détaxe)*. Some shops refund 14% of the purchase price rather than the full 17.1% you are entitled to in order to cover the time and expense involved in the refund procedure. When you leave France or another EU country, ensure that the country's customs officials validate all three pages of the invoice; the green sheet is your receipt. You will receive a transfer of funds in your home country.

If you are flying out of Nice-Côte d'Azur, Marseilles-Provence or Toulon-Hyères airports, certain stores can arrange for you to receive your refund as you're leaving the country. At the airport, validate your invoice at the customs office (☎ 04 93 21 30 80 in Nice; ☎ 04 42 14 30 70 in Marseilles; ☎ 04 94 00 83 3 in Toulon), where you will be told which customs refund window or exchange bureau to go to for your VAT refund.

POST & COMMUNICATIONS
Post

Postal services in France are fast (next-day delivery for most domestic letters) and reliable. Post offices are signposted La Poste. To mail items, go to a postal window marked *toutes opérations* (all services). Most shops that sell postcards sell stamps *(timbres)* too. Stamps bought from coin-operated machines inside post offices come out as an uninspiring, blue-coloured sticker. French stamps can be used in Monaco; Monégasque stamps are only valid in Monaco.

From France and Monaco, domestic letters up to 20g cost 3FF. Letters and postcards up to 20g cost 3FF within the EU; 3.80FF to most of the rest of Europe and Africa; 4.40FF to the USA, Canada and the Middle East; and 5.20FF to Australasia.

When addressing mail to your truffle supplier in Provence, do it the French way: write the surname or family name in capital letters first, followed by the recipient's first name in lower case letters. Insert a comma after the street number and don't capitalise 'rue', 'ave' or 'blvd'. CEDEX after the city or town name means mail sent to that address is collected at the post office rather than delivered to the door.

Poste restante is available at larger post offices.

Telephone

France has one of the most modern and sophisticated telecommunications systems in the world. Monaco has a separate telephone system to France. Neither uses area codes. Most public telephones require a phonecard *(télécarte)*, sold at post offices, tobacconists *(tabacs)*, supermarket checkout counters and SNCF ticket windows.

French telephone numbers have 10 digits. To call anywhere in Provence and the Côte d'Azur from Monaco and abroad, dial your country's international access code, followed by 33 (France's country code) and the 10-digit number, dropping the first zero. To call abroad from France, dial ☎ 00 (France's international access code), followed by the country code, area code (dropping the initial zero if necessary) and local number.

Telephone numbers in Monaco only have eight digits. To call Monaco from France and abroad, dial the international access code, followed by 377 (Monaco's country code) and the eight-digit number. To call abroad from Monaco, dial ☎ 00, followed by the country code, area code (dropping the initial zero if necessary) and local number. To call France from Monaco, dial ☎ 00-33, plus the 10-digit number.

Reverse-Charge Calls & Inquiries To make a reverse-charge (collect) call *(en PCV)*, dial ☎ 00-33, then the country code of the place you're calling (dial 11 instead of 1 for the USA and Canada). If you're using a public phone, you must insert a phonecard to place operator-assisted calls through the international operator.

To find out a country code *(indicatif pays)*, call directory inquiries (☎ 12). To find out a subscriber's telephone number abroad,

Mobile Phones

France uses GSM 900/1800, which is compatible with the rest of Europe and Australia but not with the North American GSM 1900 or the totally different system in Japan (though some North Americans have GSM 1900/900 phones that do work here). If you have a GSM phone, check with your service provider about using it in France, and beware of calls being routed internationally (very expensive for a 'local' call).

call international directory inquiries (☎ 00-3312 plus relevant country code – dial 11 instead of 1 for the USA and Canada). From abroad, this service costs 14.58/19.70FF per inquiry from a public/private phone.

International Rates The cheapest time to call home is during reduced tariff periods – weekday evenings from 7 pm to 8 am (until 1 pm to the USA and Canada), weekends and public holidays.

A phone call to Europe costs 0.74FF for the first 20-odd seconds, then 1.63FF per minute (reduced tariff 0.91FF per minute). To call the USA or Canada costs 0.74FF for the first 22 seconds, then 2.47FF per minute (reduced tariff 1.98FF). To telephone Australia, New Zealand and Japan costs 0.74FF for the first 10 seconds, and about 4.25FF per minute (reduced tariff 3.07FF per minute). Calls to other parts of Asia, non-Francophone Africa and South America cost 0.74FF for the initial five to eight seconds, then 5.45FF to 9.22FF per minute (reduced tariffs 4.26FF to 7.34FF per minute).

France Télécom's Ticket de Téléphone (a cheap calling card available at tobacconists) is handy for those on the move. The Ticket de Téléphone International costs 50/100FF and, if used exclusively during reduced-rate blue tariff periods (see Domestic Tariffs later), covers 40/80 minutes of calls to Europe, the USA and Canada; standard/reduced rates work out at 1.65/1FF per minute. An extra 0.35FF per minute is added to calls made from a public phone. To use a ticket, dial 3089, followed by the code written on the reverse side of your calling card, '#' and the subscriber's number.

Domestic Tariffs Local calls are quite cheap. The first three minutes cost 0.74FF followed by 0.28FF per minute during peak *tarif rouge* (red tariff) periods (weekdays from 8 am to 7 pm) and 0.14FF per minute at off-peak times during *tarif bleu* (blue tariff) periods (weekdays from 7 pm to 8 am and at any time at the weekend). National calls cost 0.74FF for the initial 39 seconds, plus 0.79FF per minute in tarif rouge periods and 0.39FF per minute in tarif bleu periods.

Numbers starting with '08 36' are substantially more expensive than other domestic calls and should be avoided. Ten-digit numbers starting with '06' indicate a mobile phone connected to the Itineris (France Télécom), SFR or Bouygues network.

eKno Communication Service

Lonely Planet's eKno global communication service provides low-cost international calls – for local calls you're usually better off with a local phonecard. eKno also offers free messaging services, email, travel information and an online travel vault, where you can securely store your important documents. You can join online at www.ekno.lonelyplanet.com, where you will find the local-access numbers for the 24-hour customer-service centre. Once you have joined, always check the eKno Web site for the latest access numbers for each country and updates on new features.

Minitel

Minitel is a telephone-connected, computerised information service. It is expensive to use and being given a good run for its money by the Internet. Numbers consist of four digits and a string of letters. We have not included Minitel addresses in this book. However, France Télécom has an electronic directory that you can access in some post offices. The code 3611 is used for general address and telephone inquiries. 3615 SNCF and 3615 TER give train information.

Fax

Virtually all town post offices can send and receive domestic and international faxes *(télécopies* or *téléfaxes)*, telexes and telegrams. It costs about 15/30FF to fax an A4 page within France/Europe.

Email & Internet Access

France's postal service, La Poste operates Internet stations known as Cyberposte (www .cyberposte.com) at numerous post offices across the region. A Carte Cyberposte – a rechargeable chip card – costs an initial 30FF, including one hour's online access, then 30FF per hour. Private mailboxes that can receive email messages can be set up at any Cyberposte station. Alternatively, simply set up your own Web-based email account for free with Hotmail, Yahoo or eKno (www .ekno.lonelyplanet.com). French accents in email addresses can safely be ignored. Addresses in France are often preceded by *mél*, short for *message électronique*.

Several places in the region – such as the municipality-funded Le Kiosque du Net in Arles and the State-funded youth resource centre known as Bureau d'Information Jeunesse in Nîmes – offer free Internet access. There are commercial cybercafes charging 25FF to 50FF per hour in Aix-en-Provence, Arles, Avignon, Cannes, Carpentras, Marseilles, Monaco, Nice, Nîmes, Orange, St-Tropez and Toulon.

If you plan to carry your laptop or palmtop computer with you, remember that the power supply voltage in France may vary from that at home. Invest in a universal AC adapter for your appliance. You'll also need an adapter *(adapteur)* between your telephone plug and the standard T-shaped French receptacle. You can pick these up at a local electronics shop or from a Web-based dealer such as Magellan's (www .magellans.com).

Most mid-range hotels in France are quite savvy about the Internet, although telephones hard-wired into the wall remain a common problem; if this is the case, ask the receptionist if you can plug directly into the hotel's fax line. On newer SNCF trains an 'office space' next to the luggage compartments between carriages – complete with desk and plug to hook your laptop into the electricity supply – is provided for passengers. At Marseilles-Provence international airport there are Internet hook-up stations (for which you can pay by credit card) in hall four of domestic departures. For more information on travelling with a portable computer, visit online at www .teleadapt.com or www.warrior.com.

INTERNET RESOURCES

There's no better place to start your Web explorations than at Lonely Planet's Web site: www.lonelyplanet.com, where you'll find succinct summaries on travelling to most places on earth, postcards from other travellers and the Thorn Tree bulletin board, where you can ask questions before you go or dispense advice when you get back. The sub-WWWay section links you to the most useful travel resources elsewhere on the Web.

Provence-related Web sites are plentiful. Most tourist offices have an English-French site (listed in the regional chapters), loaded with practical information. Other useful sites include:

Côte d'Azur Web News Weekly Riviera news, hot off the press from the Côte d'Azur Agency for Economic Development at Sophia-Antipolis technology park
www.cad.fr

France Holiday Store One-stop holiday shop for trips to France from the UK; everything from the latest Eurostar deals to package breaks, property searches and online bookings
www.fr-holidaystore.co.uk

Index des Sites Internet Provence, Alpes, Côte d'Azur & Monaco French site with exhaustive set of links to hundreds of useful Provence-related Web sites, including all the official tourist-office sites
www.index-paca.net

Lubéron News Events and entertainment listings, last-minute accommodation deals, weather reports, news and everything else imaginable for the Lubéron-bound traveller
www.luberon-news.fr

Provence Beyond Comprehensive site with insightful information on everything from gastronomy and astronomy to hotel/restaurant '/museum/hilltop-village listings.
www.beyond.fr

BOOKS

Most books are published in different editions by different publishers in different countries. So a book might be a hardcover rarity in one country while it's readily available in paperback in another. Fortunately, bookshops and libraries search by title or author, hence can advise you on the availability of the books recommended here. The following list is limited to works still in print and generally available in paperback. The year in brackets is the original publication date.

Lonely Planet

Lonely Planet guides to *France, Western Europe, Mediterranean Europe* and *Europe on a Shoestring* include sections on Provence and the Côte d'Azur. You might also want to check out *Paris, The Loire, Corsica, South-West France* and *World Food France*. It also publishes a handy French phrasebook and, for those who want even more action, *Walking in France* and *Cycling France*.

Guidebooks

Michelin publishes two guides to the region. Provence and the Côte d'Azur are covered in its *guide vert* (green guide) series (as two separate guides, each available in English) and Haute-Provence is included in *Alpes du Sud.*

Roman Remains of Southern France by James Bromwich is one of the few guides to unearth just what its title suggests.

General

Taurine Provence (re-published in 1994 by Alyscamps Provençal Library), by 1930s matador Roy Campbell, unravels the history of the Provençal bullfight.

The National Front and French Politics: The Resistible Rise of Jean-Marie Le Pen (1995) by then BBC World Service correspondent Jonathan Marcus.

J'Accuse: The Dark Side of Nice (1982) is a highly emotive essay by Graham Greene in which he expounds local government corruption and organised crime in Nice.

The Man Behind the Iron Mask (1988) by John Noone. An academic study on the identity of the enigmatic man behind the iron mask, immortalised by Dumas in his Three Musketeers trilogy (see Literature in the Facts About Provence chapter).

Luminous Debris: Reflecting on Vestige in Provence & Languedoc (1999) by poet and novelist Gustaf Sobin whose series of essays, inspired by the region's rich Roman heritage, address the past, the present and the grey area inbetween.

Riviera High Life

Côte d'Azur: Inventing the French Riviera (1992) by Mary Blume looks at the glamorous rise and fall of the Côte d'Azur.

Hollywood on the Riviera: The Inside Story of the Cannes Film Festival (1992) by Cari Beauchamp & Henri Béhar. A history of the festival and its stars, laced with celebrity names.

Two Weeks in the Midday Sun – A Cannes Notebook (1987) by Roger Ebert. 'Disneyland for adults' (Cannes' International Film Festival) seen through the backdoor by a festival hack.

The Grimaldis of Monaco (1992) by Anne Edwards. Detailed biography of Monaco's royal family, covering 'centuries of scandal, years of Grace' from 1215 through to 1990.

Everybody was So Young (1998) by Amanda Vaill. Beautifully evocation of American couple Gerald and Sara Murphy on the Riviera, their glamorous set of literary friends (F Scott Fitzgerald, Hemingway, Cole Porter, Picasso, etc) and the jazzy 1920s era in which they lived.

King of Cannes: Madness, Mayhem & the Movies (2000) by Stephen Walker. True story of a British filmmaker who goes to Cannes to make a movie.

Literature

Provence and the Côte d'Azur has been immortalised in foreign literature since the 18th century when the first European writers ventured here. By the early 20th century it had blossomed into a bohemia for artists seeking sunlight and social freedom.

Provençal literature is well addressed in *The Literature of Provence: An Introduction* (2000) by Marseilles-born Daniel Vitaglione. For suggested reading by Provençal writers, see Literature in the Facts about Provence chapter.

Jigsaw (1989) by Sybille Bedford. An autobiographical novel inspired by her years in Toulon during the 1920s and '30s. Bedford's earlier novels, *A Favourite of the Gods* (1963) and *A Compass Error* (1968) are both partly set on the Côte d'Azur.

Jericho (1992) by Dirk Bogarde. A sleuth novel set in rural Provence where Bogarde lived for more than 20 years. Its sequel *A Period of Adjustment* (1994) is likewise set in Provence.

An Orderly Man (1983) & *A Short Walk from Harrods* (1996) by Dirk Bogarde. The British film icon describes his renovation of a Provençal farmhouse and his subsequent retirement in Provence in the third and sixth volumes of his seven-volume autobiography.

To Die in Provence (1999) by Norman Bogner. Violent thriller set around a girl studying in the south of France.

The Mystery of the Blue Train (re-published 2000) by Agatha Christie. Hercule Poirot investigates a mysterious murder case aboard the *Train Bleu* (Blue Train) to the Riviera.

The Rock Pool (1996) by Cyril Connolly. 1930s decadence on the French Riviera.

The Rover (1923) by Joseph Conrad. Set in and around Toulon.

Little Dorrit (1857) by Charles Dickens. Classic novel which opens with Marseilles 'burning in the sun'.

Hallucinating Foucault (1996) by Patricia Duncker. Thrilling post-modern novel that sees a heterosexual Cambridge postgraduate get entwined in a passionate affair with schizophrenic, homosexual French writer Paul Michel; the novel climaxes in Nice.

The Count of Monte Cristo (1845) & *The Three Musketeers* (1844) by French novelist Alexandre Dumas (1802–70). Two classics partly set in 19th-century Marseilles.

The Avignon Quintet (1992) by Lawrence Durrell. A one-volume, awesome 1367-page edition of five Durrell novels, written 1974–85 and opening on an Avignon-bound train.

The Hairdressers of St-Tropez (1995) by Rupert Everett. Comedy of hairdressers and talking dogs that kicks off on St-Tropez's Pampelonne beach in 2042.

Tender is the Night (1934) by F Scott Fitzgerald. Vivid account of life during the decadent 1920s Jazz Age; set on Cap d'Antibes with day trips to Cannes.

Bits of Paradise (1976) by F Scott & Zelda Fitzgerald. Collection of 21 short stories by one of the Riviera's most notorious couples; Scott's 'Love in the Night' (1925), set in Cannes, really is the ultimate romance.

Loser Takes All (1955) by Grahame Greene. Short novel written in 1955 in which a young couple are manipulated into honeymooning at Monte Carlo's Hôtel de Paris.

May We Borrow Your Husband (1967) by Graham Greene. Insightful collection of short 'comedy of sexual life' stories, kicking off with two homosexuals' pursuit of a newly-wed groom while he is honeymooning in Antibes with his virgin wife. Written by Greene when he lived in Antibes. Republished by Vintage in 2000.

Garden of Eden (1987) by Ernest Hemingway. Posthumous novel set in 1920s Le Grau du Roi, near Aigues-Mortes in the Camargue. Two honeymooners pursue a hedonistic life in the sun.

The Bull that Thought (1924) by Rudyard Kipling. Short story about bullfighting in Arles, with a twist, by the winner of the 1907 Nobel Prize for literature.

Dying on the Vine – A Further Adventure of the Gourmet Detective (1998) by Peter King. A murder-mystery, set in Provence, geared to what the protagonist eats next.

The Doves' Nest & Other Stories (1923) by Katherine Mansfield. The title story disects the lives of lonely women living in a villa on the Riviera.

Collected Short Stories (1990) by Somerset Maugham. Includes a short story, 'The Facts of Life', about a tennis player taking to the gambling tables at Monte Carlo; and 'Three Fat Women from Antibes', inspired by the years Maugham lived on Cap Ferrat.

Provença (1910) & *Cantos* (1919) by imagist poet Ezra Pound. Two collections of poems based around modern adaptations of traditional Provençal songs and troubadour ballads.

The Fly-Truffler (2000) by Gustaf Sobin. Philosophical novel centred around a professor of the Provençal language and his insatiable appetite for truffles.

Perfume (1985) by Patrick Süskind. Evocation of the horrors of the 18th-century perfume industry. Much of the action – a quest to create the perfect perfume from the scent of murdered virgins – takes place in steamy Grasse.

Travelogues

Paradise & Pestilence – Aspects of Provence (1997) by Suzanne St-Albans. Autobiography of the duchess of St-Albans who moved to Vence in 1977 to restore her parents' home.

A Spell in Wild France (1992) by Bill & Laurel Cooper. A vivid portrait of the highs and lows of life on a boat moored near Aigues-Mortes in Camargue cowboy land. The couple's canal journey to Provence is recorded in *Watersteps Through France* (1996).

Cesar's Vast Ghosts: Aspects of Provence (1990) by Lawrence Durrell. Philosophical reflections on Provençal history & culture, published just a few days before the author's death in Somières, near Nîmes. Highlights include the poem 'Statue of Lovers: Aix'; the travelogue on Roman

Provence; and the close examination of the 'bullmania of the extreme south'.

Two Towns in Provence (1964) by MFK Fisher. A street-by-street, fountain-by-fountain celebration of Aix-en-Provence and Marseilles. Particularly colourful accounts of Marseillaise women.

Perfume from Provence (1935), **Sunset House** & **Trampled Lilies** by Lady Fortescue. A record of a lady's life, from the purchase of a house outside Grasse to her final flight back to the UK at the start of WWII.

A Little Tour in France (1885). Henry James vividly portrays Van Gogh's 19th-century Arles, first visited by James in 1882.

A Year in Provence (1989) and **Toujours Provence** (1991) by Peter Mayle. Best-selling accounts of life in the Lubéron that take a witty look at the Provençal through English eyes.

A Dog's Life (1995), **Anything Considered** (1996) & **Chasing Cézanne** (1997) by Peter Mayle. A look at Lubéron life through the eyes of a dog; the adventures of a flat-sitter in Monaco; the hunt for a stolen Cézanne. Beach reading.

Encore Provence (1999) by Peter Mayle. A non-fiction collection of pieces about people and other curiosities in the area.

Travels with Virginia Woolf (1993) by Jan Morris. Entertaining extracts from Woolf's journals, including observations made during visits to the Cassis home of her sister (Vanessa Bell).

Travels through France & Italy (1766) by Tobias Smollett. The Scottish author's ruthless candour caused outrage amongst local Niçois when this book was published in the late 18th century.

A Motor-Flight through France (1908) by Edith Wharton. Amusing account of the author's motor trip from Paris to Provence in 1906 and 1907; re-published in 1995 with an introduction by Julian Barnes.

Art, Artists & Architecture

Artists (Cézanne, Chagall, Matisse, Picasso, etc) and movements (impressionism, Fauvism, etc) are covered by various titles in the *World of Art* series by Thames & Hudson (☎ 020-7636 5488, ⓔ sales@ thameshudson.co.uk), 30–34 Bloomsbury Street, London WC1B 3QP. You can Visit online at www.thesaurus.co.uk/thamesand hudson. Notable books specific to Provence include *Artists and their Museums on the Riviera* (1998) by Barbara Freed; and *Lartigue's Riviera* (essay by Mary Blume,

picture selection by Martine d'Astier), which includes a stunning collection of black-and-white photographs of the coast taken by Jacques Lartigue between the 1920s and 1960s.

FILM

Watching a film either set in Provence or using the region as a backdrop is a fabulous way of getting in gear for a trip to France's southern realms. For films by Provence-born directors, see under Film in the Facts about Provence chapter.

Several 1950s classics were filmed here, among them François Truffaut's *Les Mistons* (1958) filmed exclusively in Nîmes; Jacques Démy's *La Baie des Anges* (The Bay of Angels, 1962); Henri Decoin's *Masque de Fer* (Iron Mask, 1962), parts of which were filmed in Sospel; Rohmer's *La Collectionneuse* (The Collectors, 1966) which was shot in St-Tropez; and the first in the series of Jean Girault's celebrated *Gendarme de St-Tropez* (1964). In 1972 François Truffaut filmed part of *La Nuit Américaine* (The American Night, 1972) in the Victorine studios, the Niçois hinterland and the Vésubie Valley.

The region also featured in foreign films, most notably Hitchcock's suspense thriller, *La Main au Collet* (To Catch a Thief, 1956), starring Cary Grant and Grace Kelly; John Frankenheimer's *French Connection 2*; and Disney's lovable *Herbie goes to Monte Carlo* (1977) starring Herbie the Volkswagen Beetle.

Modern French cinema has seen a renewed interest in Pagnol's great classics of Provence. In 1986 Claude Berri came up with *Jean de Florette* followed by *Manon des Sources*, modern versions of Pagnol's original works, which proved enormously popular both in France and abroad. Parts of the films were shot in the Plan-d'Aups-Ste-Baume. In 1990 Yves Robert directed *La Gloire de Mon Père* (My Father's Glory) and *Le Château de Ma Mère* (My Mother's Castle), Pagnol's autobiographical novels.

The 1998 Hollywood box office hit *The Man in the Iron Mask*, directed by screenwriter Randall Wallace, starred Gérard

Depardieu alongside Leonardo DiCaprio and Jeremy Irons. The film was a modern adaptation of the 'iron mask' mystery that occurred on the Île Ste-Marguerite near Cannes in the late 17th century and was consequently immortalised by Alexandre Dumas in his novel *Le Vicomte de Bragelonne* (the final novel in the Musketeers trilogy).

The first novel in the Dumas trilogy, *Le Comte de Monte Cristo* (The Count of Monte Cristo) – which opens with the lead character's dramatic escape from the Château d'If near Marseilles – has been adapted for cinema or television 29 times since 1907. The most recent version was Josée Dayan's TV-series adaptation (1998) starring Gérard Depardieu as the revengeful Dantès.

NEWSPAPERS & MAGAZINES

The leading regional, daily newspapers are *Nice Matin* (www.nicematin.fr), which has a separate Toulon-based Var edition, *Var-Matin*; and *La Provence* (www.laprovence-presse.fr), which is the result of a merger between *Le Provençal* and the right-wing *Le Méridional*.

The *Riviera Reporter* is a free A4-sized magazine, published every two months. It runs handy job and property listings, local gossip and other titbits and can be picked up in most English-language bookshops. Annual subscriptions (⒠ reporter@riviera-reporter.com) cost 160/210FF in Europe/USA, Canada, Australia and New Zealand. Read news online at www.riviera-reporter.com. Another English-language publication is *The News*, covering all of France but with a strong southern bias (10FF).

Reams of fantastically expensive dream properties to rent or buy fill the glossy pages of *New Riviera-Côte d'Azur*, a quarterly, 100-plus page magazine that markets itself as the 'international magazine' of the Côte d'Azur. It runs a social diary and hotel and restaurant reviews and costs 45FF. Other similar glossies loaded with fashion pics and few articles of any depth include the quarterly *Dream Homes to Rent* (50FF) and the monthly *Côte-La Revue d'Azur*

(15FF), which runs a separate Cannes edition called *Cannes Magazine-La Revue Côte d'Azur* (30FF).

English-language newspapers of the day – *International Herald Tribune, Washington Post, USA Today*, and the *Guardian* or the *Times* – are easy to pick up in Nice, Marseilles and most coastal resorts. They are practically impossible to find in Haute-Provence and other rural spots. A *Sunday Times/Herald Tribune* usually costs 25/10FF.

RADIO & TV

Monte Carlo-based Riviera Radio is an English-language radio station that broadcasts 24 hours a day and includes BBC World Service news every hour. It can be picked up on 106.3MHz FM in Monaco and on 106.5MHz FM along the rest of the Côte d'Azur. It has Internet relay at www.riviera-radio.com.

The BBC World Service can be picked up on 12095kHz (a good daytime frequency, 6 am to 7 pm), 6195kHz (6 to 9 am, 9 pm to 1 am), 9410kHz (6 to 9 am, 8 pm to midnight) and 15575kHz (last-ditch attempt, should others fail); and via Internet relay at www.bbc.co.uk/worldservice.

Indispensable for motorists, particularly in high season, is Traffic FM (107.7MHz FM), which broadcasts regular traffic news in English, French and Italian.

Local French-language radio stations include Radio Provence (103.6MHz and 102.9MHz FM), Radio Vaucluse (100.4MHz FM), Radio Lubéron (88.6MHz FM) and Cannes Radio (91.5MHz FM). Popular music channels include Nostalgie (98.3MHz FM) for golden oldies and Chérie FM (100.1MHz FM) for the latest hits.

VIDEO SYSTEMS

SECAM is used in France and Monaco (unlike the rest of Western Europe and Australia, which use PAL). French videotapes can't be played on video recorders and TVs that lack a SECAM capability.

PHOTOGRAPHY & VIDEO

Colour-print and slide *(diapositive)* film is widely available in supermarkets, photo shops and FNAC stores, as are replacement video cartridges for your camcorder.

Sunlight is extreme in southern France; avoid snapping at midday when the glare is strongest. Photography is rarely forbidden, except in museums, art galleries and some churches (such as Matisse's Chapelle du Rosaire in Vence). Snapshots of military installations are not really appreciated.

TIME
French and Monégasque time is GMT/UTC plus one hour, except during daylight-saving time (from the last Sunday in March to the last Sunday in October) when it is GMT/UTC plus two hours. The UK and France are always one hour apart – when it's 6 pm in London, it's 7 pm in Nice. New York is six hours behind Nice.

France uses the 24-hour clock and writes time like this: 15h30 (ie, 3.30 pm). Time has no meaning for many people in Provence.

ELECTRICITY
France and Monaco run on 220V at 50Hz AC. Sockets have two round prongs and a protruding earth (ground) prong.

WEIGHTS & MEASURES
France uses the metric system. When writing numbers with four or more digits, the French use full stops (periods) or spaces (as opposed to commas): one million is 1.000.000 or 1 000 000. Decimals, on the other hand, are written with commas, so 1.75 becomes 1,75.

LAUNDRY
Doing laundry while on the road is a straightforward affair. In most towns there is an unstaffed, self-service laundrette (laverie libre-service) that opens from about 7 am to 7 pm.

Laundrettes are most expensive along the coast (20FF to 30FF for a 7kg machine, then 2/5FF for five/12 minutes' drying).

TOILETS
Public Toilets
Public toilets, signposted toilettes or WC, are surprisingly few and far between, mean-

ing you can be left feeling really rather desperate. Towns that have public toilets generally tout them near the mairie (town hall) or in the port area. Expect to pay 2FF to 5FF in exchange for a wad of toilet paper (soft variety). Other towns have coin-operated, self-flushing toilet booths – usually in car parks and public squares – which cost 2FF to enter; these are highly disconcerting contraptions should the automatic mechanism fail with you inside. Some places sport flushless, kerbside urinoirs (urinals) reeking with generations of urine. Failing that, there's always McDonald's.

Restaurants, cafes and bars are often woefully under-equipped with such amenities, so start queuing ahead of time. Bashful males be warned: some toilets are semi-co-ed; the urinals and washbasins are in a common area through which all and sundry pass to get to the toilet stalls. Older establishments often sport Turkish-style toilettes à la turque – a squat toilet with a high-pressure flushing mechanism that can soak your feet if you don't step back in time.

Bidets
A bidet is a porcelain fixture that looks like a shallow toilet with a pop-up stopper in the base. Originally conceived to improve the personal hygiene of aristocratic women, its primary purpose is for washing the genitals and anal area, though its uses have expanded to include everything from hand-washing laundry to soaking your feet.

Bidets are to be found in many hotel rooms. Cheap hotels often serve rooms with a bidet and washbasin (lavabo).

HEALTH
Provence and the Côte d'Azur are healthy places. Your main risks are sunburn, foot blisters, insect bites and an upset stomach from eating and drinking too much.

Predeparture Planning
Immunisations No jabs are required to travel to France. However, there are a few routine vaccinations that are recommended whether you're travelling or not:

polio (usually administered during childhood), tetanus and diphtheria (usually administered together during childhood and updated every 10 years), and sometimes measles. All vaccinations should be recorded on an International Health Certificate. These are available from your doctor or the government health department.

Health Insurance Make sure you have adequate health insurance if you are not a citizen of an EU country; see Travel Insurance under Visas & Documents earlier. Citizens of EU countries are covered for emergency medical treatment throughout the EU on presentation of an E111 certificate, though charges are likely for medication, dental work and secondary examinations, including X-rays and laboratory tests. Ask about the E111 at your national health service or travel agency at least a few weeks before you go. In the UK, you can get the forms at post offices. Claims must be submitted to a local sickness insurance office *(caisse primaire d'assurance maladie)* before you leave France.

Other Preparations Ensure that you are healthy before you start travelling. If you are going on a long trip, make sure your teeth are OK. If you wear glasses take a spare pair and your prescription.

If you require a particular medication take an adequate supply, as it may not be available locally. Take part of the packaging showing the generic name, rather than the brand, which will make getting replacements easier. It's a good idea to have a legible prescription or letter from your doctor to show that you legally use the medication to avoid any problems.

Medical Treatment

Major hospitals are indicated on the maps in this book, and their addresses and phone numbers are mentioned in the text. Tourist offices and hotels can put you on to a doctor or dentist, and your embassy or consulate will probably know one who speaks your language. For emergency phone numbers, see Emergencies later in this chapter.

Medical Kit Check List

Following is a list of items you should consider including in your medical kit – consult your pharmacist for brands available in your country.

☐ **Aspirin** or **paracetamol** (acetaminophen in the USA) – for general pain or fever

☐ **Antihistamine** – for allergies, for example hay fever; to ease the itch from insect bites or stings; and to prevent motion sickness

☐ **Loperamide** or **Lomotil** for diarrhoea; **prochlorperazine** or **metaclopramide** for nausea and vomiting

☐ **Rehydration mixture** – to prevent dehydration, which may occur during bouts of diarrhoea; particularly important when travelling with children

☐ **Antiseptic**, such as povidone-iodine – for cuts and grazes

☐ **Calamine lotion**, **sting relief spray** or **aluminium sulphate spray** – to ease irritation from bites or stings

☐ **Bandages** and **Band-Aids (plasters)**

☐ **Scissors**, **tweezers** and a **thermometer** (note that mercury thermometers are prohibited by airlines)

☐ **Cold and flu tablets**, **throat lozenges** and **nasal decongestant**

☐ **Insect repellent**, **sunscreen**, a **chapstick**, **eye drops** and **water purification tablets**

Public Health System Anyone (including foreigners) who is sick can receive treatment in the casualty ward or emergency room of any public hospital. Hospitals try to have people who speak English in the casualty wards, but this is not done systematically. If necessary, the hospital will call in an interpreter.

Pharmacies French pharmacies are marked by a green cross, the neon components of which are lit when it's open. Pharmacists can often suggest treatments for minor ailments. If you are prescribed medication, make sure you understand the dosage. Ask for a copy of the prescription *(ordonnance)* for your records.

Pharmacies coordinate their closure so that a town isn't left without a place to buy medication. Details of the nearest weekend- or night-duty pharmacy *(pharmacie de garde)* are posted on most pharmacy doors. There are 24-hour pharmacies in Nice and Marseilles.

During the mushroom picking season (autumn), many pharmacies act as a mushroom identifying service.

24-Hour Doctor Service If your problem is not sufficiently serious to call SAMU (see Emergencies later), but you still need to consult a doctor at night, call the 24-hour doctor service, operational in most towns in the region, including in Nice (☎ 04 93 52 42 42), Aix-en-Provence (☎ 04 42 26 24 00) and Avignon (☎ 04 90 87 75 00, 04 90 87 76 00). The hospitals in all three cities also operate a 24-hour emergency service.

Basic Rules

Water Tap water all over France is safe to drink. Despite Provence's sheer abundance of fountains, the water spouting out of them is not always drinkable: *eau non potable* means 'undrinkable water'. Most fountains are signposted accordingly.

It's very easy to not drink enough liquids, particularly in summer, on hot days or at high altitude. Don't rely on thirst to indicate when you should drink. Not needing to urinate or very dark-yellow urine is a danger sign. Carrying a water bottle is a good idea.

Environmental Hazards

Fungal Infections Most fungal infections occur more often in hot weather and are usually found on the scalp, between the toes or fingers, in the groin and on the body (ringworm). You get ringworm (which is a fungal infection, not a worm) from infected animals or other people. Moisture encourages these infections.

To prevent fungal infections wear loose, comfortable clothes, avoid artificial fibres, wash frequently and dry carefully. If you do get an infection, wash the infected area at least daily with a disinfectant or medicated soap and water, and rinse and dry well. Apply an antifungal cream or powder like tolnifate (Tinaderm). Try to expose the infected area to air or sunlight as much as possible and wash all towels and underwear in hot water, change them often and let them dry in the sun.

Hay Fever Those who suffer from hay fever can look forward to sneezing their way around rural Provence in May and June when the pollen count is at its highest.

Heat Exhaustion Dehydration and salt deficiency can cause heat exhaustion. Take time to acclimatise to the high temperatures, drink sufficient liquids and do not do anything too physically demanding.

Salt deficiency is characterised by fatigue, lethargy, headaches, giddiness and muscle cramps; salt tablets may help, but adding extra salt to your food is better.

Motion Sickness Eating lightly before and during a trip will reduce the chances of motion sickness. If you are prone to motion sickness try to find a place that minimises movement – near the wing on aircraft, close to midship on boats, near the centre on buses. Fresh air usually helps; reading and cigarette smoke don't. Commercial motion sickness preparations, which can cause drowsiness, have to be taken before the trip commences. Ginger (available as capsules) and peppermint (including mint-flavoured sweets) are natural preventatives.

Prickly Heat This is an itchy rash caused by excessive perspiration trapped under the skin. It usually strikes people who have just arrived in a hot climate. Keeping cool, bathing often, drying the skin and using a mild talcum or prickly heat powder, or resorting to air-conditioning may help.

Sunburn You can get sunburnt surprisingly quickly, even through cloud. Use a sunscreen, hat, and barrier cream for your nose and lips. Calamine lotion or Stingose are good for mild sunburn. Protect your eyes with good quality sunglasses, particularly if you will be near water, sand or snow.

Infectious Diseases

Diarrhoea Simple things such as a change of water, food or climate can all cause a mild bout of diarrhoea, but a few rushed toilet trips with no other symptoms is not indicative of a major problem.

Dehydration is the main danger with any diarrhoea, particularly in children or the elderly, as it can occur quickly. Fluid replacement (at least equal to the volume being lost) is most important. Weak black tea with a little sugar, soda water, or soft drinks allowed to go flat and diluted 50% with clean water are all good. Keep drinking small amounts often. Stick to a bland diet as you recover.

AIDS & HIV The Human Immunodeficiency Virus (VIH in French), develops into AIDS, Acquired Immune Deficiency Syndrome (SIDA in French), which is a fatal disease. Any exposure to blood, blood products or body fluids may put an individual at risk. The disease is often transmitted through sexual contact or dirty needles – vaccinations, acupuncture, tattooing and body piercing can be potentially as dangerous as intravenous drug use. HIV/AIDS can also be spread through infected blood transfusions; some developing countries cannot afford to screen blood used for transfusions. Fear of HIV infection should never preclude treatment for serious medical conditions.

For information on free and anonymous HIV-testing centres *(centres de dépistage)*, ring the SIDA Info Service toll-free, 24 hours a day (☎ 08 00 84 08 00). Information is available in Nice at the Centre de Dépistage du VIH (☎ 04 93 85 12 62), 2 rue Édouard Béri (corner of Hôpital St-Roch); and in Marseilles at the Centre de Dépistage (☎ 04 91 78 43 43, metro Castellane), 10 rue St-Adrien.

CRIPS (Centres Régionaux d'Information et Prévention sur le SIDA; ☎ 04 91 13 03 40 in Marseilles, ☎ 04 92 14 41 20 in Nice) is a national chain of information centres which offer practical help and guidance. AIDES is a national organisation that works for the prevention of AIDS and assists AIDS sufferers. It has its regional head office in Marseilles (☎ 04 91 14 05 15, ✉ aidesprovence@pacman.fr), 1 rue Gilbert Dru, 13002 Marseilles. It has a Web site at www.aides.org (French only).

Sexually Transmitted Diseases Gonorrhoea, herpes and syphilis are among these diseases; sores, blisters or rashes around the genitals, discharges or pain when urinating are common symptoms. In some STDs, such as wart virus or chlamydia, symptoms may be less marked or not observed at all, especially in women. Syphilis symptoms eventually disappear completely but the disease continues and can cause severe problems in later years. While abstinence from sexual contact is the only 100% effective prevention, using condoms is also effective. The treatment of gonorrhoea and syphilis is with antibiotics. The different sexually transmitted diseases each require specific antibiotics. There is no cure for herpes or AIDS.

All pharmacies carry condoms *(préservatifs)* and many have 24-hour automatic condom dispensers outside the door. Some brasseries, discotheques, metro stations and WCs in cafes and petrol stations are also equipped with condom machines. Condoms that conform to French government standards are marked with the letters NF *(norme française)* in black on a white oval inside a red and blue rectangle.

Rabies This is a fatal viral infection found in many countries. Animals can be infected and it is their saliva that is infectious. Any bite, scratch or even lick from a warm-blooded, furry animal should be cleaned immediately and thoroughly. Medical help should be sought promptly to receive a course of injections to prevent the onset of symptoms and death.

Bites & Stings

Bee and wasp stings are usually painful rather than dangerous. However, in people who are allergic to them severe breathing difficulties may occur and they may require urgent medical care. Calamine lotion or Stingose spray will give relief, and ice packs will reduce the pain and swelling.

Jellyfish Local advice will help prevent your coming into contact with jellyfish *(méduses)* and their stinging tentacles, often found along the Mediterranean. Dousing the wound in vinegar will de-activate any stingers that have not 'fired'. Calamine lotion, antihistamines and analgesics may reduce the reaction and relieve the pain. The sting of the Portuguese man-of-war, which has a sail-like float and long tentacles, is painful but rarely fatal.

Ticks Check all over your body if you have been walking through a potentially tick-infested area, as ticks can cause skin infections and other more serious diseases. If a tick is found attached, press down around the tick's head with tweezers, grab the head and gently pull upwards. Avoid pulling the rear of the body as this may squeeze the tick's gut contents through the attached mouth parts into the skin, increasing the risk of infection and disease. Smearing chemicals on the tick will not make it let go and is not recommended.

Women's Health
Antibiotic use, synthetic underwear, sweating and contraceptive pills can lead to fungal vaginal infections when travelling in hot climates. Maintaining good personal hygiene, and wearing loose-fitting clothes and cotton underwear will help to prevent them. Fungal infections, characterised by a rash, itch and discharge, can be treated with a vinegar or lemon juice douche, or with yoghurt. Nystatin, miconazole or clotrimazole pessaries or vaginal cream are the usual treatment.

WOMEN TRAVELLERS
French men have clearly given little thought to the concept of *harcèlement sexuel* (sexual harassment). Most still believe that staring suavely at a passing woman is paying her a compliment. Women need not walk round the region in fear, however. Suave stares are about as adventurous as most French men get, with women rarely being physically assaulted on the street or touched up in bars at night.

Unfortunately, it's not French men that women travellers have to concern themselves with. While women attract little unwanted attention in rural Provence, on the coast it's a different ball game. In the dizzying heat of the high season, the Côte d'Azur is rampant with men (and women) of *all* nationalities out on the pull. Apply the usual 'women traveller' rules and the chances are you'll emerge from the circus unscathed. Remain conscious of your surroundings, avoid going to bars and clubs alone at night and be aware of potentially dangerous situations: deserted streets, lonely beaches, dark corners of large train stations, and on night buses in certain districts of Marseilles and Nice.

Topless sunbathing is not generally interpreted as deliberately provocative.

Organisations
SOS Viol is a voluntary women's group that staffs the national rape-crisis hotline (☎ 08 00 05 95 95). Its centre in Marseilles is spearheaded by SOS Femmes (☎ 04 91 42 07 00) and in Nice by Femmes Battues (☎ 04 93 52 17 81).

GAY & LESBIAN TRAVELLERS
France is one of Europe's most liberal countries when it comes to homosexuality, in part because of the long French tradition of public tolerance towards groups of people who have chosen not to live by conventional social codes. There are large gay and lesbian communities in Aix-en-Provence, Cannes, Nice and Marseilles. The latter hosts a colourful Gay Pride march in late June or early July. For more details check out www.marseillepride.org (French only). The lesbian scene is less public than its gay counterpart.

The most active gay and lesbian groups in the region are in Marseilles: they include Act Up Marseilles (☎ 04 91 94 08 43,

Vineyards and olive groves dominate the colourful Provençal landscape.

Traditional puppets take centre stage.

Visit a few different bars in Salon de Provence.

Pull up a seat and drink to the next grape harvest (or football match) in Le Panier, Marseilles.

The scent of Provence – lavender blooms in July

Bories (shepherds' stores) dot the Lubéron

Shop till you drop in Les Baux de Provence.

Dine under street lights at Place du Forum, Arles, and top the night off with a strong pastis.

actupp@compuserve.com), 40 rue Sénac, with a Web site at www.actupp.org (French only); the lesbian group, Centre Évolutif Lilith (CEL; ☎ 04 91 55 08 61), 18 cours Pierre Puget; and Arc-en-Ciel (☎ 04 91 91 01 17, e maec@france.qrd.org), 20 rue Colbert, BP 2081, 13203 Marseilles, which publishes *Le Chaperon Rouge* (a what's on guide). Visit its Web site at www.maec.net (French only).

DISABLED TRAVELLERS

The region is not user-friendly for *handicapés* (disabled people): kerb ramps are few and far between, older public facilities and budget hotels lack lifts, and the cobblestone streets typical of Provence's numerous hill-top villages are a nightmare to navigate in a wheelchair.

But all is not lost. Many two- or three-starred hotels are equipped with lifts; Michelin's *Guide Rouge* indicates hotels with lifts and facilities for disabled people. On the coast, there are beaches with wheelchair access in Cannes, Marseilles, Nice, Hyères and Ste-Maxime.

Both international airports offer assistance to disabled travellers. At Aéroport International Nice-Côte d'Azur, contact the Service Handicapés GIS (☎ 04 93 21 44 58); at Aéroport International Marseilles-Provence, call the Société d'Assistance Midi-Provence (☎ 04 42 14 27 42). TGV and regular trains are also accessible to a passenger in a wheelchair *(fauteuil roulant)*, provided they reserve by phone or at a train station at least 48 hours before departure. Wheelchair users and their travelling companion can travel in 1st class for the prices of a 2nd-class fare. Details are available in SNCF's booklet *Le Mémento du Voyageur à Mobilité Réduite* (one page in English). Alternatively, contact SNCF Accessibilité Service (☎ 08 00 15 47 53).

Particularly useful is *Gîtes Accessibles aux Personnes Handicapées*, an accommodation guide (60FF) listing *gîtes ruraux* and *chambres d'hôtes* with disabled access in the region. It's published by Gîtes de France (see Self-Catering Accommodation later in this chapter).

SENIOR TRAVELLERS

Senior travellers are often entitled to discounts on public transport, museum admission fees etc, provided they can show proof of their age (either aged over 60 or 65, depending on the establishment). At large main-line train stations such as Marseilles, SOS Voyageurs (☎ 04 91 62 12 80 in Marseilles) – a voluntary group usually run by retirees – offers help to elderly train travellers. SOS Voyageurs operates 7 am to 7 pm Monday to Saturday.

TRAVEL WITH CHILDREN

Successful travel with young children requires planning and effort. Don't overdo things; trying to see too much can cause problems. Include the kids in the planning of the trip. Balance a day traipsing around hill-top villages or the coast's art museums with time on the beach or an outing to Marineland. Many places along the coast offer special children's activities. For specific ideas on what to do with the kids, see the later boxed text 'Kidding Around'.

Most car-rental firms have children's safety seats *(sièges bébés)* for hire (80FF for the term of the rental). The same goes for highchairs and cots (cribs); they're standard in most restaurants and hotels but numbers are limited. The choice of baby food, infant formulas, soy and cow's milk, disposable nappies (diapers) and the like is as great in French supermarkets as it is back home, but the opening hours may be quite different. Run out of nappies on Saturday afternoon and you're facing a very long and messy weekend.

Most tourist offices have a list of baby-sitting services *(gardes d'enfants)* and crèches. A further information source is Lonely Planet's *Travel with Children*.

DANGERS & ANNOYANCES
Theft

Theft *(vol)* – from backpacks, pockets, cars, trains, laundrettes, beaches – is a serious problem, particularly along the Côte d'Azur. Keep an eagle eye on your bags, especially at train and bus stations, on overnight train rides, in tourist offices, in fast-food restaurants and on beaches.

Always keep your money, credit cards, tickets, passport, driving licence and other important documents in a moneybelt worn inside your trousers or skirt. Keep enough money for the day in a separate wallet. Theft from hotel rooms is less common but it's still not a great idea to leave your life's belongings in your room. In hostels, lock your non-valuables in a locker provided and cart your valuables along. Upmarket hotels have safes (coffres).

When swimming at the beach or taking a dip in the pool, have members of your party take turns sitting with everyone's packs and clothes.

At the train station, if you leave your bags at a left-luggage office or in a luggage locker, treat your claim chit (or locker code) like cash. Daypack snatchers have taken stolen chits to the train station and taken possession of the rest of their victims' belongings.

Forest Fires

Forest fires are common in heavily forested areas in July and August when the sun is hot and the land is dry. Such fires spread

---

Kidding Around

Here are some ideas on what to see and do to keep the young (and young-at-heart) smiling. See under Courses later in this chapter for details on art, craft and cookery classes designed for children. Further details on the following are included in the relevant town listings.

Amusement & Theme Parks

Acrobatic killer-whale shows at Marineland (Biot); giant waterslides at Niagara Parc Nautique (near La Môle); tortoises at the Tortoise Village in the Massif des Maures; 3-D films at the Pont du Gard.

Museums

Musée Océangraphique (Monaco); Musée du Santon and neighbouring santon (see the boxed text 'Little Saints' in the Marseilles chapter for details) workshop (Marseilles); St-Bénézet's Bridge (Avignon); Le Monde Souterrain showcasing stalactites and speleology (Fontaine de Vaucluse); Cathédrale d'Images (Les Baux de Provence); House of Butterflies (St-Tropez).

The Great Outdoors

Diving and sailing anywhere along the coast (most clubs runs classes and courses for kids); canoeing under the Pont du Gard (Collias), down the River Sorgue (the Vaucluse) or in the Gorges du Verdon (Castellane); nature walks organised by the Office National des Forêts (ONF) and Parc National du Mercantour; mountain biking at the Maison du Rafting in the Vallée de l'Ubaye (Haute-Provence); bird-watching in the Parc Ornithologique du Pont de Gau (Camargue); riding a horse like a cowboy (Camargue); cycling around the island of Porquerolles (pedal-powered chariots for kids too small to pedal themselves can be easily hired); riding the téléphérique (cable car) up Mont Faron and visiting the zoo (Toulon); skiing and snowboarding (Haute-Provence); rollerblading (Nice).

Trains & Boats

Electric tourist trains perk up sightseeing for the weary- or small-footed in Marseilles, Nice, Monaco, Mougins, Orange and a handful of other towns; they also chug through Camargais salt pans. Riding the two-car mountain railway part of the way between Nice and Digne-les-Bains is another sure bet.

By boat, sail around the Calanques (Cassis); to Château d'If to tour the fortress dungeons (Marseilles); down the River Rhône (Avignon); around Port Grimaud; or along the coast (from most coastal resorts). Glass-bottomed boats set sail from Nice, Le Lavandou, Port-Cros and Hyères.

incredibly quickly – between 20m and 30m per minute. Between 1 July and the second Sunday in September, the forest authorities close high-risk areas. Never walk in a closed zone. Tourist offices in the region can tell you if a walking path is closed. If you come across a fire, call the fire brigade immediately (see Emergencies on this page).

All forested areas are crisscrossed with road tracks enabling fire crews to penetrate the forest quickly. These roads – signposted DFCI *(défense forestière contre l'incendie)* – are closed to private vehicles but you can follow them on foot.

Lighting a camp fire or barbecue anywhere in the region is forbidden.

Rivers & Lakes

Major rivers in Provence are connected to hydroelectric power stations operated by the national electricity company, Electricité de France (EDF). Water levels rise dramatically if the EDF opens a dam. White-water sports on the Verdon river downstream of the Chaudanne dam *(barrage)* are forbidden when the water flow is less than five cubic metres/second. For information on water levels and dam releases, call ☎ 04 92 83 62 68.

Swimming is prohibited in lakes that are artificial and have steep, unstable banks (ie, Lac de Ste-Croix, south-west of the Gorges du Verdon; and Lac de Castillon and the adjoining Lac de Chaudanne, north-east of the gorges). Sailing, windsurfing and canoeing are restricted to flagged areas.

The Sea

Most larger beaches on the Côte d'Azur have a *poste de secours* (safety post) during the beach season, staffed by lifeguards. In watersport areas, a section of the sea is always sectioned off for swimmers. Always note the colour of the flag flying before diving in: a green flag means that it is safe to swim; yellow means bathing is risky but allowed; red means that swimming is forbidden; and purple means the sea water is polluted.

Poisonous Mushrooms

Wild-mushroom picking is a national pastime in Provence. Pick by all means but don't eat anything until it has been positively identified as safe by a pharmacist. Most pharmacies in the region offer a mushroom-identifying service.

The Mistral

During the balmy days of June and the steamy days of July and August, it is hard to believe that the region can be freezing cold when the mistral strikes (see the boxed text 'What a Menace' in the Facts about Provence chapter).

Thunderstorms in the mountains and hot southern plains can be extremely sudden, violent and dangerous. Check the weather report before you set out on a long walk; even then, be prepared for a sudden weather change. Storms are extremely common in August and September.

EMERGENCIES

The following numbers are toll-free:

SAMU medical treatment/ambulance	☎ 15
Police	☎ 17
Fire brigade	☎ 18
Rape crisis hotline	☎ 08 00 05 95 95

SAMU

When you ring ☎ 15, the 24-hour dispatchers of the Service d'Aide Médicale d'Urgence (Emergency Medical Aid Service) take down details of your problem and send out a private ambulance with a driver (250FF to 300FF) or, if necessary, a mobile intensive-care unit. For less serious problems, SAMU can dispatch a doctor for a house call. If you prefer to be taken to a particular hospital, mention this to the ambulance crew, as the usual procedure is to take you to the nearest one. In emergency cases (ie, those requiring intensive-care units), billing will be taken care of later. Otherwise, you need to pay in cash at the time.

LEGAL MATTERS

The police are allowed to search anyone at any time, regardless of whether there is an obvious reason to do so or not. As elsewhere in the EU, laws are tough when it comes to drinking and driving. The acceptable blood-alcohol limit is 0.05%, with drivers who exceed this amount facing fines of up to 30,000FF and even jail terms. Licences can be immediately suspended.

Importing or exporting drugs can lead to a jail sentence of up to 30 years. The fine for possession of drugs for personal use can be as high as 500,000FF.

If you litter, you risk a 1000FF fine.

Nude bathing is forbidden on St-Tropez's municipal beaches (but bathers still strip off). Since 1994 fines have been imposed in St-Raphaël, Ste-Maxime and Monaco on tourists who walk in town bare-chested or bikini-clad.

BUSINESS HOURS

Museums and shops (but not cinemas, restaurants or bakeries) are closed on public holidays. On Sunday, a boulangerie is usually about all that opens (morning only) and public transport services are less frequent. In villages, shops (including the boulangerie) close for a long lunch between 2 and 4 pm. In Provence, hotels, restaurants, cinemas, cultural institutions and shops close for their congé annuel (annual closure) in winter. Commercial banks generally open 8 or 9 am to 11.30 am or 1 pm and 1.30 or 2 pm to 4.30 or 5 pm weekdays.

Some hotels, museums and chambres d'hôtes (B&Bs) only open Pâques à la Tous- saint; this means Easter to All Saints' Day (1 November). Many places to eat and/or drink in Nice and Marseilles brandish 'open nonstop' signs. Far from meaning they open 24 hours, it actually means that the place opens nonstop – without breaking for that all-essential lunch – between the morning or evening opening hours advertised.

PUBLIC HOLIDAYS & SPECIAL EVENTS

In Provence, festivals (fêtes) and fairs (foires) are a crucial part of community life, with every city/town/village/hamlet throwing a street party at least once a year (usually more often) to celebrate everything from a good lavender or olive crop to the feast of their patron saint. An abundance of food (colossal aïolis, paellas and the like), a pétanque (boules) championship and dancing late into the night are guaranteed to stir the soul of any traveller lucky enough to witness such a joyous occasion.

French National Holidays

National public holidays (jours fériés) are often a cue for festivities to spill into the streets.

New Year's Day (Jour de l'An) 1 January
Easter Sunday (Pâques) & **Easter Monday** (lundi de Pâques) Late March/April
May Day (Fête du Travail) 1 May – buy a muguet (lily of the valley) from a street vendor for good luck
Victoire 1945 8 May– Celebrates the Allied victory in Europe that ended WWII
Ascension Thursday (L'Ascension) May – celebrated on the 40th day after Easter Mid-May to mid-June
Pentecost/Whit Sunday and Whit Monday (Pentecôte & lundi de Pentecôte) – celebrated on the 7th Sunday after Easter
Bastille Day/National Day (Fête Nationale) 14 July
Assumption Day (L'Assomption) 15 August
All Saints' Day (La Toussaint) 1 November
Remembrance Day (Le onze novembre) 11 November – celebrates the armistice of WWI
Christmas (Noël) 25 December

Though not official public holidays, numerous Provençal festivals fall on Shrove Tuesday (Mardi Gras), Maundy (or Holy) Thursday and Good Friday, and Boxing Day (26 December).

Monégasque National Holidays

Monaco shares the same holidays with France except those on 8 May, 14 July and 11 November. In addition it enjoys as public holidays:

Feast of Ste-Dévote 27 January – patron saint of Monaco
Corpus Christi June – three weeks after Ascension
Fête Nationale 19 November (National Day)
Immaculate Conception 8 December

Feasts & Festivals

Provence has a spicy cultural calendar. Most festivals celebrate a historical or folklore tradition, a performing art or, failing that, the region's most beloved pastime – food.

Indispensable is *Terre de Festivals*, a festival-listing guide for the entire region. It's free and is published annually by the Office Régional de la Culture (☎ 04 91 57 54 32, fax 04 91 57 54 40), 3 place Pierre Bertas, 13001 Marseilles. Its contents are online at www.orc-paca.net (French only).

January

Messe de la Truffe Truffle Mass, Richerenches, Sunday nearest to 17 January

Fête des Boudins Sausage festival, Cabrières d'Avignon, 22 January

Journée de la Truffe d'Aups 'Day of the Truffle' with truffle market, a truffle dog competition and demonstration of how a pig snouts truffles, Aups, 4th Sunday in January

February

Fête des Citrons Lemon festival with street sculptures constructed from lemons, Menton

Féria Primavera Three-day bullfighting Spring Festival, Nîmes

Carnaval de Nice The region's most celebrated two-week carnival with floats, masks, fireworks and flower battles, Nice, Mardi Gras

April

Baroques en Provence Three-week Baroque music festival with concerts all over the Vaucluse

Fête de la St-Marc Wine-tasting festival when the best wines of the last *millésime* (vintage) are cracked opened, Châteauneuf du Pape, 25 April

May

Fête des Gardians The day of the Camargue cowboys, Arles, 1 May

Fêtes de la Vigne et du Vin One- or two-day wine festivals in Beaumes de Venise and Sablet

Cannes International Film Festival Ten-day International Film Festival, Cannes

Bravade St-Tropez honours its patron saint with a traditional bravade, 15–17 May

Festival de Jazz en Pays d'Apt Five-day jazz festival with concerts across the Lubéron

Pélerinage des Gitans Three-day international gypsy pilgrimage, Stes-Maries de la Mer, 24–26 May

June

Fête de la Cerise Cherry Festival, Apt, Pentecost weekend

Féria de la Pentecôte Five-day Pentecost Festival, marked in Nîmes with bullfights

Fête de la Transhumance Traditional pastoral festival when shepherds lead their flocks (some 3000 sheep) to pastures new, St-Rémy de Provence, Pentecost Monday

Bravades des Espagnols St-Tropez celebrates its victory over a fleet of Spanish galleons, 15 June

Festival des Baux de Provence Month-long festival which brings a series of piano concerts to the hill-top village of Les Baux de Provence, mid-June to mid-July

Les Nuits du Théâtre Antique In June (and again in August), Orange's ancient Théâtre Antique is lit up with concerts, cinema screenings and other musical events

Fête de la Tarasque Traditional festival starring the folkloric Tarasque dragon and five days of bonfires, fireworks, street processions and carnival, Tarascon, around 24 June (midsummer's night)

Fêtes d'Arles Two-week dance, theatre, music and poetry festival in Arles, end of June

July

Fête du Fromage Cheese fair in Banon, Haute-Provence

Fête de la Sorgue Month-long music, cinema and dance festival on the banks of the River Sorgue, Fontaine de Vaucluse and L'Isle-sur-la-Sorgue

Festival International d'Art Lyrique Prestigious month-long lyrical art festival in Aix-en-Provence

Fête de la Mer et des Pêcheurs Two days honouring St Peter, patron saint of fishermen. In La Ciotat, there's a Provençal Mass, folk music, and benediction of fishing boats; in St-Raphaël local fishermen don traditional dress and joust Provençal-style from boats

Festival Provençal d'Aix et du Pays d'Aix One-week classical music, opera and ballet festival (be quick – tickets sell fast), Aix-en-Provence

Les Rencontres Internationales de la Photographie International photography festival, Arles, early July

Nice Jazz Festival One-week jazz festival with main venue being a lovely old olive grove in Cimiez, Nice

Jazz à Juan Celebrated jazz festival in and around Juan-les-Pins, from mid-July

Aix Jazz Festival Jazz, Aix-en-Provence, five days in mid-July

Danse à Aix Dance, Aix-en-Provence, last fortnight of July

Festival d'Avignon Among Europe's best-known theatre festivals, dating from 1947; tickets (available from mid-June) snapped up in seconds, Avignon, mid-July to early August

Festival Off The funkier, fringe side to the official Festival d'Avignon
Web site: www.avignon-off.org (French only)

Les Nuits Musicales de Nice Three weeks of open-air, classical music concerts in the cloisters of Cimiez Monastery, its olive grove, and in town around the Musée d'Art Moderne et d'Art Contemporain, Nice, from mid-July

Les Chorégies d'Orange Two-week classical and choral music festival held in Orange's Roman amphitheatre. Tickets are like gold dust and must reserved months in advance.
Web site: www.choregies.asso.fr

Estivales de Carpentras A two-week music, dance and theatre festival, Carpentras

Festival Mosaïque Gitane Gypsy culture celebrations, Arles and Marseilles' Plage du Prado in Marseilles, mid-July

Fête du Melon Three-day melon festival to honour the town's prized fruit, Cavaillon, mid-July

Festo Vierginenco Festival created by Provençal poet Mistral in 1904 to honour young girls from Arles who don traditional Arlésienne costume for the first time, Arles, mid-July

Festival Folklore International de Cavaillon Month-long, international folk festival which brings folk song and dance to Cavaillon, mid-July to end August

Festival des Chœurs Lauréats Polyphonic festival in the Théâtre Antique (Roman theatre) in Vaison-la-Romaine, last week of July

August

Choralies Choral Festival Two-week choral concert, the largest of its kind in Europe, held every three years in Vaison's Théâtre Antique (Roman theatre), Vaison-la-Romaine

Carreto Ramado Provençal festival which sees 50 horses pull a cart laden with local produce through town, St-Rémy de Provence, 15 August

Corso de La Lavande Five-day festival to celebrate the lavender harvest, Digne-les-Bains, first weekend in August

Festival d'Été au Théâtre Antique Dance and jazz at Orange's Roman amphitheatre, three weeks in August

September

Fête Mistralienne The birthday of literary hero Frédéric Mistral is celebrated 12–13 September

throughout Provence; Aix-en-Provence hosts particularly large celebrations

Féria des Vendanges The start of the grape harvest is celebrated with a three-day bullfighting festival in Nîmes' Roman amphitheatre, third weekend in September

Fête des Prémices du Riz Week-long festival to celebrate the start of the rice harvest with crowning of a rice ambassadress, Arles, mid-September

Fête de St-Rémy de Provence Ten-day festival in honour of St Rémy, St-Rémy de Provence, third or fourth Sunday in September

October

Fête de la Châtaigne Chestnut Festival, Collobrières, last three Sundays in October

Pélerinage des Gitans Gypsy pilgrimage, Stes-Maries de la Mer, 22 October

Fête de la Vendange et du Vin Grape Harvest & Wine Festival, third Sunday in October, Apt

November

Fête des Côtes du Rhône Primeurs Celebration of Côtes du Rhône wines, Avignon, mid-November

Fête de St-Siffrein Huge market and fair to mark the feast day of Carpentras' patron saint, Carpentras, 27 November

Journées Gourmandes Feast of the region's gastronomic pleasures, and soup *dégustation* (tasting) during the preceding Festival des Soupes (Soup Festival), Vaison-la-Romaine and surrounding villages

December

Fête de l'Huile d'Olive Nouvelle et de la Truffe Olive Oil & Truffle Festival to mark new season's oil, Aix-en-Provence

Noël Most villages celebrate Christmas with midnight Mass, traditional chants in Provençal and a ceremony in which shepherds offer a new-born lamb. Séguret is one of the few places to still celebrate Christmas with Mass and a *crèche vivant* (living crèche); see the boxed text 'A Village Christmas' in the Avignon Area chapter.

ACTIVITIES

The region lives up to its reputation as a land of sea and mountains, offering a wealth of outdoor pursuits guaranteed to thrill the most adventurous – or lazy – of travellers.

Astronomy

Observatories *(observatoires)* that welcome stargazers include the Observatoire de Haute-Provence in St-Michel l'Observatoire, west of Manosque; the Observatoire des Vallons in Bauduen, on the southern shores of Lac de Ste-Croix; and the Observatoire de Nice, in La Trinité, east of Nice. The Observatoire de la Côte d'Azur (☎ 04 93 40 54 54), at 1270m on the Plateau de Calern in Caussols, north of Grasse, is the region's highest.

Ballooning

Year round, you can take to the skies in a hot-air balloon to enjoy fabulous aerial views of Provence.

La Provence en Ballon (☎ 04 90 95 53 28, fax 04 90 95 54 50, @ jmassemin@net-up.com), BP 17, Traverse Castel Mouisson, 13570 Barbentane, operates flights across the Lubéron and the Alpilles. Flights last one hour and cost 1400FF per person (minimum three people, over 12s only). They take off early in the morning from Roussillon, and are followed by breakfast. Advance reservations are compulsory. For more details check out the Web site at www.guideweb.com/provence/ballon.

In Joucas, 5km north of Roussillon, Le Lubéron en Montgolfière (☎ 04 90 05 76 77, fax 04 90 05 74 39, @ montgolfière@infonie.fr), Le Mas Fourniquière, Joucas, 84220 Gordes, offers a one- to 1½-hour flight for 1400FF per person (minimum four people), followed by a champagne picnic. It also organises sunrise flights (2000FF per person), chateaux-ballooning (1600FF) and a 'ballooning adventure' that takes in a morning and evening flight, lunch and a canoe tour on the River Sorgue. Its Web site is at www.avignon-et-provence.com/ballooning.

Several luxurious places to stay, such as the Château Talaud near Avignon, can organise balloon flights for their guests, whom they allow to take-off from and land in their grounds.

Bird-Watching

The spectacular Camargue delta – where clouds of pink flamingos are a common sight – and the Parc National du Mercantour lure ornithologists. The spotter's guide, *Where to Watch Birds in France* (1989), written by the French League for the Protection of Birds, includes maps and marked itineraries cross-referenced to the text.

Bungee Jumping

In Haute-Provence, the brave and daring can leap off bridges in Guillaumes, in the Vallée de la Tinée, and from Europe's highest bridge in the Gorges du Verdon. Bungee jumps *(sauts à l'élastique)* cost 350FF to 590FF.

Cycling

Pedalling Provence is tremendously popular. Bar the barren slopes of Mont Ventoux in the Vaucluse, the region has few killing hills to climb, making it an ideal area to two-wheel for a couple of weeks or months. The country roads in the Lubéron, which saunter through vineyards and fruit orchards, are popular with cyclists (see the boxed text 'Lubéron by Bike' in The Lubéron chapter), as are the handful of roads that traverse the Massif des Maures. Bicycles are forbidden in the Mercantour and Port-Cros national parks, but allowed on the protected island of Porquerolles, where bikes are the only means of transport.

Cycling is less tranquil on the coast where the noisy motorway is never far away. Two-wheelers on a budget often base themselves in Nice, from where they take a train along the coast each morning with their bicycles, to avoid the trauma of cycling out of the city. Some GR and GRP trails (see Walking later in this section) are open to mountain bikes. Between Hyères and Toulon, there is a smooth-as-silk, two-lane cycling path *(piste cyclable)* that runs for 18.5km along the coast.

Details of the wealth of full- and half-day mountain-bike trips organised by Destination Nature in Châteauneuf de Grasse (see Around Vence in the Cannes Area chapter) are online at www.riviera-explorer.com/destination-nature. See Bicycle in the Getting Around chapter for information on bicycle rental and contact details of local cycling clubs and organisations.

Lonely Planet's *Cycling France* details

six cycling itineraries in the region. Didier-Richard publishes *Les Guides VTT*, a series of cyclists' topoguides (in French only). Each department publishes excellent guides for cyclotourists, detailing numerous trails (in French). Many tourist offices sell cycling itineraries (some in English) compiled by the local cycling club.

Diving & Snorkelling

The coastline and its offshore islands – Porquerolles and Embiez particularly – offer enticing diving opportunities. Experienced divers enjoy the waters around Hyères, where the seabeds are graced with numerous shipwrecks. Military WWII wrecks can be explored from St-Raphaël.

The region's most legendary and spectacular dives are around Marseilles' Calanques. Henri Cosquer, known for his discovery of prehistoric paintings in a cave around the Calanques, has his own diving school in Cassis (see the Marseilles Area chapter). There are underwater nature trails designed for amateur snorkellers at the Domain du Rayol on the Corniche des Maures (see the St-Tropez to Toulon chapter) and on the island of Port-Cros (see the Cannes Area chapter).

Diving shops and clubs where you can hire equipment and learn how to dive are listed in the relevant regional chapters. Expect to pay about 200FF for a *plongée baptême* (baptism dive), including equipment. For anything more than a baptism dive, you need to show a medical certificate and diving licence (200/300FF per year for those aged under/over 16).

Golf

Golf hit the Riviera in the 1890s. Among France's oldest golf courses – dubbed *béton vert* (green concrete) – is Golf Club de Cannes-Mandelieu (☎ 04 93 49 55 39), established by Grand Duke Michael of Russia in 1891 along what is now called route Golf.

Complete details of the region's 40-plus manicured greens are listed in the free *Golf in France* guide, available at tourist offices abroad. In Provence, contact the Ligue Régionale de Golf en Provence-Alpes-Côte d'Azur (☎ 04 42 39 86 83), Domaine de Riquetti, 13290 Les Milles.

Naturism

The region's numerous nudist camps (an *aire naturiste* in French, not to be confused with an *aire naturelle* which is a primitive farm camp site) are listed in the *Naturism in France* brochure, available at most tourist offices. Nudist spots range from small rural camp sites to large chalet villages with cinemas, tennis courts and shops. Most open April to October; visitors must have an International Naturist Federation (INF) *passeport naturiste*, available at many naturist holiday centres.

The coastline between Le Lavandou and the St-Tropez peninsula is well endowed with nudist beaches. Héliopolis on Île du Levant – an oddball island off the coast between Le Lavandou and Hyères, 90% of which is occupied by the French military – is the region's only genuine nudist colony. It dates from the 1930s and can be easily visited on a day trip by boat.

The Fédération Française de Naturisme (☎ 01 47 64 32 82), 65 rue de Tocqueville, 75017 Paris, is a good source of information.

Paragliding

St-André-les-Alpes, at the northern tip of Lac de Castillon, some 20km north of Castellane in Haute-Provence, is considered the French capital of paragliding *(parapente)*. The relaxing sport requires participants to hurl themselves off the top of a mountain, dragging a rectangular parachute behind them. As it opens, the chute fills with air and, acting like an aircraft wing, lifts you up off the ground. If the thermals are good – as in St-André – you can stay up for hours, peacefully circling the area and enjoying the breathtaking aerial views. A *baptême de l'air* (tandem introductory flight) costs 250FF to 500FF. There are paragliding schools in St-André-les-Alpes, St-Dalmas-Valdeblore and Digne-les-Bains. For information on hurling yourself from the top of Mont Ventoux, contact the Association Vaucluse Parapente (☎ 04 90 71 50 07), Maison IV de Chiffre, 84000 Avignon.

Rafting, Canoeing & Canyoning

Haute-Provence offers some exquisite white-water rafting, canoeing, kayaking and canyoning terrain. The Rivers Verdon, Vésubie, Roya and Ubaye are the region's most dramatic waters. Leading centres where you can sign up for expeditions include Castellane (for the Gorges du Verdon), St-Martin-Vésubie (for the Vésubie descent), Breil-sur-Roya (for the Vallée de la Roya) and Barcelonnette (for the Vallée de l'Ubaye). The less intrepid can try paddling the 8km along the River Sorgue from Fontaine de Vaucluse to L'Isle-sur-la-Sorgue (see the Avignon Area chapter for details).

AET Nature (☎/fax 04 93 04 47 64, ⓔ aetnature@yahoo.com), place Biancheri, Breil-sur-Roya, runs numerous white-water expeditions in the Roya Valley, aimed at all ages and abilities. One day of easy canyoning (designed for families) costs 240FF per person (330/400FF for the difficult/extreme equivalents). It runs tours of several days too (see under Organised Tours in the Getting Around chapter).

Rock Climbing & Via Ferrata

The Gorges du Verdon, the Calanques around Marseilles, the lacy Dentelles de Montmirail in the Vaucluse, Buoux in the Lubéron and the Vallée des Merveilles in the Parc National du Mercantour are just a handful of the region's numerous climbing sites *(sites d'escalade)*. Most tourist offices and branches of Club Alpin Français (CAF; listed in the regional chapters) stock lists of other spots to climb.

There are Via Ferrata (a type of rock climbing using preattached cables) courses – rigged at a dizzying height guaranteed to set your heart beating faster, and accessible to first-timers – at Tende in the Vallée de la Roya, at La Colmiane just west of St-Martin-Vésubie, and in Auron near St-Étienne de Tinée. See the Haute-Provence chapter for details of all three locations. Admission costs 20FF and equipment rental costs 40FF; guides steer amateurs around the steep course for 250FF to 300FF.

Rollerblading

Rollerblading is a tiptop way to cruise around town. A set can easily be hired in any of the larger cities as well as most resorts on the Côte d'Azur. Rates are around 50/90FF per hour/day. The most chic blading venues are Nice's promenade des Anglais, La Croisette in Cannes and La Canebière in Marseilles.

Skiing

Haute-Provence's few ski resorts are low-key, with little of the glitz and the glamour attached to the Alps' better-known resorts. They are best suited to beginners and intermediates and are marginally cheaper than their northern neighbours.

Resorts include the larger Pra Loup (1500m) and La Foux d'Allos (1800m), which share 230km of downhill pistes and 110km of cross-country trails; the pinprick sister resorts of Le Sauze (1400m) and Super-Sauze (1700m), in the Vallée de l'Ubaye, which tend to attract domestic tourists; and Barcelonnette (1300m), a small town surrounded by a sprinkling of hill-side villages. Isola 2000 (2450m) is the largest of the resorts – and the ugliest.

These resorts – all in the Parc National du Mercantour – open for the ski season from December to March/April/May (depending on the snow conditions), and for a short period in July and August for summer walkers. Buying a package is the cheapest way to ski. For online information, try www.skifrance.com.

For details of the limited skiing proffered

MARTIN HARRIS

Take to the pistes in Haute-Provence's Parc National du Mercantour

by Mont Ventoux, contact the Fédération Française de Ski's Vaucluse branch (☎ 04 90 63 16 54), Chalet Reynard, Bedoin.

Spas

Wallowing in lavender or algae baths, shiatsu massages, Mediterranean mudpacks and a rash of other self-pampering pleasures can be found at a handful of spas. A super soak in a bath at Digne-les-Bains' Établissement Thermal (see the Haute-Provence chapter) costs from 139FF. Six-day lavender stays, during which you indulge in lavender baths (bubbling thermal water laced with essential lavender oil), lavender oil massages and the like, cost 1480FF.

Les Thermes Sextius, a former Roman spa in Aix-en-Provence (see the Marseilles Area chapter), is steeped in history. It offers soothing treatments such as Zen massages (170FF), mud baths (150FF) and Camargue-salt skin scrubs (230FF), as well as one-day/one-week Energy Harmony Packages (380/1980FF).

The region's most exclusive and luxurious spa – Les Thermes Marins in Monte Carlo (see the Monaco chapter) – offers six-day slimming, stress, well-being and 'stop cellulite' packages (from 9690/3930 with/without accommodation) and some gorgeous marine treatments a la carte such as algae baths, Dead Sea mudpacks and four-hand marine massages with salt and essential oils (700FF).

Walking

The region is crisscrossed by a maze of *sentiers balisés* (marked walking paths). No permits are needed but there are restrictions on where you can camp, especially in the Parc National de Mercantour.

The best-known trails are the *sentiers de grande randonnée*, long-distance footpaths whose alphanumeric names begin 'GR' and whose track indicators are red and white stripes on trees, rocks, walls, posts etc. Some are many hundreds of kilometres long, these include the GR5, which goes from the Netherlands through Belgium, Luxembourg and the spectacular Alpine scenery of eastern France, before ending up in Nice. The GR4,

GR6 and GR9 (and their various diversions the GR99, GR98 etc) all traverse the region too.

From 1 July to 15 September, when there is a high risk of forest fire, paths in heavily forested areas – such as the section of the GR98 that follows the Calanques between Cap Croisette (immediately south of Marseilles) and Cassis – are closed. The GR51 crossing the Massif des Maures and numerous trails in Haute-Provence are also closed by the forest authorities depending on prevailing weather conditions (heat, drought and wind). See under Dangers & Annoyances earlier in this chapter for details.

Numerous walking guides cover the region – most are in French. Exceptions include Lonely Planet's *Walking in France*; *Walking in Provence* by Janette Norton, published in 2000 by Cicerone Guides; and the excellent *Walks in Provence: Lubéron Regional Nature Park*, a topoguide written by the Fédération Française de Randonnée Pédestre (FFRP; French Ramblers' Association) and translated into English (77FF).

From Digne-les-Bains, mountain guides organise walks into the mountains with a donkey (to lug your luggage); see the Haute-Provence chapter. Other walking tours available in the region are listed under Organised Tours in the Getting Around chapter.

Water Sports

Sailing is big business on the French Riviera. Antibes, Cannes, Mandelieu-La Napoule and St-Raphaël are among the largest water-sports centres where non-boat owners can hire a set of sails. Most tourist offices have a list of sailing centres *(stations violes)* that rent out gear and run courses. Count on paying 160FF per hour to rent a catamaran (600FF to 800FF for a six-day course).

Other water sports readily available on the beach include windsurfing (70FF per hour to rent a board, plus 90FF for one hour's tuition), water-skiing (130FF to 220FF per hour), jet-skiing (350FF to 400FF for 30 minutes) and parachute rides from the back of a boat (200FF for five to 10 minutes).

Between May and September, tourist offices on the coast sell the 50FF Pass

Nautique, which entitles card-holders to a 30% discount on water sports offered by Côte d'Azur sailing centres. For further information visit www.guide-azur.com.

COURSES
Arts & Crafts

Many *stages artistiques* are available, although few are conducted in English.

Association Okira (☎ 04 90 05 66 69) Usine Mathieu, 84220 Roussillon. Imaginative paper dying, wall mural painting and wood craft workshops using traditional techniques and natural dyes and pigments, extracted from the village's ochre earth (500FF per day). One- to three-hour children's workshops too (15FF to 50FF).

Ateliers de l'Image (☎ 04 90 92 51 50, e ateliers-images@pacwan.fr) 5 ave Pasteur, 13210 St-Rémy de Provence. Bilingual English-French photography workshops (from 1000FF for two days), focusing on everything from black-and-white photography to printing, portfolio presentation and bookbinding, at France's premier photography hotel. Ten-day 'Photography & Provence' courses (6600FF) and children's workshops too.
Web site: www.hotelphoto.com

Ateliers de Vitrail (☎ 04 92 68 19 06) Espace Verre Haute-Provence, Le Belvédère, 04310 Ganagobie. One-/three-/five-/10-day courses (in French only) in the art of stained glass, costing 690/1960/3080/5862FF. The courses are run by the Monastère Notre Dame (see the Haute-Provence chapter).

Ateliers du Soleil (☎ 04 42 23 08 04, fax 04 42 96 47 77) 4 traverse Notre Dame, 13100 Aix-en-Provence. One-day Impressionist painting classes in Cézanne's home town; 600/850FF for three/six hours' tuition or 1500FF for two days (excluding accommodation).

Bouches-du-Rhône – Service Loisirs Accueil (☎ 04 90 59 49 36, e sla@visitprovence.com) Domaine du Vergon, 13370 Mallemort. Two-day Impressionist painting courses 'In the Light of Cézanne', including art museum visits and practical painting classes; 1900FF package including six hours' tuition and two nights' hotel accommodation.

Lacoste School of the Arts (☎ 04 90 75 80 34) 84480 Lacoste; (☎ 914-758 7656, e lsa@bard.edu) Bard College, PO Box 5000, Annandale on Hudson, NY 12504–5000, USA. Painting, drawing, sculpture, photography, creative writing and digital imaging courses, open to under- and postgraduates. Eight-week summer sessions cost US$7250, including accommodation and meals.
Web site: www.bard.edu/lacoste

La Rade (☎ 04 42 01 02 96, e larade@hotel-cassis.com) 1 ave des Dardanelles, 13260 Cassis. Three-day photography courses organised at a Cassis hotel, September to December, costing 3300FF per person (900FF for a single room supplement).

A Taste of Provence (see under Provençal Cooking later in this chapter). Week-long workshops (US$2000 per week, including accommodation and most meals) in May, June, September and October focusing on decorative painting and how to make your own perfume.

Maison de la Céramique (☎ 04 90 72 32 61), 84220 Les Beaumettes. Five-day pottery, ceramics and faïence courses (in French only), organised by the House of Ceramics in the Lubéron. Courses cost 1500FF to 2000FF. Visit the Web site at www.ceramique.com/Luberon-Ceramique (French only)

French Language

A comprehensive list of language schools in Provence is online at www.worldwide.edu /ci/france.

Aix-en-Provence

Université d'Aix Marseille III: Institut d'Études Française pour Étudiants Étrangers (☎ 04 42 21 70 90, e iefee@iefee.u-3mrs.fr) 23 rue Gaston de Saporta. One-/two-term courses costing 6250/9500FF and month-long intensive summer courses (5000FF) in June, July and September.
Web site: www.univ-aix.fr (French only)

Avignon

Centre d'Études Linguistiques d'Avignon (CELA; ☎ 04 90 86 04 33, e acomi@avignon-et-provence.com) 16 rue Ste-Catherine. Courses from 1600FF per week (1900/1280FF in July/November and December). B&B accommodation (85FF per night). Special courses on wine, cinema, Avignon festivals and history of Cannes, etc.
Web site: www.avignon-et-provence.com/cela

Association de Langue Française d'Avignon (ALFA; ☎ 04 90 85 86 24, e alfavignon@pacwan.fr) 4 impasse Romagnoli. Courses from 1500FF per week (15 hours' tuition). Special Avignon Festival course (1870FF per week) in July and August, centred around the festival. For accommodation with local families, expect to

pay 980/1200FF per week (half-/full board).
Web site: http://perso.pacwan.fr/alfavignon
(French only)

Cannes

Cannes UFCM (☎ 04 92 19 40 40, e ufcm@
ufcm.com) Les Balladines, 1 rue de la Verrerie.
Two-week courses for 4780FF (15 hours'
weekly tuition) including homestay accommodation and meals. Thematic language classes on
wine (includes visits to vineyards and wine tasting), Provençal cuisine and 'ski and learn
French' courses.
Web site: www.ufcm.com

College International de Cannes (☎ 04 93 47 39
29, e cic@imaginet.fr) 1 ave du Docteur Pas-
cal. Two-/four-week courses (12/15 hours' tuition per week) costing 3350/4000FF in July
and August.

Cap d'Ail

Centre Méditerranéen d'Études Françaises
(☎ 04 93 78 21 59, e centremed@monte-
carlo.mc) chemin des Oliviers. School dating
from 1901 with an open-air amphitheatre designed by Cocteau. Two-/three-week courses
costing 2200/3050FF for tuition only (20 hours
per week) and 4665/6850FF for half-board
(5385/7550FF full board).
Web site: www.monte-carlo.mc/centremed

Hyères

**Institut d'Enseignement de la Langue Fran-
çaise sur la Côte d'Azur** (ELFCA; ☎ 04 94 65
03 31, e elfca@elfca.com) 66 ave de Toulon.
Courses from 1200FF per week (22 hours' group
tuition), not including homestay accommodation
(starting at 1000FF per week); 'buy' a bicycle
for 700FF and 'sell' it for 600FF when you
leave.
Web site: www.elfca.com

Marseilles

Alliance Française (☎ 04 91 33 28 19), 55 rue
Paradis. Courses for all levels. Sister schools in
Antibes (☎ 04 92 90 52 35), 3 blvd Albert 1er;
Grasse (☎ 04 93 40 17 34), 34 blvd Gambetta;
and Nice (☎ 04 93 62 67 66, e info@alliance-
francaise-nice.com), 2 rue de Paris. The latter
offers 'French through singing or theatre' workshops (650FF for eight hours per month) and private lessons for 250FF per hour.

Institut Euro'Provence
(☎ 04 91 33 90 60, e euro.provence@infonie
.fr) 69 rue de Rome. Monthly courses ranging
from 450/1750FF per month for four/20 hours'
group tuition per week; also offers thematic

courses (French politics, society, feminism etc).
Web site: http://perso.infonie.fr/euro.provence

Nice

France Langue (☎ 04 93 13 78 88, e frlang_n@
club-internet.fr) 22 ave Notre Dame. Weekly
rate for 15/22/30 hours' group tuition is 990/
1485/1980FF.
Web site: www.france-langue.fr

International House
(☎ 04 93 62 60 62, e info@ih-nice.com) 62 rue
Gioffredo. One-week courses cost 3200FF plus
a 400FF inscription fee; one-month courses cost
6800FF.
Web site: www.ih-nice.com

**Université Nice-Sophia Antipolis International
House** (☎ 04 93 37 53 94, e uie@unice.fr) 98
blvd Édouard Herriot. Four-week courses, including 20 hours' tuition costing 4200FF, plus
130FF for accommodation on campus.

Provençal Cooking

Most culinary courses for globe-trotting
gourmets revolve around markets, vineyards, olive groves – and the kitchen table.
The annual *Guide to Cooking Schools* published by Shaw Guides (online at www
.shawguides.com) and the *Guide to Cookery Courses of the British Isles & Beyond*
(2000), compiled by London's Books for
Cooks (see the Food & Wine section) have
exhaustive listings.

Association Cuisine et Tradition (ACT; ☎ 04
90 49 69 20, e actvedel@wanadoo.fr) 30 rue
Pierre Euzeby, 13200 Arles. Run by Arles-born
chef Erick Vedel, this organisation offers everything from a one-meal workshop (500FF) to
one-week culinary courses and wine-lovers
weekends.
Web site: www.cuisineprovencale.com

Hostellerie Bérard (☎ 04 94 90 11 43, e berard
@hotel-berard.comin) rue Gabriel Péri, La
Cadière d'Azur. Passport to Provence cooking
courses, including how to cook up a quintessential bouillabaisse. Four-day cooking courses
cost 6500FF per person (in a double room) and
include five nights' accommodation, morning
classes and afternoon excursions.
Web site: www.hotel-berard.com (French only)

Cooking at the Abbey (☎ 04 90 56 24 55,
e saintecroix@relaischateaux.fr) Abbaye de
Ste-Croix, place du Val de Cuech, 13300 Salon
de Provence. Three-, four- and seven-day
courses cost from 4000FF, including accommo-

dation in a former monk's cell in a Michelin-starred 12th-century abbey.

Cooking with Friends in France (☎ 04 93 60 10 56, ✉ kcookfr@aol.com) La Pitchoune, Domaine de Bramafam, 06740 Châteauneuf de Grasse; Jackson & Co (☎ 617-247 1055, ✉ kcookfr@ cookingwithfriends.com), 20 Commonwealth Ave, Boston, MA 02116. Six-day cookery sessions with accommodation in a farmhouse or cottage in May, June, September, October, November. Truffle weekends in January.
Web site: www.cookingwithfriends.com

Hostellerie de Crillon le Brave (☎ 04 90 65 61 61, ✉ crillonbrave@relaischateaux.fr) place de l'Église, 84410 Crillon le Brave. Five-day courses every November with the hotel's French chef Philippe Monti; 10,000FF per person per week, including accommodation in a double room. Organises wine workshops too.
Web site: www.crillonlebrave.com

The International Kitchen (☎ 800-945 8606, 312-803 1593, ✉ info@intl-kitchen.com) 55 East Monroe, Suite 2840, Chicago, IL 60603, USA. Various six-day courses from US$2250, ranging from scents & savours to pastry baking or biking & cooking.
Web site: www.theinternationalkitchen.com

Le Marmiton (☎ 04 90 85 93 93, ✉ mirande@ la-mirande.fr) Hôtel de la Mirande, 4 place de la Mirande, 84000 Avignon. Hotel cookery school tucked behind Avignon's Palais des Papes, with classes led by Provençal chefs from nearby restaurants. A morning class costs 550FF (1545FF to 1745FF with accommodation), following which participants dine on their culinary creations. Cookery classes for children too.
Web site: www.la-mirande.fr

Mas des Salicornes (☎ 04 90 97 83 41, ✉ contact@hotel-salicornes.com) route d'Arles, Stes-Maries de la Mer. Culinary temple of southern Provençal chef Roger Merlin.
Web site: www.salicornes.com

Mas de Cornud (☎ 04 90 92 39 32, ✉ mascornud@compuserve.com) route de Mas Blanc, 31210 St-Rémy de Provence. Cookery classes in a four-star, 18th-century farmhouse near St-Rémy. Starting at 16,100FF/750FF per person for a one-week/one-day course.
Web site: www.mascornud.com

Routas en Provence (☎ 04 94 69 96 41, ✉ frances@routas.com) Rouvière Plane, Châteauvert, Bras 83149. One-week thematic programmes, such as mushroom picking or truffle hunting, on the estate of a working chateau. Costs about 14,000FF per week, including chateau accommodation and meals.
Web site: www.routas.com

At Home with Patricia Wells (fax 214-343 1227, ✉ cookingclasses@patriciawells.com) 7830 Ridgemar Drive, Dallas, Texas 75231, USA. Summer, five-day cookery courses cost US$3000 (excluding accommodation). Black-truffle workshops, with the author of the best-selling *Food Lover's Guide to France*, are also available. Courses take place in Wells' 18th-century farmhouse near Vaison-la-Romaine. Book *at least* six months in advance.
Web site: www.patriciawells.com

A Taste of Provence (☎ 04 93 42 43 05) Le Mas du Loup, 694 chemin de St-Jean, 06620 Le Bar-sur-Loup, France; (☎/fax 04 93 42 43 05, ✉ info@tasteof provence.com), 925 Vernal Ave, Mill Valley, CA 94941, USA. Family-style cookery courses in an 18th-century farmhouse between Grasse and Vence. Courses in May, June, September and October cost from 14,000FF per person per week (including accommodation and most meals).
Web site: www.tasteofprovence.com

École de Cuisine du Soleil de Roger Vergé (☎ 04 93 75 35 70) L'Amandier, place du Commandant Lamy, 06250 Mougins. Morning or afternoon sessions (2½ hours) cost 300/1350FF for one/five sessions; reserve at least 72 hours in advance.

WORK

To work legally you need a carte de séjour (see Visas & Documents earlier in this chapter). Work *au noir* (in the black – without documents) is possible in the Côte d'Azur's tourist industry and during Provence's *vendange* (grape harvest). A useful book for those lucky enough to land a job in France is *Living & Working in France: A Survival Handbook* (1999) by David Hampshire.

Agricultural Work

To pick up a job in a field, ask around in areas where harvesting is taking place; Provence sees a succession of apple, strawberry, cherry, peach, pear and pumpkin harvests from mid-May to September.

The annual vendange happens from about mid-September to mid- or late October. The sun-soaked fruits of the Côtes de Provence vineyards are ready for harvest before those of the more northern, Châteauneuf du Pape vineyards. Increasingly, vendange is being done by machine, though mechanical picking is forbidden in some places (such as

Châteauneuf du Pape). Once the vendange starts, it lasts just a couple of weeks. The vendange start date is announced up to one week before picking starts.

Food for grape pickers *(vendangeurs)* is usually supplied but accommodation is often not (hence the reason why most pickers live locally). Tourist offices in the region have a list of producers in the region who might need an extra pair of hands, as do the different Maisons des Vins (wine houses).

Environmental

Each summer, the Station d'Observation et de Protection des Tortues des Maures (Maures Tortoise Observation and Protection Station; SOPTOM) in the Villages des Tortues, 20km north of Collobrières in the Massif des Maures, offers a limited number of placements to students aged 17 and over. The centre allows students to spend 15 days to a month working at the village, March to November. Free board and lodging is included: to apply call (☎ 04 94 78 26 41, @ soptom@compuserve.com), BP 24, 83590 Gonfaron.

Au Pair

Under the au pair system, single young people (aged 18 to about 27) who are studying in France live with a French family and receive lodging, full board and a bit of pocket money in exchange for taking care of the kids, babysitting, doing light housework and perhaps teaching English to the children.

Many families want au pairs who are native English speakers, but knowing at least some French may be a prerequisite. Association Familles & Jeunesse (☎ 04 93 82 28 22), 4 rue Masséna, 06000 Nice, is one of dozens of au pair agencies on the Côte d'Azur which arranges placements, with a Web site at www.afj-aupair.org/apfrance.htm. There's an online directory of agencies at www.europa-pages.com/au_pair.

Ski Resorts

The region's ski resorts – Isola 2000, Pra-Loup and La Foux d'Allos among them – are fairly small and offer few work opportunities. If you contact the ski resort months in advance you might be able to pick up some hospitality work in a hotel or restaurant.

Crewing on a Yacht

Working on a yacht sure looks glamorous but the reality is far from cushy. Cannes, Antibes or any other yacht-filled port on the Côte d'Azur is the place to look. Most jobs are filled by mid-April. Yacht owners often take on newcomers for a trial period of day crewing before hiring them for the full charter season. By late September, long-haul crews are in demand for winter voyages to the West Indies.

Beach Hawkers & Street Performers

Selling goods and services on the beach is one way to make a few francs, though you've got to sell an awful lot of doughnuts *(beignets)* or wrap a lot of hair with coloured beads to make a living.

One good place street musicians, actors and jugglers might try to busk is in Avignon during its May theatre festival.

ACCOMMODATION

Accommodation is notorious for being among the most expensive in France. But it is by no means unaffordable. With a bit of planning and consideration of all the options, you can stay here cheaply.

Local authorities impose a tourist tax *(taxe de séjour)* on each visitor in their jurisdiction. This is usually only enforced in the high season – Easter through to the end of September. At this time, prices charged at camp sites, hotels etc will be 3FF to 7FF per person higher than the posted rates.

Reservations

In July and August, if you don't have a reservation, don't even contemplate the coast unless you're happy to pay a fortune for the scant few rooms still available.

Calling just a couple of days before to reserve a room, or even early in the morning (8 or 9 am) on the day you intend to arrive, can save you a back-breaking hike around town upon arrival. Budget accommodation is generally snapped up by 11 am, but almost never booked up weeks in advance (unlike mid-range and top-end accommodation).

Don't turn up in Cannes, Avignon or Aix-en-Provence at festival time unless you have made a reservation months (a year in the case of Cannes) in advance.

Tourist offices usually help people who don't speak French make local hotel reservations, sometimes for a small fee. Staff have information on vacancies but are not allowed to make recommendations. You have to stop by the office to take advantage of reservation services.

Deposits Some hotels only accept reservations if they are accompanied by a deposit *(des arrhes)* in French francs. Some two- or more-starred places ask for your credit card number instead, or for a confirmation of your plans by letter or fax in clear, simple English (receipt of which is rarely acknowledged by French hoteliers). Deposits can easily be sent by postal money order *(mandat lettre)* made payable to the hotel (available from any post office).

Camping

The region has hundreds of camp sites, many set on riverbanks, near lakes, up mountains or overlooking the sky-blue sea. Most open March or April to September or October. Around St-Tropez, many open year round. Some hostels (like the Relais International de la Jeunesse on Cap d'Antibes) allow travellers to pitch tents in the back garden.

Stars reflect the facilities and amenities offered by a site. Location and seasonal demand also influence the nightly rate. Separate tariffs are usually charged for people, tents or caravans (the latter are charged extra for electricity), and cars or motorcycles. Some places have *forfaits* (fixed price deals) for two people, including tent and car. Children aged up to about 12 enjoy significant discounts. Receptions for reservations are often closed during the day; the best time to call is early morning or evening.

Camping a la ferme (camping on the farm) is coordinated by Gîtes de France which publishes the annual *Campings & Campings à la Ferme* guide (70FF); farms and other pretty places to camp are also listed in the department guides published by each local Gîtes de France office. See Self-Catering Accommodation later for further details.

Wild camping *(camping sauvage)* is illegal although it is tolerated to some degree in places (*never* ever in any of the national parks). Pitching your tent on the beach or in a meadow does make you an immediate – and easy – target for thieves.

The Comité Régional de Tourisme Provence-Alpes-Côte d'Azur (see under Tourist Offices earlier) publishes an annual booklet listing all the camp sites in the region. A handy Web site is at www .provence-campings.com.

Refuges & Gîtes d'Étape

Refuges (simple mountain shelters) and *gîtes d'étapes* (basic dorm rooms) are options in rural Provence – the Parc National de Mercantour and Haute-Provence – where undeveloped areas still exist.

Gîtes d'étapes tend to be located in towns or villages popular with walkers and mountain climbers – like Sospel, Castellane, Digne-les-Bains etc – which serve as a gateway to these areas. Refuges are in isolated wildernesses, often accessible only on foot and marked on most walking maps.

Both accommodations are basic, usually equipped with bunks, mattresses and blankets, but not sheets (sometimes available to rent). Nightly rates start at 50FF to 70FF per person per night. Meals, prepared by the *gardien* (attendant) are sometimes available. Most refuges open June to September; some are equipped with a telephone, so you can call ahead to book.

For details (and reservations) on the 10 *refuges* in the Alpes-Maritimes department, contact Club Alpin Français des Alpes-Maritimes (☎ 04 93 62 59 99, fax 04 93 92 09 55), 14 ave Mirabeau, 06000 Nice. Details on Haute-Provence *refuges* are available from the Centre d'Information Montagne et Sentiers (CIMES; ☎ 04 76 42 45 90, fax 04 76 15 23 91, e infos.montagne@ grande-traversee-alpes.com), 14 rue de la

République, BP 227, 38019 Grenoble. The latter also has information on gîtes d'étapes. Alternatively, buy Gîtes de France's annual *Alpes de Haute-Provence* guide (66FF).

Self-Catering Accommodation

Every tourist office has a list of self-catering studios, apartments and seaside villas to rent on a short- (one week) or long-term (several months) basis. The most sought-after properties are booked up a year in advance.

Some of Provence's most simple yet most sought-after self-catering accommodation – a charming, century-old *mas* (Provençal farmhouse) in an olive grove or almond and cherry tree orchard, or converted farm stables surrounded by a menagerie of farmyard animals – is represented by Gîtes de France, a 'green' organisation that liaises between owners and renters.

These idyllic little nests, known as *gîtes ruraux*, provide good-value accommodation and can be rented on a weekly basis. Gîtes de France ranks the properties it lets with a sword system: Amenities range from bathroom facilities and a kitchenette with oven, hot plates and fridge in a one-sword property to a bathroom, fully equipped kitchen, washing machine, colour TV, telephone and private garden in a four-sword place. Guests staying in many two- and three-sword pads have the use of a swimming pool. Sheets, towels and kitchen linen are not provided.

Most Gîtes de France properties are off the public-transport track and are only really suitable for travellers with a vehicle. Weekly rates for a four-person gîte start at 1750/2700FF in low/high season . Bookings can be made through the respective Gîtes de France office; a 25% deposit is required.

Alpes de Haute-Provence (☎ 04 92 31 52 39, fax 04 92 32 32 63, ℮ infos@gites-de-france-04.fr) rond point du 11 Novembre, 04001 Digne-les-Bains
Web site: www.gites-de-france-04.fr (French only)
Alpes-Maritimes (☎ 04 92 15 21 30, fax 04 93 37 48 00, ℮ gites06@crt-riviera.fr) 55 promenade des Anglais, BP 1602, 06011 Nice

Web site: www.crt-riviera.fr/gites06 (French only)
Bouches du Rhône (☎ 04 90 59 49 39, fax 04 90 59 16 75, ℮ gitesdefrance@visitprovence .com) Domaine du Vergon, 13370 Malle-mort
Var (☎ 04 94 50 93 93, fax 04 94 50 93 90, ℮ gites.de.france.var@wanadoo.fr) rond point du 4 Decembre 1974, BP 215, 83006 Draguignan
Vaucluse (☎ 04 90 85 45 00, fax 04 90 85 88 49) place Campana, BP 164, 84008 Avignon
Web site: www.itea.fr/GDF/84 (French only)

Each office publishes an annual catalogue (40FF) which lists all the gîtes ruraux in its respective department complete with a photograph of the property. Catalogues can be ordered online through the Gîtes de France Web site at www.gites-de-france.fr.

Chambres d'Hôtes

A *chambre d'hôte* (a French-style B&B) is a room in a private house rented to travellers by the night; breakfast is always included in the price while a delicious home-made evening meal is usually available for an extra fee (about 100FF). Many of Provence's chambres d'hôtes are in beautiful *châteaux* (castles), farmhouses and *moulins* (mills) and are a highly sought after option. A night's stay for two people in a double room can cost anything from 180FF to 750FF per night.

Every tourist office has a list of chambres d'hôtes available in the area, as does Gîtes de France (see under Self-Catering Accommodation earlier), which includes several dozen chambres d'hôtes in its annual department catalogues. It also publishes two national guides *Chambres et Table d'Hôtes* and *Chambres d'Hôtes Prestige et Gîtes de Charme* (both 140FF) which cover Provence; the latter lists the region's most upmarket (and expensive) B&Bs.

Unlike gîtes ruraux, an advance booking service and information about Gîtes de France chambres d'hôtes is available directly from individual property owners; you will find their contact details listed in the guides.

[continued on page 93]

Food & Wine of Provence

FOOD HIGHLIGHTS & WINE REGIONS

PROVENCE & CÔTE D'AZUR WINE-PRODUCING REGIONS

- Côteaux d'Aix-en-Provence
- Côteaux Varois
- Les Baux de Provence
- Côtes du Lubéron
- Côtes du Ventoux
- Châteauneuf du Pape
- Lirac
- Tavel
- Muscat de Beaumes de Venise
- Gigondas
- Costières de Nîmes

Côtes de Provence:
1. Les Collines du Haut Pays
2. La Vallée Intérieure
3. La Bordure Maritime
4. Le Bassin du Beausset
5. La Ste-Victoire

- Bandol
- Palette
- Cassis
- Bellet

FOOD HIGHLIGHTS

1. Olives & olive oil
2. Almond macaroons
3. Banon
4. Cantaloupe melons
5. Berlingots
6. Truffles
7. Fruits confits
8. Gâteaux secs aux amandes
9. Saucisson d'Arles
10. Rice, beef & salt
11. Oursins & violets
12. Calissons
13. Navettes
14. Pastis
15. Bouillabaisse
16. Glace aux marrons glacés, crème de marrons & marrons au sirop
17. Tarte Tropézienne
18. Chèvre & brebis
19. Fougassette
20. Socca & fruits confits

ITALY

MONACO
MONTE CARLO
Menton
NICE 20

MEDITERRANEAN SEA

Antibes
Grasse 19
CANNES
St-Raphaël
St-Tropez 17

HAUTE-PROVENCE 18

Draguignan
Collobrières 16
MASSIF DES MAURES

Brignoles
TOULON
Hyères

Banon 3
Manosque
Sault 2
Apt 7
La Ciotat
MARSEILLES 12
13
14
15

AIX-EN-PROVENCE
Carry-le-Rouet 11
Salon de Provence
Cavaillon
Étang de Berre
Golfe de Fos
Rade de Marseille

Nyons 1
Carpentras
4 5
6
AVIGNON
Orange
VAUCLUSE
VALLÉE DE LA BAUX
Tarascon
ARLES 9
CAMARGUE 10
NÎMES 8

Durance
Rhône
Étang de Vaccarès
Golfe de Beauduc

0   25   50km
0   15   30mi

FOOD

Provençal cuisine is simple. The secret of its success lies not in elaborate preparation techniques or state-of-the-art presentation, but rather in the use of fresh ingredients produced locally. Despite regional differences, some traits are upheld everywhere – oodles of olive oil and garlic. Tomatoes are another common ingredient; any dish described as *à la Provençale* is guaranteed to involve garlic-seasoned tomatoes.

JANE SMITH

Common vegetables include onions, aubergines (eggplant) and courgettes (also known as summer squash or zucchini). Tomatoes, aubergines and courgettes, stewed with green peppers, garlic and various aromatic herbs, produce the perennial Provençal favourite, *ratatouille*. The artichoke, often eaten very young, is another typical vegetable. They can all be filled with a salted pork, onion and herb mix, then baked, to become *petits légumes farcis* (little stuffed vegetables). Stuffed courgette flowers are an exquisite variation of this basic Provençal dish. Tomatoes and black olives star in many dishes, including *tian* (vegetable and rice gratin).

Another favourite way to eat vegetables is as *crudités* (raw), served as an aperitif with two of Provence's most classic dishes: *anchoïade*, a strong, anchovy paste laced with garlic and olive oil; and its dark counterpart, *tapenade*, a sharp, black olive-based dip seasoned with garlic, capers, anchovies and olive oil. Chicory tastes particularly good dipped into the latter. *Brandade de morue* is a mix of crushed salt cod, olive oil and garlic.

Strong-tasting sauces also complement soups and fish dishes. *Soupe au pistou* is a hearty vegetable, three- or four-bean and basil soup, always served with *pistou*, a spicy basil, garlic and olive oil sauce that you stir into the soup to spice it up, or spread onto small pieces of toast. *Soupe de poisson* (fish soup) also comes with crisp toast, as well as a small pot of pink *rouille* and a garlic clove. Rouille is mayonnaise combined with garlic, breadcrumbs and crushed red chilli peppers. The garlic is there to rub over the toast before dousing with the already very garlicky rouille.

Regional Savouries In seafaring Marseilles, rouille is used as a condiment for *bouillabaisse*, Provence's most famous and fishiest dish. *Bourride* is a variation of bouillabaisse. The many other fish dishes which characterise Marseillais cooking are almost always accompanied by *aïoli*, a garlicky sauce similar to rouille, but lacking the chilli peppers and thus yellow in colour. Aïoli is smeared over everything from fish to vegetables: *Aïoli Provençal complet* is a plate of vegetables (including artichokes), boiled potatoes, a boiled egg, and *coquillages* (small shellfish) to dunk in the pot of aïoli that comes with it. Many restaurants only serve aïoli Provençal complet on Friday. In small fishing ports west of Marseilles

Title page:
Feasting in true
Provençal style (photo-
graph: Greg Elms)

oursins (sea urchins) – the orange roe of which is scooped out with a spoon like a soft-boiled *egg* – and clam-like *violets* (sea squirts) – whose iodine-infused yellow flesh tastes of the sea itself – are specialities.

Niçois cooking is more Italianate in flavour, while the cuisine of the Camargue wetland – land of bulls and rice fields – is the region's meatiest. *Guardianne de taureau* is the Camarguaise equivalent of a traditional *daube Provençale*. Arles is known for its air-dried pork and beef *saucissons* (sausages). Lamb features on menus in the Alpilles hills. *Alouettes sans têtes* – far from being headless larks as a literal translation suggests – are slices of meat wrapped around a stuffing. *Pieds et paquets* (literally 'feet and packages') are sheep's feet wrapped in tripe and cooked with wine and tomatoes.

Cheese is typical of the region's rural hinterland. *Banon* is a type of *chèvre* (goat cheese) or *brebis* (sheep cheese), wrapped in a chestnut leaf.

And finally, there are *truffes* (truffles), legendary black fungi uncovered in modest amounts in the Vaucluse and as precious as gold dust to truffle aficionados.

Regional Pastries & Desserts The region's sensual choice of herbs and spices are used to create numerous sweet treats. Lavender and thyme spice up classic milk-based dishes such as creme brulee and flavoured jams and honey. Anis and orange blossom, among other things, give *navettes* (canoe-shaped biscuits from Marseilles) and *fougassettes* (sweet bread) their distinctive flavours. Almonds are turned into *gâteaux secs aux amandes* (crisp and snappy almond biscuits) around Nîmes; into *calissons* (sweets, frosted with icing sugar) in Aix-en-Provence, and into black honey nougat throughout the region.

Nice and Apt excel at *fruits confits* (glazed fruits). *Berlingots* are hard caramels originating in Carpentras, and *tarte Tropézienne* is a cream-filled sandwich cake from St-Tropez. Massif des Maures desserts generally feature *glace aux marrons glacés* (chestnut ice cream), *crème de marrons* (chestnut cream) or *marrons au sirop* (chestnuts in syrup). A popular dessert in the Vaucluse is cantaloupe melon from Carpentras doused in Muscat de Beaumes de Venise, a sweet wine.

Ethnic Cuisine Southern France's considerable immigrant population is reflected in the exceptional variety of reasonably-priced, ethnic dishes on offer in its major cities. In Marseilles, particularly, you can feast on everything from North African couscous and lamb shish kebabs to Thai, Armenian, Lebanese and Tunisian fare. Once out of the more cosmopolitan parts of Provence, there is but one – very inviting – choice: Provençal.

The Essentials

Herbs The titillating array of aromatic herbs and plants used in Provençal cooking is a legacy of the heavily scented *garrigue* (herbal scrub) covering much of the region. Its classic herbal mix of dried basil, thyme and rosemary is used to season dishes throughout Europe. In Provençal cooking, fresh basil lends its pea-green colour and strong fragrance to pistou and is used dried to flavour soupe de pistou. Sage, traditionally an antiseptic, is another pistou ingredient. Aromatic rosemary, a common Mediterranean shrub, is used fresh or dried to flavour most meat dishes. In medieval Provence it was said to possess magical powers which, if eaten regularly, ensured eternal youth.

Fresh chervil is an annual plant, the leaves of which are used in omelettes and meat dishes, while the tender young shoots of tarragon can be used to lightly flavour sauces accompanying seafood. The sensual aniseed scent of the bulbous fennel is rife in the region. Its leaves (picked in spring) are finely chopped and used in fish dishes and marinades, while its potent seeds (plucked at summer's end) form the basis of several herbal liqueurs, including pastis and the 50% alc/vol Lérina liqueur made by monks on Île St-Honorat. Equally distinctive to Provençal cuisine is the use of lavender; only its green leaves are used in the kitchen.

Olive Oil

Succulent, sun-baked black olives – born from clusters of white flowers that blossom on knotty olive trees from May to June – are harvested from 15 November to January during the *cueillette des olives* (olive harvest). Olives destined for the oil press are not picked until December; 5kg of olives produce one litre of oil.

In 1990, olive oil produced in northern Vaucluse around Nyons was granted its own recognised AOC (appellation d'origine contrôlée), followed in 1997 by the Vallée de la Baux AOC which was granted to seven communes around the Alpilles. *Oléiculteurs* (olive growers) in these regions have to comply to a rigid set of rules in order to have their bottles of oil stamped with the quality-guaranteed AOC mark.

The finest Provençal olive oil costs around 120FF per litre. It can be tasted in the same way one samples wine. An olive oil can have various degrees of sweetness or acidity, and can be clear or slightly murky (which means the oil has not been filtered). A bottle of olive oil should be kept out of direct sunlight and consumed within six months of opening. Some cooks say it loses some of its taste when heated above 80°C. Many restaurants serve a pool of olive oil in a ramekin – *beurre du soleil* (butter of the sun) – to spoon on your bread.

Olive trees only grow at an altitude of 300m to 800m. They live for an absolute age. For information on places to buy olive oil see the boxed text 'Shopping for Olive Oil' in the Facts for the Visitor chapter.

Huile d'Olive

JANE SMITH

Bouillabaisse

This dish was brewed up by the seafaring Marseillais, said to still cook the fishiest, freshest and most authentic bouillabaisse (*bouïabaisso* in Provençal). It is essentially a fish stew made with at least four kinds of fresh fish, cooked in a rockfish stock (broth) with onions, tomatoes, garlic, saffron (hence its pungent orange colour), and herbs such as parsley, bay leaves and thyme. Its name is derived from the French *bouillir* (to boil) and *baisser* (to lower, as in a flame),

Specialist Food Markets

Fish Monkfish, conger eels, sea urchins & other catch of the day – Quai des Belges (Vieux Port), Marseilles, mornings, year round; place St-François, Nice, mornings Tuesday to Sunday, year round; place aux Herbes, St-Tropez, Tuesday to Sunday, winter only

Garlic Loose or in plaits woven before your eyes – Cours Belsunce in Marseilles, daily, June and July; Èze, 24 June

Melons Mountains of sweet-fleshed cantaloupes – Cavaillon, mornings, May to September

Truffles Bring a plastic bag – Aups on Thursday, Carpentras on Friday, Richerenches and Apt on Saturday, all November to March

which reflects the cooking method required: a true bouillabaisse is rapidly brought to the boil, bubbled ferociously for some 15 minutes, and then is ready to serve!

No two cooks cook an identical bouillabaisse. There are endless debates about exactly which fresh fish constitute a true bouillabaisse, although a general consensus insists on *rascasse* (scorpion fish). A *bouillabaisse royale* touts shell fish, including *langouste* (crayfish) or *langoustine* (small saltwater lobster), while the Toulonnais throw potatoes in their bouillabaisse. Bourride is a cheap variation of bouillabaisse which contains no saffron, features cheaper white-fleshed fish, and is served with aïoli instead of rouille.

Bouillabaisse, if served correctly, is an entire meal. The *bouillon* (broth) in which the fish is cooked is served as a soup entree, accompanied by bite-sized toasts and spicy rouille. The fish flesh is then served on a platter as a main course. The pot of bouillon remains on the table, allowing you to spoon it over the fish as desired. See the boxed text 'Tasty Tip' in the Marseilles chapter for authentic bouillabaisse restaurants.

Truffles Provence's blackest gastronomic treat is the truffle. The legendary fungus is a type of mushroom (tuber melanosporum) that takes root underground at the foot of a tree, usually in symbiosis with the roots of an elm or oak tree. Tubers vary dramatically in size, from nail- to fist-sized.

Truffles are harvested November to March. *Rabassaïres* (truffle hunters) unearth the mushrooms with the aid of a dog trained to detect the smelly fungi. Once a spot has been sniffed out, the hunter carefully scrapes the top soil away to unveil the gastronomic gem.

Apparently, truffles have the same alluring pong as a male pig, which is why, traditionally, sows were used to track them down. In true pig-like fashion however, sows not only instinctively uproot, but also scoff truffles. Sows used today are generally muzzled.

Black diamonds, as they are known, are harvested in Vaucluse, around Carpentras, Vaison-la-Romaine and in the Enclave des Papes. The region's leading wholesale market is held in Richerenches and the precious fungi are canned in Puymeras (see the Avignon Area chapter later). Conserved truffles are scorned by many chefs, however, who insist on using *truffes frais* (fresh truffles) to conjure up pricey celestial treats.

Chefs of Provence

Although Provence's healthy 'n' hearty, fruit 'n' veg-inspired cuisine is not the creme de la creme of French cooking, its chefs most certainly are.

Height of Modernity – Alain Ducasse

Ducasse is the world's only chef since the 1930s to be honoured with six Michelin stars, spread between his gastronomic temples in Monaco and Paris. With this distinction, Ducasse – a former apprentice of Roger Vergé – has carved out a new-age definition of what being a chef means.

In Provence, France's most modern chef heads Le Louis XV (where stools are provided for women to rest their handbags while dining) and Bar & Bœuf in Monaco, and the Hostellerie Abbaye de la Celle in northern Var. At La Bastide de Moustiers in Moustiers Ste-Marie an army of gardeners tends a 150-variety vegetable garden.

Olive oil reigns supreme in Ducasse's kitchen. He reveals some of his secrets in the recipe book *Ducasse: Flavors of France* (1998).

Cuisine of the Sun – Roger Vergé

Hail the king of Provençal cuisine. His creation of the celebrated 'cuisine du soleil' in the 1970s – in his own words '...an art where Nature's own savours prevailed with utter simplicity...' – pioneered modern Provençal cooking. Fresh-from-the-earth ingredients sensually spiced with the sweet to tart tangs of plants and herbs remain his trademark today.

Vergé runs two Mougins restaurants, Le Moulin de Mougins in a century-old oil mill and the cheaper L'Amandier. He has published several recipe books, including *Roger Vergé's Vegetables* (1994) and *Roger Vergé's Cooking with Fruits* (1998) in English, and runs his own sun-inspired cookery school.

Provençal at Heart – Patricia Wells

Here is one of the few foreign cooks considered to have embraced the soul of Provençal cooking. The American author is a restaurant critic for the *International Herald Tribune* and has published several cookbooks. *Patricia Wells: At Home in Provence* (1999) features 175 recipes from her farmhouse kitchen in Vaison-la-Romaine.

Recipes
Mediterranean Vegetable Tourte

I cannot make the ingredients which play a primary role in my dishes. I can only exalt them.

Alain Ducasse

6 servings
Preparation: 1½–2 hours

For the Pastry
two and a half cups of flour
1 teaspoon fine sea salt
three-quarters of a cup of olive oil
2 large egg yolks
two-thirds of a cup of water

For the Filling
1 tablespoon uncooked risotto rice
4 tablespoons & 1 teaspoon olive oil
10 courgette blossoms, pistils removed and sliced into ½-inch slices
10 baby courgettes, cut into ½-inch slices
3 large Swiss card leaves or ¼lb spinach leaves, shredded
½ cup shelled fresh peas, halved
2 onions, minced
3 purple artichokes, grated
4 cups mesclun or mixed salad greens, shredded
5 spring onions (white part only), thinly sliced
1 large egg, lightly beaten
½ cup grated Parmesan cheese
¾ cup ricotta cheese
Salt and freshly ground white pepper
1 large egg yolk for glazing, beaten
Olive oil for brushing

Combine flour, salt and olive oil in a large bowl. Blend until the mixture has a crumbly texture. Add egg yolks and water and mix briskly until the ingredients just come together but the dough does not quite form a ball. Remove from the bowl and knead on an unfloured surface until the dough is smooth and supple. Divide in half; press each half into a disk, wrap with plastic film and refrigerate for at least an hour, or overnight.

JANE SMITH

Bring a small pot of water to the boil, add the rice and one teaspoon of olive oil, and cook for nine minutes. Drain. Combine courgette blossoms and vegetables in a bowl. Stir in the egg, Parmesan and ricotta cheese, 1 teaspoon salt, ½ teaspoon pepper, the rice and the remaining ¼ cup olive oil. Mix well with a wooden spoon. Adjust the seasoning.

FOOD & WINE OF PROVENCE

Preheat the oven to 325°F/160°C. Remove the dough from the refrigerator and allow to warm slightly to become malleable. On a well-floured surface, roll out one piece of dough into a 15-inch circle about 1/16 inch thick. Place the dough in a lightly greased 11-inch tart pan with a removable bottom and trim to leave a scant ¾-inch overhang. Spoon in the filling and sprinkle with salt and pepper to taste. Fold over the edges of the dough and brush with the egg-yolk glaze. Roll out the remaining dough to a 15-inch circle and place over the filling. Press down to seal, then trim the dough, leaving a 1-inch overhang. Fold this overlap over itself and make a decorative fluted edge with your fingers.

Before baking the *tourte*, cut five or six snippets in the top of the tart to allow steam to escape. Brush the top with olive oil and place in the centre of the oven. Bake for 45 to 60 minutes at 350°F/175°C until the tart turns a rich golden brown. Transfer to a wire rack and brush with olive oil again. Serve warm or cold with a crisp garden salad.

Aïoli

This marvellous sauce made of garlic, olive oil and eggs evokes the sunshine. I recommend it with any raw, poached or steamed veg-etable, and also with snails, braised fennel, baked potatoes or hard-boiled eggs. If you stir some into a cream sauce at the last minute, it adds smoothness and a vivid perfume.

Crunch a few coffee beans or parsley stems afterwards if your breath smells too aggressively of garlic or, better still, share the aïoli with your friends.

Roger Vergé

4 servings
Preparation: 25 minutes

½ medium potato
2 garlic cloves
2 egg yolks
Salt and freshly ground pepper
1 cup olive oil

Boil the half potato, unpeeled, starting it in cold, salted water. When tender, peel it, then mash with a fork on a plate.

Peel the garlic and crush in a mortar. Add the egg yolks, potato, and salt and pepper to taste. Work this mixture with the pestle until smooth. Gradually add the oil in a slow stream, mixing thoroughly with the pestle.

If you are not serving your aïoli immediately, keep it at room temperature, not in the refrigerator, lest the cold will congeal the oil and break the sauce. If this happens accidentally, put a tablespoon of hot water into a bowl and vigorously whisk in the aïoli little by little. Plenty of elbow grease will restore your sauce.

JANE SMITH

Melon & Peach Zuppetta with Provençal Honey

In Italian, zuppetta means 'small soup'. Here we are reminded of the kinship between southern French and Italian cuisine, both of which reap the benefits of wonderful orchards. In spring, do what I do: garnish your zupetta with wild strawberries.

Roger Vergé

4 servings
Preparation: 25 minutes

2 ripe cantaloupe melons
3 ripe peaches
1 vanilla bean
Juice of 1 lemon
2 tablespoons lavender honey
A few sprigs of mint

Halve the melons and remove their seeds. Using a melon ball spoon, scoop out most of the flesh into little balls. Set aside.

With a big spoon, scrape out the rest of the melon flesh and put it in a blender or food processor. Peel and pit the peaches, slicing two into wedges. Cut the third into large chunks and add to the melon. With a small knife, slice the vanilla bean lengthways. Scrape out the small seeds, add to the melon and peach mixture and puree.

In a small saucepan, heat the honey over a low flame just enough to liquefy it. Add it to the fruit puree. Stir in the lemon juice.

Divide the soup evenly among four shallow bowls. In each bowl, arrange the melon balls in the centre and the peach wedges around the outside. Garnish with a few sprigs of mint.

Tapenade

This classic spread combines the favourite flavours of Provence: the tang of the home-cured black olives in brine, the saltiness of the tiny anchovy, the briny flavour of the caper, the vibrant sharpness of garlic, the heady scent of thyme, and the unifying quality of a haunting olive oil.

Patricia Wells

Makes 1½ cups
Preparation: 25 minutes

10 anchovy fillets
4 tablespoons milk
2 cups (300g) best-quality French or
Greek brine-cured black olives, pitted
1 tablespoon capers, drained
1 teaspoon Dijon mustard

JANE SMITH

1 plump, fresh clove garlic, peeled, green germ removed, and minced
¼ teaspoon fresh thyme, leaves only
Freshly ground black pepper to taste
6 tablespoons extra-virgin olive oil

In a small shallow bowl, combine the anchovies and milk. Set aside for
15 minutes to rid the anchovies of their salt. Drain and set aside.

Mix the drained anchovies, olives, capers, mustard, garlic and thyme.
Process to form a thick paste. With the food processor running, add the
oil in a steady stream until it is thoroughly incorporated into the mixture.
Season with pepper.

WINE

Provence's wine-growing tradition dates back 2600 years. While its
wines are not France's most sought after, their making and tasting –
as with all good wines – is an art and a tradition which bears their own
unique and tasty trademark. A remarkable variety of different AOC
(appellation d'origine contrôlée) wines are produced in Provence but
each is stamped by one common trait – an exceptionally cold mistral
wind and an equally exceptional, hot ripening sun.

A crisp, Côtes de Provence rosé is Provence's classical summer drink,
drunk in abundance May to September regardless of time of day. Wine
is drunk with most meals, so much so that in many village bistros, a
bottle of house wine greets you at your table when you sit down, the
assumption being you will most certainly drink it. Cheaper house wine
– drinkable but never startling – is served in a carafe (glass jug), pichet
(pottery jug) or bouteille (bottle).

For wine-related terms see the Glossary at the back of the book.

Tasting & Buying Wine

Wine can be bought direct from the domaine (wine-growing estate) of
the producteur (wine producer) or vigneron (grower) – at a lower price
than in the shops. Most places offer dégustation (wine tasting), which
allows you to sample two or three of vintages, with no obligation to
buy. Purchasing one or two bottles or one to 20 boxes (six or 12 bottles
per box) is equally acceptable.

Tasting and buying more sought-after wines, such as Châteauneuf du
Pape, where the annual production of many estates is bought years in
advance, is more difficult. Few producers have bottles to sell and those
who do require that you make an appointment in advance (and buy a
substantial amount of their wine). Complete lists of caves (wine cellars)
open to travellers are available from the Comité Interprofessionnel des
Vins Côtes de Provence in Les Arcs-sur-Argens and the Comité Interprofessionnel des Vins Côtes du Rhône in Avignon.

FOOD & WINE OF PROVENCE

Regions

Côtes du Rhône Provence's finest (and most renowned) vintage is Châteauneuf du Pape, a full-bodied red wine grown 10km south of Orange. It is one of the many diverse wines in the highly respected Côtes du Rhône appellation, dating from 1937.

Châteauneuf du Pape vineyards were bequeathed on Provence by the Avignon popes. Its strong, well-structured reds are considered masters in their field, while the sweeter reds that have sprung up in recent years afford a lighter alternative in the summer heat. White wine, traditionally only made by the *vignerons* (wine growers) for their private use, now accounts for 7% of total annual production. Both whites and reds can be drunk young (two to three years) or old (seven years or more). Irrespective of age, whites should be served at 12°C; reds at 16 to 18°C.

Châteauneuf du Pape has a relatively high alcohol content of at least 12.5%. It was the first wine in France to be granted its own AOC in 1929, one rule being that grapes must be harvested by hand. Some vignerons claim it is the *galets* (large smooth, yellowish stones, which make the vineyards very photogenic) covering their vineyards that distinguish Châteauneuf du Pape from other vineyards. Yet there is not a stone in sight in the sandy vineyards at Château Rayas, known for its incredibly strong, typically tannic, forceful reds that are sold to US buyers three years before production. A bottle of 1989 Château Rayas easily fetches 2000FF. Exceptional Châteauneuf du Pape vintages across the board are 1988–90, 1995 and 1997.

The Tavel rosé is another popular Rhône Valley *grand cru* (literally 'great growth') in Provence. The vineyards around the Dentelles de Montmirail, some 15km east of Orange, produce notable red and rosé Gigondas, and the sweet wine, Muscat de Beaumes de Venise.

Côtes de Provence The 18 hectares of vineyards sandwiched between Nice and Aix-en-Provence produce red, rosé and white Côtes de Provence, the sixth largest appellation in France. The *terroir* ranges from sandy coastal soils around St-Tropez to chalky soils of the subalpine slopes around Les Arcs.

The appellation, awarded in 1977, is the largest in Provence with an annual production of 100 million bottles: 75% are rosé wines, 20% red and a token 5% white wines. Côte de Provence rosé is always drunk young and served at a crisp coldness of 8 to 10°C. Its luminous *robe* (colour) and delicate fruity taste is renowned for complimenting Provençal cuisine. Reds drunk young should be served at 14 to 16°C, while older red *vins de garde* – a traditional accompaniment to game, sauced meats and cheese – are best drunk at 16 to 18°C. Côte de Provence whites, a golden friend to fish, should be chilled to 8°C.

Others Six other pocket-size appellations are dotted in the Côtes de Provence wine growing area: Bandol, Cassis, Coteaux Varois, Coteaux d'Aix-en-Provence, Bellet and Palette. Of these, Bandol is the most respected, best known for its deep-flavoured reds produced from the dark-berried mourvèdre grape, which needs oodles of sun to ripen (hence its rarity). The appellation demands that grapes be harvested by hand; watch out for reds from the Domaine Tempier vineyard in Le Plan du Castellet. In neighbouring Cassis, crisp whites (75% of its production) are drunk with gusto.

Inland from Bandol is 1500 hectares of limestone soil around Brignoles, mother of the young Coteaux Varois appellation dating from 1993. Wine-lovers who prefer a drier rosé should try Coteaux d'Aix-en-Provence. Palette, east of Aix is just 20 hectares in size, dates from 1948 and produces well-structured reds from its old vines. Four out of every five Palette bottles are Château Simone. Wines from the Bellet AOC are rare outside of Nice.

LPP

The centre of Provence is carpeted with vineyards of the Côtes de Ventoux appellation (6900 hectares established in 1973) and Côtes du Lubéron (3500 hectares dating from 1988).

BONNES TABLES

Gastronomic orgasms are plentiful at these quintessential Provençal *bonnes tables* – literally 'good tables', meaning restaurants or bistros which serve delicious, exciting and enticing cuisine with flare. Advance reservations are essential.

Foodies swear by Michelin's red-jacketed *Guide Rouge* to France (150FF), known for the one, two or three stars it rates France's great restaurants with. The guide, published each March, lists countless non-starred bonnes tables too. *Guide Gault Millau France* (175FF) awards up to four red chefs' caps *(toques rouges)* to restaurants with exceptional creative cuisine; and white chefs' caps *(toques blanches)* to places with superb modern or traditional cuisine. Gault Millau is also published annually and has an English edition.

La Verre Bouteille (☎ 044 42 27 96 66, *bis rue Cabassol, Aix-en-Provence*)
Simple dishes made from market produce is the trademark of The Glass Bottle, an unassuming bistro guaranteed to please the daintiest or feistiest appetite. Salads, eggs and charcuterie platters (30FF to 58FF) encourage punters to build their own stomach-sized feasts. Tapenade and anchoïade arrives in a basket and the assiette verre bouteille (72FF) is an orgy of tastes: assorted crudités, charcuterie and cheeses, mouthwatering confiture d'ognion (a sweet onion chutney), black olives, marinated red peppers. Daily specials (dictated by the marketplace) average 50FF and a 50cL/L pichet of Coteaux d'Aix-en-Provence wine costs 38/58FF.

Le Lapin Tant Pis (☎ 04 92 75 38 88, **e** *starbrightpacific@libertysurf.fr, place Vieille, Forcalquier)*
Gérard Vives dishes up a boldly unconventional menu at his prized bistro,

challenging diners to sample olive oil as dessert and choose a wine according to gastronomic sentiment (tenderness, tradition, rarity, sensuality...). He creates titillating aperitifs from locally distilled herbal liqueurs and turns foie gras (a rich duck liver paté) into hamburgers au Muscat de Beaumes de Venise. Main courses revolve around lamb – Provence's quintessential meat – rose-pink in colour and dressed in one of a number of sauces, including truffle butter. Menus cost 175FF and 198FF (68FF lunchtime menu).

Bistrot à Michel (*☎/fax 04 90 76 82 08, Cabrières d'Avignon*)

Truffle omelettes are served here November to March. Otherwise, Michel Bosc cooks up Cavaillon melon with Muscat de Beaumes de Venise (50FF), pieds et paquets (95FF) and other memorable dishes on a flower-filled terrace behind a village bar. Pigeon roasted with garlic cloves or cooked with cinnamon and peppered turnips (135FF) is another Provençal classic. Aperitifs come with a confiture d'oignons to die for. There's a 90FF plat du jour, 100FF lunch formule and a choice of five entrees and mains a la carte.

Auberge de la Loube (*☎/fax 04 90 74 19 58, Buoux, 11km east of Lacoste*)

Chef and owner Maurice collects horse-drawn carriages but lacks the horse power to take tourists for a ride. La Loube has a 132FF lunch menu and a 165FF evening menu (175FF with cheese) which includes hors d'œuvres Provençaux de la Loube – a wicker tray filled with tapenade, anchoïade, quail eggs, melon slices, cherry tomatoes, fresh figs and other Provençal treats guaranteed to fill. Game dishes are served in season. The restaurant is closed Thursday and credit cards are not accepted.

L'Amandier (*☎ 04 93 90 00 91, place du Commandant Lamy, Mougins*)

Melon marinated in honey and lemon, garlic- and thyme-spiced lamb and duck fillet roasted with figs are among the traditional Provençal creations served at The Almond Tree, the wholly affordable place to eat run by Roger Vergé (who advises rather than cooks). An absolute must to try are the mullet fillets served with a courgette flower filled with brandade de morue (crushed salt cod, olive oil and garlic). Petits légumes farcis (little stuffed vegetables) accompany many mains. Ask for a table atop the panoramic roof terrace overlooking the Mercantour mountains. Menus 155FF, 190FF (65FF children's menu).

Chèvrerie du Peigros (*☎ 04 94 48 03 83, Col de Babaou, Collobrières*)

Goats and chestnuts are the mainstay of this goat-farm table d'hôte, off the beaten track (read: 1.8km along a gravel track, signposted from the top the Babaou mountain pass) in the Massif des Maures. The farmhouse kitchen touts one menu (130FF) – salad, chestnutty paté and charcuterie, main course (farm-killed goat or poultry, depending on the season), chèvres (goat cheeses) and dessert (often farm-made chestnut ice cream). Then try the courageous attempt to stand up. The kitchen opens lunchtime year round, evenings too in July and August. Credit cards and cheques are not accepted.

Homestays

Students, young people and tourists can stay with French families under an arrangement known as *hôtes payants* (literally 'paying guests') or *hébergement chez l'habitant* (lodging with the occupants of private homes). In general you rent a room and have access (sometimes limited) to the family's kitchen and telephone. Language schools (see Courses earlier in this chapter) often arrange homestays for their students. Students and tourists alike should count on paying upwards of 3500/1500/150FF per month/week/night for a single room, including breakfast.

Hundreds of agencies in Europe and the US arrange homestay accommodation in Provence and the Côte d'Azur; the Comité Régional de Tourisme Provence-Alpes-Côte d'Azur in Marseilles (see Tourist Offices earlier in this chapter) has a list, as do French tourist offices abroad.

Hostels

There are *auberges de jeunesse* (youth hostels) on the coast at Cap d'Antibes, Cap d'Ail, Cassis, Cannes, Fréjus-St-Raphaël, Le Trayas, Marseilles, Menton, Monaco, Nice and Stes-Maries de la Mer; in the mountains at La Foux d'Allos, La Palud-sur-Verdon and Manosque; and to the west, in Aix-en-Provence, Apt, Avignon, Arles, Nîmes, Orange, Tarascon and Fontaine de Vaucluse. Expect to pay around 70FF per night, plus 17/20FF for sheets/breakfast.

Affiliates of the Fédération Unie des Auberges de Jeunesse (FUAJ) and Ligue Française pour les Auberges de Jeunesse (LFAJ) require HI or similar cards (see Visas & Documents earlier in this chapter). The FUAJ is online at www.fuaj.fr. Privately owned hostels charge more than those affiliated to either of the latter.

Most hostels have some kitchen facilities. Most do not accept telephone reservations so turn up early, especially in July and August, if you want to ensure you get a bed for the night.

In some spots (eg, Nice and Fréjus-St-Raphaël) the hostels are a good hike out of town. If there are a couple of you it can be as cheap (or cheaper) to stay in a budget

hotel in town. Some hostels (like those at Cap d'Antibes, Cap d'Ail and Fréjus-St-Raphaël) also enforce a curfew.

Hotels

Hotels have one to four stars. Few no-star hotels (ie, that have not been rated) exist.

Breakfast *(petit déjeuner)* is never included in the room price. Count on paying an extra 25FF to 40FF (up to 100FF in four-star joints) for the privilege. Breakfast at a cafe can be cheaper.

Many hotels only operate, deplorably so, on a half-board basis in July and August, meaning you are obliged to fork out the hefty prices they set for breakfast and an evening meal in a stuffy, cramped hotel restaurant (invariably inside).

A room with a bath is always more expensive than a room with a shower. Most hotels tout neck-aching, hot-dog-shaped bolsters *(traversins)* rather than regular pillows *(oreillers)*.

Budget Expect to pay about 180FF per night for a double with washbasin (and often bidet) in your room, and a shared toilet and shower in the corridor. A shower in the hall bathroom is usually free but sometimes *payant* (10FF to 25FF per shower). Most places have more expensive rooms equipped with shower, toilet and other amenities. Prices tend to stay the same year round at budget hotels.

Budget establishments often do not have single rooms. Rather, they sport rooms fit for one or two people (ie, with one double bed) for which they charge the same price, regardless of whether it is let as a single or double. Places which do have singles (ie, with one single bed) usually charge marginally less for it than for a double (with a double bed or two singles). Triples and quads normally tout one or two beds.

In Marseilles, Nice and Toulon, there are really rock-bottom places to stay, often frequented by prostitutes and touting an hourly or half-day rate (advertised as a rate for punters 'waiting for a train or bus departure'). These are the places most unlikely to have showers, lifts or fire escapes.

Most cheap hotels demand pre-payment for the room when you check in. Don't part with any cash until you've seen the room. Do not expect any refund if you pay first, only to discover the room is an uninhabitable hovel, prompting immediate departure.

Postmodern, pressboard and plastic hotels on the outskirts of most towns, run by a hotel chain, are remarkably cheap (159FF for a room for up to three people). These sterile boxes (not listed in this guide) sport noisy views of busy roads but can be convenient for motorists. Chains include Formule 1, Fimôtel and Campanile.

Mid-Range Expect to pay 250FF to 450FF for a room in a mid-range hotel. These usually tout three sets of seasonally adjusted prices: Low-season applies October/November to February/March. Mid-season is usually March/April/May and September/October. High season, when prices rocket out of control, is July and August (sometimes June and September too).

Hotels usually close for several weeks in winter for their *congé annuel* (annual closure). Some places close straight through from September/October to March/April. The exception is in Haute-Provence's skiing resorts where hotels only open for the winter ski season.

Some 350 family-run places in the region – often in the mountains or overlooking the sea belong to Logis de France, an organisation whose affiliated establishments meet strict standards of service and amenities. The Fédération Régionale Provence and the Côte d'Azur (☎ 04 91 14 42 00), 8 rue Neuve St-Martin, BP 1880, 13222 Marseilles, issues an annual guide with details of each hotel-restaurant in the Provence and the Côte d'Azur region. The French Web site www.logis-de-france.com has more details.

Top End Provence has a wealth of four-star hotels and restaurants housed in traditional properties: farmhouses, oil mills *(moulins à huile)*, monasteries *(monastères)*, priories *(prieurés)* or restored Cistercian abbeys *(abbayes)*. Lakes, rose gardens and olive groves usually pepper the vast grounds

typical of these exclusive estates. Nightly rates start around 700FF, but can soar as high as 4850FF during world-renowned festivals like the Monaco Grand Prix. See the regional chapters for details.

Many of the region's most exclusive, expensive and unrivalled hotels fall under the umbrella of organisations such Relais & Châteaux or Châteaux & Hotels de France, the latter recently being acquired by world-renowned Provençal chef Alain Ducasse. Both publish annual guides which can be ordered online at www.relaischateaux.fr or www.chateauxhotels.com.

Chateaux

There are several wine-growing estates *(domaines)* – invariably arranged around a gorgeous chateau – in the Côtes de Provence wine region where you can stay. In addition to a comfortable bed, hearty breakfast and, upon request, an evening meal of fabulous proportions, many chateaux offer guests the opportunity to taste its wine, tour its vineyards and join in the grape harvest (in season). The Maison des Vins in Les Arcs-sur-Argens (see the St-Tropez to Toulon chapter) has a comprehensive list of such places; several are mentioned in the regional chapters.

Buying

An excellent source of information for anyone aspiring to buy a rambling old barn and convert it into a dream home is *Buying a Home in France* (1998) by David Hampshire. It includes step-by-step instructions on how to buy a property in France and has an exhaustive appendix of every possible, house-related French word you might need to know (chimney sweep, land registry, mains draining system etc).

Chateaux and *domaines viticoles* (estates with vineyards, olive groves and woods) are the speciality of real-estate agent Emile Garcin (☎ 04 90 92 01 58, ⓔ provence@emilegarcin.fr), 8–10 blvd Mirabeau, 13210 St-Rémy de Provence, with a Web site at www.emilegarcin.fr. The Riviera's *belle epoque* follies and celebrity real estates are handled by John Taylor, online at www.john-taylor.fr, and Christie's; the latter auctioned off Karl Lagerfeld's Monte Carlo pad in 2000.

FOOD

People in Provence generally think, dream and live food; most people's working day is completely geared around satisfying their insatiable appetite for dining well.

Consumer warning: Provençal cuisine oozes garlic. After consumption, munch on a sprig of parsley to avoid reeking breath.

Meals of the Day

Breakfast One of the most delightful (and coolest) times of day in Provence is *petit déjeuner*, best spent on a terrace watching the world go by or gazing out across a sea of vineyards and fruit orchards. Breakfast comprises a croissant and a piece of crusty baguette (usually with butter and jam), accompanied by a strong black coffee or *café au lait* (coffee with lots of hot milk).

Lunch & Dinner For most Provençaux, *déjeuner* (lunch) is the main meal of the day. It starts at noon on the dot, continues well into the afternoon, and entails eating (and of course drinking) a delightfully excessive amount that will leave you vowing never to eat that much again – until tomorrow.

If you turn up at a popular restaurant without a reservation later than 1 pm, the chances are you will be turned away. Most places stop serving at 2.30 pm and open again for *dîner* (dinner) from 7 or 7.30 pm to sometime around 10 pm. There is *nowhere* open to eat between 3 and 7 pm.

Most places have a *plat du jour* (dish of the day) or *formule* (fixed main course plus starter or dessert) at lunchtime as well as the *menus* available in the evening. A *menu* offers better value than ordering a la carte (hand-picking a dish for each course); it usually includes an entree, *plat principal* (main course) and *fromage* (cheese) or dessert, with drinks and coffee costing extra.

An increasing number of restaurants tout a *menu enfant* (children's *menu*), which usually costs around 40FF for minced meat,

fries, ice cream and a soft drink. Vegetarian *menus* remain non-existent.

The order of courses for a la carte dining is as follows:

apéritif – pre-dinner drink, often with olives or *tapenade* (an olive-based dip seasoned with garlic, capers, anchovies and olive oil)
amuse-bouche – complimentary morsel to whet the appetite (only in top-end restaurants)
entrée – first course/starter
plat principal – main course
salade – simply dressed green salad
fromage – cheese
dessert
café – coffee
digestif – after-dinner drink such as La Farigoule or a marc (a type of brandy made from grape pressings)

Types of Eatery

Restaurants Dining a la Provençale can mean spending anything from 70FF (in a village bistro) to 500FF or more (in one of the region's multistarred, gastronomic temples). Regardless of price, most places have a *carte* (menu) pinned up outside, allowing for a quick price and dish check for those not wanting to end up washing the dishes or dining on *pieds et paquets* (literally 'feet and packets', in reality sheep tripe).

The most authentic Provençal places to eat are in tiny hamlets off the beaten track – living proof that locals will drive any distance for a good meal. These places tout just one *menu* with *vin compris* (wine included). The *patron* (owner) of the place is often the chef who, at the end of your meal or during it, comes to your table – clad in kitchen whites – to inquire about your food. Dogs snoozing under tables are a common sight.

No restaurant can call itself truly Provençal unless it serves you a continual flow of chunky cut bread from the start to the very end of your meal (if it runs out, just ask for more – it's free). Except in the most expensive places, side plates are not provided. Don't attempt to balance your bread chunk on your main-course plate – sprinkling the table with crumbs is perfectly acceptable.

In cheaper restaurants, you might be expected to use the one set of eating utensils for the duration of your meal. Upon finishing your entree, replace your knife and fork (a subtle wipe clean with bread is allowed; licking – less cool) on the table either side of your dirty plate. If you don't, the waiter will do it for you. The waiter is also likely to add up the *addition* (bill) on your paper tablecloth.

Châteaux & Fermes Auberges The main house or building on a wine-producing estate is called a *château*, and a *ferme auberge* or *auberge de Provence* is a small, family-run inn attached to a working farm or chateau. They are two of the most delightful places to dine a la Provençale.

Typical Provençal cuisine is guaranteed at both. Dining is around shared tables with wooden benches. Portions are sufficiently hearty for those with the largest of appetites to leave in a merry state of stuffed bliss. A *menu*, comprising four courses and often wine too, can cost 120FF to 200FF.

The Maison des Vins in Les Arcs has a list of Côtes de Provence chateaux where you can eat. The Domaine de la Maurette in La Motte, 5km east of Les Arcs, (see the St-Tropez to Toulon chapter) is a prime example of a ferme auberge.

Cafes The cafe is an integral part of French society, and nowhere more so than in the sun-filled south where the cafe is the hub of village life and a highly respected institution. Many double as the village bar and bistro too. Most serve simple baguettes filled with cheese (around 25FF) or *charcuterie* (cold meats). Others have select terraces hidden out back where you can dine in the shade of overhead vines.

In towns, a cafe on a grand boulevard (or any other chic place to be seen such as the Vieux Port in St-Tropez) charges considerably more than a place fronting a quiet side street.

Les Deux Garçons in Aix-en-Provence is the region's most famous cafe. It sits on the shady side of cours Mirabeau – a street considered to be the finest in southern France. In fine cafe tradition, prices are hiked up after 10 pm.

Salons de Thé & Creperies *Salons de thé* (tearooms) are trendy and expensive establishments that offer quiches, salads, cakes, tarts, pies and pastries in addition to tea and coffee.

Creperies serve ultra-thin pancakes with a variety of sweet or savoury fillings, except in Nice where *socca* – a hearty Niçois pancake comprising chickpea flour and lashings of olive oil – is served.

Self-Catering
Provence's premier culinary delight is to stock up on breads, pastries, fruit, vegetables and prepared dishes and sit down for a gourmet *pique nique*.

When shopping, do as the locals do: spurn the supermarket and buy fresh local products from the market, followed by a stroll to the local *boulangerie* (bakery) for a baked-that-hour baguette or some *pain aux noix* (walnut bread); then on to the *pâtisserie* (pastry shop) for a *tarte Tropézienne*, *tarte aux fruits* (fruit tart), *pain au chocolat* (chocolate croissant) and other yummy cakes and pastries. Margarine-based croissants can be identified by their almost touching tips; buttery ones have their tips facing outwards.

Purchase cheese in the *fromagerie*, and ask how best to preserve the cheeses you buy, which wines are best served with them and so on. If you don't know a cheese type, ask to *goûter* (taste) it. Prewrapped cheese sold in supermarkets is unripe and utterly tasteless by comparison. Shop for slices of cold meats, seafood salads, tapenade, sweet peppers marinated in olive oil at a *charcuterie* (delicatessen) – an equally colourful experience. The catch of the day is sold at a *poissonnerie* (fishmongers), general meat can be bought from a *boucherie* (butcher) and poultry from a *marchand de volaille* (poultry seller).

Any titbits you still need are probably sold at the local *épicerie* (literally 'spice shop' but actually a grocery store) or *alimentation générale*. Backpackers wanting to stock up on shedloads of beer, bottled water and the like will – of course – find it cheaper to shop at a supermarket (Casino,

Made in Provence – colourful and hearty local produce ranges from freshly baked baguettes to olives, sausages, pumpkins and other vegetables. Visit markets throughout the region for a full menu.

JEAN-BERNARD CARILLET

JEAN-BERNARD CARILLET

JEAN-BERNARD CARILLET

GREG ELMS

JEAN-BERNARD CARILLET

With a Mediterranean coastline it's not surprising that spicy fish dishes such as bouillabaisse are traditional Provençal fare. Sniff out fresh fish, *navettes* (canoe-shaped biscuits) and Roquefort cheese.

Monoprix etc) in town or at one of the giant *hypermarchés* (Leclerc, Intermarché etc) on the outskirts of most Provençal towns.

Markets Every village, town and city in Provence has a weekly or daily market that sprawls across the central square and a neighbouring patchwork of streets. Farmers flock into town from the outlying farms and villages to sell their fresh produce and chat with friends. Bargaining is not really allowed.

The staple ingredients are fresh fruit and vegetables, olives, locally milled olive oil (see the boxed text 'Shopping for Olive Oil' later in this chapter), herbs and spices. Garlic *(aïl)* is always sold in a bunch or woven plait. A wealth of green and black olives, marinated in every imaginable concoction, are displayed in plastic tubs or buckets. Herbs are dried, mixed, and displayed in stubby coarse sacks; the classic cocktail is *herbes de Provence*, a mix of *basilic* (basil), *romarin* (rosemary), *thym* (thyme), *origan* (oregano), *sarriette* (savory) and *marjolaine* (marjoram). If you are in the Vaucluse (between November and March) you might also come across *truffes* (truffles) or, if in the Massif des Maures, *marrons* (chestnuts).

Everything from bread, cheese, cold meats, *miel* (honey), marmalade and *confiture* (home-made jam) to enticing nonedibles (art and crafts, wicker baskets, clothing etc) are sold in most markets too. Specialist food markets are listed in the special Food & Wine section earlier.

DRINKS
Alcoholic Drinks
A drink in Provence invariably means a drink of the alcoholic variety – and indulging in an aperitif on a shaded terrace is among the region's great sensual delights. Pastis (see the boxed text 'The Milk of Provence' on the following page) is the quintessential Provençal drink, closely followed by a crisp, cold Côtes de Provence rosé (see the special Food & Wine section earlier). Both are wonderfully refreshing on hot and sunny days. Beaumes de Venise, a

sweet muscat wine, is a popular aperitif in northern Vaucluse. Amandine (an almond liqueur) and Rinquinquin de Pêche (peach liqueur mixed with chilled white wine) – both from the Distillerie Domaine de Haute-Provence in Forcalquier – feature on many drinks menus in the Lubéron and neighbouring part of Haute-Provence. Liqueur de Châtaignes (chestnut liqueur) from Collobrières in the Massif des Maures can also be mixed with white wine to create a pleasant aperitif.

To ensure that appropriately 'plump and contented' feeling following a deliciously long and lazy meal, a digestif such as a *marc* or *eau de vie* (literally 'water of life') can be taken. Marc is a fiery spirit (similar to Italian grappa), distilled from grape skins and pulp left over from the wine-making process. Eaux de vie is the generic name for brandies distilled from the region's many fruits.

Ending a meal with a sweeter liqueur is considered more 'womanly'. Try Reverend Father Gaucher's Elixir, a yellow chartreuse from Tarascon elaborately blended from 30 different aromatic herbs, or La Farigoule, a thyme liqueur also distilled in Forcalquier.

Beer is not a Provençal drink and is priced accordingly; wine is, however, and likewise priced accordingly.

Nonalcoholic Drinks
Tap water in the hot south is safe to drink. Don't drink water spouting from fountains that tout a sign reading *eau non potable* (nondrinking water). In restaurants, it is perfectly acceptable to order *une carafe d'eau* (carafe of tap water) instead of a pricier soft drink, *eau de source – plate* or *gazeuse* (mineral water – still or carbonated) – or wine. Soft drinks cost about 15FF to 25FF per glass (wine can be cheaper).

The dazzling, pea-green drink you see people sipping through straws in cafes is *sirop de menthe* (mint syrup) diluted with water. Other cordials include *cassis* (blackberry), *grenadine* (pomegranate) and *citron* (lemon). The most expensive soft drink is a *citron*, *orange* or *pamplemousse pressé* – freshly squeezed lemon, orange or grapefruit mixed with iced water and sugar.

The Milk of Provence

When in Provence, do as the Provençaux do: drink pastis. The aniseed-flavoured alcoholic drink is a classic aperitif in the region, although it can be drunk at any time of day.

Amber-coloured in the bottle, it turns a milky white when mixed with water. Bars and cafes serve it straight, allowing you to decide how much water to add (roughly five-parts water to one-part pastis). It's best drunk in the sun and on the rocks.

A dash of mint cordial *(sirop de menthe)* transforms a regular pastis into a *perroquet* (literally 'parrot'). A *tomate* (tomato) is tarted up with one part grenadine, while the sweet Mauresque is dressed with *orgeat*, a smooth orange and almond syrup.

Pastis was invented in 1932 in Marseilles by industrialist Paul Ricard (1909–97). The earliest aniseed liqueur to hit the market was absinthe, a dangerous and potent liqueur distilled with wormwood oil that, from the early 1800s, was manufactured in France by Henri-Louis Pernod. The drink – which boasted an astonishing 72% alcohol content – was banned in 1915, paving the way for Ricard's 45% alc/vol pastis and other harmless (except for the alcohol) aniseed and liquorice liqueurs, such as the modern-day Pernod. Leading pastis brands are Pastis 51 (Pastis de Marseille) and Ricard, both owned by the Ricard empire (in addition to Pernod, taken over by Ricard in 1974).

JANE SMITH

Coffee costs 10FF to 20FF per cup. Unless you specify otherwise, you get a small, strong, black espresso. Those requiring a bigger caffeine fix should ask for *un grand café* (a double espresso). Milky versions include *un café crème* (espresso with steamed milk or cream) and *un café au lait* (hot milk with a dash of coffee). Coffee is never served with cold milk.

Thé (tea) and *chocolat chaud* (hot chocolate) are widely available. Most salons de thé serve a choice of *infusions* (herbal teas).

ENTERTAINMENT

Local tourist offices are the best source of information on what's on where. In addition, there is a host of regional entertainment journals and newspapers – most are free and many are in English – that contain comprehensive cinema, theatre and festival listings.

FNAC (☎ 08 36 68 93 39) is the leading hub for tickets and reservations for everything from theatre, opera and exhibitions to rock concerts, football matches and festivals. Visit online at www.fnac.fr (French only). Most stores have a *billetterie* (ticket desk) where a calendar of upcoming events is posted, advance bookings are made and tickets are sold. There is a FNAC in Avignon, Nice and Marseilles. The latter also has a Virgin Megastore with a ticket desk.

Pubs & Bars

Lively pubs and bars abound in coastal hot spots and university towns such as Marseilles, Nice, Avignon and Aix-en-Provence, where the keenest of drinkers can find plenty of places to entertain themselves, drink in hand. English- and Irish-style pubs offering a wealth of happy hours, beach parties, live bands at weekends and punters dancing on tables, are particularly rife in Marseilles and Nice. In summer, many places stay open until well into the wee hours. Come winter, last orders are called well before midnight.

Head inland into Haute-Provence and

you'll be hard pushed to find anything more adventurous than a village cafe-cum-bar.

Discos & Clubs

Discos (*discothèque* or *boîte* in French) and clubs are few and far between once you escape the coast and penetrate rural Provence. Anything goes on the Côte d'Azur however – it's engulfed in party madness from mid-June until mid-September. Nice's party season sees discos on the beach and wild dancing on tables in many of its Anglophone music bars. Music (live or recorded) ranges from jazz and rai to Latino and techno. The crowd can be gay, lesbian, straight or mixed.

Tenue correcte exigée means 'appropriate dress required'. The action doesn't hot up in most places until at least midnight. Bouncers are invariably big and paid to indulge their megalomaniacal animalistic tendencies by keeping out 'undesirables', which, depending on the place, ranges from unaccompanied men who aren't dressed right to members of certain minority groups.

Gay & Lesbian Venues

Marseilles, Nice and Aix-en-Provence have the most active gay and lesbian scenes, with a handful of homosexual venues to prove it. See the Entertainment section in the respective chapter listings for details.

Music & Theatre

Provence is a land of music and theatre, playing host to some of the country's major festivals (see Feasts & Festivals earlier in this chapter) – including the much celebrated Avignon Theatre Festival and concurrent Festival Off (fringe). The Fête de la Musique brings live music to every corner of the region on 21 June.

Cinema

You can see films in their original language (with French subtitles) in selected cinemas in Marseilles, Nice and Aix-en-Provence. Look for the letters 'VO' *(version originale)* on cinema billboards. Some spots along the coast (such as Villefranche-sur-Mer and Monaco) have outside screenings

in summer that are a joy to attend, regardless of language.

SPECTATOR SPORTS
Bullfighting

Many consider it downright cruel. Others see it as a sport or theatre, and never more so than in south-western Provence where bullfighting is regarded as a passionate celebration of Provençal tradition. Many bullfights do end with a dead bull, though the *course Camarguaise* (Camargue-style bullfight) is bloodless (see the Camargue chapter for details).

The season generally runs from Easter to September. Fights can be seen in Aigues-Mortes (mid-October), Arles (Easter weekend, last Sunday in April and 1 May), Nîmes (February, June and mid-September), Pernesles-Fontaines and Stes-Maries de la Mer. Tickets must be reserved months in advance for most events (see the relevant city listings for details).

Cycling

The three-week Tour de France, which hits the road each year in July, rarely visits Provence and the Côte d'Azur (intense heat and horrendous traffic are big deterrents). But the early season, Paris–Nice race – dubbed the 'race to the sun' and considered the official start to the professional cycling season – always does, as does the four-day Mediterranean Tour in early February.

Out of the 12 times since 1951 that the Tour de France has crossed Provence (the last was in 2000), it is 1967 that is remembered most: British cyclist Tommy Simpson suffered a fatal heart attack – triggered by the heat and a cocktail of amphetamines – on the climb up Mont Ventoux during the 211km Marseilles–Carpentras stage. The 1965 world cycling champion, who had won the Paris–Nice stage that same year, was considered one of the greats of the sport at the time.

Numerous cyclist-pilgrims continue to follow in Simpson's tracks up Ventoux's barren slopes today. A road that is tarmacked immaculately and graffitied with large-lettered slogans starting '*allez*' – such as the one up Ventoux – is a sure sign that a cycling race has recently passed by.

Football

Marseilles has long been considered the heart of French football and never more so than since France's stunning victory in the 1998 World Cup and subsequent victory in Euro 2000. The clear champion in both matches was Marseilles-born Zinedine Zidane, a midfielder of North African origin whose goal-scoring headers and extraordinary foot work earned him the titles of World Player of the Year, in 1998 and 2000, and best player of the Euro 2000 tournament. 'Zizou' Zidane has an official Web site at www.zidane.fr.

At club level, in 1991 Olympique de Marseilles (OM) became the first French team to win the European Champions League. The team was national champion for four consecutive years between 1989 and 1992, but has won no major titles since. This is, in part, due to the 1995 Bosman decision to allow European clubs to field as many European players as they wish – resulting in a great exodus of French players to better-paid clubs abroad (including Zidane, who kicked off with Cannes but plays for Juventus, Italy, today). See the boxed text 'OM' in the Marseilles Area chapter for information on visiting OM's home ground, the Stade Vélodrome, and buying tickets for matches.

The region's other strong club is AS Monaco (ASM) whose goalkeeper, Fabian Barthez (transferred to Manchester United in 2000), stole the heart of a nation with his goal-saving heroics in France 1998. Arsenal manager Arsene Wenger and star striker Thierry Henry also began their careers at ASM.

Motor Racing

The annual Monaco Grand Prix is the most glamorous race in the Formula One calendar. It is also the only race that sees F1 mean machines tear round regular town streets rather than a track solely for motor sports. The Grand Prix takes place in May and attracts some 150,000 spectators. For more details see the boxed text 'The Formula One Grand Prix' in the Monaco chapter.

Known among motorcycle enthusiasts is the Circuit du Castellet near Le Castellet. The 5.8km circuit hosts the Grand Prix de France Moto in July and the Bol d'Or in mid-September. Owned by French industrialist Paul Ricard since the early 1970s, the racing complex was sold to F1 tycoon Bernie Ecclestone in June 1999, sparking off talk that the French Grand Prix will race round Castellet after Magny Cours' current contract expires at the end of 2001. See the St-Tropez to Toulon chapter for further details.

Nautical Jousting

Joutes nautiques or *joutes Provençales* (Provençal jousting) is typical only in southern France. Spurred on by bands and a captive audience, the participants (usually male and traditionally dressed in white) try to knock each other into the water from rival boats with 2.60m-long lances. The jouster always stands balanced at the tip of a *tintaine*, a wooden gangplank protruding from the wooden boat where the rest of his team members spur him on.

The sport is particularly strong in St-Raphaël where the annual Provençal jousting championships are invariably held. Contact the Société des Joutes Raphaëloises (☎ 04 94 82 39 74, 06 09 77 89 67), 47 allée des Bruyères, Boulouris, 83700 St-Raphaël, for details. In the Vaucluse, river jousters set L'Isle-sur-la-Sorgue ablaze with colour on 14 and 26 July.

Pétanque

Pétanque (Provençal boules) is Provence's national pastime. Despite the game's humble appearance – a bunch of village men in work clothes throwing dusty balls on a gravel pitch scratched out wherever there's shade – it is a serious sport.

Pétanque was invented in La Ciotat, near Marseilles in 1910, when arthritis-crippled Jules Le Noir could no longer take the running strides prior to aiming that were demanded by the *longue* boule game. The local champion opted to stand with his feet

Polish Your Boules

The rules of *pétanque* (Provençal Boules) are precise and inviolable.

Two to six people, split into two teams, can play. Each player has three solid metal boules (two if there are six players), weighing 650g to 800g and stamped with the hallmark of a licensed boule maker. Personal initials, a name or a family coat of arms can be crafted onto made-to-measure boules. The earliest boules, scrapped in 1930, comprised a wooden ball studded with hundreds of hammered-in steel nails. Antique shops still sell them.

Pétanque revolves around the *cochonnet* (jack), a small wooden ball 25mm to 35mm in diameter. Each team takes it in turn to aim a boule at this marker, the idea being to land the boule as close as possible to it. The team with the closest boule wins the round; points are allocated by totting up how many boules the winner's team has closest to the marker (one point for each boule). The first to notch up 13 wins the match.

The team throwing the cochonnet (initially decided by a coin toss) has to throw it from a small circle, 30cm to 50cm in diameter, scratched in the gravel. It must be hurled 6m to 10m away. Each player aiming a boule must likewise stand in this circle, with both feet planted firmly on the ground. At the end of a round, a new circle is drawn around the cochonnet, determining the spot where the next round will start.

Underarm throwing is compulsory. Beyond that, players can opt between rolling the boule in a dribble along the ground (known as *pointer*, literally 'to point') or hurling it high in the air in the hope of it landing smack-bang on top of an opponent's boule, sending it flying out of position. This flamboyant tactic can turn an entire game around in a matter of seconds and is called *tirer* (literally 'to shoot').

Throughout matches, boules are lovingly polished with a soft white cloth. Players unable to stoop to pick up their boules can lift them up with a magnet attached to a piece of string.

firmly on the ground instead – a style that became known as *pieds tanques* (Provençal for 'tied feet'). Pétanque is a slurred version of pieds tanques. *Jeu Provençal* – which uses heavier balls and requires a hop before throwing – is still played in parts of Provence. See the boxed text 'Polish Your Boules' for details.

SHOPPING

Those intent on sampling a different culinary item every day should follow the Food Highlights & Wine Regions map.

Many edible products typical to Provence – such as *calissons* from Aix-en-Provence, *marrons au sirop* (chestnuts in syrup) from the Massif des Maures and rice from the Camargue – are easy to transport home. But most glass-jar products sold at markets are home-made and rarely contain preservatives. Lavender marmalade from Carpentras market, for example, lasts one month after being opened, while onion chutney

from the Lubéron – mind-blowingly delicious as it is – will not survive outside a fridge. The same goes for bread, cheese and fresh truffles. But not for wine.

Less tasty treats worth a shopping spree include perfumes from Grasse; leather sandals from St-Tropez; colourful wicker baskets and carnations from Antibes; glassware from Biot; Picasso-inspired ceramics from Vallauris; faïence from Moustiers-Ste-Marie; pipes and carpets from Cogolin; soap and *santons* (ornamental figures) from Marseilles or Salon de Provence; *courgourdons* (traditional ornaments made from dyed and hollowed marrows/squash) from Nice; lavender oil, pottery, sundials and wrought-iron pieces from the Lubéron; colourful Provençal fabrics from practically anywhere in Provence; antiques from L'Isle-sur-la-Sorgue; terracotta and ceramic tiles from Salernes; gallery art from St-Paul de Vence; or the latest *haute-couture* designs from Monaco.

Shopping for Olive Oil

The best place to buy Provence's most cherished nectar is from its source – the *moulin* (mill). Many, such as the one in Maussane-les-Alpilles, near Fontvieille, date from the 17th century. Mills are not museums however. Travellers wanting to buy are warmly welcomed by the region's busy mill owners; voyeurs are not.

Huile d'olive (olive oil) is sold by the litre, either in pretty glass bottles or in larger, plastic containers (cheaper). Expect to pay anything from 60FF to 100FF per litre. *Dégustation* (tasting) is an integral part of selecting the right oil for your needs. Most millers will pour a tiny drop of the oil onto a spoon for you to taste; the taste is unique and incomparable to bottled oil sold in supermarkets.

Mills or olive-oil cooperatives *(coopératives oléicoles)* usually open 9 am to noon and 3 to 5 or 6 pm weekdays. The best time to visit is after the olive harvest, from January through to Easter. Depending on the year's crop, mills can sell out of the year's production as early as August. Some mills are listed in the regional chapters; most tourist offices stock lists of mills in their area.

Other places to shop for oil include markets and the exclusive chains of olive-oil shops that have cropped up in recent years to pander to tourist tastes: Oliviers & Co (Cannes, St-Tropez & Valbonne), Le Comptoir des Oliviers (Aix-en-Provence) and Olive: Les Huiles du Monde (St-Rémy de Provence, Les Baux de Provence) all stock dozens of Provençal and Mediterranean olive oils to taste and buy, as well as tapenades and oily delights.

Getting There & Away

AIR

Air France, the national carrier, plus scores of other airlines link Marseilles and Nice – the region's international airports – with most European cities, as well as far-flung spots around the globe. While both airports are fiercely marketed as major international transport hubs, there are still many long-haul destinations that require a change of plane in Paris, London or another European capital. Only direct flights are mentioned below.

Airports & Airlines

Nice-Côte d'Azur airport (Aéroport International Nice-Côte d'Azur), with a Web site at www.nice.aeroport.fr, is the region's top airline hub, and the largest in France outside Paris. A 1.1 billion FF extension programme, to be completed by 2002, will raise the airport's passenger handling capacity to 11 million (16 million by 2015). From Marseilles-Provence airport (Aéroport International Marseilles-Provence), there are direct scheduled flights to 80 destinations. It has a Web site at www.marseille.aeroport.fr. Major airlines have an office at both airports.

International flights also use Nîmes-Arles-Camargue airport (Aéroport de Nîmes-Arles-Camargue) and St-Tropez-La Môle airport (Aéroport-International St-Tropez-La Môle), the region's plushest airstrip, 20km west of St-Tropez in La Môle.

Domestic routes are also served by smaller airports such as those at Avignon (Aéroport d'Avignon) and Toulon (Aéroport de Toulon-Hyères). Cannes also has an airport. For further details visit online at www.cannes.aeroport.fr.

Air France is the largest domestic carrier in France, followed by Air Liberté, Air Littoral and AOM who merged in mid-2000 under the parent wings of Swiss Air; the three are expected to re-emerge as a single carrier by 2001. Other domestic networks are operated by Corsair (run by the travel agency Nouvelles Frontières) and Corse Méditerranée.

For details on how to travel to or from town centres, see the Getting Around section in the relevant chapters.

Buying Tickets

An air ticket alone can gouge a great slice out of anyone's budget, but you can reduce the cost by finding discounted fares. Stiff competition has resulted in this widespread discounting, which is good news for travellers. The only people likely to be paying full fare these days are travellers flying in 1st or business class. Economy passengers can manage some sort of discount. But unless you buy carefully and flexibly, it is still possible to end up paying exorbitant amounts for a journey.

Before parting with any cash, always check the total fare, stopovers required (or allowed), the journey duration, the period of validity, cancellation penalties and any other restrictions. Be aware that while most firms are honest and solvent, fly-by-night outfits do exist. Don't send money (or cheques) through the post. Protection can be obtained by buying a ticket from a bonded agent, such as one covered by the Air Travel Organiser's Licence (ATOL) scheme in the UK. Visit online at www.atol.org.uk.

Better-known travel agents where you may have to pay slightly more than a rock-bottom fare in return for security and peace of mind include US-based Council Travel (www.counciltravel.com), Nouvelles Frontières (www.newfrontiers.com) and Voyageurs du Monde based in France, STA Travel (www.sta-travel.com), Canadian-based Travel CUTS (www.travelcuts.com), Irish-based USIT (www.usit.ie) and the French/Belgian-based Wasteels (French-only Web site at www.voyages-wasteels.fr).

It sometimes pays to approach the airline directly, particularly if you intend flying from a UK airport to Nice or Marseilles with a no-frill carrier such as easyJet or KLM's Buzz. These cut price airlines all accept online bookings and offer excellent fares. Visit their Web sites at www.easy jet.com or at www.buzzaway.com. Online ticket sales work well if you are doing a simple one-way or return trip on specified dates. However, online superfast fare generators are no substitute for a travel agent who knows all about special deals, has strategies for avoiding layovers and can offer advice on everything from which airline has the best vegetarian food to the best travel insurance to bundle with your ticket.

Student and Youth Fares

Full-time students and people aged under 26 have access to better deals than other travellers. The better deals may not always be cheaper fares but can include added flexibility to change flights and/or routes. You have to show a document proving your date of birth or a valid International Student Identity Card (ISIC) when buying your ticket and boarding the plane.

Travellers with Specific Needs

If they're warned early enough, airlines can often make special arrangements for travellers (such as wheelchair assistance at airports or vegetarian meals on the flight). Children under two years travel for 10% of the standard fare (or free on some airlines) as long as they don't occupy a seat. They don't get a baggage allowance. 'Skycots', baby food and nappies should be provided by the airline if requested in advance. Children aged between two and 12 can usually occupy a seat for half to two-thirds of the full fare, and do get a baggage allowance.

The disability-friendly Web site, www .everybody.co.uk, has an airline directory that provides information on the facilities offered by various airlines.

Other Parts of France

Air France is the leading carrier on domestic routes in and out of Paris to Provence; AOM and Air Liberté run a handful. From Paris there are numerous (read: 37 to 50 per day) daily flights year round to/from Nice and Marseilles – arrivals/departures every half-hour at peak times. Most use Paris Orly airport; a fraction use Roissy/Charles de Gaulle. From Paris there are up to seven daily flights to/from Toulon, Nîmes and Avignon.

To other parts of France, there are daily flights from Marseilles and Nice to most airports, including Bordeaux, Clermont-Ferrand, Lille, Lyons, Metz-Nancy, Mulhouse, Nantes, Strasbourg, Toulouse and Corsican airports at Ajaccio, Bastia, Calvi and Figari. From Toulon, there are weekly flights to Brest, Clermont-Ferrand and Lille. Corse Méditerranée flies from Nice and Marseilles to Ajaccio, Bastia, Calvi and Figari (four to six daily).

Fares vary dramatically depending on when you make the reservation and which days you intend staying in your chosen destination. Unless you are eligible for a cheaper youth or student fare, it is cheaper to train it from Paris or other cities in France to Provence and the Côte d'Azur.

Air France (☎ 08 02 80 28 02 in France) has four regular fare levels, ranging from full-fare with no restrictions to reduced fares that require advance booking and carry restrictions. Travellers aged over 60, families and couples who are married or have proof of cohabitation (eg, a French government-issued *certificat de concubinage*) get discounts. Cheaper youth/student fares (with no restrictions or advance booking requirements) are available to those aged under 25 and student-card holders aged 26 or under. The cheapest Paris–Nice return with Air France cost 970FF at the time of writing (booked 14 days in advance, with a Saturday night stay in Nice).

France has a network of student travel agencies which can supply discount tickets to travellers of all ages. OTU Voyages (French only Web site at www.otu.fr) has a central Paris office (☎ 01 44 41 38 50) at 39 ave Georges Bernanos (5e) and 42 offices around the country. Accueil des Jeunes en France (☎ 01 42 77 87 80), 119 rue St-Martin (4e), is another popular discount travel agency. In Provence, Voyages Wasteels (☎ 08 03 88 70 28) has offices in Aix-en-Provence (fax 04 42

27 06 56), 5 bis cours Sextius; Marseilles (fax 04 95 09 30 61), 67 La Canebière; Nice (fax 04 93 92 06 42), 32 rue Hôtel des Postes; and Toulon (fax 04 94 91 92 60), 3 blvd Pierre Tosca.

The UK & Ireland

With the advent of no-frills airlines such as Buzz, easyJet and Virgin Express, airfares between the UK and Nice have been slashed considerably. These airlines operate on a first-come-first-served basis, meaning the earlier you book your ticket, the cheaper the fare will be. Look out for sporadic ticket sales too when some great bargains can be scooped up.

At the time of writing, easyJet (☎ 0870 600 0000 in UK, ☎ 08 25 08 25 08 in France) was advertising one-way fares on its no-tickets-issued airline from Luton/ Liverpool to Nice for as little as UK£30/20 (maximum UK£100/100). Minimum/maximum one-way fares from Nice to Luton or Liverpool cost 210/1410FF. One-way/ return flights booked online (see the boxed text 'Electronic No Frills') are UK£2.50/ 5 less than telephone bookings; bookings can be changed for UK£10/20. easyJet currently operates two to four Nice–Luton flights a day and one daily Nice–Liverpool.

Buzz (☎ 0870 240 7070 in the UK, ☎ 01 55 17 42 42 in France), KLM's no-frills airline, was advertising one-way flights from London Stansted–Marseilles for UK£30, requiring a minimum stay of two nights or a Saturday night. A fully flexible equivalent, changeable up to 30 minutes before take-off, costs UK£119. Minimum/maximum Marseilles–London Stansted fares were advertised at 900/1500FF. Buzz operates a daily flight between Stansted and Marseilles (twice daily on Saturday). Web customers get a UK£1/2 discount on one-way/return flights.

Virgin Express (☎ 0207 744 0004 in the UK, ☎ 0800 528 528 in France) was offering promotional fares on its London–Nice flight (via Brussels) for UK£39 one-way (maximum fare UK£126) and Nice–London returns for 399/1073FF (min/max). Virgin has several fare levels: Promotional,

discounted and economy tickets can't be changed or refunded, but its more expensive, flexible ones can. From Nice, Virgin has one flight daily to/from London Gatwick, and six flights weekly to London Heathrow – both via Brussels.

Dublin-based Ryanair (☎ 01-609 7800 in Ireland, ☎ 0090 766 1000 in the UK or ☎ 03 44 11 41 41 in France) operates one daily low-fare flight between Nîmes-Arles-Camargue airport and London Stansted. One-way fares from Stansted/Nîmes currently cost UK£115.20/1076FF. Visit online at www.ryanair.com for the latest deals. Tickets can't be refunded, but they can be changed subject to flight availability.

Both Nice and Marseilles are served by regular daily British Airways flights to/from London. The cheapest London–Nice return to either airport in mid-2000 cost UK£163. Tickets are valid for one month and are also nonrefundable, nonchangeable and require a minimum Saturday night stay.

Continental Europe

There are flights two or three times daily between Nice/Marseilles and most other European cities, the cheapest fares often being available in early spring and late autumn. Air France's youth fares often cost only marginally more than charters. Virgin Express (see The UK & Ireland section earlier) has a daily flight to/from Brussels out of Nice-Côte d'Azur airport.

Between mid-April and mid-September only, Crossair flies twice weekly between

Air Travel Glossary

Alliances Many of the world's leading airlines are now intimately involved with each other, sharing everything from reservation systems and check-in to aircraft and frequent-flyer schemes. Opponents say that alliances restrict competition. Whatever the arguments, there is no doubt that big alliances are the way of the future.

Cancelling or Changing Tickets If you have to cancel or change a ticket, you need to contact the original travel agent who sold you the ticket. Airlines only issue refunds to the purchaser of a ticket – usually the travel agent who bought the ticket on your behalf. There are often heavy penalties involved; insurance can sometimes be taken out against these penalties.

Courier Fares Businesses often need to send urgent documents or freight securely and quickly. Courier companies hire people to accompany the package through customs and, in return, offer a discount ticket which is sometimes a bargain. However, you may have to surrender all your baggage allowance and take only carry-on luggage.

Fares Airlines traditionally offer 1st class (coded F), business class (coded J) and economy class (coded Y) tickets. These days there are so many promotional and discounted fares available that few passengers pay full fare.

Lost Tickets If you lose your airline ticket an airline will usually treat it like a travellers cheque and, after inquiries, issue you with another one. Legally, however, an airline is entitled to treat it like cash and if you lose it then it's gone forever. Take good care of your tickets.

Onward Tickets An entry requirement for many countries is that you have a ticket out of the country. If you're unsure of your next move, the easiest solution is to buy the cheapest onward ticket to a neighbouring country or a ticket from a reliable airline which can later be refunded if you do not use it.

Open-Jaw Tickets These are return tickets where you fly out to one place but return from another. If available, this can save you backtracking to your arrival point.

Overbooking Since every flight has some passengers who fail to show up, airlines often book more passengers than they have seats. Usually excess passengers make up for the no-shows, but occasionally somebody gets 'bumped' onto the next available flight. Guess who it is most likely to be? The passengers who check in late. If you do get 'bumped' you are normally offered some form of compensation.

Reconfirmation Some airlines require you to reconfirm your flight at least 72 hours prior to departure. Check your travel documents to see if this is the case.

Restrictions Discounted tickets often have various restrictions on them – such as needing to be paid for in advance and incurring a penalty to be altered or cancelled. Others are restrictions on the minimum and maximum period you must be away.

Round-the-World Tickets RTW tickets give you a limited period (usually a year) in which to circumnavigate the globe. You can go anywhere the carrying airlines go, as long as you don't backtrack. The number of stopovers or total number of separate flights is decided before you set off and they usually cost a bit more than a basic return flight.

Ticketless Travel Airlines are gradually waking up to the realisation that paper tickets are unnecessary encumbrances. On simple one-way or return trips, reservations details can be held on computer, and the passenger merely shows ID to claim his or her seat.

Transferred Tickets Airline tickets cannot be transferred from one person to another. Travellers sometimes try to sell the return half of their ticket, but officials can ask you to prove that you are the person named on the ticket. On an international flight tickets are always compared with passports.

Geneva and St-Tropez-La Môle airport, and three times a week to/from Zürich. Lufthansa (☎ 08 02 02 00 30 in France) operates two weekend La Môle–Munich flights from mid-April to early October, with an additional flight mid-week from mid-July until the end of August.

Across Continental Europe many have ties with STA Travel, where cheap tickets can be purchased and STA-issued tickets altered (usually for a US$25 fee). Outlets include: STA Travel (☎ 030-311 0950, fax 313 0948), Goethestrasse 73, 10625 Berlin; and Passaggi (☎ 06 474 09 23, fax 06 482 74 36), Stazione Termini FS, Galleria di Tesla, Rome. In Belgium, Connections (☎ 02-550 01 00), part of the USIT group, has several offices, including one at 19–21 rue du Midi, Brussels. Check out the Web site at www.connections.be. In Switzerland, SSR Voyages (☎ 01-297 11 11) specialises in student, youth and budget fares. It has a Web site at www.ssr.ch. In Zürich, there is a branch at Leonhardstrasse 10 and there are branches in most major Swiss cities. In the Netherlands, NBBS Reizen is the official student travel agency. You can find them in Amsterdam (☎ 020-624 50 71) at Schilphoweg 101, 2300 AJ Leiden. In Spain, try Barcelo Viajs (☎ 91 559 19) at Princesa 3, Madrid 28228.

The USA & Canada

The flight options across the North Atlantic, the world's busiest long-haul air corridor, are bewildering. The *New York Times, LA Times, Chicago Tribune* and *San Francisco Chronicle* all have weekly travel sections where you can find travel agents' ads. Council Travel (toll-free ☎ 800-226 8624), with a Web site at www.counciltravel.com, and STA (toll-free ☎ 800-777 0112), online at www.sta-travel.com, both have offices in major cities.

Canada's best bargain-hunting agency is Travel CUTS (☎ 888-835 2887), with offices in major Canadian cities and a Web site at www.travelcuts.com. You might also scan the budget travel agents' ads in the *Toronto Globe & Mail, Toronto Star* and the *Vancouver Province*. Further cheap deals are

offered by Ticket Planet, a leading ticket consolidator in the USA. For more details visit online at www.ticketplanet.com.

Delta Airlines operate one daily flight between New York and Nice, with return fares from Nice starting at 2970FF (minimum weekend stay). Beyond that, any journey to France's sunny south entails a change of plane in Paris, London or another European transport hub. A New York–Paris round trip can cost anything from US$560 in low season to US$850 with Air France or British Airways in high season. Airhitch (☎ 212-864 2000, @ airhitch@netcom.com), with a Web site at www.airhitch.org, specialises in cheap stand-by fares.

Australia & New Zealand

Saturday's travel sections in the *Sydney Morning Herald* and the *Melbourne Age* have many ads offering cheap fares to Europe. One of Australasia's best discount-air fare shops is Flight Centre (☎ 131 600), with a Web site at www.flightcentre.com.au and an office (☎ 03-9650 2899) at 19 Bourke St, Melbourne. STA Travel (☎ 131 776) has a Web site at www.statravel.com.au and offices in Sydney (☎ 02-9212 1255) and Auckland (☎ 09-309 0458). Both agencies have branch offices nationwide. Trailfinders has branches in Sydney (☎ 02-9247 7666), Brisbane (☎ 07-3229 0887) and Cairns (☎ 07-4041 1199). Visit online at www.trailfinder.com.

Airlines such as Thai Airways International (THAI), Malaysia Airlines, Qantas Airways and Singapore Airlines all have frequent promotional fares. At the time of writing, you could expect to pay around A$1650/2100 for a return fare from Australia to Paris in low/high season. From New Zealand, the cheapest fares (via Bangkok) in low season start at about NZ$1185 one-way and NZ$2049 return. Via the USA, fares in low season start at NZ$1265/2299 one-way/return. A round-the-world ticket will cost about NZ$2300.

North Africa

Marseilles is the leading hub for flights to North Africa. Air Algérie (☎ 04 42 14 22 72 in Marseilles) operates up to four flights daily to Algiers, Annaba and Constantine in Algeria. It also has weekly flights to Batna, Bejaia, Oran and Tlemcen. The cheapest return fare to Algiers is 2080FF.

To Casablanca in Morocco, there are daily flights from Nice and Marseilles with Royal Air Maroc (☎ 04 93 21 48 80 in Nice or ☎ 04 42 14 24 79 in Marseilles). The cheapest return fare costs 1850FF. Royal Air Maroc also operates direct Marseilles–Oujda flights four times weekly.

The cheapest return from Nice or Marseilles to Tunis or Monastir costs 1380FF; Tunis Air (☎ 04 93 21 35 05 in Nice, ☎ 04 42 14 21 75 in Marseilles) operates one to three flights daily to/from Tunis and weekly flights to Monastir from both airports.

LAND
Other Parts of France

Bus French transport policy is completely biased in favour of its state-owned rail system making inter-regional bus services extremely limited. Take a train.

Train France's efficient rail network, run by the state-owned SNCF (Société Nationale des Chemins de Fer), reaches almost every part of the country. The network is very Paris-centric, with key lines radiating from the capital like the spokes of a wheel. While travel between towns on different 'spokes' can be tricky and tedious, rail links between Provence and the rest of France warrant few complaints.

SNCF's pride and joy is the TGV (pronounced 'teh-sheh-veh'), short for *train à grande vitesse* (high-speed train). The TGV Sud-Est links the south-east (Nice, Marseilles, Avignon and the Alps) with Dijon, Lyons and Paris' Gare de Lyon. On this service, only the stretch of track between Paris and Valence is currently served by superfast TGV track, on which TGVs travel at a breathtaking 310km/h. From 10 June 2001, superfast TGV track will also serve Marseilles: the new high-speed service, the TGV Méditerranée, will link Valence with Avignon where the line will split – eastwards to Marseilles and westwards to

Montpellier in neighbouring Languedoc. The TGV Méditerranée, which has cost 24 billion FF to build, will cut travelling time between Paris and Marseilles (782km) from 4¼ hours to a startling three hours. A 1st-/2nd-class one-way ticket will cost 617/379FF. SNCF authorities expect the new service to boost annual traffic by 30%, upping Paris–Marseilles rail passengers to six million per year.

In addition to TGV trains, the SNCF operates less speedy rail services which are often cheaper – ideal for budget travellers with time on their hands. Both *grande ligne* (main line) trains and those operated by TER (Transport Express Régional) link smaller cities and towns with the TGV network. Many towns not on the SNCF network are linked with nearby railheads by SNCF or TER buses (see the Getting Around chapter for details). For schedules and fares for main-line trains call ☎ 08 36 67 68 69.

Sample fares from Paris include to/from Orange (399FF, four hours), Avignon (436FF, 3½ to four hours), Arles (452FF, four hours), Marseilles (379FF, 4¼ hours), Les Arcs-Draguignan (434FF, 5½ hours), Cannes (541FF, 6¼ to 7½ hours) and Nice (553FF, 7¼ to 8½ hours).

From Lille in northern France, there are two direct trains daily to Nice (679FF, nine hours), one also runs overnight. Other northern destinations such as Roissy Charles de Gaulle airport require a change of train in Lyons or Paris, as do destinations in western France. From eastern France, there are direct Strasbourg–Nice trains (496FF, 12 hours). To/from cities such as Bordeaux in southwestern France, change trains in Narbonne, Toulouse or Montpellier.

Reservations & Tickets Most trains, including TGVs, have 1st- and 2nd-class sections. In this book we quote fares for 2nd-class travel, which works out at about 50FF to 70FF per 100km for longer cross-country trips, or 70FF to 100FF per 100km for shorter hops (compare this with autoroute tolls and petrol, each costing about 40FF to 50FF per 100km). A return ticket is twice the price of a one-way ticket. Travel in 1st class costs 50% more than 2nd class. Children under four travel free; those aged four to 11 travel half-price.

A 25FF reservation fee is obligatory for TGV travellers (automatically included in the ticket price) and for non-TGV passengers on some trains during holiday periods – such as July and August on jam-packed coastal-bound trains. Most overnight trains are equipped with *couchettes* (sleeping berths) which must be reserved. A couchette costs 105FF; 2nd-class couchettes have six berths and 1st-class have four bunks.

Reservations can be made by telephone, via Minitel or the SNCF's Web site (see the boxed text 'SNCF Hotlines' below) at any SNCF ticketing office, or by using a ticket vending machine (see the Getting Around chapter for further information) at any SNCF train station. Tickets issued via machines are valid for two months. Reservations can be changed by telephone; or up to one hour before departure if you are actually at your departure station.

Tickets bought with cash can be reimbursed for cash (by you or a thief); keep them in a safe place. Alternatively, you can pay with a credit card at the ticket counter, at one of the touch-screen ticket vending machines, or online at the SNCF Web site.

SNCF Hotlines

SNCF information lines accept advance ticket reservations, dole out updated train schedules and can update you on fares and everything else you might need to know about trains within the region. Lines open 7 am to 10 pm daily.

To call from abroad dial 33 and drop the initial zero. Domestic calls are charged at 2.23FF per minute. Call ☎ 08 36 35 35 39 to contact the English-speaking information service, or ☎ 08 36 35 35 35 for information in French.

Within France, reservations can be made via Minitel (3615 SNCF) or through the SNCF Web site at www.sncf.com. SNCF don't post tickets outside France.

Prohibitive tariffs apply for tickets bought directly from the conductor on board trains.

Validating Your Ticket You risk an on-the-spot fine if you fail to validate your train ticket before boarding: time-stamp it in a *composteur*, a bizarre-looking orange post situated at the platform entrance. If you forget, find the conductor on board so he/she can punch it for you. Tickets are usually checked and punched by the conductor midway through a journey.

Tickets are valid for 24 hours after they have been time-stamped, meaning you can break your journey briefly mid-way providing you are not on a line (such as a TGV) requiring a reservation. Time-stamp your ticket again before reboarding.

Unused tickets (over 30FF) can be reimbursed (90% of the original ticket price) up to two months after the date of issue. Refunds are available from any train station ticket window.

Auto Train Under Motorail's Auto Train scheme you can travel with your car on a train. Cars are loaded on the train one hour before departure and unloaded 30 minutes after arrival. At the time of writing, this service was available at Avignon, St-Raphaël, Marseilles and Nice train stations.

Information in the UK is available from Rail Europe UK (see the boxed text 'Rail Passes & Discount Fares' later in this chapter). In France, ticketing is handled by the SNCF.

Car & Motorcycle Number one rule when motoring to Provence: avoid July and August. If this is impossible, be prepared to sit and wait in some mighty long *bouchons* (traffic jams), both on and off the *autoroute* (motorway).

The main southbound route from Paris is along the A6 and its continuation from Lyons, the A7 Autoroute du Soleil (literally the 'Road of the Sun') which continues south through Orange and Avignon to Marseilles. From Marseilles, the A8 (called La Provençale) bears east to Nice and beyond into Italy where it becomes the A10. The A9

Bis

You will often see signs at autoroute exits marked *bis* on an orange panel. This stands for *bison futé* and indicates alternative routes – generally well away from the autoroute, along national and departmental roads – which avoid areas prone to peak-period congestion.

For information on bis routes and bottlenecks to avoid call ☎ 08 36 68 20 00. An annually updated, free map of bis routes is published by the French government; contact your local automobile association or Maison de la France (see Tourist Offices in Facts for the Visitor) for a copy.

bears west from just south of Orange to Nîmes, Montpellier, and farther south to Spain. The A51 is the main road into the interior of Provence, leading north-east from Aix-en-Provence to Sisteron from where Alpes-de-Haute-Provence can be accessed. Approaching Sisteron from the north, the N85 (Route Napoléon) follows the Napoléon Bonaparte trail from Grenoble, through Gap to Sisteron, Digne-les-Bains, Castellane and farther south to Grasse and Cannes on the coast.

Road tolls are imposed on most stretches of autoroute, the exception being around major cities such as Nice or Cannes. Count on paying 40FF to 50FF per 100km (see the Road Tolls and Road Distance tables later in this chapter). Some parts of the autoroute have toll plazas every few dozen kilometres; most have a machine which issues a little ticket that you hand over at a *péage* (toll booth) when you exit. You can pay in French francs or by credit card. The toll plaza on the French side of the Italian Ventimiglia border crossing accepts French francs (11FF) or Italian lira (3000 lira).

Autoroutes in southern France are managed by either the ASF (Autoroutes du Sud de la France; ☎ 04 90 32 90 05, ☎ 01 47 53 37 00), 100 ave de Suffren, BP533, 75725 Paris, which has a French only Web site at www.asf.fr; or ESCOTA (Société des

Autoroutes Estérel Côte d'Azur-Provence-Alpes; ☎ 04 92 97 40 40), ave de Cannes, BP 41, 06211 Mandelieu-La Napoule, which has a Web site at www.escota.com. The ASFA (Association des Sociétés Françaises d'Autoroutes; ☎ 01 47 53 39 41, ℮ asfa@ autoroutes.fr) has an excellent Web site at www.autoroutes.fr with masses of traffic-related information. See the boxed text 'On the Road' on the following page for ways of getting information once on the road.

Hitching Two organisations in France put people looking for rides in touch with drivers going to the same destination. Allostop Provoya (☎ 01 53 20 42 42 in Paris, ☎ 01 53 20 42 43/44 from outside Paris and abroad, ℮ allostop@ecritel.fr) is based at 8 Rue Rochambeau, 75009 Paris, and has a French only Web site at www.ecritel.fr /allostop. Brittany-based Association Pouce (☎/fax 02 99 08 67 02, ℮ yannick@pouce .com) is online at www.pouce.com (French only).

With Allostop, passengers pay 22 centimes per kilometre to the driver plus a fee to cover any administrative expenses: 30/ 45/60/70FF for trips under 200/300/400/ 500km. Association Pouce has no cover charge.

Continental Europe

Bus Generally, buses are slower and less comfortable than trains but they are cheaper, especially if you qualify for the often well-worthwhile discounts that most companies offer to seniors, students, youths and children. Several companies include Provence and the Côte d'Azur in their European routes.

Eurolines This company (☎ 08 36 69 52 42, ℮ euroline@ imaginet.fr), with a Web site at www.eurolines.fr, is an association of companies that together form Europe's largest international bus network, linking cities such as Nice, Marseilles and Avignon with points all over Western and Central Europe, Scandinavia and Morocco. Eurolines has offices in the region at the respective bus stations in Avignon (☎ 04 90 85 27

On the Road

Motorist-friendly radio station **Autoroute FM 107.7MHz** broadcasts traffic reports in English, French and Italian every 30 minutes at peak times. It also warns motorists in advance of expected road conditions over the next few days: *rouge* (red) means 'hellish, avoid'; *orange* translates as 'busy, but tolerable' while *vert* (green) is for 'go, little traffic on the roads'.

For general information on autoroute tolls, itineraries and road conditions call **Autoroute!** on ☎ 08 36 68 09 79 or **ESCOTA** on ☎ 08 36 69 36 36. For information on tolls within the region call **ESCOTA** on ☎ 04 93 49 33 33 or the **ASF** on ☎ 04 90 32 90 05.

Plan Your Itinerary (☎ 01 47 05 90 01) advises the lost and/or helpless on where to go and how to get there.

60), Marseilles (☎ 04 91 50 57 55) and Nîmes (☎ 04 66 29 49 02); in Nice, Intercars at the bus station also sells tickets and makes reservations for Eurolines buses.

Those aged under 25, over 60 or between four and 12 qualify for a 10% to 20% discount on most routes. In summer, book tickets well in advance. Return tickets cost substantially less than two one-way tickets. In addition to the standard fare, Eurolines offers cancellation insurance (20FF) and a change-date option (25FF), which allows you to change the date on which you intend travelling after your ticket has been issued. Passengers are allowed to transport two pieces of luggage per person; a 50FF fee is charged for each additional bag.

Travelling from Nice, Cannes or Toulon, sample one-way adult fares include Amsterdam (570FF), Brussels (470FF), Rome (340FF) and Florence (270FF). At the time of writing, a one-way Nîmes–Barcelona fare was 295FF and Aix-en-Provence –Frankfurt was 350FF. Sample fares for journeys originating in Marseilles include Belgrade (700FF) and Prague (580FF).

Eurolines-affiliated companies can be found across Europe, including Amsterdam

(☎ 020-560 8787), with a Web site at www.eurolines.nl; Barcelona (☎ 93 490 40 00); Berlin (☎ 030-86 0960), online at www.deutsche-touring.com; Brussels (☎ 02-203 0707); Madrid (☎ 91 528 1105); Prague (☎ 02-2421 3420), with a Web site at www.eurolines.cz; Rome (☎ 06 44 23 39 28), online at www.eurolines.it; and Vienna (☎ 01-712 04 35), online at www.eurolines.at.

Intercars This outfit operates buses to cities in southern and central Europe and can be visited online at www.intercars.fr. Its main hub in Provence is at the bus station in Nice (☎ 04 93 80 42 20) although it has offices and buses departing from bus stations in Marseilles (☎ 04 91 50 08 66), Nîmes (☎ 04 66 29 84 22) and other stops en route.

Those aged under 26 and over 60, and children aged two to 12 years are entitled to discounted fares (approximately 5% and 10% respectively off a full adult fare). Once you have bought your bus ticket, you must pay a 50/100FF penalty if you want to change the date on which you want to travel less/more than 48 hours before your original planned departure. Passengers are allowed to transport a suitcase and one piece of hand luggage; additional bags cost 50FF a throw.

Sample one-way adult fares from Nice include those to Bratislava (490FF), Budapest (550FF) and Warsaw (765FF).

SAM Tourisme This company (☎ 04 93 54 14 49, fax 04 93 54 32 97), 5 blvd Jean Jaurès, in Nice, operates weekly buses to Casablanca (14½ hours), departing from Nice on Wednesday and Saturday at 6.30 am and stopping en route in Toulon and Marseilles. In Casablanca, tickets are sold by ASMAA Tourisme (☎ 212-248 71 00/01, fax 248 71 21, e asmaatourisme@dromadaire.com), route Ouled Ziane, Bureau 31.

Busabout This is a UK-based company (☎ 020-7950 1661, fax 7950 1662, e info@busabout.co.uk), 258 Vauxhall Bridge Road, London SW1V 1BS, that runs coaches around several loops covering a wide variety of destinations in Western and Central

Road Distances (km)

	Aix/Marseilles	Avignon	Cannes	Nice	Nimes	Menton	Monaco	Orange	Toulon
Aix/Marseilles	...								
Avignon	100	...							
Cannes	168	250	...						
Nice	196	278	28	...					
Nimes	123	45	254	280	...				
Menton	223	306	55	27	307	...			
Monaco	215	305	48	20	300	10	...		
Orange	119	26	250	276	57	302	295	...	
Toulon	64	164	125	150	187	178	170	182	...
Bordeaux	655	585	776	804	538	832	825	589	718
Calais	1075	975	1206	1234	1013	1260	1253	962	1141
Lyons	320	220	445	473	251	500	493	200	379
Paris	782	682	908	935	710	965	958	516	837
Toulouse	408	326	538	565	281	592	585	342	471

Europe, Scandinavia and Morocco. Its Web site at www.busabout.com maps out all its loops, including those that pass through France en route to northern Europe, Spain and Portugal. A Busabout pass – valid for 15 or 21 days, one to three months, or for an unlimited period – allows you to hop on and off wherever you choose, at designated pick-up points. The latter are often close to youth hostels or camp sites. Busabout operates year round, with services at each pick-up point every two or three days.

Passes are sold at major youth travel agencies throughout Europe. One-/two-/three-month passes currently cost UK£289/449/549 (UK£259/399/499 for youth or student card-holders).

Train Paris abounds with connections from all over Europe. Other major border stations in France are in Lille, Metz, Strasbourg, Bordeaux, Mulhouse and Lyons. Within the region, Nice is the major hub, sitting smartly on the Barcelona–Rome rail line – a service which gets packed out (and heavily booked well in advance) by backpackers during the summer. Day and overnight trains run in both directions. At the time of writing, a one-way Barcelona/Rome fare from Nice set you back 386/297FF (plus 90FF for a night-train couchette) for the nine-/10-hour journey. Nice is also served by direct train services to/from Milan (185FF, 4½ hours). Inland, there are regular daily TER trains between Breil-sur-Roya and Tende in Haute-Provence and Cuneo (76FF, 1¾ hours) in Italy; Turin is a further 1½-hours from Breil (107FF). Marseilles touts direct daily trains to/from Brussels (664FF, seven hours), one of which continues to Nice (749FF, 9¼ hours).

You can book tickets and get information from Rail Europe up to two months ahead (see the boxed text 'Rail Passes & Discount Fares' later in this chapter). If you intend to do a lot of train travel, consider purchasing the Thomas Cook European Timetable, up-

Road Tolls (FF)

	Aix/Marseilles	Avignon	Cannes	Nice	Nîmes	Menton	Monaco	Orange	Toulon
Aix/Marseilles	---								
Avignon	26	---							
Cannes	65.5	94	---						
Nice	80.5	109	15	---					
Nîmes	29	21	94.5	109.5	---				
Menton	98.5	127	32	30.5	140.5	---			
Monaco	101	129	35.5	20	130	10.5	---		
Orange	38	12	106	121	9	139	141	---	
Toulon	37	63	53	195	66	86	88.5	75	---
Bordeaux	245	219	313	328	216	346	348	207	282
Calais	410	384	478	493	381	511	513	372	447
Lyons	116	90	184	198	87	217	219	78	153
Paris	277	251	345	360	248	258	380	239	314
Toulouse	152	126	220	235	123	253	255	144	189

dated monthly with a complete listing of schedules, plus information on reservations and supplements. Single issues cost about UK£11 from Thomas Cook Publishing (☎ 01733-503571, fax 503596, ℮ publishing-sales@thomascook.com) in the UK.

Auto Train This arrangement (see Train under Other Parts of France earlier in this chapter) allows you to transport your car by passenger train to Avignon and St-Raphaël. In France, the SNCF offices have information; contact any Rail Europe office in other European countries. Advance bookings of at least two months are generally required.

The UK

The Channel Tunnel, inaugurated in 1994, is the first dry-land link between England and France since the Ice Age.

Bus Eurolines operates direct bus services, two to four times weekly, from London's Victoria Coach station via the Dover–Calais Channel crossing. Adult one-way fares from/to London during peak season (July and August) include Avignon (UK£63/590FF), Aix-en-Provence (UK£57/550FF), Marseilles (UK£66/590FF) and Toulon (UK£69/620FF). Coastal services from/to Nice, Cannes, Fréjus and St-Raphaël cost UK£69/630FF) in high season only. Low-season fares are about 10% less.

Bookings can be made with Eurolines UK (☎ 0870 5143 219 or ☎ 01582-404 511), through its Web site at www.eurolines.co.uk or at any National Express office.

For Busabout services from London, see Continental Europe earlier in the chapter. If you're beginning your journey in London, Busabout charges an extra UK£15 for the Channel crossing.

Train The cheapest rail route from the UK to Provence is from London to Paris on a 'rail-sea-rail' ticket (crossing the Channel

Rail Passes & Discount Fares

The following passes are available from student travel agencies, train stations in Europe, and the SNCF subsidiary Rail Europe (e europrail@eurail.on.ca), contactable in the UK (☎ 0990 848 848), 179 Piccadilly, London W1V 0BA. Information is posted on the Rail Europe Web site at www .raileurope.com.

SNCF Discounts Fares & Passes

Children under four travel free; those aged four to 11 travel for half-price. Discounted fares (25% reduction) automatically apply to travellers aged 12 to 25, seniors aged over 60, one to four adults travelling with a child aged four to 11, two people travelling on a return journey together or anyone travelling at least 200km within France and spending a Saturday night away.

Purchasing a one-year travel pass can yield a 50% discount (25% if the cheapest seats are sold out): a **Carte 12/25** aimed at travellers aged 12 to 25 costs 270FF; the **Carte Enfant Plus** for one to four adults travelling with a child aged four to 11 costs 350FF; while seniors aged over 60 can buy a **Carte Sénior** for 285FF.

The **France Rail Pass** entitles non-residents of France to unlimited travel on the SNCF system for three to six days over a one-month period. In 2nd class, the three-day version costs 1200FF (990FF each for two people travelling together); each additional day of travel costs around 200FF. A cheaper youth version is also available. France Rail Pass holders get discounts on the Eurostar and the Nice–Digne-les-Bains mountain railway.

Europe-wide Rail Passes for European Residents

The **Euro Domino Pass**, available to those who have been residents in Europe for at least six months, can be used in France for three to eight consecutive days, or non-consecutive over a one-month period, of 2nd-class travel. Adult passes cost UK£99/119/159/198 for three/four/six/eight days; passes for those aged under 26 cost UK£79/95/127/159 for three/four/six/eight days. The pass covers supplements on TGV trains, but does not include seat or couchette reservations.

by ferry or SeaCat), with a change of trains (and main-line stations) in Paris for the train journey south (see Train under Other Parts of France earlier in this chapter). Connex (☎ 0870 001 0174) handles this London –Paris route and sells tickets for the onward journey too. At the time of writing a 2nd-class, London–Marseilles/Nice adult fare was UK£131/120 and the youth fare was UK£121/111.

Eurostar This train (☎ 0870 5186 186 in the UK; ☎ 08 36 35 35 39 in France), the high-speed passenger service through the Channel Tunnel, takes three hours from London (Waterloo) to Paris. There is no direct service to Provence and the Côte d'Azur, but a direct London–Marseilles Eurostar is expected to follow hot on the heels of the TGV Méditerannée in June 2001.

Until then, you can take a Eurostar to Lille and transfer to a southbound TGV to Nice, or continue to Paris from where there are numerous southbound trains (see Train in Other Parts of France earlier in this chapter).

Full fares can be more than twice those for rail-sea-rail, but certain nonrefundable, nonexchangeable European rail tickets, which include a Eurostar Channel crossing, are competitive: a 2nd-class return ticket from London to Avignon, Marseilles, Nice, Toulon or St-Raphaël costs UK£120 (nonrefundable, nonreimbursable, includes a Saturday night stay in Provence, and must be booked a week ahead). The fare for those aged 26 or under costs the same but carries no restrictions.

In the UK, Eurostar and non-Eurostar tickets are sold at travel agents, main-line

Rail Passes & Discount Fares

With the **Inter Rail Pass**, you can travel in 29 European countries organised into eight zones; France is grouped in Zone E with the Netherlands, Belgium and Luxembourg. For 22 days of unlimited 2nd-class travel in one zone, the cost is UK£129/179 for those aged under/over 26. You also get 50% off rail travel from your home country to your zone(s) and between adjacent zones as well as discounts on Eurostar tickets and some ferry routes.

Europe-wide Rail Passes for Non-European Residents

If you are not a resident of Europe, are under 26 on your first day of travel, and anticipate clocking up more than 2400km around Provence, France and Europe, consider buying a **Eurail Youth Pass** which gives unlimited rail travel for 15/21 consecutive days or one/two/three months. One/two/three months of unlimited travel costs around US$623/882/1089; more expensive adult equivalents are also available for US$890/1260/1558.

A **Eurail Youth Flexipass** covers 10/15 non-consecutive days of travel across two months and costs around US$458/599 (US$654/862 for adult equivalents). In the USA and Canada, both types of Eurail passes can be bought by telephone (☎ 1888 667 9734) and sent to you by courier. Eurail's Web site is at www.eurail.on.ca.

The cheaper **Eurail Choice Pass** is only valid of three neighbouring European countries of your choice – eg, France, Spain and Portugal. The youth version costs US$230/252/294/334 for five/six/eight/10 days of nonconsecutive, 2nd-class travel in a two-month period. Adult equivalents covering 1st-class travel cost US$328/360/420/476.

The **Euro Pass** allows you to travel in five European countries for five to 15 non-consecutive days over a two-month period. The adult pass, good for 1st-class train travel within France, Germany, Italy, Spain and Switzerland, range from US$384 for five days to US$728 for 15 days (20% less for two adults travelling together). Cheaper **Euro Pass Youth** equivalents are only good for 2nd-class travel and cost US$233/513 for five/15 days.

train stations and SNCF-owned Rail Europe (see the boxed text 'Rail Passes & Discount Fares' above). For further details visit the Web site at www.eurostar.co.uk.

Car & Motorcycle High-speed shuttle trains operated by Eurotunnel (☎ 0870 241 2938 in the UK, ☎ 03 21 00 61 00 in France) whisk cars, motorcycles, bicycles and coaches from Folkestone through the Channel Tunnel to Coquelles, 5km southwest of Calais, in air-conditioned and soundproofed comfort. Journey time is 35 minutes. Trains run three to four times an hour (one or two per hour between midnight and 6 am). Eurotunnel has a Web site at www.eurotunnel.com.

A fully flexible return (valid for a year) for a car and passengers costs UK£355/310 in high/low season, compared to a five-day return which costs UK£249/195 in high/low season. A fully flexible fare for a motorcycle is UK£199/170 (UK£139/109 for a five-day return. Promotional fares are often available.

When calculating costs, include road tolls from Calais to Provence (see the Road Tolls table earlier in this chapter).

Bicycle European Bike Express (☎ 01642-251 440, fax 232 209, ✉ bike@bike-express.co.uk) transports cyclists and their bikes by bus and trailer from the UK to places all over Europe, including southern France. Route details and further information can be found on its Web site at www.bike-express.co.uk. Return fares start at UK£159 (UK£10 less for CTC members; see under Bicycle in the Getting Around chapter).

euro currency converter €1 = 6.56FF

SEA

Provence is linked by ferry with Corsica, Italy and North Africa, with much of the passenger traffic run by state-owned Société Nationale Maritime Corse Méditerranée (SNCM; ☎ 08 36 67 95 00), which has offices in Marseilles, Nice and Toulon (see the Getting There & Away section in those chapters) and a Web site at www .sncm.fr. Reservations and tickets for ferry travel are also available from travel agencies in France and the countries served. Prices listed are for standard one-way tickets, unless stated otherwise. Return fares are usually cheaper than two one-way fares.

The UK & Ireland

There are no direct ferries, but you can take a ferry year round from Dover to Calais or from Folkestone to Boulogne – the shortest crossings and the most competitive fares between the UK and France – and motor it south. Longer channel crossings include Newhaven–Dieppe, Poole–Cherbourg, and Portsmouth–Cherbourg/Le Havre/Ouistreham/St-Malo. Services to St-Malo and Roscoff in Brittany run less frequently than those across the Straits of Dover, particularly in winter.

Fares are wildly seasonal. Winter tickets can cost less than half as much as in high season (each company has its own complex definition of high season). Three- or five-day excursion return fares cost about the same as regular one-way tickets. Return fares generally cost less than two one-way tickets. Children aged four to 14 or 15 travel for half to two-thirds of an adult fare. Most crossings also have higher fares for lounge seats and cabins. For a list of ferry companies and ports served, see the boxed text 'Ferry 'cross the Channel' on the next page.

Corsica

Almost all ferry services between Provence – Nice, Marseilles and Toulon – and Corsica (Ajaccio, Bastia, Calvi, L'Ile-Rousse, Porto Vechio and Propriano) are handled by SNCM. Schedules and fares are comprehensively listed on the SNCM Web site at www.sncm.fr and in its pocket timetable,

freely distributed at tourist offices, some hotels and SNCM offices. At the height of summer there are up to five ferries daily to/from Nice, up to three daily to/from Marseilles and up to five times weekly to/from Toulon. In winter there are as few as one per day to/from Nice and Marseilles. Corsica–Toulon crossings only run April to October.

A one-way passage in a *fauteuil* (literally 'armchair' but in most cases a rather hard, straight-backed chair in a small cabin), costs 213/243FF in winter/June to early September on sailings to/from Nice, and 256/292FF for sailings to/from Marseilles or Toulon. Daytime crossings take about 6½ hours. For overnight trips, the cheapest/most comfortable cabin costs an additional 82/288FF per person.

Passengers aged 12 to 25, those aged over 60 and *familles nombreuses* (parents travelling with three children aged under 18) pay 186/213FF in winter/summer for all sailings to/from Nice and 224/256FF from Marseilles and Toulon. Children aged four to 12 pay 50% of the full adult fare; those aged under four travel for free. Taking a small car costs between 163FF and 612FF, depending on the season. Motorcycles under 100cc cost 136FF to transport and a 91FF fee is imposed for bicycles.

From Nice, Corsica Ferries and the SNCM also run a 70km/h express NGV (Navire à Grande Vitesse) to Calvi (2¾ hours) and Bastia (3½ hours). Fares on these zippy NGVs, which carry 500 passengers and 148 vehicles, are similar to those charged on the regular ferries. The downside of the NGV is that it cannot sail in bad weather; last-minute cancellations are not unknown.

In July and August, all Corsica-bound ferries get fully booked; reservations for vehicles and couchettes should be made well in advance. In addition to the basic fares, a port tax is levied by the French government; it ranges from 49FF (Toulon–Calvi) to 72FF (Nice–Ajaccio) per person depending on which port you sail to/from, plus 35FF (Marseilles–Bastia) to 61FF (Nice–Ajaccio) per vehicle.

In Corsica, tickets are sold from the SNCM office in Ajaccio (☎ 04 95 29 66 69,

Ferry 'cross the Channel

Ferrying it across the channel tosses up a merry assortment of routes, vessels and fares. Sample prices quoted below are for a high-season, one-way ticket for a car plus driver and one passenger.

Brittany Ferries (Roscoff ☎ 02 98 29 28 00, UK ☎ 0870 5360 360, Ireland ☎ 021-277 801). Poole–Cherbourg ferries (UK£200, four hours), Portsmouth–Ouistreham (six hours) and Portsmouth–St-Malo (UK£220, nine hours), all up to three daily. Plymouth–Roscoff (UK£170, six hours, one or two daily, mid-March to mid-November; once weekly, the rest of the year); Cork–Roscoff (IR£356, 14 hours, once weekly, April to September)
Web site: www.brittany-ferries.com

Condor Ferries (St-Malo ☎ 02 99 20 03 00, UK ☎ 01305-761551). Weymouth/Poole–St-Malo catamarans (UK£187, five/six hours, daily May to mid-October)
Web site: www.condorferries.co.uk

Hoverspeed (France ☎ 08 20 00 35 55, UK ☎ 0870 240 8070). Nippy SeaCat catamarans, Folkestone–Boulogne (UK£119, 55 minutes, four daily); Newhaven–Dieppe SuperSeaCats (UK£139, two hours, three a day)
Web site: www.hoverspeed.co.uk

Irish Ferries (Cherbourg ☎ 02 33 23 44 44, Roscoff ☎ 02 98 61 17 17, UK ☎ 0990 171 717, Ireland ☎ 053-33158, 24-hour information in Ireland ☎ 01-661 0715). Rosslare–Roscoff (IR£120, 15 hours, summer), Rosslare–Cherbourg (IR£120, 17 hours, two or four times weekly)
Web site: www.irishferries.ie

P&O Portsmouth (Cherbourg ☎ 02 33 88 65 65, Le Havre ☎ 02 35 19 78 50, UK ☎ 0870 600 3300). Portsmouth–Le Havre ferries (UK£210, six to 8¼ hours, three daily), Portsmouth–Cherbourg (UK£200, 5½ to 7½ hours, six times daily)
Web site: www.poportsmouth.com

P&O Stena Line (France ☎ 08 03 01 30 13, UK ☎ 0870 600 0612). Daily Dover–Calais ferries (1½ hours), slightly more expensive, faster and more frequent than SeaFrance

SeaFrance (Calais ☎ 08 03 04 40 45 office hours, ☎ 03 21 46 80 00 weekends and evenings, UK ☎ 0870 5711 711). Daily Dover–Calais ferries (UK£132.50 daily departures, April to June; UK£162.50 Friday to Monday, August departures)
Web site: www.seafrance.co.uk

04 95 29 66 63), 3 quai L'Herminier; in Bastia (☎ 04 95 54 66 99, 04 95 54 66 60) at the new port; and in Calvi (☎ 04 95 65 01 38, 04 95 65 17 77) on quai Landry. In France, contact the SNCM office in Nice, Marseilles or Toulon (see relevant chapters for details).

Italy

SNCM operates two or three car ferries weekly from Marseilles or Toulon to Porto Torres on the Italian island of Sardinia (Sardaigne in French). Sailing time is 15½ hours and boats depart in the afternoon or early evening.

At the time of writing a fauteuil cost 356/411FF in low/high season for a one-way passage. The equivalent fare for children aged four to 12 was 188/214FF, and 244/280FF for those aged under 22 or holders of an Inter Rail Pass (see the boxed text 'Rail Passes & Discount Fares' earlier in this chapter). A place in a two or four-berth cabin costs an additional 66/80FF in low/high season each way. To transport a bike costs 97FF and transporting a car costs 343FF to 729FF depending on the season.

Tickets and information are available from any SNCM office in Provence; in Sardinia tickets are sold by SNCF agent, Agenzia Paglietti Petertours (☎ 079-51 44 77), Corso Vittorio Emanuele in Porto Torres.

Tunisia

SNCM and the Compagnie Tunisienne de Navigation (CTN) operate two weekly car ferries (almost daily services from late June to mid-September) between Marseilles and Tunis (about 24 hours). The standard adult fare is 900FF for an armchair (those aged two to 16, 450FF), plus 50/100FF for a bunk in a four-berth cabin in low/high season. If you're taking a vehicle, which currently costs 1980/3160FF one-way/return, it is vital to book ahead, especially in summer. In Tunis, CTN's office (☎ 216-135 33 31) is at 122 rue de Yougoslavie. In Provence, ticketing is handled by SNCM.

Algeria

The regular SNCM ferry service from Marseilles to Algiers is aimed at the local North African community. Political troubles have prompted a state of emergency in Algeria since 1992 and travel is considered dangerous for foreign tourists.

SNCM operates three ferries weekly (year round) between Marseilles and Algiers. Overnight sailing time takes 24 hours. A return fare is 1690/3050FF in low/high season (930/1690FF for children aged two to 12, 1290/2580FF for students). A bunk in a cabin for four costs an additional 150/220FF and transporting a car is 2660/4280FF. Bicycles/motorcycles are an extra 130/390FF each way.

RIVER
Canal Boat

Provence is well-connected with waterways thanks to the Rhône. Cruising along its sun-flooded channels on a canal boat is one of the most exciting, relaxing and romantic ways of getting to Provence – providing time is not of the essence of course. For a first-hand account see *Watersteps Through France* (1996) listed under Travelogues in the Facts for the Visitor chapter.

The most popular canal route to Provence is via the beautiful Canal du Midi, a 240km waterway that runs from Toulouse to the Bassin de Thau between Agde and Sète, from where you continue north-east past Sète to Aigues-Mortes in the Camargue. From Toulouse, the Canal du Midi is connected with the Gardonne river leading west to the Atlantic Ocean at Bordeaux. The Midi affords great views over the sun-dried Languedoc plain and passes through more than 100 *écluses* (locks) – sometimes nine in a row, as is the case near Béziers. Canal du Midi boats can be booked in the UK through French Country Cruises (☎ 01572-821 330, fax 821 072), Andrew Brock Travel, 54 High Street East, Uppingham, Rutland LE15 9PZ. Rates for a boat for three or more people start at UK£504/910 in low/high season; one-way cruises incur a UK£70 supplement.

See under Boat in the Getting Around chapter for details on self-cruising boat rental agencies within the region.

Cruises

Many agencies offer luxury, four- to seven-day river cruises to Provence – most depart from Lyons. Year round, Alsace Croisières CroisiEurope (☎ 03 88 76 40 66, fax 03 88 32 49 96, e info@croisieurope.com), 12 rue de la Division Leclerc, 67000 Strasbourg, offers three- to seven-day cruises from Lyons to the Camargue, taking in Avignon and Martigues; starting at 1795/3995FF for three/seven days, plus 350/1000FF supplement for private cabin. The same company, which has a Web site at www.croisiere.com, also runs Mediterranean cruises from Cannes costing upwards of 6740FF for eight days). Once the new 170m-long quay at Cannes is completed in 2001, the port town should attract substantially more cruise ship traffic.

An eight-day river cruise on the four-star *MV Princesse de Provence*, from Lyons to

Warning

The information in this chapter is particularly vulnerable to change: prices for international travel are volatile, routes are introduced and cancelled, schedules change, special deals come and go, and rules and visa requirements are amended. Airlines and governments seem to take a perverse pleasure in making price structures and regulations as complicated as possible. You should check directly with the airline or a travel agent to make sure you understand how a fare (and any ticket you may buy) works. In addition, the travel industry is highly competitive and there are many lurks and perks.

The upshot of this is that you should get opinions, quotes and advice from as many airlines and travel agents as possible before you part with your hard-earned cash. The details given in this chapter should be regarded as pointers and are not a substitute for your own careful, up-to-date research.

Arles and Avignon, starts at UK£783 (including return flight from London) with Peter Deilmann Cruises Check out its Web site at www.deilmann-cruises.com. Bookings can be made in France (☎ 04 78 39 13 06), 5 rue Gentil, 69002 Lyons; and in the USA (toll-free ☎ 800-348 8287, ☎ 703-549 1741, ℮ pdcmail@deilmann-cruises.com), 1800 Diagonal Rd, Suite 170, Alexandria VA 22314. There are also offices in: London (☎ 020-7436 2931, ℮ gv13@dial.pipex .com), Albany House, Suite 404, 324–326 Regent St, London W1R 5AA; and Germany (☎ 045-613 960, fax 619 157), Am Hafensteig 17–19, 23730 Neustadt/H.

ORGANISED TOURS

For an excellent and exhaustive list of agencies worldwide offering tours to Provence and the Côte d'Azur see the Web site of the French Government Tourist Office at www.francetourism.com. French Travel Connection (☎ 02-9966 8600, fax 9966 5888), Level 6, 33 Chandos Street, St Leonards NSW 2065 and Ya'lla Tours (☎ 03-9523 1988, fax 9523 1934, ℮ yallamel@

yallatours.com.au), 661 Glenhuntly Road, Caulfield, Victoria 3162 are two leading operators in Australia.

Food & Wine

Old Ipswich Tours (☎ 887-356 5163, fax 978-356 9540, ℮ ipswichtours@mediaone.net) 8 Herrick Drive, Ipswich, MA 01938, USA. Gourmet wine tours costing from US$3599 including Boston–Paris return airfare, accommodation and tours.

Wine Trails (☎ 01306-712 111, fax 713 504, ℮ sales@winetrails.co.uk) Greenways, Vann Lake, Ockley, Dorking RH5 5NT, UK. Walking tours of Provence around Les Alpilles with a strong focus on wine and gourmet cuisine; seven-/10-day independent walking tours starting at UK£425/995, including half-board hotel accommodation.

Web site: www.winetrails.co.uk

Art & Architecture

International Study Tours (☎ 800-833 2111 or 212-563 1202, fax 594 6953) 225 West 34th Street, New York 10122, USA. Cultural and educational tours designed for the independent traveller.

Cycling & Walking

Most cycling tour operators lighten the load by taking charge of transporting cyclists' baggage by minibus between hotels. Many tours take in chateaux and other sights en route.

Cyclists' Touring Club (CTC; ☎ 01483-417 217, fax 426 994, ℮ cycling@ctc.org.uk) Cotterell House, 69 Meadrow, Godalming, Surrey GU7 3HS. The UK's biggest cycling organisation offering occasional tours to Provence among its good-value, not-for-profit tours run by and for CTC members. These and scores of commercial bicycle holiday outfits are listed in CTC's *Cycle Holiday Guide* magazine.

Web site: www.ctc.org.uk

Europeds (☎ 800-321 9552, 831-646 4920, fax 831-655 44501, ℮ europeds@aol.com) 761 Lighthouse Ave, Monterey, CA 93940, USA. Cycling, walking and hiking tours.

Explore Worldwide (☎ 01252-760 000, fax 760 001, ℮ info@explore.co.uk) 1 Frederick Street, Aldershot, Hants GU11 1LQ, UK. Eight-day walking tour around the Gorges du Verdon by the adventure specialists costs UK£474/490 in low/high season.

Web site: www.explore.co.uk

Headwater (01606-813 333, fax 813 334, <e> info @headwater.com) 146 London Road, Northwich, Cheshire CW9 5HH, UK. Seven- to 11-day walking and cycling tours in the Lubéron and northern Var; nine-day gastronomic cycling adventures, starting at UK£629 (UK£440 self-drive).
Web site: www.headwater.com

Inn Travel (☎ 01653-628 811, fax 628 741, <e> inntravel@inntravel.co.uk) – Weekend breaks, six-day discovery journeys and one-week cycling tours (UK£495/659 and upwards by self-drive/air); accommodation in family run auberges or chateaux.
Web site: www.inntravel.co.uk

Susi Madron's Cycling for Softies (☎ 0161-248 8282, fax 248 5140, <e> info@cycling-for-softies.co.uk) 2–4 Birch Polygon, Manchester M14 5HX, UK. Seven- to 14-day tours start at UK£644, includes tours of the Camargue or Lubéron; all cycling abilities.
Web site: www.cycling-for-softies.co.uk

Self-Drive Camping

Canvas Holidays (☎ 08709-022 022, fax 620 075, <e> reservations@canvas.co.uk) 12 Abbey Park Place, Dunfermline, Fife KY12 7PD, UK. Canvas and mobile home accommodation at camp sites in St-Tropez, St-Aygulf and Port Grimaud; 12 nights' tent accommodation (two adults and four kids) costing from UK£199/429/829 in low/mid-/high season, including free cycle/surf board hire.

Eurocamp (☎ 01606-78 78 78, <e> enquiries@eurocamp.co.uk) Hartford Manor, Greenbank Lane, Northwich, Cheshire CF8 1HW, UK. Numerous sites the length of the Côte d'Azur.
Web site: www.eurocamp.co.uk

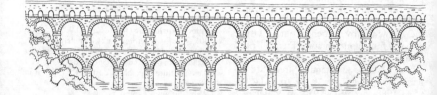

Getting Around

AIR

There are no scheduled, inter-regional plane flights within Provence but increasing numbers of high-flyers are taking to the air by helicopter.

Between March and October, Héli-Air Monaco (☎ 92 05 00 50, fax 92 05 76 17) at Héliport de Monaco (☎ 92 05 00 10) operates scheduled helicopter flights – Europe's busiest helicopter route – between Nice and Monaco (approximately every 30 minutes from 7.15 am to 8 or 9 pm). Charter flights run year round. A one-way/return fare costs 400/750FF (children aged two to 12, 200/400FF). Charters start at 2100/4700FF for up to five/10 people. Tickets in Monaco are sold at Héli-Air Voyages (☎ 97 70 80 20), 11 blvd du Jardin Exotique; and in Nice at the Héli-Air Monaco desk (☎ 04 93 21 34 32) in Terminal 1 at Nice-Côte d'Azur airport (Aéroport International Nice-Côte d'Azur). Reservations can be made online at www.heliair-monaco.com, which also posts updated flight schedules.

Héli-Inter (☎ 04 93 21 46 46), based at Nice-Côte d'Azur airport, likewise operates scheduled flights between Nice and Monaco, March to October. One-way/return fares cost 400/725FF (children aged two to 12, 30% discount or 50% for two children). It also nips between Nice and Palm Beach heliport in Cannes (400/780FF one-way/return, six minutes, at least hourly from 9 am to 6.30 pm). Héli-Inter also runs charters to/from St-Tropez heliport (☎ 04 94 97 15 12). Flying time is 20 minutes and a one-way fare for up to five passengers costs 4260FF.

Global Héli-Services (☎ 04 91 44 18 87) at Cuers airfield (Aérodrome de Cuers), 20km north of Toulon, operates chartered helicopter flights between Cuers, Giens (400FF one-way) and the island of Porquerolles (700FF one-way).

BUS

Buses are used for short-distance travel within departments, especially in rural areas such as Haute-Provence where there are relatively few train lines. However, services and routes are extremely limiting for any traveller hoping to pack in as many hill-top villages as possible. No more than one or two daily buses trundle their way from the coast to the handful of villages in the Niçois hinterland, for example. Bus services are more efficient between towns that are served by just a few trains (or no train at all). There are several daily trains between Marseilles and Aix-en-Provence but buses speed between the two towns approximately every 30 minutes.

Autocars (regional buses) are operated by a muddling host of different bus companies, most of whom usually have an office at the bus station *(gare routière)* of the cities they serve. One company usually sells tickets for all the bus companies operating from the same station.

Certain uneconomical SNCF rail lines have been replaced by SNCF buses in recent years. Routes covered by SNCF buses (known as Autocars LER) include Marseilles to Digne-les-Bains, Manosque and Sisteron; Nice, Toulon and Avignon to Aix-en-Provence; Arles to Avignon; and Carpentras to Aix and Marseilles via Cavaillon.

Few bus stations have left-luggage facilities but some have information desks that double as informal luggage rooms; you can leave your bag with the information-desk operator for 10FF.

Bus Passes

Some sights along the coast – such as the Musée Renoir in Cagnes-sur-Mer – are better served by bus. To this end, regional bus company Rapides Côte d'Azur sells the Pass Culture to holders of the Carte Musées Côte d'Azur (see Visas & Documents in the Facts for the Visitor chapter). The three-/seven-day bus pass, valid for three or seven consecutive days, costs 40/90FF and allows the holder unlimited travel on specified bus routes along the coast. You can buy your pass from the driver, upon presentation of your museum pass.

Details are available in Nice from Rapides Côte d'Azur (☎ 04 97 00 07 00), 455 promenade des Anglais, Immeuble Le Quadra, BP 253, 06205 Nice Cedex 3, or can be found online at www.rca.tm.fr.

TRAIN

The SNCF's regional rail network in Provence, served by *trains express régionaux* (TER; regional express trains), is as efficient as its national network. It comprises two routes – one that follows the coast and another that traverses the interior.

The Côte d'Azur between St-Raphaël and Ventimiglia (Vintimille in French), past the Italian border, is served by numerous daily TER trains that shuttle back and forth along the coast. From St-Raphaël the train line cuts inland to Les Arcs-Draguignan, then plunges back on to the coast at Toulon,

from where it continues its journey westwards along the coast to Marseilles and a little beyond. At Miramas, the tracks bear inland to Arles and Avignon.

Inland, the Briançon–Marseilles rail line slices through the western fringe of Alpes de Haute-Provence, linking the coast with the Provençal interior. Train stations *(gares)* from north to south include Sisteron, Château-Arnoux, Manosque and Aix-en-Provence.

In addition to SNCF routes, a narrow-gauge railway links Nice with Digne-les-Bains in Haute-Provence. Details are listed in the Haute-Provence chapter.

Information

Most train stations have separate *guichets* (ticket windows) and information or reservation offices.

Indispensable for anyone doing a lot of train travel, the *Guide Régional des Transports* is a free booklet of inter-regional rail

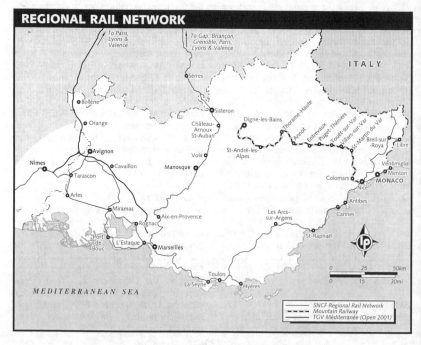

and SNCF bus schedules available at larger train stations. Alternatively, the 1045-page *Indicateur Horaires: Ville à Ville* (60FF), published twice yearly by the SNCF, features point-to-point timetables for all of France. It is sold in newsagent kiosks at some stations.

Left-Luggage

Nice, Marseilles and other larger stations will either have a *consigne manuelle* (left-luggage office), where you pay about 30/35FF per bag/bicycle for 24 hours, or a *consigne automatique*, a computerised luggage locker that issues you with a lock code in exchange for 15/20/30FF for a small/medium/large locker per 72 hours. At smaller stations you can usually leave your bag at the ticket office (30FF). Most luggage lockers/offices can be accessed from around 7 am to 10.30 pm.

Schedules

SNCF issues two sets of timetables *(horaires)* per year: a winter schedule valid from the end of September (or November on some routes) to the end of May; and a summer schedule that runs from the end of May to the end of September (occasionally November).

There are separate pocket-sized timetables (free at train stations) for regional TER trains and the *grandes lignes* (big lines) covering TGV *(train à grande vitesse;* high-speed train) and other main-line services. The footnotes at the bottom of both explain whether trains run *(circule)* Monday to Friday; until *(jusqu'au)* a certain date; or every *(tous les jours)*/except *(sauf)* Saturday, Sunday and/or holidays *(fêtes)*. Ticket attendants at Nice station speak English, as do most information-desk operators at stations along the coast.

Updated schedules are posted on the TER Web site at http://ter.sncf.fr/paca (French only).

Train Passes

Two *forfaits régionaux* (regional passes) exist, available to travellers of all ages between July and September.

The Carte Isabelle costs 60FF and is a one-day pass allowing unlimited rail travel along the coast between Théoule-sur-Mer and Ventimiglia. Inland, it covers the Nice–Tende rail line and local buses in Cagnes-sur-Mer. The pass cannot be used on TGVs and is only cost-cutting if you intend making an inland trip, in addition to visiting several coastal resorts before returning to your original destination. It also allows you to sit in 1st class for no extra supplement – a distinct advantage in July and August when the coastal trains are packed.

The more restrictive Carte Bermuda (30FF) is a one-day pass that covers return trips from Marseilles to Miramas via Port de Bouc on La Côte Bleue (The Blue Coast). It covers 1st-class travel on all trains between 11 am and 7.30 pm, and 2nd-class travel weekends only.

Other country-wide SNCF discounts and rail passes (such as the Carte 12/25, Carte Enfant Plus, Carte Senior and Découverte Séjour) are all available on regional trains. See Land – Other Parts of France in the Getting There & Away chapter.

Tickets

In most stations, you can buy your ticket at a ticket window or from an automatic, touchscreen vending machine *(billetterie automatique)*. The latter accepts credit cards for tickets costing 15FF or more and cuts down queuing time enormously.

SNCF Regional Hotlines	
Alpes de Haute-Provence	☎ 04 92 51 50 50
Alpes-Maritimes	☎ 04 93 87 30 00
Bouches du Rhône	☎ 04 91 50 00 00
Var	☎ 04 94 24 30 00
Vaucluse	☎ 04 90 27 30 00
Internet	www.sncf.com
Minitel	3615 SNCF (1.29FF per minute) or 3615 TER (1.01FF per minute)

Return tickets *(aller-retour)* are twice the price of their one-way *(aller-simple)* counterparts. Count on paying between 70FF and 100FF per 100km for short hops with 2nd-class travel. Train fares for specific routes in Provence are included in the relevant regional listings.

Reservations are neither mandatory nor necessary on most regional trains. If you intend travelling on a straight-through train however, say, from Marseilles to Avignon, it is advisable in summer to buy your ticket well in advance. Tickets are valid for two months from the date of purchase; advance reservations (20FF) are also possible for many trains, meaning you will be assured a seat for the duration of the journey.

Tickets can be purchased on board but cost 20FF to 40FF more. Moreover, unless the ticket window where you boarded was closed (quite often the case in smaller stations in Provence) *and* the station had no ticket machine (rarely the case), prohibitive tariffs apply: along the Côte d'Azur for example, ticketless passengers pay a 50FF to 100FF on-the-spot fine plus the price of a ticket purchased aboard a train; those who refuse to pay face a 150FF to 250FF fine. Finally, remember to time-stamp your ticket before boarding (see Validating Your Ticket in the Getting There & Away chapter) or you likewise risk a stiff fine.

CAR & MOTORCYCLE

Having your own wheels is the secret to discovering the region's least touched backwaters. Numerous treasures tucked in Haute-Provence's nooks and crannies are impossible to uncover by public transport. Moreover, a car or motorcycle allows you to avail yourself of cheaper places to stay on city outskirts and in the countryside.

If you're planning to drive along the coast in July or August, be prepared for it to take hours to move a few kilometres. Inland, mountain roads – laced with torturous hairpin beds *(lacets)* and dimly lit tunnels – are quiet all year.

In forested areas such as the Massif des Maures, Massif de l'Estérel and Haute-Provence, unpaved roads wend off the main

roads into the forest. These tracks are signposted DFCI (défense forestière contre l'incendie) and are for fire crews to gain quick entry to the forest when there is a fire: they are strictly off-limits to private vehicles.

Except for the traffic-plagued high season, the Côte d'Azur is easy to navigate by road. Fastest is the A8 autoroute which, travelling west to east, from near Aix-en-Provence, approaches the coast at Fréjus, skirts the Estérel range and runs parallel to the coast from Cannes to Ventimiglia. In addition to the autoroute, there are three other types of road: *routes nationales* are wide, well signposted highways; *routes départmentales* are local roads; and *chemins communaux* are narrow rural roads.

For distances between towns and cities in the region, and other motoring tips, see Car & Motorcycle in the Getting There & Away chapter.

Documents

All car drivers are required by French law to carry a national ID card or passport; a valid driving permit or licence *(permis de conduire)*; car ownership papers, known as a *carte grise* (grey card); and proof of insurance, called a *carte verte* (green card). If you're stopped by the police and don't have one or more of these documents, you risk a hefty on-the-spot fine. Never leave your car ownership or insurance papers in the vehicle.

Equipment

A reflective warning triangle, to be used in the event of breakdown, must be carried in your car. Recommended accessories – not mandatory in France but recommended in the interests of safety – are a first-aid kit, a spare bulb kit and a fire extinguisher. In the UK, contact the RAC (☎ 0870 5275 600) or the AA (☎ 0870 5500 600) for more advice. In other countries, contact the appropriate automobile association.

Road Rules

In France, as throughout continental Europe, people drive on the right side of the road and overtake on the left. Unless otherwise indicated, you must give way to cars coming from the right. North American drivers should remember that turning right on a red light is illegal in France.

Speed Limits Unless otherwise posted, a speed limit of 50km/h applies in all areas designated as built up, no matter how rural they may appear. On intercity roads, you must slow to 50km/h the moment you pass a white sign with red borders on which a place name is written in black or blue letters. This remains in force until you pass an identical sign – but with a red diagonal bar across the name – the other side of town.

Outside built-up areas, speed limits are 90km/h (80km/h if it's raining) on undivided N and D highways; and 110km/h (100km/h in the rain) on dual carriageways (divided highways) or short sections of highway with a divider strip. Speed limits are generally not posted unless they deviate from those mentioned above.

Alcohol French law is tough on drunk drivers and the police do conduct random breathalyser tests to weed out drivers whose blood-alcohol concentration (BAC) is over 0.05% (0.50g per litre of blood). Fines range from 500FF to 8000FF, and licences can be suspended.

Road Signs

Common road signs include *sens unique* (one way) and *voie unique* (one-lane road) – prevalent in Haute-Provence where there are numerous narrow bridges. Another handy one to know if you intend motoring along the famous, tunnel-linked corniches is *allumez vos feux* (switch your headlights on) and *éteignez vos feux* (switch your headlights off). A sign reading *8 lacets* means there are eight consecutive hairpin bends coming up – a sign particularly favoured in the Niçois hinterland and the Roya and Vésubie Valleys.

If you come to a *route barrée* (a closed road), you'll usually also find a yellow panel with instructions for a *déviation* (detour). Signs for *poids lourds* (heavyweights) are meant for lorries (trucks), not cars. The words *sauf riverains* on a no-entry sign

mean 'except residents' – common at the foot of most hill-top villages. Road signs with the word *rappel* (remember) featured mean you should already know what the sign is telling you (eg, the speed limit).

Petrol

Petrol *(essence)*, also known as *carburant* (fuel), is expensive in France, incredibly so if you're used to Australian or North American prices. In mid-2000, *sans plomb* (unleaded) petrol (98 octane) cost around 7.95FF per litre. *Faire le plein* (filling up) is cheapest at stations on city outskirts and at supermarkets, and most expensive at garages on the autoroute.

Parking

Finding a place to park in Nice, Marseilles or any fairly large town or touristy village, is likely to be the single greatest hassle you'll face. Public parking facilities are marked by a white letter 'P' on a blue background. *Payant*, written on the asphalt or on a nearby sign, means you have to pay. Hungry parking meters on the street or in street-level car parks swallow about 10FF per hour. Subterranean, multistorey car parks demand about 15/100FF per hour/24 hours. Motorists staying in one city for more than a few days should consider buying a short-stay parking card *(forfait courte durée)*, available at most underground car parks and costing about 320/460FF for five/10 days.

Most hill-top villages will have large, purpose-built car parks at their foot where the charge is usually at least 25FF, paid to an attendant. *Défense de stationner* means 'No Parking'.

Accidents

If you're involved in a minor accident with no injuries, the easiest way for drivers to sort things out with their insurance companies is to fill out a Constat Aimable d'Accident Automobile (jointly agreed accident report), known in English as a European Accident Statement. Such a form is automatically included in the documents you get with a rental car (see under Rental on the following page). Make sure the report includes any details that will help you prove that the accident was not your fault.

If problems arise, alert the police (☎ 17).

Car Rental

Although multinational rental agencies such as Avis, Budget, Hertz (which also rents camping cars), Europcar (Europe's largest) or National Citer can be expensive for on-the-spot rental, their prepaid promotional rates are usually reasonable. Fly-drive deals offered by Avis and Europcar are also worth looking into. For quick walk-in rental, domestic firms such as Rent-a-Système, Century or ADA usually offer the best rates. In Cannes a handful of firms rent Ferraris, Porsches and other luxury cars, while beach resorts such as Fréjus have electric car hire outlets. Companies are noted in the Getting There & Away sections for individual cities; major firms also have desks at Nice and Marseilles airports.

Most rental companies require the driver to be over 21 and have had a driving licence for at least one year. The packet of documents you are given should include a 24-hour number to call in case of a breakdown and a European Accident Statement (see under Accidents earlier in this chapter). Check how many 'free' kilometres are in the deal you're offered; *kilométrage illimité* (unlimited mileage) means you can drive to your heart's content.

Insurance *Assurance* (insurance) for damage or injury you cause to other people is mandatory, but things such as collision damage waivers vary greatly from company to company. The policies offered by some small, discount companies may leave you liable for up to 8000FF – when comparing rates, the most important thing to check is the *franchise* (excess/deductible). If you're in an accident where you are at fault, or the car is damaged and the party at fault is unknown (eg, someone dents your car while it's parked), or the car is stolen, this is the amount you are liable for before the policy kicks in.

Rates The big advantage of booking a hire car before leaving home is that you can gen-erally scoop a deal with unlimited mileage for the same (or a cheaper) cost as hiring a vehicle with limited kilometres (about 1500km per week) upon arrival in France.

At the time of writing, a Renault Twingo booked through Avis in the UK (☎ 0870 60 60 100), including unlimited mileage and a collision-damage excess of 2000FF, cost UK£154 per week, payable in advance. Budget (☎ 0541-56 56 56) was offering a similar deal for about UK£131, while the most competitive rate offered by Europcar (☎ 0870 607 5000) was UK£108. Autos Abroad (☎ 020-7287 6000), with an Web site at www.autosabroad.co.uk, charged a standard rate of UK£129 per week for a Peugeot 206, but does guarantee to be cheaper than its competitors; mail Autos Abroad a copy of a written quote from another rental agency and they will undercut it.

Within the region, the cost for an equivalent small car for a weekend/week (including 500/1750km) rented from ADA at Nice-Côte d'Azur airport was 420/1250FF. For exactly the same deal, Budget charged 575/1400FF (1125/1820FF with Avis).

All major rental companies accept payment by credit card. They also require a *caution* (deposit); most ask you to leave a signed credit card slip without a sum written on it as a deposit. If you don't like this arrangement, ask them to make out two credit card slips: one for the sum of the rental; the other for the sum of the excess. Make sure to have the latter destroyed when you return the car.

Motorcycle

Provence is superb country for motorcycle touring. Make sure your wet-weather gear is up to scratch in spring and autumn. Easy riders caught bareheaded can legally be fined 800FF and have their bike confiscated. Bikes of more than 125cc must have their headlights on during the day. No special licence is required to ride a scooter with an engine capacity of 50cc or less.

To rent a scooter or *moto* (motorcycle) you have to leave a deposit of several thousand francs, which you forfeit (up to the value of the damage) if you're in an accident and it's your fault. Since insurance companies won't cover theft, you'll also lose the deposit if the bike is stolen. Most places accept deposits made by credit card, travellers cheques or Eurocheques. Expect to pay about 300/325FF per day for a one/two person 50cc scooter and from 400/600/650FF per day for a 125/240/600cc motorcycle. Helmets *(casques)* can be rented for an extra 15FF.

Provence Moto Évasion (☎/fax 04 93 58 77 58, [e] jf@provencemotoevasion.com) at 846 Chemin de la Sine, 06140 Vence, organises motorcycle tours of Provence. Weekend/five-day tours typically cost in the region of 2600/6900FF per person or 2950/8900FF for a pilot and passenger. Fees include bikes, helmets, luggage assistance, two-star hotel accommodation and a motorcycle guide.Visit online at www.provence motoevasion.com.

BICYCLE

Provence – particularly the Lubéron – is an eminently cyclable region, thanks to its extensive network of inland secondary and tertiary roads, which carry relatively light traffic (compared to the coast). These back roads, a good number of which date from the 19th century or earlier, are an ideal vantage point from which to view Provence's celebrated rural landscapes, be it lavender fields, vineyards or olive groves. Cycling in national parks in Provence (Mercantour and Port-Cros) is forbidden.

By law, your bicycle must have two functioning brakes, a bell, a red reflector on the back and yellow reflectors on the pedals. After sunset and when visibility is poor, cyclists must turn on a white light in front and a red one in the rear.

Transporting a Bicycle

Bicycles are not allowed on most local and intercity buses, but you can take them on some trains.

On all *grandes lignes* (main line) and TGV trains, bicycles can be transported free of charge as hand luggage, *providing* they are folded up or packed, with wheels removed, in special covers (available from cycle shops) measuring no more than 120cm by 90cm. TER trains in Provence-Alpes-Côte d'Azur do not accept bikes in bags at peak travel times – between 7 and 9 am and 4.30 to 6.30 pm weekdays.

Some main-line trains – flagged on timetables with a little bicycle symbol – have a luggage van or bicycle compartment in which bicycles can be transported without being dismantled or folded up (tandems can only be transported in luggage vans). Cyclists are responsible for loading and unloading them.

Boxed bicycles can be sent as baggage between two stations in France for 195FF, or door to door for 295FF. Both services operate weekdays only. Delivery can take up to three or four days. For information call SNCF on ☎ 08 03 84 58 45. Further details are included in the multilingual SNCF brochure *Guide Train & Vélo*; pick up a free copy at any larger train station.

Cycling Organisations

The volunteer-run Fédération Française de Cyclotourisme (☎ 01 44 16 88 88), 8 rue Jean-Marie Jégo, 75013 Paris, liaises between France's cycling clubs, and will send you a free packet of general information in English. It also sells touring itineraries, cycling maps and topoguides for cyclists, and organises bicycle trips and tours that are open to visitors.

For its members, the Cyclists' Touring Club (CTC; ☎ 01483-417 217, fax 426 994, [e] cycling@ctc.org.uk), Cotterell House, 69 Meadrow, Godalming, Surrey GU7 3HS, UK, publishes a free booklet on cycling in France, plus free touring notes and itineraries for some 70 routes around the country, including several in Provence. The CTC also offers tips on bikes, spares and insurance; it sells maps and topoguides by mail order. It has a Web site at www.ctc.org.uk.

See Activities in Facts for the Visitor for more two-wheeling information; suggested maps and guides are included under Maps and Books in the same chapter. Organised Tours in the Getting There & Away chapter contains information on cycling tours.

Rental

You can hire a mountain bike *(vélo tout-terrain; VTT)* in most towns and resorts for about 100FF per day. Most places have children's bikes and some – particularly in the Lubéron and in coastal areas – have tandems and *remorques* (energetic parents can pedal their little kids along in these covered buggies). A deposit of 1000FF to 2000FF is required, which you forfeit if the bike is damaged or stolen. In general, deposits can be made in cash, with signed travellers cheques or by credit card (a passport often suffices). Rental shops are listed in the Getting Around sections of city and town listings.

Never leave your bicycle locked up outside overnight if you want to see it or most of its parts again. You can leave your bike in some train station left-luggage offices for about 35FF per day.

HITCHING

Hitching is never entirely safe in any country in the world, and we don't recommend it. Travellers who decide to hitch should understand that they are taking a small but potentially serious risk. People who do choose to hitch will be safer if they travel in pairs and let someone know where they are planning to go.

See the Hitching section in the Getting There & Away chapter for organisations within France that put drivers and hitchers in touch with each other.

BOAT
Yacht

Among the Côte d'Azur's largest pleasure ports *(ports de plaisance)* are Port Vauban in Antibes and Port Camargue in La Grau du Roi which, with 4350 moorings, claims to be Europe's biggest.

Yachts can be hired at most marinas along the coast, including the less-pompous sailing centres at Ste-Maxime and Le Lavandou. In Antibes and Juan-les-Pins, there are no less than 17 places where yachts can be hired with/without a crew. A complete list of yacht rental places is included in the free booklet *Nautisme: Riviera Côte d'Azur*

published by the Comité Régional du Tourisme Riviera Côte d'Azur.

For up-to-date marina or harbour master information, contact the Fédération Française des Ports de Plaisance (FFPP; ☎ 01 43 35 26 26), 9 rue Léopold Robert, 7501 Paris, which is represented locally by the Union des Ports de Plaisance du Levant (☎ 04 42 44 34 00), BP218, 13698 Martigues. Another useful contact is the Association des Ports de Plaisance de la Méditerranée (☎ 04 94 95 34 30), quai le Prieur, Port de Santa Lucia, 83700 St-Raphaël.

Ferry

Air France operates a ferry boat to coincide with flight arrivals/departures between Nice-Côte d'Azur airport, Cannes and St-Tropez. Details are listed under To/From the Airport in the Nice section of the Nice to Menton chapter.

A plethora of boats ply the waters from the shores of the Côte d'Azur to its various off-shore islands. Daily ferries sail to the Îles de Lérins from Cannes (year round), Juan-les-Pins (May to October) and Vallauris-Golfe Juan (May to October).

To get to Port-Cros, the national park in the Îles d'Hyères archipelago, you can take a boat from Le Lavandou or Hyères (year round); Toulon, Ste-Maxime or St-Tropez (June to September); and Port Miramar, La Croix-Valmer or Cavalaire-sur-Mer (July and August).

Its bare little sister, the Île du Levant, is accessible by boat from Le Lavandou and Hyères (year round), or Port Miramar, La Croix-Valmer and Cavalaire-sur-Mer (July and August). Porquerolles, the last in the Hyères trio, is served by regular passenger ferry from Le Lavandou and Hyères (year round); Toulon, Ste-Maxime or St-Tropez (June to September); and Port Miramar, La Croix Valmer and Cavalaire (July and August).

The Paul Ricard islands near Bandol and Toulon are equally well served by ferry. Boats to Île de Bendor depart year round from Bandol, while ferries to the larger Île des Embiez depart from Le Brusc (year round) and Sanary-sur-Mer (June to

Cathédrale de la Major dwarfs its surroundings.

Marseilles has its fair share of bells and belles.

Luxury housing in Marseilles – I'll take two

Eat, drink and be merry on Plage du Prado.

Grandiose architecture at Palais Longchamp

La Canebière glints in the early evening sun.

Reflect on Marseilles' naval history

Those net-picking Marseilles fishermen...

Stop off at Calanque d'En Vau, south-east of Marseilles, for a divine drop in the ocean.

September). From Marseilles, there are plenty of boats to the Îles du Frioul.

From St-Tropez there are additional boat services to/from St-Raphaël (April to July), Port Grimaud (June to mid-September) and Ste-Maxime (April to November).

In season, soulless boat excursions aimed solely at tourists, often with blaring music and always with loud recorded commentaries, service most hot spots along the Côte d'Azur.

Canal Boat

One of the most relaxing ways to see the region's most south-eastern corner is to rent a houseboat for a leisurely cruise along the Camargue's canals and navigable rivers. Boats usually accommodate two to 12 passengers and can be rented on a weekly basis. Anyone over 18 can pilot a river boat without a licence, and learning the ropes takes about half an hour. The speed limit is 6km/h on canals and 10km/h on rivers. The tourist cruising season runs from March to early November.

To get a boat in July and August, reservations must be made at least several months ahead. In Aigues-Mortes boats can be rented through Rive de France (☎ 04 66 53 81 21, fax 04 66 51 02 61, ℮ rdf@ i2m.fr), Péniche St-Louis, route de Grau de Roi, with a Web site at www.rive-de-france .tm.fr. Rates start at 4900FF (81455FF in July/August) per week or 2400FF (March to June and September to November only) per weekend for a six-berth boat. Farthing Holidays (☎ 0116-279 883), Holiday House, High Street, Kibworth, Leicester LE8 0DN, is its agent in the UK.

Abroad, self-cruising boats can also be hired through Crown Blue Line Camargue (☎ 04 66 87 22 66, fax 04 66 87 15 20, ℮ boating@crown-blueline.com), 2 quai du Canal, 30800 St-Gilles. You board at St-Gilles, 19km south of Nîmes, from where you cruise along the Canal du Rhône to Aigues-Mortes and farther west to the Toulouse area. Eastbound, you can cruise in three or four hours as far as Beaucaire and Tarascon, south of Avignon. Boats can be booked in the UK through Crown Travel

(☎ 01603-630 513, fax 664 298, ℮ boating @crownblueline.co.uk), 8 Ber Street, Norwich NR1 3EJ. Weekly rates for a boat for four people start at 6180/8080/9500ff in low/mid-/high season. Crown Blue Line has Web sites at www.crown-holidays.co.uk and www.crown-blueline.com.

Hoseasons (☎ 01502-500 555, fax 500 532), Sunway House, Lowestoft NR32 2LW, also organises boating holidays in southern France. It has boats moored in Beaucare, from where a southbound voyage to Aigues-Mortes (two locks, 137km) takes one week. Weekly boat hire starts at UK£690 for a four-berth boat (plus UK£60 for one-way trips). Visit its Web site at www.hoseasons.co.uk.

From Avignon, Beaucaire, Tarascon, Aigues-Mortes and Arles, there are plenty of river excursions organised along the Rhône (see the Organised Tours sections in regional chapters).

LOCAL TRANSPORT

Getting around cities and towns in Provence is a straightforward affair, thanks to excellent public transport systems. Marseilles is the only city in the region to have a metro; ultra-modern tramways are planned for Nice and Toulon. Details of routes, fares, tourist passes and so on are available at tourist offices and local bus company information counters; see Getting Around at the end of each city and town listing.

Taxis are generally expensive. Most towns have a taxi rank in front of the train station. Count on paying between 4FF and 10FF per kilometre depending on the time of day and distance you are travelling. Rates to/from the city centre and any airport are criminally expensive.

ORGANISED TOURS

Most organised tours seem to home in on the region's most frequented resorts and sights, many of which are well served by public transport. Tourist offices in larger towns and cities – such as Avignon, Aix-en-Provence, Nice and Marseilles – have a wealth of half- and full-day excursions however, which might be of interest to travellers with cash, rather than time, to spare. Aix-en-Provence tourist office organises thematic tours (in English and French) such as Ornithology and Nature in the Camargue, Lavender Roads or Villages & Castles of Lubéron. Tours typically cost 160FF to 265FF, not including admission fees.

Provence Grandeur Nature (☎ 04 90 76 68 27, ⓔ pgn@provence-gr-nature.com), 203 rue Oscar Roulet, 84440 Robion, organises tours of Provence's lavender fields. A six-night trip from Nyons to Digne-les-Bains typically costs 2550FF, including half-board hotel accommodation, farm visits, a lavender bath in Digne etc. A more active, three-day lavender tour in the Sault area, with fragrance workshops and botanical trails, costs 1630FF.

In Nice, Riviera Bus Service (☎ 04 93 37 47 37, ⓔ paris.bus@wanadoo.fr), 2 rue La Bruyère, with a Web site at www.touring-france.com/riviera, specialises in English-language day trips by bus. Its speciality is its Monte Carlo By Night tour (745FF) which takes in the Lower Corniche, the Monte Carlo skyline, dinner, casino and a glitzy cabaret show. A cheaper tour (345FF) without dinner, casino or cabaret is also available. Reception desks in most mid-range and top-end hotels take bookings.

Hyères-based Var Tours (☎ 04 94 01 37 20, fax 04 94 01 37 26), 8 ave Gambetta, runs numerous coach tours, with numerous coastal pick-up points including ones in Le Lavandou, Ste-Maxime, Fréjus, St-Raphaël and St-Tropez. Sample itineraries include

On the Path of Jean Giono (240/320FF without/with lunch), the Gorges du Verdon (240/210FF) and Village of the Petit Lubéron (340FF with lunch; children aged four to 12, 170FF). Tourist offices in the Var take bookings for Var Tours.

Sample tours focusing on the great outdoors include:

AET Nature (☎/fax 04 93 04 47 64, ⓔ aetnature @yahoo.com) place Biancheri, 06540 Breil-sur-Roya. Outdoor activity specialist in Haute-Provence, run by experienced mountain guides. Two-/three-/six-day walking tours of the Vallée des Merveilles (510/840/2550FF, including *refuge* accommodation); and two/four days of white-water sports in the Vallée de la Roya (750/1700FF, including accommodation in a *ferme-auberge*).

Agence Croisitour (☎ 04 91 14 20 30, ⓔ croisi tour@aix.pacwan.net) 9 ave des Roches, 13007 Marseilles. Seven-day 'Painters of Provence' tours that follow in the footsteps of Cézanne to Aix, Van Gogh to St-Rémy and so on; 3875FF, including accommodation in three-star hotels. Web site: www.croisitour.com

Destination Merveilles (☎/fax 04 93 73 09 07, ⓔ destination.merveilles@mageos.com) 10 rue des Mesures, 06270 Villeneuve-Loubet. Imaginative, six-day walks from the mountains to the sea through the Alpes d'Azur and plenty of hilltop villages, starting at 3150FF per person, including full board in two-star hotels.

Roya Évasion (☎/fax 04 93 04 91 46, ⓔ roya .evasion@wanadoo.fr), 1 rue Pasteur, 06540 Breil-sur-Roya. Three-day multiactivity courses in the Roya Valley, including canyoning, mountain biking, Via Ferrata and rafting. Courses start at 1450FF and include *gîte* or *refuge* accommodation.

Marseilles Area

The urban geography and atmosphere of Marseilles, utterly atypical of Provence, are a function of the diversity of its inhabitants, many of whom are immigrants (or their children and grandchildren) from Greece, Italy, Armenia, Spain, North Africa, West Africa and Indochina.

Marseilles' southern tip is kissed by some of France's most dramatic coastline. From Callelongue on the city outskirts, a series of sharp-ridged, overhanging rocks – *Les Calanques* (literally 'rocky inlets') – plunge southwards to Cassis and La Ciotat.

West of Marseilles is something of an eyesore. Rapid industrialisation has polluted the water and fast encroached on the land surrounding the Étang de Berre, a salty, 6m-deep pool which – with a surface area of 15,530 hectares and volume of 900 million cubic metres – is Europe's largest brine lake.

North of Marseilles, graceful Aix-en-Provence (pronounced like the letter 'X') is famed for its harmonious fusion of majestic public squares, shaded avenues and mossy fountains, many of which have gurgled since the 18th century. The city's eastern edge is flanked by the Aixois' much-loved Montagne Ste-Victoire, immortalised on canvas by Cézanne in the 19th century.

Salon de Provence, 10km north of the Étang de Berre and 37km west of Aix-en-Provence, marks the boundary between the soft green and purple hues of Pays d'Aix (literally 'Aix Country') and the savage cut of the barren Crau plains in the lower Rhône Valley.

Marseilles

postcode 13001 (post restante)
• pop 807,071

The cosmopolitan port of Marseilles (Marseille in French; Marsihès in Provençal) is Provence's largest city (and France's second). Notorious in the 1980s and 1990s for organised crime and racial tensions, the city

Highlights

- Rise at dawn to see Marseilles fishermen set up shop at the Vieux Port
- Walk, dive or take a boat trip around Les Calanques
- Tour Aix-en-Provence's fountains, museums and *hôtels particuliers* followed by a pastis at Les Deux Garçons
- Discover what inspired Cézanne in Aix-en-Provence and neighbouring Montagne Ste-Victoire
- Explore Cap Canaille and the panoramic route des Crètes

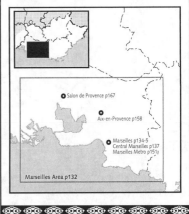

today is gaining a new dynamism. Far from being seen as the hellhole many once believed it to be, modern Marseilles – with its rejuvenated old quarters, warehouses-turned-nightclubs, cultural centres and a clutch of art museums – is increasingly seen as *the* happening place to be. Tell anyone in France you're off to La Canebière and they'll know instantly which city you mean.

Visitors who enjoy exploring on foot will be certainly rewarded with more sights, sounds, smells and big-city commotion than anywhere else in the region. Marseilles'

MARSEILLES AREA

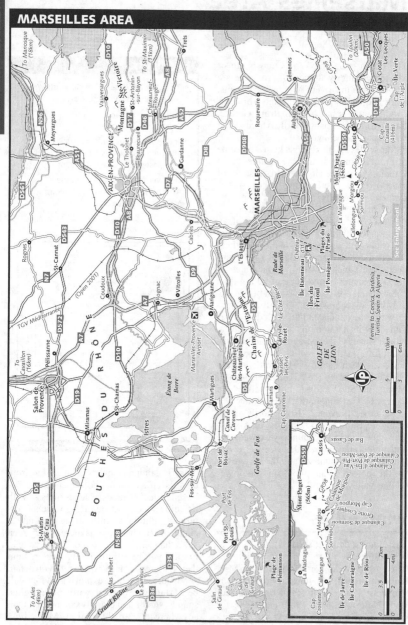

seaport is the most important in France and the third-largest in Europe after Antwerp and Rotterdam, and superspeed rail tracks will put Marseilles just three hour's train ride from Paris from June 2001.

The city's political leaning has always been more dubious. For years the extreme-right has polled about 25% citywide and a member of the fascist Front National (FN; National Front) continues to hold the mayoralty in neighbouring Marignane and Vitrolles.

Many literary figures in the 20th century turned to rough-and-ready Marseilles for inspiration, including Senegalese novelist Sembène Ousmane who portrayed his life as a black docker and African ghetto inhabitant in *Le Docker Noir* (The Black Docker, 1956). Provençal writer and film maker Marcel Pagnol was born in Aubagne, 16km east of Marseilles.

In the realm of popular culture, the best-known contemporary product 'made in Marseilles' is world-champion footballer Zinedine Zidane.

HISTORY

Massilia was founded by Greek mariners from Phocaea (a city in Asia Minor) around 600 BC. The city backed Pompey the Great in the 1st century BC, prompting Caesar's forces to capture the city in 49 BC and exact revenge by confiscating its fleet and directing Roman trade elsewhere. Massilia retained its status as a free port and was, for a while, the last western centre of Greek learning. But the city soon declined. It was revived in the 10th century by the counts of Provence.

Marseilles was pillaged by the Aragonese in 1423, but the greatest calamity in its history took place in 1720, when plague – carried by a merchant vessel from Syria – killed some 50,000 of the city's 90,000 inhabitants. Under French rule, the Marseillais quickly gained a rebellious reputation. It is after them that France's national anthem is named (see the Facts about Provence chapter).

In the 19th century, Marseilles grew prosperous from colonial trade. Commerce with North Africa grew rapidly after the French occupation of Algeria in 1830, and maritime opportunities expanded further when the Suez Canal opened in 1869. During WWII, Marseilles was bombed by the Germans and Italians in 1940 and by the Allies between 1943 and 1944.

ORIENTATION

The city's main thoroughfare, the famed wide boulevard La Canebière, stretches eastwards from the Vieux Port (old port). The train station is north of La Canebière at the northern end of blvd d'Athènes. A few blocks south of La Canebière is cours Julien, a pedestrian square dominated by a water garden and palm trees, and lined with hip cafes, restaurants and theatres. Marseilles' commercial heart is around rue Paradis. The ferry terminal is west of place de la Joliette, a few minutes' walk north from the Nouvelle Cathédrale de la Major.

Marseilles is divided into 16 *arrondissements* (districts); most travellers mingle in the first (1er), second (2e), sixth (6e) and seventh (7e). Places mentioned have the arrondissement, together with the metro stop, listed after the street address.

Maps

The tourist office distributes free city maps. If you intend venturing farther afield invest in Blay-Foldex's *Marseille et son agglo-mération* (30FF). Public transport routes are detailed on *Plan de Poche-Métro Bus Tramway*, distributed free at the Espace Infos-RTM (see Getting Around later in this section).

INFORMATION
Tourist Offices

The tourist office (☎ 04 91 13 89 00, fax 04 91 13 89 20, ⓔ destination-marseille@ wanadoo.fr; metro Vieux Port), 4 La Canebière, 1er, opens 9 am to 7.30 pm Monday to Saturday, and 9 am to 6 pm on Sunday, July to September; and 9 am to 7 pm Monday to Saturday, and 10 am to 5 pm on Sunday, the rest of the year. Its annexes (☎ 04 91 50 59 18; metro Gare St-Charles) at the train station and on place des Pistoles in Le Panier open shorter hours. Staff make hotel

MARSEILLES AREA

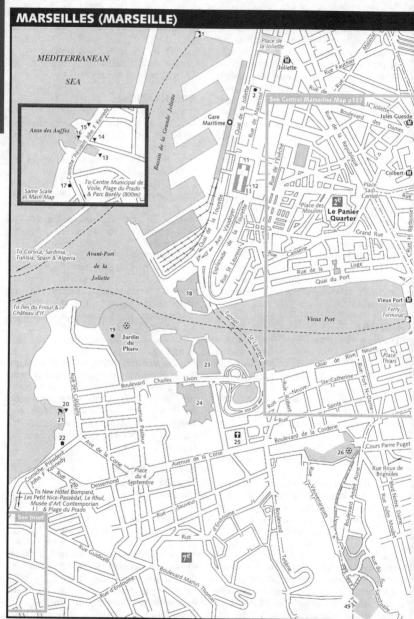

MARSEILLES (MARSEILLE)

MARSEILLES (MARSEILLE)

PLACES TO STAY
6 Hôtel Gambetta
10 Hôtel Sphinx
22 Hôtel Le Richelieu
29 Hôtel Béarn
35 Le Président
36 Hôtel Manon
37 Hôtel Massillia
38 Grand Hôtel Le Préfecture

PLACES TO EAT
9 Petit Casino Food Dispenser
13 Pizzeria Chez Jeannot
14 Chez Fonfon
15 Bistrot Plage; Restaurant de la Corniche
16 L'Épuisette
20 Pizzeria des Catalans
27 Morning Market
31 Café de la Banque; Two Cannelle
41 Le Resto Provençal
43 Marseil Café; La Passerelle
44 Djerba La Douce
46 Cubaïla Café
47 Bio-Nature

OTHER
1 Passenger Ferry Terminal
2 SNCM Ferries Office
3 Bus Station
4 Post Office
5 Taxi Stand
7 Église St-Vincent de Paul
8 New Cancan
11 Nouvelle Cathédrale de la Major
12 Ancienne Cathédrale de la Major
17 Zinedine Zidane Mural
18 Fort St-Jean
19 Palais du Pharo
21 Plage des Catalans
23 Fort St-Nicolas
24 Fort d'Entrecasteaux
25 Abbaye St-Victor
26 Jardin Pierre Puget
28 Comité Départemental du Tourisme
30 Banque de France
32 US Consulate
33 Police Headquarters
34 Préfecture
39 Bug's Café
40 Le Rézo
42 Espace Julien
45 Chocolat Théâtre
48 Au Vieux Plongeur
49 Basilique Notre Dame de la Garde

Arrondissement Boundary

euro currency converter €1 = 6.56FF

reservations and have information on organised tours (see that section later). Visit online at www.destination-marseille.com.

For information on the Bouches-du-Rhône department head to the Comité Départemental du Tourisme (☎ 04 91 13 84 13, fax 04 91 33 01 82, ℮ promotion@visitprovence.com; metro Estrangin-Préfecture), 13 rue Roux de Brignoles, 6e, or visit online at www.visitprovence.com.

The Club Alpin Français (CAF; ☎ 04 91 54 36 94; metro Vieux Port), runs a small bureau at 12 rue Fort Notre Dame, 1er. There's a Centre Régional Information Jeunesse (☎ 04 91 24 33 50; metro Noailles) at 96 La Canebière, 1er.

Money

Banque de France (metro Estrangin Préfecture), place Estrangin Pastré, 6e, exchanges currency from 8.45 am to 12.30 pm on weekdays.There are several banks and exchange bureaux west of the old port (metro Vieux Port) on La Canebière, 1er. Barclays Bank at No 34 opens 8.30 am to 12.15 pm and 1.45 to 4.30 pm weekdays. American Express agent, Canebière Change (☎ 04 91 13 71 26; metro Vieux Port), inside Canebière Voyages at No 39 opens 8.30 am to 5.30 pm weekdays, 8.30 am to noon and 2 to 5 pm on Saturday.

Post & Communications

Marseilles' postcode is '130' plus the arrondissement number (postcode 13001 for addresses in the 1st arrondissement, 1er, for example). The main post office (metro Colbert), 1 place de l'Hôtel des Postes, 1er, opens 8 am to 7 pm weekdays, 8 am to noon on Saturday.

At the port, Info Café (☎ 04 91 33 74 98, ℮ reservations@info-cafe.com; metro Vieux Port), 1 quai du Rive Neuve, 1er, charges 25/35FF per 30 minutes/hour for Internet access. It opens 8.30 am to 11 pm. Le Rézo (☎ 04 91 42 70 02, ℮ lerezo@lerezo.com; metro Notre Dame du Mont-Cours Julien), 68 cours Julien, 6e, charges 30/50FF per 30 minutes/hour and opens 10 am to 8 pm Monday to Thursday, 10 am to midnight on Friday and Saturday. Neigh-

bouring Bug's Café (☎ 04 96 12 53 43), 80 cours Julien, charges 1/50FF per minute/hour and opens 10 am to 11 pm.

Travel Agencies

Voyages Wasteels (☎ 08 03 88 70 28; metro Noailles), 67 La Canebière, 1er, opens 9.30 am to 12.30 pm and 2 to 6.15 pm weekdays, 9.30 am to 12.30 pm on Saturday.

Bookshops

Librairie Lamy (☎ 04 91 33 57 07; metro Vieux Port), 26 rue Paradis, 1er, stocks an excellent selection of English-language novels. It opens 2.15 to 7 pm on Monday, 9.30 am to 7 pm Tuesday to Saturday.

Seafaring books, maps and guides are sold at the excellent Librairie Maritime (☎ 04 91 54 79 26; metro Vieux Port), 26 quai de Rive Neuve, 1er. The Librairie-Papeterie (metro Vieux Port), 29 quai des Belges, 1er, is the best place for English- and other foreign-language newspapers. It opens 7.30 am to 8 pm weekdays, 8 am to 8 pm on Saturday, 8 am to 7 pm on Sunday.

Laundry

The laundrette (metro Vieux Port), 5 rue Breteuil, 1er, opens 6.30 am to 8 pm.

Medical Services & Emergency

The Anglo-American pharmacy, adjoining Canebière Voyages (metro Vieux Port) at 39 La Canebière, 1er, opens 8 am to 8 pm. Hôpital de la Timone (☎ 04 91 38 60 00; metro La Timone) is at 264 rue St-Pierre, 5e, south-west of place Jean Jaurès.

The police headquarters (Préfecture de Police; ☎ 04 91 39 80 00; metro Estrangin Préfecture), place de la Préfecture, 1er, opens 24 hours.

WALKING TOURS
Vieux Port & Le Panier

Marseilles grew around the old port (metro Vieux Port) where ships have docked for at least 26 centuries. The main commercial docks were transferred to the Joliette area on the coast north of here in the 1840s, but the old port remains active as a harbour for fishing boats, pleasure yachts and ferries

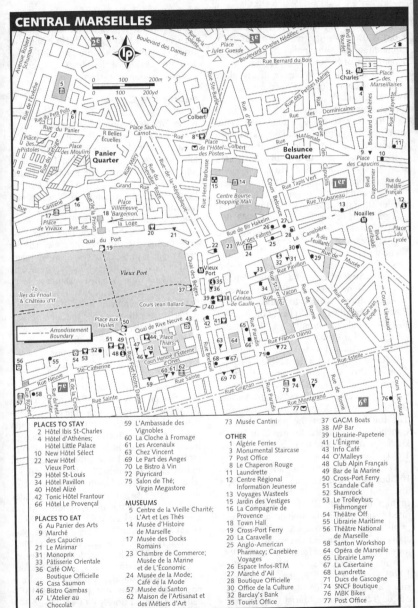

CENTRAL MARSEILLES

PLACES TO STAY
2   Hôtel Ibis St-Charles
4   Hôtel d'Athènes;
    Hôtel Little Palace
10 New Hôtel Sélect
22 New Hôtel
    Vieux Port
29 Hôtel St-Louis
34 Hôtel Pavillon
40 Hôtel Alizé
42 Tonic Hôtel Frantour
66 Hôtel Le Provençal

PLACES TO EAT
6   Au Panier des Arts
9   Marché
    des Capucins
21 Le Mirimar
31 Monoprix
33 Pâtisserie Orientale
36 Café OM;
    Boutique Officielle
45 Casa Saumon
46 Bistro Gambas
47 L'Atelier au
    Chocolat

59 L'Ambassade des
    Vignobles
60 La Cloche à Fromage
61 Les Arcenaulx
63 Chez Vincent
69 Le Part des Anges
70 Le Bistro à Vin
72 Puyricard
75 Salon de Thé;
    Virgin Megastore

MUSEUMS
5   Centre de la Vieille Charité;
    L'Art et Les Thés
14 Musée d'Histoire
    de Marseille
17 Musée des Docks
    Romains
23 Chambre de Commerce;
    Musée de la Marine
    et de L'Économic
24 Musée de la Mode;
    Café de la Mode
57 Musée du Santon
62 Maison de l'Artisanat et
    des Métiers d'Art

73 Musée Cantini

OTHER
1   Algérie Ferries
3   Monumental Staircase
7   Post Office
8   Le Chaperon Rouge
11 Laundrette
12 Centre Régional
    Information Jeunesse
13 Voyages Wasteels
15 Jardin des Vestiges
16 La Compagnie de
    Provence
18 Town Hall
19 Cross-Port Ferry
20 La Caravelle
25 Anglo-American
    Pharmacy; Canebière
    Voyages
26 Espace Infos-RTM
27 Marché d'Ail
28 Boutique Officielle
30 Office de la Culture
32 Barclay's Bank
35 Tourist Office

37 GACM Boats
38 MP Bar
39 Librairie-Papeterie
41 L'Énigme
43 Info Café
44 O'Malleys
48 Club Alpin Français
49 Bar de la Marine
50 Cross-Port Ferry
51 Scandale Café
52 Shamrock
53 Le Trolleybus;
    Fishmonger
54 Théâtre Off
55 Librairie Maritime
56 Théâtre National
    de Marseille
58 Santon Workshop
64 Opéra de Marseille
65 Librairie Lamy
67 La Casertaine
68 Laundrette
71 Ducs de Gascogne
74 SNCF Boutique
76 MBK Bikes
77 Post Office

euro currency converter €1 = 6.56FF

to Château d'If. The harbour entrance is guarded by **Fort St-Nicolas** (on the southern side) and, across the water, **Fort St-Jean**, founded in the 13th century by the Knights Hospitaller of St-John of Jerusalem.

From quai de Rive Neuve, lively place Thiars and cours Honoré d'Estienne d'Orves, with their late-night restaurants and cafes, stretch southwards. Quai de Rive Neuve is linked by ferry boat (see Getting Around later in this section) with quai du Port, its northern counterpart, which is dominated by Marseilles' 17th-century **town hall**. The Musée des Docks Romains and Musée du Vieux Marseille are a two-minute walk from here.

The increasingly trendy quarter of **Le Panier** (literally 'the basket') slinks up the slopes, north of quai du Port. In 1943 this neighbourhood – a seedy area with a strong Resistance presence – was dynamited by the Germans. It was rebuilt after the war, and since the mid-1990s has enjoyed a face-lift as its narrow streets and ageing houses strung with washing are slowly restored. Several windmills used to stand on pretty **Place des Moulins**, which lies at the heart of this so-called 'Montmartre of Marseilles'. Atop the hill sits the impressive Centre de la Vieille Charité and its museums.

Back at the port, La Canebière – derived from the Provençal word *canebe*, meaning 'hemp', after Marseilles' industrious rope industry – stretches north-eastwards to cours Belsunce (metro Vieux Port or Noailles). The tourist office at the port end of La Canebière is inside the former **Café Turc**, a key stopover for eastbound travellers in the 1950s.

The area bounded by La Canebière, cours Belsunce and rue d'Aix, rue Bernard du Bois and blvd d'Athènes is **Belsunce**, a poorer immigrant quarter slowly being rehabilitated. Future projects include a high-tech public library, due to open in 2002 on the spot where Marseilles' legendary Alcazar music hall hosted stars from 1857 until 1964.

Aubagne-born Marcel Pagnol (1895–1974) grew up in **La Pleine**, east of Belsunce around place Jean Jaurès. He lived at 52 rue Terrusse. The tourist office has information on Pagnol city tours.

Worth a stroll is the fashionable **6th arrondissement**, especially the area between La Canebière and the **préfecture** building (metro Estrangin Préfecture). Rue St-Ferréol, half a block east of the Musée Cantini, is a pedestrian shopping street.

Along the Coast

Another fine place for a stroll is along **corniche Président John F Kennedy**, 7e, which follows the coast for 4.5km. It begins 200m west of **Jardin du Pharo**, a park with breath-taking views of the old port and new ferry terminal, and home to the **Palais du Pharo**, built by Napoleon III at 58 blvd Charles Livon. The road continues southwards past the small and busy **Plage des Catalans** – which resembles a scene from *Baywatch* with its bronzed, bikini-clad volleyball players – to **Anse des Auffes**. The cove, harbour and village is presided over by a WWI memorial statue of a 'mother of liberty', framed by a giant archway. A narrow staircase leads from corniche Président John F Kennedy to the harbour around which the village nestles.

Farther south, you pass the face of Adidas – local hero **Zinedine Zidane** – who peers out in gigantic form from the side of a building at 82B corniche Président John F Kennedy. At No 271 is the fabulous **Villa Valmer** (1868) and its luxuriant gardens, a potent cocktail of pistachio, palm and pine trees that can be visited. At No 281 **Château Berger** is another fine example of the beautiful architecture that sprung up along the coast under the Second Empire; today it houses a thalassotherapy and fitness centre (☎ 04 91 52 61 61). The **propeller**, sculpted in bronze by César in 1971 to honour those who returned from North Africa, is a short walk farther south along the coast. After passing small **Plage du Prophète** and the **Centre Municipal de Voile** (☎ 04 91 76 31 60) at 2 promenade Georges Pompidou, you eventually come to **Plage du Prado**, Marseilles' heavily built-up, modern beach resort.

Overlooking this sandy, body-packed beach is **Parc Borély**, a park that encompasses the **Jardin Botanique** and 18th-century **Château Borély** (☎ 04 91 25 26 34), 134 ave Clot Bey. Art shows and exhibitions held here can be visited 2 to 7 pm on Monday, Thursday and Friday, and 11 am to 7 pm on Tuesday, Wednesday and at weekends (shorter hours in winter). Admission costs 30FF. Take bus No 19 to ave du Prado or bus No 44 to ave Clot Bey.

Along almost its entire length corniche Président John F Kennedy and its continuation promenade Georges Pompidou is served by bus No 83, which goes to the old port (quai des Belges) and the Rond Point du Prado metro stop on ave du Prado. To get to the beach from here, bear west along ave du Prado to the monumental statue of **David** – an impressive marble mimic of Michelangelo's masterpiece by Jules Cantini in 1903 – on the busy intersection of ave du Prado and promenade Georges Pompidou. The well-endowed nude is a well-known landmark among local Marseillais.

Parc Chanot sits on the south-eastern corner of rond point du Prado (Prado roundabout). From here, blvd Michelet leads south to the **stade vélodrome**, home ground since 1937 of the Olympique de Marseille football club (see the boxed text 'OM' later in this chapter). Continuing south past the stadium is Le Corbusier's **Cité Radieuse**, a 337-apartment housing block on stilts, which was hugely innovative when designed (1947–52). The estate straddles the corner of blvd Michelet and ave Guy de Maupassant. West of here is Marseilles' Musée d'Art Contemporain.

From **Plage du Prado**, promenade Georges Pompidou continues south along the coast to **La Pointe-Rouge**, **La Madrague** and **Callelongue**, a tiny harbour village on Cap Croisette from where the breathtaking **calanques** (see Les Calanques later in this chapter) can be accessed on foot. Bus No 19 from the Rond Point du Prado metro stop runs along promenade Georges Pompidou to La Madrague; from La Madrague bus No 20 continues to Callelongue.

MUSEUMS
Unless noted otherwise, museums open from 11 am to 6 pm Tuesday to Sunday, June to September; and 10 am to 5 pm Tuesday to Sunday, the rest of the year.

Admission to each museum's permanent/temporary exhibition is 12/18FF (students 6FF, seniors aged over 65 9FF); exceptions are noted in the text.

Between June and September, the Passeport Musées allows unlimited admission to all city museums over a 15-day period; it costs 50FF (children aged under 10, free) and is sold at the tourist office and museums.

Centre de la Vieille Charité
The Old Charity Cultural Centre (metro Joliette), 2 rue de la Charité, 2e, is built around Provence's most impressive Baroque church, designed by Marseilles-born architect Pierre Puget. Its stone dome is the centrepiece of Le Panier, Marseilles' oldest quarter. The centre houses superb permanent exhibits and imaginative temporary exhibitions in a workhouse and hospice built between 1671 and 1745. Before being restored, the building served as barracks (1905), a soldiers' resthome (WWI) and low-cost housing for people who lost their homes during WWII.

Today, the courtyard arcade shelters a **Musée d'Archéologie Méditerranéene** (Museum of Mediterranean Archaeology); and a **Musée des Arts Africains, Océaniens & Amérindiens** (Museum of African, Oceanic & American Indian Art). Guided tours (1½ hours) of the Centre de la Vieille Charité (☎ 04 91 14 58 80) depart from the ticket office at 3.30 pm on Tuesday and at 2 and 3.30 pm at the weekends. Complete your visit with lunch at L'Art et les Thés (see Places to Eat later in this section).

Musée Cantini
Inside a 17th-century *hôtel particulier* (private mansion) the Musée Cantini (☎ 04 91 54 77 75; metro Estrangin Préfecture), 19 rue Grignan, 6e, has an extensive permanent exhibit of 17th- and 18th-century Provençal ceramics, as well as rotating exhibitions of modern and contemporary art, and a centre dedicated to 21st-century works.

Maison de l'Artisanat et des Métiers d'Art
Contemporary photography, sculpture and calligraphy exhibitions (among others) are

Little Saints

The custom of creating a crèche (Christmas crib) with figurines of Mary, Joseph, shepherds, kings, oxen, a donkey and so on, dates from the Avignon papacy of John XII (1319–34). But it was only after the 1789 revolution and consequent Reign of Terror that these figures were cut down to size, marking the birth of the santon and the Provençal creche.

Santons (from santoùn, Provençal for 'little saint') stand no higher than 2.5cm to 15cm. The first colourfully-painted figures were created by Marseillais artisan Jean-Louis Lagnel (1764–1822), who came up with the idea of crafting clay miniatures in a plaster mould and allowing them to dry before firing the figures at 950°C. Santonniers (santon makers) still stick to Lagnel's method today.

In a traditional Provençal crib there are 55 santons ranging from the tambourine man, fishwife and miller, to tinsmith, scissors grinder, woman carrying garlic and a blowing angel. Since 1806 santonniers have flocked to Marseilles each December to take part in the Foire aux Santonniers which sees the length of La Canebière transformed into one great big santon fair.

Santons dating from the 18th and 19th centuries are displayed in Marseilles' magical **Musée du Santon** (Map C; ☎ 04 91 13 61 36, [e] carbonel@carbonel.com, metro Vieux Port), 49 rue Neuve Ste-Catherine, 7e. The museum houses the private collection of santonnier Marcel Carbonnel, who crafts santons in the adjoining atelier (workshop). The museum opens 9.30 am to 12.30 pm and 2 to 6.30 or 7 pm Monday to Saturday (free admission). Carbonnel's workshop can be visited from 8.30 am to 1 pm and 2 to 5.30 pm Monday to Thursday and 8.30 am to 1 pm Friday. Admission is free.

JANE SMITH

hosted at this House of Arts & Crafts (☎ 04 91 54 80 54; metro Vieux Port), 21 cours Honoré d'Estienne d'Orves, 1er. It opens 1 to 6 pm Tuesday to Saturday. Admission is free.

Musée d'Histoire de Marseille

Roman history buffs should visit Marseilles' Historical Museum (☎ 04 91 90 42 22; metro Vieux Port), just north of La Canebière on the ground floor of the Centre Bourse shopping centre, 1er. Exhibits include the remains of a merchant vessel – discovered by chance in the old port in 1974 – that plied the waters of the Mediterranean in the early 3rd century. The 19m-long timbers, which include five different kinds of wood, show evidence of having been repaired repeatedly. To preserve the soaked and decaying wood, the whole thing was freeze-dried right where it now sits – hidden behind glass in a very dimly lit room. The museum opens noon to 7 pm Monday to Saturday.

Roman buildings, uncovered during the construction of the Centre Bourse, can be seen just outside the museum in the **Jardin des Vestiges** (Garden of Ruins), which fronts rue Henri Barbusse, 1er.

Musée des Docks Romains

The Roman Docks Museum (☎ 04 91 91 24 62; metro Vieux Port), on ugly place de Vivaux, 2e, displays in situ part of the 1st-century Roman structures discovered in 1947 during postwar reconstruction. The huge jars on display could hold up to 2000 litres of wine or oil.

Musée de la Mode

Glitz and glamour is the name of the game at Marseilles' Fashion Design Museum (☎ 04 91 56 59 57; metro Vieux Port), 11

La Canebière, 1er. Housed in the city's Espace Mode Méditerranée (Mediterranean Fashion Centre; ☎ 04 91 14 92 00, [e] imm@ wanadoo.fr), the museum traces fashion trends from 1930 to the present day and displays some 2000 items of clothing and accessories. Several original Chanel designs (many worn by Mademoiselle herself) are on display, along with more contemporary pieces by Gaultier, Dior, Yves St-Laurent and funky British designer Alexander McQueen. The museum opens noon to 7 pm; free guided tours (in French only) depart at 4 pm at the weekends. Admission costs 18FF (students and seniors aged over 65, 9FF).

Chambre de Commerce

A few doors from the Musée de la Mode along on La Canebière is the colonnaded Chamber of Commerce (also known as Palais de la Bourse), built from 1854 to 1860. It houses the **Musée de la Marine et de l'Économie** (Naval & Economic Museum; ☎ 04 91 39 33 33; metro Vieux Port). For about half the year, the ship models and engravings are replaced by an art exhibition (35FF). Both open 10 am to 6 pm. Admission costs 10FF (students and those aged over 65, 5FF).

Palais Longchamp

Colonnaded Longchamp Palace (metro Cinq Avenues Longchamp), constructed in the 1860s, is at the eastern end of blvd Longchamp on blvd Philippon, 4e. It was designed in part to disguise a water tower built at the terminus of an aqueduct from the Durance River. The palace's two wings house the **Musée des Beaux-Arts** (☎ 04 91 14 59 30), Marseilles' oldest museum, whose speciality is 15th- to 19th- century paintings. A **Musée d'Histoire Naturelle** (☎ 04 91 14 59 90) captures prehistoric Provence.

Musée d'Art Contemporain

Marseilles' Museum of Contemporary Art (MAC; ☎ 04 91 25 01 07), 69 blvd de Haïfa, 8e, is north of the Prado beach area and Parc Borély. On display are works by Christo, new realists Ben and Klein, pop artist Andy Warhol and Marseilles' very own César who designed the little statue handed to stars at the Césars (the French cinema awards that bear his name).

Take bus No 44 from the Rond Point du Prado metro stop to the place Bonnefons stop, from where it is a short walk along ave de Hambourg to rond point Pierre Guerre – easily recognisable by a giant metal thumb (César's doing) that proudly sticks up from the middle of the roundabout.

BASILIQUE NOTRE DAME DE LA GARDE

Not to be missed, especially if you like overwrought 19th-century architecture or great panoramas, but count on a stiff walk up to the enormous Roman-Byzantine basilica, 1km south of the old port. It stands on a hill top (162m) – the highest point in the city – and provides staggering views of sprawling Marseilles.

The domed basilica, ornamented with all manner of coloured marble, intricate mosaics, murals and gilded objects, was erected between 1853 and 1864. The bell tower is topped by a 9.7m-tall gilded statue of the Virgin Mary on a 12m-high pedestal. The great bell inside is 2.5m high and weighs a hefty 8.3 tonnes (the clapper alone weighs 387kg). Bullet marks from Marseilles' Battle of Liberation (15–25 August 1944) scar the cathedral's northern wall.

The basilica and crypt open 7 am to 7 or 8 pm (free admission). Dress respectably. Bus No 60 links the old port (from cours Jean Ballard) with the basilica. Count on 30 minutes each way by foot.

NOUVELLE CATHÉDRALE DE LA MAJOR

Marseilles' Roman-Byzantine New Cathedral of the Major, also called Basilique de Ste-Marie Majeure (metro Joliette), on place de la Major, just off quai de la Tourette, 2e, is topped with cupolas, towers and turrets of all shapes and sizes. The structure, built between 1852 and 1893 (a period not known for decorative or architectural understatement) is enormous: 140m long and 60m high. It dwarfs the nearby old cathedral, **Ancienne Cathédrale de la Major**, a mid-11th-century Provençal Romanesque structure that stands on the site of what was once a temple to the goddess Diana.

The new cathedral opens 9 am to noon and 2.30 to 6 pm Friday to Sunday; its old counterpart can only be visited (free) by appointment (☎ 04 91 90 53 57).

ABBAYE ST-VICTOR

The twin tombs of 4th-century martyrs and a 3rd-century sarcophagus are among the sacred objects that rest in the imposing Romanesque 12th-century Abbaye St-Victor (metro Vieux Port), 3 rue de l'Abbaye, 7e, set on a hill (162m) above the old port. Each year on 2 February the statue of the Black Virgin inside the abbey is carried through the streets in a candle-lit procession. Marseilles' annual sacred music festival is also held here. The abbey opens 8 am to 7 pm. Admission costs 10FF.

The weary footed, not fussed about viewing the abbey interior, can hop aboard the **Petit Train de Notre Dame de la Garde**, an electric train that takes tourists on a 50-minute sightseeing tour around Abbaye St-Victor. A second circuit runs between the port, cathedral and Centre de la Vieille Charité. Trains depart from quai des Belges every 30 minutes between 10 am and 12.30 pm and 2 to 6.30 pm, April to September; less frequently and weekends only, the rest of the year. Rides cost 30FF (children 18FF).

CHÂTEAU D'IF

Château d'If (☎ 04 91 59 02 30), the 16th-century fortress-turned-prison made famous by Alexandre Dumas' classic work of fiction, *Le Comte de Monte Cristo*, is on a three-hectare island 3.5km west of the entrance to the old port. Among the people incarcerated here were political prisoners, hundreds of Protestants, the revolutionary hero Mirabeau, who served a stint here in 1774 for failing to pay debts, some 1848 revolutionaries and the Communards of 1871.

The fortress was built between 1524 and 1528. It opens 9.30 am to 6.30 pm, April to September; and 9.30 am to 5.30 pm Tuesday to Sunday, the rest of the year. Admission costs 25FF (children 15FF); free on the first Sunday of the month.

Boats run by GACM (☎ 04 91 55 50 09; metro Vieux Port), 1 quai des Belges, 1er, leave for Château d'If from outside the GACM office at the old port. Hourly boats run between 9 am and 7 pm (until 8.30 pm in July and August). Sailing time is 20 minutes and a return fare costs 50FF. Return boats depart from Île d'If hourly between 9.30 am and 6.30 pm (early morning crossing at 7.15 am).

ÎLES DU FRIOUL

The islands of Ratonneau and Pomègues, each of which is about 2.5km long, are a few hundred metres west of Château d'If. They were linked by a dike in the 1820s. From the 17th to 19th centuries the islands were used as a place of quarantine for those suspected of carrying plague or cholera. Today the rather barren islands (total area about 200 hectares) shelter seabirds, rare plants and bathers, and are dotted with fortifications (used by German troops during WWII), the ruins of the old quarantine hospital, **Hôpital Caroline**, and **Fort Ratonneau**.

GACM boats to Château d'If also serve the Îles du Frioul. A return fare is 50FF (80FF to stop at Château d'If too).

BEACHES

Marseilles' main beach, 1km-long Plage du Prado is about 5km south of the city centre. Take bus No 19 or 72 from the Rond Point du Prado metro stop or bus No 83 (No 583 at night) from the old port (quai des Belges) and get off at either La Plage or Plage David. On foot, follow corniche Président John F Kennedy, which runs along the coast, past short **Plage des Catalans**. The latter, open 7 am to 7 pm, costs 25FF to access (walk down the steps signposted 'Bains des Catalans').

If you don't like sand between your toes, spread yourself out on one of the wooden sundecks built atop the rocky seafront near **Anse des Auffes**, from where bathers climb down short ladders to take a dip in the sea. **Bains de Mer du Petit Pavillon** (☎ 04 91 31 00 38), 54 corniche Président John F Kennedy, charges 30FF admission, plus 20FF for a big comfy sun-lounger. About

100m farther along the corniche at No 60 is **Plage de la Corniche** (☎ 04 91 31 62 12), which has a lovely bistro (see Places to Eat later in this sectio) and plush mattresses (50FF) on which to sprawl. By bus, get off at the Vallon des Auffes stop.

DIVING
The Calanques (see Les Calanques later in the chapter), islands and wrecks off the shores offer spectacular diving. Equipment can be hired or bought at Au Vieux Plongeur (☎/fax 04 91 48 79 48, ⓔ vieuxplongeur@ vieuxplongeur.com; metro Notre Dame du Mont), 116 cours Lieutaud, which also runs a diving school. Abyss Adventures (☎ 04 91 91 98 07, 06 12 66 74 50, ⓔ abyssadv@ aol.com), inside Bains de Mer du Petit Pavillon at 54 corniche Président John F Kennedy, is another diving school worth trying. See Diving & Snorkelling under Activities in the Facts for the Visitor chapter.

ORGANISED TOURS
The tourist office offers guided tours (40FF to 90FF), including old-town walks and thematic tours (Baroque Marseilles, Botanical Marseilles etc), departing from the main tourist office at 1 am or 2.30 pm. From 1 July to mid-September, it runs nocturnal port tours at 9.30 pm on Friday. All tours should be booked (☎ 04 91 13 89 00) in advance.

The tourist office also sells tickets for Marseilles' Histobus Tour (☎ 04 91 10 54 71), a three-hour city tour (75FF) run by local bus company RTM. Tours depart from the old port at 2.30 pm on Sunday in June, and at 2.30 pm daily, July to 1 October.

From Easter to September, GACM (☎ 04 91 55 50 09), 1 quai des Belges, runs return boat trips from the old port to Cassis (120FF, four hours), which pass by the stunning Calanques – dramatic coastal rock formations that attract a large amount of unusual wildlife (see Les Calanques later in this chapter). A glass-bottomed boat sails on Saturday.

PLACES TO STAY
Marseilles has some of France's cheapest hotels although many are filthy dives in dodgy

areas whose main business is renting out rooms by the hour. Those we list appeared, at the time, to be relatively clean and reputable. Map M refers you to the Marseilles map; Map C to the Central Marseilles map.

PLACES TO STAY – BUDGET
The tourist office has a list of a dozen or so chambres d'hôtes in Marseilles, some of which offer B&B for as little as 150/200FF for one/two people.

Camping
Tents can usually be pitched on the grounds of the *Auberge de Jeunesse Château de Bois Luzy* (see Hostels below) for about 30FF per person. Marseilles' closest camp sites are in Aubagne and Cassis (see Cassis later in this chapter).

Hostels
About 4.5km south of the town centre is the *Auberge de Jeunesse de Bonneveine* (☎ 04 91 17 63 30, fax 04 91 73 97 23, ⓔ marseille-bonneveine@fuaj.org, Impasse du Docteur Bonfils, 8e). It opens February to mid-December and charges 88/69FF for B&B in a dorm/double room. It rents bikes for 70FF per day. Take bus No 44 from the Rond Point du Prado metro stop and get off at the place Bonnefons stop. Alternatively take bus No 19 from the Castellane metro stop or bus No 47 from the Ste-Marguerite Dromel metro stop.

Auberge de Jeunesse Château de Bois Luzy (☎/fax 04 91 49 06 18, allées des Primevères, 12e), opens year round and is 4.5km east of the centre in the Montolivet neighbourhood. B&B costs 63FF, plus 7FF per week for sheets. Reception opens 7.30 am to noon and 5 to 10.30 pm. A hostelling card is mandatory. Take bus No 6 from near the Réformés-Canebière metro stop or bus No 8 from La Canebière.

Hotels – Train Station Area
The hotels around the train station are convenient if you arrive by train, but there is better value elsewhere.

Two-star *Hôtel d'Athènes (Map C; ☎ 04 91 90 03 83, fax 04 91 90 72 03, 37 blvd*

MARSEILLES AREA

d'Athènes, 1er; metro Gare St-Charles), at the foot of the monumental staircase leading from the train station to town, has well-kept singles and doubles with shower and toilet costing 220FF to 320FF. Shower-equipped rooms for one or two in its adjoining one-star annexe, *Hôtel Little Palace* (*Map C; ☎ 04 91 90 12 93, 39 blvd d'Athènes*) cost 160FF.

Hotels – North of La Canebière

Overlooking the bustling old port, *New Hôtel Vieux Port* (*Map C; ☎ 04 91 90 51 42, fax 04 91 90 76 24, e marseil-levieux-port@new-hotel.com, 3 bis rue Reine Elisabeth, 1er; metro Vieux Port*) is a large renovated complex with modern singles/doubles for 430/470FF. Rooms at *New Hôtel Select* (*Map C; ☎ 04 91 50 65 50, fax 04 91 50 45 56, e marseilleselect@new-hotel.com, 4 allées Léon Gambetta, 1er; metro Réformés-Canebière*), run by the same company, are slightly cheaper.

Hôtel Gambetta (*Map M; ☎/fax 04 91 62 07 88, 49 allées Léon Gambetta, 1er; metro Réformés-Canebière*) has singles for 105FF (145FF with shower) and shower-equipped doubles for 145FF. Hall showers cost 15FF.

Hotels – South of La Canebière

There are many rock-bottom, very sleazy hotels along rue Sénac de Meilhan, rue Mazagran and rue du Théâtre Français and around place du Lycée (all near metro Réformés-Canebière, 1er). Slightly to the west, rue des Feuillants (metro Noailles) has several one-star hotels.

A cut above its neighbours, *Hôtel Sphinx* (*Map M; ☎ 04 91 48 70 59, fax 04 91 7 74 54, 16 rue Sénac de Meilhan, 1er; metro Réformés-Canebière*) has well-kept doubles with toilet for 130FF (170FF with shower). Hall showers cost 17FF.

Nearby, cheap *Hôtel Pavillon* (*Map C; ☎ 04 91 33 76 90, 27 rue Pavillon, 1er; metro Vieux Port*) touts rock-bottom singles/doubles with no perks for 99/101FF (139/149FF with shower).

Pretty-in-pink *Hôtel St-Louis* (*Map C; ☎ 04 91 54 02 74, fax 04 91 33 78 59, 2 rue des Récollettes*) is an elegant old pile over-looking rue de Rome in the hub of Marseilles' shopping district. The wrought-iron balconies add an ornate touch. Bathroom-equipped singes/doubles start at 220/260FF.

Just a few blocks south-east of the old port on a busy shopping street, *Hôtel Le Provençal* (*Map C; ☎ 04 91 33 11 15, 32 rue Paradis, 1er; metro Vieux Port*) has one-star singles/doubles/triples with shower for 145/185/230FF. Reception is on the 1st floor.

Hotels – Préfecture Area

All the hotels in this section (metro Estrangin Préfecture, 6e) appear on the Marseilles map (Map M).

Blvd Louis Salvator, in a decent neighbourhood, has several two-star hotels touting bright rooms and modern decor. At No 9 is friendly *Grand Hôtel Le Préfecture* (*☎ 04 91 54 31 60, fax 04 91 54 24 95*) which has beautifully clean and modern rooms with shower, toilet and TV for 200FF (230FF with bath). Opposite at No 12, *Le Président* (*☎ 04 91 48 67 29, fax 04 91 94 24 44*) charges 190FF for shower-equipped doubles with toilet and TV (240FF with bath, toilet and TV).

Farther uphill at No 25, one-star *Hôtel Massilia* (*☎ 04 91 54 79 28*) has doubles with shower for 140FF (160FF with shower and toilet). Guests punch in a *code confidentiel* to enter. Rooms can also be rented on a weekly/monthly basis. Almost opposite, nonclassified *Hôtel Manon* (*☎ 04 91 48 67 01, fax 04 91 47 23 04*) at No 36 charges 200/240/320FF for a single/double/triple with shower and toilet.

Single-star *Hôtel Béarn* (*☎ 04 91 37 75 83, fax 04 91 81 54 98, 63 rue Sylvabelle*) is quiet with colourfully decorated singles/doubles for 120/130FF with shower (180/200FF with shower and toilet). Guests can watch TV in the common room. Reception closes at 11 pm or midnight.

PLACES TO STAY – MID-RANGE & TOP END

Hôtel Ibis St-Charles (*Map M; ☎ 04 91 95 62 09, fax 04 91 50 68 42, e h1390@accorhotels.com, 1 square Narvik, 1er; metro Gare St-Charles,*), on the southern side of the train terminal building is clean, large and could be anywhere in the world. Unexciting rooms for one or two kick off at 370FF.

At the port, atmospheric *Hôtel Alizé* (*Map C; ☎ 04 91 33 66 97, fax 04 91 54 80 06, 35 quai des Belges, 1er; metro Vieux Port,*) is an elegant pile wedged between cafes. Pleasant singles/doubles cost 285/ 305FF (375/395FF with port and sea view).

Neighbouring *Tonic Hôtel Frantour* (*Map C; ☎ 04 91 55 67 49, fax 04 91 55 67 56, e franrout.tonichotel@wanadoo.fr, 43 quai des Belges, 1er, metro Vieux Port*) is another beautifully restored old building which shelters McDonald's on its ground floor. Air-conditioned doubles on the 1st floor, a three-star portside pad cost 440FF.

Built into the rocks to offer idyllic sea and beach views is two-star *Hôtel Le Richelieu* (*Map M; ☎ 04 91 31 01 92, fax 04 91 59 38 09, 52 corniche Président John F Kennedy, 7e),* near Plage des Catalans. Rooms for one or two cost 235FF to 360FF. Don't miss breakfast (34FF or 39FF) on the terrace.

Sea breezes also blow on *New Hôtel Bompard* (*☎ 04 91 52 10 93, fax 04 91 31 02 14, e marseillebompard@new-hotel .com, 2 rue des Flots Bleues, 7e),* just off corniche Président John F Kennedy. Come here for sea views, a swimming pool, extensive grounds and three-star singles/ doubles with all the gadgets for 400/440FF on weekdays (390/430FF at weekends and in July and August).

Among Marseilles' most prestigious pads are *Le Rhul* (*☎ 04 91 52 01 77, fax 04 91 52 49 82, 269 corniche Président John F Kennedy, 7e),* known as much for its legendary bouillabaisse as its lovely three-star rooms overlooking the water; and *Le Petit Nice-Passédat* (*☎ 04 91 59 25 92, fax 04 91 59 28 08, e hotel@petitnice-passedat.com, Anse de Maldormé, 7e),* built atop rocks above a little cove. Doubles costs at least 500FF at Le Rhul, 1000FF at Le Petit Nice.

PLACES TO EAT

This lively port city offers an incredible variety of restaurants. Unless noted otherwise, the places listed appear on the Central Mar-

seilles map. Map M refers to the Marseilles map.

Restaurants – French

Fish predominates, whether it's *huîtres* (oysters), *moules* (mussels) or other *coquillages* (shellfish), all of which are plentiful. Quai de Rive Neuve, 1er, is plastered with cafes and touristy restaurants; those on quai du Port on the northern side of the old port are slightly more expensive but still a fair bet (*plats du jour* from 65FF). To the south, the pedestrian streets around place Thiars overflow with yet more terraces where you can wine and dine.

Place aux Huiles (metro Vieux Port, 1er) offers several places worth a pitstop. Those with a fetish for king prawns should dive into *Bistro Gambas* (*☎ 04 91 33 26 44, 29 place aux Huiles)* where plates of *gambas* (king prawns) are accompanied by a wild choice of sauces. Its lunchtime *menu* (85FF) and spicy Gambas Go-Go *menu* (104FF) are both lip-smacking and finger-licking (finger bowl provided) good. Lovers of salmon are catered for at *Casa Saumon* (*☎ 04 91 54 22 89, 22 rue de la Paix-Marcel),* where salmon-stuffed *menus* start at 74FF.

Chocolate in all its guises is the speciality of *L'Atelier au Chocolat* (*☎ 04 91 33 55 00, 18 place aux Huiles).* Marseilles' self-professed Ambassador of Vineyards, *L'Ambassade des Vignobles* (*☎ 04 91 33 00 25, 42 place aux Huiles)* allows diners to sample a different vintage with each course (160/210FF *menu* without/with wine).

Cours Honoré d'Estienne d'Orves, a skip and a jump east of place aux Huiles, is equally laden. Eat cheese, cheese and cheese – 70 types in fact – at *La Cloche à Fromage* (*☎ 04 91 54 85 38)* at No 27, or opt for a table amid historic splendour at *Les Arcenaulx* (*☎ 04 91 59 80 30),* a restaurant-cum-*salon de thé* wrapped around an interior courtyard at No 25.

A block south, *Le Bistro à Vin* (*☎ 04 91 54 02 20, 17 rue Sainte)* is a top lunchtime spot. All the old favourites – *pieds et paquets* (sheep tripe, literally 'feet and packages') and *alouettes sans têtes* (meat slices wrapped around a stuffing, literally 'headless larks') –

Tasty Tip

No trip to Marseilles is complete without trying *bouillabaisse* (a traditional fish stew, pronounced 'bwee-a-bezz'). Although many touristy restaurants around the port advertise Provence's signature dish for as little as 100FF, a truly authentic bouillabaisse – evident from the manner in which it is served and its fresh fish content – will cost you at least 250FF per person.

Kosher bouillabaisse restaurants generally don't dish up the stew to solo diners (minimum two people). Among the 16 places to have signed the Charte de la Bouillabaisse Marseillaise – a charter aimed at safeguarding the century-old culinary creation – are Marseilles' best known bouillabaisse restaurants. These are delightful *Chez Fonfon* (Map M; ☎ 04 91 52 14 38, 140 Vallon des Auffes); portside *Le Mirimar* (Map C; ☎ 04 91 91 10 40, ⓔ contact@bouillabaisse.com, 12 quai du Port, 1er; metro Vieux Port), with a fishy Web site at www.bouillabaisse.com; and hotel restaurant *Le Rhul* (off Map M; ☎ 04 91 52 54 54, 269 corniche Président John F Kennedy, 7e). Advance reservations are essential at all three.

More intimate details about bouillabaisse are uncovered in the special Food & Wine section earlier in the book.

are dished up at this authentic bistro that oozes charm. Mains average 75FF and there's a 59FF *assiette du jour* (dish of the day).

Don't confuse the latter with *Le Part des Anges* (☎ 04 91 33 55 70, 33 rue Sainte), a *bar à vins* (wine bar) farther along the same street where you can taste regional wine and nibble on Provençal dishes until 2 am. Near the opera, traditional French *Restaurant O'Stop* (☎ 04 91 33 85 34, place de l'Opéra) is the best (and almost only) bet for late diners; it opens 24 hours.

Pizzeria *Chez Vincent* (☎ 04 91 33 96 78, 25 rue des Glandeves, 1er; metro Vieux Port) is like no other. It is small, simple and ruled with a heart of gold by 76-year-old Rosie – chef, patron and legendary grandmother of this Marseillais establishment. Pizzas average 40FF and pasta/meat dishes cost 50/85FF. Rosie does not accept credit cards.

In Le Panier, *Au Panier des Arts* (☎ 04 91 56 02 32, 3 rue du Petit Puits, 2e; metro Vieux Port) is a cosy and colourful spot serving simple and delicious *menus* (98FF) without pretention. *L'Art et les Thés* (☎ 04 91 14 58 71), nestled in the courtyard of the Centre de la Vieille Charité, serves mains such as ginger-spiced chicken brochettes (50FF to 75FF).

There are some colourful places to eat on cours Julien (Map M; metro Notre Dame du Mont-Cours Julien, 6e). Tasty choices include *Le Resto Provençal* (☎ 04 91 48 85 12), at No 64, and *Le Sud du Haut* (☎ 04 91 92 66 64), a brightly painted place with an eclectic interior at No 80. Both places serve lunchtime/evening *menus*, averaging 65/80FF, on an idyllic sky-topped terrace.

Restaurants – Ethnic Cuisine

For Vietnamese and Chinese fare, the many restaurants on, or just off, rue de la République (metro Vieux Port, 1er) are worth a nibble. Other than that, cours Julien (Map M; metro Notre Dame du Mont-Cours Julien, 6e) – Marseilles' trendy and bohemian patch of town – is lined with fun and funky restaurants offering a tantalising variety of other ethnic cuisines. Rue des Trois Mages alone has a Greek, an Indian, a Lebanese and a Spanish restaurant, as well as the fabulously popular *Cubaïla Café*, a Tex-Mex restaurant at No 40, which come midnight turns into a pulsating nightclub where salsa and Latino rule (open Thursday to Saturday).

Restaurants – By the Beach

Famed for its exquisite bouillabaisse is *Chez Fonfon* (Map M; ☎ 04 91 52 14 38, 140 Vallon des Auffes, 7e), overlooking the harbour of Anse des Auffes. Fish dishes are the house speciality: bouillabaisse du pêcheur costs 266FF per person and oysters/clams/prawns are 10/26/66FF per half-dozen. Reservations are essential at this chic seaside spot.

Equally worth the wallet-crunch is elegant *L'Épuisette (Map M; ☎ 04 91 52 17 82, Vallon des Auffes, 7e)*, a concrete-and-glass edifice built astride a rock looking out to sea. *Soupe de poissons* (fish soup) is 80FF and *menus* swim in at 195FF.

Not pricey but always packed, thanks to its great location, is *Pizzeria Chez Jeannot (Map M; ☎ 04 91 52 11 28, 129 Vallon des Auffes, 7e)*. Jeannot serves fresh salads, pasta, oysters and shellfish as well as pizza. Her terrace restaurant is a great boat-watching spot.

Other sea-breeze spots include *Pizzeria des Catalans (Map M; ☎ 04 91 52 37 82)* which touts an enviable terrace next to the beach-volley courts on Plage des Catalans. A small/medium/large pizza here averages 46/57/71FF. Farther south along the corniche, *Bistrot Plage & Restaurant de la Corniche* (see Beaches later in this section) serves an 87FF lunchtime *menu* in its restaurant (☎ 04 91 31 80 32) and imaginative salads costing about 70FF in its seaside bistro. Both offer unbeatable views of the coast and Château d'If.

Cafes & Fast Food

Cafes crowd quai du Port, quai de Rive Neuve and cours Honoré d'Estienne d'Orves, 1er, a long open square two blocks south of the latter. There is a less touristy cluster overlooking the fountain on place de la Préfecture, at the southern end of pedestrianised rue St-Ferréol, 1er.

Locally favoured is *Café de la Banque (Map M; ☎ 04 91 33 35 07, blvd Paul Reytal, 1er; metro Estrangin Préfecture)*, which has outside seating on the sunny side of the street and attracts a young shades 'n' attitude type of crowd. It serves a handy 20FF and 30FF breakfast and wholesome lunchtime salads and pasta (40FF). At No 28 *Two Cannelle (Map M; ☎ 04 91 54 96 95)* serves similar fare on its pavement terrace, as well as sweet home-made tarts, pastries and tea.

The trendy *Salon de Thé (Map C; ☎ 04 91 55 55 00, 75 rue St-Ferréol, 1er; metro Estrangin Préfecture)*, inside the Virgin Megastore, opens 9.30 am to 9 pm weekdays, and 9.30 am to midnight on Saturday. Chocoholics should aim for the 1st-floor tea room in the *Puyricard* chocolate shop (Map C; see Self-Catering below) where calorie-killer treats are served noon to 6 pm Monday to Saturday.

Dressed to kill? Then head for elitist *Café de la Mode (Map C; ☎ 04 91 91 21 36, 11 La Canebière, 1er; metro Vieux Port)*, inside the Musée de la Mode; it has a 50FF lunchtime *formule*.

Cours Julien (Map M; metro Notre Dame du Mont-Cours Julien, 6e) has a cluster of great cafes. *Marseil Café* on rue des Trois Mages is a popular bohemian cafe-cum-bar inside La Passerelle, a comic-strip bookshop, where you can read, giggle and glug, all at the same time. It opens 5 pm to 2 am.

Self-Catering

Marseilles has a wholesome array of markets, the most aromatic being the daily *fresh fish market* which fills quai des Belges at the old port from 8 am to noon. The *fishmonger (Map C; ☎ 04 91 33 76 09, 24 quai de Rive Neuve)* opens from 5 am to 1 pm. Equally aromatic is the *marché d'ail* (garlic market) held in season on cours Belsunce. Fruit, vegetables, fish and dried products are sold at the *Marché des Capucins (Map C; place des Capucins, 1er; metro Noailles)*, daily from 8 am to 7 pm, and at the *morning market* on cours Pierre Puget *(Map M; 6e; metro Estrangin Préfecture)* on Monday, Wednesday and Friday.

Organic groceries are sold at *Bio-Nature (Map M; 64 cours Lieutaud)*. The *Monoprix* supermarket (Map C) at the northern end of rue de Rome opens 8.30 am to 8.30 pm Monday to Saturday. The shop-sized *Petit Casino food dispenser (Map M; 96 La Canabière)* functions 24 hours.

For *foie gras* (duck liver paté) and Provençal wines, shop at *Ducs de Gascogne (Map C; 39 rue Paradis, 1er)*. *Puyricard (Map C; 25 rue Francis Davso, 1er)* sells chocolate, while *La Casertaine*, an Italian *épicerie* (grocery shop) at 71 rue Francis Davso, 1er, specialises in authentic pasta, artichoke hearts and so on.

Traditional breads and pastries are baked

at *Boulangerie-Pâtisserie Aixoise (45 rue Francis Davso, 1er)*. For baklava and other calorie-loaded pastries, try *Pâtisserie Orientale (Map C; 28 rue Pavillon)* or *Djerba La Douce (Map M; 36 rue des Trois Mages)*, two Middle Eastern patisseries.

ENTERTAINMENT

Cultural event listings appear in the monthly *Vox Mag* and weekly *Taktik*, which has a Web site at www.taktik.presse.fr (French only). Both can be picked up for free at the tourist office, cinemas and at the following *billetteries* (ticket counters) where you can buy tickets for most cultural events: in FNAC (☎ 04 91 39 94 00; metro Vieux Port) on the top floor of the Centre Bourse shopping mall, 1er; the Virgin Megastore (☎ 04 91 55 55 11; metro Estrangin Préfecture), 75 rue St-Ferréol, 1er; and the Office de la Culture (☎ 04 96 11 04 61, 04 96 11 04 70, e office.culture. marseille.com@wanadoo.fr; metro Vieux Port), 42 La Canebière, 1er.

Espace Julien (Map M; ☎ 04 91 24 34 14, 39 cours Julien, 6e; metro Notre Dame du Mont-Cours Julien) is a leading venue for rock concerts, opérock, alternative theatre, reggae festivals, hip hop, Afro-groove and other cutting-edge entertainment.

Pubs & Bars

Quai de Rive Neuve (Map C; 7e; metro Vieux Port) is lined with places to drink and be merry: *O'Malleys* at No 9 and *Shamrock* at No 17 are two Irish watering holes. Pagnol drank at *Bar de la Marine* at No 15, while *Scandale Café*, also at No 17, lures a young and bolshy crowd which drinks beer until 5 am at weekends. Across the water (take the ferry boat), *La Caravelle (Map C; ☎ 04 91 90 36 64, 34 quai du Port, 2e)* is less in-your-face but just as trendy. The boat-inspired bar, hidden on the 1st floor of Hôtel Bellevue, hosts live jazz concerts.

There are more bohemian pubs and bars around cours Julien (Map M; metro Notre Dame du Mont-Cours Julien, 6e). *Marseil Café* inside La Passerelle (see Cafes & Fast Food earlier in the section) is among the most popular.

Discos & Clubs

Play pétanque underground at *Le Trolleybus (Map M; ☎ 04 91 54 30 45, 04 91 48 71 84, 24 quai de Rive Neuve, 7e; metro Vieux Port)*, a nightclub in an 18th-century warehouse, open 11 pm to 6 am Thursday to Saturday. For salsa, Latino and other hot jives, try *Cubaïla Café* (see Restaurants – Ethnic Cuisine earlier in the section), a trendy Tex-Mex restaurant which hosts a disco from Thursday to Saturday. *La Machine à Coudre (☎ 04 91 55 62 65, 6 rue Jean Roque, 1er; metro Noailles)*, tucked in a small street off the southern end of blvd Garibaldi, plays funk, punk, blues and rap from 10 pm to 2 am Tuesday to Saturday.

Gay & Lesbian Venues

Le Chaperon Rouge is the name of a bi-monthly gay listings magazine and the name of a gay cafe *(Map C; ☎ 04 91 91 01 17, e maec@france.qrd.org, 20 rue Colbert)*.

Popular gay spots for a drink include *L'Énigme (Map C; ☎ 04 91 33 79 20, 22 rue Beauvau, 1er; metro Vieux Port)* and *MP Bar (☎ 04 91 33 64 79)* at No 10 on the same street. Camper than a row of tents and full of fun is *New Cancan (Map M; ☎ 04 91 48 59 76, 3 rue Sénac de Meilhan, 1er; metro Noailles or Réformés-Canebière)*, Marseilles' best-known gay nightclub, open until 6 am.

Opera & Ballet

The lovely *Opéra de Marseille (Map C; ☎ 04 91 55 11 10, 2 rue Molière, 1er; metro Vieux Port)* is an Art Deco building dating from 1921. Tickets for performances cost between 55FF and 340FF. In June and July, performances are staged at *Théâtre Silvain*, an open-air amphitheatre midway between plage des Catalans and plage du Prophète on corniche Président John F Kennedy, 7e.

Theatre

Marseilles has an active alternative theatre scene. Venues include *Chocolat Théâtre (Map M; ☎ 04 91 42 19 29, 59 cours Julien, 6e; metro Notre Dame du Mont-Cours Julien)*, a comedy theatre which doubles

OM

Olympique de Marseille (OM) is not just another football team – it's an institution backed by a cityful of fans who sing *'Nous sommes les Marseillais! Et nous allons gagner!'* ('We are the Marseillais! And we will win!') both in and out of the stadium.

Guided tours of OM's home ground, the **Stade Vélodrome** (metro Pond Point du Prado), 3 blvd Michelet, 8e, kick off from the stadium six times per day Monday to Saturday, mid-June to 31 August. Tours cost 30FF (students and those aged five to 18, 15FF) and last one hour. Built in 1930, the stadium can seat up to 60,000 screaming spectators. Outside the stadium is **Musée-Boutique de l'OM** (☎ 04 91 71 46 00), a museum that unravels the history of the club from its creation in 1899. The museum opens 2 to 7.30 pm on Monday, and 9 am to 7. 30 pm Tuesday to Saturday (free admission).

Tickets for matches (about 100FF to 250FF), the club's blue-and-white shirts, scarves and other OM paraphernalia are sold at the Musée-Boutique at the stadium; or at Boutiques Officielles OM in town (metro Vieux Port, 1er) at 44 La Canebière (☎ 04 91 33 52 28), open 2.30 to 7 pm on Monday, and 10 am to 7 pm Tuesday to Saturday; and 3 quai des Belges (☎/fax 04 91 33 96 75), open 10.30 am to 7 pm. The latter adjoins **Café OM** (☎ 04 91 33 80 33), the club cafe-cum-bar where supporters who fail to score a ticket can be found during matches staring agog at the TV screen.

OM has an official Web site at www.olympiquedemarseille.com.

as a restaurant; pocket-sized *Théâtre Off (Map C; ☎ 04 91 33 12 92, 16 quai de Rive Neuve, 7e; metro Vieux Port)*, with performances (60FF) most evenings at 8.30 pm; and cafe theatre *Le Quai du Rire (☎ 04 91 54 95 00 16, quai de Rive Neuve, 7e; metro Vieux Port)* where you can watch comedy while you dine (250FF including dinner).

Mainstream dramas are hosted at *Théâtre National de Marseille (Map C; ☎ 04 91 54 70 54, e tnmlacriee@wanadoo.fr, 30 quai de Rive Neuve, 7e; metro Vieux Port)*, inside Marseilles' old fish auction house dating to 1909. The repertoire at the municipal theatre, *Odéon (☎ 04 91 92 79 44, 162 La 'Canebière, 1er; metro Vieux Port)*, is varied.

Cinema

The two cinemas, *Cinéma Variétés (☎ 04 96 11 61 61, e cesarvarietes@intfrance.com, 37 rue Vincent Scotto, 1er; metro Noailles)* and sister *Cinéma César (☎ 04 91 37 12 80, 4 place Castellane, 6e; metro Castellane)*, show foreign films in their original language. Tickets cost about 38FF.

SHOPPING

Cours Julien (Map M; metro Notre Dame du Mont-Cours Julien), 6e, hosts various morning markets: fresh flowers on Wednesday and Saturday, fruit and veg on Friday, antique books every second Saturday; and stamps or antique books on Sunday. Stalls laden with everything from second-hand clothing to pots and pans fill nearby place Jean Jaurès on Saturday from 8 am to 1 pm.

The best place to shop for traditional Provençal santons is the boutique inside the Musée du Santon (see the boxed text 'Little Saints' earlier in this chapter). Marseillais soaps can be bought at La Compagnie de Provence (Map C; ☎ 04 91 56 20 94; metro Colbert or Vieux Port), 1 rue Caisserie, 2e, which specialises in self-pampering products made from Provençal herbs, plants and ochre. Its lavender shower-gel, thyme- and rosemary-scented *eau de linge*, shaving cream with clay, body lotion with olive oil and tasty choice of soaps (almond, vanilla, honeysuckle, honey, rose) are all irresistible.

GETTING THERE & AWAY
Air

Marseilles-Provence airport (Aéroport International Marseille-Provence; ☎ 04 42 14 14 14) is 25km north-west of Marseilles in Marignane. It has a Web site at www .marseilleaeroport.fr,

Bus

The bus station (Gare Autocars de Marseille; Map M; ☎ 04 91 08 16 40; metro Gare St-Charles), place Victor Hugo, 3e, is 150m to the right as you exit the train station. The information counter doubles as a left-luggage office (10FF per day). Tickets are sold at the ticket counters or by bus drivers. Some buses from Bandol, La Ciotat and Cassis use place Castellane (metro Castellane), south of the centre, 6e.

Marseilles is served by buses from Aix-en-Provence (26FF, 35 minutes via the autoroute/one hour via the N8, every 15 minutes between 5 am and 8.15 pm). Other services include two to four buses daily to/from Cassis (22FF, 1¼ hours), La Ciotat (25FF, one hour to 1½ hours), Draguignan (three hours), Digne-les-Bains (80FF, 2½ hours), Manosque (53FF, 1½ hours), Sisteron (82FF, 2½ hours), Carpentras (two hours), Cavaillon (60FF, one hour) and other destinations. There are some seven buses per day to/from Avignon (93FF, two hours). Buses to/from Arles (26FF, two hours, five daily except Sunday) stop in Salon de Provence (1¾ hours), Les Baux de Provence (1½ hours) and Fontvieille (1¾ hours).

During the ski season, SCAL (☎ 04 92 51 06 05 in Gap) runs a daily bus in either direction to Pra-Loup (124FF, 3¾ hours) via Digne-les-Bains and Barcelonnette (124FF, 2½ hours).

At the bus station, Eurolines (☎ 04 91 50 57 55) opens 9 am to 6 pm Monday to Saturday and Intercars (☎ 04 91 50 08 66, e intercars.marseille@wanadoo.fr) opens 9.15 to 11.30 am and 2 to 5.30, 5.45 or 6 pm weekdays, and 10 to 11.45 am and 2 to 4.40 pm on Saturday. Route and fare details are included in the Getting There & Away chapter.

Train

Marseilles' passenger train station, served by both metro lines and under renovation until 2003, is called Gare St-Charles (metro Gare St-Charles). The information and ticket reservation office is one level below the tracks, next to the metro entrance, and opens 9 am to 8 pm Monday to Saturday. The luggage lockers, next to the tracks on platform A, are accessible from 7.15 am to 10 pm (15/20/30FF for a small/medium/large locker per 72 hours). The toilets (2.80FF) and showers on the same platform open 6.30 am to 8 pm and cost 18FF.

In town, train tickets can be bought at the SNCF Boutiques at 17 rue Grignan, 1er, and in the Centre Bourse shopping centre, both open 9.30 am to 5 pm weekdays.

There are direct trains to Aix-en-Provence (59FF, 40 minutes, 16 to 24 daily), Nîmes (116FF, 1½ hours, 10 daily) via Arles (81FF, 50 minutes), Orange (109FF, 1½ hours, five to seven per day), Avignon (102FF, one hour, hourly) and numerous other destinations. Heading east along the coast, over two dozen trains per day chug on the Marseilles–Ventimiglia (Vintimille in French) line, linking Marseilles with Toulon, Les Arcs-sur-Argens, St-Raphaël (135FF, 1¾ hours), Cannes (113FF, two hours), Antibes (159FF, 2¼ hours), Nice (169FF, 2½ hours), Monaco (179FF, three hours) and Menton (180FF, 3¼ hours).

The Marseilles–Hyères train (72FF, 1¼ hours, four daily) stops en route at Cassis, La Ciotat, Bandol, Ollioules, Sanary-sur-Mer and Toulon. Hourly trains from Marseilles to Les Arcs-sur-Argens (121FF, 1½ hours) stop in Toulon (78FF, 45 minutes).

Trains to other destinations in France and Europe are listed in the Getting There & Away chapter.

Car & Motorcycle

Avis (☎ 04 91 64 71 00) has a desk at the train station. ADL-Thrifty (☎ 04 91 95 00 00) is at 8 place Marseillaises, Eurloc Rent-a-Car (☎ 04 91 50 12 00) is at No 10 on the same square, Europcar (☎ 04 91 99 40 90) is at 7 blvd Maurice Bourdet and Hertz (☎ 04 91 14 04 24) is at 16 blvd Nédelec.

Boat

Marseilles' passenger ferry terminal (Gare Maritime; ☎ 04 91 56 38 63, fax 04 91 56 38 70; metro Joliette) is 250m west of place de la Joliette, 2e.

SNCM ferries (Map M; ☎ 08 36 67 95 00, fax 04 91 56 35 86) link Marseilles with

Corsica, Sardinia, Tunisia, Spain and Algeria. SNCM's office (metro Joliette), 61 blvd des Dames, 2e, opens 8 am to 6 pm weekdays and 8.30 am to noon on Saturday.

Algérie Ferries (Map C; ☎ 04 91 90 64 70; metro Joliette), 29 blvd des Dames, 2e, opens 8.15 to 11.45 am and 1 to 4.45 pm weekdays. Ticketing and reservations for the Tunisian ferry company, Compagnie Tunisienne de Navigation (CTN), are handled by SNCM. For more information see Sea in the Getting There & Away chapter.

GETTING AROUND
To/From the Airport
Shuttle buses operated by Transports Routiers Passagers Aériens (TRPA; ☎ 04 91 50 59 34 in Marseilles, ☎ 04 42 14 31 27 at the airport) link Marseilles–Provence airport with Marseilles train station (47/27FF for adult/child aged six to 10). Buses to the airport leave from in front of the train station's main entrance at 5.30 and 5.55 am and then every 20 minutes from 6.10 am to 9.50 pm; buses from the airport depart at 6.15 am, every 20 minutes from 6.30 am to 8.50 pm, and at 9.15, 9.40, 10, 10.20 and 10.50 pm. The journey time is 25 minutes.

Bus & Metro
Marseilles has two fast, well-maintained metro lines called Métro 1 and Métro 2, a tramline, and an extensive bus network. They are all operated by Régie des Transports de Marseille (RTM), which runs an Espace Infos-RTM (☎ 04 91 91 92 10, metro Vieux Port) at 6 rue des Fabres, 1er. It opens 8.30 am to 6 pm weekdays and 9 am to 5.30 pm on Saturday. RTM has a Web site at www.lepilote.com (French only).

The metro (which began operation in 1977), trams and most buses run from about 5 am to 9 pm. From 9.25 pm to 12.30 am, metro and tram routes are covered every 15 minutes by surface bus Nos M1 and M2, and tramway No 68; stops are marked with fluorescent green signs reading *métro en bus* (metro by bus). Most 'Fluobus' night buses begin their runs in front of the Espace Infos-RTM office.

Bus/metro tickets (9FF) can be used on

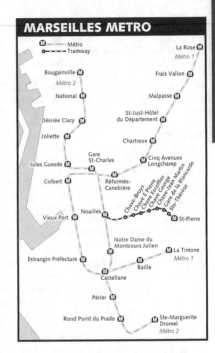

any combination of metro, bus and tram for one hour after they've been time-stamped (no return trips). A six-day carnet/one-day pass costs 42/25FF. Tram stops have modern blue ticket distributors to time-stamp your ticket before you board.

Taxi
There's a taxi rank in front of the train station (Map M). Marseille Taxi (☎ 04 91 02 20 20), Radio Taxi France (☎ 04 91 85 80 00) and Taxi Blanc Bleu (☎ 04 91 51 50 00) dispatch taxis 24 hours a day.

Boat
The hot and bothered who can't face walking another footstep can indulge in the shortest boat ride on the Riviera, a trip immortalised by Marcel Pagnol. Between June and August, a ferry (Ligne au Ferryboat; ☎ 04 91 55 31 32) yo-yos between the town hall on quai du Port and place aux Huiles on quai de Rive Neuve. It sails 8 am

to 6.30 pm Sunday to Friday, and 8 am to 8.30 pm on Saturday. A single/return fare costs 3/5FF (children aged under seven, free). Sailing time is about two minutes.

Boat taxis operate a 24-hour service (☎ 04 91 55 50 09 or 06 09 95 89 26 after 8.30 pm) from the eastern end of quai du Port.

Bicycle

MBK-Cycles DO (☎ 04 91 54 33 14 or 04 91 33 65 57), 68–76 cours Lieutaud, has mountain bikes and scooters to rent. It opens 10 am to 7 pm Tuesday to Saturday. Near Plage du Prado, Cycles Ulysse (☎ 04 91 77 14 51), 3 ave du Parc Borély, and Tandem (☎ 04 91 22 64 80) at No 6 on the same street, are two other rental outlets.

Les Calanques

Since 1975, this 20km strip of coast, and inland Massif des Calanques covering 5000 hectares, has been protected as a natural monument.

Summer forest fires are a continual threat to the semi-arid flora that skirts the limestone coastline, and the Office National des Forêts closes the massif interior each year from the third weekend in June until the second Saturday in September (see Ecology & Environment in the Facts about Provence chapter for more information).

Despite its barren landscape, the massif shelters an extraordinary wealth of flora and fauna – including 900 plant species of which 15 are protected, such as the dwarf red behen, Marseilles astragalus and tartonraire sparrow wort. Myrtle and wild olive trees grow in the warmer valleys. The Bonnelli eagle is a frequent visitor to Les Calanques, which give shelter to Europe's largest lizard and longest snake – the eyed lizard (60cm) and the Montpellier snake (2m) – in their darker cracks and crevices.

Les Calanques offer ample walking opportunities, including the coastal **GR98** which leads south from the Marseilles suburb of **La Madrague** to Callelongue on **Cap Croisette**, and then eastwards along the

coast to Cassis. Count on 11 to 12 hours at least to walk this 28km stretch. See Along the Coast in the Marseilles Walking Tours section earlier in this chapter for bus information from Marseilles to Callelongue.

Boat excursions in Les Calanques set sail from Marseilles, Cassis and La Ciotat, as well as Bandol, Sanary-sur-Mer and Le Brusc (see the St-Tropez to Toulon chapter).

SORMIOU & MORGIOU

There are plenty of shorter, marked trails (inaccessible from late June to mid-September), the most popular being those that lead to **Calanque de Sormiou** and neighbouring **Calanque de Morgiou**.

Sormiou, the largest calanque, hit the headlines in October 1991 when Henri Cosquer, a diver from Cassis (see that section on the next page) discovered an underwater cave here. Its interior was adorned with prehistoric wall paintings dating from around 20,000 BC. The only access to the cave was a narrow, 150m-long passage, 36m underwater. Named the Grotte Cosquer, the cave is protected as a historical monument and closed to the public today. Many more are believed to exist here.

To get here by car from place Louis Bonnefon (next to Château Borély) in Marseilles, follow the southbound ave de Hambourg past César's thumb on rond point Pierre Guerre to chemin de Sormiou. From the end of this road, the route du Feu forest track (a 45-minute walk) leads to Sormiou's small fishing port and beach in the Calanque. By bus, take No 23 from the Rond Point du Prado metro stop to La Cayolle stop, from where it is a 3km walk to Sormiou.

Sormiou and Morgiou are separated by the headland Cap Morgiou. **Calanque de Morgiou** nestles on the eastern side of the cape. During the 17th century, Louis XIII came to Marseilles to fish for tuna in the bay. From ave de Hambourg, follow the Morgiou road signs past Marseilles' infamous prison in Les Beaumettes. Morgiou beach is one hour's walk from the car park. By bus, take No 23 and continue past La Cayolle. Get off at the Morgiou-Beauvallon bus stop.

EN VAU, PORT PIN & PORT MIOU

Continuing eastwards along the stone sculptured coast you come to **Calanque d'En Vau** which, with its emerald waters encased by cliffs occasionally studded with dangling rope-clad climbers, is the most photographed calanque. Its entrance is guarded by **Doigt de Dieu**, a giant rock pinnacle, and its beach is pebbly. En Vau is accessible by foot. There is a three-hour marked trail starting from the car park on the Col de la Gardiole (south off the D559), 5km from Cassis on a wiggly dirt road into the Forêt de la Gardiole. Approaching from the east, it is a good 1½-hour walk on the GR98 from Port Miou. En route you pass neighbouring **Calanque de Port Pin**, a 30-minute walk from Port Miou.

In summer, boats sail from Cassis to En Vau. **Calanque de Port Miou**, immediately west of Cassis, is one of the few inlets accessible by car; the tourist office in Cassis distributes free maps featuring the three Calanques plus the various walking trails which lead to them.

CASSIS

postcode 13260 • pop 8070

Sweet little Cassis is best known for its white wines, of which Provençal poet Frédéric Mistral wrote 'the bee does not have a sweeter honey, it shines like an untroubled diamond...' Quality aside, the neat picture-postcard appearance of Cassis' terraced vineyards, which climb up the slopes in little steps against a magnificent backdrop of sea and cliffs, can hardly be disputed.

Unfortunately, the fishing port – complete with a 14th-century chateau, views of Baie de Cassis and France's highest cliff – is a hub for summer boat trips along the Calanques and gets overrun with camera-happy tourists. An open-air market fills place du Marché on Wednesday and Friday morning. Stalls to look out for include one which sells the sweetest, moistest, freshest sultana bread in Provence, and another which displays a rainbow of scented soaps.

Cassis (pronounced ca-see) has nothing to do with the blackcurrant liqueur (pronounced ca-sees) which is mixed with white wine to create an aperitif called kir.

Orientation & Information

Cassis train station, ave de Gare, is just over 3km east of the centre. Buses stop at rond point du Pressoir, five minutes' walk along ave du Professeur René Leriche and rue de l'Arène to the port. The old town surrounds the port. Its medieval chateau – privately owned and closed to visitors – peers down on the port atop a rocky outcrop. Quai St-Pierre, from where boat trips depart, runs alongside the port to the beach, sandy Plage de la Grande Mer. Pebbly Plage de Bestouan is 700m north-west of the port.

To get to the tourist office from quai St-Pierre, walk southwards along rue Barthélemy, across place Clémenceau, then continue farther south along rue de l'Arène, and cut through the Jardin Public to place Baragnon. The tourist office (☎ 04 42 01 71 17, fax 04 42 01 28 31, e omt-cassis@enprovence.com) opens 9 am to noon and 2.30 to 5.30 pm weekdays and 9 am to noon on Saturday. In 2001 a new tourist office will open in the portside Oustaou Calendal, a 14.5 million FF reconstruction of the infamous casino at the port where hearts were won and lost following its opening in 1951. The tourist office has a Web site at www.cassis.enprovence.com.

There's a 24-hour banknote change machine at the port end of rue de l'Arène, outside Crédit Mutuel.

Boat Excursions

Year round, boats take tourists on trips around Les Calanques. Tickets for the 15-odd daily boats are sold at the kiosk on square Gilbert Savon, the gravel area that doubles as a pétanque pitch opposite the boats moored alongside quai St-Pierre: a 45-minute trip to three Calanques (Port Miou, Port Pin and En-Vau) costs 50FF; a 65-minute trip covering the latter plus Oule and Devanson Calanques is 70FF; and a 1½-hour trip taking in seven Calanques (including Morgiou) costs 90FF. A ticket for a child aged under 10 costs 30/50/70FF respectively (children aged under two, free).

In addition to the circular boat trips, you can disembark at En Vau, spend a couple of hours on the beach here, then sail back to Cassis on a later boat. A return fare costs 70FF (children aged two to 10, 50FF). Wear sturdy shoes as the climb from the boat to the beach is across rocks, a scramble not recommended for young children.

Between July and early September, a glass-bottomed boat (☎ 04 42 73 11 15, 06 13 23 88 42) sails from quai St-Pierre every evening at 10.30 pm. The 1¼-hour trip costs 60FF (children aged two to 10, 50FF) and includes an underwater *son et lumière* (sound-and-light show).

Diving

Diving expeditions are organised by the Centre Cassidain de Plongée (☎ 04 42 01 89 16, fax 04 42 01 23 76, ⓔ henri .cosquer@cassis-services-plongee.fr), 3 rue Michel Arnaud. It's Web site is at www .cassis-services-plongee.fr. The school is run by Henri Cosquer (see Sormiou & Morgiou earlier in this chapter for details). A baptism dive costs 300FF. Half-/full-day and night dives, and shipwreck expeditions are available.

Wine Tasting

There is no better time to taste the local vino than at the annual Fête des Vendanges et du Vin Cassis, celebrated to mark the grape harvest on the first Sunday in September. Failing that, you can visit one of the 13 *domaines* (wine-producing estates) that produce the Cassis appellation (AOC). Just 168 hectares of land are carpeted with terrace vineyards which yield 600,000 to 700,000 bottles of whites, reds and rosés a year. Heading south-eastwards along route des Crêtes (the D141), you pass **Domaine du Bagnol** (☎ 04 42 01 78 05), 12 ave de Provence. There are more estates on route de La Ciotat; the tourist office can provide you with a list.

Cassis white wine is particularly tasty drunk with oursins (sea urchins). See the Cap Couronne & Carry-le-Rouet section later in this chapter for more details about that delicacy.

Places to Stay

Cassis has one camp site, ***Camping Les Cigales*** (☎ 04 42 01 07 34, ave de la Marne), 1km uphill from the port off route de Marseille. It charges 76FF per night for two people with tent and car, and opens March to mid-November. Buses to/from Marseilles will stop outside if you ask.

Isolated in the heart of the Massif des Calanques is the ***Auberge de Jeunesse*** (☎ 04 42 01 02 72), 3km west of Cassis centre. It has no running water, is one hour's walk from the nearest road and you have to bring your own food. By car, follow the signs off the D559 from Marseilles, park and then follow the trail from the end of ave des Calanques in Port Miou. Reception opens 8 to 10 am and 5 to 9 pm; the hostel opens year round and charges 69FF per night (50FF to HI card-holders).

Hôtel du Commerce (☎ 04 42 01 09 10, fax 04 42 01 14 17, 1 rue St-Clair), 20m north of the port, has one-star doubles costing 200FF. Rooms for two at ***Hôtel Le Liautaud*** (☎ 04 42 01 75 37, fax 04 42 01 12 08, 2 rue Victor Hugo), overlooking the port, or pretty ***Hôtel Cassitel*** (☎ 04 42 01 96 31, fax 04 42 01 83 44, place Clémenceau) cost around 350FF.

Cassis' classiest joint is ochre-coloured ***Le Jardin d'Émile*** (☎ 04 42 01 80 70, fax 04 42 01 80 55), set beneath trees opposite Plage de Bestouan. Six doubles with garden/sea view cost 450/650FF and its restaurant has 180FF and 295FF *menus*; bouillabaisse royale costs 245FF per person (order 24 hours in advance). Next door, white ***Hôtel de la Plage*** (☎ 04 42 01 05 70, fax 04 42 01 34 82, ⓔ plage-bestouan@ enprovence.com) offers a sweeping vista of Plage de Bestouan from its ocean-view rooms (500/650FF in low/high season).

The quays overlooking the port are lined with touristy places to eat, all with outside terraces.

Getting There & Away

Cassis (☎ 04 42 08 41 05) is on the Bandol–Marseilles and La Ciotat–Aix-en-Provence bus routes. Buses from Marseilles/Aix arrive at rond point du Pressoir on ave du 11

Novembre 1918; buses to Marseilles/Aix depart from the stop around the corner on ave de Provence. Cassis is served by four to six buses daily on each route; a single fare to Marseilles costs 22FF (1¼ hours).

Cassis is on the Marseilles–Hyères rail line and has regular daily trains in both directions including to/from La Ciotat (13FF, 7 minutes), Bandol (26FF, 20 minutes), Toulon (40FF, 30 minutes) and Marseilles (29FF, 22 minutes).

Getting Around

Carnoux Bikes (☎ 04 42 01 79 20), inside the Renault Garage des Calanques on route de la Ciotat, overlooking rond point du Pressoir, rents bicycles/scooters/mopeds for 60/190/290FF per day.

CAP CANAILLE & ROUTE DES CRÊTES

The south-western side of Baie de Cassis is dominated by imposing **Cap Canaille**, a rocky limestone cape from which one of Europe's highest maritime cliffs (416m) rises. Its hollow peak hides **Grotte des Espagnols** (Spaniards' Cave), which is filled with a magical assortment of stalactites and stalagmites, and cannot be visited. From the cliff there are magnificent views of Cassis and Mont Puget (565m), the highest peak in the Massif des Calanques.

From Cassis, well-maintained **route des Crêtes** (literally 'road of crests') wiggles along the top of the cliff-caked coastline to La Ciotat, 16km east. En route there are numerous spots to pull in, park up and partake in the awesome panorama that unfolds as you drive along.

LA CIOTAT

The rusty old cranes cranked up over the shipyards of La Ciotat (pop 30,620; La Ciéutat in Provençal), 16km east of Cassis, lost their glean long ago. The naval shipyards, which enjoyed their heyday in the interwar period, have since closed. Facing the shipyards is La Ciotat's quaint Vieux Port (old port), a favourite of Braque (1892–1963) who painted it several times. Behind the yards rises the imposing **Bec d'Aigle**

(155m), a rocky massif on Cap de l'Aigle, the peak of which resembles the head of a bird of prey – hence its name (literally 'eagle's beak'). The ensemble – protected under the Parc Marin de la Ciotat – is best viewed from **Île Verte** (Green Island), a minuscule island offshore from the cape's south-eastern tip.

The world premier of the first ever movie was screened in La Ciotat in September 1895, courtesy of the pioneering Lumière brothers who filmed the motion picture at La Ciotat train station and then showed it for the first time at their father's chateau in the town. The history of the film, called *L'arrivée d'un train en gare de La Ciotat* (The arrival of a train at La Ciotat station), comes to life in the **Espace Simon Lumière** (☎ 04 42 71 61 70), an exhibition hall dedicated to filmography on rue du Maréchal Foch. La Ciotat remains home to the world's oldest picture house, the Eden Théâtre, overlooking the modern pleasure port from the corner of blvd Anatole France and blvd Jean Jaurès.

The tourist office (☎ 04 42 08 61 32, fax 04 42 08 17 88, ⓔ info@asther.com), blvd Anatole France, on the headland separating the old port from the new pleasure port, distributes a free English-language brochure which guides visitors around La Ciotat *In the Footsteps of the Lumière Brothers*.

La Ciotat hosts a morning market on Tuesday on place Evariste Gras, the square in front of the modern Cinéma Lumière. A nocturnal arts and crafts market (8 pm to 1 am) fills the old port quays in July and August. Pétanque – Provence's favourite game – was invented by boules player Jules Lenoir in La Ciotat in 1907 (see the boxed text 'Polish Your Boules' under spectator sports in the Facts for the Visitor chapter).

Getting There & Away

The train station is a 5km trek from La Ciotat centre. La Ciotat is served by frequent trains on the Marseilles–Hyères line (see Cassis earlier in this chapter). Buses use the more convenient bus station (☎ 04 42 08 90 90), adjoining the tourist office at the western end of blvd Anatole France. There are regular buses (☎ 04 42 08 41 05) to Marseilles via Cassis and Aix-en-Provence.

La Ciotat is midway between Marseilles and Toulon; from Cassis the most direct route is the inland D559 (bypassing route des Crêtes).

North of Marseilles

AROUND THE ÉTANG DE BERRE

Oil refineries adorn the port area around the waters of Étang de Berre, while **Marignane** (pop 34,238), on its south-eastern shore, is dominated by Marseilles-Provence airport. **Istres**, on the western shore of Étang de Berre, is best known for its military airport which has been here since 1914.

A horrifying view of this vast industrial landscape can be scowled at from the ruins of an 11th-century Saracen tower bizarrely perched on top of a rock in **Vitrolles** (pop 37,087). Across the waters, the Canal de Caronte links the reasonably attractive fishing port of **Martigues** (pop 44,256), on the south-western corner of Étang de Berre, with Golfe de Fos in the Mediterranean. It is from Martigues (tourist office ☎ 04 42 42 31 10, e ot.martigues@visitprovence.com) that the national French flag originates. Unattractive **Fos-sur-Mer** is a starting point for guided forays into this industrial heartland; the tourist office (☎ 04 42 47 71 96, e tourismefossurmer@visitprovence.com) can arrange tours (30FF) of the Solomat Merex industrial waste processing plant, the Shell oil refinery, Elf's chlorine and sodium works, and the distillation site of petroleum magnet Esso. It also takes bookings for jolly boat rides around Fos-sur-Mer's industrial port (60FF).

Pockets of crystal clear skies and blue waters still exist thanks to the **Chaîne de l'Estaque**, a harsh, uninhabitable massif which forms a natural blockade between industrial Étang de Berre and the Mediterranean. The rocky limestone coastal stretch on the protected southern side of the massif from Cap Couronne to Marseilles is known as Côte Bleue (Blue Coast).

Cap Couronne & Carry-le-Rouet

From Martigues the D5 leads 10km south to **Cap Couronne**, a cape with a large sandy beach that draws plenty of Marseillais at weekends. The waters around it are protected by the Parc Régional Marin de la Côte Bleue, one of the region's first marine reserves set up in 1983 to safeguard and revive marine life. The protected zone – which does not actually touch the coastline – is marked with yellow buoys topped with St-Andrew's crosses. The park headquarters (☎ 04 42 45 45 07), Club de la Mer, BP 37, 13960 Sausset-les-Pins, organises guided snorkelling expeditions for free departing at 9.30, 10.30 and 11.30 am on Tuesday, Thursday and Saturday in July and August. Advance reservations are recommended.

One of the region's most unique gastronomic delights – *oursins* (sea urchins) – can be sampled in **Carry-le-Rouet** (pop 6107), a busy harbour town favoured by French comic actor Fernandel in the 1930s. The oprickly little creatures – dubbed *châtaignes de mer* (sea chestnuts) – are only caught between September and April (fishing for them is forbidden in summer when the urchins reproduce).

Each year, on the first three Sundays of February, Carry-le-Rouet celebrates **L'Oursinade**, its annual sea urchin festival which sees a giant open-air picnic spill across the quays around the old port. Restaurants and hotels set up stalls selling urchin platters, allowing everyone – tourists and locals alike – to indulge in a *dégustation* (tasting) session around shared tables. The creatures are reportedly best served with chilled Cassis white wine.

Carry-le-Rouet tourist office (☎ 04 42 13 20 36, fax 04 42 44 52 03, e ot.carrylerouet @visitprovence.com), near the port on ave Aristide Briand, has details on Cap Couronne's numerous camp sites, Carry's three hotels and surrounding *chambres d'hôtes*.

L'Estaque

East of Carry-le-Rouet by 17km is L'Estaque, a once-untouched fishing village adjoining Marseilles' northern suburbs, which, like St-Tropez, lured artists from the impressionist, Fauvist and cubist movements. Renoir, Cézanne, Dufy and Braque painted numerous canvases during their sojourns here, although the only piece that remains in the region is Dufy's *L'Usine à L'Estaque* (Factory at L'Estaque), displayed in Marseilles' Musée Cantini. The English-language brochure entitled *L'Estaque and the Painters*, distributed for free by Marseilles' tourist office, is handy for travellers interested in the artists' trail.

Snacks unique to L'Estaque and ideal for a munch while strolling the water's edge include *chichi freggi* (sugar-coated doughnuts) and *panisses* (chickpea flour cakes). Both are sold at kiosks around the harbour.

Getting There & Away

From Marseilles there are more than a dozen trains daily (less in winter) along La Côte Bleue as far as Port de Bouc (44FF, 55 minutes), from where the train line heads inland to Miramas on the northern shore of the Étang de Berre. From Marseilles trains stop at L'Estaque (13FF, 10 minutes),Carryle-Rouet (27FF, 20 minutes), La Couronne (35FF, 40 minutes) and Miramas (49FF, 1¼ hours).

See the Getting Around chapter for details of train passes available on this route.

AIX-EN-PROVENCE

postcode 13100 • pop 137,067

Aix (Ais in Provençal) was founded as a military camp under the name of Aquae Sextiae (the Waters of Sextius) in 123 BC on the site of thermal springs, which still flow. Fortunately for stuck-up Aix the settlement consequently became known as Aix – not Sex. The city reached its zenith as a centre of art and learning under the enlightened King René (1409–80), a brilliant polyglot who brought painters to his court from all around Europe. The city remains an academic centre today thanks to the University of Aix-Marseilles, whose forerunner was established in 1409 and which attracts a student population of about 30,000.

Some 200 elegant *hôtels particuliers* (private mansions) grace Aix's squares and avenues. Many, exhibiting the unmistakable influence of Italian Baroque and coloured a distinctive Provençal yellow, date from the 17th and 18th centuries. Tree-covered cours Mirabeau is generally considered to be Provence's most beautiful street.

Orientation

Cours Mirabeau, Aix's main boulevard, stretches from La Rotonde, a roundabout with a huge fountain on place du Général de Gaulle, eastwards to place Forbin. The oldest part of the city, Vieil Aix, is north of cours Mirabeau; most of the streets, alleys and public squares in this part of town are closed to traffic. South of cours Mirabeau is the Quartier Mazarin, whose regular street grid was laid out in the 17th century. The entire city centre is ringed by a series of one-way boulevards.

Information

Tourist Offices Aix's tourist office (☎ 04 42 16 11 61, fax 04 42 16 11 62, [e] infos@ aixenprovencetourism.com), 2 place du Général de Gaulle, opens 8.30 am to 8 pm (to 10 pm in July and August) Monday to Saturday, and 10 am to 1 pm and 2 to 6 pm on Sunday. Staff can advise you on accommodation options (☎ 04 42 16 11 84/85, [e] resaix@aixenprovencetourism.com) and make hotel reservations for you. It has Web sites at www.aix-en-provence.com and www.aixenprovencetourism.com.

The Maison de la Nature et de l'Environnement (☎ 04 42 93 15 80), 2 place Jeanne d'Arc, is a green source for those seeking information on the environment and ways to explore it (nature walks, discovering Mediterranean flora and so on). It opens 10 am to noon and 2 to 7 pm Monday to Saturday.

The Provence-Alpes-Côte d'Azur's Office National des Forêts (ONF; ☎ 04 42 17 57 00) is at 15 ave Paul Cézanne.

Money Banque de France, 18 rue du 4 Septembre, changes currency from 9.15 am to 12.15 pm weekdays.

Commercial banks amass along cours Mirabeau and cours Sextius which runs

MARSEILLES AREA

AIX-EN-PROVENCE

PLACES TO STAY
7 Hôtel du Globe
28 Hôtel des Arts
42 Hôtel de France
46 Grand Hôtel
Nègre Coste
54 Hôtel Cardinale
57 Hôtel Cardinale
58 Hôtel des
Quatre Dauphins
75 Hôtel St-Christophe

PLACES TO EAT
8 Le Marais Provençal
13 Autour d'une Tarte
17 Boulangerie du Coin
19 Le Fournil de Maître Pains
23 Le Dernier Bistrot
30 Jacquèrres
32 Aux Pâtes Fraîches
32 Chez Maxime
38 Le Bistro Latin; Le Saf
39 Le Poivre d'Âne
40 Les Bacchanales

45 Monoprix
48 Les Deux Garçons
49 Boulangerie Tournefort
52 L'Épicerie Italienne
63 La Verre Bouteille
64 Gu et Fils
71 Yôji

MUSEUMS
3 Musée des Tapisseries
14 Musée du Vieil Aix
15 Galerie du Festival
44 Espace 13
56 Musée Granet
61 Musée Paul Arbaud

OTHER
1 Aix Micro
2 Cathédrale St-Sauveur
4 Institute of French
Studies
5 Thermes Sextius
6 Pavillon de
Vendôme

9 Cellier du 31
10 Virtu@lis
11 Cave du Felibrige
12 Town Hall
16 Le Comptoir des Oliviers
18 Laundrette
20 Aix G@mes
21 Cycles Zammit
22 Chapelle du Ste-Catherine
24 Hublot CyberCafe
25 Puyricard
26 Église de la Madeleine
27 Laundrette
32 Justice Palace
33 La Truffe Cendrée
34 Galaxy Pub
35 The Red Clover
36 Laundrette
37 Laundrette
41 Maison de la Nature et
de l'Environnement
43 L'Agence
47 Goulard Bookshop
50 Rich Art

51 Théâtre du
Jeu de Paume
53 Bremond
55 Église St-Jean de
Malte
59 Paradox Librairie
Internationale
60 Banque de France
62 Hôtel de Caumont
65 Hôtel d'Isoard
de Vauvenargues
66 Cinéma Renoir
67 John Taylor
68 Béchard
69 Cinéma Mazarin
70 Le Cézanne
72 Tourist Office
73 La Rotonde
74 Post Office
76 Pétanque
Court
77 Parc Jourdan;
Boulodrome Municipal
78 Bus Station

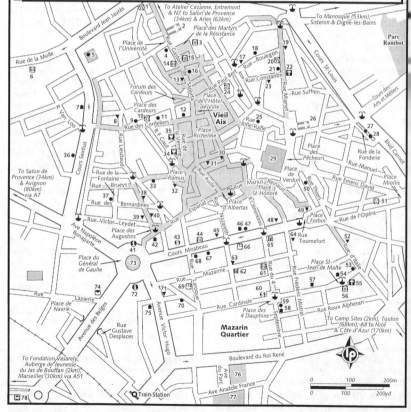

north–south to the west of La Rotonde. American Express agent, L'Agence (☎ 04 42 26 84 77), 15 cours Mirabeau, opens 9 am to 7.30 pm Monday to Saturday, and 10 am to 2 pm on Sunday, July and August; and 9 am to 6.30 pm weekdays, and 9 am to 1 pm and 2 to 5 pm on Saturday, the rest of the year.

Post & Communications The post office on the corner of ave des Belges and rue Lapierre opens 8.30 am to 6.45 pm weekdays, 8.30 am to noon on Saturday.

Hublot CyberCafe (☎ 04 42 21 37 31, ⓔhub1@mail.vif.fr), 15–27 rue Paul Bert, opens 9 am to 8 pm weekdays, and 10 am to 8 pm on Saturday. It charges 45/25FF per hour before/after 7 pm.

Virtu@lis (☎ 04 42 26 02 30, ⓔ virtualis @netcourrier.com), 40 rue des Cordeliers, charges 25FF per hour and opens 11 to 1 am Tuesday to Saturday, and 2 pm to 1 am Sunday and Monday. Both Aix Micro (☎ 04 42 23 48 84) at 2 blvd Jean Jaurès (open 10 to 1 am) and Aix G@mes (☎ 04 42 21 01 34), 31–33 rue Mignet (open 9 am to 10 pm) tout a 20FF hourly rate.

Bookshops Paradox Librairie Internationale (☎ 04 42 26 47 99), 15 rue du 4 Septembre, sells English-language novels and guidebooks, including Lonely Planet guides, and buys/sells second-hand books. It opens 9 am to 12.30 pm and 2 to 6.30 pm Monday to Saturday.

The Goulard bookshop, 35 cours Mirabeau, has a handful of English-language novels.

Libraries The American Library in Aix (☎ 04 42 23 02 82), 2 bis rue du Bon Pasteur, opens 2 to 7 pm Monday to Thursday and 2 to 6 pm on Friday.

Laundry Laundrettes abound: 3 rue de la Fontaine, 34 cours Sextius, 3 rue de la Fonderie and 60 rue Boulegon. All open 7 or 8 am to 8 pm.

Walking Tour

Aix's social scene centres on the pleasant cours Mirabeau, laid out during the latter half of the 1600s and named after the heroic revolutionary comte de Mirabeau. Trendy cafes adorned with young beauties basking in the shade of their sunglasses spill out onto the pavements on the sunny northern side of the street, which is crowned by a leafy rooftop of green plane trees. The shady southern side shelters a string of Renaissance hôtels particuliers. **Hôtel d'Espargnet** (1647) at No 38, which today houses the Tribunal de Commerce, is among the most impressive. The Marquis de Entrecasteaux murdered his wife in their family home, the **Hôtel d'Isoard de Vauvenargues** (1710), at No 10 (an estate agency today). More fabulous properties and *châteaux du soleil* (castles of the sun) feature in the window of estate agent **John Taylor** (☎ 04 42 91 54 00), 14 cours Mirabeau.

The cast-iron fountain at the western end of cours Mirabeau, **Fontaine de la Rotonde**, dates from 1860 and personifies justice, agriculture and fine arts. The fountain at the avenue's eastern end on place Forbin is decorated with a 19th-century statue of King René holding a bunch of Muscat grapes, a variety he is credited with introducing to the region. Moss-covered **Fontaine d'Eau Chaude**, at the intersection of cours Mirabeau and rue Clémenceau, spouts 34°C water.

Other streets and squares lined with aristocratic 17th- and 18th-century townhouses include **rue Mazarine**, south of cours Mirabeau; **place des 4 Dauphins**, two blocks farther south, where the fountain (1667) does indeed feature four *dauphins* (dolphins); the eastern continuation of cours Mirabeau, **rue de l'Opéra** (at Nos 18, 24 and 26); and stunning, cobblestoned **place d'Albertas,** created just west of place St-Honoré for the Marquis d'Albertas in 1745. Sunday strollers should not miss a jaunt to **place de l'Hôtel de Ville** where the city brass band trumpets out a host of jolly tunes most Sunday mornings to the delight of the smiling crowds. From place de l'Hôtel de Ville, rue Gaston de Saporta leads to the **Cathédrale St-Sauveur**. Opposite the cathedral is the Institute of French Studies for Foreign Students, in the former Université d'Aix (1741).

South of the historic centre lies pleasing **Parc Jourdan**, a spacious green area dominated by Aix's largest fountain and home to the town's **Boulodrome Municipal** where men gather beneath the shade of the trees to play pétanque on sunny days. Pétanque is also the name of the game on the tree-studded court, opposite the park entrance on ave du Parc. Spectators are welcomed.

Westbound city walkers can take a leafy stroll to the **Pavillon de Vendôme** (☎ 04 42 27 57 35), 32 rue Célony, which languishes amid a manicured French garden. Contemporary art and digital exhibitions are held in the 18th-century mansion.

Museums

The tourist office sells a Passeport Musées costing 50FF (seniors and students 40FF, those aged under 18, free) that gets you into Musée Granet, Musée des Tapisseries and Pavillon de Vendôme; and a 60FF version that also covers admission to the Atelier Paul Cézanne.

Aix's finest is the **Musée Granet** (☎ 04 42 38 14 70), place St-Jean de Malte, in a 17th-century priory of the knights of Malta. Exhibits include Celtic statues from Entremont and Roman artefacts, while the museum's collection of paintings boasts 16th- to 19th-century Italian, Dutch and French works, plus some lesser-known paintings and watercolours by Aix-born Cézanne. The museum opens 10 am to noon and 2 to 6 pm Wednesday to Monday. Admission costs 10FF to 50FF (depending on what's on).

An unexceptional collection of artefacts pertaining to the city's history is in the **Musée du Parlement de Provence et du Vieil Aix** (☎ 04 42 21 43 55), inside Hôtel d'Estienne de St-Jean at 17 rue Gaston de Saporta. It opens 10 am to noon and 2 to 5 pm Tuesday to Sunday, November to March; and 2.30 to 6 pm Tuesday to Sunday, the rest of the year. Admission costs 15FF (seniors, students and children aged 14 to 18, 10FF).

The **Musée des Tapisseries** (Tapestry Museum; ☎ 04 42 23 09 91), in a former archbishop's palace at 28 place des Martyrs de la Résistance, opens 10 to 11.45 am and 2 to 5.45 pm Wednesday to Monday. The **Musée Paul Arbaud**, 2a rue du 4 Septembre, displays books, manuscripts and a collection of Provençal *faïence* (earthenware); it opens 2 to 5 pm Monday to Saturday. Admission to both costs 15FF (students 10FF).

Art lovers should not miss the **Petit Musée Cézanne** (☎ 04 42 23 42 53), 24 rue Gaston de Saporta. **Galerie Moscato** (☎ 04 42 21 07 51), next door at No 22, hosts unusual art exhibitions; as does **Espace 13** (☎ 04 42 93 03 67), an art gallery in 17th-century Hôtel de Castillon at 21 bis cours Mirabeau.

Cathédrale St-Sauveur

Aix's cathedral incorporates architectural features representing every major period from the 5th to the 18th century. The main Gothic structure, built from 1285 to 1350, includes the Romanesque nave of a 12th-century church as part of its southern aisle. The chapels were added in the 14th and 15th centuries. There is a 5th-century sarcophagus in the apse. The cathedral opens 8 am to noon and 2 to 6 pm. Sunday mass is celebrated at 10.30 am and 7 pm. Soulful Gregorian chants and organ concerts are sometimes sung here.

The 15th-century *Triptyque du Buisson Ardent* (Triptych of the Burning Bush) in the nave is by Nicolas Froment. It is usually only opened for groups. Near it is a triptych panel illustrating Christ's passion. The tapestries encircling the choir date from the 18th century and the fabulous gilt organ is Baroque. There's a son et lumière at 9.30 pm most evenings in summer.

Fondation Vasarely

The Vasarely Foundation (☎ 04 42 20 01 09, @ fondation.vasarely@wanadoo.fr), 1 ave Marcel Pagnol, is about 4km west of town near the hostel. It is the creation of Hungarian-born artist Victor Vasarely, the 'father of Op Art', who sought to brighten up grey urban areas with huge, colourful works that integrated art with architecture. Vasarely's works are displayed here in 14 hexagonal spaces recognisable from afar by their contrasting black-and-white, geo-metrical designs.

The foundation opens 10 am to 1 pm and 2 to 7 pm, mid-March to October; 9.30 am to 1 pm and 2 to 6 pm weekdays, and 9.30 am to 6 pm weekends, the rest of the year. Admission costs 40FF (seniors over 60, students and those aged seven to 18, 25FF). Take bus No 4 to the Vasarely stop.

Paul Cézanne Trail
Cézanne (1839–1906), Aix's most celebrated son (at least after his death), did much of his painting in and around the city. If you're interested in the minute details of his day-to-day life follow the **Circuit de Cézanne**, marked by round bronze markers in the pavement that begin at the tourist office. The markers are coordinated with an English-language guide entitled *In the Footsteps of Cézanne*, available free from the tourist office. Cézanne was a close friend of the French novelist Émile Zola (1840–1902) who also spent his youth in Aix.

Cézanne's last studio, atop a hill about 1.5km north of the tourist office at 9 ave Paul Cézanne, has been left exactly as it was when he died. Although none of his works are displayed in the **Atelier Cézanne** (☎ 04 42 21 06 53, 📧 atelier.cezanne@wanadoo.fr), his tools are. In the audio-visual room, films and CD-Roms recreate the artist's life and works. The studio opens 10 am to noon and 2.30 to 6 pm daily, June to September; and 10 am to noon and 2 to 5 pm, the rest of the year. Admission costs 16FF (students 10FF). Take bus No 1 to the Cézanne stop.

Thermes Sextius
Discover Aix's sexy past at the thermal spa (☎ 04 42 23 81 82, fax 04 42 95 11 33, 📧 thermes.sextius@wanadoo.fr), 55 cours Sextius, built on the site of the warm springs that soothed weary feet in Roman Aquae Sextiae in the 1st century BC. The excavated archaeological remains of the Roman spa are displayed beneath glass in the reception of Aix's contemporary spa, inside an 18th-century hôtel particulier today.

See Activities in Facts for the Visitor for more spa details.

Organised Tours
The tourist office offers a wealth of thematic walking tours (in English from July to November). A tour costs 50FF (students, those aged over 60 and under 25, 25FF) and a 'Visa for Aix' valid for three tours is 120FF (no reductions). Between April and mid-October, it also runs a packed schedule of bus excursions; see Organised Tours in the Getting Around chapter.

Special Events
Aix has a sumptuous cultural calendar. The most sought-after tickets are for July's week-long Festival Provençal d'Aix et du Pays d'Aix, which brings classical music, opera and ballet to a myriad of city venues, including Cathédrale St-Sauveur. Buskers bring a festive spirit to cours Mirabeau.

Other festivals include the two-day Festival du Tambourin (Tambourine Festival) in mid-April; the Aix Jazz Festival, Danse à Aix and Festival International d'Art Lyrique in July; and the Fête Mistralienne which marks the birthday of Provençal hero Frédéric Mistral on 13 September.

Aix's Fête de l'Huile d'Olive Nouvelle et de la Truffe, held on place Jeanne d'Arc in December to mark the season's new olive oil, is Aix's main gastronomic celebration.

Places to Stay
Despite being a student town, Aix is not cheap. In July and August, when hotel prices rise precipitously, it may be possible to stay in the university dorms – the tourist office has details or you can call the student accommodation outfit CROUS (☎ 04 42 93 47 70), ave Jules Ferry, in the Cité des Gazelles.

The tourist office has details on chambres d'hôtes and *gîtes ruraux* in and around Aix; it publishes an updated list of all accommodation, including studios and farmhouses, to rent on a longer-term basis each week.

Places to Stay – Budget
Camping At Pont des Trois Sautets, 2km south-east of town on route de Nice, is

Camping Arc en Ciel (☎ 04 42 26 14 28), open mid-March to mid-October. A tent site costs 90FF per person. Take bus No 3 to Les Trois Sautets stop.

Hostels Almost 2km west of the centre is the *Auberge de Jeunesse du Jas de Bouffan (☎ 04 42 20 15 99, fax 04 42 59 36 12, 3 ave Marcel Pagnol)*, which opens mid-January to mid-December. B&B costs 82FF for the first night, then 69FF for each subsequent night. Rooms are locked between 10 am and 5 pm. Take bus No 4 from La Rotonde to the Vasarely stop.

Hotels On the city centre's eastern fringe, laid-back *Hôtel des Arts (☎ 04 42 38 11 77, fax 04 42 26 77 31, 69 blvd Carnot & 5 rue de la Fonderie)* is away from the milling crowds. It has 16 doubles with a shower and toilet costing 220/190FF for a quiet/noisy room overlooking an empty backstreet/cafe-filled square.

Just out of the pedestrianised area, *Hôtel du Globe (☎ 04 42 26 03 58, fax 04 42 26 13 68, 74 cours Sextius)* has basic singles/doubles for 180/200FF (295FF for one or two people with shower and toilet). Garage parking costs 49FF per night.

Places to Stay – Mid-Range & Top End

Hôtel Cardinale (☎ 04 42 38 32 30, fax 04 42 26 39 05, 24 rue Cardinale) is a charming place, in a charming street, with very charming rooms including shower, toilet and a mix of modern and period furniture. Singles/doubles cost 300/350FF and it has small self-catering suites in an annexe at 12 rue Cardinal.

Hôtel de France (☎ 04 42 27 90 15, fax 04 42 26 11 47, 63 rue Espariat), in another old building bang in the heart of things, has atmospheric doubles with washbasin costing 250FF (270FF with shower, 320FF with shower and toilet).

Good places close to the centre include the friendly, 12-room *Hôtel des Quatre Dauphins (☎ 04 42 38 16 39, fax 04 42 38 60 19, 54 rue Roux Alphéran)*, charging 295/375/520FF for two-star singles/

doubles/triples with period furnishings and shower or bath.

Aix is well-endowed with three- and four-star hotels, although many sit on the outskirts of town. *Hôtel St-Christophe (☎ 04 42 26 01 24, fax 04 42 38 53 17, [e] saintchristophe@francemarket.com, 2 ave Victor Hugo)*, conveniently near the tourist office, serves breakfast (47FF) on a lovely street terrace from 7 to 10.30 am and has comfortable singles/doubles costing 380/420FF.

In a prime location with a prime view of slick cours Mirabeau is *Grand Hôtel Nègre Coste (☎ 04 42 27 74 22, fax 04 42 26 80 93, 33 cours Mirabeau)* where, so the story goes, Louis XIV played tennis in 1660. Fanciful rooms with 18th-century furnishings, for one or two, cost 420FF to 800FF.

Places to Eat

Aix has many lovely places to dine, but prices do little to moderate the town's upmarket gastronomic image. Aix's cheapest dining street is rue Van Loo which is lined with tiny restaurants offering Chinese, Thai, Italian and other Oriental cuisines.

Aix's pastry speciality is the *calisson* (see the boxed text 'Calissons' on the next page).

Restaurants Numerous cafes, brasseries and restaurants line place des Cardeurs and place de l'Hôtel de Ville in the city's heart. *Le Dernier Bistrot (☎ 04 42 21 13 02, 19 rue Constantin)* sports a good-value lunchtime *formule express/du chef* costing 52/65FF and serves giant-sized salads for 50FF. Evening *menus* are 125FF and 149FF. Another informal spot is *Le Marais Provençal*, on the corner of rue Lirutasa and rue des Musletiers, where lunchtime/evening *menus* cost 55/65FF.

Just off cours Mirabeau, next to the historic Hôtel de Caumont (1715–42) at 1 bis rue Cabassol, *La Verre Bouteille* is a straightforward family affair that should not be missed; see the special Food & Wine section earlier for details.

Place des Augustins and the fan of pedestrian streets north of the square are also restaurant-laden. *Le Poivre d'Âne (☎ 04 42*

Calissons

These sweet almond and fruit biscuits, frosted white with icing sugar on top, have made mouths water since 1473 when privileged guests at the wedding banquet of King René dined on calissons. Today, a handful of Aixois *calissonniers* (calisson makers) still bake these sweets, which must be 40% ground almonds and 60% melon and fruit syrup, according to tradition.

Traditional calisson makers include **Béchard** (☎ 04 42 26 06 78), an upmarket patisserie and calissonnerie, at 12 cours Mirabeau; **Brémond** (☎ 04 42 38 01 70), 16 rue d'Italie, dating to 1830; and **Roy René** (☎ 04 42 26 67 86), 10 rue Clémenceau. Expect to pay about 20FF per 100g (eight or nine calissons); ornately boxed calissons cost slightly more.

93 45 56, 7 rue de la Couronne) is quintessentially Provençal. It serves strictly local cuisine, mirrored in the tastebud-tickling treats – fig compote, chestnut confit, truffle oil – sold in the épicerie that it runs across the street. The latter sells hearty slices (16FF) of savoury tarts (the tomato, basil and pine kernel tart is irresistible) to take away.

Another hip choice is *Le Bistro Latin* (☎ 04 42 38 22 88, 18 rue de la Couronne), which specialises in traditional French cooking. Simple but savoury lunchtime *menus* start at 55FF. Come evening, the two-floor bistro has a 129FF *menu du marché* (market menu) and an imaginative *menu à l'huile d'olive* (olive oil menu).

Next door at No 16, *Le Saf* (☎ 04 42 26 94 25) dishes up Senegalese dishes. Sun-inspired *menus* sell for 100FF and 130FF. French *Les Bacchanales* (☎ 04 42 27 21 06) at No 10 is a classical favourite which dons a delectable *menu gourmand* (295FF) and less rich *menu* for 145FF.

Nearby rue de la Verrerie and rue Félibre Gaut flaunt various Vietnamese and Chinese options. Place Ramus, off pedestrian rue Annonciade, is a tiny restaurant-filled square where buskers perform. Known for

the 500-odd different *crus* (wines) on its wine list is upmarket *Chez Maxime* (☎ 04 42 26 28 51, place Ramus) which has *menus* costing between 135FF and 270FF. Waiter service is formal.

Off cours Mirabeau, *Yôji* (☎ 04 42 38 48 76, 7 ave Victor Hugo) is a Japanese sushi bar offering succulent evening *menus* ranging from 125FF to 205FF (59FF to 89FF at lunchtime).

A heavy scent of lavender fills the air at *Gu et Fils* (☎ 04 42 26 75 12, 3 rue Frédéric Mistral), or rather 'Chez Gu' as Peter Mayle called the place in *A Year in Provence*. Gu – known as much for his handsome moustache as culinary skills – serves purely Provençal dishes and wonderful aperitifs *à la composition secrète*. He has a 140FF *menu*, translated into English.

Cafes No visit to Aix is complete without a quick pose and peering session at *Les Deux Garçons* (☎ 04 42 26 00 51, 53 cours Mirabeau). Dating from 1792, this renowned cafe-cum-brasserie – a former intellectual hangout with a stunning interior – is an Aixois hot spot designed purely for the sort of people-watching and pastis-drinking that is not free of pretension. Its lunchtime *menu* costs 129FF and its plat du jour hovers at 75FF. In summer an astonishing number of people spend entire evenings simply strolling up and down the crowded street.

Not quite so conspicuous are the terraces which sprawl across Aix's backstreet squares: place des Cardeurs, forum des Cardeurs, place de Verdun, place Richelme and place de l'Hôtel de Ville are all safe bets for a coffee or cocktail.

Autour d'une Tarte (☎ 04 42 96 52 12, 13 rue Gaston de Saporta) is a cosy tart shop which specialises in delicious sweet *(sucrées)* and savoury *(salées)* tarts, to eat in or takeaway.

Self-Catering Aix is among Provence's premier market towns. A mass of fruit and vegetable stands are set up every morning on place Richelme, just as they have been for centuries. Another *marché d'alimentation* (grocery market) fills place des

Pêcheurs on Tuesday, Thursday and Saturday morning.

The next best thing after bread from the market is a warm loaf from *Boulangerie du Coin (4 rue Boulegon)*, *Le Fournil de Maître Pains (30 rue Mignet)* or *Boulangerie Tournefort* on rue Tournefort, which opens 24 hours. Buy cheese, cold meats, sausages and any of the pick of 300 types of whisky at *Jacquèrres (☎ 04 42 23 48 64, 9 rue Mejane)*, a traditional épicerie. Fresh pasta is sold at *Aux Pâtes Fraîches (10 rue Laurent Fauchier)* and *L'Épicerie Italienne (9 rue d'Italie)*. *La Corbeille d'Orient (28 rue Cordeliers)* sells nuts, grains, rice and dried fruits.

Monoprix supermarket *(cours Mirabeau)* opens 8.30 am to 8 pm Monday to Saturday.

Entertainment

Pick up a free copy of the monthly *Le Mois à Aix* at the tourist office to find out what's on when.

Rue de la Verrerie is lined with bars: Irish *The Red Clover* at No 30 hosts a happy hour from 6 to 8 pm, and *Galaxy Pub* at No 38 has live bands playing on Thursday, Friday and Saturday evening.

Stunning *Théâtre du Jeu de Paume (☎ 04 42 99 12 12, 17–21 rue de l'Opéra)* was built in 1756 on the site of a royal tennis court; the curtain rises in the ornate Italianate auditorium at 8.30 pm. *Chapelle du Ste-Catherine (☎ 04 42 23 42 79, 20 rue Mignet)* hosts classical music concerts.

Cinema The Aixois are fond of *le septième art* (the seventh art), and two cinemas are dedicated solely to screening nondubbed films: *Cinéma Mazarin (6 rue Laroque)* and *Cinéma Renoir (24 cours Mirabeau)*. Twelve-screen *Le Cézanne (1 rue Marcel Guillaume)* hosts dubbed and nondubbed films. Programme details (☎ 08 36 68 72 70) in French are online at www.lecezanne.com.

Shopping

A flower market sets place des Pêcheurs ablaze with every colour of the rainbow on Sunday mornings. On Tuesday, Thursday and Saturday morning another flower market fills place de Hôtel de Ville and a flea market occupies place de Verdun.

Aix's chic shops (designer clothes, hats, accessories etc) cluster along pedestrian rue Marius Reinaud which winds it way behind the Palais de Justice on place de Verdun.

Santons (see the boxed text 'Little Saints' earlier in this chapter) can be admired and bought at several *ateliers* (workshops), including Santons Fouque (☎ 04 42 26 33 38), 65 cours Gambetta, where the thumbalina figures have been crafted since 1934. The tourist office has a complete list of ateliers.

La Truffe Cendrée, 9 rue Aumône Vieille, is the place to shop for luxury food products typical to the region, including truffles in season. Chocolate olives are among the sweet delights sold at Puyricard, 7 rue Rifle Rafle, and Rich Art, 8 rue Thiers, two designer chocolatiers. Olive oil can be tasted and bought at Le Comptoir des Oliviers (☎ 04 42 96 21 28, 14 rue Gaston de Saporta). For wine, try Cave du Felibrige, 18 rue des Cordeliers; Cellier du 31, 31 rue des Cordeliers or Bacchus, 27 rue d'Italie.

Getting There & Away

Air Marseilles-Provence airport is 25km from Aix-en-Provence. See Marseilles earlier in this chapter for details of flights.

Bus From the bus station (☎ 04 42 91 26 80), ave de l'Europe, there are buses to Marseilles (26FF, 35 minutes via the autoroute/one hour via the N8, every five to 10 minutes), Arles (80FF, 1¾ hours, twice daily), Avignon (88FF, one to 1½ hours, six to 10 daily) and Toulon (88FF, one hour, four daily).

Sumian buses serve Apt, Castellane and the Gorges du Verdon via La Palud (see the Haute-Provence chapter for details).

Train Aix's tiny train station, at the southern end of ave Victor Hugo leading from La Rotonde, runs frequent services to Marseilles (59FF, 35 minutes, about 20 daily).

Getting Around

To/From the Airport COMETT (☎ 04 42 14 31 27) operates buses every 30 minutes between 8 am and 10 or 11 pm (less frequent on Sunday) between Aix bus station and Marseilles-Provence airport (45FF, 30 minutes).

Bus The city's 14 bus and three minibus lines are operated by Aix en Bus (☎ 04 42 26 37 28), whose information desk inside the tourist office opens 8.30 am to 7 pm Monday to Saturday.

La Rotonde is the main bus hub. Most services run until 8 pm. A single-/10-ticket carnet costs 7/44FF. Minibus No 1 links the train and bus stations with La Rotonde and cours Mirabeau. Minibus No 2 starts at the bus station and then follows much the same route.

Taxi Cabs lurk outside the bus and train stations. To order a cab, call Taxi Radio Aixois (☎ 04 42 27 71 11).

Bicycle Cycles Zammit (☎ 04 42 23 19 53), 27 rue Mignet, rents road and mountain bikes and opens 9 am to 12.30 pm and 3 to 7.30 pm Tuesday to Saturday.

MONTAGNE STE-VICTOIRE

Among Cézanne's favourite haunts was Montagne Ste-Victoire, a mountain ridge immortalised on canvas numerous times by artists over the centuries. Garrigue covers its dry slopes and its foot is carpeted with 3200 hectares of vineyards, from which the local Coteaux d'Aix-en-Provence white, red and rosé wines originate.

Contemporary art exhibitions are hosted in the **Moulin de Cézanne**, a restored mill in Le Tholonet, 5km east of Aix on the D17. The village is dominated by the 17th-century **Château du Tholonet**, a green-shuttered mansion that cannot be visited. Continuing eastwards on the D17, you pass local artists at their easels in the roadside pine forests trying to reproduce works painted by Cézanne along this stretch. *La Montagne Ste-Victoire au Grand Pin* (1887) is one of his best known paintings.

Some 10km south of Le Tholonet off the D6 in the **Arc Valley** – the inspiration for Cézanne's cubist *Les Baigneurs* and *Les Baigneuses* (The Bathers) – is **Gardanne**

(pop 19,679). Traditionally a mining town, just 900-odd miners remain employed in the mines which are slated for closure by 2005. The **Écomusée de la Forêt Méditerranéenne** (☎ 04 42 65 42 10, [e] fondation-foret @en provence.com), set in a 13-hectare park off chemin de Roman (the D7), is run by the people responsible for the reforestation in the Provence-Alpes-Côte d'Azur region and is well worth the 30FF admission (children aged under 15, 15FF). The centre opens 10 am to 7 pm daily, July and August; and 9 am to 6 pm, the rest of the year.

St-Antonin-sur-Bayon, 4km east of Le Tholonet, is home to the Maison de Ste-Victoire (☎ 04 42 66 84 40), converted stables sheltering an **Écomusée**, restaurant, terrace cafe and shop that sells walking guides and maps. It opens 10 am to 7 pm.

Returning to Aix-en-Provence via the westbound D10, you pass through **Vauvenargues**. Picasso, who spent most of his creative life on the Côte d'Azur, is buried on the estate of his 14th-century **Château de Vauvenargues,** which dominates the village. The red-brick castle, purchased by the artist in 1958, still belongs to the Picasso family; a sign outside the main gate bluntly states *Le château n'est pas à visiter. N'insistez pas, merci. Le musée est à Paris* (This castle cannot be visited. Do not insist. The museum is in Paris).

Places to Stay & Eat

Camping Ste-Victoire (☎ 04 42 66 91 31, fax 04 42 66 96 43, quartier Paradou) in Beaurecueil opens year round. In Puyloubier, *Camping Le Cézanne* (☎ 04 42 66 36 33, 06 80 32 11 10, fax 04 42 66 35 46, ave Noclercq) opens April to November. Both sites charge about 60FF per night for two campers with tent and car. The tourist office in Aix has details on chambres d'hôtes in the area.

In Le Tholonet, *Le Relais Cézanne* (☎ 04 42 66 91 91, ave Cézanne) is a family run place with doubles costing 230FF. In Vauvenargues, one-star *Moulin de Provence* (☎ 04 42 66 02 22, fax 04 42 66 01 21, 33 ave des Maquisards) has singles/doubles from 120/220FF.

A superb place to dine is *La Petite Auberge du Tholonet* (☎ 04 42 66 84 24), beautifully set at the end of a country lane overlooking neighbouring fields and Montagne Ste-Victoire. House specialities include *tarte aux olives et chèvre chaud* (olive and goat's cheese tart) and *menus* cost upwards of 85FF; it opens at lunchtime Tuesday to Sunday. Book in advance.

SALON DE PROVENCE
postcode 13300 • pop 38,137
Salon de Provence (Seloun in Provençal), 35km west of Aix and 40km east of Arles, is known for its olive oil production and *savon de Marseille* (Marseilles soap) industry. Medieval Salon served as the residence of the Arles archbishops. The philosopher Nostradamus (1503–66) lived and died here.

Since 1936 France's military flying school, the École de l'Air et École Militaire de l'Air, has been stationed here, although it is very difficult to catch the Patrouille Aérienne de France – France's equivalent of the UK's Red Arrows – in flight. The school is closed to the public and France's aerial acrobatic showmasters are, more often than not, on tour around the world.

An open-air morning market fills place Morgan on Wednesday.

Orientation & Information
Salon de Provence is small. Banks, the tourist office and most sights are in the Vieille Ville (old town) or on cours Gimon, cours Victor Hugo and cours Carnot which circle it. From place Crousillat, the train station is a straight 1km-walk west along blvd de la République.

The tourist office (☎ 04 90 56 27 60, fax 04 90 56 77 09, ⓔ ot.salon@visitprovence .com), 56 cours Gimon, opens 9 am to noon and 2 to 7 pm Monday to Saturday, and 10 am to noon on Sunday (until 6.30 pm and closed Sunday in winter). It sells the 50FF Passeport Visite des Musées de Salon (children aged under seven, free), which covers admission to all Salon museums. The tourist office has a Web site at www .salon-de-provence.org (French only).

Banque de France, 281 bvd Maréchal Foch, exchanges currency between 9.30 am and noon on weekdays. The post office is on the corner of blvd Maréchal Foch and rue Massenet, and you can send emails from Colisée Oriental Cybercafe (☎ 04 90 56 00 10), place Crousillat.

Walking Tour
A giant, moss-covered mushroom of a fountain, **Fontaine Moussue**, dominates place Crousillat, Salon's prettiest square tucked just outside the walled old town. To enter the old city, bear east beneath the **Tour d'Horloge** (1626). The bells atop the clock tower have chimed every 15 minutes since 1664.

Pedestrian rue de l'Horloge brings you to place de Ancienne Halle, a large square from which rue Nostradamus leads to the **Maison de Nostradamus** (☎ 04 90 56 64 31) at No 11. Nostradamus lived here from 1547 until his death in 1566. The family home is now a museum with 10 tableaux depicting scenes from the philosopher's life. Nostradamus wrote his famous prophecies, published in Lyons in 1555, here. His house opens 9 am to noon and 2 to 6 pm on weekdays, and 2 to 6 pm at weekends. Admission costs 20FF (students, seniors aged over 60 and children aged under 7, 15FF).

Nostradamus is buried in the Chapelle Centrale de la Vierge inside the imposing **Collègiale St-Laurent**, built in 1344 on place St-Laurent. The side chapel dedicated to the Virgin Mary, where his tomb lies, is opposite the side entrance to the collegiate church.

From the southern end of place de Ancienne Halle, steps lead to the **Château-Musée de l'Empéri** (☎ 04 90 56 22 36), one of Provence's oldest remaining castles. It served as residence to the archbishops of Arles from the 9th to 18th centuries. Some 30 of its spacious medieval halls are filled with over 10,000 exhibits dedicated to French military history up to WWI. Napoleon I steals the limelight. It opens 10 am to noon and 2.30 to 6.30 pm Wednesday to Monday, April to September; and 2 to 6 pm Wednesday to Monday, the rest of the year.

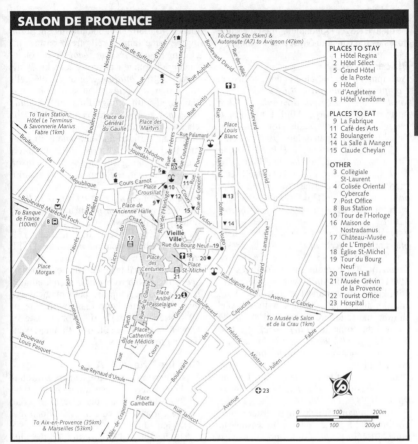

SALON DE PROVENCE

To Camp Site (5km) &
Autoroute (A7) to Avignon (47km)

To Train Station,
Hôtel Le Terminus
& Savonnerie Marius
Fabre (1km)

To Banque
de France
(100m)

To Musée de Salon
et de la Crau (1km)

To Aix-en-Provence (35km)
& Marseilles (53km)

Vieille
Ville

PLACES TO STAY
1 Hôtel Regina
2 Hôtel Sélect
5 Grand Hôtel
  de la Poste
6 Hôtel
  d'Angleterre
13 Hôtel Vendôme

PLACES TO EAT
9 La Fabrique
11 Café des Arts
12 Boulangerie
14 La Salle à Manger
15 Claude Cheylan

OTHER
3 Collégiale
  St-Laurent
4 Colisée Oriental
  Cybercafe
7 Post Office
8 Bus Station
10 Tour de l'Horloge
16 Maison de
  Nostradamus
17 Château-Musée
  de L'Empéri
18 Église St-Michel
19 Tour du Bourg
  Neuf
20 Town Hall
21 Musée Grévin
  de la Provence
22 Tourist Office
23 Hospital

0   100   200m
0   100   200yd

More local lore and legend is unravelled with 54 life-size waxworks at the **Musée Grévin de la Provence** (☎ 04 90 56 36 30), place des Centuries, open the same hours as the Château-Musée de l'Empéri.

Tour du Bourg Neuf, at the eastern end of rue du Bourg Neuf, is part of the fortified ramparts built around the city in the 12th century. In the 13th century, young women wanting to conceive venerated the statue of the Black Virgin tucked in the gate. A rare treat are the solemn Gregorian chants sung at Sunday Mass (9 am) in 13th-century **Église St-Michel**, place St-Michel, every

first and third Sunday of the month from September to June.

One of Salon's two remaining *savonneries* (soap factories), the **Savonnerie Marius Fabre** (☎ 04 90 53 24 77), 148 ave Paul Borret, with a Web site at www.marius-fabre.fr, can be visited at 10.30 am on Monday and Thursday (by appointment only). Exit the train station, turn right along ave Émile Zola, left along blvd Maréchal Foch, then right onto ave Paul Borret.

The history of Salon's soap and olive industries and its popular traditions are explained in the **Musée de Salon et de la Crau**

(☎ 04 90 56 28 37), 500m east of the centre on ave Roger Donnadieu, open the same hours as the Château-Musée de l'Empéri.

Places to Stay

Accommodation in Salon is not expensive. *Camping Nostradamus* (☎ 04 90 56 08 36, fax 04 90 56 65 05, route d'Eyguières), 5km north of Salon, charges 80FF for two people with a car, and 12.20FF for each additional person. It opens March to October.

Closer to the city heart, *Hôtel Vendôme* (☎ 04 90 56 01 96, fax 04 90 56 48 78, 6 blvd Maréchal Joffre) markets itself as a 'garden in town' and has two-star doubles with washbasin for 225FF (255FF to 300FF with toilet and shower). Family rooms cost 420FF.

Near the imposing Collègiale St-Laurent, one-star *Hôtel Regina* (☎ 04 90 56 28 92, fax 04 90 56 77 43, 245 rue des Frères Kennedy) has bargain singles/doubles for 100/110FF (130/140FF with shower, 140/150FF with shower and TV, 160/190FF with shower and toilet). Triples with shower/ shower and toilet are a steal at 190/270FF. Around the corner, at *Hôtel Sélect* (☎ 04 90 56 07 17, fax 04 90 56 42 48, 35 rue Suffren), more upmarket rooms for one or two cost 225FF.

In the heart of town overlooking Tour de l'Horloge is *Grand Hôtel de la Poste* (☎ 04 90 56 01 94, fax 04 90 56 20 77, 1 rue des Frères Kennedy), filled with two-star rooms costing 160FF for a double with washbasin and 230/260FF for singles/doubles with shower and toilet.

Hôtel d'Angleterre (☎ 04 90 56 01 10, fax 04 90 56 71 75, 98 cours Carnot) has modern rooms off spacious landings costing 230/260/345/385FF for one/two/three/four.

Places to Eat

Among the many terraces on pedestrian rue de l'Horloge, one stand-out is bohemian *La Fabrique* (☎ 04 90 56 07 39, 75 rue de l'Horloge), a charming Italian place with brilliantly painted walls and delicious pasta dishes from 50FF. The adjoining shop, run by the same family, sells fresh pasta – including *tagliatelles au chocolat* (chocolate-flavoured spinach pasta) – to take away. Opposite, the *boulangerie* at No 96 sells Marseillais *navettes* (boat-shaped biscuits flavoured with orange blossom). *Claude Cheylan*, at 154 cours Victor Hugo, sells cheese.

Elegant, refined and unbeatable in summer is chic *Café des Arts* which has a terrace overlooking the mossy fountain on place Crousillat. Light snacks start at 55FF (85FF *menu*).

La Salle à Manger (☎ 04 90 56 28 01, 6 rue du Maréchal Joffre) is in a 19th-century hôtel particulier wrapped around a secret garden where you can dine in summer. It serves an 89FF lunchtime menu; the 135FF version includes choice of entree and main dish. An unusual lavender dip accompanies aperitifs and the rose petals sprinkled atop its cold Indian soup are both magical and tasty. Complete your feast with one of 40 desserts (from 28FF); for a taste of Provence, opt for the trio of thyme, lavender and rosemary sorbet.

Getting There & Away

Bus Inter-regional buses share Autobus Aréliens' intercity bus station (☎ 04 90 56 50 98), which adjoins place Jules Morgan, on the corner of blvd Maréchal Foch and blvd Victor Joly.

The bus timetable is posted on the blue panel, in front of which intercity buses stop. There are daily services from Aix-en-Provence (hourly 8 am to 6 pm Monday to Saturday, less frequently on Sunday), Arles (45FF, 1¼ hours, four to nine daily) and Avignon (two to four daily).

Train From the train station on ave Émile Zola there are some eight trains daily to Marseilles (56FF, two hours) and Avignon (49FF, 50 minutes).

The Camargue

The sparsely populated, 780 sq km delta of the River Rhône, known as the Camargue (Camargo in Provençal), is famed for its desolate beauty and the incredibly varied bird life that its wetlands support. Over 400 species of land and water birds inhabit the region, including storks, bee-eaters and some 160 other migratory species. Most impressive of all are the huge flocks of *flamants roses* (pink flamingos) that come here to nest during the spring and summer; many set up house near the Étang de Vaccarès and Étang du Fangassier. In 1999, some 30,000 flamingos wintered in the Camargue and 24,000 couples hatched and raised their offspring in spring 2000.

The Camargue has been formed over the ages by sediment deposited by the River Rhône as it flows into the Mediterranean. In the southern Camargue, the areas between the *digues à la mer* (sea-wall embankments) that line water channels are taken up by shallow salt marshes, inland lakes and lagoons whose brackish waters shimmer in the Provençal sun. The northern part of the delta consists of dry land, and in the years following WWII huge tracts were desalinated as part of a costly drainage and irrigation programme designed to make the area suitable for large-scale agriculture, especially the cultivation of rice. Rice production has dropped sharply since the 1960s but is still a very important part of the Camarguais economy: almost 70% of France's annual rice yield is produced here.

At some places along the coast, the delta continues to grow, sweeping one-time seaside towns kilometres from the Mediterranean. Elsewhere, sea currents and storms have, in recent centuries, washed away land that had been around long enough for people to build things on it. The course of the Rhône has changed repeatedly over the millennia, but the Grand Rhône (which carries 90% of the river's flow) and the Petit Rhône have followed their present channels for about 500 years.

Highlights

- Follow Vincent van Gogh's footsteps, see Picasso sketches in the Musée Réattu and discover what the Romans called fun at the Roman amphitheatre in Arles

- Party on down at a rice or cowboy festival in Arles or at a Roma pilgrimage at Sts-Maries de la Mer

- View pink flamingos at close quarters in the Parc Ornithologique de Pont de Gau

- Walk atop the walled city of Aigues-Mortes

- Explore the wetlands on foot or by horse; bird-watch (& watch out for mosquitoes!)

- Take a walk on the wild side – along the Digue à la Mer in the Camargue's untamed southern realm

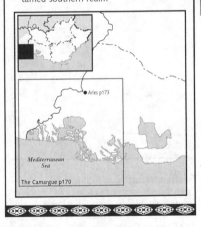

Most of the Camargue wetlands are within the Parc Naturel Régional de Camargue (PNRC), established in 1970 to preserve the area's fragile ecosystems by maintaining an equilibrium between ecological considerations and the region's economic mainstays: agriculture, salt production, hunting, grazing, and tourism. The central, 6000-hectare Étang de Vaccarès has been protected by the

169

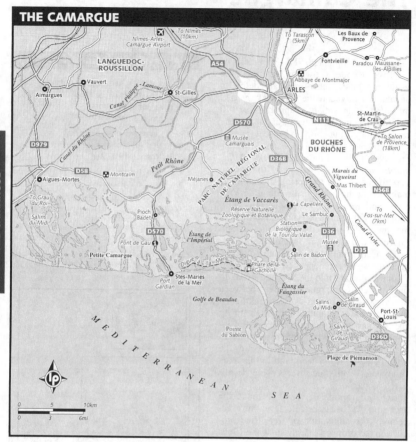

THE CAMARGUE

Réserve Nationale de Camargue – a 135 sq km nature reserve embracing the lagoon and its nearby peninsulas and islands – since 1927. Another 2000 hectares between Arles and Salin de Giraud in south-eastern Camargue is managed by the Conservatoire de l'Espace Littoral et des Rivages Lacustres.

The Camargue's famous herds of cream-coloured *cheveaux* (horses) and black *taureaux* (bulls) which roam free under the watchful eyes of the mounted *gardians* (Camarguaise cowboys) can still be seen. An equally likely sight is bulls grazing in fenced-in fields and horses saddled and tethered,

waiting in rows under the blazing sun for tourists to pay for a ride. The *cheval de Camargue* – always grey-cream in colour, with a square-shaped head and about 13.1 hands in size – has been recognised as a breed in its own right since 1978. Most bulls are raised for bullfighting.

At least one traditional Camargue phenomenon is alive and well: the area's savage mosquitoes are flourishing, feeding on the blood of hapless passers-by just as they have for countless aeons. Pack *plenty* of insect repellent – then pack more.

Camarguaise cuisine tends to be extremely

meaty: *guardianne de taureau* (literally 'bull's herdsman') is a heart-warming beef stew.

ORIENTATION

Shaped like a giant croissant, the 850 sq km PNRC is enclosed by the Rivers Petit Rhône and Grand Rhône. The protected Étang de Vaccarès is bang in its centre.

Inland, the Roman town of Arles rides on the croissant's back and is the gateway to the park. The Camargue's other two towns, both on the coast, are the resort of Stes-Maries de la Mer, 39km south-west, and the walled town of Aigues-Mortes, 34km north-west.

Rice is cultivated in the northern sections of the delta. Enormous salt evaporation pools lie around the Salin de Giraud and Aigues-Mortes.

PARK OFFICES

The PNRC has an information centre, called Centre de Ginès (☎ 04 90 97 86 32, fax 04 90 97 70 82, ⓔ info@parcs-naturels-regionaux.tm.fr), in Pont de Gau, 4km north of Stes-Maries de la Mer off the D570. Exhibits focus on environmental issues. From the glassed-in foyer you can watch birds in the nearby marshes through powerful binoculars. The centre opens 9 am to 6 pm, April to 30 September; and 9.30 am to 5 pm Saturday to Thursday, the rest of the year.

The Réserve Nationale de Camargue has an information centre (☎ 04 90 97 00 97, fax 04 90 97 01 44, ⓔ snpn.reserve.de .camargue@wanadoo.fr) at La Capelière on the D36B. Many trails and paths fan out from the centre; see South-Eastern Camargue later in this chapter for details.

BIRD-WATCHING & WALKING

The Parc Ornithologique du Pont de Gau (☎ 04 90 97 82 62, ⓔ parc.pont-de-gau@ provnet.fr), next to the PNRC information centre on the D570 in Pont du Gau, should be the first port of call for anyone keen to peek at the area's winged creatures or walk in the wetland. Within the ornithological park, several kilometres of paths wend their way through reed beds and marshes. Schools of pink flamingos fly overhead or wade through the watery landscape, making it the best place in the Camargue to view the graceful birds. The 60-hectare park opens 9 am (10 am from October to March) to

THE CAMARGUE

Pretty in Pink

The pink or greater flamingo (phoenicopterus ruber) in flight is a breathtaking sight. Equally majestic is the catwalk stance – neck high, breast out – adopted by this elegant, long-legged creature when strutting through shallow waters.

Flamingo courtship starts in January, with mating taking place from March to May. The single egg laid by the female in April or May is incubated in a mud-caked nest for one month by both parents. The young chicks shakily take to the skies when they are about three months old. By the time they reach adulthood (around five years old), their soft grey down has become a fine feather coat of brilliant white or pretty rose-pink.

This well-dressed bird lives to the grand old age of 34 (longer if kept in captivity). It stands between 1.5m to 2m tall and has an average wing span of 1.9m. When the flamingo feels threatened, its loud hiss is similar to the warning sound made by a goose. It feeds on plankton, sucking in water and draining it off with a disproportionately heavy, curved bill.

Some flamingos remain in the Rhône delta year round. Come September, several thousand take flight to Spain, Tunisia and Senegal where they winter in warmer climes before returning to the Camargue in February in time for early spring.

JANE SMITH

sunset. Admission costs 28FF (students 22FF; children aged under 10, 16FF). Guided walks (48FF) around the park are available (students 32FF, children aged under 10, 26FF). Salin de Badon in south-eastern Camargue (see that section later in this chapter) is the Camargue's other prime bird-watching spot.

There are numerous other walking trails in the PRNC, the Réserve Nationale, along the sea embankments and the coast. One of the most dramatic paths is atop the dike between Stes-Maries and Salin de Giraud (see the South-Eastern Camargue section later in this chapter). Shorter nature trails start from the Musée Camarguais south-west of Arles and from La Palissade (1½ to four hours) and La Capelière (1½ hours), both in South-Eastern Camargue.

Park offices sell detailed maps of the area, including the 1:25,000 IGN Série Bleue maps, Nos 2944E and 2944O.

CYCLING

As long as you can put up with the insects and stiff sea breezes, bicycles are the finest way to explore the very flat Camargue. East of Stes-Maries, areas along the seafront and farther inland are reserved for walkers and cyclists. Cycling is forbidden on beaches, but you can two-wheel along the dike footpath (see the previous section). Le Vélo Saintois or Le Vélociste in Stes-Maries de la Mer distribute a list of cycling itineraries – 20km to 70km in length – with route explanations in English. Both places deliver bicycles to your hotel door and open Easter to early October. See Stes-Maries later for details.

Le Vélociste organises guided bicycle rides and also runs combined cycling and canoeing/horse-riding day trips. Its one-day Vélo+Canoe *formule* (schedule; 180FF) includes a 20km bike ride and 8km paddle in a canoe. Its Vélo+Cheval *formule* (210FF) includes a 25km cycle and a two hours' horse ride.

Rental agencies in Arles and other towns are listed in the respective Getting Around sections. Mas de Méjanes (see Horse-riding later) rents mountain bikes for 25/40/50/80FF for one/two/four/eight hours.

HORSE RIDING

Numerous farms offer *promenade à cheval* (horse riding); there are plenty along the D570 into Stes-Maries. Expect to pay 80/350FF per hour/day. You can also ride at the Auberge de Jeunesse in Pioch Badet near Stes-Maries, and at Mas de Méjanes (☎ 04 90 97 10 62), a Paul Ricard leisure complex (also called Domaine Paul Ricard) isolated on the north-eastern bank of the Étang de Vaccarès in Méjanes, 20km south-west of Arles. Accompanied rides cost 75/140FF for one/two hours (215/360FF per half/full day). The Domaine de la Palissade organises scenic rides in the wilder south-eastern Camargue (see the that section later in this chapter).

For more information on equestrian activities contact the Association Camarguaise de Tourisme Équestre (☎ 04 90 97 86 32), in the Centre de Ginès at Pont de Gau.

ORGANISED TOURS

Boat excursions can be picked up in Aigues-Mortes and Stes-Maries. Les Guides du Terroir Camprolan (☎ 04 90 97 96 82), 17 place des Gitans, Stes-Maries, organises all types of activities including fishing trips (195FF, three hours) and bird-watching tours with a local ornithologist (95FF). La Maison du Guide (☎/fax 04 66 73 52 30, ☎ 06 12 44 73 52, ⓔ guide.camargue@wanadoo.fr) in Montcalm, 10km west of Stes-Maries on the D58, organises guided tours by foot, boat and bicycle.

A couple of companies in Arles and Stes-Maries organise trips by jeep into the Camargue heartland; see Organised Tours in those sections.

ARLES

postcode 13200 • pop 54,614

The attractive city of Arles (Arle in Provençal), at the northern tip of the Camargue alluvial plain, lies on the River Grand Rhône just south of where the Petit Rhône splits off from it. Avignon is 36km north-east and Nîmes is 31km north-west.

Arles began its ascent to prosperity and political importance in 49 BC, when the victorious Julius Caesar – who the city had

ARLES

PLACES TO STAY
2 Hôtel de France
3 Hôtel Terminus
   et Van Gogh
6 Hôtel Régence
8 Hôtel de Paris
9 Hôtel Voltaire
10 Hôtel Le Rhône
13 Hôtel du Musée
18 Hôtel d'Arlatan
29 Grand Hôtel Nord Pinus
32 Hôtel de la Muette
39 Hôtel Le Calendal
43 Hôtel de l'Amphitheatre
48 Hôtel St-Trophime
55 Hôtel Jules César

PLACES TO EAT
4 Monoprix Supermarket
14 L'Olivier
15 La Cuisine
16 Pierre Milhau
   Charcuterie
19 La Paillotte
21 L'Entrevue
30 Café La Nuit
40 Salon de Thé &
   Entrance to Hôtel Le Calendal

OTHER
1 Inter-Regional Bus Station
5 Viewpoint where Van Gogh
   painted Starry Night
7 Laundrette

11 Musée Réattu
12 Thermes de Constantin
17 Boutique des Passionnés
20 Banque de France
22 Peugeot Cycles
23 La Farandole (Sausage Maker)
24 Regional Bus Station
25 Espace Van Gogh
26 Librairie Van Gogh
27 Musée Arlaten
28 Cryptoporticus du Forum
31 Huiles Jamard
33 École Nationale de
   la Photographie
34 Rencontres Internationales
   de la Photographie
35 La Boutique Provençal
36 Entrance to Les Arènes
   & Ticket Office
37 Les Arènes
38 Église de la Major
41 Théâtre Antique
42 Entrance to Théâtre Antique
44 Fondation Vincent Van Gogh
45 La Rose des Vents
46 En Camargue
47 Église St-Trophime
49 Town Hall
50 Cloître St-Trophime
51 Le Kiosque du Net
52 Europcar
53 Police Station
54 Post Office
56 Tourist Office

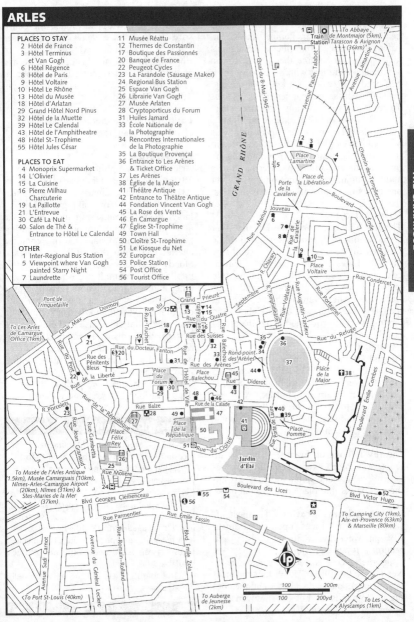

THE CAMARGUE

supported – captured and plundered Marseilles, which had backed Caesar's rival, the general and statesman Pompey the Great. Arles soon replaced Marseilles as the region's major port and became the sort of Roman provincial centre that within a century and a half needed a 20,000-seat amphitheatre and a 12,000-seat theatre to entertain its citizens. Today, the two imposing structures stage cultural events and Camarguaise bullfights.

The Arlésiens' most famous resident was Vincent van Gogh (1853–90) who settled in the town for a year in 1888, immortalising many of the city's most picturesque streets and surrounding rural areas on canvas. Not one of his original works remains in Arles.

Orientation

The centre of Arles is enclosed by the River Grand Rhône to the north-west, blvd Émile Combes to the east and, to the south, by blvd des Lices and blvd Georges Clémenceau. It is shaped like a foot, with the train station, place de la Libération and place Lamartine (where Van Gogh once lived) at the ankle, Les Arènes at the anklebone and the tourist office squashed under the arch.

Information

Tourist Offices The tourist office (☎ 04 90 18 41 20, fax 04 90 18 41 29, ⓔ ot.arles @visitprovence.com), esplanade Charles de Gaulle, opens 9 am to 7 pm Monday to Saturday, April to September; and 9 am to 6 pm the rest of the year. Its Web site is at www .arles.org (French only).

Money Banque de France, 35 ter rue du Docteur Fanton, exchanges currency between 8.30 am and noon weekdays. Commercial banks line place de la République.

Post & Communications The post office, 5 blvd des Lices, opens 8.30 am to 6.30 pm weekdays, 8.30 am to 12.30 pm Saturday. It has Cyberposte.

Internet access is free at Le Kiosque du Net (☎ 04 90 49 37 75, ⓔ kiosquedunet @arles.org), place de la République, but log-in slots must be booked in advance. It opens 1 to 7 pm weekdays.

Bookshops The Librairie Van Gogh (☎ 04 90 96 86 65), wrapped around the courtyard of the Espace Van Gogh at 1 place Félix Rey, has an extensive range of English-language art, history, culture and cookery books pertaining to Provence. It opens 10 am to 12.30 pm and 2 to 6.30 pm Tuesday to Saturday.

Laundry The laundrette at 6 rue de la Cavalerie opens 7 am to 9 pm.

Les Arènes

Arles' Roman amphitheatre (☎ 04 90 96 03 70), built in the late 1st or early 2nd century AD to host an audience of 25,000, measures 136m by 107m, making it marginally larger than its counterpart in Nîmes. Like other such structures around the Roman empire, it was built to stage sporting contests, chariot races and the wildly popular and bloody spectacles so beloved by the Roman public. Wild animals were pitted against other animals or gladiators (usually slaves or criminals), who fought each other until one of them was either killed or surrendered (in the latter case their throat was usually then slit). Executions were carried out either by the executioner or by pushing the victim into the arena with a wild animal.

In the early medieval period, during the Arab invasions, Les Arènes was transformed

---

Pass Monuments

The Pass Monuments (Monuments Pass) costs 70FF (students and those aged 12 to 18, 55FF) and is valid for three months. It covers admission to all Arles' museums and Roman relics.

Those with less time to spare can buy a cheaper 55FF Circuit Arles Antique (students and those aged 12 to 18, 40FF) which covers all the sights *except* the Église St-Trophime, Les Alyscamps, Musée Réattu and Musée Arlaten.

The tourist office and the museums sell both passes.

Bulls & Cowboys

In *mise à mort* bullfighting *(corrida)*, which is popular in Spain, Latin America and parts of southern France, a bull bred to be aggressive is killed in a bloody ceremony involving picadors, toreadors, matadors and horses. But not all bullfighting ends with a dead bull.

In a *course Camarguaise* (Camargue-style bullfight), white-clad *raseteurs* try to remove ribbons or *attributs* (rosettes) tied to the bull's horns with hooks held between their fingers. It originates from the 15th century when dogs, lions and bears were let loose in a ring to chase a bull. Finally slammed as cruel in the 19th century, the other animals were then banished from the ring, leaving man alone to pit his wits alone against the bull *(taureau)*.

Bulls are bred, fed and tended by *gardians*, Camargue cowboys who herd the region's cattle. These mounted herdsmen are honoured by the Fête des Gardians in Arles in May, during which they parade through town on horseback – clad in leather hats, chequered shirts and dusty boots. Long ago, gardians lived in *cabanes de gardians*, white-washed cottages crowned with a thatched roof and sealed with a strip of mortar.

Courses Camarguaises are common in Arles but not so popular in Nîmes where *férias* (bullfighting festivals) sport corridas and novilladas in which young bulls, less than four years old, are thrown in the ring to fight.

into a fortress; three of the four defensive towers can still be seen around the structure. These days the amphitheatre holds over 12,000 and still draws a full house during the bullfighting season.

Unless there's a performance on, Les Arènes opens 9 am to 7 pm, mid-June to mid-September; 9 am to 12.30 am and 2 to 7 pm, April to mid-June and the last fortnight in September; and 10 am to noon and 2 to 4.30, 5 or 5.30 pm, the rest of the year. Admission costs 20FF (students and those aged 12 to 18, 15FF). Les Arènes' *bureau de location* (ticket office; ☎ 04 90 96 03 70), adjoining the main entrance to the amphitheatre on rond point des Arènes, opens 9 am to noon and 2.30 to 6 pm weekdays, and 9 am to 1 pm Saturday.

Théâtre Antique

For centuries, the Roman theatre (☎ 04 90 96 93 30), dating from the 1st-century BC, was used as a convenient source of construction materials. Nowadays little of the original structure (measuring 102m in diameter) remains, except for two imposing columns. Entered through the **Jardin d'Été** (Summer Garden) on blvd des Lices, it hosts open-air dance, film and music festivals. It shares the same opening hours and

admission costs as Les Arènes (see the previous section).

Église St-Trophime

This austere Romanesque church, once a cathedral (Arles was an archbishopric from the 4th century until 1790), stands on the site of several earlier churches. It was built in the late 11th and 12th centuries – perhaps using stone cut from the Théâtre Antique – and was named after St-Trophimus, a late 2nd- or early 3rd-century bishop of Arles.

Unlike the almost unadorned (save for a few tapestries) interior, the western portal facing place de la République is richly decorated in 12th-century stone carvings. Two lateral chapels were added in the 14th century. The choir and the ambulatory are from the 15th century, when the structure was significantly enlarged. Across the courtyard is the serene **Cloître St-Trophime**, a cloister surrounded by superbly sculptured columns. Church and cloister open the same hours and has the admission costs as Les Arènes (see that section earlier in this chapter).

Les Alyscamps

This large necropolis, 1km south-east of Les Arènes, was founded by the Romans and taken over by Christians in the 4th century.

Les Alyscamps became a popular last resting place because of the presence of Christian martyrs among the dead, said to work miracles.

The necropolis was treated badly during and after the Renaissance, making it a shadow of its former self. Both Van Gogh and Gauguin painted Les Alyscamps with great vividness. It opens the same hours and has the same admission costs as Les Arènes (see that section earlier in this chapter).

Other Roman Sites

The **Thermes de Constantin**, Roman baths built in the 4th century near the river on rue du Grand Prieuré, are only partly preserved. The **Cryptoporticus du Forum** – underground storerooms, most of which were carved out in the 1st century BC – can be accessed though a 17th-century Jesuit chapel on rue Balze. Both keep the same hours and has the admission fee as Les Arènes (see that section earlier in this chapter).

Museums

The **Musée de l'Arles Antique** (☎ 04 90 18 88 88) brings together the rich collections of the former museums Musée d'Art Païen (Museum of Pagan Art) and the Musée d'Art Chrétien (Museum of Christian Art). Exhibits include Roman statues, artefacts, marble sarcophagi and a renowned assortment of early Christian sarcophagi from the 4th century. The museum is 1.5km south-west of the tourist office at ave de la Première Division Française Libre on the Presqu'île du Cirque Romain. It opens 9 am to 7 pm, March to 31 October; and 10 am to 5 pm, the rest of the year. Admission costs 35FF (students and those aged 12 to 18, 25FF).

The **Musée Arlaten** (☎ 04 90 96 08 23), 29 rue de la République, founded by Provençal poet Frédéric Mistral in 1896, is dedicated to preserving and displaying everyday objects related to traditional Provençal life: furniture, crafts, costumes, ceramics, wigs, a model of the Tarasque (a human-eating amphibious monster of Provençal legend) and so on. It occupies a 16th-century townhouse constructed around Roman ruins and opens 9.30 am to 1 pm

and 2 to 6.30 pm daily, June to August; and 9.30 am to 12.30 pm and 2 to 6 pm Tuesday to Sunday, April, May and September; and 9.30 am to 12.30 pm and 2 to 5 pm Tuesday to Sunday, the rest of the year. Admission costs 25FF (students and those aged 12 to 18, 20FF).

The **Musée Réattu** (☎ 04 90 96 37 68), inside a 15th-century priory at 10 rue du Grand Prieuré, exhibits works by some of the world's finest photographers, modern and contemporary works of art, and paintings by 18th- and 19th-century Provençal artists. It also has 57 Picasso drawings, sketched by the artist between December 1970 and November 1971. The conventional portrait of his mother Maria, painted in Côte d'Antibes in 1923, is particularly fine. The museum opens the same hours as Les Arènes. Admission costs 25FF (students and those aged 12 to 18, 20FF).

Contemporary art exhibits can be seen at the **Rencontres Internationales de la Photographie** (☎ 04 90 96 63 69, ℮ r.i.p.arles@ pacwan.fr), 10 rond point des Arènes, a photography centre that also organises photography courses and an international photography festival (see Feasts & Festivals in the Facts for the Visitor chapter). It opens 9 am to noon and 2 to 6 pm weekdays. Some shows are also held in the **Exposition Galerie Arènes** at the École Nationale de la Photographie (National School of Photography) inside elegant 18th-century Hôtel Quiqueran de Beaujeu at 16 rue des Arènes.

Van Gogh

The **Fondation Vincent van Gogh** (☎ 04 90 49 94 04), inside Palais de Luppé at 24 bis rond point des Arènes, displays paintings by artists inspired by Van Gogh. The centre opens 10 am to 7 pm, April to October; and 10 am to 5.40 pm, the rest of the year. Admission costs 30FF (students 20FF).

The gallery **La Rose des Vents** (☎ 04 90 96 15 85), 18 rue Diderot, displays various Van Gogh reproductions and letters written by him. In 1888 Van Gogh wrote to his sister Willemien, 'nature in the south cannot be painted with the palette of a mauve for instance which belongs to the north...now

Candles burn brightly in honour of St Sarah in the crypt of the old church, Stes-Maries de la Mer.

The Grand Rhône sweeps past the old Roman town of Arles.

From gladiatorial combat in Roman times to bullfights today, Les Arènes in Arles has hosted it all.

The tranquil Cloître St-Trophime, Arles

The tables turn in a traditional bullfight.

Wild white horses roam the Camargue.

Be swept off your feet by a *gardian*.

A throng parades the Stes-Maries to the sea.

the palette is distinctly colourful, sky blue, orange, pink, vermilion, a very bright yellow, bright green, wine red and violet'. The gallery opens 10.30 am to 12.30 pm and 3 to 7 pm Tuesday to Saturday, and 3 to 7 pm on Sunday.

Various art exhibitions take place at the modern **Espace Van Gogh** (☎ 04 90 49 39 39), in the former hospital on place Félix Rey where Van Gogh spent some time.

Musée Camarguais

Inside a sheep shed built in 1812, the Camargue Museum (☎ 04 90 97 10 82) at Mas du Pont de Rousty (10km south-west of Arles on the D570 to Stes-Maries) is an excellent introduction to the history, ecosystems, flora and fauna of the Camargue river delta. Much attention is given to traditional life in the Camargue (sheep and cattle raising, salt production at Salin de Giraud, local arts). A 3.5km nature-trail leads from the museum to an observation tower.

The museum opens 9.15 am to 5.45 pm (to 6.45 pm in July and August) Wednesday to Monday, April to October; and 10.15 am to 4.45 pm Wednesday to Monday, the rest of the year. Admission costs 25FF (students 13FF). The museum can be reached from Arles by bus (see Getting There & Away later in this section).

Abbaye de Montmajor

Montmajor Abbey (☎ 04 90 54 64 17), some 5km north-east of Arles on route de Fontvieille (the D17) is a medieval ensemble featuring an 11th-century main building and crypt, a Romanesque cloister built by Benedictine monks in 12th century and a hermitage dedicated to St Peter. The edifice, steadily restored since 1892, hosts occasional photography exhibitions. It opens 9 am to 7 pm daily, April to October; and 10 am to 1 pm and 2 to 5 pm Wednesday to Monday, the rest of the year. Admission costs 32FF (students 21FF) and is free on the first Sunday of the month.

Organised Tours

En Camargue (☎ 04 90 96 94 44, fax 04 90 49 67 55), 14 bis rue de la Calade, runs English-language 4WD tours in the Camargue, from March to the end of October. Half-/full-day jeep tours cost 150/195FF (children aged under 12, 80/100FF). It opens 9.30 am to noon and 2 to 6 pm. Reservations can also be made at La Boutique Provençal (☎ 04 90 49 84 31), a souvenir shop at 8 rond point des Arènes.

Special Events

In early July, Les Rencontres Internationales de la Photographie (International Photography Festival) attracts photographers and aficionados from around the world. The two-week Fêtes d'Arles at the end of June brings dance, theatre, music and poetry readings to Les Arènes. For more information contact Festiv'Arles (☎ 04 9 96 81 18), 35 place de la République; tickets cost 110FF to 315FF.

Other fascinating events include the Festo Vierginenco in mid-July, celebrated since 1904 to honour young girls who don the traditional Arlésienne costume for the first time. The week-long Fête des Prémices du Riz in September marks the start of the rice harvest.

Places to Stay – Budget

Camping Arles' nearest camp site is two-star *Camping City* (☎ 04 90 93 08 86, fax 04 90 93 91 07, 67 route de Crau), 1km southeast of Arles' centre on the road to Marseilles. It opens April to 30 Setember and charges 24/17/10FF per adult/child/dog plus 25/18FF per tent/car. Take bus No 2 to the Hermite stop.

Hostels The 100-bed *Auberge de Jeunesse* (☎ 04 90 96 18 25, fax 04 90 96 31 26, 20 ave Maréchal Foch), which charges 80FF for B&B, is 2km south of the centre. Take bus No 3 from blvd Georges Clémenceau or No 8 from place Lamartine to the Fournier stop.

Hotels The *Hôtel de France* (☎ 04 90 96 01 24, fax 04 90 96 90 87, 1–3 Lamartine) has rooms for one or two people, with shower and toilet, starting at 185FF. Next door, *Hôtel Terminus et Van Gogh* (☎/fax 04 90 96 12 32, e hotelvangogh@aol.com, 5 place

THE CAMARGUE

Lamartine) has singles/doubles with shower for 200FF (240/270FF with toilet too). Triples/quads with shower cost 290/340FF.

Heading into town you come to a cluster of cheapies, including *Hôtel Régence* (☎ 04 90 96 39 85, fax 04 90 96 67 64, 5 rue Marius Jouveau) which has rooms with shower (some with a view of the River Rhône) for 170FF (starting at 200FF with shower and toilet). Nearby *Hôtel de Paris* (☎ 04 90 96 05 88, 8 rue de la Cavalerie) adjoins a bar (popular with locals) and has rooms with shower and TV for 180/240FF (200/260FF with toilet too).

Flower box-adorned *Hôtel Voltaire* (☎ 04 90 96 49 18, fax 04 90 96 45 49, 1 place Voltaire) has serviceable doubles, some overlooking the pretty square, for 160FF with washbasin (180FF with shower, 200FF with bathroom). Old-fashioned and cluttered *Hôtel Le Rhône* (☎ 04 90 96 43 70, fax 04 90 93 87 03, 11 place Voltaire) has basic rooms costing 130FF (170FF with shower, 210FF with shower and toilet). Two-star triples with shower cost 190FF (220FF with toilet too).

Places to Stay – Mid-Range

Appealing, 20-room *Hôtel du Musée* (☎ 04 90 93 88 88, fax 04 90 49 98 15, 11 rue du Grand Prieuré) occupies a 12th- to 13th-century building, and is spacious, calm and has a terrace garden out back. Doubles with shower/bath and toilet start at 230/320FF.

Family run, two-star *Hôtel de la Muette* (☎ 04 90 96 15 39, fax 04 90 49 73 16, e hotel.muette@wanadoo.fr, 15 rue des Suisses) is part of the Logis de France chain and has prettily furnished rooms with toilet and shower for 320FF. Rooms with shower only (no toilet) cost 240FF.

A refined option is *Hôtel St-Trophime* (☎ 04 90 96 88 38, fax 04 90 96 92 19, 16 rue de la Calade), in a 17th-century mansion. Singles/doubles with shower, toilet and TV cost 215/295FF and triples/quads cost 390/430FF. Equally charming is *Hôtel Le Calendal* (☎ 04 90 96 11 89, fax 04 90 96 05 84, e contact@lecalendal.com, 5 rue Porte de Laure), with its lovely palm tree-studded summer garden off place Pomme.

Elegant rooms with shower start at 250FF (from 380/440FF with garden view/terrace). Triples/quads/rooms for five cost 450/490/530FF.

Arty *Hôtel de l'Amphithéâtre* (☎ 04 90 96 10 30, fax 04 90 93 98 69, e contact@hotelamphitheatre.fr, 5 rue Diderot) is decked out in a contemporary fashion to contrast with its 17th-century exterior. Singles/doubles start at 250/290FF.

Places to Stay – Top End

A hotel since 1920, historic *Hôtel d'Arlatan* (☎ 04 90 93 56 66, fax 04 90 49 68 45, e hotel-arlatan@provnet.fr, 26 rue du Sauvage) has lavish doubles costing from 598FF to 850FF in the former private residence of the counts of Arlatan de Beaumont.

Big spenders can try Relais et Châteaux's four-star *Hôtel Jules César* (☎ 04 90 93 43 20, fax 04 90 93 33 47, e julescesar@calva.net, 9 blvd des Lices), inside a former convent with Roman-style portico, private chapel, outdoor swimming pool and sumptuous Provençal-style rooms costing upwards of 750FF.

Overlooking place du Forum at No 14 is *Grand Hôtel Nord Pinus* (☎ 04 90 93 44 44, fax 04 90 93 34 00, e info@nordpinus.com). Fancy singles/doubles start at 770/840FF.

Places to Eat

Blvd Georges Clémenceau and blvd des Lices are lined with plane trees and terraced brasseries – fine for a meal if you don't mind dining a la traffic fumes. In Arles' historic heart, place du Forum is an intimate square shaded by eight large plane trees and filled with restaurant terraces. The bright yellow facade of *Café La Nuit* (☎ 04 90 96 44 56) at No 11 mimics the canary yellow house on place Lamartine which Van Gogh painted for his canvas *Café de Nuit* (1888). *Menus* cost 75FF and 95FF.

Absolutely devoid of pretension is bohemian *La Cuisine*, at the northern end of pedestrian rue Réattu. Cheap, cheerful and full of fun, 'The Kitchen' dishes up a no-frills soupe/plat/salade du jour for around 50FF a throw. Oil drums mark the entrance.

THE CAMARGUE

Despite its name, Hôtel Calendal's *Salon de Thé* on place Pomme is one of Arles' finest places to lunch. Imaginative 48FF salads – salmon and grapefruit, cheese and *saucisson d'Arles* (Arles sausage) – and other light bites are served beneath the shade of trees in its peaceful and beautiful, bird-twittering walled garden. Diners can limber up with a game of giant-sized chess.

By the river, calm and cool *L'Entrevue* (☎ 04 90 93 37 28, 23 quai Max Dormoy) is in an artsy cinema, bookshop and restaurant complex and serves Oriental and Caribbean cuisine in a stylish laid-back atmosphere. Choose between 11 tajines, six types of couscous, a 55FF plat du jour or 130FF *menu*, followed by a pot of wonderfully refreshing mint and pine kernel tea.

La Paillotte (☎ 04 90 96 33 15, 26 rue du Docteur Fanton) dishes up great *aïoli Provençal* (see the special Food & Wine section earlier in the book) for 78FF and has *menus* for 94FF and 148FF. *L'Olivier* (☎ 04 90 49 64 88, [e] olivier@provnet.fr, 1 bis rue Réattu) is one of Arles' more upmarket choices, serving tasty Provençal- and Mediterranean-inspired *menus* starting at 148FF (108FF at lunchtime). Period furnishings and a patio add a distinctive touch.

Self-caterers can shop at the Wednesday-morning *market* on blvd Émile Combe, or the Saturday morning market on blvd des Lices and blvd Georges Clémenceau.

Shopping

Local *saucisson d'Arles* is sold at sausage makers *La Farandole (11 rue des Porcelets)* and at *Pierre Milhau Charcuterie (11 rue Réattu)*. Olive oil is sold by the bottle or litre at rustic *Huiles Jamard (46 rue des Arènes)*, run by the same team as La Cuisine (see the previous Places to Eat section).

Getting There & Away

Air Nîmes-Arles-Camargue airport (Aéroport de Nîmes-Arles-Camargue; ☎ 04 66 70 49 49), also called Aéroport Garons, is 20km north-west of the city on the A54 to Nîmes.

Bus The inter-regional bus station (☎ 04 90 49 38 01) is at the end of ave Paulin Talabot,

---

Bamboleo et al

Roma bands such as Los Reyes, Arles' very own Gypsy Kings (discovered while busking in St-Tropez), Chico & the Gypsies (founded by former Gypsy King, Chico Bouchikki) and Manitas de Plata have all sung on the streets of Arles and Stes-Maries de la Mer at some point in their vibrant careers. For an outstanding collection of tracks by these and other artists, shop at **La Boutique des Passionnés** (Boutique of the Passionates; ☎ 04 90 96 59 93, [e] contact@passionnes.com), a fabulous music shop at 14 rue Réattu, which opens 2 to 7 pm Monday, 9 am to 7 pm Tuesday to Saturday. It has an online boutique at www.passionnes.com (French only).

The best time to watch Roma bands perform on the streets is during the Festival Mosaïque Gitane in Arles in mid-July and the Stes-Maries de la Mer pilgrimages in May and October. The musicians (exclusively male) are usually encircled by Roma women dancing Camargue flamenco.

---

about 1km north of Les Arènes. The regional bus company, Les Cars de Camargue, has an office at 14 blvd Georges Clémenceau (☎ 04 90 18 96 33) – the bus stop for intercity buses – and at 4 rue Jean Mathieu Artaud (☎ 04 90 96 94 78). It runs services to Tarascon (18FF, 30 minutes, four daily during term-time only), Nîmes (32FF, 50 minutes, six daily) and Marseilles (88FF, two hours, three to five daily) via Fontvieille (12.50FF, 20 minutes), Les Baux de Provence (29FF, 35 minutes), Salon de Provence (45FF, 1¼ hours) and Aix-en-Provence (80FF, 1¾ hours, twice daily).

Les Cars de Camargue buses link Arles with other parts of the Camargue, including Stes-Maries de la Mer (37FF, one hour, six to nine daily in summer, two in winter), Salin de Giraud (38FF, 40 minutes, five to seven daily), Port St-Louis (28FF, 50 minutes, four to six daily) and many places en route such as Mas du Pont de Rousty, Pioch Badet (28FF, 40 minutes) and Pont de Gau.

Ceyte Tourisme Méditerranée (CTM; ☎ 04 90 93 74 90), 21 chemin du Temple, runs

THE CAMARGUE

buses to Aix-en-Provence, Marseilles and Avignon (40FF, 45 minutes, five daily Monday to Saturday).

Eurolines (☎ 04 90 96 94 78) sells tickets for European destinations at 14 blvd Georges Clémenceau.

Train Arles train station is opposite the bus station and serves major rail destinations including Nîmes (41FF, 30 minutes), Marseilles (81FF, 40 minutes) and Avignon (56FF, 20 minutes).

Car & Motorcycle Car rental companies with offices in Arles include Avis (☎ 04 90 96 82 42) and National Citer (☎ 04 90 93 02 17) on ave Paulin Talabot; and Europcar (☎ 04 90 93 23 24) and Hertz (☎ 04 90 96 75 23), both on blvd Victor Hugo.

Getting Around

To/From the Airport CTM (☎ 04 90 93 74 90) runs bus services to Nîmes-Arles-Camargue airport from 14 blvd Georges Clémenceau.

Bicycle Bikes can be hired from Peugeot Cycles (☎ 04 90 96 03 77), 15 rue du Pont, which opens 8 am to noon and 2 to 7 pm Monday to Saturday. It offers road and mountain bikes costing upwards of 80/300F per day/week to rent. Students get a small discount.

The newspaper kiosk adjoining the tourist office on esplanade Charles de Gaulle, is an agent for EuropBike SARL (☎/fax 04 90 49 52 85, ⒠ europbike@wanadoo.fr), 1 rue Philippe Lebon, and has bikes to rent for 60/80FF per half-/full day. The kiosk opens 7 am to 7 pm (shorter hours in winter).

STES-MARIES DE LA MER

postcode 13460 • pop 2200

Stes-Maries de la Mer (Li Santo in Provençal) is no more than a seaside village, marooned between the Étang de l'Impérial and the sea in the Camarguaise outback. It is best known for its magnificent fortified Romanesque church, which has for centuries served as a pilgrimage site for Europe's colourful *gitan* (Roma) population.

The coastline is lined with 30km of uninterrupted sandy beaches. Nudists frequent the patch near Phare de la Gacholle, a lighthouse 11km east of the village.

Orientation & Information

The amphitheatre, the tourist office and Port Gardian are lined up between ave Van Gogh and the sea. From the bus stop on ave d'Arles (the southern end of the D570), bear south along ave Frédéric Mistral then east across place des Remparts and place Portalet to get to place de l'Église.

The tourist office (☎ 04 90 97 82 55, fax 04 90 97 71 15, ⒠ saintes-maries@enprovence.com), 5 ave Van Gogh, opens 9 am to 8 pm, July and August; 9 am to 7 pm April, May, June and September; and 9 am to 5 or 6 pm, the rest of the year. Visit the Web site at www.saintes-maries-camargue.enprovence.com (French only). There is an ATM outside the tourist office and a laundrette at 24 ave d'Arles.

Things to See

The donjon-style **Église des Stes-Maries**, built between the 12th and 15th centuries on place de l'Église, dominates the village. Its sober, dim interior shelters a beautiful elevated choir and a crypt where the statue of St Sarah is religiously kept. Year round, a sea of smoky candles burns at the foot of the over-dressed black statue, which at pilgrimage time is showered with at least 40 or 50 brightly colourful dresses (see the boxed text 'The Roma Pilgrimage' on the next page). St Sarah's relics – discovered in the crypt by King René in 1448 – are enshrined in a gaudy wooden chest, stashed away in a hole cut in the sturdy stone wall above the choir. In summer, pay 10FF for a panoramic view of the Camargue wetlands from the roof terrace. The church opens 8 am and 6 pm (to 7 pm March, April and October).

Roma culture is unravelled in a series of eight *roullettes* (caravans) from the 1930s to 1960s at **Le Panorama du Voyage** (☎ 04 90 97 52 85), next to the hostel in Pioch Badet, 8km north of Stes-Maries on the D570. Admission costs 20FF (children aged under 14, 18FF). About 2km farther north along the

D570 is **Château d'Avignon** (☎ 04 90 97 58 60), an 18th-century chateau furnished almost exactly as it was by wealthy Marseilles merchant Louis Noilly Prat, who used the place as a hunting lodge in the 1890s. He kitted out the castle with hot and cold running water, central heating and other gadgets – all revolutionary at the time. The chateau can be visited by guided tour (45 minutes), hourly between 10 am and 5 pm Wednesday to Monday. Admission costs 20FF (students and children aged under 14, 10FF).

Back in Stes-Maries, the **Musée de Baroncelli** (☎ 04 90 97 10 82) in the 19th-century city hall on rue Victor Hugo is dedicated to the Marquis of Baroncelli (1869–1943) – a *manadier* (herdsman) who devoted his life to reviving local Camarguaise culture when not herding his *manades* (herds of bulls and horses). It opens 10 am to noon and 2 to 6 pm, April to mid-November. Admission costs 10FF and a combined ticket for museum and church terrace is available for 15FF.

Les Arènes (☎ 04 90 97 85 86), the amphitheatre next to Port Gardian, can only be visited during bullfights; the tourist office has details on buying tickets. Bullfights are also held on Sunday, Easter to mid-July, at the **Arènes de Méjanes** (☎ 04 90 97 10 60), an open-air theatre at Mas de Méjanes (☎ 04 90 97 10 10), the Paul Ricard complex 30km north in Méjanes.

Boat Trips

Several companies offer boat excursions, including Bateau de Promenade (☎ 04 90 97 84 72), 5 rue des Launes, and En Camargue (☎ 04 90 97 70 10), 36 ave Théodore Aubanel. Both have boats departing from **Port Gardian**, March to November. *Tiki III* (☎ 04 90 97 81 68, e tiki3@wanadoo .fr) plies the delta's shallow waters (70FF, 1½ hours) and is docked at the mouth of the Petit Rhône 1.5km west of Stes-Maries.

Kayak Vert (☎ 04 90 97 88 89 06 09 56 06 47), based at the Cabanes de Cambon, 14km north of Stes-Maries, on the banks of the Petit Rhône off the picturesque D38, is a canoeing centre where you can explore Camargue's waterways by paddle power. It hires canoes and organises half-/full-day guided expeditions.

THE CAMARGUE

The Roma Pilgrimage

Europe's Roma population is said to have its roots in Camargue's shifting waters, and Roma people from all over Europe flock to Stes-Maries de la Mer to honour their patron saint, Sarah, each May and October. According to Provençal legend, Sarah was the servant of Mary Jacob and Mary Salome who (along with other New Testament figures) fled the Holy Land by boat and drifted in the open sea until landing near the River Rhône in AD 40.

Pilgrimages set the streets of Stes-Maries ablaze with song, music and dance. The May festivities last for three days, the first two of which celebrate the feast day of Mary Jacob (25 May) and see Roma party with great gusto. Many hit the road for the long journey home on the third day, which honours the Marquis de Baroncelli Jaron (1869–1943), a local herdsman who revived many Camarguaise traditions in the 19th century. Fewer travel to the autumn pilgrimage, which falls on the Sunday nearest to Mary Salome's feast day (22 October).

In anticipation of a pilgrimage, a wooden chest above the choir in Église des Stes-Maries is lowered to the altar so the pilgrims can touch it and pray by its side. The chest is believed to contain the skeletons of Sarah, Mary Jacob and Mary Salome, discovered in the church in 1448. Following a solemn mass, a statue of black Sarah is carried from the church crypt, through the streets and down to the sea, to symbolise the arrival of the Roma patron saint. The procession is led by *gardians* (Camargue cowboys) on horseback who usher the statue to the seashore, where it is placed in a wooden fishing boat in the sea and blessed. The pilgrims pour into the sea fully clothed. The same ritual is showered upon statues of Mary Jacob and Mary Salome on 25 May when, following the benediction of the sea, the sacred relics in the church are winched back up to their safe hidey-hole.

Organised Tours

Le Gitan (☎ 04 66 70 09 65) organises photographic safaris by 4WD (jeep tours) in the delta from its office (☎ 04 90 97 89 33) on the seafront at 13 ave de la Plage.

For information on other tours and activities see Organised Tours at the start of this chapter.

Special Events

The village bursts with life during its annual Roma pilgrimages on 24–25 May and 17–18 October. Bullfights animate Les Arènes most Sundays in May and June, in mid-June for the village's five-day Fête Votive, in mid-August during the Fête Biou y Toros and during pilgrimages. The tourist office has an updated schedule.

Places to Stay & Eat

Camping North-east of the centre by the seashore, *Camping La Brise (☎ 04 90 97 84 67, fax 04 90 97 72 01, ℮ saintes-maries @enprovence.com, rue Marcel Carrière)* has a swimming pool. *Camping Le Clos du Rhône (☎ 04 90 97 85 99, fax 04 90 97 78 85, route d'Aigues-Mortes)* opens April to September. Count on paying about 85FF for a tent, car and two adults at either.

Hostels There's an *Auberge de Jeunesse (☎ 04 90 97 51 72, fax 04 90 97 54 88)* in Pioch Badet, 8km north of Stes-Maries on the D570 to Arles. Half-board is obligatory and costs 130FF. Reception opens 8.30 to 11 am and 5 to 10 pm (later in July and August). The hostel has bicycles to rent (60FF per day) and can organise horse-riding. A hostelling card is obligatory.

Les Cars de Camargue buses from Arles to Stes-Maries drop you at the door in Pioch Badet; see Getting There & Away in the Arles section earlier in this chapter.

Cabanes Aspiring cowboys can rent a *cabane de gardian* (see the boxed text 'Bulls & Cowboys' earlier in this chapter); the tourist office has details. Most cabanes sleep up to five people and can be rented on a weekly basis, April to September. There is a cluster for hire on ave Riquette Aubanel,

a narrow lane (the D38) leading from Stes-Maries past the port to Aigues-Mortes.

Farmhouses Numerous *mas* (farmhouses) surround Stes-Maries. *Mas de la Grenouillère (☎ 04 90 97 90 22, 06 80 25 68 58, fax 04 90 97 70 94, route d'Arles)*, 1.5km along a dirt track signposted off the D570 1km north of Stes-Maries, has small but comfortable rooms with a terrace overlooking open fields and a choir of frogs singing guests to sleep at night. Doubles/triples/quads start at 260/380/460FF. La Grenouillère (literally 'Frog Farm') has a swimming pool and organises horse-riding.

Even more idyllic – if you can afford it – is nearby *L'Étrier Camarguais (*the Camargue Stirrup; ☎ 04 90 97 81 14, fax 04 90 97 88 11)*, a farmhouse-hotel made from 'a dream, flowers and the sun'. It is 500m before La Grenouillère along the same dirt track. Doubles cost 400/500FF in low/high season. It opens April to 30 September.

B&B *Mas des Colverts (☎ 04 90 97 83 73, fax 04 90 97 74 28)* and two-star hotel complex *Mas des Salicornes (☎ 04 90 97 83 41, fax 04 90 97 85 70, ℮ les-salicornes @wanadoo.fr)* are other lovely farmhouses accessible via the D570. Both are run by Provençal chef Roger Merlin who also hosts cookery courses (see Courses in the Facts for the Visitor chapter). Doubles start at 245/290FF in low/high season.

Hotels Heaps of hotels – mostly three- or four-star and costing at least 300FF per night – line the D570, the main road (called route d'Arles) from Arles to Stes-Maries. In the village, the cheapest rooms are at one-star *Les Vagues (☎/fax 04 90 97 84 40, 12 ave Théodore Aubanel)* on the road running along the port, west of the tourist office; or *Le Delta (☎ 04 90 97 81 12, fax 04 90 97 72 85, 1 place Mireille)* on the right as you enter Stes-Maries from the north. Doubles at Les Vagues start at 250FF. Le Delta has singles/doubles for 185/205FF and triples/quads for 245/275FF, all with showers.

If you want to be closer to the birds, *Hostellerie du Pont de Gau (☎ 04 90 97 81 53, fax 04 90 97 98 54)*, a Logis de France hotel

THE CAMARGUE

with an excellent restaurant (*menus* from 95FF) next to the Parc Ornithologique on the D570, is for you. Doubles cost 255FF. It opens mid-February to January.

Getting There & Away

Stes-Maries has no real bus station; buses use the shelter at the northern entrance to town on ave d'Arles (continuation of route d'Arles and the D570).

For bus details to/from Arles (via Pont du Gau and Mas du Pont de Rousty), see Getting There & Away in the Arles section. In summer there are two buses daily from Stes-Maries to Nîmes (1¼ hours) via Aigues-Mortes.

Getting Around

Le Vélo Saintois (☎/fax 04 90 97 74 56), 19 ave de la République, opens 8.30 am to 7 pm (8 am to 10 pm in July and August). It charges 90/220FF for one/three days' bike rental. It rents children's bicycles (90FF per day) and tandems (180FF per day). Ask for a copy of its free English-language tour brochure before pedalling off.

Le Vélociste (☎ 04 90 97 83 26) ,opposite the town hall on place des Remparts, opens 9 am to 7.30 pm and charges the same. It has a brochure detailing scenic rides and organises cycling, canoeing and horse-riding trips.

The Pioch Badet hostel rents wheels for 60FF per day.

AIGUES-MORTES

postcode 30220 • pop 5000

On the Camargue's western edge, 28km north-west of Stes-Maries in the Gard department, is the curiously named walled-town of Aigues-Mortes (literally 'Dead Waters'; Aigo-Morto in Provençal). Sleepy Aigues-Mortes was established on marshy flat land in the mid-13th century by Louis IX so the French crown would have a Mediterranean port under its direct control. At the time, the area's other ports were governed by various rival powers, including the counts of Provence. In 1248, Louis IX's ships – all 1500 of them – gathered here before setting sail to the Holy Land for the Seventh Crusade.

Aigues-Mortes' sturdy, rectangular ramparts – the tops of which afford great views over the marshlands – can be easily circumambulated from the **Tour de Constance** (☎ 04 66 53 61 55). Count on 30 minutes for the 1.6km wall-top walk. Inside the impregnable fortress, with its 6m-thick walls, you can visit the 32m-tall tower which served as a Huguenot women's prison following the revocation of the Edict of Nantes in 1685. The word *register* ('to resist' in old French) on the millstone in the centre of the prison was carved by heroine inmate Marie Durand, jailed here for 38 years. The Tour de Constance (named by Louis VII after his sister) opens 9.30 am to 8 pm, June to August; 10 am to 6 pm in February, April and October, 9.30 am to 7 pm in May and September; and 10 am to 5 pm the rest of the year. Ticket booths close one hour before closure. Admission costs 35FF (those aged 18 to 21, 21FF).

The tourist office (☎ 04 66 53 73 00, fax 04 66 53 65 94, e office.tourisme .aigues.mortes@wanadoo.fr), inside the walled city at Porte de la Gardette, opens 9 am to 8 pm in July and August; and 9 am to noon and 2 to 6 pm weekdays, and 10 am to noon and 2 to 6 pm on weekends, the rest of the year. It has a Web site at www .ot-aiguesmortes.fr.

Salins du Midi

There are magnificent views of the pink-hued saltpans that stretch south from the top of Aigues-Mortes' southern ramparts. By road, the lone D979 follows the narrow land bar that cuts across the still pools. Alternatively, hop aboard the salt train (☎ 04 66 53 85 20) that salt producer La Baleine operates in summer. Trains depart at 10 am and 6.30 pm, April to September (additional departures at 11.15 am and 2.30, 3.45 and 5.15 pm in June, July and August). Tickets for the informative, one hour's train ride (with commentary in English), cost 35FF (children aged four to 12, 20FF). Heading towards the Salins du Midi, La Baleine train stop is clearly flagged on the left just before the bridge.

Between May and August, tours of the

salt works and marshes are possible. The tourist office has details.

Boat Excursions

Between March and November, boats line up at Aigues-Mortes port to take tourists on 2½-hour safaris around the wild Camargue waters; tickets cost 60FF (children aged four to 13, 35FF). You can also **hire boats** of your own (170FF per hour for four people).

Places to Stay

The cheapest place to stay in Aigues-Mortes is *Hôtel Carrière* (☎ 04 66 53 73 07, fax 04 66 53 84 75, 18 rue Pasteur), with rooms from 200FF. *Hôtel Le St-Louis* (☎ 04 66 53 72 68, fax 04 66 53 75 92, 10 rue Amiral Courbet) has rooms costing 290FF to 490FF.

Three-star *Hôtel des Ramparts* (☎ 04 66 53 82 77, fax 04 66 53 73 77, 6 place France), overlooking Tour de Constance, has singles/doubles with shower and toilet for 265/280FF. Next door, *Le Victoria* (☎ 04 66 51 14 20, fax 04 66 51 14 21) has two-star doubles with shower and toilet costing 268FF. Neighbouring rough-and-ready *Café de la Bourse* has a handful of bargain-basement rooms above its busy bar.

Places to Eat

The walled city is loaded with places to eat. Pretty place St-Louis, at the southern foot of Grand rue, has heaps of open-air cafes and terrace restaurants, most of them sporting *menus* averaging 80FF and *guardianne de taureau* (a traditional meaty beef stew from the Camargue) for 50FF.

Simple but elegant *La Salicorne* (☎ 04 66 53 62 67, 9 rue Alsace Lorraine) stands out. Quintessential Provençal dishes with an imaginative twist are served a stylish, old-world yet jazzy setting. Its *menu* costs 145FF.

Food shops, grocers, boulangeries and boucheries bespeckle Grand Rue. *Le Moulin de Pauline* (22 rue Emile Zola) specialises in olive oils, spices, rice and other regional delights.

Getting There & Away

From Aigues-Mortes' tiny train station (☎ 04 66 53 74 74), route de Nîmes, there are a handful of trains to/from Nîmes (39FF, 45 minutes). Many scheduled trains are replaced by SNCF buses.

SOUTH-EASTERN CAMARGUE

The wetland is at its most savage around the eastern shores of the Étang de Vaccarès. Much of this area is protected and off limits to tourists. A memorable day trip is to head southwards along the D570 from Arles, turn left onto the D36, then bear right (west) along the narrow D36B to La Capelière and beyond to Salin de Giraud. Return to Arles via the northbound D36, a larger road which shadows the Grand Rhône.

Arles to Digue à la Mer

Mid-way along this 48km stretch – where the road kisses Vaccarès' eastern shores – is **La Capelière**, a minuscule hamlet where the Réserve Nationale de Camargue runs its excellent **Centre d'Information Nature** (Nature Information Centre; ☎ 04 90 97 00 97). As well as exhibitions, a 1.5km-long **Sentier des Rainettes** (nature trail), studded with four wildlife observatories, enables you to discover flora and fauna typical to fresh-water marshes. The centre opens 9 am to 1 pm and 2 to 6 pm daily, April to September; and 9 am to 1 pm and 2 to 5 pm Wednesday to Monday, the rest of the year. Admission costs 20FF (students and those aged 12 to 18, 10FF).

The centre runs three observatories at **Salin de Badon**, former royal salt pans about 7km farther south along the D36B. Unlike at La Capelière, the bird-watching towers fall within the Réserve Nationale de Camargue. Photography is therefore forbidden and visitors need a 20FF permit (issued at the Centre d'Information Nature in La Capelière) to enter. The site is accessible to permit holders from 4 pm (3 pm November to 28 February) to sunset on Wednesday, and from sunrise to 10 am (11 am November to 28 February) and 4 pm (3 pm November to 28 February) to sunset Thursday to Tuesday.

A beautiful stroll along what seems to be the edge of the world can be enjoyed on the **Digue à la Mer**, a sea dike built in the 19th century to cut the delta off from the sea. A 18km-long walking and cycling track runs along the length of the dike; there's also a shorter 10km circuit and a 2.3km footpath that cuts down to a lovely sandy beach. Walking on the fragile sand dunes is forbidden. To access the dike, follow the D36B for 10km south-west to Parking de la Gochelle where motorists have no choice but to park. The **lighthouse** (phare) cannot be visited. The dike can be accessed 9 am to 1 pm and 2 to 6 pm (to 5 pm October to March).

Salin de Giraud & Beyond

The chequered evaporation saltpans (marais salants) of **Salin de Giraud** cover 14,000 hectares and produce about 1,000,000 tonnes of salt per year, making them one of Europe's largest. *Sel* (salt), which takes three years to produce, is harvested in September and then stored in giant mountains. Pass the entrance to Salin de Giraud on the D36 and continue south along the D36D for a stunning panorama of the marsh village, the saltpans and the salt mountains. A couple of kilometres south of here is a **point de vue** (view point) where you can pull up, breathe in the salty sea air and hop aboard the tiny **tourist train** that takes tourists on scenic three-hour rides through the saltpans. Trains depart at 11 am, noon, 2 and 6 pm, Easter to mid-September. Tickets cost 30FF (children aged under 10, 15FF).

The final 12km leg of this southbound journey is unforgettable. Drive slowly to enjoy the views and stop to see pink flamingos wading through the water. Approximately 8km south of Salin de Giraud is the badly signposted **Domaine de la Palissade** (☎ 04 42 86 81 28), a nature centre run by the Conservatoire de l'Espace Littoral et des Rivages Lacustres, which organises forays in the marshes on foot and horse back. It opens 9 am to 5 pm, April to October.

The road reaches the Mediterranean about 4km farther south. Caravans and camper vans can park overnight in the camp site on the sand here, overlooking **Plage de Piémanson**. Bear east (left) from the car

park and walk 1400m to get to the nudist section of the very windy beach.

Salin de Giraud is 15km east of the Digue à la Mer via the winding D36C. En route you pass the **Mas de St-Bertrand** (☎ 04 42 48 80 69, route de Vaccarès), an idyllic gîte which rents rooms and bicycles from February to mid-November. The tourist office (☎ 04 42 86 80 87), situated in a traditional gardian's cabane on place des Gardians (the central square in Salin de Giraud) has information on the few other accommodation options in this isolated part of the world. It opens June to mid-September.

Back to Arles

Some 8km north of Salin de Giraud is the **Musée du Riz du Petit Manusclat** (☎ 04 90 97 20 29) in Petit Manusclat. The history of the Camargue rice industry dating from the 13th century is explained. The wetland yields 8 million *quintaux* (400,000 tonnes) of rice per year. Museum opening hours are sporadic; call in advance to arrange a visit.

In **Le Sambuc**, 6km north along the D36, there are several places where you can horse-ride for 80/290FF per hour/day. *Hôtel Longo Maï* (☎ 04 90 97 21 91, fax 04 90 97 22 92, e jray13200@aol.com), 1.5km south of the small hamlet, is a Logis de France hotel with nice singles/doubles costing 278/294FF.

The **Station Biologique de la Tour du Valat** (☎ 04 90 97 20 13), just west of here, is a research station. It covers an area of 2500 hectares and opens to the public one day per year (in January). In 1970 it instigated the construction of the artificial **Étang du Fangassier**. The 4000 sq metre island serves as a flamingo breeding colony, which a few years previously had started to breed less in the region.

On the eastern bank of the Grand Rhône is the Mas Thibert, from where the **Marais du Vigueirat** – an extensive marshland – can be explored with a local guide. Eight heron species frequent these dense swamps. Expeditions (four to six hours, April to September) have to be booked in advance through the tourist office in Arles.

Avignon Area

Avignon, the capital of the Vaucluse department (Van Cluso in Provençal), acquired its ramparts and reputation as a city of art and culture during the 14th century, when Pope Clement V and his court, fleeing political turmoil in Rome, established themselves near Avignon. From 1309 to 1377, the Holy See was based in Avignon, under seven French-born popes, and huge sums of money were invested in building and decorating the papal palace and other important church edifices.

North of Avignon, fan-shaped Vaucluse – with Avignon at its hinge – spreads out into a multitude of contrasting landscapes, climaxing with the stark summit of Mont Ventoux (1912m), the region's highest mountain, where the legendary mistral wind often blows at speeds of 250km/h. Walking and cycling opportunities are abundant here.

South of Avignon are a cluster of towns, first settled by the Greeks, then by the Romans who left behind a trove of archaeological treasures. The fortified village of Les Baux de Provence rakes in 2.5 million tourists a year, ranking it as among France's most visited tourist attractions.

Avignon & Around

AVIGNON
postcode 84000 • pop 88,312
• elevation 21m

Avignon (Avignoun in Provençal) continues its traditional role as a patron of the arts, most notably through its annual performing arts festival. Avignon's other attractions include its fine Côtes du Rhône wines, its bridge, a historic walled city and several interesting museums, including some across the River Rhône in the town of Villeneuve-lès-Avignon (sometimes written Villeneuve-lez-Avignon; Vilo-Novo-Avignoun in Provençal).

Orientation
The main avenue, cours Jean Jaurès – south

Highlights

- See how the popes lived at Avignon's Palais des Papes
- Follow in the footsteps of the Romans through Orange, Vaison-la-Romaine, Carpentras, St-Rémy de Provence and Nîmes
- Climb or cycle up Mont Ventoux or around the Dentelles de Montmirail
- Shop for olives in the Enclave des Papes and fresh truffles at the weekly markets in Aups, Carpentras and Richerenches (November to March)
- Sample France's most potent wine at Châteauneuf du Pape
- Think purple! Follow the lavender road

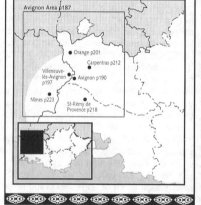

of the tourist office and rue de la République – is inside the walled city and runs northwards from the train station to place de l'Horloge.

Place de l'Horloge is 200m south of place du Palais, which abuts Palais des Papes. The rehabilitated Quartier des Teinturiers (dyers' quarter), around rue des Teinturiers and south-east of place Pie, is Avignon's bohemian part of town.

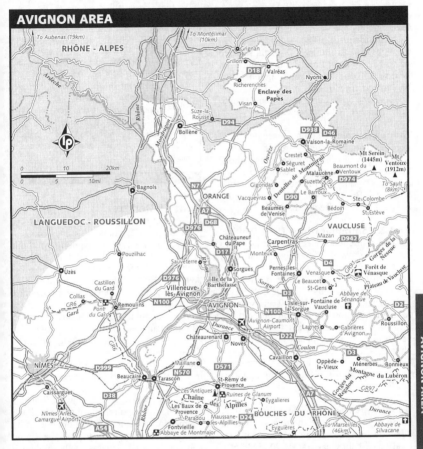

AVIGNON AREA

Villeneuve-lès-Avignon, the suburb on the right bank of the Rhône, is reached by crossing the two branches of the river and Île de la Barthelasse, the island that divides them.

Information
Tourist Offices Avignon's main tourist office (☎ 04 32 74 32 74, fax 04 90 82 95 03, ⓔ information@ot-avignon.fr), 41 cours Jean Jaurès, opens 9 am to 6 pm weekdays, 9 am to 1 pm and 2 to 5 pm Saturday, and 10 am to noon Sunday (9 am to 1 pm and 2 to 5 pm Sunday, April to September). Hours

during the Avignon Festival are 10 am to 8 pm Monday to Saturday, and 10 am to 5 pm Sunday. The tourist office annexe (same ☎) at Pont St-Bénézet opens 9 am to 7 pm, May to September. They share a Web site at www.ot-avignon-tourisme.fr.

In Villeneuve-lès-Avignon, the tourist office (☎ 04 90 25 61 33, fax 04 90 25 91 55, ⓔ villeneuve.lez.avignon@wanadoo.fr), 1 place Charles David, opens 10 am to 7 pm weekdays, 10 am to 1 pm and 2.30 to 7 pm weekends, July; 9 am to 12.30 pm and 2 to 6 pm, August; and 9 am to 12.30 pm and 2 to 6 pm Monday to Saturday, the rest of the year. Its Web site is at www.villeneuve-lez-avignon.com.

Avignon tourist office (☎ 04 3 74 32 72) arranges walking tours (50FF; those aged 12 to 18, 30FF) in English on Tuesday and Thursday, April to October. Avignon's Bureau Information Jeunesse (☎ 04 90 82 29 56), 102 rue de la Carreterie, opens 9 am to noon and 2 to 5.30 pm weekdays.

Money Banque de France, place de l'Horloge, exchanges currency from 8.35 am to 12.05 pm weekdays. There is a 24-hour banknote exchange machine outside Lyonnais de Banque, 13 rue de la République, and Caixa Bank, 67 rue Joseph Vernet (opposite the Musée Requien).

Post & Communications The post office, cours Président Kennedy, opens 8 am to 7 pm weekdays, 8 am to noon on Saturday. It has Cyberposte.

Internet access costs 30FF per hour at Cyber Highway (☎ 04 90 27 02 09), 30 rue Infirmières. It opens from 10 am Monday to Saturday, and from noon on Sunday. Nearby, La Pomme Bleue (☎ 04 90 14 00 15), 5 place Carmes, opens 11 to 2 am and charges 45FF per hour. The hourly rate at Cyberdrome (☎ 04 90 16 05 15), 68 rue Guillaume Puy, open 8 am to midnight, is 35FF.

Bookshops The Maison de la Presse (☎ 04 90 86 57 42), opposite the tourist office at 34 cours Jean Jaurès, stocks maps. Alternatively try Shakespeare (☎ 04 90 27 38 50), 155 rue de la Carreterie, an English-language bookshop open 9.30 am to 12.30 pm and 2 to 6.30 pm Tuesday to Saturday.

Laundry Laundrettes at 27 rue du Portail Magnanen and 66 place des Corps Saints open 7 am to 7.30 or 8 pm.

Medical Services The hospital (Centre Hospitalier; ☎ 04 90 80 33 33), 305 rue Raoul Follereau, is 2.5km south of the train station, at the southern terminus of bus line No 1 or 3 (marked on bus maps as Hôpital Sud).

Museum Passes

Avignon and Villeneuve-lès-Avignon tourist offices doll out a *pass gratuit* (free pass) that, after visiting one museum, entitles you and your family to a 20% to 50% discount on every subsequent museum or monument. The pass is valid for two weeks.

A Passeport pour l'Art (Passport for Art) costs 45FF and covers admission to all the Villeneuve-lès-Avignon sights included in this guide. Villeneuve-lès-Avignon tourist office sells it.

Pont St-Bénézet

St-Bénézet's Bridge (☎ 04 90 85 60 16, e| monument@palais-des-papes.com) – better known as Pont d'Avignon – was built between 1177 and 1185 to link Avignon with what later became Villeneuve-lès-Avignon. By tradition, the construction of the bridge began when Bénézet (Benedict the Bridge Builder), a pious lad from Savoy, was told in three visions to get the Rhône spanned at any cost.

Yes...this is the **Pont d'Avignon** mentioned in the French nursery rhyme, although people did not dance *sur le pont d'Avignon* (on the bridge of Avignon) but rather *sous* (under) it.

The 900m-long structure was originally made of wood and rebuilt in stone by Pope Clement VI around 1350. All but four of its 22 spans – over both channels of the Rhône and Île de la Barthelasse in the middle – were washed away by floods in 1669.

Admission to the bridge via cours Châtelet costs 19FF (seniors and students 15FF, children aged under eight, free) and includes an excellent audioguide in English. A *billet jumelé* (combination ticket) covering admission to Pont d'Avignon and Palais des Papes costs 55FF (seniors and students 45FF). The bridge can be visited 9 am to 7 pm, March to July and October; 9 am to 9 pm July; 9 am to 8 pm August and September; and 9 am to 1 pm and 2 to 5 pm Tuesday to Sunday, the rest of the year.

AVIGNON AREA

Walled City

Avignon's most interesting bits are within the roughly oval walled city – 151 hectares of history surrounded by 4.3km of ramparts built between 1359 and 1370. They were restored during the 19th century but the original moats were not re-dug, leaving the crenellated fortifications looking less imposing than they once did. Even in the 14th century this defence system was hardly state-of-the-art: the towers were left open on the side facing the city and machicolations (openings in the parapets to drop things such as boiling oil or to shoot arrows at attackers) are missing in many sections.

There's an interesting **trompe l'œil portrait** of Avignon's nine popes in their fashionable garbs of the day on the side of the *conseil général* (general council) building, off rue Viala.

Palais des Papes This huge Gothic palace (☎ 04 90 27 50 74, [e] monument@ palais-des-papes.com), place du Palais, was built in the 14th century as a fortified palace for the pontifical court. Its undecorated stone halls, though impressive, are practically empty save the occasional exhibition. Papal banquets held here were of tremendous proportions. A feast to celebrate Clement VI's coronation in 1342 comprised 7428 chickens, 50,000 sweet tarts, 39,980 eggs and 95,000 loaves of bread, among numerous other things.

The best view of Palais des Papes is from Villeneuve-lès-Avignon. The cours d'Honneur – the palace's main courtyard – has hosted the Avignon theatre festival since 1947. The complex opens from 9.30 am to 5.45 pm, November to mid-March; 9.30 am to 6.30 pm, mid-March to 1 April; and 9 am to 7 pm, the rest of the year. Visiting the interior costs 45FF (seniors and students, 36FF) and includes a user-friendly, English-language audioguide. A combination ticket covering admission to Pont d'Avignon is available.

From Palais des Papes, a signposted tourist trail leads along narrow rue Vice Legat to **Jardins des Papes**, the gardens where the popes grew sweet-smelling plants and herbs, and kept exotic animals such as ostriches and lions (in cages).

Musée du Petit Palais This museum (☎ 04 90 86 44 58), at the far northern end of place du Palais, served as a bishop's and archbishop's palace during the 14th and 15th centuries. Today it houses an outstanding collection of 13th- to 16th-century Italian religious paintings. The Little Palace Museum opens 9.30 am to 1 pm and 2 to 6 pm Wednesday to Monday (5.30 pm September to June). Admission costs 30FF (those aged under 18, 15FF in July and August, free admission the rest of the year).

Rocher des Doms Just up the hill from unexciting Romanesque Cathédrale Notre Dame des Doms, on the northern side of Palais des Papes, is Rocher des Doms, a delightful bluff-top park that affords wonderful views of the Rhône, Pont St-Bénézet, Villeneuve-lès-Avignon and the Alpilles.

Conservatoire de Musique Avignon's Conservatory of Music, across place du Palais from Palais des Papes, occupies the former Hôtel des Monnaies (mint), built in 1619 to house a papal legation led by Cardinal Scipione Borghese. His enormous coat of arms decorates the ornate Baroque facade.

Musée Calvet & Musée Lapidaire Avignon's fine arts museum, Musée Calvet (☎ 04 90 86 33 84) is in elegant Hôtel de Villeneuve-Martignan (1741–54) at 65 rue Joseph Vernet. It displays an archaeological collection of artefacts from prehistorical to Roman times as well as 16th- to 20th-century paintings. It opens 10 am to 1 pm and 2 to 6 pm Wednesday to Monday. Admission costs 30FF (students and those aged 12 to 18, 15FF).

Musée Lapidaire (Statuary Museum; ☎ 04 90 85 75 38), 27 rue de la République, is inside a 17th-century chapel of a former Jesuit college. Collections include stone carvings from the Gallo-Roman, Romanesque and Gothic periods. It opens 10 am to 1 pm and 2 to 6 pm Wednesday to Monday.

AVIGNON AREA

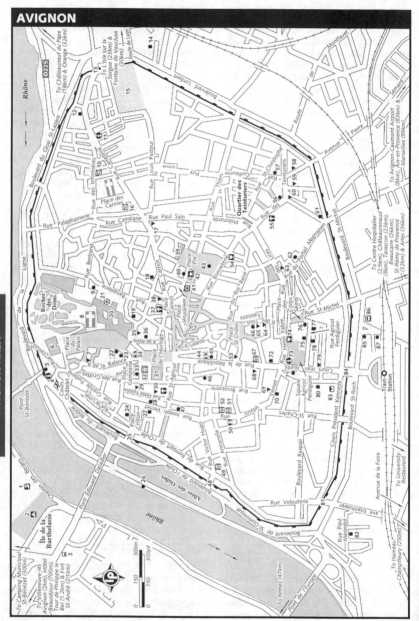

AVIGNON

PLACES TO STAY					
2	Camping Bagatelle; Auberge Bagatelle	68	Monoprix Supermarket	32	Opéra Théâtre d'Avignon
14	Avignon Squash Club (Hostel)	69	La Cuisine de Reine; Boutique du Cloître	33	Maison des Pays de Vaucluse
18	Hôtel Médiéval	79	Erio Convert	34	Banque de France
19	Hôtel de la Mirande			36	Bureau du Festival
23	Hôtel du Palais des Papes	**MUSEUMS**		37	Église St-Pierre
24	Hôtel L'Europe	6	Musée du Petit Palais	39	Palais de Justice
27	Hôtel Mignon	49	Musée Louis Vouland	40	TCRA Bus Information Kiosk
28	Hôtel Le Provençal	51	Musée Requien	41	Synagogue
61	Hotel Le Magnan	52	Musée Calvet	42	Police Station
70	Hôtel Innova	67	Musée Lapidaire	43	Les Halles
72	Hôtel Central			44	24-hour Banknote Exchange Machine
75	Hôtel du Parc	**OTHER**		45	FNAC
77	Hôtel Colbert	1	Swimming Pool	46	Trompe l'Oeil Painting of Popes
78	Hôtel Le Splendid	3	La Barthelasse Bus Stop		
80	Cloître St-Louis; Restaurant Le St-Louis	4	Tourist Office Annexe	47	Puyricard
82	Hôtel St-Roch	5	Tour de Châtelet; Entrance to Pont St-Bénézet	48	Porte Ste-Dominique
		8	Cathédrale Notre Dame des Doms	50	24-hour Banknote Exchange Machine
PLACES TO EAT		9	La Manutention (Le Grand Café; Le Bistrot d'Utopia; AJMI; Cinéma Utopia)	54	Pub Z
7	Le Brunel			55	Chapelle des Pénitents Gris
17	Pick-Up Café	10	Cyber Highway	56	Salle Benoît XII
29	Simple Simon	11	Bureau Information Jeunesse	57	Cyberdrome
30	Le Brantes	12	Shakespeare Bookshop	62	Lavmatic
35	Christian Étienne	13	Porte St-Lazare	66	Maison des Vins
38	Le Belgocargo	15	Université d'Avignon	71	Maison de la Presse
53	Maison Nani	16	La Pomme Bleue	73	Tourist Office
58	Restaurant au 19ème	20	Palais des Papes	74	Koala Bar
59	Café-Théâtre Tache d'Encre	21	Jardins des Papes	76	Laverie La Fontaine
60	Woolloomooloo	22	Conservatoire de Musique	81	Porte St-Roch
63	Le Petit Comptoir	25	Porte de l'Oulle	83	Post Office
64	Thiérry Piedoie	26	Boat Excursions	84	Porte de la République
65	Le Caveau du Théâtre	31	Town Hall	85	Transhumance Voyages
				86	Bus Station
				87	Car Rental Agencies

AVIGNON AREA

Admission costs 10FF (students 5FF; those aged 12 to 18, free).

Musée Requien This museum (☎ 04 90 82 43 51), neighbouring Musée Calvet at 67 rue Joseph Vernet, explores the city's natural history. It opens 9 am to noon and 2 to 6 pm Tuesday to Sunday. Admission is free.

Musée Louis Vouland This small but interesting museum (☎ 04 90 86 03 79), 17 rue Victor Hugo, displays a fine collection of 17th- and 18th-century decorative arts. It opens 10 am to noon and 2 to 6 pm Tuesday to Saturday, June to September; and 2 to 6 pm Tuesday to Saturday, the rest of the year. Admission costs 35FF (students and seniors 25FF).

Synagogue The synagogue (☎ 04 90 85 21 24), 2 place Jérusalem, was first built in 1221. A 13th-century oven used to bake unleavened bread for Passover can still be seen, but the rest of the present round, domed, neoclassical structure dates from 1846. It can be visited 10 am to noon and 3 to 5 pm Monday to Thursday, mornings only on Friday. Visitors must be modestly dressed and men have to cover their heads as is custom.

Quartier des Teinturiers Stone-paved rue des Teinturiers follows the course of the River Sorgue through Avignon's old dyers' district which, until the 19th century, was a hive of activity. Some of the water wheels can still be seen. Beneath the plane trees lining the narrow street is 16th-century **Chapelle des Pénitents Gris**. From the northern end of rue des Teinturiers, turn left along rue des Lices, right onto rue Noël Biret, then left onto rue Roi René. At No 22 on this street is **Chapelle St-Clare**, the church where the poet Petrarch first cast eyes on Laura, his muse. Laura is buried in the **Couvent des Cordeliers**, near the corner of rue des Lices and rue des Teinturiers.

Wine Tasting For information on where to taste Côte du Rhône wines, including the Avignon popes' favourite tipple, Châteauneuf du Pape (see that section later), head to the Maison des Vins (☎ 04 90 27 24 00, 🅔 export@vivarhone.com), 6 rue de Trois Faucons. Its free 66-page booklet entitled *Wine Routes in Côtes du Rhône* is invaluable for anyone intent on touring this wine region.

Boat Excursions

Les Grands Bateaux de Provence (☎ 04 90 85 62 25), based at the *embarcadère* (landing stage) on allées de l'Oulle, opposite Porte de l'Oulle, runs boat excursions down the River Rhône from Avignon to Arles and the Camargue (four to seven hours, starting at 180FF).

In July and August, Bateau Bus (same details as Les Grands Bateaux) makes less-ambitious return trips (1¼ hours, six daily) between Avignon and Villeneuve-lès-Avignon. A return fare costs 40FF (children 20FF). Boats dock in Avignon/Villeneuve-lès-Avignon at the jetty on allées de l'Oulle/ in front of Tour de Philippe le Bel.

L'Odyssée (☎ 04 90 49 86 08, 06 07 50 55 17), Berge du Rhône, Quartier du Moulin, runs cruises in July and August from the Tour de Philippe le Bel jetty in Villeneuve-lès-Avignon to Arles, Tarascon and Châteauneuf du Pape.

Special Events

The world famous Festival d'Avignon, founded in 1947, is held every year from early July to early August. It attracts hundreds of actors, dancers, musicians and other artists who perform some 300 shows a day in every imaginable venue. Alongside this expensive, prestigious, and government-subsidised official festival runs the fringe Festival Off. A Carte Public-Adhérent (75FF) gets you a 30% discount on all Festival Off performances. For more details see www.festival-off.org (French only).

Tickets for official festival performances cost 140FF to 200FF. Programme and ticket information is available from the Bureau du Festival (☎ 04 90 14 14 26), 8 bis rue de Mons. During the festival there is a bureau de location inside Espace St-Louis at 20 rue Portail d'Avignon and on place du Palais des Papes (both open 11 am to 8 pm). From early June, tickets can be reserved by telephone (☎ 04 90 14 14 14), via its Web site at www.festival-avignon.com or at branches of FNAC.

Places to Stay

During the festivals, it is impossible to find a hotel room unless you've reserved months in advance. The tourist office has information on dorm accommodation. Hotel rooms are readily available in August, however, when places in the rest of the Vaucluse are at a premium.

Places to Stay – Budget

Camping Shaded *Camping Bagatelle (☎ 04 90 86 30 39, fax 04 90 27 16 23)* is north of Pont Édouard Daladier, 850m from the walled city on Île de la Barthelasse. Charges are 17.80/8.50/15FF per adult/ child/tent and car in low season (23.80/ 10/18FF in high season). Reception opens 8 am to 9 pm. Take bus No 10 from the main post office to La Barthelasse stop.

Camping Municipal St-Bénézet (☎ 04 90 82 63 50, fax 04 90 85 22 21, chemin de la Barthelasse) is slightly farther north. It opens late March to October and charges 60/80FF in low/high season for two campers with a tent and car.

Hostels The *Auberge Bagatelle (☎ 04 90 86 30 39, fax 04 90 27 16 23)* is part of a large, park-like area on Île de la Barthelasse that includes Camping Bagatelle. A bed in a four- to eight-person room costs

58.90FF; it also has 15 doubles costing 130FF to 180FF per person. Breakfast costs 20FF.

A bunk in a converted squash court at *Avignon Squash Club* (☎ *04 90 85 27 78, fax 04 90 82 90 84, 32 blvd Limbert)* costs 60FF. It also has two- to four-bed rooms for 110FF per person per night. A sheet can be hired for 16FF. Reception opens 9 am to 10 pm; the club closes on Sunday, October to 30 June. Take bus No 7 from the train station to the Université stop.

Hotels Within the city walls, *Hôtel du Parc* (☎ *04 90 82 71 55, 18 rue Agricol Perdiguier)* has basic singles/doubles costing 160/185FF (195/240FF with shower, 220/265FF with shower and toilet). Bathroom-equipped triples cost 315FF and hall showers cost 10FF.

Friendly *Hôtel Le Splendid* (☎ *04 90 86 14 46, fax 04 90 85 38 55, 17 rue Agricol Perdiguier)* offers shower-equipped costing 160/240FF (220/290FF with toilet too).

The third in the trio, *Hôtel Colbert* (☎ *04 90 86 20 20, fax 04 90 85 97 00, 7 rue Agricol Perdiguier)*, sports rooms with shower costing 230/260FF (320FF with a toilet too).

Popular *Hôtel Innova* (☎ *04 90 82 54 10, fax 04 90 82 52 39, 100 rue Joseph Vernet)* has bright, comfortable and well soundproofed rooms costing 140/160FF (180FF with shower, 200FF with shower and TV, 260FF with shower and toilet). Reception is on the 1st floor.

Nearby, less-than-friendly *Hôtel Central* (☎ *04 90 86 07 81, fax 04 90 27 99 54, 31–33 rue de la République)* has uninspiring rooms costing 124/149FF (294FF with shower and toilet).

One-star *Hôtel Mignon* (☎ *04 90 82 17 30, fax 04 90 85 78 46, 12 rue Joseph Vernet)*, tucked amid designer clothes shops, has spotless, well-kept and soundproofed singles with shower for 160FF and bathroom-equipped doubles for 230FF.

Charming, two-star *Hotel Le Magnan* (☎ *04 90 86 36 51, fax 04 90 85 48 90, 63 rue Portail Magnanen)*, overlooking the city walls, is part of the Logis de France chain and has doubles with TV, bath and toilet starting at 205FF.

In Villeneuve-lès-Avignon, *Hôtel Beau-séjour* (☎ *04 90 25 20 56, 61 ave Gabriel Péri)* has bargain-basement rooms for one or two costing 148FF (200FF with shower, 225FF with shower and toilet).

Places to Stay – Mid-Range
Two-star *Hôtel Le Provençal* (☎ *04 90 85 25 24, fax 04 90 82 75 81, 13 rue Joseph Vernet)*, adjoining a snack bar, has rooms for one or two with shower costing 251/310FF in low/high season (201/360FF with shower and toilet). Prices include breakfast; mind the step when entering/exiting.

Very charming, old-worldly *Hôtel du Palais des Papes* (☎ *04 90 86 04 13, fax 04 90 27 91 17, 1 rue Gérard Philippe)* has doubles with shower, TV and toilet for 320FF; pricier rooms sporting a view of Palais des Papes peak at 850FF.

Splendid two-star *Hôtel Médiéval* (☎ *04 90 86 11 06, fax 04 90 82 08 64, 15 rue Petite Saunerie)*, in a restored 17th-century mansion, has doubles from 240FF to 350FF. It also rents studios on a weekly/longer-term basis.

Outside the walls, *Hôtel St-Roch* (☎ *04 90 16 50 00, fax 04 90 82 78 30, 9 rue Paul Mérindol)*, open January to November, has airy doubles equipped with shower, toilet and TV for 280FF; it has a handful of triples and quads too.

Places to Stay – Top End
'A place of pilgrimage for men and women of taste' is how French newspaper *Le Figaro* summed up *Hôtel de la Mirande* (☎ *04 90 85 93 93, fax 04 90 86 26 85,* e *mirande @la-mirande.de, 4 place de la Mirande)*, Avignon's most exclusive hotel in a 14th-century cardinal's palace behind Palais des Papes. Fabulous rooms cost upwards of 1700FF. There's a cooking school too.

Hôtel L'Europe (☎ *04 90 14 76 76, fax 04 90 14 76 71,* e *reservations@hotel-d-europe.fr, 12 place Crillon)* is cheap in comparison: four-star rooms for one or two start at 690FF.

AVIGNON AREA

Another fine spot to languish is *Cloître St-Louis* (☎ 04 90 27 55 55, fax 04 90 82 24 01, e hotel@cloitre-saint-louis.com, 20 rue du Portail Boquier), a stunning four-star hotel in a Jesuit school dating from 1589. Its ultra-modern new wing – which touts a rooftop swimming pool – was designed in 1991 by French architect Jean Nouvel (best known for his Institut du Monde Arabe in Paris). Exquisite doubles cost upwards of 550/800FF in low/high season.

Places to Eat
Restaurants – Around Place de l'Horloge
Excellent-value *Le Brantes* (☎ 04 90 86 35 14, 2 rue Petite Fusterie) is a pizza-grill place with 70FF, 87FF and 99FF *menus*. Pizzas/pasta dishes cost 44/33FF upwards and there is a 35FF kids' *menu*. Don't miss its flower-filled courtyard out back.

Hearty salads (55FF), meat dishes (56FF to 64FF) and other simple, sunny bistro-style dishes are served with a typical Provençal flourish at *Maison Nani* (☎ 04 90 82 60 90, 29 rue Théodore Aubanel), a busy place that markets itself as 'the restaurant of the Avignonnais'. Bold prints, paintings and murals add a flamboyant splash to its ochre-painted interior.

Delicious cuisine is served in a magnificent setting at *Le Grand Café* (☎ 04 90 86 86 77, 4 rue des Escaliers Ste-Anne, La Manutention), tucked to one side of Palais des Papes. Contemporary creations hang from the red-brick, former warehouse ceiling and tantalising *menus* cost 160FF.

In front of the palace, *Le Brunel* (☎ 04 90 85 24 83, 46–48 rue de la Balance) is a contemporary spot with a designer interior, a plat du jour for 65FF and tasty 65/98FF lunchtime/evening *menus*. Enter through the archway.

Le Caveau du Théâtre (☎ 04 90 82 60 91, Rue des Trois Faucons) is a fine spot for tasting local Côtes du Rhône wine. The theatrical wine cellar has a 65FF lunchtime *formule* (savoury tart plus dessert) and an 110FF evening *menu* in its repertoire.

Nearby, chef *Thiérry Piedoie* (☎ 04 90 86 51 53, 26 rue des Trios Faucons) cooks

up Provençal classics with a twist at his self-named restaurant. Highlights on his 190FF discovery *menu* include goat cheese-stuffed tomatoes and thyme-spiced creme brulee.

Belgian *Le Belgocargo* (☎ 04 90 85 72 99, 7 rue Armand de Pontmartin), behind Église St-Pierre, serves mussels (54FF to 68FF) in a variety of ways: *moules de Marseille* are laced with saffron, fennel and pastis.

Restaurants – Quartier des Teinturiers
Rue des Teinturiers is bespeckled with bohemian-style restaurants and is Avignon's most fun street. Each week at *Woolloomooloo* (☎ 04 90 85 28 44, 16 bis rue des Teinturiers), next to the old paper mill, a jumble of eclectic antique and contemporary furnishings are rearranged to create a 'new look'. During festival time Woolloomooloo lets rip with its eccentric furniture antics spilling out onto the street. *Menus* cost 67FF to 89FF and it has vegetarian and Antillean dishes too.

On the western fringe of the dyers' quarter is *Le Petit Comptoir* (☎ 04 90 86 10 94, 52 rue des Lices), an eight-table place offering a choice of main course plus dessert or starter for 40FF (three for 70FF). The lemon and ginger-scented pork brochette is particularly tasty.

For a more classical approach, try *Restaurant Au 19ème* (☎ 04 90 27 16 00, e au19eme@yahoo.com, 75 rue Guillaume Puy), in the 19th-century townhouse where absinthe inventor Jules Pernod lived. It hosts live jazz on Saturday evenings, harp recitals on Friday evening, and has lunch/dinner *menus* starting at 95/200FF.

Restaurants – Fine Dining
Elegant *La Cuisine de Reine* (☎ 04 90 85 99 04, rue Joseph Vernet), in Le Cloître des Arts, is a restaurant wrapped around an 18th-century courtyard and cloister. *Menus* start at 110FF and include a complimentary *pique nique à la maison* (house picnic) comprising smoked meats, olives and bread.

Equally worth the splurge are the gastronomic feasts served at *Restaurant Le St-*

AVIGNON AREA

Louis (☎ *04 90 27 55 55, 20 rue du Port ail Boquier*), overlooking a 16th-century cloister and huge moss-covered fountain. Lunch/dinner *menus* start at 130/200FF (98FF lunchtime *formule*).

Avignon's best-known chef *Christian Étienne* conjures up culinary creations from his eponymous rooftop restaurant (☎ *04 90 86 67 09,* [e] *contact@christian-etienne.fr, 10 rue de Mons*) overlooking Palais des Papes. Dining a la Étienne costs around 500FF per head.

Cafes Most pedestrian streets and squares, including place du Palais and place de l'Horloge, ring with the chink of coffee cups and clink of beer glasses in summer.

Behind place de l'Horloge, *Simple Simon* (☎ *04 90 86 62 70, 26 rue Petite Fusterie*) is a *très anglais* place for an afternoon cuppa (15 tea types starting at 20FF) with cake, crumble, scones, bakewell tart and salads.

A perfect spot for one of 26 types of tea, calorie-killer cakes and the gooiest chocolate brownies around is *Boutique du Cloître* (☎ *04 90 82 70 60, rue Joseph Vernet*), a trendy tea salon adjoining La Cuisine de Reine.

Pick-Up Café (☎ *04 90 85 49 77, 22 rue du Portail Matheron),* a student haunt crammed with bric-a-brac, is popular for its 10FF breakfast (8 am to midnight). Tummy-filling *menus* range from 27FF to 37FF.

Self-Catering The food market in *Les Halles* (*place Pie*) opens 7 am to 1 pm Tuesday to Wednesday.

Erio Convert (*45 cours Jean Jaurès*), spitting distance from the train station, is one of Provence's top boulangeries with a superb range of breads and filled baguettes. There's a *Monoprix* supermarket opposite Musée Lapidaire on the same street.

Entertainment

Tickets for cultural events are sold at the tourist office and at FNAC (☎ *04 90 14 35 35*), 19 rue de la République. Event listings fill the free weekly *César* magazine and fortnightly *Rendez-vous d'Avignon*. The tourist office distribute both.

Pubs & Bars A cool hang-out is *Le Bistrot d'Utopia* (☎ *04 90 27 04 96, 4 rue des Escaliers Ste-Anne*) inside La Manutention, a hip entertainment and cultural centre with a jazz club, restaurant and cinema. The arty bar opens noon to 1 am.

Koala Bar (*2 place des Corps Saints*), founded by an Australian ex-rugby player, is another hang-out popular with Anglophones. At *Pub Z* (*58 rue Bonneterie*) a life-sized zebra greets punters who enter the striped bar.

Classical Music, Opera & Ballet From October to June, *Opéra Théâtre d'Avignon* (☎ *04 90 82 23 44, place de l'Horloge*), in an imposing structure built in 1847, stages operas and operettas, plays, symphony concerts, chamber music concerts and ballet. The box office opens 11 am to 6 pm Monday to Saturday, and 11 am to 12.30 pm and from 2 pm Sunday and performance days.

Jazz La Manutention arts centre hosts *AJMI* (☎ *04 90 86 08 61, 4 rue des Escaliers Ste-Anne*), an abbreviation for Association pour Le Jazz & La Musique Improvisée. This cool jazz club has concerts most Thursdays at 9 pm, October to June.

Cinema For new and old nondubbed films, try visiting *Cinéma Utopia* (☎ *04 90 82 65 36, 4 rue des Escaliers Ste-Anne*) at La Manutention.

Theatre Avignon has numerous theatres. Venues include *Théâtre du Chien qui Fume* (☎ *04 90 85 25 87, 75 rue des Teinturies*); *Théâtre du Bourg Neuf* (☎ *04 90 85 17 90, 5 bis rue du Bourg-Neuf*); and *Théâtre des Halles* (☎ *04 90 85 52 57, 4 rue Noël Biret*).

Avignon also has a lively cafe-theatre scene. Try *Café-Théâtre Tache d'Encre* (☎ *04 90 85 97 13, 1 rue Tarasque*) in the Teinturiers quarter.

Shopping

Avignon's classiest shopping streets, rue St-Agricol and the northern part of rue Joseph Vernet, are just west of place de l'Horloge. Art and antique shops decorate rue de Limas.

AVIGNON AREA

Galerie Ducastel at 9 place Crillon is a contemporary art gallery.

Puyricard at 33 rue Joseph Vernet sells designer chocolates.

Getting There & Away

Air Avignon-Caumont airport (Aéroport d'Avignon-Caumont; ☎ 04 90 81 51 51), 8km south-east of Avignon, is served by domestic flights. See Getting Around for details.

Bus Avignon bus station (☎ 04 90 82 07 35) is in the basement of the building down the ramp to the right as you come out of the train station on blvd St-Roch. The information window opens 8 am to noon and 1.30 to 6 pm Monday to Saturday noon. You can leave luggage there (10FF). Tickets are sold on the buses, which are run by about 20 different companies.

Services include two to five daily to/from Aix-en-Provence (86FF via national roads/the autoroute, one to 1½ hours), Apt (43.50FF, 1¼ hours), Arles (38FF, 1½), Cavaillon (20FF, one hour), Châteauneuf du Pape (20FF, 35 minutes), Vaison-la-Romain (42.50FF, 1¼ hours), Nîmes (65FF, 1¼ hours, 10 or more daily) and Pont du Gard (35FF, 45 minutes). Orange (30.50FF) and Carpentras (23FF) are both served by some 20 buses daily (45 minutes). Most lines operate on Sunday at a reduced frequency.

Long haul bus companies Linebus (☎ 04 90 85 30 48) and Eurolines (☎ 04 90 85 27 60) have offices at the far end of the bus platforms.

Train The train station, across blvd St-Roch from Porte de la République, is served by numerous daily trains to/from Arles (56FF, 15 minutes), Marseilles (102FF, one hour), Nice (226FF, 2½ hours), Nîmes (46FF, 30 minutes) and Orange (29FF, 15 minutes).

Car & Motorcycle Most car rental agencies are signposted from the train station: Europcar (☎ 04 90 85 01 40) is in the Hôtel Ibis building. Budget (☎ 04 90 27 34 95) is down the ramp to the right as you exit the station.

Getting Around

Bus Local TCRA bus tickets cost 6.50FF each if bought from the driver; a five-ticket carnet (for 10 rides) costs 48FF at TCRA offices. Buses run from 7 am to about 7.40 pm (8 am to 6 pm and less frequently on Sunday). The two most important bus transfer points are the Poste stop at the post office and place Pie. Carnets and free bus maps (plan du réseau) are available at the TCRA office (☎ 04 32 74 18 32), ave de Lattre de Tassigny.

Villeneuve-lès-Avignon is linked with Avignon by bus No 10, which stops in front of the main Avignon post office and on the western side of the walled city near Porte de l'Oulle.

Taxi Pick up a taxi from in front of the train station or call the place Pie taxi rank (☎ 04 90 82 20 20), open 24 hours.

Bicycle Transhumance Voyages (☎ 04 90 27 92 61, e transvoy@pacwan.fr), 200m from the train station at 52 blvd St-Roch, rents town/mountain bikes for 30/100FF per day. It also has 50/125cc scooters for 220/290FF per day; it organises cycling tours too.

VILLENEUVE-LÈS-AVIGNON
postcode 30400 • pop 12,078

Villeneuve-lès-Avignon, across the Rhône from Avignon, was founded in the late 13th century. It became known as the City of Cardinals because many primates affiliated with the papal court built large residences (known as livrées) in the town, despite the fact that it was in territory ruled by the French crown and not the pope.

Things to See & Do
Chartreuse du Val de Bénédiction The Val de Bénédiction Charterhouse (☎ 04 90 15 24 24), 60 rue de la République, was founded in 1356 by Pope Innocent VI and, with its 40 cells and three cloisters, was once France's largest Carthusian monastery. **Cloître St-Jean** gives you an idea of the architecture and layout of the charterhouse. In the 14th-century church, the delicately

AVIGNON AREA

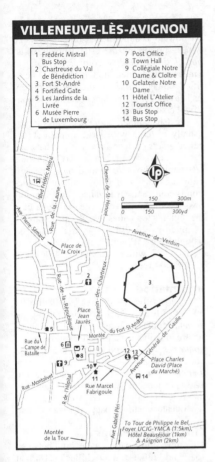

VILLENEUVE-LÈS-AVIGNON

1 Frédéric Mistral Bus Stop
2 Chartreuse du Val de Bénédiction
3 Fort St-André
4 Fortified Gate
5 Les Jardins de la Livrée
6 Musée Pierre de Luxembourg
7 Post Office
8 Town Hall
9 Collégiale Notre Dame & Cloître
10 Gelaterie Notre Dame
11 Hôtel L'Atelier
12 Tourist Office
13 Bus Stop
14 Bus Stop

the Revolution, including paintings from the 15th to 17th centuries. The museum's most exceptional objects include the *Vierge en Ivoire* (Ivory Virgin), a superb 14th-century Virgin carved from an elephant's tusk; the 15th-century *Vierge Double Face*, a marble Virgin whose two faces point in opposite directions; and *Couronnement de la Vierge* (Coronation of the Virgin), painted by Enguerrand Quarton in 1453, displayed on the 1st floor.

The museum opens 10 am to 12.30 pm and 3 to 7 pm, April to September; and 10 am to noon and 2 to 5.30 pm Tuesday to Sunday, October to December, February and March. Admission costs 20FF (students 12FF; children aged under 10, free).

Tour de Philippe le Bel This 32m-tall defensive tower (☎ 04 32 70 08 57) was built in the 14th century at what was, at the time, the western end of Pont St-Bénézet. The platform on top, reached after a dizzying climb up 172 steps of spiral staircase, affords a magnificent panorama of Avignon. The tower can be scaled 10 am to 12.30 pm and 3 to 7 pm, April to September; and 10 am to noon and 2 to 5.30 pm Tuesday to Sunday, October to December, February and March. Admission costs 10FF (students and those aged 12 to 18, 6FF).

Fort St-André This lumbering 14th-century fortress (☎ 04 90 25 45 35), built on Mont Andaon by the king of France to keep an eye on events across the river in the papal domains, affords lovely views. The **fortified gate** is a fine example of medieval military architecture. It opens 10 am to 12.30 pm and 2 to 6 pm, April to September; and 10 am to noon and 2 to 5 pm, the rest of the year. Admission costs 25FF (those aged 18 to 25, 15FF; those aged under 18, free).

Places to Stay & Eat

A night's sleep at Villeneuve's *Foyer UCJG-YMCA* (☎ 04 90 25 46 20, fax 04 90 25 30 64, **e** *info@ymca-avignon.com*, 7 bis chemin de la Justice) costs 80/100FF per person in a three-bedded room in low/high season, 88/110FF in a double room,

carved **mausoleum** of Pope Innocent VI (died 1362) is an extraordinary example of Gothic artisanship. It was removed during the Revolution and returned in 1963. The monastery opens 9 am to 6.30 pm, April to September; and 9.30 am to 5.30 pm, the rest of the year. Admission costs 32FF (students aged 18 to 25, 21FF; those aged under 18, free).

Musée Pierre de Luxembourg This museum (☎ 04 90 27 49 66), 3 rue de la République, has a fine collection of religious art taken from the Chartreuse during and 136/170FF in a single. Breakfast costs 20/25FF and small/large sheets can be hired for 10/15FF. Take bus No 10 to the Pont d'Avignon stop.

Hôtel L'Atelier (☎ 04 90 25 01 84, fax 04 90 25 80 06, 5 rue de la Foire) has charming doubles costing upwards of 250FF. Equally idyllic is small, select **Les Jardins de la Livrée** (☎ 04 90 26 05 05, 4 bis rue du Camp de Bataille), a chambre d'hôte with a stone terrace, swimming pool, Provençal kitchen and rooms costing 290FF to 520FF.

For authentic Italian ice cream and sorbet try **Gelaterie Notre Dame** (☎ 04 90 26 04 15, 8 rue Fabrigoule), a stylish ice-cream parlour that draw crowds across the bridge.

North of Avignon

Vaucluse fans out northwards, from the lucrative vineyards of Châteauneuf du Pape and the Roman treasures of Orange, through to the rocky Dentelles de Montmirail, the slopes of Mont Ventoux and the harsh and uninhabitable Albion plain in the Vaucluse's easternmost corner.

If you don't have access to a car, it is possible to labour from town to town by local bus, but the frequency and pace of services are in keeping with the relaxed tempo of Provençal life.

CHÂTEAUNEUF DU PAPE
postcode 84230 • pop 2098
• elevation 87m

Wealthy Châteauneuf du Pape, 18km north of Avignon, was once a humble mining hamlet, called Calcernier after its limestone quarries. Then in 1317 Pope John XXII (ruled 1316–34) had a pontifical residence built in the village, around which he established a papal vineyard. Today the village is renowned worldwide for its rich, full-bodied Châteauneuf du Pape red wines that boast a minimum alcoholic strength of 12.5% (France's highest).

The wine produced in the 18th century was called *vin d'Avignon* and Châteauneuf du Pape-Calcernier in the 19th century. In 1923 Baron Le Roy de Boiseaumarié, a local *vigneron* (wine grower), wrote rules on how to produce Châteauneuf du Pape wine – prompting the establishment of an *appellation d'origine contrôlée* (AOC) in France. Châteauneuf du Pape became a certified vintage in 1929, distinguishable by its heavily embossed label bearing the pontifical coat of arms.

The Châteauneuf du Pape vineyards – usually covered with large smooth stones called *galets* – cover 3200 hectares between Avignon and Orange, on the River Rhône's left bank. They are tended by some 350 vignerons, many of whose annual production is sold years in advance, making it impossible for tourists to taste, let alone buy, the region's top wines, which can command as much as 2000FF per bottle. Count on paying from 75FF for a run-of-the-mill bottle of 1997 white and 80/80/74FF for a 1996/95/94 red.

Information
The tourist office (☎ 04 90 83 71 08, fax 04 90 83 50 34, [e] tourisme-chato9-pape @wanadoo.fr) on place du Portail, the central square, distributes maps and a list of 80-odd *domaines* (wine producing estates) where you can taste and buy wine. The office opens 9 am to 7 pm, July and August; and 9 am to 12.30 pm and 2 to 6 pm Monday to Saturday, the rest of the year. Its Web site is at www.chateauneuf-du-pape.enprovence.com.

Château des Papes
The ruins of this papal castle, built between 1317 and 1333, stand on a hillock (118m) at the northern end of the village. It was plundered and burnt during the Wars of Religion, and further destroyed by German troops on 20 August 1944.

From the foot of the castle there are sweeping views of Avignon, the Vaucluse plateau, the Lubéron, the River Rhône and beyond. From the car park next to the castle, steps lead to the old town.

Tasting & Buying Wine
A good place to start is the **Musée des Outils de Vignerons** (☎ 04 90 83 70 07, [e] brottw@wanadoo.fr), ave Louis Pasteur.

AVIGNON AREA

The Museum of Wine Producers' Tools is essentially a ploy to sell wine from the Caves Brotte-Père Anselme. However, it's still a good opportunity to soak up the pungent smell of wine and ask 'beginner-level' questions without feeling stupid. It opens 9 am to noon and 2 to 6 pm.

Most producers allow wine cellar visits and offer *dégustation gratuite* (free wine-tasting). However, some can only be visited *sur rendez-vous* (*sur RV*; by appointment) and are closed at the weekend, and others only cater to groups. Opening hours and visiting requirements are detailed in the list of producers available at the tourist office.

Château Mont Redon (☎ 04 90 83 72 75), 4km north of Châteauneuf du Pape on route d'Orange (D68), is among the largest and oldest producers of Châteauneuf du Pape. A *circuit touristique* cuts through part of its 163 hectares of galet-crusted vineyards – each row flagged with a rose bush – to Châteauneuf du Pape village. This is a particularly beautiful cycle ride.

Château de Beaucastel (☎ 04 90 11 12 00), chemin de Beaucastel, and Château de Vaudieu (☎ 04 90 83 70 31) are both worth visiting, simply for a peek at the grandiose chateau on each estate.

All known for producing good, typically strong, well-structured reds are: Domaine Chante Cigale (☎ 04 90 83 70 57), ave Louis Pasteur; Domaine Font de Michelle (☎ 04 90 33 00 22), 14 impasse des Vignerons; Clos du Mont Olivet (☎ 04 90 83 72 46), 15 ave St-Joseph; Le Clos des Papes (☎ 04 90 83 70 13), 13 ave Pierre de Luxembourg; and Château Fortia (☎ 04 90 83 72 25), still in the hands of the AOC-founding Le Roy family on route de Bédarrides.

Special Events
Not surprisingly, Châteauneuf du Pape celebrates a string of wine-inspired festivals. The Fête de la St-Marc – the feast day of the patron saint of wine growers – is on 25 April; a Fête de la Véraison is held the first weekend in August to mark the ripening of the grapes; and the Fête des Vendanges fills the streets with merry-making in mid-

September to celebrate the start of the grape harvests.

Places to Stay & Eat
Open June to October, *Camping Caravaning de L'Isle St-Luc* (☎ 04 90 83 56 36, fax 04 90 83 76 77) charges 80FF for two people with tent and car. The site is 2km south of the village along route de Sel.

In the village, *Hôtel La Garburie* (☎ 04 90 83 75 08, fax 04 90 83 52 34, e garbure @wanadoo.fr, 3 rue Joseph Ducos) offers doubles with bath/shower for 320/365FF.

Nearby *La Mère Germaine* (☎ 04 90 83 54 37, fax 04 90 83 50 27, place de la Fontaine) oozes charm. It has eight well-furnished rooms with shower and toilet costing upwards of 320FF, and a flowery terrace restaurant touting several excellent-value *menus*. These range from a 95FF brasserie *menu* to a splendid *menu pontifical* – seven courses accompanied by seven different Châteauneuf du Pape wines (380/310FF with/without wine).

Le Verger des Papes (☎ 04 90 33 50 94, e papeverger@aol.com), at the foot of the chateau, likewise has a shady terrace offering stunning Rhône-and-vineyard views and delicious cuisine. Its house speciality is *aïoli Provençal complet*, served strictly on Friday.

South of the village, amid sprawling vineyards off the Avignon-bound D17, is dreamlike *Hostellerie du Château des Fines Roches* (☎ 04 90 83 70 23, fax 04 90 83 78 42, e finesroches@enprovence .com). A night's stay in this made-in-heaven, turreted castle costs upwards of 850FF for two.

Shopping
Chocoholics can spend a fortune at Bernard Castelain's Chocolaterie Artisanale (☎ 04 90 83 54 71, e chbcm@wanadoo.fr), a chocolate factory south of the village on the Avignon-bound D17. It opens 9 am to noon and 2 to 7 pm Monday to Saturday, and 10 am to noon and 3 to 6 pm Sunday.

Getting There & Away
From Châteauneuf du Pape, Rapides du Sud-Est (☎ 04 90 34 15 59 in Orange) operates

buses Monday to Saturday to/from Avignon (20FF, 35 minutes, one or two daily) and Orange (15FF, 15 minutes, one or two daily). In Châteauneuf, buses use the stop on ave du Général de Gaulle.

ORANGE
postcode 84100 • pop 28,889
• elevation 97m
Through a 16th-century marriage with the German House of Nassau, the House of Orange – the princely dynasty that had ruled Orange since the 12th century – became active in the history of the Netherlands and later, through William III (William of Orange), Britain and Ireland. Orange (Arenjo in Provençal), which had earlier been a stronghold of the Reformation, was ceded to France in 1713 by the Treaty of Utrecht, but to this day many members of the royal house of the Netherlands are known as the princes and princesses of Orange-Nassau.

Orange is best known for its magnificent Roman relics and less-than-magnificent National Front mayor.

Thursday is market day.

Orientation
The train station is about 1km east of place de la République, the city centre, along ave Frédéric Mistral and rue de la République. Rue St-Martin links place de la République and nearby place Georges Clémenceau with the tourist office, 250m west. The Théâtre Antique – Orange's Roman theatre – is two blocks south of place de la République. The tiny River Meyne lies north of the centre.

Information
The tourist office (☎ 04 90 34 70 88, fax 04 90 34 99 62, ℮ officedetourisme@free .fr, orangetourisme@hotmail.com), 5 cours Aristide Briand, opens 9 am to 6 or 7 pm, April to September; and 9 am to 1 pm and 3 to 6 pm Monday to Saturday, the rest of the year. Between April and September, it runs an annexe on place des Frères Mournet, open 10 am to 1 pm and 2 to 7 pm Monday to Saturday (10 am to 6 pm Sunday in July and August). Its Web site is at www .provence-orange.com (French only).

The branch of Banque de France at 5 rue Frédéric Mistral exchanges currency from 8.30 am to noon weekdays. The post office is opposite the bus station on blvd Édouard Daladier.

Théâtre Antique
Orange's Roman theatre (☎ 04 90 51 17 60), designed to seat about 10,000 spectators, was probably built during the time of Augustus Caesar (ruled 27 BC to AD 14). Its **stage wall** *(mur de scène)* – the only such Roman structure still standing in its entirety (minus a few mosaics and the roof) – is 103m wide and almost 37m high. Its plain exterior can be viewed from adjacent place des Frères Mounet to the north.

For a panoramic view of the Roman masterpiece, follow montée Philbert de Chalons or montée A Lambert to the top of **Colline St-Eutrope** (elevation 97m). En route you pass the **ruins** of a **12th-century château**, the former residence of the princes of Orange.

The theatre opens 9 am to 6.30 pm, April to September; and 9 am to noon and 1.30 to 5 pm, the rest of the year. Guided tours in English depart at 11 am in July and August. In the 17th-century Hôtel Can Cuyl opposite on rue Madeleine Roch is the unexciting **Musée Municipal** known – yawn – for its Roman cadastres (land-survey registers). It opens 9.30 am to 7 pm, April to September; and 9 am to noon and 1.30 to 5.30 pm, the rest of the year. Admission covering entrance to both sights costs 30FF (seniors, students and children aged 10 to 16, 25FF); tickets are only sold at the theatre.

Arc de Triomphe
Orange's Roman triumphal arch is at the northern end of plane tree-lined ave de l'Arc de Triomphe about 450m from the centre. Probably built around 20 BC, it is 19m in height and width and 8m deep/thick. The exceptional friezes commemorate Julius Caesar's victories over the Gauls in 49 BC. The arch has been restored several times since 1825.

Overlooking the eastern side of the arch is a **pétanque** court. If you don't have a set,

ORANGE

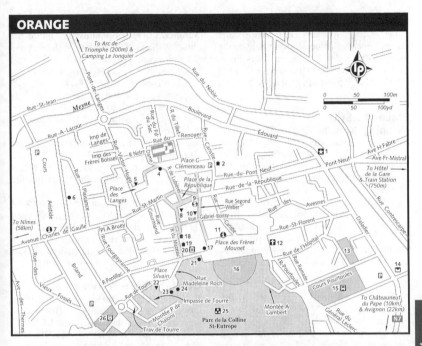

ORANGE

PLACES TO STAY
2   Le Milan
18 Hôtel Arcotel
19 Hôtel St-Florent

PLACES TO EAT
5   Le Garden
8   Le Sangria; La Saladerie-
    Crêperie
10 Chez Daniel
22 L'Aigo Boulido

OTHER
1   Police Station
3   Cathédrale Notre Dame de
    Nazareth
4   Town Hall
6   Pêche Chasse Bourgeois
    (Bowls Shop)
7   Tourist Office
9   Banque de France
11 Tourist Office Annexe
12 Église St-Florent

13 Palais des Princes
14 Post Office
15 Bus Station
16 Théâtre Antique
17 Tourist Train
20 Musée Municipal
21 Entrance to Théâtre Antique
23 Location Théâtre Antique
24 Service Culturel
25 Chateau Ruins
26 Municipal Theatre

deck yourself out at Pêche Chasse Bourgeois, 20 cours Aristide Briand.

Special Events

In June and August, the Théâtre Antique comes alive with concerts, cinema screenings and musical events throughout Les Nuits du Théâtre Antique. During the last fortnight in July, it hosts Les Chorégies d'Orange, a series of weekend operas, classical concerts and choral performances. Seats (20FF to 990FF) must be reserved months beforehand, though it's possible to catch a free glimpse of the action from the lookout atop Colline St-Eutrope.

Tickets for Théâtre Antique events can be reserved at Location Théâtre Antique (☎ 04 90 34 24 24), 14 place Silvain, open

9 am to 7 pm Monday to Saturday. FNAC branches also sell tickets. For tickets to other cultural events (including those held at the modern Palais des Princes on cours Pourtoules), go next door to the Service Culturel (☎ 04 90 51 57 57), open 8.30 am to 5.30 pm weekdays.

Places to Stay
Camping Near the Arc de Triomphe is *Camping Le Jonquier* (☎ 04 90 34 49 48, fax 04 90 51 16 97, @ joeldenis@waika9 .com, 1321 rue Alexis Carrel), open April to October. It charges 94.50/109.50FF for two people with a tent and car in low/high season. Take bus No 1 from the République stop (on ave Frédéric Mistral 600m from the train station) to the Arc de Triomphe. From here, walk 100m back, turn right onto rue des Phocéens and right again onto rue des Étudiants. The site is across the football pitch.

Hotels The cheapest joint is *Le Milan* (☎ 04 90 34 13 31, 22 rue Caristie), which has very basic rooms costing 146/156FF with shower/shower and toilet for one or two people. Reception is the downstairs bar. Also cheap is *Hôtel de le Gare* (☎ 04 90 34 00 23, fax 04 90 34 91 72, 60 ave Frédéric Mistral), next to the train station. Doubles start at 180FF.

Near the Théâtre Antique, welcoming *Hôtel Arcotel* (☎ 04 90 34 09 23, fax 04 90 51 61 12, @ jor8525@aol.com, 8 place aux Herbes) has one-star singles/doubles costing 110/150FF (220FF with shower and toilet) and 300FF rooms for four with toilet and shower.

Around the corner, *Hôtel St-Florent* (☎ 04 90 34 18 53, fax 04 90 51 17 25, @ stflorent @yahoo.fr, 4 rue du Mazeau) has rooms with wall murals and fantastic *belle epoque* wooden beds adorned with crushed and studded velvet. Singles with washbasin cost 120FF and shower-equipped doubles go for 210FF (280FF with toilet and TV too).

Places to Eat
La Sangria (☎ 04 90 34 31 96, 3 place de la République) has a 50FF lunch *menu* and evening ones for 115FF. Next door, *La Saladerie-Crêperie* claims to capture the 'blue of the sky, the yellow of the sun and the colours of Provence' in its crepe- and salad-inspired *menus* (starting at 60FF).

Chez Daniel (☎ 04 90 34 63 48, rue Segond Weber) dishes up oysters, mussels and other shellfish by the bowlful or dozen and serves fish platters to eat in or takeaway (65FF to 150FF).

For the ultimate Provençal feast, head for *Aïgo Boulido* (☎ 04 90 34 18 19, 20 place Silvain), where you can sample its namesake, *aïgo boulido* (garlic soup), on the 95FF *menu*.

For a splurge, head for *Le Garden* (☎ 04 90 34 64 47, 6 place de Langes), adjoining three-star Hôtel Arène, a block west of place Georges Clémenceau. The restaurant is furnished 1930s-style and specialises in truffles. Pricey fungi aside, *menus* start at 105FF.

Getting There & Away
Bus Orange bus station is south-east of the city centre on cours Pourtoules. Buses operated by Rapides du Sud-Est (☎ 04 90 34 15 59) run from here to Avignon (30.50FF, 45 minutes, about 20 daily), Châteauneuf du Pape (15FF, 15 minutes, one or two daily), Carpentras (25FF, 40 minutes), Marseilles and Vaison-la-Romaine (28FF, 45 minutes).

Train The train station, at the eastern end of ave Frédéric Mistral, is a 1.5km walk east of the tourist office. Trains run southwards to Avignon (29FF, 15 minutes, 17 daily), Marseilles (109FF, 1½ hours, 10 daily) and beyond.

VAISON-LA-ROMAINE
postcode 84110 • pop 5986
• elevation 193m

Vaison-la-Romaine, 23km and 47km northeast of Orange and Avignon respectively, is endowed with extensive Roman ruins, a picturesque medieval old city and too many tourists.

In the 2nd century BC, the Romans conquered an important Celtic city on this site and renamed it Vasio Vocontiorum. The Roman city flourished, in part because it was granted considerable autonomy, but around the 6th century the Great Migrations forced the population to move to the hill across the river, which was easier to defend. The counts of Toulouse built a castle atop the hill in the 12th century. The resettlement of the original site began in the 17th century. The Roman remains unearthed here include mosaic-decorated villas, colonnaded streets, public baths, a theatre and aqueduct; the latter brought water down from Mont Ventoux.

Like Malaucène and Carpentras, 10km and 27km respectively to the south, Vaison is a good base for exploring the Dentelles de Montmirail and Mont Ventoux region. A *grand marché Provençal* fills place Franois Cevert every Tuesday morning; smaller markets are held on Thursday and Saturday mornings.

Orientation & Information

Vaison is bisected by the ever-flooding River Ouvèze. The Roman city centre, on top of which the modern city centre has been built, is on the river's northern bank; the medieval Haute Ville is on the southern bank. In the modern city, pedestrian Grand rue heads north-westwards from Pont Romain (bridge), changing its name near the Roman ruins to ave du Général de Gaulle.

To get from the bus station to the tourist office (☎ 04 90 36 02 11, fax 04 90 28 76 04, ⓔ ot-vasion@axit.fr) on place du Chanoine Sautel, exit the station and turn left, then left again into rue Colonel Parazols, which leads past the Puymin excavations along rue Burrus to place du Chanoine Sautel. It opens 9 am to noon and 2 to 6.30 pm Monday to Saturday, 10 am to 1 pm Sunday, and has a Web site at www .vaison-la-romaine.com (French only).

Gallo-Roman Ruins

Vaison's Gallo-Roman ruins can be visited at two sites: **Fouilles de Puymin**, the excavations on the eastern side of ave du Général de Gaulle; and **Fouilles de la Villasse**, to the west of the same road.

Fouilles de Puymin (entrance signposted 'Site Archéologique de Puymin-Musée' op-

posite the tourist office), the more interesting of the pair, includes houses, mosaics and a theatre (designed to accommodate 6000 people) built around AD 20 during the reign of Tiberius. Among the artefacts displayed in the onsite **Musée Archéologique** is a hefty collection of statues, including the silver bust of a 3rd-century patrician and likenesses of Hadrian and his wife Sabina. At Fouilles de la Villasse you can visit the mosaic- and fresco-decorated house in which the bust was discovered.

Both sites open 9 or 9.30 am to 12.30 pm and 2 to 6 or 7 pm, March to October; and 10 am to noon and 2 to 4.30 pm Wednesday to Monday, the rest of the year. Admission costs 41FF (students 22FF; those aged 12 to 18, 14FF). Guided tours (included in the admission fee) in English run April to October.

Medieval Quarter

Across the **Pont Romain**, on the south bank of the Ouvèze, lies the **Haute Ville**, which dates from the 13th and 14th centuries. Narrow, cobblestone alleys lead uphill past restored houses. At the summit is the imposing 12th-century **château**, modernised in the 15th century only to be later abandoned.

Wine Tasting

Local wines (AOC Villages des Côtes du Rhône, Gigondas, Châteauneuf du Pape), honey and other *produits du terroir* (local food products) can be tasted and bought at the Maison des Vins, in the basement of the tourist office.

Special Events

The two-week Choralies choral festival, held every three years in August in Vaison's Théâtre Antique (Roman theatre), is the largest of its kind in Europe. The next takes place in 2001. During the polyphonic festival some 3000 voices from across Europe sing in unison. Tickets are available from the Centre à Cœur Joie (see Hostels on the following page) or the Mouvement Choral à Cœur Joie (☎ 04 72 19 83 40, fax 04 78 43 43 98), 24 ave Joannès Masset BP 317, 69337 Lyons Cedex 09.

AVIGNON AREA

The latter also has details on the Festival des Chœurs Lauréats, a smaller polyphonic festival held during the last week of July.

Places to Stay

Camping Open mid-March to October, *Camping du Théâtre Romain (☎/fax 04 90 28 78 66, chemin de Brusquet)* is opposite the Théâtre Antique in the northern section of the Fouilles de Puymin. It charges 25/40FF per person/tent. South-east of the centre, *Le Carpe Diem (☎ 04 90 36 02 02, fax 04 90 36 36 90, route de St-Marcellin)* opens April to October and charges 22/27FF per person/tent in low season and 25/43FF in high season. Both sites have a pool and rent bikes.

Hostels Quiet but expensive *Centre à Cœur Joie (☎ 04 90 36 00 78, fax 04 90 36 09 89, [e] centracj.france@wanadoo.fr, ave César Geoffray)*, 500m south-east of town along the river, has great views of Mont Ventoux. A minimum of half-board, which costs 215/190FF per person for those staying in a double/triple room, is obligatory. Rates in July and August/winter are 10% more/less.

Hotels Decent places are few and far between. Opposite the tourist office *Hôtel Le Théâtre Romain (☎ 04 90 28 71 98, fax 04 90 28 86 96, ave Général de Gaulle)* has basic doubles costing 155FF (230FF with shower, 260FF with shower and toilet).

Two-star *Hôtel Le Burrhus (☎ 04 90 36 00 11, fax 04 90 36 39 05, 2 place Montfort)* and eight-room *Hôtel des Lis (same ☎/fax, 20 cours Henri Fabre)*, owned by the same team, charge 290FF and 450FF respectively for a shower- and toilet-equipped double.

Getting There & Away

The bus station (☎ 04 90 36 05 22) is east of the modern town on ave des Choralies. There are limited services from Vaison-la-Romaine to/from Carpentras (22FF, 45 minutes) via Crestet (8FF, five minutes), Malaucène (17FF, 15 minutes) and Le Barroux (17FF, 25 minutes); Orange (28FF, 45 minutes) and Avignon (42.50FF, 1¼ hours).

ENCLAVE DES PAPES

French king Charles VII (ruled 1422–61) refused point-blank to sell any of his kingdom to the papacy, the result being the Enclave des Papes – a papal enclave in France which, from 1318 until the French Revolution in 1789, belonged to the Pope. Part of the Vaucluse since 1791, this bizarre ball of land measuring no more than 20km in diameter remains an enclave today – wholly surrounded by the Drôme department.

Medieval **Valréas** (postcode 84600, pop 9500, elevation 250m), 29km north of Vaison-la-Romaine, is the primary town in Provence's Enclave des Papes. During the 19th century, the town was known for its cardboard production, the history of which unfolds in the world's only **Musée du Cartonnage et de l'Imprimerie** (Cardboard & Printing Museum; ☎ 04 90 35 58 75), ave Maréchal Foch. Each year, during the Nuit du Petit St-Jean on 23 June, Valréassiens in traditional dress and bearing torches parade through the old-town streets to crown a three- to five-year-old boy the new Petit St-Jean (Little St-John).

Lavender fields and treasure troves of truffles buried underground (see the boxed text 'Black Diamonds' on the next page) surround Valréas. Fortified **Grillon, Visan** and **Richerenches**, the first three to be bought by the Avignon Popes in 1318, are the only other villages in the enclave. From here, age-old olive groves stretch across the border south to Vaison-la-Romaine and east to **Nyons** (pop 6948), 14km from Valréas, where the harvested black fruits are turned into olive oil. *Saucissons aux olives de Nyons* (Nyon olive sausages) are sold at *Boucherie Guy Dineile* at 2 rue de la Résistance. Hop 3km across the enclave's western border to **Suze-la-Rousse** (pop 1591) to learn about wine at France's Université du Vin (University of Wine; ☎ 04 75 97 21 30, [e] universite-du-vin@wanadoo.fr), inside flamboyant **Château de la Suze**, a 12th- to 14th-century feudal structure.

Valréas tourist office (☎/fax 04 90 35 04 71, [e] enclavedespapes@pacwan.fr), place Aristide Briand, stocks information on accommodation in the enclave. The tourist

AVIGNON AREA

office in Nyons (☎ 04 75 26 10 35, ⓔ ot
.nyons@wanadoo.fr), place de la Libération, has a wealth of information on everything to do with olives and oils (growing,
harvesting, tasting, buying and so on). Alternatively, contact the Confrérie des Chevaliers de l'Oliviers (literally 'Brotherhood
of Knights of the Olive Tree'; ☎ 04 75 26
16 77), 40 place de la Libération.

DENTELLES DE MONTMIRAIL
Immediately south of Vaison-la-Romaine
loom the pinnacles of the Dentelles de
Montmirail, a series of limestone rocks
that thrust into the sky like needles. Vineyards cling to the lower parts of the rocky

slopes, while climbers dangle perilously
from the south-facing rocks around Gigondas. This area, stretching as far west as
Mont Ventoux, makes great walking terrain; Régis at the Gîte d'Étape des Dentelles de Gigondas (see Places to Stay
later) arranges guided walks, rock climbs
and bike rides.

Looping the lacy outcrop of the Dentelles
by car or bicycle is a good day trip: from Vaison-la-Romaine take the southbound D938
to Carpentras, which snakes around the eastern side of the Dentelles to Le Barroux. Just
south of here, follow the westbound D21 to
Beaumes de Venise from where you can continue north to Gigondas, Sablet, Séguret and

Black Diamonds

Provence's cloak-and-dagger truffle trade is far from glamorous. In fact, the way these diamond
dealers operate – out of a car trunk, payment exclusively by cold hard cash – is a remarkably black
business.

Little known Richerenches, a deceptively wealthy village shielded within the thick walls of a 12th-
to 13th-century Templar fortress, is the congruous setting for Provence's leading wholesale **truffle
market**. Once a year, villagers celebrate a **truffle Mass** in the village church, during which parish-
ioners offer truffles instead of cash. The Mass (☎ 04 90 28 02 00 at the town hall) falls on the closest Sunday to 17 January, the feast day of Antoine, the patron saint of truffles and their harvesters.

Crisp, cold Saturday mornings from November to March (10 am to noon) see ave de la
Rebasse – Richerenches' main street – resound with the furtive whisperings of local *rabassaïres* (truffle hunters) gearing up to sell their weekly harvest to a big-time dealer from Paris, Germany, Italy
or beyond. No more than four or five cash-laden dealers attend the weekly market. Each sets
up shop – the trunk of their car – on the street, from where they carefully in-
spect, weigh and invariably buy kilos of the precious black fungi. Their
courtiers (brokers) mingle with the truffle hunters to scout out the
best truffles and keep tabs on deals being cut by rival dealers.

Truffle hunters, harvesters and dealers alike store the ugly,
mud-caked truffles in grubby white plastic bags. Individuals
seeking black diamonds generally have their own dealer
whom they telephone to place an order. **Trufficulteurs**
in Richerenches include Maurice Escoffier (☎ 04 90 28 02
11) and Monsieur Ruat (☎ 04 90 28 00 90).

At the world's largest **truffle cannery** (☎ 04 90 46 41 44)
in Puymeras, 7km north-east of Vaison-la-Romaine, the fungus is
conserved in jars for year-round consumption. The cannery, signposted 'Plantin' just west of
Puymeras village on the D46/D938 junction, opens 8 am to noon and 1.30 to 5.30 pm weekdays.
The history of truffles is unearthed in the **Musée de la Truffe et du Tricastin** (Truffle Museum; ☎ 05
75 96 61 29), 14km west of Richerenches in St-Paul Troix Châteaux. Truffles are sold in the village,
November to March, at the *épicerie fine* (grocery shop; 3 Grande Rue).

JANE SMITH

AVIGNON AREA

back to Vaison-la-Romaine. Bicycles can be hired from Location VTT (☎ 04 90 46 83 25), 55 bis Grand Rue, in Sablet. **Cycling routes** are mapped out on a noticeboard on the square front of Sablet tourist office (☎ 04 90 46 82 46), 8 place du Village.

Malaucène (pop 2581, elevation 350m) is 10km south of Vaison-la-Romaine and the place where many people begin their forays into the Dentelles and the surrounds of Mont Ventoux, 21km to the east. Its tourist office (☎/fax 04 90 65 22 59, ⓔ omalaucene@axit.fr), place de la Mairie, opens 10 am to noon and 2 to 6 pm Monday to Saturday.

Crestet
postcode 84110 • pop 441

Signposted west off the D938 is Crestet, 14km south of Vaison-la-Romaine. What must be the narrowest streets in Provence lead from the car park at the top of the village to the **Panoramic Café**, which affords breathtaking views of the Dentelles and Mont Ventoux.

Art in nature and nature in art is the thematic leaning of contemporary works displayed at **Crestet Centre d'Art** (☎ 04 90 36 35 00, ⓔ crestet.centre.art@wanadoo.fr), signposted from the foot of the village along chemin de la Verrière. A one-hour walking trail wends its way around 12 sculptures exhibited in the woods. Works by artists in residence are displayed in the centre, open 11 am to 7 pm, April to August, and 11 am to 6 pm, the rest of the year.

Le Barroux
postcode 84330 • pop 574
• elevation 325m

Yellow-stone Le Barroux tumbles down the hillside around medieval **Château du Barroux** (☎ 04 90 62 35 21), the hill-top village's crowning glory. The castle was built as a watchtower to protect the plain from Saracen attacks in the 12th century. During WWII it was occupied by German troops who set fire to it when they left; the castle burnt for 10 days. The restored 16th-century *salle des gardes* (guards' hall) above the chapel hosts classical music concerts. The

castle opens 2 to 6 pm, Easter to October. Admission costs 15FF.

From the northern end of the village, route de Suzette leads to **Abbaye Ste-Madeleine** (☎ 04 90 62 56 31), a Romanesque monastery surrounded by lavender gardens. Each morning at 9.30 am (10 am on Sunday and holidays) the Benedictine monks – whose life revolves around hard work, poverty and prayer – sing Gregorian chants and celebrate Mass in the chapel. The shaven-headed monks get up at 3.15 am and are back in bed by 8.30 pm.

Beaumes de Venise & Gigondas

At the foot of the loop around the Dentelles sits **Beaumes de Venise** (pop 2070), 10km south-west of Le Barroux at the crossroads of the D21 and the D90, which leads northwards into the massif. The village is best known for its fruity and sweet, golden **Muscat wines** – best drunk young, chilled to 6°C or 8°C and served as a digestif. Juicy melons from Cavaillon form the perfect partner to Beaumes de Venise's Or Blanc. The tourist office (☎ 04 90 62 94 39), cours Jean Jaurès, has a list of estates where you can taste and buy the nectar. Expect to pay 60FF per bottle.

The yellow-stone village of **Gigondas**, 15km north-east, offers ample wine-tasting opportunities. Wine cellars stud the central square, place du Village, from where rue du Corps de Garde climbs upwards to Gigondas' ruined chateau, church with its campanile, and cemetery. Contemporary sculptures en route form **Le Cheminement de Sculptures**; ask for a map of the sculpture trail at the tourist office (☎ 04 90 65 85 46, ⓔ ot-gigondas@axit.fr) on rue du Portail, off place du Village. Its free *Circuits VTT* brochure details three circular **cycling routes** (13km to 21km long) from Gigondas.

Places to Stay & Eat

Camping On the D974 towards Mont Ventoux, 1.5km east of Malaucène, *Camping du Groseau* (☎ 04 90 65 10 26, route du Ventoux) opens Easter to 30 September and charges 50FF for a tent, two people and car.

Some 4km north of Malaucène, *Aire*

AVIGNON AREA

A Village Christmas

Nowhere is a traditional Provençal Christmas celebrated more than in **Séguret** (pop 912), a quaint yellow-tinged village that clings to a rocky outcrop 9km south of Vaison-la-Romaine.

Festivities open with **Cacho Fio** at nightfall on Christmas Eve. During this Provençal ceremony, a log – usually cut from a pear, olive or cherry tree – is placed in the hearth, doused with fortified wine, blessed thrice by the youngest and oldest family members, then set alight. In keeping with tradition, this fire has to burn until the three kings arrive on 6 January.

Although many still celebrate Cacho Fio in the privacy of their own homes, it is only in Séguret that the entire village gathers to bless and burn a log. This takes place in the Salle Delage, adjoining Chapelle Ste-Thecle on rue du Four. Later, villagers wend their way up to Église St-Denis at the top of the village where, during **Li Bergié de Séguret**, the Christmas nativity scene is brought to life with real-life shepherds, lambs and a (relatively) newborn baby in a manger. This **crèche vivant** (living creche) starts at 10 pm; seats (60FF) can be reserved from 1 November by calling ☎ 04 90 46 91 08 (French only). It is followed by midnight Mass, celebrated in Provençal.

After Mass, families rush home for **Caleno vo Careno**, the traditional feast of 13 desserts, which symbolises Jesus and the 12 apostles. Among the culinary delights are *pompe ahuile* (leavened cake baked in olive oil and flavoured with orange blossom), sweet black-and-white nougat (home-made from honey and almonds) and an assortment of dried and fresh fruits.

Naturelle La Saousse (☎ 04 90 65 23 52) offers lovely views in an unspoilt neck of the woods. The site opens Easter to October and charges 20/10/10FF per person/tent/car. From Malaucène, head northwards along the D938, turn right onto the D13, then right again at the first crossroads.

Gîtes d'Étape In Gigondas, *Gîte d'Étape des Dentelles de Gigondas* (☎ 04 90 65 80 85, fax 04 90 65 84 63, e regis@provence-treking.com), next to the fire station, charges 70/80FF for a bed in a dorm/double or triple room with shared bathroom. Sheet hire costs 20FF.

Chambres d'Hôtes Many sleepy-eyed *mas* open their doors to B&B guests in summer. Particularly recommended is delightful *Le Mas de la Lause* (☎ 04 90 62 32 77, e maslause@francemel.com, chemin de Geysset), off route de Suzette in Le Barroux. Modern rooms in the renovated farmhouse, dating from 1883, cost 300FF for two or 470/550FF for a split-level, mezzanine suite for three/four. Prices include a breakfast of fresh bread, croissants and home-made jam. Evening meals at a shared table cost 95FF per person. It opens April to October.

In Crestet *La Respelido* (☎/fax 04 90 36 03 10) has just two guest rooms in a former oil mill. A double/triple with Mont Ventoux view costs 350/450FF (with private bath and toilet), including a lavish breakfast on the terrace or courtyard. Speak sweetly to host Monsieur Veit and (in season) he might just agree to accompany you to Richerences truffle market. La Respelido opens February to December.

There are several chambres d'hôtes on the northbound D23 to Séguret. Some 6km south of Beaumes de Venise, signposted off the D107 just south of Loriol du Comtat, is *Château Talaud* (☎ 04 90 65 71 00, e chateautalaud@avignon-et-provence.com), a castle with rooms named after different colours and costing 750FF to 1000FF.

Hotels In Malaucène, *Hôtel Le Venaissin* (☎ 04 90 65 20 31, fax 04 90 65 18 03, cours des Isnards) has comfortable doubles with shower costing 210FF (230FF with shower and toilet). Opposite, *Hôtel Origan* (☎ 04 90 65 27 08, cours des Isnards) charges 230/300FF per double/triple.

Les Géraniums (☎ 04 90 62 41 08, fax 04 90 62 56 48) in Le Barroux is a charming, yellow-stone hotel with luxurious doubles

AVIGNON AREA

furnished in traditional Provençal style for 250FF. In summer half-board is obligatory. Its in-house restaurant is also worth a nibble.

Three-star *Hôtel Montmirail* (☎ *04 90 65 84 01, fax 04 90 65 81 50)* is a 19th-century mansion located in a remote spot midway between Gigondas and neighbouring Vacqueyras. It has doubles from 410/425FF in low/high season.

Séguret has two hotels. On the plains, wine-producing *Domaine de Cabasse* (☎ *04 90 46 91 12, fax 04 90 46 94 01,* e *info@ domaine-de-cabasse.fr, route de Sablet)* has singles/doubles for 400/550FF (half-board only costs 610/980FF for one/two people in July and August). At the top of the village, eight-room *La Table du Comtat* (☎ *04 90 46 91 49, fax 04 90 46 94 27)* charges between 470FF and 610FF for a double.

MONT VENTOUX

The 25km narrow ridge, dubbed the *désert de pierre* (stone desert) – immediately east of the Dentelles de Montmirail – is Mont Ventoux. It is Provence's most prominent geographical feature thanks to its height (1912m) and supreme isolation. The mountain's stone-capped top gives it the appearance from afar of being snow-capped, which it is from December through to April. The radar and antenna-studded peak, accessible by road for just a few months in summer, affords spectacular views of Provence, the southern Alps and beyond. The mountain and its surrounds fall under the protection of the Réserve de Biosphère du Mont Ventoux, headquartered in Carpentras (see that section later in this chapter).

Mont Ventoux is the boundary between the fauna and flora of northern France and those of southern France. Some species, including the snake eagle, numerous spiders and a variety of butterflies, are found only here. The mountain's forests were felled 400 years ago to build ships, but since 1860 some areas have been reforested with a variety of species, including the majestic cedar of Lebanon. The mix of deciduous trees makes the mountain especially colourful in autumn. The broken white stones that cover the top are known as *lauzes*.

Since the summit is considerably cooler than the surrounding plains – there can be a difference of up to 20°C– and receives twice as much precipitation, bring warm clothes and rain gear. Areas above 1300m are generally snow-covered from December to April. With winds of up to 300km/h recorded you could say that Mont Ventoux is breezy.

Near the western end of the Mont Ventoux massif is the agricultural village of **Bédoin** (postcode 84410, pop 2657, elevation 295m) and, 4km farther east along route du Mont Ventoux (D974), neighbouring **Ste-Colombe**. Road signs here tell you if the *col* (mountain pass) over the summit is closed. At the eastern end of the Mont Ventoux massif is **Sault** (pop 1190, elevation 800m), which is surrounded by a patchwork of purple lavender in July and August. In winter **Mont Serein** (1445m), 16km east of Malaucène and 5km west of Mont Ventoux's summit on the D974, is transformed into a bustling ski station.

Maps

Didier-Richard's 1:50,000 scale map No 27, entitled *Massif du Ventoux*, includes Mont Ventoux, the Monts du Vaucluse and the Dentelles de Montmirail. More detailed is IGN's Série Bleue No 3140ET 1:25,000 *Mont Ventoux* (58FF).

Information

Tourist Offices Malaucène tourist office (see the earlier Dentelles de Montmirail section) stocks information on exploring Mont Ventoux by bicycle or on foot, including night climbs up Ventoux in July and August. Its efficient counterparts in Bédoin (☎ 04 90 65 63 95, e ot-bedoin@axit.fr), place du Marché, and Sault (☎ 04 90 64 01 21), ave de la Promenade, likewise organise guided mountain walks.

In Sault, the Maison de l'Environnement et de la Chasse (☎ 04 90 64 13 96) on ave de l'Oratoire houses the Centre Découverte de la Nature. The Nature Discovery Centre opens 10 am to noon and 3 to 7 pm Tuesday to Sunday in summer; and 10 am to noon and 2 to 6 pm, Tuesday to Sunday the rest

AVIGNON AREA

Bloody contests have been staged at Les Arènes, the Roman ampitheatre in Nîmes, for centuries.

Sur le pont d'Avignon – St-Bénézet Bridge, of nursery rhyme fame, is reflected in the Rhône.

Fort St-André and its snaking walls are remnants of Villeneuve-lès-Avignon's papal past.

Canoe or just drift along at L'Isle-sur-la-Sorgue.

Spectacular Fontaine de Vaucluse river canyon

of the year. Admission costs 12FF (children aged under eight, free).

Walking

The GR4, running from the Ardèche to the west, crosses the Dentelles de Montmirail before climbing up the northern face of Mont Ventoux. It then joins the GR9, and both trails follow the bare, white ridge before parting ways, with the GR4 winding eastwards to the Gorges du Verdon. The GR9, which takes you to most of the area's ranges (including the Monts du Vaucluse and Lubéron ranges) is arguably the most spectacular trail in Provence. The first person to climb to the top of Mont Ventoux was the Italian poet Petrarch, who scaled the mountain with a donkey in 1336, leaving everyone convinced he was mad.

Camping du Mont Serein (see Places to Stay & Eat later) organises nature walks and thematic trails (flora, fauna, geology, photography etc). Half-/full-day walks cost 90FF (children aged under 12, 50FF).

At Chalet Reynard, mountain guide Jean-Pierre Bianco (☎ 06 62 50 95 14, ☎/fax 04 90 60 48 25) leads walks for 50/100FF per half-/full day (half-day for children aged under 10, 35FF).

Cycling

In summer cyclists labour up the sun-baked slopes of Mont Ventoux (from Chalet Reynard on the westbound D974) to the summit. Many who make the journey are inspired by the British world champion cyclist Tommy Simpson (1937–67) who suffered a fatal heart attack here during the 1967 Tour de France. Most pedal to the top, then backtrack to add their water bottle to the cycling memorabilia surrounding the roadside memorial to Tommy Simpson, 1km east of the summit and 1km west of Chalet Reynard. The epitaph on the grey stone tablet reads 'There is no mountain too high'.

In Malaucène, ACS Cycles (☎/fax 04 90 65 15 42), ave de Verdun, repairs and rents road and mountain bikes (from 50/70FF per half-/full day). In Sault, Albion Cycles (☎ 04 90 64 09 32), route de St-Trinit, has wheels to rent. Bédoin's local cycling club arranges

weekly bike rides, departing from Camping Pestory (see Places to Stay & Eat below).

Skiing

Between December and March, locals flock up Ventoux to ski down its slopes. **Chalet Reynard** (☎ 04 90 61 84 55), at the intersection of the D974 and the eastbound D164 to Sault, is a small ski station (1440m) on the southern slopes. It has two drag lifts *(téléskis)* up to two blue runs – both about 900m long. You can hire a set of skis, boots and poles here (100FF per day); cross-country skiing is also popular. Non-skiers can test the luge (50FF).

Mont Serein (1400m), 5km west of the summit on the colder northern side, is the main ski station served by six drag lifts. Skis, ski schools, piste maps and ski passes are available from Chalet d'Accueil (☎ 04 90 63 42 02), in the centre of the resort. A half-/full- day ski pass costs about 62/82FF (children aged under six, 30FF). Chalet Liotard (see Places to Stay & Eat) is a mid-station, 100m farther uphill.

Places to Stay & Eat

Places listed in the Dentelles de Montmirail section (earlier in this chapter) also serve as a good base to explore Mont Ventoux.

In Beaumont du Ventoux, 15km north-east of Malaucène off the D974, is *Camping du Mont Serein* (☎ 04 90 60 49 16, 06 83 79 73 38, route du Mont Ventoux), 5km east of the Ventoux summit at 1400m. It costs 10/25FF per person/tent and has four-person chalets to rent (starting at 1800FF per week).

Nearby *Chalet Liotard* (☎ 04 90 60 68 38, fax 04 90 60 12 08) is practically Alpine in its cosiness, warming cuisine (lunch/evening *menus* 50/95FF) and roaring winter fire. Comfortable doubles cost 280FF (330FF in July, August and December to February).

In Bédoin, *Camping Pastory* (☎ 04 90 12 85 83, route de Malaucène), at the western end of the village on the D19, charges 10/10/13/7FF per tent/car/adult/child aged under seven. Reception opens 8 am to noon and 3 to 7 pm; the site opens mid-March to October.

AVIGNON AREA

AVIGNON AREA

The Perfume of Provence

If there's one aroma associated with Provence, it's *lavande* (lavender). Lavender fields – once seen, never forgotten – include those surrounding Abbaye de Sénanque near Gordes and the Musée de la Lavande in Coustellet, and those carpeting the arid Sault region, east of Mont Ventoux on the Vaucluse plateau. The vast lavender farms that sweep across the Plateau de Valensole and those at Lagarde d'Apt, are particularly memorable.

The sweet purple flower is harvested when it is in full bloom, between 15 July and 15 August. It is mechanically harvested on a hot dry day, following which the lorry-loads of cut lavender, known as *paille* (straw), are packed tight in a steam still and distilled to extract the sweet essential oils.

Authentic lavender farms, all the rage in Provence in the 1920s, are a dying breed today. Since the 1950s, lavandin – a hybrid of fine lavender and aspic, cloned at the turn of the century – has been mass produced for industrial purposes. Both blaze the same vibrant purple when in flower, but lavandin yields five times more oil than fine lavender (which produces 1kg of oil from 130kg of cut straw).

Approximately 80% of Provence's lavender farms produce lavandin today. The few remaining traditional lavender farms – such as Château du Bois, which can be visited (see the Lubéron chapter) – usually colour higher areas. Wild lavender needs an altitude of 900m to 1300m to blossom, unlike its common sister, which can grow anywhere above 800m.

A complete list of lavender farms, distilleries and gardens open to visitors are listed in the English-language brochure *Les Routes de la Lavande* (The Lavender Roads), available free from tourist offices or the Association Routes de la Lavande (☎ 04 75 26 65 91, fax 04 75 26 32 67, ⓔ routes .lavande@educagri.fr), 2 ave de Venterol, BP 36, 26111 Nyons. The latter also has information on lavender tours; some are listed in this guide under Organised Tours in the Getting Around chapter.

Fêtes de la Lavande (lavender festivals) are celebrated in Valensole (3rd Sunday in July), Sault (15 August), Digne-les-Bains and Valréas (first weekend in August).

Sault offers appealing *Hôtel Le Louvre* (☎ 04 90 64 08 88, place du Marché), which has double rooms overlooking the village square for 300FF and an excellent Provençal kitchen. About 2km north along the D950 towards St-Trinit is *Hostellerie du Val de Sault* (☎ 04 90 64 01 41, fax 04 90 64 12 74) – a haven of peace and tranquillity. 'Gourmet stays' cost 480/590FF per person in low/high season for half-board; in season, the chef cooks up numerous truffle treats.

Shopping

Don't leave Sault without indulging in a slab of its sweet lavender-honey and almond-flavour nougat or bitter-sweet macaroons. Both are sold at André Boyer (☎ 04 90 64 00 23, ⓔ infos@nougat-boyer.fr) on place de l'Europe, a nougat maker featured in the *Guinness Book of Records* for cooking up the largest bar of nougat (12.45m long and 180kg in weight). Factory visits can be arranged.

Equally delectable are the unusual mixes of dried Provençal herbs and herbal liqueurs sold at Le Jardin des Lavandes (☎ 04 90 64 10 74) on route de la Lavande, a shop dedicated to Provence's sweetest-smelling flower. Savoury dishes such as curried goat cheese, duck thighs and ginger jam are sold at L'Épicerie Paysanne, on the corner of rues des Esquiche Mouches and rue Porte des Aires.

Getting There & Away

If you've got a car, the summit of Mont Ventoux can be reached from Sault via the tortuous D164 or, in summer, from Malaucène or St-Estève via the switchback D974, built in the 1930s. This mountain road is often snow-blocked until as late as April. See the Carpentras section later for bus details.

CARPENTRAS

postcode 84200 • pop 27,249
• elevation 102m

Drowsy Carpentras, an important trading centre in Greek times and later a Gallo-Roman city, became the capital of the papal territory of the Comtat Venaissin in 1320. It flourished in the 14th century, when it was visited frequently by Pope Clement V. At the same time, Jews expelled from territory controlled by the French crown (especially in Provence and Languedoc) sought refuge in the Comtat Venaissin, where they could live under papal protection – subject to certain restrictions. The Comtat Venassin became part of France in 1791 after the French Revolution. Today, Carpentras' 14th-century synagogue is France's oldest such structure still in use.

Carpentras is equidistant (25km) from Avignon and Orange. Easy to navigate on foot, the agricultural town is best known for its bustling Friday morning market on place Aristide Briand, which sells everything from truffles (November to March) to *berlingots* (hard-boiled sweets). The streets fanning out from the square – rue de la République and ave Jean Maréchaux – tout tables laden with nougat, cheese, orange and lavender marmalade, cauldrons of paella, buckets of olives and flowers galore, as well as the usual knock-off jeans and generic T-shirts.

Orientation

In the 19th century, the city's 16th-century fortifications and walls were replaced by a ring of boulevards: ave Jean Jaurès, blvd Alfred Rogier, blvd du Nord, blvd Maréchal Leclerc, blvd Gambetta and blvd Albin Durand. Inside, is the partly pedestrianised old city. Northern Porte d'Orange (1560) still stands.

If you arrive by bus, walk north-eastwards to place Aristide Briand, a major traffic intersection at the southernmost point on the heart-shaped ring of boulevards. Ave Jean Jaurès leads to the tourist office, while pedestrian-only rue de la République heads northwards to the cathedral and Palais de Justice. The town hall is a few blocks northeast of the cathedral.

Information

Tourist Offices The tourist office (☎ 04 90 63 00 78, fax 04 90 60 41 02, ℮ tourist .carpentras@axit.fr), 170 ave Jean Jaurès, sells maps and organises 25FF city tours (those aged 10 to 18, 15FF). It also arranges wine-tasting of Côtes du Ventoux vintages and tours to a berlingot factory. The office opens 9 am to 7 pm Monday to Saturday, 9.30 am to 1 pm Sunday, June to September; and 9 am to 12.30 pm and 2 to 6 or 6.30 pm Monday to Saturday, the rest of the year.

The headquarters of the Réserve de Biosphère du Mont Ventoux (☎ 04 90 63 22 74, fax 04 90 67 09 07, ℮ ventoux .biosphere@wanadoo.fr) is at 1260 ave des Marchés.

Money Banque de France, 161 blvd Albin Durand, exchanges currency between 9 am and 12.15 pm weekdays. Commercial banks line place Aristide Briand and blvd Albin Durand.

Post & Communications The post office, 65 rue d'Inguimbert, opens 8 am to 7 pm weekdays, 8 am to noon Saturday. It has Cyberposte. Web Center (☎ 04 90 67 32 62), 290 blvd Albin Durand, charges 1/50FF per minute/hour. It opens 10.30 am to 8.30 pm Monday to Saturday.

Laundry Lavomatique, 112 rue Porte de Monteux, opens 7 am to 7.30 pm.

Synagogue

Carpentras synagogue – inconspicuous as it is – was founded on this site in 1367, rebuilt 1741–3 and restored in 1929 and 1954. The 1st-floor sanctuary is decorated with wood panelling and liturgical objects from the 18th century. Down below, there's an oven that was used until 1904 to bake matzo *(pain azyme* in French), the unleavened bread eaten at Passover.

The synagogue, on place Juiverie, can be identified by a stone plaque positioned high on the wall that is inscribed with Hebrew letters. It can be visited 10 am to noon and 3 to 5 pm (4 pm on Friday) weekdays; ring the bell.

AVIGNON AREA

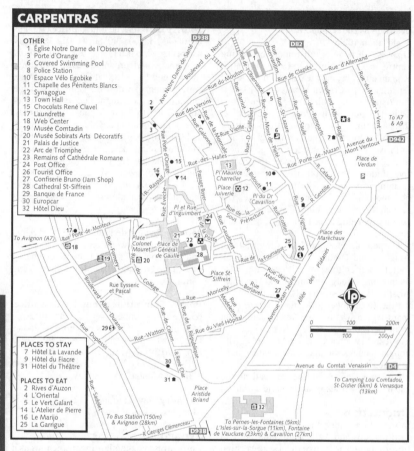

CARPENTRAS

OTHER
1 Église Notre Dame de l'Observance
3 Porte d'Orange
6 Covered Swimming Pool
8 Police Station
10 Espace Vélo Egobike
11 Chapelle des Pénitents Blancs
12 Synagogue
13 Town Hall
15 Chocolats René Clavel
17 Laundrette
18 Web Center
19 Musée Comtadin
20 Musée Sobirats Arts Décoratifs
21 Palais de Justice
22 Arc de Triomphe
23 Remains of Cathédrale Romane
24 Post Office
26 Tourist Office
27 Confiserie Bruno (Jam Shop)
28 Cathedral St-Siffrein
29 Banque de France
30 Europcar
32 Hôtel Dieu

PLACES TO STAY
7 Hôtel La Lavande
9 Hôtel du Fiacre
31 Hôtel du Théâtre

PLACES TO EAT
2 Rives d'Auzon
4 L'Oriental
5 Le Vert Galant
14 L'Atelier de Pierre
16 Le Marijo
25 La Garrigue

AVIGNON AREA

Cathedral St-Siffrein

Carpentras' one-time cathedral, which dominates place Charles de Gaulle, was built in the Méridional (southern French) Gothic style between 1405 and 1519. The doorway, whose design is classical, was added in the 17th century. Inside, the **Trésor d'Art Sacré** (Treasury of Religious Art) displays liturgical objects and reliquaries from the 14th to 19th century, including **St-Mors**, the Holy Bridle-bit supposedly made by St-Helen for her son Constantine from a nail taken from the True Cross.

The cathedral opens between 10 am and noon and between 2 and 4 or 6 pm, Wednesday to Monday. Sunday Mass is celebrated at 9 and 10.30 am.

Arc de Triomphe

Hidden in a corner off rue d'Inguimbert – next to the cathedral and behind the **Palais de Justice** in an episcopal palace built in 1801 – what's left of this triumphal arch is the town's only Roman relic. Built under Augustus in the 1st century AD, it is little more than a convenient public urinal today. One of the carvings on the eastern side depicts two Barbarian captives (note the beards and chains), their faces all but worn away by time and the weather.

Facing the arch on the opposite side of the square are the paltry remains of a 7th-century **Cathédrale Romane**, most of which was destroyed in 1399.

Carpentras' northern outskirts are crossed by its most impressive stone relic, the remains of a 10km-long **aqueduct** that brought water to the city between 1745 and 1893. For a heady glimpse of its 48 arches, follow the Orange road signs from the town centre.

Museums

Museums open 10 am to noon and 2 to 6 pm (4 pm in winter) Wednesday to Monday. The **Musée Comtadin**, which displays artefacts related to local history and folklore, and the **Musée Duplessis**, which houses a bunch of paintings, are at 234 blvd Albin Durand.

The **Musée Sobirats Arts Décoratifs**, a block west of the cathedral at 112 rue du Collège, is an 18th-century private residence crammed with furniture, faïence and *objets d'art* in the Louis XV and Louis XVI styles. Admission costs a token 2FF; ring the bell to enter.

The 18th-century **Hôtel Dieu**, place Aristide Briand, has an old-time pharmacy, open 9 am to 11.30 am, Monday, Wednesday and Thursday. Admission costs 8FF.

Swimming

Art Deco fans who enjoy taking a plunge should head for the lovely covered swimming pool (Piscine Couverte Renovée; ☎ 04 90 60 92 03), overlooking place Capponi on rue Mont de Piété. was built by the Caisse d'Épargne in 1930 and has since been restored to its geometric glory. The water temperature is 20 C. Hours vary, but it generally opens 3 to 5.15 pm and 6 to 8 pm. Admission costs 15FF (seniors and children aged three to 15, 9FF).

Places to Stay

Camping Outside town, *Camping Lou Comtadou* (☎ 04 90 67 03 16, ave Pierre de Coubertin) opens Easter to October. It charges 65FF for a tent, car and two people.

Hotels Arguably the best place in town to stay for travellers watching their wallets is one-star *Hôtel du Théâtre* (☎ 04 90 63 02 90, 7 blvd Albin Durand), a friendly establishment overlooking place Aristide Briand. Large doubles cost 170FF (190FF with shower, 210FF with shower and toilet).

Eight-room *Hôtel La Lavande* (☎ 04 90 63 13 49, 282 blvd Alfred Rogier), straddling a busy road, has 155FF doubles (185FF with shower/205FF with shower and toilet).

Hôtel du Fiacre (☎ 04 90 63 03 15, fax 04 90 60 49 73, 153 rue Vigne), above a restaurant and piano bar, has bathroom-equipped doubles costing 190FF to 390FF.

Places to Eat

Regional fare rules at *Le Marijo* (☎ 04 90 60 42 65, 73 rue Raspail), which serves up superb three- and four-course *menus* for 98FF and 142FF. The pick of its entrees is local melon served with Muscat de Beames de Venise, followed by a truffle omelette. Finish with goat cheese marinated in herbs and olive oil and sprinkled with *marc*, a local eau de vie.

La Garrigue (☎ 04 90 60 21 24), behind the tourist office, has a flower-filled terrace. Besides its abundance of pizzas (from 65FF), Serge also concocts a wide variety of Provençal dishes that change daily. His plat du jour costs 59FF.

Carpentras' finest terrace sits at the foot of a 16th-century belfry, topped by an ornate campanile dating from 1572. *L'Atelier de Pierre* (☎ 04 90 60 75 00, 30 place de l'Horloge) has 150FF and 198FF *menus* worth every centime for the setting alone.

Equally palatable are the truffles served at *Le Vert Galant* (☎ 04 90 67 15 50, 12 rue de Clapiès). Expect to pay at least 100FF to sample the precious bits of black fungi dished up by chef Michel Castelain. His lunchtime/evening *menus* cost 120/149FF.

Another prized restaurant is colourful *Rives d'Auzon* (☎ 04 90 60 62 62, 47 blvd du Nord), opposite the Porte d'Orange. *Menus*, which change every two months, cost 140FF, 165FF and 190FF.

L'Oriental (☎ 04 90 63 19 57, 26 rue de la Monnaie) specialises in Moroccan

AVIGNON AREA

couscous, costing 65FF to 120FF a plateful. Tajines average 75FF.

Shopping

Chocolats René Clavel (☎ 04 90 63 07 59), 30 rue Porte d'Orange, is packed with fantastical sculptures carved from berlingot, a hard caramel candy created in Carpentras in 1844. The largest weighs 56kg and was a *Guinness Book of Records* record-breaker in 1992. It sells *calissons* (almond and fruit biscuits) and chocolate olives too.

Almond and pine kernel meringues are sold at Jouvard Pâtissier, 40 rue Éveche. For unusual home-made jams (quince, kiwi fruit and so on) and candied fruits shop at Confiserie Bruno (☎ 04 90 63 04 99), 280 ave Jean Jaurès.

Getting There & Away

The bus station, place Terradou, is 150m south-west of place Aristide Briand. Schedules are available from Cars Comtadins (☎ 04 90 67 20 25), 38 ave Wilson, open 8 am to noon and 2 to 6 pm weekdays.

There are hourly services to/from Avignon (23FF, 45 minutes) and less frequent runs to/from Orange (25FF, 40 minutes), Cavaillon (28FF, 45 minutes), L'Isle-sur-la-Sorgue (20FF, 20 minutes), Vaison-la-Romaine (22FF, 45 minutes) via Le Barroux (17FF, 20 minutes), Malaucène (17FF, 30 minutes) and Crestet (20FF, 40 minutes).

Getting Around

Bicycle Espace Vélo Egobike (☎ 04 90 67 05 58), 64 rue Vigne, is a mountain-bike specialist, open 10 am to noon and 2.30 to 7 pm weekdays, and 2.30 to 7 pm Saturday. It rents bikes for 50/70/110FF (plus 3500FF deposit) per two hours/half-day/full day. A guide for up to 12 cyclists costs 350/800FF per half-day/day. The centre can also transport you and your bike to the top of Mont Ventoux (275FF for one to six people), allowing you to whizz downhill in unexhausted splendour.

AROUND CARPENTRAS

From Carpentras, a circular day trip takes travellers through a waterworld of fountains and water wheels, gushing springs and breathtaking gorges.

Pernes-les-Fontaines

postcode 84210 • pop 10,309
• elevation 75m

A former capital of Comtat Venaissin, Pernes-les-Fontaines, 5km south of Carpentras, is named after the 40 fountains that spring from its stone walls and decorate its squares. Upon discovering the Font de Bouvery source in the 18th century, the town mayor graced the town's four quarters with a monumental mushroom of a fountain, extravagantly decorated and sprouting from a 3.20m-wide base. The grandiose, moss-covered fountains – Fontaine du Cormoran, Fontaine Reboul (also called La Grand Font) and Fontaine du Gigot – are the result.

The tourist office (☎ 04 90 61 31 04, 04 90 66 47 27, fax 04 90 61 33 23) on place du Comtat Venaissin distributes city maps marked up with a fountain tour.

L'Isle-sur-la-Sorgue

postcode 84800 • pop 17,443

A farther 11km south sits L'Isle-sur-la-Sorgue, a chic spot known for its antique shops and graceful waterways. L'Isle dates from the 12th century when villagers built huts on stilts above what was then a swampy marshland. By the 18th century it was a thriving silk-weaving centre surrounded by canals ploughed by water wheels powering its paper mills and silk factories.

On Sunday morning the quays are swamped with book and antique sellers, and a host of market stalls selling other wares. A food market fills the streets on Thursday morning. Le Quai de la Gare (☎ 04 90 20 73 42), 4 ave Julien Guigue, is an old warehouse housing 25 antique dealers. Another 90 or so can be found in Le Village des Antiquaires (☎ 04 90 38 04 57), an antique shopping mall fronted by an 18th-century mill at 2 bis ave de l'Égalité. Don't expect any bargains. Antique wines dating to 1900 are sold at Antiq'Vins (☎ 04 90 38 91 62), cours René Char.

The tourist office (☎ 04 90 38 04 78, fax 04 90 38 35 43), place de l'Église, opens

9 am to 12.30 pm and 2.30 to 6 pm Monday to Saturday, and 9 am to 12.30 pm Sunday. It has plenty of information on **canoeing** the 8km along the Sorgue from neighbouring Fontaine de Vaucluse to L'Isle-sur-la-Sorgue. Between May and September, Canoë Évasion (☎ 04 90 38 26 22), next to Camping La Coutelière on the D24, and Kayak Vert (☎ 04 90 20 35 44) in Fontaine de Vaucluse, rent canoes and organise river expeditions for 110FF (children aged seven to 14, 70FF).

Fontaine de Vaucluse

postcode 84800 • pop 61 • elevation 75m

The mighty spring that gives Fontaine de Vaucluse (Vau-Cluso La Font in Provençal) its name is the spot where the Sorgue River ends its subterranean course and gushes to the surface. At the end of winter and in early spring, up to 200 cubic metres of water per second spill forth from the base of the cliff, forming one of the world's most powerful springs. During drier periods, the reduced flow seeps through the rocks at various points downstream from the cliff and the spring becomes little more than a still, very deep pond. Following numerous unsuccessful human and robotic attempts to reach the bottom, an unmanned submarine touched the 315m-deep base in 1985.

Some 1.5 million visitors descend upon Fontaine de Vaucluse each year to stroll its streets and throw pebbles in its pond. The tourist office (☎ 04 90 20 32 22, fax 04 90 20 21 37, e officetourisme.vaucluse@ wanadoo.fr), south-east of central place de la Colonne on chemin de la Fontaine, opens 10 am to 6 or 7 pm Monday to Saturday.

Museums Fontaine's three museums – all on chemin de la Fontaine – deal with: the Resistance movement, **Musée d'Histoire 1939–45** (☎ 04 90 20 24 00) adjoining the tourist office; justice and punishment, **Musée Historique de la Justice et des Châtiments** (☎ 04 90 20 24 58); and stalactites and speleology, **Le Monde Souterrain** (Subterranean World; ☎ 04 90 20 34 13).

The **Moulin à Papier Vallis Clausa** (☎ 04 90 20 34 14), opposite the tourist office on chemin de la Fontaine, is a reconstruction of a paper mill, built where Fontaine de Vaucluse's old mill was from 1522 to 1968. Flower-encrusted paper, made by hand as it was in the 16th century, is sold in its boutique. In the neighbouring Galerie Vallis Clausa (☎ 04 90 20 20 83) there's a **Musée du Santon**.

The Italian Renaissance poet Petrarch (Pétrarque in French) lived in Fontaine de Vaucluse from 1337 to 1353 where he immortalised his true love, Laura, wife of Hugues de Sade, in verse. The **Musée Pétrarque** (☎ 04 90 20 37 20) on the left bank of the Sorgue is devoted to his work, sojourn and broken heart. Admission costs 20FF (seniors, students and those aged 12 to 18, 10FF).

Pays de Venasque

The hill-top villages sprinkled around Venasque are beautiful yet seldom explored. The area is crossed with parts of **Le Mur de la Peste** (literally 'Wall of Plague'), a 1.5m-high, dry stone wall built under Papal orders in 1721 to prevent (unsuccessfully) the plague from penetrating Comtat Venaissin.

The village baptistery in **Venasque** (pop 980, elevation 320m), 13km south-east of Carpentras, was built in the 5th century on the site of a Roman temple and is one of France's oldest structures. Ventoux Sport (☎ 04 90 66 61 26, 04 90 82 76 75), place de Tours, guides 10- to 35km-long mountain-bike rides (40FF) in Pay de Venasque.

The fortress village of **Le Beaucet** (pop 354, elevation 300m), tumbles down the hillside 6km south via the winding D314. Two kilometres south along chemin des Oratoires (the D39A) in the hamlet of **St-Gens** is a small Romanesque basilica, rebuilt in 1884. The hermit Gens, who lived with wolves and performed rain-making miracles, died here in 1127.

The **Forêt de Vénasque**, crossed by the GR91 walking trail, lies to the east of Venasque. From here the GR91 heads north to the foot of the magnificent **Gorges de la Nesque**, from where Sault and the eastern realms of the Ventoux can be accessed.

Venasque tourist office (☎ 04 90 66 11 66),

AVIGNON AREA

Grande Rue, has information on Pays de Venasque.

Places to Stay
This part of Provence can also be easily explored from the villages of Cabrières d'Avignon and Lagnes in the Lubéron (see that chapter), both of which offer attractive places to stay.

Camping In Fontaine de Vaucluse *Camping Municipal Les Prés (☎ 04 90 20 32 38, route de Cavaillon)* is west of the village centre near the car park. You can also camp in the Auberge de Jeunesse grounds (see Hostels below).

Riverside *Camping Municipal La Sorguette (☎ 04 90 38 05 71, fax 04 90 20 84 61, ⓔ sorguette@wanadoo.fr, route d'Apt)* in L'Isle-sur-la-Sorgue, opens mid-March to mid-October. It charges 84FF for two campers with a tent and car.

Hostels The *Auberge de Jeunesse (☎ 04 90 20 31 65, fax 04 90 20 26 20, chemin de la Vignasse)* is 800m south of Fontaine de Vaucluse towards Lagnes (walk uphill from the bus stop). B&B/sheets cost 67/ 17FF. Campers can pitch their tent here for 27FF per person and hire a bike for 60FF per day. If you don't have an HI card, you need to pay an extra 19FF for a nightly stamp. Reception opens 8 to 10 am and 5 to 10 pm The hostel opens February to mid-November.

Hotels Avoid L'Isle-sur-la-Sorgue; it's stupidly expensive. The most affordable of Fontaine de Vaucluse's three hotels is 12-room *Hôtel Les Sources (☎ 04 90 20 31 84, fax 04 90 20 39 09, route de Cavaillon)*, which has doubles costing 170FF.

Getting There & Away
Fontaine de Vaucluse is 21km south-east of Carpentras and about 7km east of L'Isle-sur-la-Sorgue. From Avignon, Voyages Arnaud (☎ 04 90 38 15 58 in L'Isle-sur-la-Sorgue) runs three to four buses daily to L'Isle-sur-la-Sorgue (15FF, 40 minutes), Fontaine de Vaucluse (25FF, one hour); the

bus then continues to Lagnes (28FF, 1¼ hours) in the Lubéron. There are also Arnaud buses from Carpentras to L'Isle-sur-la-Sorgue (20 minutes). A one-way L'Isle-sur-la-Sorgue–Fontaine de Vaucluse fare is 12FF.

L'Isle-sur-la-Sorgue train station is not served by passenger trains.

Getting Around
In L'Isle-sur-la-Sorgue, you can hire a bicycle for 85FF per day from Cycles Peugeot-Christophe Tendil (☎ 04 90 38 19 12), 8 ave Julien Guigue.

Out of town, try Plein Air Location (☎ 04 90 38 25 80), at Canoë Évasion's riverside base on route de Fontaine de Vaucluse (D24), south of Fontaine de Vaucluse. It charges 100FF per day.

Les Alpilles

South of Avignon is the Chaîne des Alpilles, a barren chain of wild limestone rocks, carpeted in parts with herbal *garrigue* (scrubland) and studded with oil mills. To the north and south sits St-Rémy de Provence and Maussane-les-Alpilles respectively, a town and a village linked by the Vallée des Baux, which safeguards its own culinary secret. Les Alpilles stretch eastwards to the River Durance and westwards to the River Rhône.

ST-RÉMY DE PROVENCE
postcode 13210 • pop 10,007
• elevation 60m
St-Rémy de Provence – the main starting point for forays into the Chaîne des Alpilles – is a colourful place with a colourful past. The Greeks and then the Romans settled Glanum on the city's southern fringe. Philosopher Nostradamus (1503–66) was born in a house on rue Hoche in St-Rémy, only later moving to Salon de Provence to compile his influential prophecies. Three centuries on, a tormented Vincent van Gogh (1853–90) sought refuge in St-Rémy, painting some of his best known works here in 1889–90.

Sheep, sheep and more *moutons* fill the streets each year on Pentecost Monday during the Fête de la Transhumance, which marks the movement of the flocks to pastures new. On 15 August St-Rémy celebrates its Carreto Ramado, during which 50 horses lug a cart laden with local produce through town. September closes with a 10-day festival in honour of St-Rémy's patron saint.

More recently, St-Rémy has become something of a gastronomic mecca, luring some notables and one of France's best *chocolatiers* (chocolate makers) into its fold. The famed, smooth, rich oils from the Vallée des Baux – credited with their own *appellation d'origine contrôllée* (AOC) since 1997 – can also be tried and tasted here. Wednesday is market day.

Orientation & Information

Glanum is 2km south of the centre. From the ruins, ave Vincent van Gogh (D5) and its continuation, ave Pasteur, leads northwards to place Jean Jaurés and farther to blvd Victor Hugo, the street encircling the old town. Maps are sold at the Maison de la Presse, 19 blvd Marceau. The Librairie des Arts (☎ 04 90 92 12 38), 24 blvd Victor Hugo, is the place to go for guides and English-language novels.

The tourist office (☎ 04 90 92 05 22, fax 04 90 92 38 52, e webmaster@st-remy .fr), place Jean Jaurés, organises 1½-hour guided tours costing 35FF (students 20FF; children aged under 12, free), including one that follows in Van Gogh's footsteps. It also offers appealing nature walks in the Alpilles. The office opens 9 am to noon and 2 to 7 pm Monday to Sunday noon, June to October; and 9 am to noon and 2 to 6 pm Monday to Saturday, the rest of the year.

Site Archéologique de Glanum

The Glanum archaeological site sits at the foot of Mont Gaussier. It was uncovered in 1921 and comprises excavated remains dating from the Gallo-Greek era (3rd to 1st centuries BC) to the Gallo-Roman era (1st century BC to 3rd century AD). The Celto-

Ligurians first inhabited the site, which they called Glaniques. Among the archaeological finds uncovered were parts of Glanum's temple, enabling archaeologists to partially reconstruct the columned edifice, complete with its decorative upper mouldings. Other Roman buildings clearly evident are the public baths dating from 50 BC and the forum. Smaller fragments of treasure dug up are displayed in the Renaissance **Hôtel de Sade** (☎ 04 90 92 64 04), rue du Parage, in the centre of St-Rémy, open 10 am to noon and 2 to 5 or 6 pm..

Glanum archaeological site (☎ 04 90 92 23 79) opens 9 am to 7 pm, April to September; and 9 am to noon and 2 to 5 pm, the rest of the year. Admission costs 32FF (those aged 12 to 25, 21FF). Alternatively, a combined ticket covering admission to Hôtel de Sade costs 36FF (those aged 12 to 25, 25FF).

The roadside opposite the archaeological site entrance on ave Van Gogh (the southbound D5) is dominated by Provence's two most spectacular Roman monuments: the **triumphal arch** and **mausoleum**. **Les Antiques**, as the majestic pair is known, date from AD 20 and 30–20 BC respectively.

Van Gogh

The Dutch-born artist retreated to **Monastère St-Paul de Mausole**, a monastery that served as an asylum from the 18th century. Van Gogh voluntarily admitted himself on 3 May 1889 and stayed here until 16 May 1890. During this time, he accomplished 100 drawings and about 150 paintings, including the well-known *Les Irises* (Still life with Iris, 1890) and *Le Champ de Blé au Cyprès* (Yellow Cornfield, 1889). During WWI, the building was a prison camp. Today it is a clinic, but the 11th- to 12th-century church and adjoining Romanesque cloister can be visited, 9.30 am to 6 pm weekdays, and 10.30 am to 6 pm weekends. Admission costs 15FF (students and those aged 12 to 16, 10FF).

From the monastery entrance, coloured information boards mark the route of the *Promenade sur les lieux peints par Van Gogh* – a trail which leads you to the places

AVIGNON AREA

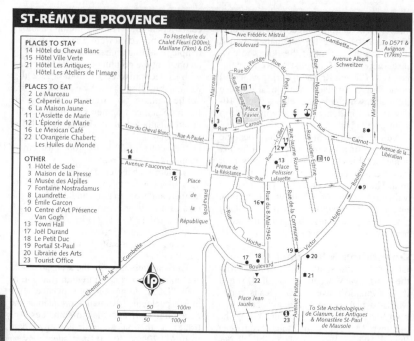

ST-RÉMY DE PROVENCE

PLACES TO STAY
14 Hôtel du Cheval Blanc
15 Hôtel Ville Verte
21 Hôtel Les Antiques;
   Hôtel Les Ateliers de l'Image

PLACES TO EAT
2 Le Marceau
5 Crêperie Lou Planet
6 La Maison Jaune
11 L'Assiette de Marie
12 L'Épicerie de Marie
16 Le Mexican Café
22 L'Orangerie Chabert;
   Les Huiles du Monde

OTHER
1 Hôtel de Sade
3 Maison de la Presse
4 Musée des Alpilles
7 Fontaine Nostradamus
8 Laundrette
9 Émile Garcon
10 Centre d'Art Présence
   Van Gogh
13 Town Hall
17 Joël Durand
18 Le Petit Duc
19 Portail St-Paul
20 Librairie des Arts
23 Tourist Office

where Van Gogh painted some of his most famous works. Next to the Glanum archaeological site entrance, he painted *Les Oliviers* (Olive Trees) and *Montagnes de St-Rémy* (St-Rémy Mountains) in July 1889.

In town, the life and works of Vincent van Gogh are unravelled at the **Centre d'Art Présence Van Gogh** (☎ 04 90 92 34 72), 8 rue Estrine.

Frédéric Mistral

The Provençal poet and 1904 winner of the Nobel Prize for Literature was a native of less-than-momentous **Maillane**, a village 7km north-west of St-Rémy de Provence. Frédéric Mistral (1830–1914) was born in the Mas du Juge, a farmhouse on its outskirts. After his father's death, he and his mother moved into the centre of the village. Upon marrying, 46-year-old Mistral left home – moving with his new wife (aged 19) into a house opposite his mother's.

The house at 11 rue Lamartine, where he spent his married life, is a museum today, open 9.30 to 11.30 am and 2.30 to 6.30 pm Tuesday to Sunday, April to September; and 10 to 11.30 am and 2 to 4.30 pm Tuesday to Sunday, the rest of the year. You can also see the lizard and short verse written in Provençal that he engraved on his mother's house opposite. Mistral is buried in the village cemetery.

Places to Stay

Charming, pool-endowed *Hôtel Ville Verte* (☎ 04 90 92 06 14, fax 04 90 92 56 54, 18 place de la République) has 37 doubles with shower overlooking the street/courtyard for 200/225FF (240/260FF with shower and toilet). It also has 17 self-catering studios, costing upwards of 2100/2450FF per week in low/high season. It opens from March to January.

Around the corner, *Hôtel du Cheval Blanc* (☎ 04 90 92 09 28, fax 04 90 92 69 05, 6 ave Fauconnet) is a large, green-

AVIGNON AREA

A Tasty Shopping Spree

Shop for...

...chocolates to die for at Joël Durand's boutique (☎ 04 90 92 38 25), 3 blvd Victor Hugo, open 9.30 am to 12.30 pm and 2.30 to 7.30 pm Tuesday to Saturday. His astonishing use of Provençal herbs and plants – lavender, rose petals, violet, thyme etc – makes him one of France's top 10 *chocolatiers* (chocolate makers). Flavoured squares are numbered one to 32 (110FF for 32 squares).

...historical biscuits baked by food historian Anne Daguin using old Roman, Renaissance, Alpine and Arlésien recipes. Her shop, Le Petit Duc (☎ 04 90 92 08 31), 7 blvd Victor Hugo, opens 10 am to 1 pm and 3 to 7 pm Thursday to Tuesday.

...olive oil from Provence and the Mediterranean at Les Huiles du Monde (☎ 04 90 92 53 93), 16 blvd Victor Hugo. Tucked in a *hôtel particular*, it offers *dégustation* of 30 different oils. It opens 10 am to 1.30 pm and 3 to 8 pm, March to November (shorter hours, weekends only, the rest of the year). Enter via the courtyard.

shuttered place with 22 rooms costing 250/280/310/360FF per single/double/triple/quad. It opens from mid-December to mid-November; dogs and parking are free.

A short stroll north is cosy **Hostellerie du Chalet Fleuri** (☎ 04 90 92 03 62, fax 04 90 92 60 28, 15 ave Frédéric Mistral), part of the Logis de France chain. Prettily furnished doubles with shower cost 230FF (290FF with shower and toilet). Provençal cuisine is served in the flowery garden restaurant.

Grand old **Hôtel Les Antiques** (☎ 04 90 92 03 02, fax 04 90 92 50 40, 15 ave Pasteur) has grand old doubles costing 370FF to 590FF. The four-star hotel opens mid-April to mid-October.

Outpacing them all in innovation and design is **Hôtel Les Ateliers de l'Image** (☎ 04 90 92 51 50, fax 04 90 92 43 5, e ateliers-images@pacwan.fr, 5 ave Pasteur), a photography hotel that runs photography workshops (see Courses in the Facts for the Visitor chapter). It has 16 air-conditioned doubles – all architectural gems – costing 560FF to 660FF.

Places to Eat

Crêperie Lou Planet (☎ 04 90 92 19 81, 7 place Favier) is a pleasant spot to sit in the sun and munch on a sweet or savoury crepe after museum-visiting or old-town strolling.

Le Mexican Café ☎ 04 90 92 17 66, 4 rue du 8 Mai 1945), down a narrow alley, is a bright and cheerful joint where you can

tuck into tacos (68FF), enchiladas (60FF) and fajitas (90FF).

Highly recommended for local cuisine in an old-world Provençal setting is **L'Assiette de Marie** (☎ 04 90 92 32 14, 1 rue Jaume Roux). The eclectic bistro, cluttered with knick-knacks from another era, has a 135/189FF lunch/evening *menu*. Advance bookings are essential. Around the corner, self-caterers can stock up on Marie's treats at **L'Épicerie de Marie** (☎ 04 90 92 12 37, 1 place Isdores Gilles), open 9 am to noon Tuesday to Thursday, and 9 am to noon and 4 to 7 pm Friday and Saturday.

Upmarket **L'Orangerie Chabert** (☎ 04 90 92 05 95, 16 blvd Victor Hugo) has a gorgeous, flower-filled terrace out back. Its plat du jour costs 69FF and it has 114FF (lunch), 162FF and 218FF *menus*, crammed with tasty Provençal temptations.

Alain Assaud is one of many big chefs lured to trendy St-Rémy: sample his culinary creations at **Le Marceau** (☎ 04 90 92 37 11, 13 blvd Marceau), a simple yet refined place where you can dine beneath age-old beams. *Anchoïade* and *aïoli* star on Assaud's 150FF and 230FF *menus*.

La Maison Jaune (☎ 04 90 92 56 14, e lamaisonjaune@wanadoo.fr, 5 rue Carnot) is another recommended gastronomic stop. Traditional throughout, from the blue-shuttered exterior, its interior is decked out in a stark, contemporary style. lunchtime/evening *menus* start at 120/180FF.

AVIGNON AREA

Getting There & Away

Buses to Tarascon and Nîmes operated by Cévennes Cars (☎ 04 66 29 27 29) depart from the bus stop outside the Bar du Marché on place de la République. Avignon-bound buses run by Sociétés Rapides du Sud Est (☎ 04 90 14 59 00) leave from in front of the École de la République on blvd Victor Hugo.

LES BAUX DE PROVENCE

postcode 13520 • pop 443
• elevation 185m

Some 10km south of St-Rémy de Provence is Les Baux de Provence – a hill-top village that gave its name to bauxite, the chief ore of aluminium first mined in the village in 1822. In Provençal, *baou* means 'rocky spur'.

The most pleasant time to visit **Château des Baux** (☎ 04 90 54 55 56), a former feudal home of Monaco's Grimaldi royal family, whose ruins sprawls across some seven rocky hectares, is early evening after the caterpillar of tourist coaches has evacuated the village. The castle affords fantastic views of the surrounding Chaîne des Alpilles. It opens 9 am to 7.30 pm, March to November (until 9.30 pm July and August); and 9 am to 5 or 6 pm the rest of the year. Admission costs 37FF (students 28FF, children 20FF) and includes an informative, English-language audioguide.

A dramatic portrait of Provence is projected across 4000 sq metres of rock at **Cathédrale d'Images** (☎ 04 90 54 38 65, e catimage@club-internet.fr), route de Maillane, at the northern foot of Les Baux. The museum, in a redundant quarry, screens 3000 different images during its 30-minute sound-and-light show. The Image Cathedral – chilly year round, so bring a sweater – opens 10 am to 7 pm, March to October; 10 am to 6 pm, the rest of the year. Admission costs 43FF (those aged under 19, 27FF).

For information on Les Baux's limited (expensive) accommodation contact the tourist office (☎ 04 90 54 34 39, fax 04 90 54 51 51, e tourisme@lesbauxdeprovence.com), with a Web site at www.lesbauxdeprovence .com, at the end of cobbled Grande Rue. Taste and buy wine from one of Baux's 12 vineyards (which have their own AOC) at the **Maison des Vins** (☎ 04 90 54 34 70), lower downhill on Grande Rue, and oil from **Olive: Les Huiles du Monde** opposite.

Maussane-les-Alpilles

postcode 13520 • pop 2003
• elevation 35m

Maussane-les-Alpilles, 3km south of Les Baux de Provence on the Alpilles' southern fringe, shelters some of Provence's best-known *moulins d'huile* (oil mills), where freshly harvested olives are pummelled and pressed into smooth, golden olive oil. You cannot tour the mills here, but you can buy olive oil.

The **Coopérative Oléicole de la Vallée des Baux** (☎ 04 90 54 32 37, e covb@ com puserve.com) was established in 1924. It is in a 17th-century mill, also called Moulin Oléicole or Moulin Jean Marie Cornille after the original mill owner. Its fine olive oil – just 120,000L of which are produced each year – costs 110FF per litre. Depending on the harvest, it can sell out by mid-August. New stock goes on sale from 15 December. From the village centre, bear northwards along ave Jean Marie Cornille. The mill opens 8 am to noon and 2 to 6 pm weekdays.

The **Moulin du Mas des Barres** (☎ 04 90 54 44 32), on the eastern edge of the village (signposted off the D78, which runs through the village), sells oil for 125FF per 75cl bottle. Complete the day with lunch at *Le Bistrot du Paradou* (☎ 04 90 54 32 70), an authentic Provençal bistro 3km west along the D78 in Paradou. Every table is snapped up by 12.30 pm by courageous diners, determined to savour every last morceau of the fixed *menu* (200FF), which includes wine, a choice of entrees and home-made desserts, a no-choice main course and a fantastic array of ponging cheeses.

From Maussane, **stunning views** of the fierce, silver-ridged Alpilles can be enjoyed. By bicycle or car, follow the D78 east out of town for 8km, then bear northwards along the D24 towards Eygalières. After 5km you meet a road junction where you can continue north (left) to **Eygalières** or south-east (right) along the D25 to **Eyguières**, a village dominated by the Alpilles' highest point (493m). Both routes are scenic. By foot, the GR6 traverses the Alpilles' entire length.

Maussane tourist office (☎ 04 90 54 52 04, e contact@maussane.com), place Laugier de Monblan, opens 9 am to noon and 2 or 3 to 6 or 7 pm Monday to Saturday.

Fontvieille
postcode 13990 • pop 3566
• elevation 20m

Sleepy Fontvieille, 10km west of Maussane-les-Alpilles along the D17, is famed for its windmill immortalised by Alphonse Daudet in his collection of short stories *Lettres de mon Moulin* (Letters from my Windmill), published in 1869. Despite the French author being born in Nîmes and spending most of his life in Paris, he shared a strong spiritual affinity with Provence and is regarded as a Provençal writer.

Contrary to popular belief, Le Moulin de Daudet (Daudet's windmill), which dates back to 1814 and houses the **Musée de Daudet**, is not the windmill where the writer spent hours sunk in literary thought. From the windmill-museum, a trail (signposted *'sur les traces de Daudet'*) leads past ruined **Moulin Ramet** to **Moulin Tissot-Avon** – Daudet's true haunt, defunct since 1905. The trail continues to **Château de Montauban** (☎ 04 90 54 75 12) – home to Daudet's cousins with whom he stayed when in town. It hosts local history exhibitions and art shows.

Musée de Daudet opens 9 am to 7 pm, June to September; and 10 am to noon and 2 to 5 pm, the rest of the year (except January). Château Montauban opens 9.15 am to 7.30 pm, February to December. Dual admission costs 10FF (those aged seven to 12, 5FF).

In town, Fontvieille tourist office (☎ 04 90 54 67 49, fax 04 90 54 69 82, e ot .fontvieille@visitprovence.com), 5 rue Marcel Honorat, opens 9 am to noon and 2 to 6 pm Monday to Saturday. Tucked amid trees behind the chateau is *Camping Municipal Les Pins (☎ 04 90 54 78 69, fax 04 90 54 81 25, rue Michelet)*, which is open from Easter to mid-October and has a pool.

TARASCON & BEAUCAIRE

The mighty chateaux of Tarascon (Tarascoun in Provençal; pop 12,991) and Beaucaire (Bèucaire in Provençal; pop 13,940) stare at each other across the murky grey waters of the Rhône. Each year during June's Fête de la Tarasque, a Chinese-style dragon parades through Tarascon to celebrate St-Martha's slaying of Tarasque, a dragon that lurked in the Rhône according to Provençal legend.

Louis II had **Château de Tarascon** (☎ 04 90 91 01 93) built in the 15th century to defend Provence's political frontier marked by the Rhône. The interior was richly decorated under King René, but later stripped and used as a mint, then, from the 18th century until 1926, as a prison. Inmates' wall scratchings are still evident in the king's salon: 'here is 3 Davids in a mess/prisoners we are in distress/by the French we was caught/and to this prison we was brought/ taken in the xephyr strop of war (1778)'. The fortress opens 9 am to noon and 2 to 5 pm, October to March; and 9 am to 7 pm, the rest of the year. Admission costs 32FF (those aged 18 to 25, 21FF; those aged under 18, free).

According to legend, shabby and dusty Beaucaire was also plagued by a dragon, Drac de Beaucaire, who slept in the Rhône but prowled the streets of Beaucaire by day disguised as a man. One day he snatched a washerwoman and took her back to his filthy hole where she tended Drac's baby son, Le Draconnet, for seven years. Years after her release, she spotted Drac in Beaucaire. Upon greeting him, Drac was so horrified to have his disguise blown that he poked out the woman's eyes. A sculpture of him can be seen on place de la République. Falconry displays (☎ 04 66 59 26 72) are held mid-March to November in the grounds of ruined 11th-century **Château de Beaucaire**.

Accommodation in both towns is limited. Beaucaire tourist office (☎ 04 66 59 26 57), 24 cours Gambetta, and its counterpart in Tarascon (☎ 04 90 91 03 52, e tourisme @tarascon.org), 59 rue des Halles, with a Web site at www.tarascon.org, have details.

Camping Tartarin (☎ *04 90 91 01 46*), open April to October next to Château de Tarascon, charges 20/18/10FF per person/tent/car. Tarascon's *Auberge de Jeunesse* (☎ *04 90 91 04 08, fax 04 90 91 54 17, 31 blvd Gambetta*) charges 67FF for B&B.

Across The River Rhône

On the western bank of the River Rhône sits the Roman town of Nîmes and the Roman aqueduct known as the Pont du Gard – two fabulous sights which, though not part of Provence-Alpes-Côte d'Azur *région* (both are in Languedoc-Roussillon), make an easy day trip from Avignon.

NÎMES
postcode 30000 • pop 137,740
• elevation 40m

Lazy, laid-back Nîmes, a little bit Provençal but with a soul as Languedocien as *cassoulet*, is graced by some of Europe's best-preserved Roman public buildings. Founded by Augustus, Roman Colonia Nemausensis reached its zenith during the 2nd century, receiving its water supply from a Roman aqueduct system that included the Pont du Gard, an awesome bridge 23km to the north-east. The sacking of the city by the Vandals in the early 5th century began a downwards spiral, from which Nîmes never recovered.

The city is also known for its contemporary architectural creations, notably its Carrée d'Art. Nîmes' coat of arms, featuring a palm tree and a crocodile, was re-designed by Philippe Starck in 1987. The French designer, best known for his furniture creations, also designed *Abribus*, Provence's most attractive bus stop, on ave Carnot. Fountain-decorated **place d'Assas** (1989) is the creation of new realist painter Martial Raysse.

Nîmes, just 44km south-west of Avignon, becomes more Spanish than French during its *férias*, the city's bullfighting festivals. The surrounding countryside is composed of vineyards and garrigue – whose herbal vegetation gives off a powerful fragrance in spring and early summer.

Orientation
Everything, including the traffic, revolves around Les Arènes. Just north of the amphitheatre, the fan-shaped, largely pedestrianised old city is bounded by blvd Victor Hugo, blvd Amiral Courbet and blvd Gambetta. North of place aux Herbes, one of the main squares, lies carefully preserved Îlot Littré, the old dyers' quarter. Rue Général Perrier is the spot to shop for mainstream fashion.

South-east of Les Arènes is esplanade Charles de Gaulle, a large open square, from where ave Feuchères leads southwards to the train and bus stations.

Information
Tourist Offices Nîmes tourist office (☎ 04 66 67 29 11, fax 04 66 21 81 04, ℮ info@ot-nimes.fr), 6 rue Auguste, opens 8.30 am to 7 pm weekdays, November to March; and 8 am to 7 or 8 pm weekdays, 9 am to 7 pm Saturday, and 10 am to 6 pm Sunday, the rest of the year. Visit online at www.ot-nimes.fr.

The Bureau Information de Jeunesse (☎ 04 90 82 29 56), 102 rue de la Carreterie, opens 9 am to noon and 2 to 5.30 pm weekdays.

For information on the Gard department, go to the Comité Départemental du Tourisme (☎ 04 66 36 96 30, fax 04 66 36 13 14, ℮ cdt.gard@imaginet.fr), 3 place des Arènes, open 8.45 am to 6 pm weekdays, 9.30 am to noon Saturday. Gîtes de France (see Places to Stay later in this section) is on the 1st floor here.

Money Banque de France, Square du 11 Novembre 1918, exchanges currency from 8.30 am to 12.15 pm weekdays. Commercial banks are on Blvd Victor Hugo and blvd Amiral Courbet.

Post & Communications The post office, 1 blvd de Bruxelles, opens 8 am to 6.30 pm weekdays, and 8 am to noon Saturday. It has Cyberposte facilities. The Cybercentre

NÎMES

PLACES TO STAY
5 Hôtel Royal
10 New Hotel La Baume
13 Hôtel Central
14 Hôtel Temple
37 Hôtel de la Mairie
42 Hôtel de France
43 Hôtel Amphithéâtre
44 Hôtel Le Lisita
45 Hôtel Concorde

PLACES TO EAT
4 Le Haddock Café
7 Côte Bleue
11 Le Magister
15 Le Menestrel
17 Le Pétrin
20 Aux Plaisirs des Halles
24 L'Assiette
25 Café Carré
34 Boulangerie
41 Grand Café de la
   Bourse et du Commerce
46 Prisunic (Supermarket)
51 Les Olivades & Vinothèque

OTHER
1 Post Office
2 La Coupole des Halles;
   FNAC
3 Laundrette
6 Tourist Office
8 Les Halles
9 Brandade Raymond
12 Église St-Baudille
16 O'Flaherty's Irish Pub
18 Cathédrale de St-Castor
19 Cafés Nadal
21 Bureau Information
   de Jeunesse
22 Maison Carrée
23 Carrée d'Art; Musée
   d'Art Contemporain
26 Net Games
27 Théâtre de Nîmes
28 La Maison Villaret
29 Au Petit Gourmand
30 L'Atelier du Chocolat
31 L'Huilerie
32 Cafés Nadal
33 Musée du Vieux Nîmes
35 Musée d'Archéologie
36 Musée de Nîmes
38 Town Hall
39 Cycles Rebour
40 Laundrette
47 Abribus Bus Stop
48 Justice Palace
49 Matador Statue
50 Les Arènes
52 Bureau de Locations des Arènes
53 Comité Départemental
   du Tourism; Gîtes de France
54 Banque de France
55 Post Office
56 Musée des Beaux-Arts
57 Police Station
58 Bus Station

inside the Bureau Information de Jeunesse (see Tourist offices earlier in this section) offers a free hour online per week.

At 25 rue de l'Horloge, Net Games (e abl .computer@wanadoo.fr) charges 25FF per hour and opens 10 am to 1 am, May to mid-September; and 10 am to 9.30 pm Monday to Saturday, and 2 to 9.30 pm Sunday, the rest of the year.

Two blocks north of the post office at 17 rue Porte d'Alès, Le Pluggin (☎ 04 66 21 49 51, e info@lepluggin.com) charges 40/175FF for one/five hours. It opens 2 pm to 1 am.

Laundry The laundrettes at 30 rue du Grand Couvent and 26 rue Porte de France open 7 or 8 am to 8.30 or 9 pm.

Les Arènes

This superb Roman amphitheatre, reminiscent of the Colosseum in Rome, was built around AD 100 on place des Arènes to seat 24,000 spectators. It is better preserved than any other such structure in France, even retaining its upper storey – unlike its Arles counterpart. The interior has four tiers of seats and a system of exits and passages designed so patricians attending the animal and gladiator combats never had to rub shoulders with the plebeians.

Throughout the year Les Arènes, which is covered by a high-tech removable roof from October to April, is used for theatre performances, music concerts and bull-fights. Unless there's something on, it opens 9 am to 6 pm (7 pm in summer). Admission costs 28FF (students 20FF). Tickets, available until 30 minutes before it closes, are sold at the ticket office (☎ 04 66 21 80 52), tucked in the amphitheatre's northern walls, directly opposite Hotel Lesita.

Maison Carrée & Carré d'Art

The rectangular, Greek-style temple known as the Maison Carrée (Square House; ☎ 04 66 36 26 76), place de la Maison Carrée, is one of the world's most remarkably preserved Roman temples. Built around AD 5 to honour Augustus' two nephews, it survived the centuries as a meeting hall (dur-

Denim de Nîmes

During the 18th century, Nîmes' sizeable Protestant middle class, barred from government posts and various ways of earning a living, turned its energies to trade and manufacturing. Among the products made in the Protestant-owned factories was a twilled fabric known as *serge*. The soft but durable material became very popular among workers and, stained blue, was the 'uniform' of the fishermen of Genoa.

When Levi Strauss (1829–1902), a Bavarian-Jewish immigrant to the USA, began producing trousers in California during and after the gold rush of 1849, he soon realised that miners needed garments that would last. After trying tent canvas, he began importing the *serge de Nîmes*, now better known as 'denim'.

ing the Middle Ages), a private residence, a stable (in the 17th century), a church and, after the Revolution, an archive.

The Maison Carrée, entered through six symmetrical Corinthian columns, sits at the end of rue Auguste. It opens 9 am to noon or 12.30 pm and from 2.30 to 7 pm; until 6 pm in winter. Admission is free.

The striking glass-and-steel building to the west at 15 place de la Maison Careé, dating to 1993, is the modern **Carrée d'Art** (Square of Art; ☎ 04 66 76 35 77, e ecm .nimes@wanadoo.fr), which houses the municipal library and mediatheque, and Musée d'Art Contemporain (see Museums on the following page). It is the work of British architect Sir Norman Foster, who designed the seminal Hong Kong Bank building in Hong Kong. It perfectly reflects the Maison Carrée and is everything modern architecture should be: innovative, complementary and beautiful.

Jardins de la Fontaine

The Fountain Gardens, home to Nîmes' other important Roman monuments, were laid out around the Source de la Fontaine (the site of a spring, temple and baths in

Roman times). They retain an elegant air, with statue-adorned paths running around deep, slimy-green waterways. Don't miss the **Temple de Diane** to the left of the main entrance.

A 10-minute walk uphill through the terraced gardens takes you to the crumbly white shell of **Tour Magne**, the largest of the many towers that once ran along the city's 7km-long Roman ramparts. A spiral staircase of 140 exhausting steps lead to the top of the tower, from where there is a fine panorama; it can be scaled from 9 am to 6 pm (7 pm from July to mid-September). Admission costs 15FF (students and those aged under 16, 12FF). A combination ticket allowing admission to the Arènes as well costs 34FF (students and those aged under 16, 28FF). The gardens open 7.30 am to 6.30 pm (10 pm between April and mid-September).

The gardens are almost 1km north-west of the amphitheatre. The main entrance is on quai de la Fontaine, the city's classiest thoroughfare, laden with fine architecture. Men gather to play pétanque beneath the trees at the eastern end of this quay. The gravel square is strictly reserved for veteran players, but spectators are welcome. Wine buffs keen to learn more about the local vintage should make nearby **Espace Costières** (☎ 04 66 36 96 20), 19 place Aristide Briand, their port of call.

Museums

Museums open 11 am to 6 pm Tuesday and Sunday. Admission costs 28FF (students 20FF; children aged under 10, free) at each. Museum buffs should buy a three-day pass, covering admission to all museums. It costs 60FF (students 30FF); the tourist office or any museum sells it.

The **Musée du Vieux Nîmes** (Museum of Old Nîmes; ☎ 04 66 36 00 64) is in the 17th-century episcopal palace, south of the unimpressive **St-Castor Cathedral** on place aux Herbes. Themes change but the emphasis is always on the city's history.

The **Musée d'Archéologie** (Archaeological Museum; ☎ 04 66 67 25 57), 13 bis blvd Amiral Courbet, brings together columns, mosaics, sculptures and personal effects from the Roman and pre-Roman periods that have been unearthed around Nîmes.

A wonderful Roman mosaic uncovered in Nîmes and an unsurprising collection of Flemish, Italian and French works can be viewed at the **Musée des Beaux-Arts** (Fine Arts Museum; ☎ 04 66 67 38 21), rue de la Cité Foulc between Nos 20 and 22.

For a dazzling collection of modern art, look no further than the **Musée d'Art Contemporain** (Contemporary Art Museum; ☎ 04 66 76 35 70), lodged on the 2nd floor of the Carrée d'Art. A peek inside this striking building and the views it offers of the Roman temple across the square make a trip here an absolute must.

Férias & Bullfights

The three férias – the three-day Féria Primavera (Spring Festival) during the last weekend in February, the five-day Féria de Pentecôte (Pentecost Festival) in June, and the three-day Féria des Vendanges to mark the start of the grape harvest on the third weekend in September – revolve around a series of *corridas* (bullfights), one or two of which are held on each of the days. Tickets to a corrida cost 95FF to 545FF; reservations must be made months in advance through the Bureau de Location (☎ 04 66 67 28 02), 1 rue Alexandre Ducros, on the south-western side of the Arènes. The bureau opens 10 am to 12.30 pm and 3 to 6 pm Monday to Saturday. It accepts telephone bookings.

Courses Camarguaises (see the boxed text 'Bulls & Cowboys' in the Camargue chapter) are held on the weekend before a féria and at other times during the bullfighting season. Tickets cost between 60FF and 120FF. The best bulls are rewarded with a couple of bars from the opera *Carmen* as they leave the arena.

Places to Stay – Budget

Camping About 4km south of town on the D13, heading towards Générac, is *Domaine de la Bastide* (☎ 04 66 38 09 21, route de Générac). Two people with a tent pay 74FF. From the train station, take bus No 1 in the

AVIGNON AREA

Caremeau direction. At the Jean Jaurès stop, change to bus D and get off at La Bastide.

Hostels The 80-bed *Auberge de Jeunesse* (☎ 04 66 68 03 20, fax 04 66 68 03 21, e nimes@fuaj.org, 257 chemin de l'Auberge de Jeunesse) is 3.5km north-west of the train station. A bed costs 52FF (71FF to non-HI card-holders) and sheets/breakfast cost 17/19FF. Internet access, laundry and bicycle rental likewise cost extra. From the train station, take bus No 2 (Alès or Ville-verte direction) to the Stade stop, in front of the Marché U supermarket on route d'Alès, from where it is a 500m walk uphill; follow the hostel signs.

Hotels A warm welcome awaits budget travellers at *Hôtel Concorde* (☎/fax 04 66 67 91 03, e hotel.concorde@wanadoo.fr, 3 rue des Chapeliers), a pleasant place with basic rooms costing 120/150FF (140/160FF with shower, 160/180FF with shower and toilet *or* TV).

Hôtel de France (☎ 04 66 67 23 05, fax 04 66 67 76 93, 4 blvd des Arènes) has an assortment of dreary rooms and a pricing policy not unlike that used by the Romans at the amphitheatre: the higher you climb, the less you pay. Fourth-floor (no lift) singles/triples/quads with washbasin cost 110/175/175FF, 3rd-floor singles/doubles/triples with shower cost 140/145/190FF, while 1st-floor doubles/triples clock in at 150/280FF. *Hôtel Le Lisita* (☎ 04 66 67 66 20, fax 04 66 76 22 30), next door at No 2, is similarly priced.

Unexciting, two-star *Hôtel de la Mairie* (☎ 04 66 67 65 91, 11 rue des Greffes) has doubles with washbasin/shower starting at 135/170FF and doubles/quads with shower and toilet costing upwards of 200/230FF.

Places to Stay – Mid-Range

Just up from its namesake, 17-room *Hôtel Amphithéâtre* (☎ 04 66 67 28 51, fax 04 66 67 07 79, e hotel-amphitheatre@wanadoo.fr, 4 rue des Arènes) is one of the loveliest options. Rooms have eclectic furnishings, and most have a shower and toilet. Rooms start at 185/240FF.

Equally colourful is *Hôtel Central* (☎ 04 66 67 27 75, fax 04 66 21 77 79, 2 place du Château), which has creaky floorboards and wild flowers painted everywhere. Singles/doubles/triples with bathroom start at 190/210/230FF. Opposite, cheerful *Hôtel Temple* (☎ 04 66 67 54 61, fax 04 66 36 04 36, 1 rue Charles Babut), has been run by the same family since 1960. Its bathroom-equipped singles/doubles/triples/quads cost 175/210/260/280FF and warrant no complaints. Private parking at either costs 40FF per night.

Three-star *Hôtel Royal* (☎ 04 66 58 28 27, fax 04 66 58 28 28, 3 blvd Alphonse Daudet) has good-value rooms costing 220/280FF and a lovely terrace-restaurant overlooking place d'Assas.

Places to Stay – Top End

Sumptuous choices include *New Hotel La Baume* (☎ 04 66 76 28 42, fax 04 66 76 28 45, e nimeslabaume@new-hotel.com), 21 rue Nationale, where period-furnished rooms (some with frescoed ceilings) are wrapped around a 17th-century courtyard. Rooms cost upwards of 450/510FF.

Four-star *Imperator Concorde* (☎ 04 66 21 90 30, fax 04 66 67 70 25, e hotel .imperator@wanadoo.fr, quai de la Fontaine) is a dreamy four-star, honeymoon-ers' type of pad, with Nîmes' most exquisite garden-restaurant. Rooms for two cost from 550FF to 1000FF.

Places to Eat

Restaurants Just west of place des Arènes is packed *Les Olivades* (☎ 04 66 21 71 78, 18 rue Jean Reboul), which specialises in local wines. It has *menus* for 92FF and 128FF (66FF lunchtime *formule*).

L'Assiette (rue Corneille) offers startling views of the Carrée d'Art, good-value build-your-own-salads (around 40FF) and five types of carpaccio (28FF to 38FF).

Tucked close to Église St-Baudille is *Le Menestrel* (☎ 04 66 67 54 45, 6 rue École Vieille). The Minstrel conjures up *menus* for 60FF, 85FF and 125FF. Equally small, but blue, on the corner of rue Littré and rue du Grand Couvent, is *Côte Bleue*. The Blue

Coast serves local dishes inside and outside on a straw-covered terrace.

The chef at *Aux Plaisirs des Halles* (☎ 04 66 36 01 02, *4 rue Littré*) conjures up succulent cuisine, served on a peaceful terrace save a trickling fountain and clinking wine glasses. Its 88FF lunchtime *menu* , which is honoured with a 50cl pichet of wine (40FF) makes for some memorable dining.

Several cosy little spots cooking up traditional French cuisine are hidden on place Esclafidous, a fountain-decorated square, which is a real gem once found. Splurging lovers seeking romance should dine at *L'Enclose de la Fontaine*, a beautiful garden inside the Imperator Concorde hotel (see Places to Stay – Top End earlier in this section). *Menus* cost 150FF to 365FF.

Cafes Place aux Herbes is one big cafe in summer. Equally bustling is place du Marché, another charming square pierced with a statue of a crocodile at one end and an extraordinarily large palm tree in its centre. Younger bohemians hang out in the pavement cafes lining the western length of place de la Maison Carrée; the smarter-dressed languish on the terrace of *Le Ciel de Nîmes* (☎ 04 66 36 71 70), the 3rd-floor cafe of Carré d'Art, which offers a stunning view of the Roman temple.

Le Haddock Café (13 rue de l'Agau) hosts a variety of jolly theme nights and has excellent-value salads/lunchtime *formules* averaging 35/60FF.

Ideal for breakfast or a quick coffee inside or outside is *Grand Café de la Bourse et du Commerce* (☎ 04 66 67 21 91, *2 blvd des Arènes*), opposite the Arènes ticket booth.

For a lazy breakfast (30FF) in the early morning sun, head for *Café Carré*, on the western side of place de la Maison Carré; breakfast is served from 7 to 11 am.

Self-Catering Nîmes plays host to colourful *street markets* in the old city on Thursday in July and August. *Les Halles*, the indoor food market between rue Guizot and rue des Halles, opens 6 am to noon.

Entertainment

What's-on listings fill *Nîmescope*, a fortnightly entertainment magazine freely distributed at the tourist office and hotels.

Plays, ballets, modern dance and musical recitals take place at *Théâtre de Nîmes (place de la Calade)*. The box office (☎ 04 66 36 65 10) inside the theatre opens 10 am to 1 pm and 2 to 6 pm Tuesday to Friday, and 2 to 6 pm Saturday.

FNAC's Billetterie de Spectacles (☎ 04 66 36 33 33), in La Coupole des Halles indoor shopping centre at 22 blvd Gambetta, sells tickets for most other cultural events.

O'Flaherty's Irish Pub (21 blvd Amiral Courbet) is the No 1 spot to meet other travellers and foreign students; local bands play regular gigs here.

Shopping

Shop for chocolate at L'Atelier du Chocolat (☎ 04 66 21 56 93) on rue de l'Aspic. For bread shaped like a bull's head, go to the *boulangerie* on Grande rue. Traditional breads are also sold at Le Pétrin on rue de la Curaterie. *Caladons* – hard, honey-and-almond biscuits, typical to Nîmes – are sold at Au Petit Gourmand, 27 rue de la Madeleine. *Croquants de villaret* – a finger-shaped variation on the latter – have been baked with pride at La Maison Villaret (☎ 04 66 67 41 79), on the corner of rue de la Madeleine and place de l'Horloge, since 1775.

Local herbs, oils and spices are sold at quaint Cafés Nadal on 4 rue Marchands and at nearby L'Huilerie (☎ 04 66 67 37 24), 10–12 rue Marchands. Coffee beans are the speciality of Cafés Nadal at 7 rue St-Castor. Local wines sold by knowledgeable staff can be found at the Vinothéque adjoining Les Olivades (see Restaurants earlier).

Brandade de Nîmes is the trademark of Brandade Raymond at 34 rue Nationale, a veteran traiteur who occasionally gives free demonstrations in his shop on how to make the much-loved fishy paste. A 125g tin costs around 12.50FF.

Getting There & Away

Air Nîmes-Arles-Camargue (Aéroport de Nîmes-Arles-Camargue; ☎ 04 66 70 49 49),

AVIGNON AREA

also called Aéroport Garons, is 10km south-east of the city on the A54 to Arles.

Bus The bus station is behind the train station on rue Ste-Félicité. At the other end, the general bus information counter (☎ 04 66 29 52 00) for domestic services opens 8 am to noon and 2 to 6 pm weekdays.

Destinations served include five buses per day to Pont du Gard (35FF, 45 minutes, five to six daily), Avignon (65FF, 30 minutes, 10 or more daily) and Arles (34FF, 30 to 45 minutes, four to eight daily). STD Gard organises day excursions to Nice, Menton and other coastal destinations in summer.

The international bus operators Eurolines (☎ 04 66 29 49 02) and Linebus (☎ 04 66 29 50 62) have neighbouring offices at the far end of the terminal.

Train The train station is at the south-eastern end of ave Feuchères. The information office opens 8 am to 6.30 pm Monday to Saturday. Tickets can be bought here or at the SNCF automatic ticket machine, next to the Billetterie de Spectacles in FNAC (see Entertainment earlier in this section).

Destinations include Arles (41FF, 30 minutes, nine daily), Avignon (46FF, 30 minutes, 10 or more daily) and Marseilles (116FF, 1¼ hours, 12 daily). Some SNCF buses and trains head to Aigues-Mortes (39FF, one hour) in the Camargue.

Getting Around
To/From the Airport Airport shuttle buses (☎ 04 66 67 94 77) depart from the bus station to coincide with flight times (30 minutes).

Bicycle Cycles Rebour (☎ 04 66 76 24 92), 38 rue de l'Hôtel Dieu, rents bikes for 100FF per day. Information on weekend cycle rides organised by local cycling afficionados, Cyclotourisme Nîmois (☎ 04 66 29 45 38, 04 66 63 19 13), are posted in its window.

The Auberge de Jeunesse (see Places to Stay earlier in this section) rents bikes for 50FF per day.

PONT DU GARD
The exceptionally well-preserved, three-tiered Roman aqueduct known as the Pont du Gard – photographs of which consistently appear in textbooks on Western European history – was once part of a 50km-long system of canals built around 19 BC by Agrippa, Augustus' powerful deputy and son-in-law, to bring water from near Uzès in Languedoc to Nîmes. The 35 small arches of the 275m upper tier of the pont, 49m above the River Gard, contain a 1.2m by 1.75m water course that was designed to carry 20,000 cubic metres of water a day. The Romans built the aqueduct with stone from the nearby Vers quarry. The largest boulders weigh over five tonnes.

From large car parks on either side of the river, paths lead through scented garrigue to the shores of the River Gard, from where you can view both the aquaduct and the road bridge, built in 1743 alongside the top of the aqueduct's lower tier on the Gard's upstream side. Recent renovations have seen 280 cubic metres of stone replaced. The best views of the Pont du Gard are, in fact, to be had from the hill on the northern side (left bank) of the river.

On hot days you can swim in the river. The Pont du Gard – the fifth most-visited site in France – is frequented by two million people a year (averaging 5000-plus visitors a day). Admission to the site is free, but you have to pay 25FF to join a guided tour if you want to cross the bridge or amble along the aqueduct's three tiers. English-language tours (25FF, one hour) depart from Le Portal (☎ 08 25 01 30 30), a huge modern building designed by French architect Jean Paul Viguier on the left (northern) river-bank, which houses a film studio where educational films relating to the Pont du Gard are screened several times daily on a 45 sq m screen (30FF; those aged five to 21, 15FF). The building also houses several places to eat, shops, the Ludo children's entertainment centre and – by mid-2001 – a museum and multimedia resource centre.

On the opposite (right/southern) river-bank is La Baume, another visitor centre, where silent panoramic shows (30 minutes) entitled *The Way of the Wind* can be viewed in 3D on a screen that stretches beneath the audience's feet. Admission costs 35FF (those aged five to 21, 20FF).

Information

Information on Le Portal and La Baume is available from the Accueil du Pont du Gard (☎ 04 66 37 50 08) which also sells tickets for both attractions, on the left (northern) bank of the River Gard. A one-day pass covering admission to the museum, multimedia centre and both film centres costs 60FF (those aged five to 21, 30FF).

Information on the Gard department is doled by the Richesses du Pont du Gard (☎ 04 66 37 03 77), directly opposite. It opens 10 am to 6 pm (longer hours in July and August). There is a tiny tourist office in Remoulins, 3km east of Pont du Gard on the N86. Camping La Sousta sells walking maps.

Canoeing

The beautiful, wild River Gard, which descends from the Cévennes mountains, flows through the hills in a long gorge, passing under the Pont du Gard. Hire canoes to paddle around beneath the aqueduct from Kayak Vert (☎ 04 66 22 80 76) or Canoë Le Tourbillon (☎ 04 66 22 85 54), both based in neighbouring **Collias** (pop 852), 6km upstream, under the village's single bridge.

You can paddle from Collias to the Pont du Gard with a group in half a day (175/ 100FF for a canoe/kayak for two) or arrange to be dropped off 22km upstream at **Russan**, from where there's a great descent back. The latter is a full-day trip and is usually available between March and May only. Canoes/kayaks cost about 50/35FF per hour to rent (145/90FF per day).

The region is known for its unpredictable weather. Torrential rains rapidly raise water levels by 2m to 5m, while during long dry spells, the Gard can almost disappear.

Places to Stay

Three-star *Camping La Sousta* (☎ 04 66 37 12 80, ave du Pont du Gard), open March to 1 November, is a five-minute walk from the aqueduct on the southern side (follow the D981). It charges 65FF for two people with a tent/caravan and car. Reception opens 8 am to noon and 2 to 7 pm.

Within walking distance of the aquaduct, on the D981 on Remoulins' western fringe is *Le Colombier* (☎ 04 66 37 05 28, fax 04 66 37 35 75, ave du Pont du Gard), a rambling building with a terracotta-tiled roof, sunny terrace and doubles costing upwards of 240FF. Breakfast is an extra 38FF.

Near the car park on the northern side, *Le Vieux Moulin* (☎ 04 66 37 14 35, fax 04 66 37 26 48), an attractive inn with truly splendid views of the Pont du Gard, will have rooms costing 500FF to 1000FF when it reopens after its extensive revamp.

Getting There & Away

The Pont du Gard is 23km north-east of Nîmes and 26km west of Avignon. Buses from Avignon and Nîmes stop 1km north of the bridge. To get to Collias (35FF, one hour) take bus No 168 (two daily) from Nîmes' bus station – or hitch.

Parking in one of the car parks on either riverbank costs 20FF for two hours, then 5FF per following hour (30FF, then 10FF in July and August).

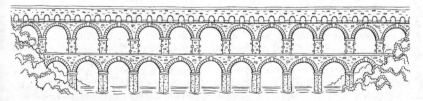

euro currency converter €1 = 6.56FF

The Lubéron

The Lubéron hills stretch from Cavaillon in the west to Manosque in the east, and from Apt southwards to the River Durance and the Romanesque Abbaye de Silvacane. The area is named after the main range, a compact massif with the gentle summit of Mourre Nègre (1125m). Its oak-covered northern face is steep and uneven, while its southern face is drier and more Mediterranean in both climate and flora. Fruit orchards and vineyards carpet the lower slopes. The Combe de Lourmarin divides the Petit Lubéron in the west with the Grand Lubéron in the east. The entire region is crisscrossed with great walking trails and its 100km-long, marked cycle route makes it an excellent place for a bike ride.

Much of the Lubéron (Leberoun in Provençal) is protected by the Parc Naturel Régional du Lubéron. The 1200-sq-km regional park created in 1977 encompasses 67 villages (pop 155,000), desolate forests, unexpected gorges and age-old *mas* (farmhouses) – many restored by fans of British novelist Peter Mayle, whose purchase of a mas outside Ménerbes in the late 1980s formed the basis of his witty *A Year in Provence*. Mayle, who later fled Provence and the droves of over-eager readers flocking to his Ménerbes home, returned to the Lubéron – this time to a mas between Lourmarin and Vaugines – in 1999.

The Lubéron is greener, less densely populated and extremely affluent compared to the rest of the Vaucluse department, of which it is a part. Unlike Haute-Provence, most of its lower lying land is farmed, forming a rich manicured patchwork of vineyards, olive groves and fruit farms as toy-like (and lucrative) as the perfectly restored, golden-stone mas. The northern part of the region around Apt is dotted with *bories* (archaic dry stone huts). Its fire-red ochre sands, sculpted by the wind and rain over the centuries to form fantastic formations, have been exploited since the mid-19th century.

Highlights

- Take a colourful walk: through red rocks in Rustrel, purple lavender fields in Lagarde d'Apt, and around silver-stone bories (shepherds' huts) in Viens
- Tour the dramatic gorges and grand fortresses of the Grand Lubéron
- Shop for melons and fresh bread in Cavaillon, wine and honey in Bonnieux, cherries in Apt and olive oil in Oppède-le-Vieux
- Learn how Cistercian monks live at the Romanesque Abbaye de Sénanque
- Explore the Petit Lubéron by bicycle

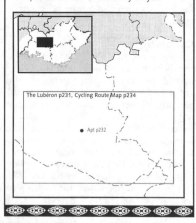

The Lubéron p231, Cycling Route Map p234

● Apt p232

APT

postcode 84400 ● pop 11,488
● elevation 250m

Apt (Ate in Provençal), an excellent base for exploring the Lubéron, is largely unexceptional beyond its grapes, cherries and *fruits confits* (candied fruits), all of which are well worth a nibble. The town throws a Fête de la Cerise (Cherry Festival) in May or June, a jazz festival to mark Ascension in May, and the fabulous, three-day Cavalcade d'Apt to celebrate Pentecost in June.

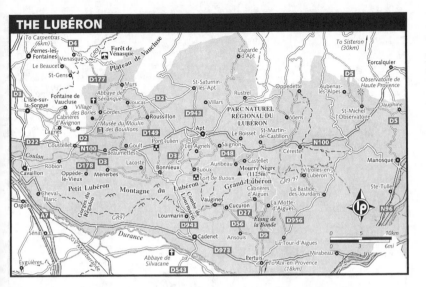

THE LUBÉRON

The Saturday morning market, which fills rue St-Pierre, and the Tuesday morning farmers' market (May to October) are, depending on the season, the perfect place to shop for goat cheese, truffles, marinated olives, fruit and vegetables.

The GR9 links Apt with the hill-top villages of Buoux, 8km south, and Villars, 10km north.

Orientation & Information

Tourist Offices In July and August, the tourist office (☎ 04 90 74 03 18, fax 04 90 04 64 30, e tourisme.apt@pacwan.fr), 20 ave Philippe de Girard, organises weekly city tours and takes bookings for guided walks and mountain-bike rides in the Lubéron. It opens 9 am to 1 pm and 3 to 7 pm Monday to Saturday, and 9 am to noon on Sunday, July and August; and 9 am to noon and 2 to 6 pm Monday to Saturday, and 9 am to noon on Sunday, the rest of the year.

Park Offices Information on the Parc Naturel Régional du Lubéron, including details about the park's two dozen *gîtes d'étape*, is available from the Maison du Parc (☎ 04 90 04 42 00, fax 04 90 04 81 15,

e pnr.luberon@wanadoo.fr), 60 place Jean Jaurès. The centre has information on walking and cycling in the park, and sells an excellent range of guides including the recommended topoguide *Le Parc du Lubéron à pied* (PN07; 77FF). This book details 24 walks including the GR6, GR9, GR92 and GR97 trails (available in English too); and the topoguide *Walks in Provence* (PN04; 77FF), which outlines 24 shorter walks (3–20km) and includes fascinating 'heritage discovery' features on the park's flora, fauna, ochre production and so on. The centre, which also houses a **Musée de Paléontologie** (Palaeontology Museum) focusing on prehistoric history, flora and fauna, opens 8.30 am to noon and 1.30 to 7 pm Monday to Saturday, April to September; and 8.30 am to noon and 1.30 to 6 pm Monday to Saturday noon, the rest of the year.

An excellent choice of maps and walking guides are sold at the Maison de la Presse (☎ 04 90 74 23 52), 28 rue des Marchands, and at nearby Librairie Dumas, 16 rue des Marchands.

Money Commercial banks frame the western side of place de la Bouquerie.

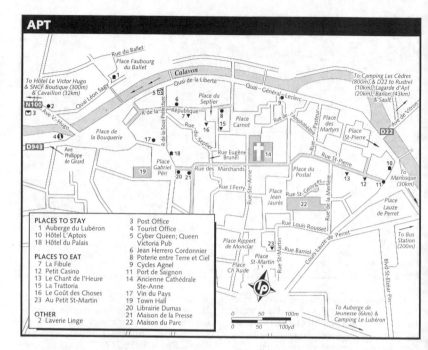

APT

PLACES TO STAY
1 Auberge du Lubéron
10 Hôtel L'Aptois
18 Hôtel du Palais

PLACES TO EAT
7 La Fibule
12 Petit Casino
13 Le Chant de l'Heure
15 La Trattoria
16 Le Goût des Choses
23 Au Petit St-Martin

OTHER
2 Laverie Linge

3 Post Office
4 Tourist Office
5 Cyber Queen; Queen Victoria Pub
6 Jean Herrero Cordonnier
8 Poterie entre Terre et Ciel
9 Cycles Agnel
11 Port de Saignon
14 Ancienne Cathédrale Ste-Anne
17 Vin du Pays
19 Town Hall
20 Librairie Dumas
21 Maison de la Presse
22 Maison du Parc

Post & Communications The post office, 105 ave Victor Hugo, opens 9 am to noon and 2 to 7.30 pm on weekdays, and 8.30 am to noon on Saturday.

Download your emails at Cyber Queen, inside the Queen Victoria Pub (☎ 04 90 04 67 30) at 94 quai de la Liberté, which opens 5.30 to 1.30 am. It charges 1/50FF per minute/hour.

Laundry Wash your whites at Laverie Linge at 4 quai Léon Sagy. It opens from 7 am to 7.30 pm.

Places to Stay
Camping By the river out of town, *Camping Les Cèdres* (☎ 04 90 74 14 61, *route de Rustrel*), opens mid-February to mid-November. It charges 13/10FF per person/tent or car. *Camping Le Lubéron* (☎ 04 90 04 85 40, *route de Saignon*), south-east of Apt, opens April to September and charges similar rates.

Hostels Apt's nearest hostel, *Auberge de-Jeunesse Regain* (☎ 04 90 74 39 34, fax 04 90 74 50 94) is 6km south-east, on a farm in the hamlet of Le Colombier. From Apt, follow the southbound D48 through the village of Saignon, then turn right (west) onto the westbound D232 to Bonnieux. A bed in a three- to nine-bed room costs 80F and includes breakfast. Dinner/sheets cost an extra 60/10FF. The hostel opens from mid-February to mid-January. To get there without a car, use your feet or thumb.

Hotels The welcoming *Hôtel du Palais* (☎/fax 04 90 04 89 32, place Gabriel Péri) provides basic doubles with washbasin for 180FF (210FF with shower, 230FF with shower and toilet).

Cyclist-friendly *Hôtel L'Aptois* (☎ 04 90 74 02 02, fax 04 90 74 64 79, 289 cours Lauze de Perret) touts doubles costing 170FF (250FF with shower and toilet).

Cosy *Auberge du Lubéron* (☎ 04 90 74

12 50, fax 04 90 04 79 49, e *serge.peuzin@ free.fr, 8 place Faubourg du Ballet)*, on the opposite side of the river, is part of the Logis de France chain and its restaurant is said to serve superb cuisine. Doubles cost upwards of 295FF and it has delectable *menus* starting at 240FF.

Heading west out of town, two-star *Hôtel Le Victor Hugo (☎ 04 90 04 74 60, 67 ave Victor Hugo)* has 15 doubles with shower and toilet costing 195FF. Reception is through the ground-floor brasserie.

Places to Eat

Place de la Bouquerie buzzes with cafes and restaurants when the sun shines. Rue St-Pierre is another hot spot with plenty of shops, bars and places to eat.

A fine place for lunch in the shade is *Le Goût des Choses (☎ 04 90 74 27 97, 3 place du Septier)*, a rustic, unpretentious *salon de thé* (tearoom) and *saladerie* in a courtyard wrapped around a small fountain. Around the corner, Moroccan *La Fibule (☎ 04 90 74 05 29, 28 rue de la République)* serves spicy tajines and couscous in a warm, ochre-painted interior. Evening reservations are essential.

Irresistible home-made pasta is cooked up at *La Trattoria (☎ 04 90 04 63 68, place Carnot)*, an authentic Italian bistro. Its sauces, oils and *pâtes fraîches* are sold in the adjoining delicatessen, behind the restaurant at 50 rue Eugène Brunel.

Au Petit St-Martin (☎ 04 90 74 10 13, 24 rue St-Martin) is a tiny back-street restaurant with a 96FF *menu Provençal*, a 45FF plat du jour and lots of crepes. *Le Chant de l'Heure (☎ 04 90 74 08 38, 23 rue St-Pierre)* has *menus crêpes* for 68FF, 74FF and 90FF.

Self-caterers can shop in town at *Petit Casino (130 rue St-Pierre)* and out of town at the giant-sized *Leclerc* or *Adac* supermarkets, both on the westbound N100 towards Avignon.

Shopping

Côtes du Lubéron wine is sold at rustic Vin du Pays, 70 rue du Docteur Gros. For fruits confits and *miel* (honey), head for La Bonbonnière, 47 rue de la Sous Préfecture.

Unusual pottery is sold at Poterie entre Terre et Ciel, 144 rue de la République. Jean Herrero Cordonnier (☎ 04 90 74 09 17), 24 rue de la République, sells handmade leather sandals (350FF).

Getting There & Away

Bus Buses leave from the bus station (☎ 04 90 74 20 21), 250 ave de la Libération, east of the centre. Daily bus services include to/from Avignon (43.50FF, 1¼ hours, five daily) via Coustellet (27FF, 40 minutes) and Cavaillon (36FF, 50 minutes); Digne-les-Bains (62FF, two hours); and Manosque (42FF, one hour, twice daily). Twice-daily buses between Apt and Marseilles (60FF, 2½ hours) stop in Bonnieux, Lourmarin, Cadenet, Pertuis and Aix-en-Provence.

Train Apt does not have a train station but advance reservations can be made and tickets bought at the SNCF boutique (☎ 04 90 74 00 85), 26 blvd Victor Hugo. It opens 8.30 am to 6 pm on weekdays, and 8.30 am to 5 pm on Saturday.

Getting Around

Bicycle Cycles Agnel (signposted 'Cycles Raleigh'; ☎ 04 90 74 17 16), 86 quai Général Leclerc, hires mountain or road bikes per day/week for 80/400FF. The shop opens Wednesday to Saturday. Posters advertising weekly group rides organised by VTT Lubéron plaster its windows.

Hôtel L'Aptois (see Places to Stay on the previous page) has regular road bikes (80FF per day) and tandems (120FF per day) to hire. It makes up picnic hampers for cyclists (40FF to 65FF) and will transport your luggage from A to B for 3FF per km (minimum 50FF charge for return journeys less than 20km).

AROUND APT

From Apt a good day trip is to head north-westwards to rocky red Roussillon, Gordes and the Abbaye de Sénanque – three of Provence's hottest tourist spots – and return via the pretty villages of **Murs** (pop 420), with its marvellous views of the region, **Joucas** (pop 321), **St-Saturnin-lès-Apt**

Lubéron by Bike

Cyclists can cross the Parc Naturel du Lubéron by following a marked route that stretches for just over 100km. The itinerary uses roads – steep in places – that have little traffic, except for fellow cyclists, and pass through some of the region's many beautiful villages.

Hardened cyclists who enjoy a stiff climb should follow the route east to west, signposted with white markers. Freewheelers should opt for the easier westbound route, which is marked by orange signs. The final 42km leg of the itinerary from Apt to Cavaillon through Bonnieux, Lacoste and Ménerbes – Peter Mayle country – pedals cyclists past vineyards and olive groves, lavender fields and fruit farms. The restored Moulin St-Pierre, on the banks of the Cavaillon-Carpentras canal in Les Taillades, 5km east of Cavaillon, was built in 1849 to produce madder dye and later flour.

For day-trippers already in Cavaillon, the 40km round-trip to Ménerbes and back again makes for an exhilarating – and not *too* exhausting – bike ride. Cyclists pedalling off from Forcalquier should take to the skies at the observatory in St-Michel l'Observatoire, just 14km west.

Colourful information boards posted along the way provide details on accommodation, places to eat, and sights in and around the 19 villages included in the two-wheel itinerary.

Alternatively, contact Vélo Loisir en Lubéron (☎ 04 92 79 05 82, [e] vll@pacwan.fr), BP 14, 04280 Céreste, which gives information on accommodation and bicycle rental, and also provides technical support to saddle-sore cyclists following the Lubéron cycle route.

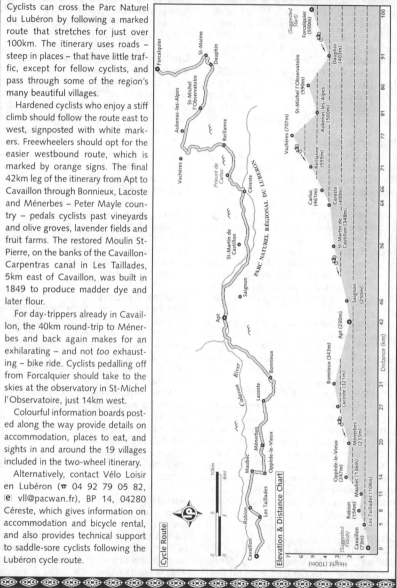

Cycle Route

Elevation & Distance Chart

(pop 2393) and **Villars** (pop 700), a hill-top village that hosts a Sunday-morning market, June to mid-September.

In St-Saturnin-lès-Apt, shop for honey, lavender and truffles (in season), and learn how olives are turned into oil (90FF per litre) at the **Moulin à Huile Jullien** (☎ 04 90 75 45 80), 1 rue Albert Trouchet. The actual mill can only be visited in November during the olive harvest. Lovely views of the village rooftops and beyond can be enjoyed from the **17th-century windmill**, signposted 'Les Château Les Moulins', 1km north of St-Saturnin off the Sault-bound D943.

Gordes
postcode 84220 • pop 2127
• elevation 372m

On the white, rocky southern face of the Vaucluse plateau, the tiered village of Gordes (Gordo in Provençal), 20km west of Apt on the Lubéron slopes, forms an amphitheatre overlooking the Rivers Sorgue and Calavon. The village is crowned by a sturdy 11th-century chateau, rebuilt in 1525. It houses **art exhibitions** and a small museum today. The bright blue piece of monumental art at the foot of the village is the creation of Hungarian sculptor Vasarely, an honorary citizen of Gordes since 1983.

This once typical Provençal village is overrun with tourists in summer but it's still worth a wander if you've got the wheels to get you there. Gordes tourist office (☎ 04 90 72 02 75, fax 04 90 72 02 26, ⒠ office .gordes@wanadoo.fr), place du Château, opens 9 am to noon and 2 to 6 pm Monday to Saturday, and 10 am to noon and 2 to 6 pm on Sunday.

South of Gordes, 3.5km along route de St-Pantaleon (D148) and just west of St-Pantaleon, is the **Musée du Moulin des Bouillons** (☎ 04 90 72 22 11), a preserved oil mill complete with a 10m-long press weighing seven tonnes. The gastronomic thrill of locally milled oil (and some 200 wines) can be sampled at *Mas de Tourteron* (☎ 04 90 72 00 16, chemin de St-Blaise), an upmarket restaurant serving typical Provençal cuisine against a backdrop of opulent, flower-laden gardens. Count on paying

at least 170/200FF for a lunchtime or dinner *menu*.

Camping Les Sources (☎ 04 90 72 12 48, route de Murs) is a large site open March to October. It charges 46FF for two people with tent and car. At the other extreme, heavenly *La Bastide (☎ 04 90 72 12 12, fax 04 90 72 05 20, ⒠ bastide-gordes@ avignon.pacwan.net)* has four-star doubles with village/valley view from 790/1070FF.

Buses, operated by Les Express de la Durance (☎ 04 90 71 03 00 in Cavaillon), link Gordes with Cavaillon twice a day except Sunday.

Village des Bories
The walled Village des Bories (☎ 04 90 72 03 48) is 4km south-west of Gordes off the D2 towards Cavaillon. *Bories* are one- or two-storey beehive-shaped huts constructed without mortar using thin wedges of limestone. They were first built in the area in the Bronze Age and were continuously lived in, renovated and even built anew until as late as the 18th century. It is not known what purpose they first served but over the centuries they have been used as shelters, workshops, wine cellars and storage sheds. The 'village' contains about 20 such structures, restored to the way they were about 150 years ago. Some say that the bories remind them of Ireland's *clochán*. The site opens 9 am to sunset. Admission costs 35FF (those aged 10 to 18, 20FF).

Abbaye Notre-Dame de Sénanque
Some 4km north-west of Gordes off the D177 is the Cistercian Abbaye Notre-Dame de Sénanque (☎ 04 90 72 05 72, ⒠ ndsenanque@aol.com) which, in July, is framed by fields of lilac lavender. The abbey, founded in 1148 and inhabited by six young monks today, opens 10 am to noon and 2 to 6 pm Monday to Saturday, and 2 to 6 pm on Sunday, March to October; and 10 am to noon and 2 to 6 pm on weekdays, and 2 to 5 pm on weekends, November to February. Admission costs 30FF (those aged six to 18, 12FF). Mass is celebrated in the abbey at noon on weekdays and 9 am Sunday.

THE LUBÉRON

Roussillon

postcode 84220 • pop 1190
• elevation 360m

Some two millennia ago, the Romans used the distinctive ochre earth around Roussillon, situated in the valley between the Vaucluse plateau and the Lubéron range, for producing pottery glazes. These days the whole village – even gravestones in the cemetery – is built of the reddish local stone, making it a popular place for painters eager to try out the range of their palettes. The red and orange hues are especially striking given the yellow-white bareness of the surrounding area and the green conifers sprinkled around town.

From the village, a 1km-long **Sentier des Ocres** (Ochre Trail) leads you through fairytale groves of chestnuts, maritime pines and scrub to the bizarre and beautiful ochre formations created by erosion and fierce winds over the centuries. The trail, which starts next to the cemetery and Parking des Ocres (off place de la Poste), is accessible 9 am to 7.30 pm daily, July and August; 10 am to 5.30 pm daily, September to mid-November and March to June; and 9 am to noon and 1 to 5 pm, Tuesday to Sunday, the rest of the year. Admission costs 10FF (children aged under 10, free). Avoid wearing white; you'll return rust-coloured. Smoking during the 35-minute trail is forbidden.

Innovative work shops exploring the colouring properties of ochre, first realised in the 18th century, are held at **Usine Mathieu** (☎/fax 04 90 05 66 69). Guided tours (in French only) of the Conservatoire des Ocres et Pigments Appliqués (Applied Pigment and Ochre Conservatory; ☎/fax 04 90 05 66 69, e info@okhra.com), route d'Apt, depart at 2, 3, 4 and 5 pm daily, July to October; and once or twice a month, the rest of the year. Tours last 45 minutes and cost 25FF (children aged under 10, free). The centre opens 10 am to 7 pm.

Roussillon tourist office (☎ 04 90 05 60 25, fax 04 90 05 63 31, e ot-roussillon@axit.fr), place de la Poste, opens 10 am to noon and 2 to 6.30 pm Monday to Saturday, and 2 to 6 pm on Sunday. It has a list of hotels and *chambres d'hôtes* pinned outside. Roussillon, 9km east of Gordes, is inaccessible by public transport. The GR6 footpath passes through.

Rustrel & Around

The main reason for visiting Rustrel (pop 621), 10km north-east of Apt, is to gaze in awe at the breathtaking rock formations at the **Colorado Provençal** (see the boxed text 'Provence's Colorado' below). For an aerial

---

Provence's Colorado

Men are known to stare wistfully at the **Cheminée de Fées** (literally 'chimney of fairies'), a fiery pillar that protrudes in all its magnificence from a savage landscape of red ochre sands. It is part of an extraordinary collection of rock formations at the **Colorado Provençal**, a disused quarry in Rustrel where ochre was mined from the 1880s until 1956.

Although ochre has been used in the Lubéron since Roman times, it was not until 1785 that large deposits of the hydrated oxidised iron-and-clay sands were unearthed. These were exploited industrially from 1830 until 1930 when, with the increasing use of synthetic pigments, the ochre industry collapsed. At its peak in 1929 it yielded 40,000 tonnes of ochre annually.

Traditionally used as a pigment (extracted from the ochre sands through a simple washing process) to colour pots and buildings, ochre comes in some 25 shades, ranging from delicate yellow to vivid orange and fire red. Many of these hues can be discovered first-hand along seven short walking trails that wind through the colorado. The trails for two of the most dramatic – the **Sentier des Cheminées de Fées** (1km, 30 minutes) and the **Sentier du Sahara** (1.5km, 45 minutes) – start from the municipal car park in Bouvène, immediately south of Rustrel village along a narrow road signposted off the D22. Parking costs 12FF and includes a free map detailing all seven walks.

---

view, head for paragliding school Rustr'aile Colerado (☎/fax 04 40 04 96 53); a tandem flight costs about 400FF. In the village, you can visit the working **Moulin à Huile de Rustrel** (Rustrel Oil Mill; ☎ 04 90 04 98 49), open noon to 6 pm, July and August; and 2 to 5 pm, June and September.

Equally dramatic walking can be enjoyed at **Château du Bois** (☎ 04 90 76 91 23), an 80-hectare lavender farm, 15km north of Rustrel in Lagarde d'Apt (pop 27). A 2km trail, signposted 'Parcours Lavande', leads visitors past field upon field of purple lavender, abuzz with bees and aflutter with butterflies from late June until mid-July when the sweet-smelling flower is harvested.

The eastbound D22 and winding D33 links Rustrel with **Viens** (pop 500), a good starting point for forays into the **Gorges d'Oppedettes**, a limestone canyon. From the northern end of the village, a circular footpath (4km, 1½ hours) marked with yellow blazes takes strollers past several bories. The GR4 passes through **Céreste** (pop 1045, elevation 370m), 8km south. In Roman times the Via Domitia passed through the village. Its tourist office (☎ 04 92 79 09 84) on central place de la République has mountain bikes to rent for 100/500FF per day/week.

From Céreste the N100 pushes on east to Haute-Provence (see that chapter). Lavender fiends might want to access this neighbouring region via the northbound D14, a scenic road strung with purple in season (see the boxed text 'Perfume of Provence' in the Avignon Area chapter for details).

These villages are inaccessible by public transport: walk, cycle or drive.

Places to Stay & Eat

There is a *camp site* (☎/fax 04 90 75 20 11, @ denis.mangeot@wanadoo.fr) with swimming pool in St-Martin de Castillon, 7km south of Viens; the site is signposted off the D48 west of St-Martin. Isolated *Hôtel St-Paul* (☎ 04 90 75 21 47, fax 04 90 75 30 80), 1km north of Viens along the narrow D201 to Oppedette, is a perfect get-away-from-it-all spot if you have your own wheels. Bathroom-equipped doubles/triples

with panoramic green views cost 310/390FF and half-board is 320FF per person. The hotel sports a swimming pool and tennis court. In Céreste *Hôtel Aiguebelle* (☎ 04 922 79 00 09, place de la République) is a quintessential village inn, offering doubles for 210FF (295FF with shower and toilet) and *menus* starting at 89FF; the grilled duck with lavender honey is worth the trip.

LE PETIT LUBÉRON

The rocky landscape of the 'little Lubéron' embraces the western part of the massif and is studded with a maze of *villages perchés*. These villages, perched aloft stony spurs, offer good views of the region's lower-lying treasures, including its thick cedar forests.

Côtes du Lubéron vineyards – covering 3500 hectares – line southbound route de Bonnieux (D3) from Apt to Bonnieux. *Domaines* (wine-producing estates) you pass en route include Château de L'Isolette (☎ 04 90 74 16 70) and Domaine de Mayol (☎ 04 90 74 14 80), known for its great reds. Both offer *dégustation* (tasting); expect to pay upwards of 40FF per bottle. Lubéron wine has enjoyed its own *appellation d'origine contrôlée* (AOC) since 1988. See the Food & Wine section for more details.

The Lubéron's other nectar is *meil* (honey). Taste and buy the region's sweetest product from **Le Mas des Abeilles** (☎ 04 90 74 29 55, @ info@mas-des-abeilles.com), a farmhouse on the Col du Pointu (accessed via the D943, which runs parallel to the D3), on Bonnieux's northern fringe. Visit their Web site at www .mas-desabeilles.com (French only).

Bonnieux
postcode 84220 ● pop 1436
● elevation 425m

Bonnieux, 11km south-west of Apt and 26km east of Cavaillon, is Le Petit Lubéron's best-known hill-top village. Eighty-six steps lead from place de la Liberté and rue de la Mairie to its 12th-century **Église Vieille** (old church). Bonnieux's **Musée de la Boulangerie** (Bakery Museum; ☎ 04 90 75 88 34) unravels the history of bread.

Pont Julien, 6km north on the D149, is a three-arched Roman bridge built between

THE LUBÉRON

27 BC and AD 14. Five kilometres north towards Goult (D36) is **La Gare de Bonnieux**, home to the local wine cooperative, the old village train station and a contemporary art gallery.

From Bonnieux, a *route forestière* (forestry road) leads south-westwards to **Forêt des Cèdres**, a protected cedar forest dating back to 1861. Parts of its 250 hectares are crossed by a two-hour **Sentier Botanique** (botanical trail). Bonnieux tourist office (☎ 04 90 74 91 90, fax 04 90 75 92 94, e ot-bonnieux@axit.fr), place Carnot, has information on guided walks and accommodation lists for the surrounding villages. It opens 9.30 am to 12.30 pm and 2.30 to 7 pm Monday to Saturday, April to September. Visit the office's Web site at www .provenceguide.com.

Places to Stay On route de Ménerbes, *Camping Le Vallon (☎/fax 04 90 75 86 14, e camping@bonnieux.com)* charges 13.50/11/9FF per adult/tent/car. *Les Termes Blanches (☎ 04 90 75 88 42, route de Ménerbes)* is a *gîte d'étape* with dorm beds for 100FF and breakfast/half-board for 20/180FF. Both places are on the westbound D3 to Lacoste.

Bonnieux's cheapest hotel is six-room *Hôtel Le César (☎ 04 90 75 80 18, place de la Liberté)*, which charges 200/250FF for a single/double with shower (280FF with shower and balcony, 450FF with bathroom and terrace). Bathroom-equipped triples cost 600FF.

Count on paying upwards of 390/560FF for a double with shower/bath and toilet at three-star *Hostellerie du Prieuré (☎ 04 90 75 80 78, fax 04 90 75 96 00, rue Jean Baptiste Aurard)*, a charming, 18th-century priory with a peaceful walled garden.

Signposted off the eastbound D232 from Bonnieux is *Bastide de Capelongue (☎ 04 90 75 89 78, fax 04 90 75 93 03)*, a plush modern mas with doubles designed for the bottomless wallet. A night's sleep for two costs upwards of 1000FF.

Places to Eat Pizza, truffles, game and *pain de chèvre* (goat-cheese bread) and cooked up at *La Flambée (☎ 04 90 75 82 20, 2 place du 4 Septembre)*, a simple restaurant well-worth frequenting for the stunning panorama that can be enjoyed from its 1st-floor terrace. Its has 89FF and 130FF *menus*.

A cut above the average village restaurant is *Le Fournil (The Bakehouse; ☎ 04 90 75 83 62, 5 place Carnot)*, next to the tourist office. Its interior is cut around a rock face and its exterior around a trickling fountain. Provençal highlights served with a flourish include a tasty courgette *gâteau* garnished with tiny prawns, thyme-dressed shoulder of lamb, and *soupe de cerise au vin rouge* (cherry and red wine soup). *Menus* cost 98FF (lunch only), 130FF and 190FF. Advance reservations are essential. It opens Tuesday evening to Sunday.

Dining spots that are an easy cycle or drive away include *Restaurant de la Gare (☎ 04 90 75 82 00)* in La Gare de la Bonnieux, 5km north along the D36 to Goult. It serves delicious lunchtime/evening *menus* costing from 60/120FF and rents bicycles for guests to wobble around the countryside on afterwards. Advance reservations are essential so the chef knows how many to cook for.

Upmarket diners can splurge a la Provençale at *Auberge de l'Aiguebrun (☎ 04 90 04 47 00)*, a remote *bastide* (country house) set in the dramatic heart of the Combe de Lourmarin, 6km south of Bonnieux off the D943 towards Lourmarin. Lunch/evening *menus*, served Thursday to Tuesday from March to mid-November, start at 180/250FF. Auberge de l'Aiguebrun also has 10 double rooms, costing upwards of 750FF.

Getting There & Around Buses to/from Apt and Marseilles stop in Bonnieux (see Apt earlier in this chapter).

In the centre of Bonnieux, near the tourist office, Mountain Bike Lubéron (☎ 04 90 75 94 23, 06 83 25 48 07, e mtbikeluberon@ aol.com), 7 rue Jan Baptiste Aurard, has road and mountain bikes to rent for 50/90/330FF per half-day/day/four days.

To call a taxi in Bonnieux dial ☎ 04 90 72 31 41 or ☎ 06 07 86 23 88.

Sadism

The Marquis de Sade (1740–1814) was a sadist, hence the word. His sexually explicit novels – *120 Journées de Sodome* (120 Days of Sodom; 1785), *Justine* (1791) and *Juliette* (1798) – caused an outrage and were banned when published in the late 18th century. Equally shocking were the sex scandals surrounding de Sade's own life, 27 years of which were spent in prison.

De Sade lived in Lacoste with his wife and three children from 1771, following his ostracism by Parisian society for accosting and flagellating a woman who took him to court for rape. De Sade spent much of his childhood in Provence where his family had owned Château de Lacoste since 1627. Among the de Sade family members were Hugues de Sade and his wife Laura, a lifelong muse for the Italian poet Petrarch.

The Marquis de Sade wed at the age of 22 but never allowed his marriage to Parisian bourgeoisie, Renée Pélagie de Montreuil, tamper with his love of orgies. In Lacoste he was brought to trial on charges of sodomy and attempted poison after indulging in a whipping session with four prostitutes and his manservant in Marseilles.

The chateau was looted by revolutionaries in 1789, and subsequently sold by de Sade who spent the last 11 years of his life in a mental asylum where he died, far from mad, aged 74. It was only after WWII that his works were freely published.

Lacoste

postcode 84220 • pop 417
• elevation 320m

It was to the 9th-century **Château de Sade** atop Lacoste, 6.5km west of Bonnieux, that the notorious Marquis de Sade retreated in 1771 when his writings became too scandalous for the Parisians. His 45-room palace, once cared for by 20 servants, is just an eerie ruin today. The steep climb is rewarded with unbeatable views of the valley. The village visible from the sunny terrace of **Cafe de France** is Bonnieux.

Places to Stay & Eat At the foot of the village, *Café de Sade (☎ 04 90 75 82 29, fax 04 90 75 95 68, rue Basse)*, open mid-February to December, runs a gîte d'étape with 32 dorm beds costing 75FF, plus 25/32FF for sheets/breakfast. It also has a handful of basic double rooms for 200FF (290FF with shower and toilet).

Excellent-value *Hôtel de France (☎ 04 90 75 82 25)*, in the village centre, has six simple but charming doubles costing 190FF (240FF with shower, 290FF with shower and toilet).

Bonnieux tourist office has information on chambres d'hôtes in Lacoste. Upmarket *Relais du Procureur (☎ 04 90 75 82 28, rue Basse)* with a terrace and pool, offers B&B in luxury doubles/triples for 500/700FF. Adjoining *Table du Procureur (☎ 04 90 75 84 78)* is Lacoste's loveliest spot to dine; lunchtime/evening *menus* kick off at 58/119FF.

Ménerbes

postcode 84560 • pop 1007
• elevation 230m

Continue 6km west on the D109 to Ménerbes, a pretty hill-top village marked firmly on the tourist trail by British novelist Peter Mayle who lived here between 1986 and 1993 (since 1999 he has made neighbouring Lourmarin his home). On place Albert Roure, the central square, Café du Progrès (☎ 04 90 72 22 09) sells glossy tourist guides (35FF) to the incoming coachloads and doles out directions to Mayle's former mas, which is 2km southeast on the D3 to Bonnieux (second house on the right after the football pitch). The massive car and coach parks at the foot of the village and the bounty of souvenir shops in its heart have all sprung up since Mayle's *A Year in Provence* was first published in 1989; the bestseller sold four million copies and has been translated into 22 languages.

Sample local Côtes du Lubéron wine and

THE LUBÉRON

stare agog at over 1000 different corkscrews at the **Musée du Tire Bouchon** (Corkscrew Museum; ☎ 04 90 72 41 58), in the chateau of Domaine de la Citadelle, at the village's western foot on the D3 to Cavaillon. The museum is the brain child of Yves Rousset-Rouard, village mayor and French MP who resides in the restored chateau at the top of Ménerbes village. In the 1970s he produced films, notably the soft porn *Emmanuelle* (1974). The museum also displays César's *Compression de Tire-Bouchons*, comprising a block of compressed corkscrews. Admission costs 25FF (students 19FF; children aged under 15, free).

Oppède-le-Vieux
postcode 84580 • pop 1246
• elevation 300m

Large car parks designated for tourist traffic sit at the foot of Oppède-le-Vieux, 6km south-west of Ménerbes. This medieval village was abandoned around 1910 by the villagers who moved down the valley to the cultivated plains. A steep rocky path leads to the **ruins** that cling to the hillside. The 16th- to 18th-century church, where French comedian Michel Lebb wed in June 2000, is slowly being restored and opens to visitors 10 am to noon and 2 to 5 pm at weekends (daily in July and August), May to November. The church hosts musical concerts in August and celebrates mass in honour of Oppède's patron saint on 10 August. The new village, Oppède les Poulivets, is 1km north of Oppède-le-Vieux.

Locally milled olive oil is sold at the **Moulin à Huile d'Olives** (☎ 04 90 76 90 66), between the two Oppèdes on route du Four Neuf. Mill tours are available between 15 November and Christmas when the freshly harvested olives are being pressed.

Coustellet

Coustellet, on busy route de Gordes (N100) about 6km north of Oppède les Poulivets, is uninspiring beyond its **Musée de la Lavande** (☎ 04 90 76 91 23). The museum has *stills* used to extract the sweet-smelling scent, and a boutique selling lavender-scented products. The most informative part is a short video (in English), which explains how the purple flower is harvested and distilled (see the boxed text 'The Perfume of Provence' in the Avignon Area chapter). The museum opens 10 am to noon and 2 to 6 or 7 pm, March to December. Admission costs 15FF (children aged under 15, free).

Thirsty travellers can fill up their water bottles with local Côtes du Lubéron wine for 10.70FF per litre or even cheaper table wine for 6.20FF per litre at the large **Cave du Lubéron** (☎ 04 90 76 90 01), at the southern end of Coustellet on the D2. *Maison Gouin* (☎ 04 90 76 90 18), at the intersection of the D2 and N100 in the village centre, is a traditional *boucherie* (butcher), *traiteur* (caterer) and *crèmerie* (dairy) dating to 1928. Its delicious meats, dairy produce and salads can be eaten in – its 65FF lunchtime *menu* includes 25cl of table wine – or taken away.

Cabrières d'Avignon & Lagnes

Five kilometres north of Coustellet, Cabrières d'Avignon (pop 1431, postcode 84220, elevation 167m), was one of 11 Lubéron villages destroyed by troops under the terms of the Aix Parliament's *Arrêt de Mérindol* in 1545 that condemned Vaudois heretics to death. The Vaudois (Waldenses) were a minority group who sought refuge in the Lubéron hills following the excommunication of their leader, Valdès, from the Church by Pope Lucius III in 1184. The Vaudois joined the Reformation in 1532, leading to their eventual massacre on the 19 and 20 April 1545 – 3000 people were murdered and a further 600 sent to the galleys. In Cabrières d'Avignon, troops stormed the 12th-century **chateau** (1182). The castle, since restored, is private property and can't be visited.

The northern part of the village is shrouded with beautiful pine and cedar forests, crisscrossed with walking paths, picnic tables and a small amphitheatre made from the same dry stone as the region's bories.

Le Bistrot à Michel (☎/fax 04 90 76 82 08) in Cabrières d'Avignon village centre has nine delightful rooms costing upwards of 450FF, and an even more delightful *restaurant* renowned for its exquisite and excellent Provençal cuisine (reviewed in the Food & Wine section). Rooms/tables need to be booked months/days in advance.

Yellow-brick **Lagnes** (pop 1509, postcode 84220, elevation 110m), 5km west, offers little to do beyond strolling its cobbled streets and visiting art exhibitions hosted in its *vieux lavoir* (old wash house) off place du Fontaine. Lagnes has two lovely chambres d'hôtes: *Le Grand Jas* (☎ 04 90 20 25 12) and *Le Mas du Grand Jonquier* (☎ 04 90 20 90 13), both in restored, pool-equipped Provençal mas with doubles costing 330FF to 485FF. Traditional *Le Mas des Grès* (☎ 04 90 20 32 85, fax 04 90 20 21 45, e mas.de.gres@ wanadoo.fr, route d'Apt) is a 14-room hotel, likewise set in a restored farmhouse and open mid-March to mid-November. Doubles cost 395FF to 850FF.

Getting There & Away From Lagnes, Voyages Arnaud (☎ 04 90 38 15 58 in L'Isle-sur-la-Sorgue) operates three to four buses daily to/from L'Isle-sur-la-Sorgue (15FF, 25 minutes) and Avignon (28FF, 1¼ hours).

CAVAILLON
postcode 84300 • pop 25,058
• elevation 75m

Acting as the Lubéron's western gateway, Cavaillon (Cavaioun in Provençal) is 28km south-east of Avignon. The market town is best known for its sweet melons, mountains of which are sold at the early morning Monday market in season, May to September. Melons abound during mid-July's Fête du Melon.

Information
The tourist office (☎ 04 90 71 32 01, fax 04 90 71 42 99, e o.t.cavaillon@wanadoo.fr), place François Tourel, organises various guided tours in July and August, including cycling, walking and melon-tasting tours (35FF, children aged under 12, free). It opens 9 am to 12.30 pm and 2 to 7 pm Monday to Saturday, May to September; and 9.30 am to 12.30 pm and 1.30 to 6.30 pm, the rest of the year. It also opens until lunchtime on Sunday, year round.

The post office on place du Cros, which adjoins place François Tourel, has a currency exchange and Cyberposte. Various commercial banks dot cours Bournissac and cours Gambetta.

Things to See & Do
An **arch** built by the Romans in the 1st century BC adorns place François Tourel, the square in front of the tourist office, at the western end of cours Bournissac, Cavaillon's main shopping street. Three blocks north is 12th-century **Cathédrale St-Véran** with its fine Roman *cloître* (cloister). Cavaillon's beautiful **synagogue** (1772) and adjoining **Musée Juif Comtadin** (Jewish Museum; ☎ 04 90 76 00 34), on rue Hébraïque, are likewise worth a visit.

Cheval-Blanc, 3km south of Cavaillon, is the starting point for walks into the majestic **Gorges de Régalon**. The gorges, up to 30m high and as narrow as 50cm in places, are protected by a geological nature reserve. A footpath leads from the car park in La Tuillie, 9km east of Cheval-Blanc off the D973.

Places to Stay & Eat
Camping La Durance (☎ 04 90 71 11 78, fax 04 90 71 98 77, Digue des Grands Jardins), opens April to October and charges 25/11FF per person/tent or car. There are also *camp sites* in Robion, 6km east, and Maubec, 9km east.

Out of town, *Auberge Ferme La Bastide* (☎ 04 90 71 01 81, fax 04 90 78 16 85, Quartier des Faysses) is a working farm with a hearty Provençal kitchen and seven chambres d'hôtes, costing 180FF to 250FF per double. The farm is signposted off the westbound D973 to Caumont.

Central hotels in Cavaillon that won't break the bank include *Hôtel Le Provence* (☎ 04 90 78 03 38, 9 cours Bournissac), which has nine doubles above a simple snack bar that cost 110FF; and *Hôtel Le Forum* (☎ 04 90 78 37 55, 68 place du

THE LUBÉRON

Clos), which has 18 rooms costing 130FF to 300FF.

Le Fin de Siècle (☎ 04 90 71 28 85, 42 place du Clos) is a popular brasserie, dating from 1900, with a lovely people-watching pavement terrace and a 69FF *menu*. Head southwards along ave Gabriel Peri and its continuation, ave de Verdun, to get to the melon-flesh coloured *restaurant (☎ 04 90 71 32 43, 353 ave de Verdun)* of Jean Jacques Prévôt, Cavaillon's best-known chef who has authored several books on his greatest passion – melons. Between mid-May and mid-October, during the melon season, Prévôt serves a melon-inspired *menu* (from 290FF), featuring fantastic creations such as wild boar and melon procciutto or langoustines roasted in melon and served in a fishy soup. Lunchtime/evening *menus* start at 160/290FF.

Master baker *Auzet Cavaillon (☎ 04 90 78 06 54, 61 cours Bournissac)* bakes 15 types of bread (garlic, walnut, wholemeal, bran, rye and so on) plus an additional clutch of more exotic loafs, including Roquefort, thyme and onion, which have to be ordered in advance. Eat *pain bouillabaisse* with Provençal fish soup, and make sandwiches from *pain de miel*. Auzet also serves a 40FF breakfast and sells well-filled baguettes and creamy quiches to eat in or take away.

Provençal honey, wine, melon liqueur, biscuits and cheese are sold at delectable *Le Clos Gourmand (☎ 04 90 78 05 22, 8 place du Clos)*, a superbly stocked *épicerie* (grocery) and *fromagerie* (cheese shop).

Getting There & Away
Bus From the bus stop beside the train station, there are daily bus services (call ☎ 04 90 63 01 82 for information) to/from L'Isle-sur-la-Sorgue (19FF, 15 minutes, three or four daily), Aix-en-Provence (46FF, 1½ hours, three daily) and Marseilles (60FF, one hour, three daily). Avignon is served by five to 10 daily (call ☎ 04 90 71 03 00 for information; 20FF, one hour). There are two or three buses daily to/from Gordes (call ☎ 04 90 73 23 59 for information; 15FF, 30 minutes).

Train The train station, place de la Gare, is at the eastern end of ave Maréchal Joffre. Walk to the end of this street, turn right onto ave Gabriel Péri, then left onto cours Bournissac to get to the centre. From Cavaillon there are trains to Marseilles (71FF, 1¼ hours) and Avignon (33FF, 30 minutes).

Getting Around
You can hire a bike from Bouti Cycle (☎ 04 90 71 45 55), 200m west of the train station at 25 ave Maréchal Joffre (open Wednesday to Monday); or from friendly and efficient Cyclix Cavaillon (☎ 04 90 78 07 06, ⒠ cyclix@wanadoo.fr), 166 cours Gambetta, where tandems and regular bikes rent for 100/180/450FF per day/weekend/week. It opens Monday to Saturday.

LE GRAND LUBÉRON
The deep **Combe de Lourmarin,** which cuts through the massif in an almost perfect perpendicular from Bonnieux to Lourmarin, marks the great divide between Le Petit and Le Grand Lubéron. Dramatic gorges and grand fortresses are the trademarks of the 'Big' Lubéron.

Buoux
postcode 84480 • pop 117
Several kilometres north-east of Bonnieux and 8km south of Apt is Buoux, dominated by the splendid hill-top **ruins of Fort de Buoux** (550m). As a traditional Protestant stronghold, Buoux was destroyed in the 1545 Vardois massacres and again in 1660. The fort and old village ruins, perilous in places due to loose rocks and so on, can be explored on foot. From the watchtower at the far end of the fort there are magnificent views of the valley. White arrows painted on rocks mark an optional return route via a magnificent 'hidden' spiralling staircase cut in the rock.

Places to Stay & Eat Midway between Castellet and Le Boisset is *Les Monguets (☎ 04 90 75 28 62)*, a lovely farm and cherry orchard where you can camp *à la ferme* (on the farm). A tent pitch for one or two people costs 60FF. Les Monguets also

Lavender Trail

From **Buoux**, an invigorating cycling/driving route takes you north on the D113 to a set of crossroads straddled by lavender fields, which in July and August blaze blue. At the crossroads you can bear west along the D232 to Bonnieux; east to the hill-top village of **Saignon** and farther east along the D48 to **Auribeau** (4.3km), **Castellet** (7km) and **Le Boisset** (from where you can link up with the N100); or continue on a northbound lavender trail for a further 9km to Apt.

After passing more lavender fields, the D113 climbs to **Les Agnels**, from where there are good views of stone-capped Mont Ventoux. In Les Agnels, visit **Distillerie Agnel** (☎ 04 90 74 22 72, route de Buoux), a distillery where essential oils have been made from lavender, cypress leaves, rosemary and other aromatic plants since 1895. Guided tours of the distillery depart at 11 am, 3.30 and 5.30 pm daily in July and August; and at the same times, Tuesday to Sunday, in May, June and September.

has a couple of *gîtes ruraux* (country cottages) to rent on a weekly basis and sells home-made lavender honey. The farm is on the D223, 500m east of the D48 junction. It opens Easter to October.

In Buoux, rambling *Auberge des Seguins* (☎ 04 90 74 16 37, fax 04 90 74 03 26), signposted from Buoux village centre, is a gîte d'étape, set in the middle of nowhere and charging 180FF per person for half-board. It opens from March to mid-November.

The place to eat in Buoux is *Auberge de la Loube* (☎/fax 04 90 74 19 58), an atmospheric inn, surrounded by flowers and a couple of horse-drawn carriages collected by Maurice, the chef and owner. It has lured a chic, sports-car set since Mayle mentioned it. La Loube has a 135FF lunch *menu* and a three-course evening 165FF *menu* (175FF with cheese), which includes hors d'œuvres Provençaux de la Loube – a wicker tray filled with Provençal treats such

as tapenade, *anchoïade* (anchovy sauce), quail eggs, melon slices, cherry tomatoes and fresh figs. It opens Friday to Tuesday and does not accept credit cards.

Saignon, 5km north-east, has a hostel (see Places to Stay under Apt earlier) and the pretty *Auberge de Presbytère* (☎ 04 90 74 11 50, fax 04 90 04 68 51, ⓔ auberge .presbytere@provence-luberon.com, place de la Fontaine), which has doubles costing 390FF to 570FF. Its serves a 175FF *menu* on a pavement terrace, overlooking the old village wash house on a fountain-decorated square.

Lourmarin
postcode 84160 • pop 1127
• elevation 230m

Little Lourmarin – the site of a massacre in 1545 during the Reformation – lies 6.5km south of Bonnieux. Its main draw is its Renaissance **chateau** (☎ 04 90 68 15 23), which can be visited by guided tour. The schedule (every half-hour between 10 am and 5.30 pm in July and August) is pinned outside the tourist office (☎/fax 04 90 68 10 77), across the field opposite the castle at 9 ave Philippe de Giraud.

Nobel Prize winning writer Albert Camus (1913–60) – who lived here for a number of years before his death in a car accident – and his wife are buried in the village cemetery; his tombstone is planted with rosemary, hers with lavender. Henri Bosco (1888–1976), best known for his children's books, is also buried here. From the chateau, continue along rue du Temple past a converted windmill, turn left onto the D27, then right down the narrow street that leads to the cemetery. In recent years, Lourmarin gained fame as the setting for French car manufacturer Renault's 'Papa! Nicole!' Clio TV commercials and as the adopted home of novelist Peter Mayle.

La Ferme de Gerbaud (☎ 04 90 68 11 83, ⓔ cgerbaud@aol.com), 3km north-east of Lourmarin along chemin d'Aguye and chemin de Gerbaud, is an organic farm that grows medicinal and aromatic herbs, and plants from which dyes are produced. Informative English-language tours of the

THE LUBÉRON

25-hectare estate depart at 5 pm daily, April to October; and at 3.30 pm at weekends, the rest of the year. Admission costs 30FF (children aged under 12, free). Dried herbs, essential oils and honey are sold in the farm shop.

Back in Lourmarin, grandiose *Moulin de Lourmarin* (☎ 04 90 68 06 69, fax 04 90 68 31 76, e lourmarin@francemarket.com), has doubles in a restored 18th-century oil mill, costing upwards of 800/1100FF in low/high season.

Vaugines & Cucuron

From Lourmarin the D56 follows the G97 footpath 5km east to Vaugines (pop 469), a charming village where parts of Claude Berri's Pagnol films *Manon des Sources* and *Jean de Florette* (1986) were shot. Take one look at the giant horse-chestnut tree and fabulous moss-covered fountain that fills central place de la Fontaine and you'll understand why.

Cucuron, 2km farther east, is the starting point for walks up **Mourre Nègre**. The tourist office (☎ 04 90 77 28 37, fax 04 90 77 17 00), rue Léonce Brieugne, stocks maps and guides.

Abbaye de Silvacane

The lovely Silvacane abbey is the third in the trio of the medieval Provence abbeys built in an austere Romanesque style in the 12th century. It sits south of the River Durance, 7km south of **Cadenet** (pop 3937). The Cistercian monks responsible for the magnificent architectural creations built Silvacane Abbey between 1175 and 1230. Work on the large refectory that adjoins the cloister's northern side did not begin until 1420. The abbey (☎ 04 42 50 41 69) opens 9 am to 7 pm daily, April to September; and 10 am to 1 pm and 2 to 5 pm, Wednesday to Monday, the rest of the year. Admission costs 32FF (students aged under 26, 21FF; those aged under 17, free). The abbey hosts various classical music concerts in summer.

Pays d'Aigues

Many consider rugged Pays d'Aigues the last remaining stronghold in Lubéron yet to be colonised by *résidence secondaire* (second home) owners.

Swimmers and sunbathers can bathe on the shores of the **Étang de la Bonde**, a small lake and beach 3km south of Cabrières d'Aigues on the D9.

Château d'Ansouis (☎ 04 90 09 82 70) in Ansious (pop 1057) was built between the 10th and 18th centuries. The castle is still inhabited by the original de Sabran family and can be visited by guided tour between 2.30 and 6 pm daily in summer; and Wednesday to Monday in winter. Its lovely gardens only open in June and July.

Eccentrics will adore Ansouis' **Musée Extraordinaire** (☎ 04 90 09 82 64), set up by Marseilles-born Georges Mazoyer whose passion for the sea and its prehistoric past is reflected in the museum's fossilised exhibits. It opens 2 to 6 or 7 pm. Admission costs 22FF (students 18FF; children 10FF).

La Tour d'Aigues (pop 4010), 10km farther east, is dominated by the Renaissance **Château de la Tour d'Aigues** (☎ 04 90 07 50 33), a substantial part of which (including its roof) was destroyed by fire in 1792. The 12th- to 15th-century castle houses a **Musée des Faïences**, in which 18th-century earthenware made in La Tour is exhibited. In summer, a rich pageant of concerts are held in its *cour d'honneur* (court of honour). Sud Lubéron Tourisme (☎ 04 90 07 30 00, fax 04 90 07 59 72, e provence.luberon @wanadoo.fr), in the chateau, provides tourist information and organises gastronomic, walking and cycling trips. Its Web site is at www.provence-luberon.net.

MANOSQUE
postcode 04100 • pop 20,309
• elevation 387m

Part of the Alpes de Haute-Provence department but still in the Parc Naturel Régional du Lubéron, Manosque (Manosco in Provençal) is a perfect stepping stone between toy-town Lubéron and its wilder eastern neighbour. Accommodation is cheaper here, making it a good base to explore the Lubéron. On the opposite bank of the River Durance, a stunning carpet of lavender fields covers the Valensole plateau, conveniently crossed by the eastbound D6 from Manosque.

Provençal writer Jean Giono (1895 –1970) was born and bred here. **Mont d'Or** (Mount d'Auro in Provençal, meaning 'mount of the wind'), immediately north of Manosque, offers good views of the town's red rooftops and Lubéron hills beyond. There are unparalleled panoramic views from **Montforon** (elevation 600m), 10km west of Manosque.

A dozen picturesque cycling and driving routes are detailed on a board in front of Manosque tourist office (☎ 04 92 72 16 00, fax 04 92 72 58 98, **e** otsi@ville-manosque.fr), place du Docteur Joubert, open 9 am to 12.15 pm and 1.30 to 6.30 pm Monday to Saturday, and 10 am to noon on Sunday. The tourist office's Web site is at www.ville-manosque.fr.

Giono & Carzou

Art exhibitions frequent **Centre Jean Giono** (☎ 04 92 70 54 54), 3 blvd Elémir Bourges, an arts centre dedicated to the Manosque-born writer. The small cottage on the corner of rue Grande and rue Torte, where Giono lived his whole life, still stands.

The frescoes, covering 670 sq metres of wall, inside the adjoining 19th-century **Chapelle de la Congrégation** (1840), 7 blvd Elémir Bourges, are a shock. The serial paintings – entitled *L'Apocalypse* and intended to portray a frightening 21st century – were painted by contemporary Armenian-born artist Jean Carzou between 1985 and 1991. Hitler, the Holocaust, Stalin and Pol Pot all feature on the chapel walls, as does the 'great whore' and 'lustful immoral couples'. The chapel, run by **Fondation Carzou** (☎ 04 92 87 40 49, **e** carzou@karatel.fr), opens 10 am to noon and 2.30 to 6.30 pm, Friday to Sunday. Admission costs 25FF (students 15FF).

Places to Stay

Manosque has several camp sites and an *Auberge de Jeunesse (☎ 04 92 87 57 44, fax 04 92 72 43 91, ave de l'Argile, Parc de la Rochette)*. Dorm beds here cost 48FF.

Fusty *Hôtel François 1er (☎ 04 92 72 07 99, fax 04 92 87 54 85, 18 rue Guilhempierre)*

charges 140/160FF for singles/doubles (240/310FF with shower and toilet).

Downtrodden *Hôtel du Terreau (☎ 04 92 72 15 50, fax 04 92 80 42, **e** hotelduterreau @wanadoo.fr, 21 place du Terreau)*, above a noisy bar, has rooms costing 130/160FF (210/250FF with shower).

Two-star *Grand Hôtel de Versailles (☎ 04 92 72 12 10, fax 04 92 72 62 5717 ave Jean Giono)*, has good-value doubles costing 130FF (170FF with shower, 220FF with shower and toilet).

Manosque's most prestigious pad is pretty *Hostellerie de la Fuste (☎ 04 92 72 05 95, fax 04 92 72 92 93, **e** lafuste@aol.com, route d'Oraison)*, 6km east on the D4. Regal doubles cost 650FF to 1000FF.

Places to Eat

Open-air restaurant terraces, cafes and bars – such as *St-Patrick Irish Pub (2 rue Mont d'Or)* and adjoining *Cantina Tex Mex,* which specialises in Texan fondue and beef slabs – fill place de l'Hôtel de Ville in the heart of the old town. From the square, pedestrian rue des Marchands leads to *La Cigogne d'Or (☎ 04 92 72 59 94)* at No 19, which has a terrace. Provençal and Alsacian cuisine, including *pieds et paquets* (68FF; see the Food & Wine section) and *choucroute* (sauerkraut), are its specialities.

Buy home-made pasta at *Aux Mille Pâtes (45 rue Grande)* and organically grown fruit and veg at *Le Blé en Herbe*, a biological co-operative at 7–9 rue des Marchands.

Hostellerie de la Fuste (see Places to Stay above) is Manosque's most sought-after kitchen. From this luxurious mansion, set amid sunflower fields and vineyards, the southbound D4 leads up to **Château Rousset**, a turreted fairytale castle, where you can taste and buy olive oil and wine.

Getting There & Away

Bus Manosque bus station, on blvd Charles de Gaulle, is 500m from the centre. Exit the station, turn left along blvd Charles de Gaulle, then right on to ave Jean Giono.

Buses are operated by Société des Cars Alpes Littoral (☎ 04 92 51 06 05 in Gap) and Digne-based Société des Autocars

THE LUBÉRON

Dignois (☎ 04 92 31 50 00). There are 10 or so daily buses to/from Aix-en-Provence (35FF, 50 minutes) and Marseilles (53FF, 1½ hours); and twice daily to/from Apt (42FF, one hour) and Avignon (96FF, 3¼ hours); three daily to/from Forcalquier (35 miutes); and two to four daily to/from Digne-les-Bains (32FF, 1¼ hours).

Train The train station, place Frédéric Mistral, is 2km south of the centre. Walk or bus it along ave Maréchal de Lattre de Tassigny and its continuation, ave Jean Giono. There are about six daily trains to/from Marseilles (83FF, 1½ hours), Aix-en-Provence (60FF, 1¼ hours) and Sisteron (56FF, one hour).

Haute-Provence

Haute-Provence is Provence at its rawest. Mass tourism has yet to touch these mountainous 'Alpes d'Azur', and peace, tranquillity and isolation are not hard to find. The splendid snowcapped peaks of the southern Alps dominate the north, while its south-eastern valleys, are sprinkled with hill-top villages, where the tempo of life has barely shifted gear since medieval times. South-west lies the land of lakes, gorges and Europe's grandest canyon. Lavender is a purple trait of the lower-lying Plateau de Valensole, on the left bank of the River Durance (Durènço in Provençal), which skirts the region's western side.

A large part of the Alpes-de-Haute-Provence department is protected by the **Parc National du Mercantour** (see National Parks in the Facts about Provence chapter). Spreadeagled in an arc along the French–Italian border, it is Provence's largest national park and offers a rich variety of outdoor activities including walking, cycling and white-water rafting in summer, and skiing in winter.

The Monte Carlo Rally tears round Haute-Provence's overdose of hairpin bends in January. Part of the region is also crossed by an enchanting narrow-gauge railway, a steam train huffs and puffs along a small section of it. Exploring is tough without your own wheels and a sturdy set of walking boots.

GORGES DU VERDON

The gorgeous 25km of Gorges du Verdon (also called the Grand Canyon du Verdon), Europe's largest canyon, slice through the limestone plateau midway between Avignon and Nice on the southernmost fringe of Haute-Provence. The green gorges begin at **Rougon** (pop 85) – near the confluence of the Rivers Verdon (Vervoudon in Provençal) and Jabron – until the river flows into **Lac de Ste-Croix**. The villages of **Castellane** (pop 1539), at the eastern end of the gorges, and **Moustiers Ste-Marie** (pop

Highlights

- Discover Europe's grandest gorges – on foot, by canoe or by bicycle
- Take a ride into the wild side of Provence with Digne-les-Bains' mountain railway – stunning views guaranteed!
- Track down prehistoric rock drawings in the Réserve Géologique de Haute-Provence
- Sniff Provence's perfumes at Salagon priory
- Scale new heights – cross Europe's highest bridge (182m) and highest mountain pass (2802m)

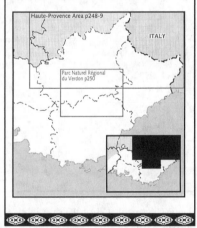

635) at their western end, are the main gateways into the region's most fabulous sight. There are plenty of accommodation options (especially camp sites) across the entire area.

Since 1997 the Parc Naturel Régional du Verdon has protected the 250m- to 700m-deep gorges, carved by the greenish waters of the River Verdon. The gorges are 8m to 90m wide at the bottom and the rims are 200m to 1500m apart. It is the water's unusually high

HAUTE-PROVENCE

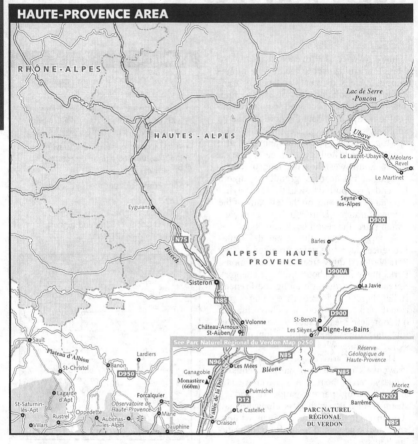

HAUTE-PROVENCE AREA

fluorine content that gives the river its magnificent green colour.

Information

Tourist Offices The best information source is Castellane tourist office (☎ 04 92 83 61 14, fax 04 92 83 76 89, ✉ office@castellane .org), rue Nationale; or its counterpart in Moustiers Ste-Marie (☎ 04 92 74 67 84, fax 04 92 74 60 65, ✉ moustiers@wanadoo .fr), rue de la Bougade.

The Castellane office organises summer excursions into the gorges and stocks an endless stream of information on outdoor activities in the area. It opens 9.15 am to noon and 2 to 6 pm weekdays, and 10 am to noon and 3 to 6 pm on Saturday. The busy Moustiers office sells excellent English-language guides and provides a wealth of information on the Parc Naturel Régional du Verdon (☎ 04 92 74 63 95, fax 04 92 74 63 94, ✉ parc.regional.verdon@wanadoo .fr), BP 14, 04360 Moustiers Ste-Marie. It opens from 10 am to 12.30 pm and from 2 to 7.30 pm.

There are small, seasonal tourist offices in La Palud-sur-Verdon (☎/fax 04 92 77 32 02) and Trigance (☎/fax 04 94 85 68 40).

HAUTE-PROVENCE AREA

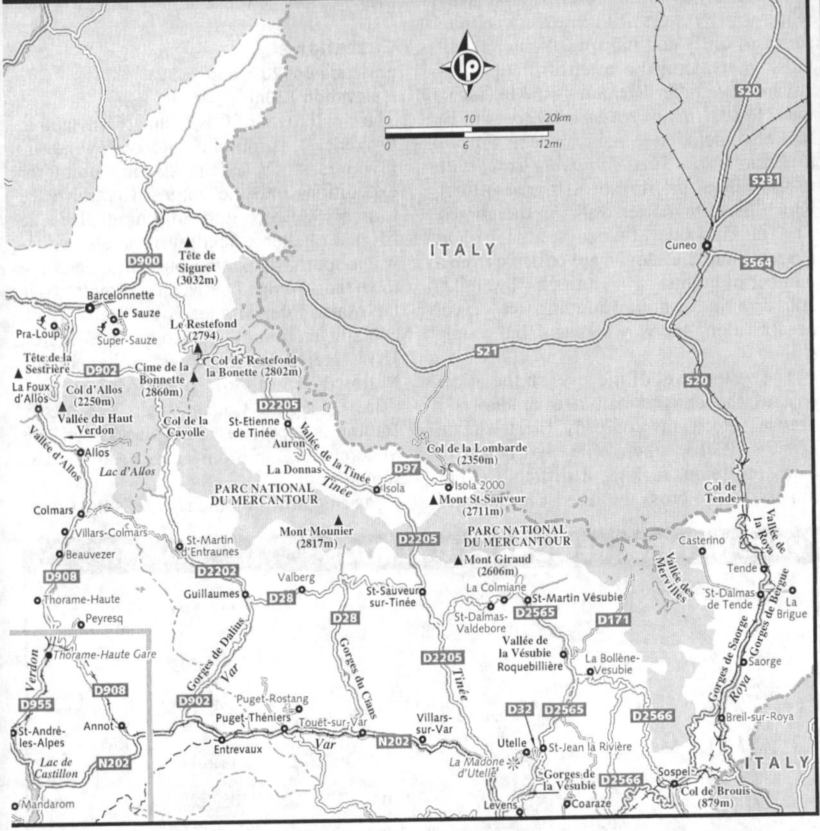

The Canyon

The bottom of the gorges can be visited on foot or by raft. Motorists and cyclists can enjoy spectacular (if dizzying) views from two cliff-side roads which link Moustiers Ste-Marie and Castellane.

The **route des Crêtes** (the D952 and D23) follows the northern rim and passes the **Point Sublime** viewpoint at the canyon's entrance, from where the GR4 trail leads to the bottom of the canyon.

The **corniche Sublime** (the D19 to the D71) skims the southern rim and takes you to such landmarks as **Balcons de la Mescla** (Mescla Terraces) and **Pont de l'Artuby**, Europe's highest bridge (182m), from which the fearless leap (see Bungee Jumping later in this chapter).

A complete circuit of the Gorges du Verdon involves about 140km of driving (around relentlessly narrow hairpins for much of the time). Castellane tourist office stocks a free English-language brochure that outlines 11 driving itineraries in the region. The only real village en route is **La Palud-sur-Verdon**, 2km north-east of the northern bank of the gorges. In summer, heavy traffic slows to a crawl.

The bottom of the canyon, first explored in its entirety in 1905, presents walkers and white-water rafters with an overwhelming series of cliffs and narrows. You can walk most of it along the often difficult GR4, covered by Didier-Richard's 1:50,000-scale map No 19, *Haute-Provence-Verdon* (70FF). It is also included in the excellent, *Canyon du Verdon – The Most Beautiful Hikes* (25FF at Castellane or Moustiers tourist office), which lists 28 shorter walks in the gorges. The full GR4 takes two days, though short descents into the canyon are possible from a number of points. Bring a torch (flashlight) and drinking water. Camping on gravel beaches along the way is illegal, but people still do it.

The water level of the river in the upper part of the canyon can rise suddenly if France's electricity company, Electricité de France (EDF), opens the hydroelectric dams upstream, making it difficult, if not impossible, to cross the river. Check water levels and weather forecasts with the tourist office before setting out.

Castellane
postcode 04120 • pop 1539
• elevation 730m

The small town of Castellane (Castelano in Provençal) is unmomentous beyond its favoured status as the starting point for expeditions into the gorges. Central place Marcel Sauvaire and adjoining place de l'Église shelter a handful of hotels, white-water sports shops, the post office and the town hall. Wedged between the latter two is the **Maison des Sirènes & Siréniens** which explains mermaid mythology. On 3 March 1815, Napoleon I stopped off at 34 rue Nationale (north off place Marcel Sauvaire), today the **Conservatoire des Arts & Traditions Populaires**. Both places open 9am to noon and 2 to 6 pm Tuesday to Sunday, summer only.

Peering down on the square is the **Chap-**

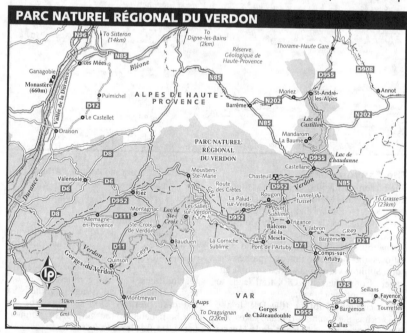

elle Notre Dame du Roc (elevation 903m), dating from 1703 and perched precariously on the 180m needle-shaped rock. A walking trail leads from place de l'Église to the rock top and chapel. Each year on 15 August (Assumption Day), pilgrims proceed up to the rock to celebrate Mass.

Four kilometres north of the town is Lac de Chaudanne and, 4km north again, Lac de Castillon (see the Lacs du Verdon section later). About 10km south of Castellane on the picturesque D955 to Trigance, is the **Moulin des Soleils** (☎ 04 94 76 92 62), one of Provence's few remaining flour mills still in operation. You can visit between 3 and 6 pm in summer. Don't leave without sampling freshly baked bread.

Moustiers Ste-Marie
postcode 04360 • pop 635
• elevation 634m

Pretty little Moustiers Ste-Marie (Moustié Santo Mario in Provençal) comprises a quaint crop of houses that nestle on a rocky shelf beneath a backdrop of two towering cliffs. A 227m-long gold chain bearing a star hangs between the rocks. The 12th-century **Chapelle Notre Dame de Beauvoir**, with its nearby waterfall, is perched on a ledge on one of the limestone cliffs. Numerous stone bridges grace the village below, through which the **Ravin de Notre Dame** streams.

In the 17th century, Moustiers earned itself European recognition for its decorative Provençal *faïence* (earthenware), a tradition that is kept alive today by a handful of potters who tend to turn out tourist souvenirs rather than works of art. The latter can be admired in the **Musée de la Faïence** (☎ 04 92 74 61 64), rue Bourgade, open 9 am to noon and 2 to 6 pm Wednesday to Monday (to 7 pm in July and August). Admission costs 10FF (seniors, students and those aged 12 to 18, 5FF).

A steep trail, with countless steps, leads from rue Bourgade to the Chapelle Notre Dame de Beauvoir, passing 14 stations of the cross en route. Count on at least one hour's walking to get to the top, from where there are breathtaking views.

JANE SMITH

Enjoy life on an inflatable in the Gorges du Verdon.

River & White-Water Sports
Most outdoor activity places have a base in Castellane: Aboard Rafting (☎/fax 04 92 83 76 11, ⓔ info@aboard-rafting.com), 8 place Marcel Sauvaire, runs two-day white-water cocktails which combine **rafting**, **canoe-rafting** and **canyoning** (650FF), six-day discovery expeditions (1290/1490FF in low/high season), and half-day canyoning, **hot-dogging** (in an inflatable canoe) and hydrospeed trips (200FF to 360FF). For adventurous cyclists, it organises **water-rambling trips** with mountain bikes (200/350FF per half-/full day). Trips must be booked in advance and you have to know how to swim but no white-water experience is necessary. Trips run April to September.

Other Castellane-based outlets, all offering similar deals, include Aqua Viva Est (☎/fax 04 92 83 75 74), 12 blvd de la République; Montagne & Rivière (☎/fax 04 92 83 67 24, ⓔ montagneriviere@wanadoo .fr), 20 rue Nationale; and Aqua Verdon (☎ 04 92 83 72 75) at 9 rue Nationale.

On route des Gorges du Verdon (the D952), 4km west of Castellane, is Acti-Raft (☎ 04 92 83 76 64, 04 92 83 76 64, ⓔ acueil @actiraft.com), an activity centre that organises rafting (200/300FF for a half-day and 500FF for a full-day expedition), hot-dogging (250FF for a half-day), canyoning (270/300FF for a half-day discovery/perfection trip), canoe-kayaking (180FF) and water-trekking (200FF).

Bungee Jumping
Marseilles-based Latitude Challenge (☎ 04 91 09 14 10), 40 ave de St-Antoine, arranges

bungee jumps off Pont de l'Artuby. A leap off Europe's highest bridge (182m) costs 590FF for the first jump, then 370FF for each subsequent jump. Jumps, which take place at 8 am, must be booked in advance; transport to the bridge is not included. You can also bungee jump in Guillaumes (see Vallée de la Tinée later in this chapter).

Places to Stay & Eat

Camping Along the approach to Castellane, the river is lined with some 15 crowded and pricey seasonal camp sites. Count on paying about 19/20/9FF per tent/person/car.

Hostels At the start of route des Crêtes, *Auberge de Jeunesse Le Trait d'Union* (☎/fax 04 92 77 38 72, route de la Maline), 500m south of La Palud-sur-Verdon, opens April to November. B&B costs 68FF or you can pitch your tent for 28FF per person per night. Non HI card-holders have to buy a one-night stamp for an extra 19FF. Sheets are 17FF. The hostel closes from 10 am to 5 pm.

Gîtes d'Étape In Trigance, *Gîte d'Étape de Fontaine Basse* (☎ 04 94 85 68 36, 04 94 85 68 60, fax 04 94 85 68 50), 16km south-east of Castellane, charges 85FF for a dorm bed (110FF for B&B) and 20FF for sheets.

In Castellane, a dorm bed at *L'Oustaou* (☎ 04 92 83 77 27, chemin des Listes) costs 75FF. It also does B&B for two/four people (220/420FF).

Chambres d'Hôtes Pays du Verdon offers ample B&B opportunities; ask at the tourist office. In the 16th-century hill-top village of Chasteuil (elevation 900m), 8km south-west of Castellane along the D952 and 2.5km north on a narrow lane, is *Gîte de Chasteuil* (☎/fax 04 92 83 72 45, ⓔ gchasteuil@apol.com). Here you can enjoy B&B in the former village schoolhouse for 225/275/365FF for one/two/three people. An evening meal without/with drinks costs an extra 65/95FF per person.

Hotels – Castellane If you are seeking wholesome mid-range accommodation then

Castellane is your place. *Grand Hôtel du Levant* (☎ 04 92 83 60 05, fax 04 92 83 72 14, place Marcel Sauvaire) is an impressive pile with particularly good-value comfortable doubles for 220FF. The equivalent at *Hôtel La Forge* (☎ 04 92 83 62 61, fax 04 92 83 65 81, place de l'Église) costs 220FF to 310FF. *Hôtel du Roc* (☎ 04 92 83 62 65), next door, touts almost identical rates.

On rue de la République, off place Marcel Sauvaire, *Hôtel du Verdon* (☎ 04 92 83 62 02, fax 04 92 83 73 80) has basic doubles costing 190FF (210FF with shower, 260FF with shower and toilet). On the same street, *Ma Petite Auberge* (☎ 04 92 83 62 06, fax 04 92 83 68 49) has bathroom-equipped doubles for 260FF.

Hotels – Moustiers Ste-Marie This village has three hotels that fill up fast and charge upwards of 280/350FF for a double in low/high season: *La Bonne Auberge* (☎ 04 92 74 66 18, route de Castellane); *Le Belvédère* (☎ 04 92 74 66 04, ave de Lérins); and pretty *Le Relais* (☎ 04 92 74 66 10, fax 04 92 74 60 47, ⓔ le.relais@wanadoo.fr, place du Couvent), which has some terrace-connected rooms with stunning views.

One of the region's most refined places to stay, which offers a rare glimpse of Provence at its most luxurious, is less than 1km from Moustiers and signposted off northbound route de Riez (the D952). *La Bastide de Moustiers* (☎ 04 92 70 47 47, fax 04 92 70 47 48, ⓔ contact@bastide-moustiers.com, chemin de Quinson), with a Web site at www.bastide-moustiers.com, is run by the French chef Alain Ducasse. The gorgeous 17th-century country house has 12 poetically named rooms (costing 900–1750FF, depending on the room and season) – the 'Poppy' room has a Starck-designed bathtub and the 'Pigeon Loft' room is in the former pigeon house. Chefs pack gourmet picnic-hampers, offer cooking lessons upon request and welcome guests to stroll around their vegetable garden. Painting and pottery workshops and truffle hunts are also possible, and there are bikes and horses on which to explore the surrounding countryside.

euro currency converter 10FF = €1.52

Hotels – South of Castellane About 10km south-east of the canyon in Comps-sur-Artuby, **Grand Hôtel Bain** (☎ 04 94 76 90 06, fax 04 94 76 92 24) has been run by the same family since 1737. Fine rooms cost 250FF to 370FF.

Big spenders should head for three-star **Château de Trigance** (☎ 04 94 76 91 18, fax 04 94 85 68 99), 16km south-east of Castellane in hill-top Trigance. Rooms with valley view in the 10th-century castle cost 750FF and the upmarket restaurant has delicious menus costing about 250FF.

Getting There & Away
Bus Public transport is limited. Autocars Sumian (☎ 04 42 67 60 34 in Jouques) runs buses from Marseilles to Castellane via Aix-en-Provence (116FF, 3½ hours, once or twice weekly), La Palud and Moustiers. VFD (☎ 04 93 85 24 56 in Nice) operate a daily bus from Grenoble to Nice via Digne-les-Bains and Grasse, stopping in Castellane en route. Tourist offices have schedules.

LACS DU VERDON
The Verdon lakes – all creations of the national electricity company – are a spectacular, sparkling green.

Lac de Ste-Croix
Pretty little **Bauduen** (pop 276) sits on the south-eastern banks of the Verdon's largest lake, Lac de Ste-Croix, which stretches for 10km south of Moustiers Ste-Marie. The huge lake, covering 2200 hectares, was created in 1974. Camp sites are dotted along the lakeside D71 and D249, which lead to the village. From the **Observatoire des Vallons** (☎ 04 94 84 39 19), on the lake's southern shore (D71) 2km west of Bauduen, you can stargaze. The small tourist offices in Bauduen (☎/fax 04 94 84 39 02), rue de Juterie, and Les Salles-sur-Verdon (☎ 04 94 70 21 84, [e] verdon83@clubinternet.fr), place Fontfreye, have details.

Ste-Croix de Verdon (pop 103, elevation 525m) is the only village on the lake's western banks. From its centre a road leads to the lake shores, where you can hire electric

boats, sailboards and catamarans. Note that Swimming from the pebble beach here is forbidden.

Lac de Quinson
Lake Quinson sits at the southernmost foot of the Basse (lower) Gorges du Verdon. The lake is crossed by the D11, the main road that cuts through **Quinson** (pop 354). A museum complex devoted to the gorges' prehistoric past and archaeological treasures, the **Musée de la Préhistoire des Gorges du Verdon** (☎ 04 02 74 09 59) is set to open in April 2001. It covers 4274 sq metres and is located at the southern end of the village (on the D11). Quinson tourist office (☎ 04 92 74 01 12) has details.

The endearing village of **Montagnac** (pop 326), 11km north of Quinson off the D11, is known for its fresh truffles, available from November to March. Eight kilometres west of Montagnac on the D111 is **Allemagne-en-Provence** (pop 384). The village adopted its German-influenced name during the Wars of Religion when the baron d'Allemagne (baron of Germany) besieged the place. Its centrepiece is the privately owned 12th- to 16th-century Château d'Allemagne (☎ 04 92 77 46 78). The donjon-style building – part fortress, part pretty palace – can be visited by guided tour at 4 and 5 pm Wednesday to Sunday, July to mid-September; and at 4 and 5 pm on weekends, April to June and mid-September to the end of October. The castle remains inhabited year round (see Chambres d'Hôtes under Places to Stay later in this section).

Lacs de Chaudanne & Castillon
The eastern end of the Gorges du Verdon is adorned with **Lac de Chaudanne**. At Chaudanne, it is possible to visit the EDF's central hydroelectric plant in July and August. Book a free guided tour of the dam (barrage) through Castellane tourist office.

Four kilometres north is **Lac de Castillon**, a steep-banked lake with little water-sport activity. You can only swim and hire paddle boats from the banks of the lake's south-western tip. From here, the single-track D402 cuts into the mountains to the walled

Cité Ste-de Mandarom Shambhasalem (Holy City of Mandarom Shambhasalem; ☎ 04 92 83 63 83, e mandarom@aumisme .org), with a Web site at www.aumisme.org. The oversized relics that glitter and sparkle from Castillon's western shores are worshipped by the Aumist cult (founded in 1969). Its burgundy robed, shaven-headed members adhere to a cocktail of world religions, considered drug-induced by locals who won their bid in August 2000 to get the cult's largest statue (33m tall) levelled. There are guided tours of the park in Eng-lish from 10 am to noon and 3 to 5 pm in summer and during school holidays, and 3 to 4 pm on weekends only in winter.

St-André-les-Alpes (postcode 04170, pop 832, elevation 914m) kisses the northern tip of Lac de Castillon and is among France's leading paragliding centres. Amateurs and experts alike can spread their wings at Aérogliss (☎ 04 92 89 11 30, fax 04 92 89 02 36, e aerogliss@aerogliss.com) on chemin des Iscles at the southern end of the village. Initiation courses cost 2400/2600FF in low/high season for five days.

Along the Mountain Railway

The *Chemin de Fer* Digne–Nice railway chugs from the sea to the mountains, crossing five valleys en route and affording breathtaking views of dramatic landscapes scarcely navigable by road.

The 150km narrow-gauge track was built between 1890 and 1911, and passes through 25 tunnels, across 16 viaducts and 15 metal bridges on its adventurous mountain journey. From May to October, passengers can enjoy a blast from the past along part of the route with the **Train des Pignes**, a steam locomotive dating from 1909. It used to be fuelled by pine cones *(pignes)*, hence its pretty name.

Eastbound, the scenic journey takes you from Digne-les-Bains through **St-André-les-Alpes** (50 minutes), stopping at a sprinkling of tiny villages on the way. In St-André, you can paraglide, walk around Lac de Castillon and feast on wild boar sausages (see the Lacs de Verdon section earlier in this chapter). The next stop is **Thorame-Haute** (11 minutes), a village (pop 174, elevation 1012m) at the foot of the Vallée du Haut Verdon, which despite its pinprick size serves as a vital link on bus routes between southern Provence and the Allos ski resorts. The bus stop is in front of the crumbling old train station on the D955. After Thorame-Haute, the Col de St-Michel (1431m) and the ancient shepherdry village of **Peyresq** flash past the train window. The 3.5km-long tunnel here took 400 workers some two years to construct.

Annot (pop 1020, elevation 700m) is the next halt. The village is known for its *grès d'Annot*, a haphazard arrangement of bizarre rock formations that can be explored on foot. Exploratory walks are featured in the free brochure *Rando Train: Les Randonées des Chemins de Fer de Provence*. Annot tourist office (☎ 04 92 83 23 03) is five minutes' walk from the station on blvd St-Pierre.

Entrevaux (pop 752), 7km farther east, is an impressive hill-top village that tumbles down the steep hillside from the Vauban-built citadel. Across the drawbridge, outside the 17th-century fortifications surrounding the village, is an oil and flour mill that can be visited. Ask the tourist office (☎ 04 93 05 46 73), inside the old city gate, for details.

The elegant *train à vapeur* (steam train) is stationed at **Puget-Théniers** (pop 1624), eight minutes east of Entrevaux and 25 minutes from Annot. Between May and October it shunts its way between Puget and Annot (110FF return, 50 minutes). Annot tourist office has details. In Puget, passengers seeking some hearty Haute-Provence fodder should head for the charming *Auberge des Acacias* (☎ 04 93 05 05 25), 1km from the village on the N202 (get off at 'Le Planet' train stop).

Picking up the eastward trail again, you reach the mountain villages of **Touët-sur-Var** (pop 445) and **Villars-sur-Var** (pop 584) before plunging south along the Var through **St-Martin du Var** and **Colmars** (pop 385) to Nice. The entire trip from Digne-les-Bains to Nice (111/218FF one-way/return) takes 3¼ hours.

Further course details are posted on its Web site at www.aerogliss.com; alternatively contact St-André tourist office (☎ 04 92 89 02 39, fax 04 92 89 19 23), place Marcel Pastorelli. Local culinary specialities sold at the Maison du Saucisson (☎ 04 92 89 03 16), place du Verdun, include *âne* (donkey) and *sanglier* (wild boar) sausage.

St-André is linked with eastern Provence and the coastal resort of Nice by the narrow-gauge **Chemin de Fer** (see the boxed text 'Along the Mountain Railway' on the previous page for details).

Places to Stay & Eat
Camping There are numerous camp sites in and around Ste-Croix de Verdon. Castellane tourist office has details.

Campers wanting to bare it all can try the *Centre Naturiste* (☎/fax 04 92 83 64 24, fax 04 92 83 68 79, La Grande Terre), signposted off the D402 in La Baume. The nudist centre charges 44FF per person to pitch a tent or park a caravan (20/10% less in low/mid-season). It also has four-berth caravans to rent (206FF for two people). The camp site opens Easter to September.

Camping Les Iscles (☎ 04 92 89 02 29, chemin des Iscles), in St-André-les-Alpes next to the paragliding school, charges 59FF for a car, tent and two people. It opens April to September.

Gîtes d'Étape In La Baume (elevation 1150m), 2km south of the 'Holy City' on the D402 and 9km north of Castellane, is *Au Soleil Gourmand* (☎/fax 04 92 83 70 82). The gîte affords lovely views of Lac de Castillon and has dorm beds for 60FF; doubles/quads cost 200/400FF.

St-André-les-Alpes has a well-located gîte d'étape, *Les Cougnas* (☎ 04 92 89 18 78), from where you can watch paragliders plop down from the sky. A bed costs 65FF and breakfast costs 25FF.

Some 3km to the west along the N202 in Moriez is *Le Château* (☎/fax 0 92 89 13 20, 🄴 moriez@club-internet.fr), a large gîte d'étape with dorm beds for 70FF and breakfast/dinner for 25/75FF (including a 25cl pichet of wine).

Chambres d'Hôtes & Hotels *Château d'Allemagne* (☎ 04 92 77 46 78, fax 04 92 77 73 84), in Allemagne-en-Provence, offers B&B in a well-preserved 12th- to 16th-century chateau. Its three luxurious doubles cost 600FF to 900FF.

Bauduen, Ste-Croix de Verdon and Montagnac each have a couple of hotels. In St-André, *Hôtel de France* (☎ 04 92 89 02 09, place de l'Église) has shower-equipped singles/doubles for 130/160FF. Lakeside *Hôtel Lac et Forêt* (☎ 04 92 89 07 38, fax 04 92 89 13 88, route de Nice), just south of the village, has unbeatable doubles for 150FF with toilet and washbasin, 250FF with shower, 280FF with shower and lake view. Rooms for three or four cost 300FF. The hotel opens from mid-December to mid-November.

DIGNE-LES-BAINS
postcode 04000 • pop 17,680
• elevation 608m
The land of snow and melted cheese meets the land of sun and olives around Digne-les-Bains (Digno in Provençal). The town is named after its thermal springs, visited annually by 11,000 people seeking a water cure for rheumatism, respiratory ailments and other medical conditions.

Digne itself is unremarkable, although it was home to a remarkable woman, Alexandra David-Neel, whose travels to Tibet brought her wide acclaim. The shale around Digne is rich in fossils and is protected by the Réserve Géologique de Haute-Provence (150,000 hectares). The area is also known for its production of *lavande* (lavender), usually harvested in July or August and honoured in Digne with the five-day Corso de la Lavande, starting the first weekend of August. Throughout the region the little purple flower is celebrated with Les Journées Lavande in mid-August. In spring, flowering poppies sprinkle the green fields with blood-red buttons.

Route Napoléon (the N85), which Bonaparte followed in 1815 on his way to Paris after his escape from Elba, passes though Digne-les-Bains. The northbound D900 takes you past the mountain village of **La**

Javie to **Seyne-les-Alpes** (pop 1230, elevation 1200m), 42km north in the Vallée de la Blanche, where you can ski in winter.

Orientation

Digne-les-Bains is built on the eastern bank of the shallow River Bléone. The major roads into town converge at rond point du 11 Novembre 1918, 400m north-east of the train station. The main street is blvd Gassendi, which heads north-eastwards from the roundabout and passes large place du Général de Gaulle, the town's main public square.

Information

The tourist office (☎ 04 92 36 62 62, fax 04 92 32 27 24, ⓔ info@ot-dignelesbains.fr), on place du Tampinet (overlooking rond point du 11 Novembre 1918), opens 8.45 am to noon and 2 to 6.30 pm Monday to Saturday, and 10.30 am to noon on Sunday, May to October; 8.45 am to noon and 2 to 6 pm Monday to Saturday, the rest of the year. Its Web site is at www.ot-dignelesbains.fr.

Banque de France, 16 blvd Soustre, exchanges money 8.45 am to noon weekdays. The post office is at 4 rue André Honnorat and opens 8 am to 8.30 pm weekdays, 8 am to noon on Saturday. You can log-in for 40FF per hour at Cyber Games Café (ⓔ cyber .games@wanadoo.fr), 48 rue de l'Hubac, open 10 am to 8 pm Tuesday to Saturday.

Musée Alexandra David-Néel

Paris-born writer and philosopher Alexandra David-Néel (1868–1969), who spent her last years in Digne (reaching the ripe old age of 101), is known for her early-20th-century incognito voyage to Tibet. Her memory and all-consuming passion for Tibet are kept alive by the Musée Alexandra David-Néel (☎ 04 92 31 32 38, ⓔ neel@ alexandra-david-neel.org), which occupies her erstwhile residence at 27 ave Maréchal Juin. The Journées Tibetaines, an annual celebration of Tibetan culture, is held in August.

The museum is just over 1km from town on the Nice-bound N85. Guided tours depart at 10.30 am, and 2, 3.40 and 5 pm, July

to September; and at 10.30 am, 2 and 4 pm, the rest of the year. Admission is free. By bus, take TUD bus No 3 to the Stade Rolland stop.

Réserve Géologique de Haute-Provence

Digne-les-Bains is in the middle of the Réserve Géologique de Haute-Provence, whose spectacular fossil deposits include the footprints of prehistoric birds as well as ammonites (spiral shells that look something like a ram's horn). You'll need a detailed regional map or topoguide (sold at the tourist office) to the Digne and Sisteron areas and your own transport (or a patient thumb) to get to the 18 sites. Most of the sites are around **Barles** (pop 114), 24km north of Digne, and **Barrême** (pop 442), 28km south-east. There's an impressive limestone slab with some 500 ammonites 3km north of Digne on the road to Barles.

The reserve is headquartered in the **Centre de Géologie** (☎ 04 92 36 70 70, ⓔ regeol@calvanet.calvacom.fr), 2km north of town off the road to Barles in St-Benoît. Its mineral and geological exhibits can be viewed 9 am to noon and 2 to 5.30 pm weekdays (to 4.30 pm on Friday), April to October; and 9 am to noon and 2 to 5.30 pm weekdays (to 4.30 pm on Friday), the rest of the year. Admission costs 25FF (students 18FF, children aged seven to 15, 15FF). Take TUD bus No 2 to the Champourcin stop (across the bridge), then take the road to the left. Cars aren't allowed up, making it a 15-minute walk along the rocky overhang above the river.

Activities

Between mid-February and early December, you can enjoy a **thermal bath** (29° to 49°C) at Digne's Établissement Thermal (☎ 04 92 32 32 92, ⓔ thermes_digne@ wanadoo.fr), 3km east of Digne centre. Voyeurs rather than *curistes* (people taking the waters) can join a free tour at 2 pm on Thursday, March to August and November. The thermal establishment also organises **cycling** trips around Digne.

The more active can take to the skies, solo

Cyclists get everywhere in the Lubéron.

Sip a Côte du Lubéron in hill-top Menerbes.

Walk among cliffs of red ochre in the Lubéron – Provence's Colorado.

INGRID RODDIS

Gorges du Verdon is Europe's largest canyon.

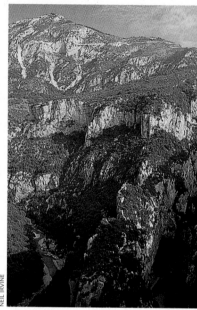

NEIL IRVINE

Giddy heights at the Balcons de la Mescla

NICOLA WILLIAMS

The town of Saorge sits snugly in its hillside cradle, Haute-Provence.

or in tandem, with Une Autre Dimension (☎/fax 04 92 32 42 06, e parapente .dinovol@wanadoo.fr), a **paragliding** school, which has an office in town at 9 rue de Provence and its base at 10 ave du Maréchal Juin (route de Nice). A full-day's paragliding (*parapente*) costs 450FF. A *vol biplace découverte* (tandem discovery flight), which allows you an approximate 15-minute aerial view of Digne-les-Bains, costs 300/450FF.

Mountain walks and **guided walks** with donkeys are also arranged by *Refuge-Hôtel Le Chalet (☎ 04 92 35 04 08, fax 04 92 35 7 46, Le Grand Puy)* in the mountain resort of Seyne-les-Alpes, 41km north of Digne.

Places to Stay & Eat
Bookings for gîtes ruraux and chambres d'hôtes in the Alpes de Haute-Provence department can be made through Gîtes de France (☎ 04 92 31 52 39, fax 04 92 32 32 63), in the tourist office building. It opens 8 am to noon and 2 to 6 pm (to 5 pm on Friday) weekdays, 9 am to noon and 2 to 6 pm on Saturday.

Camping du Bourg (☎ 04 92 31 04 87, route de Barcelonnette), almost 2km northeast of Digne, opens April to October and charges 65FF for two people with a car and tent or caravan (60FF if you're taking a cure at the Éstablissement Thermal). Take bus No 2 to the Notre Dame du Bourg stop, from where it is a 600m walk.

Camping des Eaux Chaudes (☎ 04 92 32 31 04, route des Thermes) touts similar rates.

Walkers can use *Gîte du Château des Sièyes (☎ 04 92 31 20 30, ave Georges Pompidou)* in Les Sièyes, 1.5km north-west of the centre off the road to Sisteron. A dorm bed costs 55FF. Take Sisteron-bound bus No 1 to the Pompidou stop.

Hotel-wise, *Hôtel du Petit St-Jean (☎ 04 92 31 30 04, fax 04 92 36 05 80, 14 cours des Arès)* has singles/doubles for 120/140FF (130/150FF with washbasin and bidet, 160/190FF with shower). Triples cost 190/240FF without/with shower. *Menus* in its terrace restaurant overlooking place du Général de Gaulle start at 57FF; it serves *aïoli Provençal complet* on Friday. See the

Food & Wine special section earlier in the book for details.

Two-star *Hôtel Central (☎ 04 92 31 31 91, fax 04 92 31 49 78, 26 blvd Gassendi)* has doubles costing 150FF (195FF with shower, 260FF with shower and toilet). Reception is on the 1st floor; guests need a code to enter after dark. *Hôtel Le Coin Fleuri (☎ 04 92 31 04 51, fax 04 92 32 55 75, 9 blvd Victor Hugo)* sports functional doubles costing 220FF (300FF including shower). It also has a garden.

A *food market* fills place du Général de Gaulle on Wednesday and Saturday mornings.

Getting There & Away
Bus The bus station (☎ 04 92 31 50 00), place du Tampinet, is behind the tourist office. Several companies operate buses to/from Nice (83FF, 2¼ hours, one or two daily), Aix-en-Provence (63FF, 2¼ hours) and Marseilles (80FF, two hours, two to four daily).

Services inland include to/from Castellane (65FF, one hour, twice daily) via St-André-les-Alpes; La Foux d'Allos (65FF, two hours, two or three weekly during the ski season, July and August) via Colmars and Allos; Barcelonnette (51FF, 1½ hours, one bus daily); Manosque (32FF, 1¼ hours, two to four daily); and Apt (63FF, two hours, twice daily).

Between Christmas and Easter (during the ski season), SCAL (☎ 04 92 51 06 05 in Gap) runs a daily bus in either direction between Marseilles and Pra-Loup (124FF, 3¾ hours), via Digne-les-Bains and Barcelonnette. Transporting a pair of skis costs 15FF.

Train From the train station, a 10-minute walk west of the tourist office on ave Pierre Sémard, four daily trains serve Marseilles (115FF, 2¼ hours).

In addition to SNCF trains, Digne-les-Bains is served by two-car diesel trains, operated by the privately owned Chemins de Fer de la Provence (☎ 04 92 31 01 58 in Digne), which chug along a scenic and winding narrow-gauge line from Digne to

Nice, stopping at various lovely villages en route (see the boxed text 'Along the Mountain Railway' earlier in this chapter).

VALLÉE DE LA DURANCE

The Durance Valley ploughs along Haute-Provence's western fringes. The River Durance, an affluent of the Rhône, follows a 324km course from its source in the southern Alps to the Camargue delta. Its impetuous waters, slammed by Frédéric Mistral in the 19th century as one of Provence's great three curses (along with the Aix Parliament and the mistral wind), were partly tamed by the EDF in the 1960s. Canals snake the length of the Vallée de la Durance, as does the noisy A51 autoroute.

Manosque, on the eastern edge of the Lubéron (see that chapter) and **Sisteron**, 50km farther north on the confluence of the Rivers Durance and Buëch, are the two main towns along this 100km stretch. East of Manosque is the **Plateau de Valensole**. The D6 cuts across the plateau to **Valensole** (pop 2358) and offers sweeping views of the vast lavender farms for which the area is famed. Valensole celebrates a Fête de la Lavande on the 3rd Sunday in July; its annual Fête du Goût (literally 'festival of taste') in October or November is a good chance to taste lavender honey.

Sisteron (pop 7232, elevation 485m) is shabby and unstartling beyond its 13th- to 16th-century **Château de Sisteron**, perched on a rock above the *cluse* (transverse valley) in which sunken Sisteron sits. It hosts open-air concerts during the Nuits de la Citadelle (☎ 04 92 61 06 00 for information) in July and August. The only other lure is its **Musée Terre & Temps** (Museum of Earth & Time; ☎ 04 92 61 61 30), 6 place du Général de Gaulle, which is part of the Réserve Géologique de Haute-Provence (see that section earlier). The museum opens April to September.

In Les Mées (pop 2973), 20km south of Sisteron, is the **Rocher des Mées**, a geological wonder comprising a row of rocky pinnacles that stand 100m tall. According to legend, the rock formations, also called Les Pénitents des Mées, were created from a gaggle of monks who were turned to stone for lusting after Saracen women. Walking trails lead around the rocks, signposted from the village square in Les Mées. The 10th-century **Monastère Notre Dame** (☎ 04 92 68 00 04) in Ganagobie (pop 94), 10km south on the western bank of the Durance, is also worth visiting. The 12th-century floor mosaic, the largest of its kind in France, which carpets the altar in its chapel is exquisite. The Benedictine monastery opens 3 to 5.30 pm Tuesday to Sunday in summer, and 3 to 5 pm Tuesday to Sunday in winter. It hosts stained-glass workshops (see Ateliers de Vitrail under Courses in the Facts for the Visitor chapter).

Forcalquier
pop 4375 • elevation 550m

Forcalquier sits atop its rocky perch 20km south-west of Ganagobie. Fields of sunflowers blossom at its feet. Steep steps lead to the citadel and octagonal shape chapel, at the top of the village, where carillon concerts are held in summer. The tourist office (☎ 04 92 75 10 02, ℮ oti.forcalquier@wanadoo.fr), 8 place du Bourget, overlooking the Gothic **Église Notre Dame**, has details. Forcalquier's **cemetery** – sectioned off with 5m-high hedges, 1km north of the centre on place du Souvenir Français – is France's only *cimitière classé* (listed cemetery).

Fiery liqueurs such as La Farigoule (thyme liqueur), *amandine* (almond liqueur) and *eau de vie de poires* (pear brandy) have been distilled at the **Distillerie Domaine de Haute-Provence** since 1898. Buy a bottle at the distillery shop, 9 ave St-Promasse, or sample one as an aperitif at *Le Lapin Tant Pis*, an inspired village restaurant run by quirky French chef Gérard Vives (see the Food & Wine special section earlier in the book for details).

The **Prieuré de Salagon** (☎ 04 92 75 70 50), 4km south in Mane, is a 13th-century priory on a farm estate. It houses the Musée-Conservatoire Ethnologique de la Haute-Provence, which works towards the preservation of the region's ethnographical heritage. Aromatic herbs used for traditional remedies grow in its medieval garden

A Delicious Detour

From Forcalquier, a tasty detour can be made to the cheesy town of **Banon** (pop 940), unremarkable save its culinary pleasures and blazing lavender fields that carpet its southern foot.

Banon is a type of cheese that comes exquisitely wrapped in a chestnut leaf. Traditionally made from goats' milk *(chèvre)* in summer and sheep's milk *(brebis)* in winter, the 6cm- to 8cm-diameter and 3cm-thick cheese patties can taste mild *(doux)* or strong *(fort)*, depending on the ripening process. A *Banon à la feuille* is dipped in *eau de vie* before being packaged in its leaf. In July each year Banon celebrates a Fête du Fromage (cheese fair).

The **Fromagerie de Banon** (☎ 04 92 73 25 03), route de Carniol, makes the best Banon. Its cheeses are sold in town at **Chez Melchio** (☎ 04 92 73 23 05), a not-to-be-missed charcuterie and épicerie on place de la République, the central square. Cheese-aside, Maurice Melchio cooks up *brandilles* – extraordinary, long (about 60cm) and skinny goat or donkey sausages, flavoured with pine kernels, walnuts or herbs. The sausages weigh in at 160FF per kilo and can be bought by mail order (140/250FF for five/10 sausages), within France. Chez Melchio opens 7 am to 12.30 pm and 2.30 to 7 pm on Monday and Wednesday to Saturday.

Delicious homecooking – often Banon-inspired – can be tucked into at rural *Le Moulin* (☎ 04 92 73 38 54), an old farmhouse 15km east of Banon along the D950 and D12 in Lardiers. B&B costs 140/240FF for one/two people (half-board costs 250FF per person). The Mill has bikes to rent (30FF per hour) and horses to ride (50FF per hour). In Banon itself, *Hôtel Les Voyageurs (☎ 04 92 73 21 022, place de la République)* has basic doubles costing 180FF (250FF with bathroom).

Banon is 25km north-west of Forcalquier along the winding D950; the two towns are not linked by public transport.

and *senteurs* (perfumes) typical to Provence – lavender, mint, mugwort, sage – fill its Jardin de Senteurs. Unique exhibitions are held in the priory, open 10 am to noon and 2 to 7 pm, May to September; 2 to 6 pm in October; and 2 to 6 pm, weekends only, the rest of the year. Admission costs 28FF (students 16FF).

Observatories

The **Observatoire de Haute-Provence** (☎ 04 92 70 64 00, fax 04 92 76 62 95), 10km south-west of Forcalquier at the end of the D305 from St-Michel l'Observatoire, is a national research centre that can be visited by a 30-minute guided tour at 2 and 4 pm on Wednesday, April to September; and at 3 pm on Wednesday, the rest of the year. Tours cost 15FF (children aged six to 12, 10FF). The observatory has a Web site at www.obs-hp.fr (French only).

From St-Michel l'Observatoire, the eastbound D5 races past the **Centre d'Astronomie** (☎ 04 92 76 69 09, e centre.astro @wanadoo.fr), an astronomy centre that or-

ganises star-filled, multimedia events and educational workshops in summer. Learn how to watch stars with the naked eye and through telescopes at 8.30 pm or 9 pm on Tuesday, Thursday and Friday, in July and August. It costs 50FF (children aged six to 12, 40FF); wear warm clothes. More details are on the Internet at www.astrosurf.com /centre.astro (French only).

Accommodation is available in St-Michel l'Observatoire at friendly *Hôtel l'Observatoire (☎/fax 04 92 76 63 62, place de la Fontaine)*. Singles/doubles cost 150/180FF, and its simple yet satisfying dishes served on its pavement terrace are well worth a nibble.

Getting There & Away

There are buses from Sisteron bus station (☎ 04 92 61 22 18) to/from Marseilles (82FF, two hours, four daily), Aix-en-Provence (65FF, 2½ hours, four daily), and Nice (111FF, 3¾ hours, one daily) via Digne-les-Bains (23FF to 42FF, 45 minutes).

From Forcalquier, Autocars Sumian (☎ 04 91 49 44 25 in Marseilles) runs three daily buses to/from Manosque (35 minutes, three daily), Aix-en-Provence (52FF, 1½ hours) and Marseilles (60FF, two hours). There are other daily services to/from Sisteron (☎ 04 92 75 33 74) and Avignon (two hours).

St-Michel l'Observatoire is accessible by one daily bus from Manosque (25FF, 30 minutes) and Forcalquier (12FF, 15 minutes).

PARC NATIONAL DU MERCANTOUR

The Mercantour National Park is Provence at its most majestic. Its uninhabited heart covers 68,500 hectares in the north-east of the region and embraces six valleys. The park kisses Italy's Parco Naturale delle Alpi Marittime to the east and is surrounded by a 146,500-hectare partially protected and inhabited peripheral zone.

Europe's highest mountain pass *(col)* strides through the Vallé de l'Ubaye, the park's most northern and wildest valley. Come winter, the Ubaye and its southern sisters, the Haut Verdon and Tinée Valleys, offer fine skiing. Farther south sits the Vésubie, Merveilles and Roya Valleys – a heady mix of gorges, ageless rocks and white waters, all within easy reach of the Côte d'Azur.

The national park has information offices in Barcelonnette, St-Martin-Vésubie and Tende, and summer bureaux in St-Sauveur-sur-Tinée and at Lac d'Allos. The park's headquarters are in Nice (see the Nice to Menton chapter). It has a Web site at www.parc-mercantour.fr.

Vallée de L'Ubaye

The River Ubaye, a tributary of the Durance, skirts Provence's northern tip between Lac de Serre-Poncon and Barcelonnette. Along with the Verdon, it offers some top white-water rafting. The Ubaye Valley, a desolate place shielded by the southern Alps, is sandwiched between the Parc Régional du Queyras to the north and the Parc National du Mercantour to the south. It is crossed by

the D900, which closely shadows the river-banks.

Barcelonnette (postcode 04400, pop 3316, elevation 1135m), founded by the count of Barcelona in 1231, is the only town in the valley and is a good base for expeditions up the surrounding ski slopes and down the River Ubaye. From the 18th century until WWII, some 5000 Barcelonnetais followed in the footsteps of the enterprising Arnaud brothers who emigrated to Mexico in 1805 to seek their fortunes in the silk and wool-weaving industry. Their colourful history, and that of the valley, unfolds in the **Musée de la Vallée** (☎ 04 92 81 27 15), in a sumptuous Mexican-inspired villa (1878–80), built by a returned emigré, at 10 ave de la Libération.

Information In Barcelonnette, the Maison de la Vallée de l'Ubaye (☎ 04 92 81 03 68, fax 04 92 81 51 67, e ubaye@laposte.fr), 4 ave des Trois Frères Arnaud, has information on the valley, also available on its Web site at www.ubaye.com. Barcelonnette tourist office (☎ 04 92 81 04 71, fax 04 92 81 22 67, e info@barcelonnette.net), place Frédéric Mistral, opens 9 am to noon and 2 to 6.30 pm Monday to Saturday. Its Web site is at www.barcelonnette.net.

The tourist office has a list of guides who organise walks, VTT and canoeing trips. From 15 June to 15 September, the Parc National du Mercantour (☎ 04 92 81 21 31) has an office on the ground floor of the Musée de la Vallée, 10 ave de la Libération, open 10 am to noon and 3 to 7 pm.

River & White-Water Sports Numerous canoe-rental places line the D900 between Le Lauzet-Ubaye (pop 207) and Barcelonnette. In **Le Martinet**, just south of the D900, 8km east of Le Lauzet-Ubaye, is AN Rafting (☎ 04 92 85 54 90) and the Maison du Rafting (☎ 04 92 85 53 99), with a Web site at www.maison-du-rafting.fr (French only). Both bases arrange rafting (210/190FF for 2½ hours in low/high season), hot-dogging (210FF), canyoning (370FF a day) and so on from April to October. Adventure Rio Raft (☎ 04 92 81 91 15), next to Camping du Rioclar in **Méolans-Revel**

(pop 293), 12km west of Barcelonnette, sports similar rates.

Cycling The Vallée de l'Ubaye is linked to the outside world by seven mountain passes. Cyclists tough enough to conquer them all, including Col de Restefond la Bonette – Europe's highest road at 2808m – are given a medal; the Maison de la Vallée de l'Ubaye in Barcelonnette has details.

Hire a mountain bike in Le Lauzet-Ubaye from Le Relais du Lac (☎ 04 92 85 51 07) for 30/100FF per hour/day. In Le Martinet, both white-water sports bases (see the previous section) rent mountain bikes (50/30FF per hour for adults/children) and offer guided trips (180FF); Maison du Rafting has a special mini-VTT course for kids aged five to 11; and 20km of forest trails, 1.7km of downhill tracks and a 500m bi-cross (scramble) circuit for adult riders. Camping du Rioclar, in Méolans-Revel, rents regular bikes for 120FF per day.

Skiing Pra-Loup is the main resort, 8.5km south-west of Barcelonnette, connected by a lift system across the Vallon des Agneliers with La Foux d'Allos ski resort in the Vallée du Haut-Verdon (see that section later). Pra-Loup has 167km of runs, served by 53 lifts best suited for intermediate and advanced skiers. Neighbouring Super-Sauze (1400m) has 65km of pistes, three chair lifts and 21 drag lifts.

A six-day Ski Pass Vallée covering the above resorts plus Ste-Anne La Condamine (1800m) costs 692/841FF in low/high season (those aged over 60 and children aged five to 12, 533/631FF). The École du Ski Français (ESF; ☎ 04 92 84 11 05 in Pra-Loup, ☎ 04 92 81 05 20 in Sauze) charges around 600FF for six group lessons. Skis, boots and poles can be hired for 150FF per day.

Pra-Loup tourist office (☎ 04 92 84 10 04, fax 04 92 84 02 93, einfo@praloup.com) in the Maison de Pra-Loup opens 9 am to 7 pm. Visit online at www.praloup.com.

Places to Stay You can pitch your tent by the river next to the Maison du Rafting in Le Martinet for 30FF per person (free hot showers). In Méolans-Revel, *Camping du Rioclar* (☎ 04 92 31 20 30, ave Georges Pompidou) opens in summer only. *Domaine Loisirs de l'Ubaye* (☎ 04 92 81 01 96, 04 92 81 92 53) has four-person chalets to rent for 1800/1400FF per week in. A double room in a chalet with a shower costs 200FF per night.

The tourist offices have accommodation lists for the ski resorts. Hotels in Barcelonnette include *Grand Hôtel* (☎ 04 92 81 03 14, 6 place de la Poste) where doubles with washbasin cost 170FF; and 18-room *Hôtel du Cheval Blanc* (☎ 04 92 81 00 19, fax 04 92 81 15 39, 12 rue Grenette), which has bathroom-equipped doubles costing 280FF.

Getting There & Away The nearest train station is Gap (outside Provence), 60km north, from where there are a couple of buses daily to Pra-Loup (50FF, 1½ hours) via Barcelonnette.

SCAL (☎ 04 92 81 00 20 in Barcelonnette, ☎ 04 92 51 06 05 in Gap) runs buses from Barcelonnette to Gap, Marseilles and Digne-les-Bains. From Christmas and Easter during the ski season, there are direct buses between Pra-Loup and Marseilles (124FF, 3¾ hours), departing daily from Marseilles at 7 am and from Pra-Loup at 3.55 pm. Transporting skis costs 15FF.

Buses in the Vallée de l'Ubaye are operated by Autocars Maurel (☎ 04 92 81 20 09). There are three Barcelonnette–La Martinet buses a day, and four daily shuttle buses between Barcelonnette and Sauze (10FF). Shuttle buses between Sauze (3.5km south of Barcelonnette) and Super-Sauze (5km farther south) are free.

Vallée du Haut Verdon

The breathtaking **Col d'Allos** (2250m) links Vallée de l'Ubaye with its southern neighbour, the Vallée du Haut Verdon, which penetrates the Parc National du Mercantour. The mighty River Verdon has its source here at La Tête de la Sestrière (2572m).

Immediately after crossing the mountain pass (snow-blocked in winter), you arrive at the unattractive ski resort of **La Foux d'Allos** (elevation 1800m), 23.5km south of Pra-Loup and connected by cable car. The tourist office (☎ 04 92 83 02 81, fax 04 92 83 86 27), in the Maison de la Foux on the main square, posts information on its Web site at www.valdallos.com. In the upper part of the village near the main lift stations, the *Auberge de Jeunesse (☎ 04 92 83 81 08, fax 04 92 83 83 70)* charges 90FF for a dorm bed in summer and around 2000FF for a one-week skiing package.

Allos (pop 650, elevation 1400m), 8km farther south on the D908, bears the same architectural stamp as its ugly sister and is as deserted outside of the ski season, with the exception of July and August when hotels reopen their doors to walkers. Call ☎ 92 83 02 81 for the tourist office.

Lac d'Allos, 12km east of Allos along the D226, is the valley's main draw in summer. From Parking du Laus, the car park at the end of the road on Plateau du Laus, trails lead to Lac d'Allos (2226m), which is Europe's largest Alpine lake, at 62 hectares. Smaller **Lac de la Petite Cayolle** and **Lac des Garrets** are also accessible on foot. Route maps and walking information are available from the Parc National du Mercantour office that operates from the car park in July and August. Guided nature walks can be booked through the tourist office in Allos or La Foux d'Allos.

Lower down the valley, the villages of **Colmars** (pop 385) and **Beauvezer** (pop 287) are ideal retreats for walkers or skiers keen to escape the crowds. Colmars, 24km south of Allos and 28km north of St-André-les-Alpes (see the Lacs du Verdon section earlier in this chapter), is a pretty fortified village graced by high thick walls built by Vauban.

For regional information, go to the Maison de Pays de Haut Verdon (☎ 04 92 83 47 84, fax 04 92 83 50 43) in Beauvezer.

Getting There & Away Autocars Girieud (☎ 04 92 83 40 27 in Colmar-les-Alpes) runs buses from Digne-les-Bains to La Foux d'Allos (two hours, twice daily), 9km south-east of the actual resort, stopping at St-André, Thorame-Haute Gare, Colmars and Allos.

From Nice, you can take the Chemin de Fer railway to Thorame-Haute Gare (see the boxed text 'Along the Mountain Railway' earlier in this chapter), from where you can get a bus. In addition to the two Digne–La Foux buses, there are three daily buses between Thorame-Haute Gare and Allos.

Vallée de la Tinée

Europe's highest mountain pass, the **Col de Restefond la Bonette**, which peaks at 2802m, links Barcelonnette and the Vallée de l'Ubaye with the tamer, more southern Vallée de la Tinée. In winter, when the snowy pass is closed (November to June most years), the 149km-long Tinée Valley can only be accessed up its southern leg from Nice. The narrow road (D2205) is laced with hairpins and wiggles along the French-Italian border for the duration of its journey from the mountain pass to **Isola** (875m), where it plummets sharply south towards the coast.

The steep D97 makes an eastbound climb to **Isola 2000** (pop 536, elevation 2000m), a horrible purpose-built ski resort from where the **Col de la Lombarde** (2350m) crosses into Italy. It offers good skiing, although the snow can be heavy. Isola 2000, 15km of hairpins from Isola and 93km north of Nice, opens December to May and in summer from mid-June to early September. Its 120km of pistes are served by 23 lifts and are suitable for skiers and snowboarders of all levels. A five-day ski pass costs 490/570FF in low/high season.

St-Étienne de Tinée (pop 1684), 15km north of Isola village on the D2205, is a lovely Alpine village offering endless walking opportunities in summer around the Cime de la Bonette (2860m). Thrill-seekers can scale new heights here at the **Via Ferrata d'Auron**; Auron tourist office (☎ 04 93 23 02 66) has details. Southbound, the road twists through the beautiful Gorges de Valabres to **St-Sauveur-sur-Tinée** (pop 459, elevation 490m), a gateway to the Parc National du Mercantour. Three kilometres south on the D2205 is the **Ouvrage de la Frassinea**, a bunker cut in the rock during WWI to control the entrance to the valley.

West from St-Sauveur along the torturous D30, you can access the spectacular **Gorges du Cians** and parallel **Gorges de Dalius**. Both gorges are carved from burgundy-coloured rock. The Gardienne des Gorges, a rock naturally shaped to form a woman's head, guards the northern entrance to the Dalius gorges. Nearby, thrill-seekers **bungee jump** from Pont de la Mariée, an 80m-high stone footbridge across the gorges. In April, May, June and September, jumps must be booked in advance (☎ 04 93 73 50 29, 06 07 56 07 30). In July and August, jumpers can jump for 350FF between 9 am and 5 pm; just turn up at the bridge.

Information Isola 2000 tourist office (☎ 04 93 23 15 15, fax 04 93 23 14 25, e isola@cote-dazur.com) is inside the Galerie Marchande high rise complex, which also houses the ESF (☎ 04 93 23 28 00) in winter and a Parc National du Mercantour bureau in summer. Visit online at www .isola-2000.com (French only). The ESF organises ski-touring in the park and also heli-skiing.

In summer, the Mercantour has an office in St-Sauveur-sur-Tinée (☎ 04 93 02 01 63), on the banks of the Tinée at 11 ave des Blavets.

Places to Stay Nine *gîtes ruraux* around Isola can be booked through the Gîtes de France office in Nice (see Accommodation in the Facts for the Visitor chapter); gîtes for two/four people start at 860/1387FF per week. The tourist office makes bookings for self-catering studios (from 1600/2000FF per week for two/four people).

Isola 2000 has a host of unappealing concrete blocks. Down the valley in Isola village, one-star *Hôtel de France* (☎ 04 93 02 17 04), part of the Logis de France chain, has doubles without/with shower for 220/260FF per person (half-board).

In St-Sauveur-sur-Tinée, *Au Relais d'Auron* (☎ 04 93 02 00 03), above the village tobacconist, at 18 ave des Blavets (the D2205) has rooms from 150FF. Guillaumes, 44km west at the northern mouth of the Gorges de Dalius, has rooms for 200FF

at *Hôtel La Renaissance* (☎ 04 93 05 12), opposite the sheep folds where the weekly village sheep fair takes place.

Getting There & Away There are three daily buses between Nice and Isola 2000 (90FF, 2½ hours), December to April, and one or two daily the rest of the year. Call ☎ 04 93 85 92 60 for information. During the ski season, buses serve Nice-Côte d'Azur airport (90FF, two hours).

Vallée de la Vésubie

The Vésubie, a dead-end valley that has to be accessed from the south, is less wild that its north-western neighbours, primarily due to its proximity to Nice and the Côte d'Azur. Its calming lack of life still comes as a breath of fresh air after the tourist circus on the coast however.

The hairpin-laced **Gorges de la Vésubie** weaves its way from the Vésubie's southern foot, which kicks off at Plan du Var, 20km north of Nice on the busy N202. For a stunning aerial view of the gorge and surrounding valley, head for **La Madone d'Utelle** (1181m), a pilgrimage site settled by Spanish sailors in the 9th century, which since 1806 has been crowned with a chapel. Pilgrims come here each year on 15 August (Assumption Day) and 8 September (Nativité de la Vierge). From the mountain village of **St-Jean la Rivière** (D2565), a stone bridge crosses the River Var, from where a steep, curvaceous mountain pass (D32) leads west to **Utelle** (pop 489), 6km north of La Madone.

Small, old **St-Martin-Vésubie** (pop 1102, elevation 964m), 24km north of St-Jean, is the valley's main outdoor activity base. The Parc National du Mercantour (☎ 04 93 03 23 15) has an office inside the Maison du Parc at 8 rue Kellermann Sérurier. For guided walks and ski tours, go to one of the two Bureau des Guides (☎ 04 93 03 31 32 or ☎ 04 93 03 56 60) on rue Cagnoli. St-Martin tourist office (☎ 04 93 03 21 28), place Félix Faure, has details of other mountain guides.

A good map for walks in the area is Didier-Richard's No 9 or IGN's Série Bleue map No 3741OT *(Vallée de la Vésubie, Parc National du Mercantour)*, which costs 45FF.

Activities The small **ski** station of La Colmiane, 7km west of St-Martin across the Col de St-Martin, has one chair lift that whisks skiers and walkers up to Pic de la Colmiane (1795m). From here, 30km of pistes and many more kilometres of **walking** trails can be accessed. A single ride (for skiers only) costs 23FF and a one-day pass costs 82/96FF (those aged 12 to 18, 72/80FF, those aged under 12, 72FF year round) for low season weekdays/weekends year round and every day in high season.

La Colmiane is graced with a **Via Ferrata** (a type of rock climbing using preattached cables), which takes intrepid wannabe climbers on a breathtaking journey up sheer rock faces and over mind-blowingly high rope-bridges. Anyone (with guts) can do it. You can hire all the necessary equipment (harness, ropes, karabiners, helmet etc) from Igloo Sports (☎ 04 93 02 83 43) for 30/60FF per half-/full day. It also rents skis/snowboards/mountain bikes (85/129/120FF per day). The Via Ferrata is about 3km from the ski station along an unpaved track; access costs 20FF. The Bureau des Guides (☎ 04 93 02 84 16) in La Colmiane arranges guided climbs (250FF) and ski-treks (380FF) The tourist office (☎ 04 93 02 88 59) has details.

St-Dalmas-Valdeblore (1350m), 5km farther west, is a leading **paragliding** centre. The tourist office (☎ 04 93 23 25 90) in La Roche Valdeblore has a list of schools.

Places to Stay On La Madone d'Utelle, *Refuge Agapé* (☎ 04 93 03 19 44) next to the ochre-painted chapel opens year round. Full board costs 180FF to 240FF per person. Wild camping (for free) is allowed. Snow cuts off the gîte most winters for about 10 days.

In St-Martin, *La Rouguière* (☎ 04 93 03 29 19, rue Kellermann Sérurier), next to the Maison du Parc, opens year round and charges 63FF per person (no heating). Lakeside *Gîte d'Étape du Mercantour*

(☎ 04 93 03 27 27, 04 93 03 34 82) in Le Boréon, 5km north-west of St-Martin on the D89, overlooks Lac du Boréon and offers half-board for 180FF.

Camping St-Dalmas (☎ 04 93 02 88 90) in St-Dalmas charges 10/22/9FF for a tent/adult/child aged under 12. Its *gîte d'etape* (☎ 04 93 02 83 96) has dorm beds for 45FF. Both open year round.

St-Martin and St-Dalmas each have a handful of hotels.

Places to Eat Two kilometres west of St-Jean la Rivière on the D32 is the *Auberge del Campo* (☎ 04 93 03 13 12), a charming farmhouse inn run by a very humorous patron. The stone farmhouse dates from 1785, and offers sweeping views of the gorges and village from its hillside terrace. A roaring fire warms the place in winter. *Menus* oozing local fresh produce cost 105FF, 140FF and 160FF. The bill is delivered to the table by Hubert, the Alsatian dog.

Getting There & Away Transport Régional des Alpes-Maritimes (TRAM; ☎ 04 93 03 20 23 in St-Martin; ☎ 04 93 89 41 45 in Nice) runs three daily buses between Nice and St-Martin (48.50FF, 1¾ hours) via St-Jean la Rivière. In summer, the same company operates a daily bus between Nice and La Colmiane (62.50FF, two hours) and St-Dalmas-Valdeblore (62.50FF, 2¼ hours).

Vallée des Merveilles

Sandwiched between the Vésubie Valley to the west and the Roya Valley to the east, is the 'Valley of Wonders'. It lies at the heart of the Parc National du Mercantour and protects one of world's most precious collections of Bronze Age petroglyphs. The rock engravings of human figures, bulls and other animals, spread over 30 sq km around Mont Bégo (2872m), date from 1800 and 1500 BC and are thought to have been done by a Ligurian cult. The area is sprinkled with lakes.

The moonscape valley is snowcovered much of the year and the best time to visit is July to September. Access is restricted. Walkers can only use authorised footpaths and are encouraged by park authorities to only visit the valley with a guide. Guideless walkers have little chance of uncovering the wondrous petroglyphs. AET Nature in Breil-sur-Roya (see the next section) runs one-day guided walks in the valley (130FF per person, five-hours walking), June to September. For information on longer expeditions, see Organised Tours in the Getting Around chapter.

The main access routes into the valley are the eastbound D91, which can be picked up in St-Dalmas de Tende in the Vallée de la Roya, or the dead-end D171 which leads north to the valley from **Roquebillière** (pop 1513) in the Vallée de la Vésubie. From the car park at the end of the road, it is a 1km walk along the left bank of the river (signposted 'Refuge de Nice via L'Éstrech') to the **Cascade de L'Éstrech**. The GR52 links the Refuge de Nice (2232m) with the rest of the Vallée des Merveilles. The Club Alpin Français in Nice (see the Nice to Menton chapter) takes bookings for Refuge de Nice (check in before 6 pm) and others.

IGN's Série Bleue map No 3841OT *(Vallée de la Roya, Vallée des Merveilles)* covers the area in a scale of 1:25,000 (45FF).

Vallée de la Roya

The Roya Valley once served as a hunting ground for King Victor Emmanuel II of Italy and only became part of France in 1947. In this valley is the pretty village of **Breil-sur-Roya** (pop 2023, elevation 280m), 62km north-east of Nice. There are good views of the village from the Col de Brouis (879m), which links **Sospel** (pop 2937), 21km south, with the Roya Valley.

The dramatic **Gorges de Saorge**, 9km north of Breil, lead to the fortified village of **Saorge** (pop 398, elevation 520m), overlooking the valley and set in a natural amphitheatre. The village is a maze of narrow, stepped streets and 15th- to 17th-century houses.

Immediately north of here, the **Gorges de Bergue** lead to **St-Dalmas de Tende**, the main gateway into the Vallée des Merveilles. From St-Dalmas de Tende, the D91 winds 10km west to **Lac des Mesches**

(1390m), from where trails lead into the valley past the Refuge des Merveilles (2111m). Alternatively, continue for 5km to **Casterino** at the end of the D91 where more northern trails start.

In neighbouring **Tende** (pop 1890, elevation 815m), 4km north of St-Dalmas de Tende, the **Musée des Merveilles** (☎ 04 93 04 32 50), ave du 16 Septembre 1947, unravels the natural history of the valley and exhibits numerous archaeological finds. Just 5km north of Tende, the **Tunnel de Tende** (engineered in 1882) provides a vital link into Italy.

Activities Breil-sur-Roya is a popular water-sports base. Roya Évasion (☎ 04 93 04 91 46, **e** roya.evasion@wanadoo.fr), 1 rue Pasteur, organises **kayaking**, **canyoning** and **rafting** trips on the River Roya, as well as walks and mountain-bike expeditions. AET Nature (☎/fax 04 93 04 47 64, **e** aetnature@yahoo.com), on central place Biancheri, is run by knowledgeable mountain guides who organise a multitude of white-water and walking trips. Breil-sur-Roya tourist office (☎/fax 04 93 04 99 76), on the same square, sells maps and guides. See Organised Tours in the Getting Around chapter for information on activity tours.

Guides for the Vallée des Merveilles can be hired in St-Dalmas de Tende and Tende. In Tende, the tourist office (☎ 04 93 04 73 71), ave du 16 Septembre 1947, and the Bureau des Guides du Val des Merveilles (☎ 04 93 04 77 73, 04 93 04 78 56), 18 rue de France, have details on 4WD jeep expeditions and walks. The latter also rents equipment and sells tickets. Tickets cost 20FF (those aged under 18, 15FF) for the dizzying **Via Ferrata des Comtes Lascaris** in Tende.

In Sospel, the tourist office (☎ 04 93 04 15 80), inside the city gate on the old bridge, stocks reams of information on walking and canoeing around Sospel and the Vallée de la Roya.

Places to Stay & Eat

USBTP Municipal Azur & Merveilles (☎ 04 93 04 46 66, quai de l'Aigara) is a

HAUTE-PROVENCE

camp site with a pool, signposted from Breil-sur-Roya train station. Nightly rates start at 14/10/11FF per tent/adult/car.

Refuge des Merveilles (☎ *04 93 04 64 64)* opens mid-June to the end of September. Half-board costs 192FF. *Neige et Merveilles* (☎/*fax 04 93 04 62 40)*, in St-Dalmas de Tende, is a mountain activity centre that opens April to October. Half-board costs 175/200FF in a dorm/double room.

Hotel-wise, the valley boasts two lovely places. Breil-sur-Roya's *Hôtel Le Roya* (☎ *04 93 04 48 10, place Biancheri)* is in a 16th-century mill. The old millstone and grinding mechanisms adorn the basement restaurant, which specialises in trout. Doubles start at 200FF.

Lakeside *Le Prieuré* (☎ *04 93 04 75 70, fax 04 93 04 71 58)*, in an old priory in St-Dalmas de Tende, hosts organ recitals and also prides itself on its gastronomy. Singles/doubles cost upwards of 287/379FF, including breakfast.

Getting There & Away There is an SNCF train station in Sospel, Breil-sur-Roya, St-Dalmas de Tende and Tende – all served by the Nice–Turin line that run several times per day from the coast, along the Roya Valley and into Italy.

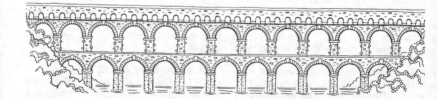

Nice to Menton

Nice and Menton (and the 30km of towns in between) are linked by three *corniches* (coastal roads), each higher and more hazardous than the last. They are particularly celebrated for their breathtaking sea views, luxurious seaside villas and – in July and August – hellish traffic, which moves at a snail's pace in the searing heat. In the 1920s motorists raced the coastal *Train Bleu* (Blue Train) from Paris along these roads. Speed fiends today should opt for the inland A8, which continues east to Ventimiglia (Vintimille in French) in Italy.

Nice makes an ideal base for exploring the rest of the Côte d'Azur. The city has plenty of relatively cheap places to stay and is only a short train or bus ride from Monaco (see the Monaco chapter), Cannes and other Riviera hot spots. Away from the coast's body-packed beaches, is the Niçois hinterland, an inland maze of remote *villages perchés* (hill-top villages) and hairpin mountain passes, guaranteed to send a chill through the raciest of drivers.

Nice

postcodes 06000 & 06300 • pop 345,892
Nice is nice. So it's apt that Nice (Nissa in Niçois, Niço in Provençal, Nizza in Italian) – the fifth largest town in France – should be dubbed the Côte d'Azur's capital. This fashionable but relaxed city is fun fun fun, and never more so than in the height of summer when backpackers flock here in their droves to dip their toes in its sparkling waters and sample the best of southern France's sky-blue coast.

The city's pebble beach may not be worth a postcard home, but the city's fantastical architecture from the turn-of-the-century *belle epoque*, art museums and buzzing cultural scene most certainly are. The famous Nice Carnival sets the streets ablaze each year at Mardi Gras with a merry-go-round of masked parades and colourful floats.

Highlights

- Discover Nice's wedding-cake mansions and *belle epoque* follies
- Find out what made Matisse tick in Cimiez; visit his modern friends at the Musée d'Art Moderne et d'Art Contemporain in Nice
- Follow in Le Corbusier's footsteps in Cap Martin-Roquebrune
- See how the rich lived: visit the lush interiors and gardens of Cap Ferrat's Villa Rothschild and the Villa Grecque Kérylos in Beaulieu-sur-Mer
- Take a three-hour stroll along the coastal path from Cap Martin to Monte Carlo

ITALY

Nice to Menton p268

Menton p298

MONACO

Nice p270-1

Mediterranean Sea

Nice was founded by seafaring Greeks, who named the colony Nikaia to commemorate a victory *(nike* in Greek) over a nearby town. The Romans followed in 154 BC and settled Cemenelum (now Cimiez). The city become part of France in 1860.

ORIENTATION

Ave Jean Médecin runs southwards from near the train station to place Masséna. The modern city centre, the area north and west

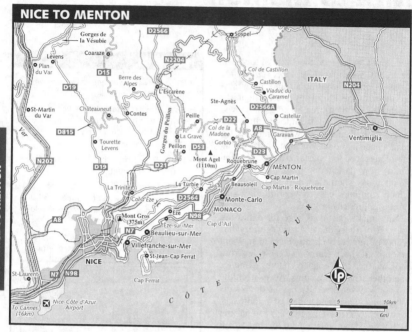

of place Masséna, includes the pedestrian streets of rue de France and rue Masséna. The bus terminal on square Général Leclerc and the local bus station are east of place Masséna.

Famous promenade des Anglais follows the gently curved beachfront westwards from the port area, past the city centre to the airport, 6km to the west. Vieux Nice (Old Nice) is delineated by blvd Jean Jaurès, quai des États-Unis and, to the east, the hill known as Le Château. Place Garibaldi is at the north-eastern tip of Vieux Nice.

The wealthy residential neighbourhood of Cimiez, home to several outstanding museums, is just north of the city centre.

INFORMATION
Tourist Offices
The tourist office (☎ 04 93 87 07 07, fax 04 93 92 82 98, @ otc@nice-coteazur.org) adjoining the train station on ave Thiers opens 8 am to 8 pm, June to September; and 8 am to 7 pm, the rest of the year. The beachfront annexe (☎ 04 92 14 48 00), 5 promenade des Anglais, opens 8 am to 8 pm Monday to Saturday, and 9 am to 6 pm Sunday. At the airport, the tourist office runs an information desk (☎ 04 93 21 44 11) in the arrivals hall of terminal 1, open 8 am to 10 pm. All three offices dole out free city maps and make hotel reservations. It has a Web site at www.nice-coteazur.org.

The Comité Régional du Tourisme Riviera-Côte d'Azur (CRT; ☎ 04 93 37 78 78, fax 04 93 86 01 06, @ crt06@crt-riviera.fr), 55 promenade des Anglais, with a Web site at www.crt-riviera.fr, opens 8.30 am to noon and 2 to 6 pm weekdays. It also runs a desk (☎ 04 93 21 80 95) at the airport (next to the Nice tourist office desk), open 8 am to 10 pm.

In town, the Centre Information Jeunesse (☎ 04 93 80 93 93, @ crij.cote.dazur@ wanadoo.fr), 19 rue Gioffrédo, opens from 8.45 am to 6.45 pm weekdays.

National Park Offices

The headquarters of the Parc National du Mercantour (☎ 04 93 16 78 88, fax 04 93 88 79 05, ✉ mercantour@wanadoo.fr), at 23 rue d'Italie, opens 9 am to 6 pm weekdays. It stocks numerous guides, including the free *Les Guides Rand Oxygène* series, which details 120 walking trails, 30 canyoning routes, 30 mountain-bike trails and in separate editions. The park has a Web site at www.parc-mercantour.fr.

Money

Banque de France, 14 ave Félix Faure, exchanges currency from 8.45 am to noon weekdays. American Express (☎ 04 93 16 53 53), 11 promenade des Anglais, opens 9 am to 9.50 pm, May to September; and 9 am to noon and 2 to 6 pm Monday to Friday (Saturday morning only), the rest of the year.

At the train station, there is a Thomas Cook exchange bureau (☎ 04 93 82 13 00) in the car rental building (to the right as you exit the station) and another at the top of the stairs leading from ave Thiers to blvd de Belgique and ave de Durante. Both open 7 or 8 am to 9.30 pm.

Change (☎ 04 93 88 56 80), facing the station at 17 ave Thiers, offers commission-free exchange 7 am to midnight. Other branches, open equally long hours, are at 64 ave Jean Médecin and 10 rue de France. There's a 24-hour currency exchange machine outside branches of Banque Populaire de la Côte d'Azur at 17 ave Jean Médecin and 20 blvd Jean Jaurès.

Post & Communications

The postcode for central Nice north and west of blvd Jean Jaurès and ave Galliéni is 06000. The postcode for Vieux Nice and the ferry port is 06300.

The main post office – a fantastic red-brick building at 23 ave Thiers – opens 8 am to 7 pm weekdays, and 8 am to noon Saturday. In Vieux Nice, there is a branch office at 2 rue Louis Gassin.

France's Telecom's Espace Internet (☎ 08 01 02 22 14), 8 rue Foncet, offers free Internet access and opens 10 am to 7 pm Tuesday to Friday,. Web Nice (☎ 04 93 88

72 75), promenade des Anglais, charges 50FF per hour and opens 10 am to 8.30 pm.

In Vieux Nice, L'Arob@s (☎ 04 93 62 64 59), 22 rue Benoît Bunico, opens 11.30 to 12.30 am Tuesday to Sunday. Email Café (☎ 04 93 62 68 86, ✉ email.cafe@wanadoo .fr), 8 rue St-Vincent, opens 10.30 am to 11.30 pm. Both charge a 40FF hourly rate.

Near the train station, Web Store (☎ 04 93 87 87 99, ✉ info@webstore.fr), 12 rue de Russie, opens 10 am to noon and 2 to 7 pm Monday to Saturday (50FF an hour). 3WO-World Wide Web (☎ 04 93 80 51 12), 32 rue Assalit, charges 10FF per 15 minutes.

Travel Agencies

USIT Voyages (☎ 08 25 08 25 25) has branches at 10 rue de Belgique and 17 rue de France. Both open 9.30 am to 6.30 pm Monday to Saturday. Voyages Wasteels (☎ 08 03 88 70 28) is at 32 rue Hôtel des Postes.

Bookshops

A good choice of new and second-hand English-language novels and guides are sold at The Cat's Whiskers (☎/fax 04 93 80 02 66), 30 rue Lamartine, open 9.30 am to noon and 2 to 6.45 pm weekdays, and 9.30 am to noon and 3 to 6.30 pm Saturday.

The travel bookshop, Magellan Librairie de Voyages (☎ 04 93 82 31 81), 3 rue d'Italie, has an excellent selection of IGN maps, Didier-Richard walking maps, topoguides and travel guides (including Lonely Planet) in English. It opens 9.30 am to 1 pm and 2 to 7 pm Tuesday to Saturday. Papeterie Rontani at 5 rue Alexandre Mari and the Maison de la Presse, 1 place Masséna, also sell maps and guides.

Cultural Centres

The ornate Holy Trinity Anglican Church (☎ 04 93 87 19 83) at 11 rue de la Buffa, functions as an Anglophone cultural centre. Sunday Mass is held at 11 am. Among the 'pioneer' expatriate graves from the 19th and 20th centuries in the adjoining cemetery is that of Henri Francis Lyte (1793–1847), a British vicar from Devonshire who wrote the hymn *Abide with Me*

NICE

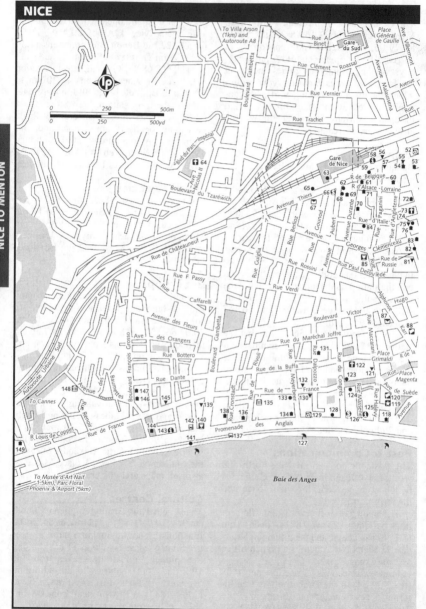

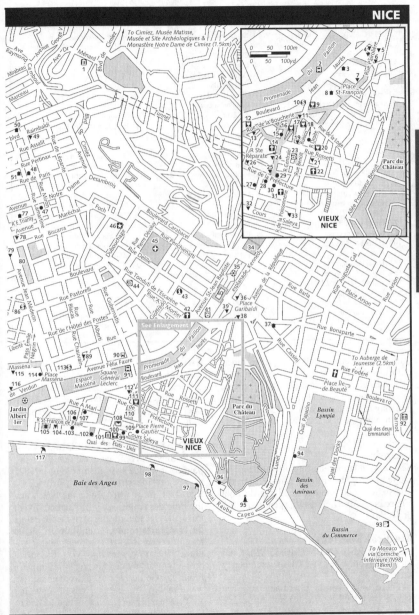

NICE

NICE TO MENTON

To Cimiez, Musée Matisse,
Musée et Site Archéologiques &
Monastère Notre Dame de Cimiez (1.5km)

0   50   100m
0   50   100yd

VIEUX
NICE

See Enlargement

VIEUX
NICE

Baie des Anges

Bassin
Lympia

Bassin
des
Amiraux

Bassin
du Commerce

To Auberge de
Jeunesse (2.5km)

To Monaco
via Corniche
Inférieure (N98)
(18km)

Parc du
Château

NICE

PLACES TO STAY
3 Hôtel au Picardy
8 Hôtel St-François
37 Hotel Genève
48 Hôtel Plaisance
50 Pado Tourisme Hostel
51 Hôtel Alexandra
53 Backpackers' Hôtel; Le Faubourg Montmartre
54 Hôtel Darcy; Restaurant de Paris
60 Hôtel de la Gare
61 Hôtel d'Orsay
69 Hôtel Belle Meunière
70 Hôtel Les Orangers
71 Hôtel du Piemont
72 Hôtel du Centre
76 Hôtel Lyonnais; Hôtel Notre Dame
77 Hôtel Le Petit Louvre
83 Hôtel Clémenceau
105 Hôtel Beau Rivage
118 Hôtel Méridien
131 Hôtel les Cigales
134 Hôtel Westminster
136 Hôtel Négresco; Chantecler
138 Hôtel Cronstadt
144 Melia Elysée Palace
146 Hôtel Carlone
147 Résidence Hôtelière Astoria

149 Centre Hébergement Jeunes

PLACES TO EAT
4 Chez René
5 Comptoir aux Épices
6 L'Escalinada
7 Chez Auguste
11 Lou Philha Leva
13 À L'Écurie
19 La Fanny
21 Chez Thérésa
24 Gelateria Azzurro
25 Nissa Socca
26 Le Braconnier
32 Fruit & Vegetable Market
33 L'F 2000
36 L'Olivier; 4 Wheels Skate Shop
38 Café de Turin
39 Prisunic
49 Chez Mireille
55 China Fast Food
56 Flunch Cafétéria
57 Mondial Buffet
75 L'Allegria; Restaurant au Soleil
78 Prisunic
79 Au Bretzel Chaud
81 Crêperie Bretonne
89 Le Latinos

104 Le Comptoir
112 L'Art Gourmand; No-Name Boulangerie
115 Boccaccio
116 Scotch Tea House
121 Aux Spécialités Belge
130 La Trattoria
132 Manoir Café
139 Intermarché
145 La Ronde des Pains

MUSEUMS
1 Musée National Message Biblique Marc Chagall
40 Musée d'Art Moderne et d'Art Contemporain; Grand Café des Arts
92 Musée de Paléonthologie Humaine de Terra Amata
96 Musée de la Marine; Tour Bellanda & Lift
135 Musée Masséna
148 Musée des Beaux-Arts Jules Chéret

OTHER
2 Intercity Bus Station
9 William's Pub
10 Banque Populaire de la Côte d'Azur

only three weeks before dying from tuberculosis in Nice.

The English-American library, 12 rue de France, opens 10 to 11 am and 3 to 5 pm Tuesday to Thursday, and 3 to 5 pm Friday. Cut through the passageway opposite 17 rue de France.

Laundry

Self-service laundrettes are plentiful and include one on blvd Jean Jaurès near the bus station; and another at 13 rue du Pont Vieux in Vieux Nice. Both open 7 am to 8 or 10 pm.

Medical Services

Hôpital St-Roch (☎ 04 92 03 33 75), 5 rue Pierre Dévoluy, has a 24-hour emergency service.

There is a 24-hour pharmacy at 7 rue Massé (☎ 04 93 87 78 94) and at 66 ave Jean Médecin (☎ 04 93 62 54 44).

Emergency

The police headquarters (☎ 04 92 17 22 22), 1 ave Maréchal Foch, has a special foreign tourist department (☎ 04 92 17 20 31). It opens 8 to noon and 2 to 6 pm. Be prepared to queue.

PROMENADE DES ANGLAIS

Palm-lined 'Promenade of the English', paid for by Nice's English colony in 1822 as a shoreside strolling path, provides a fine stage for a walk along the beach and the Baie des Anges (Bay of Angels). Don't miss the facade of the Art Deco **Palais de la Méditerranée**, crumbling in all its magnificence at 13–17 promenade des Anglais. The 1930s casino was the prize property of its owner American millionaire Frank Jay Gould, whose seafront enterprise was France's top-earning casino until the 1970s when his luck changed and he had to shut up shop. Plans to turn it into a com-

12 McMahons Pub	65 Sports Évasion	103 Moulin à Huile d'Olive Alziari
14 Cathédrale Ste-Réparate	66 Change	106 Town Hall
15 Laundrette	67 Main Post Office	107 Papéterie Rontani
16 Pub Oxford; De Klomp	68 JML Location	108 Branch Post Office
17 Jonathan's Live Music Pub	73 Église Notre Dame	109 Chapelle de la Miséricode
18 Palais Lascaris	74 Magellan Librairie de	110 Justice Palace; Préfecture
20 O'Hara's	Voyages	111 Wayne's; Master Home
22 Église St-Jacques Le Majeur	80 Centre Commercial Nice	113 Banque de France
23 L'Arob@s	Étoile	114 Maison de la Presse
27 Shoemaker's *Atelier*	82 Web Store	117 Plage Publique de
28 La Poulette	84 Parc National du Mercantour	Beaurivage
29 Chez Gilles	Headquarters	119 Police Station
30 Caves Caprioglio	85 La Palousa	120 US Consulate
31 Église St-Giaume	86 24-Hour Currency Exchange	122 Holy Trinity Anglican Church
34 Acropolis	Machine	123 English-American Library
35 Jardin Maréchal Juin	87 Branch Post Office	124 USIT Voyages
41 Théâtre de Nice	88 UK Consulate	125 Tourist Office Annexe
42 Église du Voeu	90 Sunbus	126 American Express
43 Centre Information Jeunesse	91 Station Centrale	127 Lido Plage
44 Espace Internet	93 Ferry Terminal;	128 Palais de la
45 Hôpital St-Roch	SNCM Office	Méditerranée
46 Police Headquarters	94 Trans Côte d'Azur	129 Web Nice
47 The Cat's Whiskers	95 WWI Memorial	133 Sapori Italiani
52 3WO-World Wide Web	97 Plage Publique des	137 Airport Buses
58 Tourist Office	Ponchettes	140 Forum
59 Nicea Location Rent	98 Plage Publique de l'Opéra	141 Public Showers & Toilets
62 Rent a Car Système	99 Flower Market	142 Airport Buses
63 Car Rental Agencies	100 Thor Pub	143 Comité Régional du
64 Cathédrale Orthodoxe Russe	101 Galérie des Ponchettes	Tourisme Riviera-Côte
St-Nicolas	102 Opéra de Nice	d'Azur

mercial centre appear to have also taken a tailspin.

Heading east towards Vieux Nice and the port, promenade des Anglais becomes **quai des États-Unis**, named after the United States in honour of President Wilson's decision in 1917 for the USA to join WWI. A colossal memorial commemorating the 4000 Niçois who died in the war is carved in the rock at the eastern end of the quay.

At 77 quai des États-Unis is **Galérie des Ponchettes** (☎ 04 93 62 31 24), a 19th-ntury, vaulted hall that hosts contemporary art exhibitions. The building was used as an arsenal for the Sardinian navy, then as a fish market until 1950 when Matisse persuaded the council to revamp it. It opens 10 am to noon and 2 to 6 pm Tuesday to Saturday, and 2 to 6 pm Sunday. Admission is free.

At the southern end of **ave Jean Médecin**, Nice's main commercial street, sits **place Masséna**, whose early 19th-century, neo-

classical arcaded buildings are painted in various shades of ochre and red. This is Nice's largest public square. Its western end is dominated by the 19th-century **Jardin Albert 1er**, in which a giant arc designed by sculptor Bernar Venet elegantly reclines. The sculpture, called **Arc 115°5**, commemorates the centenary of the appellation 'Côte d'Azur', the brainchild of French poet Stéphane Liégeard (1830–1925).

Espace Masséna, a public square enlivened by fountains, a rollerblading dome and ornamental gardens, straddles the eastern side of place Masséna.

VIEUX NICE

This area of narrow, winding streets wedged between quai des États-Unis and the Musée d'Art Moderne et d'Art Contemporain has looked pretty much the same since the 1700s. Arcade-lined **place Garibaldi**, built during the latter half of the 18th century, is named after one of the great heroes of Italian unification, Giuseppe Garibaldi (1807–82), born in Nice and buried in the cemetery in Parc du Château.

Cours Saleya and rue de la Préfecture, the old city's main artery, are dominated by the imposing **Palais de la Préfecture**, built at the beginning of the 17th century for the princes of Savoy.

Interesting churches in Vieux Nice include Baroque **Cathédrale Ste-Réparate** (1650–80) built in honour of the city's patron saint on place Rossetti; blue-grey and yellow **Église St-Jacques Le Majeur** (1650), place du Gésu (close to rue Rossetti), whose Baroque ornamentation dates from the mid-17th century; **Église St-Giaume**, 1 rue de la Poissonnerie; and **Chapelle de la Miséricorde** (1740-80), next to place Pierre Gautier on cours Saleya.

Rue Benoît Bunico, which runs perpendicular to rue Rossetti, served as Nice's Jewish ghetto after a 1430 law restricted where Jews could live. Gates at each end were locked at sunset. Heading southwards along parallel rue Droite, you come to the 17th-century, Baroque **Palais Lascaris** (☎ 04 93 62 05 54) at No 15. The arms and motto of the Lascaris-Ventimiglia family who owned the house can still be seen above the entrance hall. The motto between the two-headed eagles reads 'Not even lightning shall strike me'. The monumental staircase leads up to state apartments, the ceilings of which are richly decorated with elaborate frescoes depicting ancient mythology. Fine Flemish tapestries line the walls. Lascaris Palace opens 10 am to noon and 2 to 6 pm Tuesday to Sunday. Admission is free.

PARC DU CHÂTEAU

At the eastern end of quai des États-Unis, atop a 92m hill, is this shady public park, where people come to stroll, admire the panoramic views of Nice and the sparkling Baie des Anges, or visit the **Cascade Donjon**, an artificial waterfall crowned with a spacious viewing platform. It's a great place to escape the heat on a summer afternoon (open 7 am to 8 pm). Open-air concerts are held here on summer evenings.

The 12th-century castle, after which the hill and park are named, was razed by Louis XIV in 1706. In the one remaining tower, 16th-century **Tour Bellanda**, above the eastern end of quai des États-Unis, is the **Musée de la Marine** (☎ 04 93 80 47 61), with naval exhibits for dyed-in-the-wool Sinbads. It opens 10 am to noon and 2 to 7 pm, June to September; and 10 am to noon and 2 to 5 pm, the rest of the year. Admission costs 15FF (students 9FF; those aged under 18, free). The cemetery where Garibaldi is buried covers the north-western area of the park.

To get to the top of Le Château, take the lift, the **ascenseur du château** from under the Tour Bellanda, rue des Ponchettes. It operates 9 am to 7.50 pm in summer (5.50 pm the rest of the year). A one-way/return ticket costs 3.80/5.50FF (children aged four to 10, 2/4FF). Alternatively, plod up the staircase on montée Lesage or at the eastern end of rue Rossetti.

MUSÉE D'ART MODERNE ET D'ART CONTEMPORAIN

The Museum of Modern and Contemporary Art (MAMAC) is Nice's pride and joy architecturally speaking. It specialises in European and American avant-garde works

---

Museums in Nice

Museums in Nice are free to everyone on the first Sunday of the month (those aged under 18, year round). Beyond that, you have to pay to view Matisse's *Blue Nude*, Warhol's *Dollar Sign* or Christo's wrapped shopping trolley.

The tourist offices sell **Le Passe Musées**, costing 40FF (no reduced rate) and allowing its holder one visit to each of Nice's museums during seven consecutive days. Museum aficionados can invest in the 120FF version (students 60FF), which is valid for a year and allows card-holders 15 museum visits.

If you intend straying farther afield, invest in La Carte Musées Côte d'Azur (see the Facts for the Visitor chapter for details).

from the 1960s to the present. Glass walkways connect the four marble towers, topped with a rooftop garden and gallery featuring works by Nice-born Yves Klein (1928–62). The sweeping views of Nice are equally stunning.

Temporary exhibitions fill the ground and 1st floors of the giant building. Highlights in its 2nd- and 3rd-floor permanent exhibitions include Andy Warhol's *Campbell's Soup Can* (1965), a shopping trolley wrapped by Christo, **Entablature** (1971) by pop artist Roy Lichtenstein, and a pea-green model-T Ford compressed to a 1.60m-tall block by French sculptor César.

The hall, dedicated to the 1960s new realism movement, features works by Romanian Daniel Spoerri and Arman. Spoerri's **La Table Bleue** (The Blue Table) features the remnants from a table in a Parisian restaurant – unwashed cutlery and crockery stuck behind glass. Arman is best known for encasing mountains of mundane objects such as kitchen trash, letters or children's toys in monumental perspex containers, some of which are on display in the museum. Arman, born in Nice as Armand Fernandez in 1928, studied at the city's École Nationale d'Art Décoratif. A printer's mistake inspired him to drop the 'd' from his name in 1958.

MAMAC (☎ 04 93 62 61 62), promenade des Arts, opens 10 am to 6 pm Wednesday to Monday. Admission costs 25FF (students 15FF; those aged under 18, free). Art films and cult movies are screened twice a month in the auditorium. The **Jardin Maréchal Juin**, a modernist red concrete garden on the eastern side of the Musée d'Art Moderne et d'Art Contemporain, is worth a stroll.

Take bus No 17 from the train station to the bus station, from where the museum is a five-minute walk.

MUSÉE NATIONAL MESSAGE BIBLIQUE MARC CHAGALL

The Marc Chagall Biblical Message Museum (☎ 04 93 53 87 20) is close to blvd de Cimiez across the street from 4 ave Docteur Ménard. It houses the largest public collection of works by Russian painter Marc

Chagall (1887–1985), who lived in St-Paul de Vence from 1950 until his death.

Floating humans, goats and green-headed violins characterise Chagall's work. His *Biblical Message Cycle*, displayed in the severe, purpose-built museum, includes 12 canvases illustrating scenes from the Old Testament. Don't miss the second version of the **Blue Rose** mosaic (1958) of the rose window at Metz Cathedral, viewed through a plate-glass window and reflected in a small pond.

The museum opens 10 am to 6 pm Wednesday to Monday, July to September; and 10 am to 5 pm Wednesday to Monday, the rest of the year. Admission costs 30FF (those aged 18 to 25 and everyone on Sunday, 20FF; those aged under 18, free). Take bus No 15 from place Masséna to the stop in front of the museum; or walk (signposted from ave de L'Olivetto).

MUSÉE MASSÉNA

The Masséna Museum (☎ 04 93 88 11 34), also known as the Musée d'Art et d'Histoire, is in Palais Masséna, 65 rue de France. It is currently closed for renovation. When it reopens in mid-2001, expect to view an eclectic collection of paintings, furniture, icons, ceramics and religious art – all in a marvellous Italian-style villa dating from 1898.

The palm tree-studded gardens behind the museum (off promenade des Anglais) are equipped with the same blue chairs as promenade des Anglais, making for a shady hideaway from the posing crowds on the packed prom. The gardens open until 7 pm in summer.

MUSÉE DES BEAUX-ARTS JULES CHÉRET

The Jules Chéret Fine Arts Museum (☎ 04 92 15 28 28), 33 ave des Baumettes, is in a fantastic cream and apricot 19th-century villa built for Ukrainian princess Elisabeth Vassilievna Kotschoubey in 1878. Its decorative stucco friezes and six-column rear terrace overlooking luxuriant gardens are typical of houses dating from Nice's *belle epoque*.

The collection includes works by Dutch artist Kees van Dongen (1877–1968) and

NICE TO MENTON

Fauvist Raoul Dufy; several Flemish tapestries; Pierre Bonnard's 20th-century *Window Opening onto the Seine at Vernonnet*; some late impressionist pieces by Monet and Sisley; a large number of works by Jules Chéret (1836–1932), the creator of modern poster art; and locally produced works of art by Alexis Mossa (1844–1926) – a Niçois artist better known for introducing wildly decorated floats to the Nice Carnival than for his watercolours.

The museum opens 10 am to noon and 2 to 6 pm Tuesday to Sunday. Admission costs 25FF (students 15FF; those aged under 18, free). Bus No 38 from the local bus station stops outside.

CIMIEZ & THE MUSÉE MATISSE

The Matisse Museum (☎ 04 93 81 08 08), 164 ave des Arènes de Cimiez, which houses a fine collection of works by Henri Matisse, is 2.5km north-east of the train station in the bourgeois district of Cimiez. The museum's permanent collection is displayed in a red-ochre, 17th-century Genoese villa overlooking an ancient olive grove and the **Parc des Arènes**. Temporary exhibitions are hosted in the futuristic basement building, which leads through to the stucco-decorated villa. The reception hall of the museum is dominated by a colourful, 4.10 x 8.70m, paper cut-out frieze entitled *Flowers and Fruits* and designed by Matisse for the inner courtyard of a Californian villa in 1953.

Well-known pieces in the permanent collection include Matisse's blue paper cut outs of *Blue Nude IV* (1952) and *Woman with Amphora* (1953). Numerous Indian ink drawings and sombre oil paintings, representative of Matisse's early career from 1890 until 1905, are also on display.

The museum opens 10 am to 6 pm, April to September (5 pm the rest of the year). Admission costs 25FF (students 15FF;

Matisse – the Essential Elements

Henri Matisse (1869–1954) was passionate about pure colour. His paintings epitomised the radical use of violent colour, heavy outlines and simplified forms characteristic of Fauvism. Fauvism – which rose to prominence around 1905 – was a short-lived movement but Matisse clung to the method of setting striking, complementary colours against one another throughout his career.

Matisse was a latecomer compared to other influential painters, not becoming interested in painting until he was 20. By the time he was 22 however he had given up his law career in his home region, Picardy, and had gone to Paris.

Matisse studied art for many years under the symbolist painter Gustave Moreau. While visiting Brittany, he met an Australian artist, John Russell, who introduced him to the works of Van Gogh, Monet and other impressionists, prompting (so it is believed) Matisse's change from a rather sombre palette to brighter colours. He also spent time in Corsica, whose clear and rich Mediterranean light was to have a lasting influence on his work. By the early 1900s he was well known in Paris among followers of modern art and his paintings were being exhibited, but he was still struggling financially. It wasn't until the first Fauvist exhibition in 1905, which followed a summer of innovative painting in the fishing village of Collioure in Roussillon, that his financial situation improved. By 1913 he had paintings on display in London and New York.

In the 1920s Matisse moved to the Côte d'Azur but still spent much time travelling – to Ètretat in Normandy and abroad to Italy and Tahiti. During these years he painted prolifically but was less radical; his work's characteristic sensuality and optimism, however, were always present. The 1930s saw him return to more experimental techniques and a renewed search for simplicity, in which the subject matter was reduced to essential elements. In 1948 he began working on a set of stained-glass windows for the Chapelle du Rosaire in Vence, run by Dominican nuns. He ended up designing not just the windows but the entire chapel – a project which took several years. He died and was buried in Nice three years later.

Absolutely Fabulous

Belle epoque Nice was ab fab. The wedding-cake mansions, palaces and pastel-painted concrete gateaux that sprung up in abundance were not just fabulous: they were fantastical.

The Cimiez quarter remains the pearl of this lavish, turn-of-the-century legacy. The Haussmann-style **Conservatoire de Music**, 8 blvd de Cimiez, dates from 1902. At No 46 is **L'Alhambra** (1901), an opulent private mansion set on a small, palm tree-studded mound and surrounded by a high wall, though not high enough to hide the Moorish minarets that rise from the sparkling white building. **Villa Raphaeli-Surany** (1900), opposite at No 35, is adorned with intricate mosaic reliefs. The boulevard's crowning jewel is **Hôtel Excelsior Régina**, 71 ave Régina, built in 1896 to welcome Queen Victoria to Nice (a statue of her stands in front). Henri Matisse later lived here.

The pink confection you see from Nice ferry port, atop star-studded Mont Boron, where celebrities such as Elton John reside, is **Château de l' Anglais**, built in 1859 for an English engineer called Robert Smith, renowned at the time as being the only foreigner to live in Nice year round. Locals quickly dubbed his castle – protected today a historical monument – Smith's folly.

those aged under 18, free). Take bus No 15, 17, 20 or 22 from the local bus station to the Arènes stop.

Matisse is buried in the cemetery of the 16th-century **Monastère Notre Dame de Cimiez** (Cimiez Monastery). The artist's grave is signposted *sépulture Henri Matisse* from the graveyard's main entrance (next to the monastery's Église Notre Dame on ave Bellanda). The grave of Raoul Dufy (1877–1953), who spent many years in Nice, is also here. Stairs lead from the eastern end of the olive grove (on allées Miles Davis) to ave Bellanda.

Inside the monastery is the **Musée Franciscain** (☎ 04 93 81 00 04), a small museum run by, and unravelling the history of,

the monastery's Franciscan monks. Three pieces of precious medieval art by Nice artist Louis Bréa hang in the adjoining Église Notre Dame. The monumental Baroque altar, carved in wood and decorated with gold leaf, dates from the 17th century. The beautifully landscaped **Jardin du Monastère** surrounding the monastery offers a sweeping panorama of the Baie des Anges. The garden, studded with cypress trees and an abundance of sweet-smelling roses, opens until 6, 7 or 8 pm. The museum opens 10 am to noon and 3 to 6 pm Monday to Saturday; the church art can be viewed from 3 to 7 pm (free admission).

Bus No 32 links the train station and Cimiez; in Cimiez get off at the Monastère stop.

MUSÉE ARCHÉOLOGIQUE

Behind the Matisse museum, on the eastern side of the Parc des Arènes, lie the ruins of the ancient Roman city of Cemenelum, the focus of the Archaeology Museum (☎ 04 93 81 59 57) at 160 ave des Arènes de Cimiez. Both the public baths and the amphitheatre – the venue for outdoor concerts during the Nice Jazz festival – can be visited.

The museum opens 10 am to noon and 2 to 6 pm Tuesday to Sunday, April to September; and 10 am to 1 pm and 2 to 5 pm Tuesday to Sunday, the rest of the year. Admission costs 25FF (students 15FF, those aged under 18, free). To get here from Parc des Arènes, turn left out of the main park entrance on ave des Arènes de Cimiez, walk 100m, then turn left again onto ave Monte Croce where the main entrance to the archaeological site is.

VILLA ARSON

Some wonderful temporary contemporary art and photographic exhibitions can be enjoyed at the Centre National d'Art Contemporain (☎ 04 92 07 73 73), 20 ave Stéphane Liégeard, housed in the 18th-century Villa Arson.

It opens 1 to 7 pm, July to September; and 1 to 6 pm Tuesday to Sunday, the rest of the year. Take bus No 36 to the Villa Arson

NICE TO MENTON

NICE TO MENTON

stop, or bus No 4, 7 or 26 to the Fanny stop on blvd de Cessole.

CATHÉDRALE ORTHODOXE RUSSE ST-NICOLAS

The multicoloured Russian Orthodox Cathedral of St-Nicolas (☎ 04 93 96 88 02), crowned by six onion domes, was built between 1903 and 1912 in early 17th-century style and is an easy 15-minute walk from the train station. Step inside and you are transported to Imperial Russia. The cathedral, on ave Nicolas II opposite 17 blvd du Tzaréwich, can be visited 9, 9.15 or 9.30 am to noon and 2 or 2.30 to 5.30 pm Monday to Saturday. Admission costs 12FF. Shorts, miniskirts and sleeveless shirts are forbidden.

MUSÉE INTERNATIONAL D'ART NAÏF ANATOLE JAKOVSKY

A collection of naive art from all over the world can be seen at the Anatole Jakovsky International Naive Art Museum (☎ 04 93 71 78 33), ave du Val Marie, less than 2km west of the city centre. The very pink Château Ste-Héléne, in which the museum is housed, was built in the 19th century atop Mont Fabron by François Blanc, who founded the casino in Monte Carlo; it later served as the country home of a perfume manufacturer. The collection – which includes the works of 200 artists from 27 countries – was donated to the museum by Romanian art critic, Anatole Jakovsky (1909–83), who lived in southern France with his wife Renée from 1932. The museum opens 10 am to noon and 2 to 6 pm Wednesday to Monday. Admission costs 25FF (students 15FF; those aged under 18, free).

To get to the museum, take bus No 10 or 12 from the local bus station to the Fabron stop, then walk or take bus No 34 to the Musée Art Naïf stop.

PARC FLORAL PHOENIX

At 7000 sq metres, the greenhouse in Nice's floral Phoenix Park, 405 promenade des Anglais (near the airport), is said to be Europe's largest. Seven different climates are

reproduced inside the gigantic glass house, known as the *diamant vert* (green diamond), which contains everything from an exotic orchid garden to an insectarium, Australian garden, 25m-tall palmier and butterfly house. Some 1500 different plant species are represented in the seven-hectare park, which sports a small lake, zoo, Mayan temple and tacky theme park. It opens 9 am to 7 pm, April to September (to 5 pm the rest of the year). Admission costs 40FF (those aged six to 18, 20FF).

The modernist white-marble building in the park, designed by Japanese architect Kenzo Tange, houses the **Musée des Arts Asiatiques** (☎ 04 92 29 37 00), which showcases Oriental Art. It opens 10 am to 6 pm (5 pm from October to April) Wednesday to Monday. Admission costs 35FF (students 25FF; those aged six to 18, 15FF).

MUSÉE DE PALÉONTHOLOGIE HUMAINE DE TERRA AMATA

Just east of Bassin Lympia (the port), this museum (☎ 04 93 55 59 93, @ mgoudet @nice-coteazur.org), 25 blvd Carnot, displays objects from a site inhabited some 400,000 years ago by the predecessors of *Homo sapiens*. It opens 9 am to noon and 2 to 6 pm Tuesday to Sunday. Admission costs 25FF (students 15FF; those aged under 18, free). Bus No 32 links the local bus station and the museum; alight at the Carnot stop.

ACTIVITIES

If you don't like the feel of sand between your toes, Nice's **beaches** – covered with smooth round pebbles – are for you. Sections of beach open to the public without charge alternate with 15 private beaches, which you have to pay for by renting a sun lounger (50FF to 70FF per day). **Lido Plage** (☎ 04 93 87 18 25, @ lidoplage@wanadoo .fr), opposite 13-17 promenade des Anglais, hosts everything from romantic candle-lit dinners (110FF) to discos and salsa evenings on the beach. **Plage Publique des Ponchettes**, opposite Vieux Nice, gets the most packed with oiled bodies laid out to bake.

On the private sections of beach you can hire catamaran paddleboats (around 90FF per hour) or sailboards and jet skis (350FF for 30 minutes), take a parachute ride (250FF for 15 minutes) or water-ski (from 150FF for 10 minutes). The tourist office has a list of **diving** schools.

Trans Côte d'Azur (☎ 04 92 00 42 30), quai Lunel, runs **boat excursions** (one hour) along the coast, departing from the port at 3 pm Sunday to Friday, mid-June to mid-September. Tickets cost 60FF (children aged four to 10, 30FF). It also runs excursions in a glass-bottomed boat (70FF; children 45FF) and weekly trips to the Îles de Lérins (135FF; children 100FF) and St-Tropez (210FF; children 120FF), mid-June to September; and to Monaco (110FF; children 80FF) and San Remo (190FF; children 100FF) in neighbouring Italy, in July and August.

For details of **mountain-biking** and **walking** trails in the region, go to the headquarters of the Parc National du Mercantour (see the earlier Information section) in Nice or to Club Alpin Français des Alpes-Maritimes (☎ 04 93 62 59 99, fax 04 93 92 09 55), 14 ave Mirabeau, 06000 Nice. Nice-based Destination Merveilles (☎/fax 04 93 73 09 07, e destination.merveilles@mageos.com), 34 corniche Frère Marc, specialises in guided walks in the national park.

Promenade des Anglais is the hot spot to **rollerblade**. Near the train station, Nicea Location Rent (see Car & Motorcycle later in this section) rents rollers for 90/50FF per day/half-day. On promenade des Anglais, Web Nice (see Email & Internet Access earlier) has blades to hire for 50FF per hour. Roller fashion is sold at the 4 Wheels Skate Shop (☎ 04 92 04 94 66), 4 place Garibaldi.

ORGANISED TOURS
Several companies arrange Riviera bus tours; see Organised Tours in the Getting Around chapter for details.

SPECIAL EVENTS
The celebrated two-week Carnaval de Nice (Nice Carnival) has been held each year around Mardi Gras (Shrove Tuesday) since 1294. The highlight is its *bataille de fleurs* (battle of flowers), when hundreds upon thousands of fresh flowers are tossed into the crowds from processing floats. A mock carnival king is burned and fireworks are lit on promenade des Anglais.

The week-long Nice Jazz Festival jives through town in July, its main venue being the olive grove behind the Musée Matisse in Cimiez. Equally atmospheric is the two-day Fête au Château, an outdoor music festival held in Parc du Château in mid-June. During the Festival de Musique Sacrée (Festival of Sacred Music), Russian sacred chants meet with Mozart's *Requiem* for two weeks in late June. During the three-week Les Nuits Musicales de Nice in mid-July/early August, classical musical concerts are held in the cloisters of Cimiez Monastery, the olive grove in Cimiez and in the gardens around the Musée d'Art Moderne et d'Art Contemporain.

PLACES TO STAY
Nice has a surfeit of reasonably priced places to stay, although cheap accommodation can be hard to find during the Easter holidays and in July and August when most hostels brandish a *complet* (full) sign by 10 am. Sleeping on the beach is illegal.

The information desk at the bus station (see Getting There & Away later) has a list of Logis de France hotels (☎ 04 93 80 80 40) in the region. For self-catering accommodation, contact Gîtes de France des Alpes-Maritimes (☎ 04 92 15 21 30, fax 04 93 37 48 00, e gites06@crt-riviera.fr), 55 promenade des Anglais, with a French-only Web site at www.crt-riviera.fr/gites06.

PLACES TO STAY – BUDGET
Hostels
Touting a tree-studded garden with tables and chairs for guests to lounge on is busy *Hôtel Belle Meunière (☎ 04 93 88 66 15, 21 ave Durante)*. A place in a four- or five-bed dorm costs 78FF (82FF in a triple), including breakfast. It also has 98/112FF dorm beds in three- or four-/five-bed rooms with private shower and toilet. Belle Meunière is run by a young, fun crowd. Safety

NICE TO MENTON

deposit boxes (12FF per day) are available at reception, open 7.30 am to midnight. The hotel opens February to November.

Almost opposite is equally popular *Hôtel Les Orangers* (☎ *04 93 87 51 41, fax 04 93 87 57 82, 10 bis ave Durante)* in a turn-of-the-century townhouse. A dorm bed in a snug four- to six-bed room with shower and big windows, costs 85FF. The cheerful owner speaks English, Spanish and Italian – the result of dealing with backpackers for the past 21 years. Les Orangers opens December to October. Nearby, *Hôtel Darcy* (see Hotels – Train Station Area below) has dorm beds for 102FF.

Just off ave Jean Médecin, *Backpackers' Hotel* (☎ *04 93 80 30 72, 06 13 25 29 31,* e *chezpatrick@voila.fr, 32 rue Pertinax)*, above the Faubourg Montmartre restaurant, charges 80FF per night. Cheery Patrick, who runs the place, is said to be an absolute darling. Internet and laundry facilities are available.

Nice's *Auberge de Jeunesse* (☎ *04 93 89 23 64, fax 04 92 04 03 10, route Forestière de Mont Alban)* is 5km east of the train station. A dorm bed costs 68.50FF. Curfew is at midnight and rooms are locked from 10 am to 5 pm. Take bus No 14 from the local bus station (linked to the train station by bus Nos 15 and 17) and get off at L'Auberge stop.

The *Centre Hébergement Jeunes* (☎ *04 93 86 28 75, fax 04 93 44 93 22, 31 rue Louis de Coppet)* has dorm beds available mid-June to early September. A bed in a six-person room costs 50FF. Reception opens 8.30 am to 12.30 pm and 2 pm to midnight on weekdays and 8.30 to 11.30 am and 6 pm to midnight at weekends. There's a midnight curfew and by day, bags must be stored in the luggage room (10FF).

Hotels – Train Station Area
The quickest way to get to these hotels is to cut down the steps opposite the train station onto ave Durante. As well as dorm beds, warm and welcoming *Hôtel Belle Meunière* (see Hostels earlier) has a variety of rooms with high ceilings; doubles cost from 164FF (shared bathroom) to 290FF (private

shower and toilet). There's free private parking in the front courtyard.

Highly recommended *Hôtel Les Orangers* (see Hostels) has doubles/triples/quads with shower (some with balcony), overlooking palm-tree gardens, for210/285/360FF. Rooms are gloriously sunlit and come with fridge (and free hotplate upon request).

Hôtel Darcy (☎ *04 93 88 67 06, 28 rue d'Angleterre)* has basic singles/doubles/triples for 135/160/225FF. Shower-equipped singles/doubles cost 180/200FF and doubles/triples/quads with shower and toilet are not bad value at 230/288/340FF.

Opposite, *Hôtel de la Gare* (☎/*fax 04 93 88 75 07, 38 rue d'Angleterre)* has modern bright singles/doubles with washbasin for 150/155FF, doubles/triples with shower costing 245/300FF and also doubles/triples/quads with shower and toilet for 250/350/400FF. Hall showers cost 13FF.

Rue d'Alsace-Lorraine is dotted with several two-star hotels. Among the cheaper few is *Hôtel du Piemont* (☎ *04 93 88 25 15)*, down an alley at No 19. Singles/doubles/triples/quads with washbasin cost 110/130/190/240FF. Singles/doubles/triples including shower cost 120/150/210FF (200/220/270FF with shower, toilet, fridge and a hotplate). Quads with all the gadgets are available for 380FF. The Piemont rents rooms on a longer-term basis too.

At No 20 on the same street, *Hôtel d'Orsay* (☎ *04 93 88 45 02, fax 04 93 82 30 28)* has 32 rooms costing 135/165/230/280FF for a basic single/double/triple/quad (165/210/280/350FF with shower and toilet). From May to September, prices jump by 20FF to 30FF per night.

Hotels – City Centre
Midway between the sea and the train station is colourful *Hôtel Le Petit Louvre* (☎ *04 93 80 15 54, fax 04 93 62 45 08, 10 rue Emma Tiranty)*, a backpacker favourite run by a humorous musician. A faceless Mona Lisa greets guests as they enter and corridors are adorned with an eclectic mix of paintings. Singles/doubles with shower, washbasin, fridge and hotplate cost 180/

210FF (210/240FF with toilet too). Triples are 249FF. Breakfast (30FF) comprises cereal and fruit as well as the usual baguette, croissant and coffee. It opens February to October.

Prices at one-star *Hôtel Lyonnais* (☎ 04 93 88 70 74, fax 04 93 16 25 56, 20 rue de Russie) reflect the season and type of washing facilities: singles/doubles/triples/quads with washbasin and bidet cost 145/190/240/320FF (180/200/255/340FF in high season). Singles/doubles with shower cost 190/200FF (225/235FF in high season), and rooms with shower, toilet and TV rock in at 240/250/300/390FF per night (260/280/350/480FF in high season). The Lyonnais has yet another set of cheaper rates for long-term stays.

A safe bet is *Hôtel Clémenceau* (☎ 04 93 88 61 19, fax 04 93 16 88 96, 3 ave Georges Clémenceau). Basic singles/doubles cost 150/200FF (200/230FF July and August) and rooms with shower and toilet cost 200/250FF (250/310FF July and August). It also has good-value three-/four-/five-bed rooms for 300/400/500FF per night (350/450/550FF July and August). Reception is at the top of the marble staircase.

Hotels – Vieux Nice

Hôtel St-François (☎ 04 93 85 88 69, fax 04 93 85 10 67, 3 rue St-François) has 19 basic rooms costing 140/170FF. Showers cost 15FF.

Hôtel au Picardy (☎ 04 93 85 75 51, 10 blvd Jean Jaurès) has basic rooms with washbasin and bidet starting at 120/230FF for one or two/three or four people. Shower-equipped doubles for up to three/four people start at 220/250FF (179/250FF with shower and toilet). Hall showers cost 10FF.

By the port, little-known *Hôtel Genève* (☎ 04 93 56 73 73, 1 rue Cassini), above a simple bar, has singles/doubles/triples costing upwards of 200/250/350FF.

PLACES TO STAY – MID-RANGE

Near the train station, there are plenty of two-star hotels on rue d'Angleterre, rue d'Alsace-Lorraine, rue de Suisse, rue de Russie and ave Durante.

In the centre, *Hôtel Plaisance* (☎ 04 93 85 11 90, fax 04 93 80 88 92, 20 rue de Paris) is a pleasing two-star pile with air-conditioned rooms for 340/450FF.

Named after its location near Église Notre Dame is clean and modern *Hôtel Notre Dame* (☎ 04 93 88 70 44, fax 04 93 82 20 38, 22 rue de Russie). Spacious singles/doubles/triples with shower and toilet cost 200/250/320FF. Another good-value place on the other side of Église Notre Dame is modest, 28-room *Hôtel du Centre* (☎ 04 93 88 83 85, fax 04 93 82 29 80, e hotel-centre@webstore.fr, 2 rue de Suisse). Basic doubles cost 180FF (260FF with shower, 300FF with shower, toilet and TV). After 11.30 pm guests need a door code to enter.

A stone's throw from the sea and the Musée des Beaux-Arts is good-value *Hôtel Carlone* (☎/fax 04 93 44 71 61, 2 blvd François Grosso). Light and airy rooms for one or two/three/four cost 320/440/540FF. *Résidence Hôtelière Astoria* (☎ 04 95 15 25 45), almost next door, has two-room studios with bathroom, fridge and hotplate to let on a nightly/weekly/monthly (or longer) basis. Rates start at 170/1000/3000FF in low season and peak at 230/1600FF per night/week (no monthly rentals) in August. The Astoria also has a pretty garden where guests breakfast (30FF).

Just like home and equally close to the sea is welcoming, 10-room *Hôtel Cronstadt* (☎ 04 93 82 00 30, 3 rue Cronstadt), hidden inside a *belle epoque* mansion with a marble-decorated garden. Quiet and graceful singles/doubles/triples cost 286/290/370FF in low season (316/320/400FF in high season). Press the buzzer to enter via the porch.

Three-star *Hôtel Alexandra* (☎ 04 93 62 14 43, fax 04 93 62 30 34, 41 rue Lamartine) is everything you would expect of a hotel managed by the Best Western group. Rooms cost 480/570FF.

There are a couple of small, family run options in upmarket Cimiez. Two-star *Hôtel Le Floride* (☎ 04 93 53 11 02, fax 04 93 81 57 46, 52 blvd de Cimiez) has rooms with shower, toilet and views of Cimiez' opulent mansions starting at 190/260FF. Next door at No 54, **Hôtel Hélios** (☎ *04 93 53 04 55, fax 04 93 81 41 40),* towering over the absolutely fabulous L'Alhambra mansion, charges upwards of 200/220FF for a room with shower.

PLACES TO STAY – TOP END
Legendary pink-domed, green-shuttered and four-starred **Hôtel Négresco** (☎ *04 93 16 64 00, fax 04 93 88 35 68,* e *reservations@ hotel-negresco.com, 37 promenade des Anglais)* is Nice's fanciest hotel. Rooms with sea view cost upwards of 1900/2350FF in low/high season. Van Loo paintings, Aubusson carpets and crystal chandeliers are among its lavish *belle epoque* furnishings. Reception staff , porters and doormen wear knickerbockers and caps with feathers.

Stylish four-star **Hôtel Méridien** (☎ *04 93 82 25 25, fax 04 93 16 08 90,* e *reserv@ lemeridien-nice.com, 1 promenade des Anglais)* with its rooftop pool and **Hôtel Westminster** (☎ *04 92 14 86 86, fax 04 93 82 45 35,* e *westminster@french-riviera.fr, 27 promenade des Anglais)* both offer a touch of class for a little less cash. Doubles average 1000FF.

Matisse stayed at **Hôtel Beau Rivage** (☎ *04 92 47 82 82, fax 04 92 47 82 83,* e *nicebeaurivage@new-hotel.com, 24 rue St-François de Paule)* when he was in town in 1916. Before that, in 1891, Russian playwright Anton Chekhov (1860–1904) graced the place with his presence. Sea views from the four-star hotel remain superb. Doubles start at 750/950FF in low/high season.

The modern face of Nice is reflected in the black-glass walls of **Melia Elysée Palace** (☎ *04 93 97 90 90, fax 04 93 44 50 40,* e *reservation@elysee-palace.com, 59 promenade des Anglais).* The building's concrete rear is adorned with a giant statue of Venus baring a breast to passers-by on rue de France. Doubles start at 900/1300FF in low/high season.

PLACES TO EAT
Restaurants – Train Station Area
All the places to eat listed here are cheapish, within five minutes' walk of the train station and best suited for hungry backpackers and travellers seeking a cheap fill.

The unpretentious **Restaurant au Soleil** (☎ *04 93 88 77 74, 7 bis rue d'Italie)* has been run by the same husband-and-wife team since 1960. The smiling pair serve local cuisine at unbeatable prices, including an all-day omelette breakfast for 35FF and a hearty 70FF *menu,* (translated into many languages), which includes a 25cL pichet of wine.

Another cheap favourite is bustling **Restaurant de Paris** (☎ *04 93 88 99 88, 28 rue d'Angleterre),* adjoining Hôtel Darcy, which touts a 45FF *menu* and giant-sized salads for 38FF.

You can taste a cheap version of bouillabaisse at **Le Faubourg Montmartre** (☎ *04 93 62 55 03, 32 rue Pertinax),* another popular place, which serves the fishy stew for two for a mere 120FF and has a 68FF *menu.*

There are over a dozen Vietnamese and Chinese restaurants on rue Paganini, rue d'Italie and rue d'Alsace-Lorraine. Don't expect miracles, except perhaps at **China Fast Food**, a clean fast-food place, open 9 am to midnight on the corner of ave Thiers and ave Jean Médecin.

Another option is **Mondial Buffet** (☎ *04 93 16 15 51, 7 ave Thiers),* opposite the station. The cafeteria-style place specialises in Asian dishes and offers a buffet *à volonté –* which means serve yourself as much as like – costing 75FF. Smaller appetites can get a good-value fill on a 23FF *plat du jour* (dish of the day) or 32FF *menu.*

Tasty options for diners seeking a midrange option near the station include Corsican **L'Allegria** (☎ *04 93 87 42 00, 7 rue d'Italie),* which hosts energetic guitar duets and other Île de Beauté musical delights some weekends; **Chez Mireille** (☎ *04 93 85 27 23, 19 rue Raimbaldi),* which offers paella for 120FF per person (20 minutes to prepare); and **La Ferme Fromagerie** *(27 rue Lépante),* a cheesy restaurant adjoining a top-rate fromagerie. It serves cheese fondues (60/100FF for 150/250g), Lyonnaise *cervelle de canut* (a creamy cheese with chives) as well as salads, omelettes (45FF to 60FF) and Alpine *tartiflette* (80FF).

NICE TO MENTON

Restaurants – City Centre

Pedestrian rue Masséna and its nearby streets and squares, including rue de France and place Magenta, are crammed with touristy cafes and restaurants. Most don't offer particularly good value, although *La Trattoria* (☎ 04 93 88 20 07, 37 rue de France) is worth a nibble. It specialises in pizza *au feu de bois* (cooked over a wood fire).

Nearby *Boccaccio* (☎ 04 93 87 71 76, e *bocaccio@club-internet.fr, 7 rue Masséna*) serves fabulous *plateaux de fruits de mer* (seafood platters) and fish dishes on an atmospheric street terrace. The polka-dotted fish, which swims about in a tank inside, is purely for decorative purposes.

A chic spot in the centre is refined *Manoir Café* (☎ 04 93 16 36 16, 32 rue de France). Much of the original decor from 1908 remains; the fantastic sculpted wood panelling was added in 1947. Jazz bands play here some evenings and table reservations – for dining or drinking – are essential. *Menus* cost 89FF and 129FF.

Not far from the port, *L'Olivier* (☎ 04 93 26 89 09, 2 place Garibaldi) is a small, simple and local spot. Starters (such as hot goat cheese *à la tapenade*) and mains (such as salmon-filled ravioli with sea-urchin sauce) average 45FF and 65FF respectively.

Café de Turin (☎ 04 93 62 66 52, e *bdudoignon@aol.com, place Garibaldi*) sports an authentic 1900 interior and is one of Nice's nicest seafood spots. Oysters/sea urchins start at 80/50FF per dozen. Shellfish are prepared beneath the arches on the cool pavement terrace.

Graceful *Le Comptoir* (☎ 04 93 92 08 80, 20 rue St-François de Paule) is close to the seashore. The restaurant has an adjoining nightclub and terrace and is decked out in Art Deco style. Pasta/fish/meat dishes start at 60/89/98FF and it has a 69FF lunchtime *menu*.

Just north of Vieux Nice, *Le Latinos* (☎ 04 93 85 01 10, 6 rue Chauvain) is a stylish tapas place, open 8 pm to midnight Wednesday to Monday. Tapas costs 15FF per dish and mains – which include several types of grilled fish – average 75FF.

For a mind-blowing extravaganza, dine in style at *Chantecler* inside Hôtel Négresco. Impeccable service and tantalising cuisine add up to 500FF per head (at least).

Restaurants – Vieux Nice

Vieux Nice's narrow streets are lined with restaurants, cafes, pizzerias and so on that draw locals and visitors alike. In summer, the numerous outdoor places to eat and drink on cours Saleya, place Pierre Gautier and place Rossetti buzz with activity until well past midnight.

This is the spot to sample *socca*, a giant-sized chickpea flour and olive oil pancake fried on a griddle above a wood-stoked fire. A perennial favourite is *Chez René (1 rue Pairolière)*, an unpretentious spot with seating both sides of rue Miralhet. Select a plateful of socca (12FF) to eat with other typical Niçoise treats such as *beignets de courgettes* (slices of zucchini fried in batter), *beignets d'aubergines* (battered eggplant slices) or *pissaladière* (onion, anchovy and black olive tart). Wash the whole down with a 12FF glass of Côtes de Provence wine.

Lou Philha Leva (place Centrale) is a similar spot, always crammed. Buy your food at the bar before sitting down; waiters only serve drinks. Socca costs 10FF a plateful and beignets or *farcis* (stuffed vegetables) cost 25FF.

Sedate diners who prefer to sample Nice's culinary pleasures in a more refined setting can eat at *L'Escalinada* (☎ 04 93 62 11 71, 22 rue Pairolière). This enchanting place, with smiling staff and a candlelit terrace, serves all of the above delicacies plus its house speciality – perhaps not to everyone's taste – *testicules de mouton panés* (sheep testicles in batter).

Nearby, charming *Le Braconnier* (☎ 04 93 80 85 45) has tables, chairs and twittering bird cages spilling out – and filling – place Vieille, a tiny square off rue Centrale. It serves a 48FF Niçoise platter and includes tripe in its house specials. *La Fanny* (☎ 04 93 80 70 63, 2 rue Rossetti) is another recommended place for traditional Niçoise cooking.

Snails are among the delights waiting to

be sampled at busy *À L'Écurie* (☎ 04 93 62 32 62, 4 rue du Marché), run by the same family since 1945. Its thin cheesy pizzas average 50FF and it has a 130FF *menu*.

And then there is *Nissa Socca* (☎ 04 93 80 18 35, 5 rue Ste-Réparate), whose *salade niçoise* (green salad with tuna, egg and anchovies), ratatouille and other traditional dishes have drawn the crowds here for years.

Cafes & Fast Food

There are numerous sandwich stalls and snack bars around the train station. *Flunch Cafétéria*, to the left as you exit the station building, doles out uninspiring but edible fast food from 11 am to 10 pm. Among the deluge of sandwich joints on ave Jean Médicin, *Au Bretzel Chaud* at No 27 touts a 12FF drink-and-sandwich combination, well-filled *moricettes* (15FF) and the most sugary *beignets* (donuts) in town. It opens 6.15 am to 7.30 pm Monday to Saturday.

Terrace cafes and bars just made for beer quaffing and cocktail sipping abound. In Vieux Nice, try *L'F 2000* (place Charles Félix). The designer chairs here overlook the spot where motorcyclists park up their mean machines for passers-by to stroke and admire.

Down-to-earth *Chez Thérésa* (☎ 04 93 85 00 04, 28 rue Droite) doles out socca through a hole in the wall, 8 am to 1 pm Tuesday to Sunday. The socca maker, whose family business dates to 1925, has a stall at the cours Saleya food market (see Self-Catering).

For cream teas and home-made tarts, head for cosy but chic *Scotch Tea House* (☎ 04 93 87 75 62, 4 ave de Suède), tucked between designer clothes shops. As well as sweet treats and 34 types of tea, it serves eggs, salads and a hot *plat du jour*, making it a busy lunchtime spot.

Aux Spécialités Belges (3 rue Maccarani) is a small *salon de thé* (tea room) with plenty of naughty-but-nice treats. It opens 7.15 am Monday to Saturday, making it a good breakfast spot. *L'Art Gourmand* (☎ 04 93 62 51 79, 21 rue du Marché) is an ice-cream and chocolate shop that has a small tea salon too.

Sweet crepes, savoury galettes, punchy

ciders and ice creams are beautifully presented at *Crêperie Bretonne* (☎ 04 93 16 02 98, 3 rue de Russie).

Those seeking to escape the city heat should head for *Grand Café des Arts* (☎ 04 93 80 58 58, place Yves Klein, a shaded rooftop cafe atop MAMAC.

Self-Catering

The *fruit and vegetable market* (cours Saleya) opens 7 am to 1 pm Tuesday to Sunday. The *fresh fish market* (place St-François) operates 6 am to 1 pm Tuesday to Sunday.

The no-name *boulangerie* at the southern end of rue du Marché sells sandwiches, pizza slices, traditional *michettes* (savoury bread stuffed with cheese, olives, anchovies and onions) and local breads. Otherwise take a mouthwatering stroll along rue du Collet and its continuation, rue Pairolière, which is lined with *fromageries*, *boulangeries* and *fruit shops*. Don't miss *Chez Auguste*, a fromagerie at 37 rue Pairolière; or *Comptoir aux Épices* (2 rue Pairolière), which sells some 50 different spices, olives, pulses, dried tomatoes and salted sardines. Shop for bread at *La Ronde des Pains* (78 rue de France) or *J Militari* (2 rue Alphonse Kerr).

Cooked chickens are sold, hot from the spit, at *La Poulette* on the corner of rue de la Préfecture and rue Gaétan. *Gelateria Azzurro* (1 rue Ste-Réparate) sells all-Italian ice cream in all flavours (peanut butter, grapefruit, chewing gum etc); two scoops in a crunchy cone cost 18FF.

There is an *Intermarché* supermarket at the southern end of blvd Gambetta and a *Prisunic* supermarket, opposite 33 ave Jean Médicin.

ENTERTAINMENT

The tourist office has detailed information on Nice's abundant cultural activities. Cinema and theatre schedules are on the Web at http://nice.webcity.fr (French only).

Tickets for most events are sold at FNAC (☎ 04 92 17 77 74), inside the Centre Commercial Nice Étoile (see Shopping later in the Nice section).

JANE SMITH

Anyone for pétanque? Try your hand at Provence's favourite pastime.

Pubs & Live Music

Nice boasts a rash of pubs that sport a happy hour, host live bands and lure Anglophones like bees to a honey pot.

Best known is *Wayne's* (☎ 04 93 13 46 99, 15 rue de la Préfecture), which has live music from 9.30 pm and is always rammed. In summer it throws DJ-driven beach parties (100FF including one free drink) 11 pm to 4 am (watch out for flyers); the pub opens 2.30 pm to 1 am. Upcoming events are posted on its Web site at www.waynes.fr. *Master Home* next door is a good spot to sit outside, watch the crowds pile into Wayne's and relax over a pint between busy pubs.

Pub Oxford (☎ 04 93 92 24 54, 4 rue Mascoïnat) sells itself as a traditional English pub. It has live music from 10 pm (open until 4 am). Next door at No 6, Dutch *De Klomp* (☎ 04 93 92 42 85) lures punters with 18 beers on tap (40/75FF per 50/100cL), 100 bottled beers, 60 whiskies and a Little-Cafe-of-Amsterdam slogan. It opens 5.30 pm to 2.30 am.

Jonathan's Live Music Pub (☎ 04 93 62 57 62, 1 rue de la Loge) has live bands (country, boogie-woogie, Irish folk and so on) every night in summer. A pint/pichet/metre of the house draft beer here costs 18/30/150FF.

William's Pub (☎ 04 93 85 84 66, 4 rue Centrale) has live music most evenings from 9 pm and opens until 4 am. It has pool, darts and chess in the basement. *Thor Pub*

(☎ 04 93 62 49 90, 32 cours Saleya) has a terrace on cours Saleya and also throws a weekly beach party.

Nice has three Guinness-serving Irish pubs: *McMahons Pub* (☎ 04 93 13 84 00, 50 blvd Jean Jaurès), close to the bus station; fireplace-ornamented *O'Neill's* (☎ 04 93 80 06 75, 40 rue Droite), which runs the occasional pub quiz; and nearby *O'Hara's* (☎ 04 93 80 43 22, 22 rue Droite), where pint prices are translated into US dollars and British pounds for the predominantly Anglophone clientele. It serves pub grub, shows BBC on the box, and opens 4 pm to 2.30 am.

Nightclubs

Unlike its pub and bar scene, Nice's clubs are tough to track down for those not in the know. In Vieux Nice, young 'n' fun partiers hit *Subway* (☎ 04 93 80 56 27, 19 rue Droite).

La Palousa (☎ 04 93 82 37 66, 29 rue Alphonse Kerr) markets itself as the French Riviera's biggest nightclub. It hosts various theme nights including salsa on Sunday, and opens 11 pm to 6 am Thursday to Sunday. Admission is free with a flyer before 1 am; otherwise face a stiff 100FF admission fee, plus upwards of 50FF per drink.

By the beach, flashy *Forum* (☎ 04 93 96 68 00, 45–47 promenade des Anglais) lets women through its steel doors for free before 1 am; after that everyone pays a hefty 100FF admission (including one 'free' drink). Ouch.

Blue Boy Enterprise (☎ 04 93 44 68 24, 9 rue Spinetta) just off blvd François Grosso is a gay nightclub close to the centre, open 11 pm to 6 am.

Opera, Ballet & Classical Music

Operas and orchestral concerts are held at the Garnier-designed *Opéra de Nice* (☎ 04 92 17 40 40, ℮ opera@nice-coteazur.org, 4–6 rue St-François de Paule), dating to 1885. The box office (☎ 04 9 13 98 53) opens 10 am to 5.30 pm Tuesday to Saturday, September to mid-June.

Cinemas

Nice has two cinemas that screen original-language films, many in English. *Cinéma*

NICE TO MENTON

Nouveau Mercury (☎ *08 36 68 81 06, 16 place Garibaldi),* and *Cinéma Rialto* (☎ *04 93 88 08 41, 4 rue de Rivoli).* Art films (usually in French or with French subtitles) are shown in the cinema at MAMAC (see that section earlier in this chapter).

Theatre

The modern *Théâtre de Nice* (☎ *04 93 80 52 60, esplanade des Victoires),* a block west of place Garibaldi, hosts first-rate plays and concerts. Tickets cost 50FF to 200FF. The information desk opens 1 to 7 pm Tuesday to Saturday, and an hour before each performance. A new, 6850-seat theatre, estimated to cost 100 million FF, is planned for 2001.

SHOPPING

Cours Saleya hosts a colourful flower market, 6 am to 5.30 pm, Tuesday to Sunday lunchtime. There are a number of vendors selling *fruits glacés* (glazed or candied fruits), a speciality of the region. The figs, tangerine slices and pears have to be tasted to be believed. To tour, taste and buy chocolate-coated orange slices, cocoa-covered almonds and the like, visit the Confiserie Florian (☎ 04 93 55 43 50), 14 quai Papacino; free factory tours run 9 am and noon and 2 to 6.30 pm.

Numerous shops sell fresh pasta: try Chez Gilles at 6 rue Ste-Réparate, which dates from 1816; or Sapori Italiani, a divine Italian épicerie on the corner of rue de France and rue Meyerbeer. Fill your water bottle with wine (from 7.80FF per litre) at Caves Caprioglio, 16 rue de la Préfecture. For olive oil (from 50FF per litre) shop at Moulin à Huile d'Olive Alziari, 14 rue St-François de Paule.

In Vieux Nice, rue du Collet and rue Pairolière offer bargains galore for shoppers in search of cheap clothes, hats and trinkets. Handmade leather sandals are sold by the shoemaker's *atelier* (workshop; ☎ 04 93 80 79 98) at 6 rue Gaétan.

Designer names abound above the beautiful fashion boutiques that line rue Paradis, rue de Suède, rue Alphonse Karr, and rue du Maréchal Joffre. Mainstream fashion shops, FNAC and so on are in the Centre Commercial Nice Étoile, an indoor shopping centre at 30 ave Jean Médecin, open 10 am to 7.30 pm Monday to Saturday. The Galeries Lafayette department store on place Masséna opens 9 am to 7 or 7.30 pm Monday to Saturday.

Close to the train station, Sports Évasion (☎ 04 93 16 88 44), 16 ave Thiers, is a top-rate outdoor activities shop that sells all the gear to walk, climb etc, including maps.

GETTING THERE & AWAY
Air

You can Kiss & Fly (as the drop-off point outside Terminal 1 departure hall is called) from Nice-Côte d'Azur international airport (Aéroport International Nice-Côte d'Azur; ☎ 04 93 21 30 30, 04 93 21 30 12), 7km west of Nice city centre. The airport has a Web site at www.nice.aeroport.fr.

Bus

Lines operated by some two dozen bus companies use the intercity bus station, 5 blvd Jean Jaurès. The information counter (☎ 04 93 85 61 81) opens 8 am to 6.30 pm Monday to Saturday. Small/large pieces of luggage can be left for 10/15FF per hour at the Intercars desk.

Most coastal services – slow but frequent – are operated by Rapides Côte d'Azur (☎ 04 93 85 64 44, 04 97 00 97 00), with a Web site at www.rca.tm.fr. It runs at least 15 buses daily to/from Cannes (line No 200; 32FF, 1¼ hours) via Marineland in Biot (35FF return, 40 minutes), Antibes (25.50FF, 50 minutes) and Golfe-Juan (30FF, one hour); to/from Menton (line 100 or 110; 28FF return, 1¼ hours) stopping at all villages en route (see the Corniche Inférieure section later in this chapter); and twice daily to/from Hyères (130FF, two hours) and Toulon (132FF, 2½ hours). The sporadic bus line No 115 serves the Grande Corniche (see that section later in this chapter).

If you intend visiting Vence (line No 400/410; 20FF, one hour, buses every half-hour); Cagnes-sur-Mer (16FF, 25 minutes) and St-Paul de Vence (45 minutes), buy a one-day 35FF *billet circulaire*, which allows you to stop in all three places. Most buses to/from Grasse (line No 500; 37FF, 1¼ hours, eight to 10 buses daily) stop in Cagnes-sur-Mer too.

Heading northwards to Haute-Provence, Transport Régional des Alpes-Maritimes (TRAM; ☎ 04 93 89 41 45 in Nice) runs buses to/from St-Martin-Vésubie (48.50FF, 1¾ hours, three daily), La Colmiane (62FFF, two hours, one daily summer only) and St-Dalmas-Valdeblore (48.50FF, one daily summer only) in the Vallée de la Vésubie. Société des Cars Alpes-Littoral (SCAL; ☎ 04 92 51 06 05) operates buses to/from Gap (133FF, 4½ hours, one daily Monday to Saturday) via Sisteron (104FF, 3¾ hours), St-André-les-Alpes (60FF, two hours) and Digne-les-Bains (83FF, three hours, one or two daily). Buses to/from Isola 2000 (90FF, 2½ hours) depart three times daily, December to April, and once or twice daily the rest of the year.

The daily bus from Nice to Geneva (565FF, 9¾ hours) operated by Cars VDF (☎ 04 76 87 90 31 in Grenoble) stops in Castellane (74FF, 2¼ hours) and Digne-les-Bains (83FF, 2½ hours). The bus leaves Nice at 7.30 am and from Geneva at 7 am.

For longer-haul travel, Intercars (☎ 04 93 80 42 20) at the bus station, takes you to various European destinations. It opens 2 to 6 pm Monday, 9 am to noon and 2 to 6 pm Tuesday to Thursday, and 9 am to noon Friday. SAM Tourisme (☎ 04 93 54 14 49), also at the bus station, runs buses to Morocco; for details see the Getting There & Away chapter.

Train

Nice's main train station, Gare de Nice (also called Gare Thiers; ☎ 08 36 35 35 35), ave Thiers, is 1200m north of the beach. Only tickets for same-day departures are sold at the windows opposite the main entrance; all other tickets are sold at the information and reservations office, at the far end of the ticket hall, open 8.30 am to 6.30 pm Monday to Saturday, and 8.50 to 5.45 pm Sunday. For simple queries, try the small information desk (accueil) next to the main entrance.

There is a fast, frequent service – up to 40 trains daily in each direction – to towns along the coast between St-Raphaël and Ventimiglia across the Italian border, including Antibes (22FF, 25 minutes), Cannes (32FF, 40 minutes), Menton (26FF, 35 minutes), Monaco (20FF, 20 minutes) and St-Raphaël (76FF, 45 minutes).

The left luggage lockers in the ticket hall can be accessed 7 am to 10.30 pm (15/20/30FF for a small/medium/large locker; maximum deposit 72 hours). Lost luggage and other problems are handled by SOS Voyagers (☎ 04 93 82 62 11), open 9 am to noon and 3 to 6 pm weekdays. Toilets and showers, at the foot of the escalator to the tracks, open 8 am to 12.30 pm and 1.30 to 7.45 pm (19/2.80FF for use of shower/toilet).

The ever-popular two-car diesel trains operated by Les Chemins de Fer de la Provence (☎ 04 93 88 34 72 in Nice; 04 92 31 01 58 in Digne-les-Bains; [e] trainpigne @aol.com) make the scenic trip four times daily from Nice's Gare du Sud (☎ 04 93 82 10 17), 4 bis rue Alfred Binet.

destination	FF	hours
Villars-sur-Var	40	1
Puget-Théniers	53	1¼
Entrevaux	55	1½
Annot	64	1¾
St-André-les-Alpes	93	2½
Digne-les-Bains	111	3¼

Seniors aged over 55 get a 25% discount; children aged four to 12 pay half price (children aged under four travel free).

Boat

The fastest SNCM ferries from mainland France to Corsica (see the Getting There & Away chapter) depart from Nice's ferry terminal (Gare Maritime; ☎ 04 93 13 66 66), quai du Commerce. SNCM has a ticketing office here (☎ 04 93 13 66 99), open 8 am to 7 pm weekdays, 8 to 11.45 am Saturday, and two hours before scheduled departures on Sunday. Many travel agencies in town likewise sell ferry tickets.

From ave Jean Médecin take bus No 1 or 2 to the Port stop.

GETTING AROUND
To/From the Airport

Sunbus No 99 provides a speedy link between Nice train station and the airport, departing every half-hour between 8 am and 9 pm. Journey time is 15 minutes. Buy your ticket (23FF) from the bus driver, from window No 5 at the train station, or at the ticket desk in terminal 1 bus station at the airport. Snail-slow bus No 23 also runs to/from the airport every 20 or 30 minutes on weekdays from 6 am to 8 pm. It stops at the train station or on blvd Gambetta, rue de France or rue de la Californie. Journey time is 35 minutes and a one-way fare is 8.50FF.

From the airport bus station (☎ 04 93 85 30 83), next to Terminal 1 at Nice airport, there are daily buses to countless other destinations, including Avignon (150FF, 4¾ hours), Cannes via the coastal N7 (48.50FF, one hour) or via the A8 (70FF, 50 minutes), Grasse (54.50FF, one hour), Isola 2000 (90FF, ski season only, two hours), Monaco (80/140FF one-way/return, 45 minutes) and Vence (25FF, 45 minutes).

Between June and October, Air France (☎ 08 02 80 28 02) runs boats from the airport to Cannes/St-Tropez. Tickets cost 200/375FF one-way (children aged two to 12, 50% discount). Departures are from the Air France desk in Terminal 2 and from platform No 6 at the Terminal 1 bus station. In 2000 there was one boat daily to/from Cannes (40 minutes) and three boats daily to/from St-Tropez (2¼ hours). Further information is on the Air France Web site at www.airfrance.fr (French only).

A taxi from the airport to Nice centre costs between 120FF and 200FF, depending on the time of day, which terminal you're at and whether you're being ripped off or not.

Bus

City buses are run by Sunbus, which has its main hub (the Station Centrale) on square Général Leclerc, sandwiched between ave Félix Faure and blvd Jean Jaurès. Tickets (34/55FF for a five-/10-ticket carnet) are sold at the Sunbus information office (Sunboutique; ☎ 04 93 16 52 10), 10 ave Félix Faure, open 7.15 am to 7 pm weekdays, and

7.15 am to 6 pm Saturday. Passes allowing unlimited travel for one/five/seven days cost 25/85/110FF. Holders of La Carte Musées Côte d'Azur can buy a three-/seven-day bus pass for 40/90FF. Bus drivers sell single tickets for 8.50FF. After you time-stamp your ticket, it's valid for one hour and can be used for one transfer.

Bus No 12 links the train station with promenade des Anglais and the beach. To get from the train station to Vieux Nice and the local bus station, take bus No 2, 5 or 17. At night, Noctambuses run north, east and west from place Masséna.

Plans are afoot for a tramway in Nice.

Car & Motorcycle

Most car rental agencies – ADA (☎ 04 93 82 27 00), Budget (☎ 04 97 03 28 00), Europcar (☎ 04 93 82 17 34), Hertz (✆ 04 93 03 01 20) and National Citer (☎ 04 93 16 01 48) – have an office in the annexe adjoining the train station at 12 ave Thiers, as well as an office in town and at the airport. Rent a Car Système (☎ 04 93 88 69 69), opposite the station at 38 ave Aubert, offers exceptionally competitive rates, as does JML Location (☎ 04 93 16 07 00, ✉ holidaybikes.nice@wanadoo.fr), 34 ave Aubert. Car/scooter/125cc motorcycle rental costs from 196/210/330FF per day. Agencies open 8 am to 7 pm.

Nicea Location Rent (☎ 04 93 82 42 71, fax 04 93 87 76 36, ✉ nicealocation@aol.com), 12 rue de Belgique, rents 50cc scooters for one/two people for 290/325FF per day, 100cc scooters for 425FF, and 125/240/600cc motorcycles for 440/600/620FF per day. Helmets are an extra 15FF. The office opens 9 am to 6 pm (Monday to Saturday only in winter).

Taxi

Nice has numerous taxi ranks (☎ 04 93 13 78 78), including outside the train station, near place Masséna on ave Félix Faure and on promenade des Anglais.

Bicycle

Nicea Location Rent (see Car & Motorcycle) rents mountain bikes for 85/100FF per day/

Going Greek at Villa Grecque Kérylos, Beaulieu-sur-Mer

Mother and child, Menton

Keeping a watchful eye on the princely Palais de la Préfecture, Nice

Baring it all on the Côte d'Azur: it's nice in Nice...

The unspoilt harbour of Villefranche-Sur-Mer

A touch of the contemporary at Théâtre de Nice

Baroque-style Cathédrale Ste-Réparate, Nice

An eye-widening array of regional gastronomy

In the pink at Villa Ephrussi de Rothschild

Trees and arcades line Place Garibaldi, Nice.

24 hours. JML (see Car & Motorcycle on the previous page) is an agent for Holiday Bikes and has road bikes for 45/65FF per four hours/day and mountain bikes for 56/69FF.

The Three Corniches

The Corniche Inférieure (also called the Basse Corniche or Lower Corniche; the N98) sticks closely to the nearby train line and villa-lined waterfront. The Moyenne Corniche, the middle and least exciting coastal road (N7), clings to the hillside, affording great views if you can find somewhere to pull over. The Grande Corniche, whose panoramas are by far the most spectacular, leaves Nice as the D2564 and passes the **Col d'Èze** (512m), La Turbie and Le Vistaëro, all of which offer breathtaking coastline views.

Accommodation here is pricey and limited. The cheapest option is to stay in Nice from where easy day or half-day trips can be made. The Corniche Inférieure, the lowest of the trio, is well served by train from Nice; the higher two roads, and the entire Niçois hinterland, are practically inaccessible by public transport.

CORNICHE INFÉRIEURE

Heading eastwards from Nice to Menton, the Corniche Inférieure – built in the 1860s – passes through Villefranche-sur-Mer, St-Jean-Cap Ferrat, Beaulieu-sur-Mer, Èze-sur-Mer, Cap d'Ail and Monaco. Look for pretty pink Château de l'Anglais (see the boxed text 'Absolutely Fabulous' in the Cimiez & the Musée Matisse section earlier in this chapter), 176 blvd Carnot, on Mont Boron, on the right as you flash past leaving Nice.

Getting There & Away

The lower coastal road is well served by bus and train. Bus No 100 operated by Rapides Côte d'Azur (☎ 04 93 85 64 44 for information) runs the length of the Corniche

Inférieure between Nice and Menton, stopping at all the villages along the way (every 15 minutes between 6 am and 7.45 pm Monday to Saturday, and every 20 or 30 minutes between 6 am and 7.50 pm Sunday and holidays). To/from Nice, bus No 111 serves St-Jean-Cap Ferrat (12.50FF, 25 minutes, hourly between 7 am and 7 pm Monday to Saturday); and bus No 117 serves Villefranche-sur-Mer (9FF, 15 minutes, 11 buses between 7.30 am and 7.30 pm).

Trains – speedier, easier and generally more convenient – run from Nice along the coast to Ventimiglia, Italy, every 10 to 20 minutes between 6 am and 6 pm (every 30 to 50 minutes from 6 pm to 1 am). Most trains stop at:

destination	FF	minutes
Villefranche-sur-Mer	9	8
Beaulieu-sur-Mer	12	14
Èze-sur-Mer	13	17
Cap d'Ail	16	21
Monaco	20	25
Cap Martin-Roquebrune	23	32
Carnolès	25	36
Menton	25	38

Between July and September, buy a Carte Isabelle (see Train Passes in the Getting Around chapter) if you intend making several train trips along the coast in one day. If you intend to make a return day-trip to Menton, stopping en route in Villefranche-sur-Mer and Beaulieu-sur-Mer, it is cheaper however to buy a straightforward Nice–Menton return ticket.

Villefranche-sur-Mer
postcode 06230 • pop 6877

Set in one of the Côte d'Azur's most charming – and unspoilt – harbours, this port village overlooks the Cap Ferrat peninsula. It has a well-preserved, 14th-century old town. Steps break up the tiny streets, the most interesting and evocatively named of which is arcaded **rue Obscure**.

Keep a lookout for occasional glimpses of the sea as you wander through the streets that lead to quai Amiral Courbet, the **port** where fishermen tend their nets remains a common sight. The cottages overlooking the harbour through wooden shutters are painted in a rainbow of muted colours, ranging from bedtime-pink to sea blue and peppermint green. On Sunday morning, an art and antique **market** fills place Amelie Pollonais.

From the fishing port, a narrow **coastal path** runs around the citadel to Port de la Darse, Villefranche-sur-Mer's modern pleasure port. En route there are picture-taking opportunities and good views of Cap Ferrat and the wooded slopes of the Gulf of Villefranche, which served as a naval base for the Russians during their conflicts with the Turks in the 19th century.

Orientation From Villefranche-sur-Mer train station, steps lead to quai Amiral Corbet and Plage des Marinières, a shallow shingle beach. To get to rue Obscure, walk up the staircase at 7–9 quai Amiral Colbert (between La Mère Germaine and L'Oursin Bleu restaurants), then turn immediately right onto rue Obscure. Follow it to its dark and eerie end and you come out on rue du Poilu, the main street in the old town.

Citadel Imposing Fort St-Elme (1557), place Emmanuel Philibert, was built by the duke of Savoy at the end of the 16th century to defend the gulf. Its thick walls today shelter Villefranche's town hall; the open-air Théâtre de la Citadelle, where films are screened daily at 9.30 pm in July and August (35FF); public gardens; and the **Musée Volti** (☎ 04 93 76 33 27), an art museum which displays bronze sculptures of voluptuous female forms in all shapes, sizes and postures. Most are the work of sculptor Antoniucci Volti (1915–89), who was born in Villefranche-sur-Mer.

The citadel opens 9 or 10 am to noon and 2 or 3 pm to 5, 6 or 7 pm Wednesday to Saturday, and 2 or 3 to 5, 6 or 7 pm Sunday. Admission is free. During Les Petits Matins de la Citadelle (☎ 04 93 01 73 68), every Friday between April and September, you can indulge in breakfast in the museum garden at 9 am, followed by a guided tour of

the citadel and old town from 9.30 am. Tickets cost 50FF.

Chapelle de St-Pierre Villefranche was a favourite of Jean Cocteau (1889–1963), who sought solace here in 1924 following the death of his companion Raymond Radiguet. In 1957 Cocteau decorated the inside of Chapelle de St-Pierre, a derelict 14th-century Romanesque chapel used by local fishermen to store their nets until the 68-year-old artist got his hands on it. The engraving above the entrance to the waterfront chapel reads 'Enter this building as if it were made of living stone'. The interior, pastel-coloured frescoes, the altar – carved out of a rock from La Turbie – and its cloths, crucifix and candelabra inside the waterfront chapel were all designed by Cocteau.

Mass is celebrated in the chapel (☎ 04 93 76 90 70) once a year – on 29 June, the feast day of St-Peter, the patron saint of fishermen. The chapel can be visited 10 am to noon and 4 to 8.30 pm Tuesday to Sunday, June to September. Hours the rest of the year are sporadic. Admission costs 12FF.

When in town, Cocteau stayed at Hôtel Welcome, a restored 17th-century convent opposite the chapel on quai Courbet. He wrote the play *Orphée* (Orpheus), and the libretto for Stravinsky's *Oedipus Rex* here.

Places to Stay & Eat Two-star *Hôtel de la Darse* (☎ 04 93 01 72 54, ave Général de Gaulle), at the pleasure port, has doubles with shower for 290FF (320FF with toilet too, 380FF with sea view).

Cocteau's *Hôtel Welcome* (☎ 04 93 76 27 62, fax 04 93 76 27 66, e reservation@ welcomehotel.com, 1 quai Amiral Courbet), overlooking the old port, has doubles which cost upwards of 570/690FF in low/high season. Rooms with a balcony, where you can breakfast overlooking the sea, cost 710/ 820FF.

Quai Amiral Courbet is lined with terrace restaurants: Eat the catch of the day at *La Fille du Pêcheur* (☎ 04 93 01 90 09) at No 13, or if you prefer your fish sliced try *Carpaccio* at No 17; the tuna carpaccio melts in your mouth.

St-Jean-Cap Ferrat
postcode 06230 ● pop 1907

Once a fishing village, St-Jean-Cap Ferrat (Sant Jouan Cau Ferrat in Provençal) lies on the spectacular wooded peninsula of Cap Ferrat, which conceals a bounty of million-aires' villas and a star-studded past. Charlie Chaplin, Churchill and Cocteau all holi-dayed here. King Leopold II of Belgium and *Pink Panther* actor David Niven (1910–83) retired here. Writer Somerset Maugham lived – never without house guests – and died at the luxurious Villa Mauresque; Noël Coward, Ian Fleming, TS Eliot and Evelyn Waugh were among his regular guests. British film director Michael Powell ran a hotel at the port. In 1938 Murray Burnett wrote the play *Everybody Comes to Rick's* here, which was the basis for the classic film *Casablanca*.

Several coastal paths *(sentiers pédestres)* wend their way around Cap Ferrat. One leads from sandy **Plage de Passable** on the cape's western shore to the cafe-lined port on the eastern side of the cape, from where it is an easy 30-minute stroll to Beaulieu-sur-Mer. An 8km-walk (two to three hours) takes you right around the cape. Routes are marked on a map distributed at the tourist office (☎ 04 93 76 08 90, fax 04 93 76 16 67), 59 ave Denis Séméria. On clear days scale the 164 steps of the *phare* (lighthouse) on the cape's most southern tip for a stun-ning panorama of the coast from Italy to the Ésterel.

Villa Ephrussi de Rothschild
On the narrow isthmus of Cap Ferrat is the Musée de Béatrice Ephrussi de Rothschild (☎ 04 93 01 33 09, [e] message@villaephrussi .com), in a *belle epoque* villa built for the Baroness de Rothschild in 1912. Her house was designed in the style of the great Re-naissance houses of Tuscany and took 40 architects seven years to build. It abounds with paintings, tapestries, porcelain and an-tique furniture and is surrounded by seven hectares of beautiful gardens, each mani-cured in a different style. The central garden was landscaped like a ship's deck so that the baroness could imagine herself aboard the *Île de France* ship after which she named the villa. On her ship's prow, stands an en-chanting temple of love, behind which sprawl Spanish, Japanese, Florentine, cac-tus and oriental gardens. Different herbs, lauriers roses and an olive grove adorn the Jardin Provençal.

The villa opens 10 am to 7 pm in July and August; 10 am to 6 pm, mid-February to June, September and October. The rest of the year, the villa opens 10 am to 6 pm weekends, and the gardens only between 2 and 6 pm weekdays. Admission to the gar-dens and ground-floor collection costs 49FF (those aged seven to 17, 37FF). A ticket to the collection on the 1st floor is an extra 14FF.

Bus No 111 linking Nice and St-Jean-Cap Ferrat stops at the foot of the driveway leading to Villa Rothschild, at the northern end of ave Denis Séméria (the D25). The stop is called 'Passable'. By train, get off at Beaulieu-sur-Mer from where it is 20 min-utes' walk: from the seafront, follow prom-enade Maurice Rouvier southwards and turn right along the 2nd alleyway (just be-fore the melon pink villa built on the rocks). Continue uphill along ave Honoré Sauvan (note the round-shaped villa on the left through the trees) to the D25.

Places to Stay
Among the cheapest is one-star *La Frégate* (☎ 04 93 76 04 51, fax 04 93 76 14 93, 11 ave Denis Séméria), on the western side of the port, which touts 10 shower-equipped rooms costing 230FF (310FF with toilet too). *L'Oursin* (☎ 04 93 76 04 65, fax 04 93 76 12 55, [e] oursin@ wanadoo.fr, 1 ave Denis Séméria) is another 'cheapie'.

The most expensive is Michael Powell's former haunt, *La Voile d'Or* (☎ 04 93 01 13 13, fax 04 93 76 11 17, [e] reservation@ lavoiledor.fr, ave Mermoz), overlooking the port from its eastern quay. Today it boasts four stars with sky-high prices to match (starting at 1100/1980FF in low/high sea-son). Similar rates are charged at *Grand Hôtel du Cap Ferrat* (☎ 04 93 76 50 50, fax 04 93 76 04 52, 71 blvd Général de Gaulle), an equally dreamy paradise.

NICE TO MENTON

Beaulieu-sur-Mer
postcode 06310 • pop 3701

Upmarket Beaulieu-sur-Mer never witnessed such a grand time as during the turn-of-the-century's flamboyant *belle epoque*, when Europe's wealthy and aristocratic flocked to the resort.

French architect Gustave Eiffel lived at the waterfront Villa Durandy from 1896 until his death in 1923; the Florentine-style villa was consequently converted into luxury holiday apartments (see Places to Stay & Eat). Next door is the Villa Grecque Kérylos, Beaulieu's main draw.

Tamer remnants of the resort's golden age include the **Grand Casino**, 4 ave Fernand Dunan, built in 1928 and still drawing wild cards until 4 or 5 am daily; and the neighbouring La Rotonde (1899), a dome structure built as a hotel, used as a hospital during WWII and today home to the **Musée du Patrimoine Berlugan**, dedicated to local history. Across from the harbour are the **Jardins de L'Olivaie**, the venue for a two-week Jazz Parade in August.

Beaulieu's shingle **beach** overlooks Baie des Fourmis (Bay of Ants). From here, narrow **promenade Maurice Rouvier** leads south-westwards beneath a hedgerow of lauriers roses to the port of St-Jean-Cap Ferrat, making for a pleasant 30-minute stroll (2.5km). From St-Jean-Cap Ferrat, several more walking paths are marked.

The tourist office (☎ 04 93 01 02 21, fax 04 93 01 44 04, ℮ tourisme@ot-beaulieu-sur-mer.fr), next to the train station on place Georges Clémenceau, opens 9 am 12.30 pm and 2 or 3 to 7 pm Monday to Sunday lunchtime. It is online at www.ot-beaulieu-sur-mer.fr. From the tourist office, walk down the steps that lead beneath the rail tracks and along pedestrianised rue du Marché. At the road junction, continue straight along pedestrianised rue Gallieni to central blvd du Maréchal Leclerc and the seafront. Villa Kérylos is 15 minutes' walk south-west from here.

Villa Grecque Kérylos This luxurious villa, perched on the rocky Baie des Fourmis peninsula, is a reconstruction of an ancient Greek dwelling, built in 1902 for scholar and archaeologist Théodore Reinach (1860–1928). The villa took seven years to complete and is a near-perfect reproduction of an Athenian villa from the 1st and 2nd centuries BC.

The rooms retain their original Hellenic name and purpose. From the marble bath tub decorated with mosaics of splashing dolphins in the *balanéion* (bathroom), Reinach's male guests retired to the *triklinos* (dining room) and afterwards to the *andron*, a large parlour clad in yellow marble from Siena. It appears Reinach saw no need to invite women to the villa where he lived, given it has no *gynaeceum*, the parlour to which women retired after dinner in ancient Greece. In the gardens, a botanical trail highlights the ancient uses of plants typical to Greece and the French coast.

Villa Grecque Kérylos (☎ 04 93 01 61 70, ℮ vkerylos@libertysurf.fr), ave Gustave Eiffel, opens 10.30 am to 7 pm in July and August; 10.30 am to 6 pm, September to November and mid-February to July; and 2 to 6 pm weekdays, and 10.30 am to 6 pm weekends, the rest of the year. Admission costs 45FF (students and children aged under eight, 25FF). In summer, concerts are held here. Tickets (100FF) are only sold on the day of the concert, but advance reservations by telephone are accepted.

Places to Stay & Eat Beaulieu's bargain-basement hotel is one-star *Hôtel Rivièra* (☎ 04 93 01 04 92, fax 04 93 01 19 31, 6 rue Paul Dommer), north off blvd du Maréchal Leclerc. Singles/doubles with washbasin and bidet cost 180/190FF; doubles/ triples/ quads with shower and toilet are 280/360/ 440FF.

Famed, four-star and very pink *La Réserve de Beaulieu* (☎ 04 93 01 00 01, fax 04 93 01 28 99, ℮ reservebeaulieu@ relaischateaux.fr, 5 blvd du Maréchal Leclerc) has been Beaulieu's decadent hangout since its grand opening in the 1870s. Its cheapest rooms cost from 980/2420FF in low/high season.

At the former family home of Gustave Eiffel, *Résidence Eiffel* (☎ 04 93 76 46 46, *fax 04 93 76 46 00,* e *info@ residence-eif-fel.com, rue Gustave Eiffel),* weekly rates for a four-person self-catering studio start at 3745/5950FF in low/high season. Anyone can feast on the magnificent sea views its terrace restaurant and salon de thé offer.

Cap d'Ail
postcode 06320 • pop 4565

There is little to do on unpoetically named Cape of Garlic – a lush, heavily vegetated headland of palm trees and pines, bespeckled with villas – except stroll or swim.

Greta Garbo and Valentina Schlee both hung out on here in the 1960s. Cocteau's spectacular **amphitheatre** on chemin des Oliviers is used as a youth theatre by the Centre Méditerranéen d'Études Françaises (☎ 04 93 78 21 59).

Smoking and dogs are banned on **Plage La Réserve de La Mala**, Cap d'Ail's shingle beach tucked in a small cove. To get here from Cap d'Ail train station, walk down the steps to ave Raymond Gramaglia, a promenade from where the coastal path can be accessed. Bear west (right) for a 20-minute stroll around rocks to the beach, or east (left) for a more strenuous 3.5km-walk to Monaco. Information panels explain the flora and fauna. During rough seas, the path is closed.

The tourist office (☎ 04 93 78 02 33, fax 04 92 10 74 36, e cap-dail@monte-carlo.mc), 87 bis ave du 3 Septembre, at the eastern end of the village on the N98, has details on other walks in the area.

Cap d'Ail's other attraction is its seaside hostel, *Relais International de la Jeunesse* *(☎ 04 93 78 18 58, 26 ave Scuderi),* signposted from ave Raymond Gramaglia. A bed in a four-, six- or 10-bed dorm costs 70FF per night, including breakfast and sheets. Travellers have to vacate their rooms between 9.30 am and 5 pm (curfew is at 11 pm). It opens April to 30 September.

Cap Martin
Cap Martin is the coastal quarter of Cap Martin-Roquebrune. This green headland is best known for its sumptuous villas, presumptuous collection of royal honorary

citizens and famous past residents – among them, Winston Churchill, Coco Chanel, Marlène Dietrich, the architect Le Corbusier, designer Eileen Gray and the Irish poet WB Yeats.

Cap Martin-Roquebrune tourist office (☎ 04 93 35 62 87, fax 04 93 28 57 00), 20 ave Paul Doumer, is at the northern end of the cape, midway between Carnolès and Cap Martin-Roquebrune train stations. It stocks information on the medieval hill-top village of Roquebrune (see Grande Cornich later in this section) and arranges guided tours to its 10th-century chateau and visits to Corbusier's seashore studio and Eileen Gray's former coastal abode.

Things to See & Do Exploring on foot is one of the most pleasurable pastimes on Cap Martin. The closest beach to Cap Martin-Roquebrune train station, ave de la Gare, is **Plage du Buse**, two minutes' walk from the station and accessible from ave Le Corbusier.

Ave Le Corbusier follows the coast eastwards, around Baie de Roquebrune to the northern end of the cape where it turns into promenade Le Corbusier. It runs past **Cabanon Le Corbusier**, a wooden chalet used by Le Corbusier as his studio in summer. In 1965 the architect suffered a heart attack while diving off Cap Martin and died. He is buried in Roquebrune cemetery. The tourist office runs a once-weekly visit (advance reservations only) to the cabanon.

Another fine walk is from Cap Martin to Monte Carlo (three hours). Inland, Roquebrune hill-top village is one hour's walk (up numerous staircases) from Cap Martin-Roquebrune train station (1½ hours from Carnolès).

Places to Stay The most affordable place on Cap Martin is one-star *Hôtel Europe Village (☎ 04 93 35 62 45, 04 92 10 13 10, fax 04 93 57 72 59, 242 ave Virginie Hériot),* which has simple rooms costing 280/390FF. Two-star *Hôtel Westminster (☎ 04 93 35 00 68, fax 04 93 28 88 50,* e *westmins@imaginet.fr, 14 ave Louis Laurens-Cabbé),* about 500m west of Cap

Martin-Roquebrune train station, has rooms costing upwards of 210/310FF.

MOYENNE CORNICHE

Cut through rock in the 1920s, the Moyenne Corniche takes you from Nice past the Col de Villefranche (149m), Èze and Beausoleil, the French town up the hill from Monte Carlo in Monaco.

Getting There & Away

To/from Nice, bus No 112 operated by Rapides Côte d'Azur (☎ 04 93 85 64 44 for information) serves the Moyenne Corniche, stopping at Èze and Beausoleil.

By train from Nice, get off at Èze-sur-Mer train station on the Corniche Inférieure, from where shuttle buses transport tourists up and down the hill between May and October (20FF, eight buses in either direction daily, timed to coincide with train arrivals/departures). Failing that, it's a 3km uphill trudge on foot to Èze village.

Èze

postcode 06360 ● pop 2526
● elevation 390m

Perched on a rocky peak is picturesque Èze (Ezo in Provençal), a village once occupied by Ligurians and Phoenicians and grossly overrun with tourists today. Below is its modern coastal counterpart, Èze-sur-Mer, accessible by road or train from the Corniche Inférieure.

The German philosopher Friedrich Nietzsche (1844–1900) spent some time here, during which he started to write *Thus Spoke Zarathustra*; the path that links Èze-sur-Mer and Èze is named after him. Walt Disney also holidayed here once.

The tourist office (☎ 04 93 41 26 00, fax 04 93 41 04 80, e eze@webstore.fr), place Général de Gaulle, also has information on its Web site at www.eze-riviera.com.

Vieille Ville The steep narrow streets leading up to the top of the medieval hill-top village are crammed with art galleries, souvenir shops and pricey cafes. The chateau ruins which crown Èze are surrounded by a cactus-laden **Jardin Exotique**, open 9 am to

noon and 2 pm to dusk. Those keen to savour the marvellous panorama of Cap Ferrat to the Massif de l'Ésterel have no choice but pay the cheeky 12FF admission fee.

Perfumeries Perfumery Fragonard (see Grasse in the Cannes Area chapter) has an outlet in Èze where the subtleties of its sweet-smelling products can be discovered. The Fragonard factory (☎ 04 93 41 05 05), on the eastern edge of Èze on the Moyenne Corniche, can be visited by free guided tour. Rival perfumery Galimard (☎ 04 93 41 10 70), place de Gaulle, also has an outlet here.

Places to Stay There is a camp site and good-value auberge above Èze village on the Col d'Èze (see Observatoire de Nice on the following page).

In Èze village the cheapest option, always booked months in advance, is 11-room *Hôtel du Golf* (☎ 04 93 41 18 50, fax 04 93 41 29 93, place de la Colette), which has rooms for one or two costing 160FF (350/450FF with shower/shower and toilet). Booked out by a dramatically different clientele is four-star *Château de la Chèvre d'Or* (☎ 04 92 10 66 66, fax 04 93 41 06 72, e chevredor@relaischateaux.fr, rue du Barri). Its nine luxurious rooms kick off at 1800FF.

GRANDE CORNICHE

The Grande Corniche was built by Napoleon along part of the Roman via Julia Augusta. Its entire length is shot through with spectacular (dangerous) tunnels and blinding hairpin bends – all of which proved sufficiently cliff-hanging in the 1950s to act as a backdrop to Hitchcock's film *To Catch a Thief* (1956), starring Cary Grant and Grace Kelly. Ironically, the Hollywood actress, who met her Monégasque Prince Charming while shooting the film, died in 1982 after crashing her car on this same road.

Getting There & Away

This road is practically impossible to explore without your own wheels. To/from Nice, bus No 115 stops at La Trinité and La

Turbie en route to Peille (one hour, four buses daily Monday to Saturday).

Observatoire de Nice

This 19th-century, classical-domed observatory, 5km east of Nice centre atop Mont Gros (375m), was designed by French architects Gustave Eiffel and Charles Garnier. It sits amid 35 hectares of landscaped parkland. When the observatory opened in 1887, its telescope – 76cm in diameter – was among the largest in Europe. It has a Web site at www.obs-nice.fr (French only).

Guided 1½-hour tours (30FF) of the observatory (☎ 04 92 00 31 45, 04 93 85 85 58) are possible at 3 pm on Saturday; at other times, you must make an appointment. Stargazers keen to observe the skies should head instead to Astrorama (☎ 04 93 41 23 04), a planetarium and astronomy centre 8km farther east along the Grande Corniche in La Trinité. On the Col d'Èze, turn left along a fairly small road signposted 'Parc Départemental de la Grande Corniche-Astrorama'. Astrorama opens 6 pm to 10 or 11 pm Monday to Saturday, June to August; and from 6 pm Friday and Saturday only, the rest of the year. Admission costs 40FF (children aged seven to 10, 30FF).

Places to Stay & Eat The Col d'Èze offers a couple of excellent value places to stay. *Camping Les Romarins* (☎/fax 04 93 01 81 64), at the western end of the Col d'Èze, charges 105FF for two people with tent and car. It opens April to October.

From Les Romarins, it is a short walk to 10-room *Hermitage du Col d'Èze* (☎ 04 93 41 00 68, fax 04 93 41 24 05), an old-style inn spectacularly set at the top of the mountain pass and touting unbeatable views from its terrace restaurant. A night's sleep costs upwards of 170FF for a double (310FF with shower and toilet).

La Turbie

postcode 06320 • pop 3043

La Turbie teeters on a promontory directly above Monaco and offers a stunning nighttime vista of the principality. By day, an unparalleled aerial view can be had from the gardens of the **Trophée d'Auguste**, a trophy monument on the highest point of the old Roman road. It was built by Roman Emperor Augustus in 6 BC to celebrate his victory over the Alps. The 45 Alpine tribes he conquered are listed on the 9m-wide inscription carved on the western side of the monument.

Restoration work started on the trophy in the 1920s. Steps lead to the top of the shoddily reconstructed monument and there is a history museum at its base. The site (entrance on place Théodore de Banville) opens from 9.30 am to 6 pm, April to mid-June; 9.30 am to 7 pm, mid-June to mid- September; and from 10 am to 5 pm Tuesday to Sunday, the rest of the year. Admission costs 25FF (students and those aged 12 to 18, 15FF).

La Turbie village is unexciting bar its small but intact old town, neatly packed around the Baroque-style **Église St-Michael** (1777). From the village, a perilously steep mountain road leads to the top of **Mont Agel** (1110m), the slopes of which are graced with the greens of Monte Carlo Golf Club, a members-only club at a heady height of 810m.

Places to Stay Simple *Hôtel Le Cesarée* (☎ 04 93 41 16 08, fax 04 93 41 19 49, 16 cours Albert 1er), opposite the entrance to the Trophée d'Auguste, has rooms for 310/360FF.

Rooms for one or two at *Hôtel Napoléon* (☎ 04 93 41 00 54, fax 04 93 41 28 93, 7 ave de la Victoire) cost a straight 300FF.

Cap Martin-Roquebrune

postcode 06190 • pop 11,966
• elevation 70m

Cap Martin-Roquebrune, sandwiched between Monaco and Menton, became part of France in 1861; prior to that it was a free town following its revolt against Grimaldi rule in 1848. The town is neatly divided into four quarters, stretching northwards from the exclusive suburb of Cap Martin on the coast, accessible from the Corniche Inférieure (see that section earlier), to the medieval hill-top town of Roquebrune (300m), which straddles the Grande Corniche. The less touristy quarters of St-Roman and Carnolès border Monaco and Menton respectively.

NICE TO MENTON

Medieval Roquebrune This is a donjon complete with a re-created feudal castle dating from the 10th century. The mock-medieval **Tour Anglaise** (English Tower) near the entrance was built by wealthy British lord, William Ingram, who bought the chateau in 1911. His fairytale tower caused such an outrage in the village that the state almost immediately classified the chateau as a historical monument to protect it from further fantastical modifications. The tortuous little streets leading up to it are lined with souvenir shops and overrun with tourists in summer. Don't miss impressive rue Moncollet, with its arcaded passages and stairways carved out of the rock.

Cemetery Swiss architect Le Corbusier is buried with his wife in the old cemetery at the top of the village. The grave – designed by Corbusier before his death – is adorned by a cactus and the epitaph, *ici repose Charles Édouard Jeannet (1887–1965)*, painted in Corbusier's cursive hand on a small yellow, red and blue ceramic tile. Until 1948 William Butler Yeats (1865–1938) was also buried in Roquebrune cemetery. The writer died in 1938 in Cap Martin-Roquebrune while wintering on Cap Martin. His remains were moved to his native Ireland in 1948.

To get to the cemetery from central place des 2 Frères, walk eastwards to the end of rue Grimaldi, turn left onto rue d'Église, right onto rue de la Fontaine, then left onto chemin de Gorbio from where 160 steps lead to Le Corbusier's grave (section J).

The Cap Martin-Roquebrune tourist office (see under Corniche Inférieure earlier in this chapter) arranges visits to the architect's summer house on Cap Martin.

Arrière-Pays Niçois

The Niçois hinterland stretches inland from Nice to Menton. It is studded with medieval hill-top villages, which were perched aloft rocky crags as a safeguard and lookout point.

GETTING THERE & AWAY
The region is practically impossible to explore without your own transport. To/from Nice, there are two or three buses daily Monday to Saturday to Coaraze (line No 303; one hour) via Contes, and two buses daily Monday to Saturday to Berre-les-Alpes (line No 302; 55 minutes). From Menton, there are buses to/from Ste-Agnès (line No 902; 45 minutes, three daily) and Gorbio (line No 901).

CONTES & COARAZE
Roman Contes (pop 6644, postcode 06390) sits on a rock shaped like a ship above the River Paillon de Contes. **Châteauneuf de Contes**, 6km south-west, is a small hamlet at the foot of the overgrown ruins of an older village, abandoned prior to WWI. A path, occasionally barred by a territorial pack of goats, leads from the road to the crumbling ruins, which (goats allowing) can be freely explored.

To get to the **ruines de Châteauneuf** from Châteauneuf de Contes, follow the route de Châteauneuf (D815) through the village, then bear left at the wrought-iron roadside cross along route des Chevaliers de Malte. The ruins are 2km from here. Continuing westwards along the D815, you come to **Tourrette Levens**, a particularly dramatic hilltop village crowned with a chateau, which houses a collection of exotic butterflies.

Coaraze (postcode 06390, pop 659, elevation 640m), 9km north of Contes on the Col St-Roch (D15), is known as the *village du soleil* (village of the sun) after the ceramic **sun dials** that adorn its cobbled streets. The Provençal poem, engraved in stone next to the green lizard mosaic on place Félix-Giordan, tells the tale of how villagers trapped the devil and demanded he sacrifice his lizard-like tail to be set free. Coaraze is derived from the Provençal words '*coa raza*' meaning 'cut tail'. The village celebrates an olive festival on 15 August.

Places to Stay & Eat
In Berre-les-Alpes (675m), 7km north-east of Contes, rooms with shower, toilet and mountain view for one or two people at

one-star *Hôtel des Alpes* (☎ 04 93 91 80 05, fax 04 93 91 85 69, 2 ave Borriglione) cost 250FF. Uphill on central place Bellevue, *Hôtel Beauséjour* (☎ 04 93 91 80 08) has seven doubles costing 200FF to 250FF.

In Coaraze, Logis de France's *Auberge du Soleil* (☎ 04 93 79 08 11, fax 04 93 79 37 79), tucked in the village's heart, has 10 doubles with bathroom costing 370FF to 520FF. The auberge opens mid-March to mid-November. Both Contese and Coaraze have a handful of places to eat.

PEILLE & PEILLON
Quaintly restored Peille (postcode 06440, pop 2055, elevation 630m) is quite un-touched by tourism tack despite the raving reports it gets as being among the hinter-land's most intact hill-top village. Its east-ern entrance is guarded by the 12th-century **Chapelle St-Roch**, place Jean Mioul.

Captions are written in Pelhasc in the **Musée du Terroir**, open 2 to 6 pm summer weekends. This is a dialect specific to Peille and distinguishable from the Niçois dialect by its absent R's and silent L's – the Peil-lasques say *carriea* instead of *carriera* (Niçois for *rue*, meaning street). Peille cele-brates a wheat and lavender festival in August.

Six kilometres of hairpins south-west of Peille on the D53 towards Peillon, is **La Grave** (pop 516), a blot-on-the-landscape cement works where the hinterland's lime-stone is turned into cement. The best aerial view of Peille and La Grave is from the **Col de la Madone** (927m), a beautiful, stone-tunnelled mountain pass (the D22) that runs eastwards from Peille to Ste-Agnès.

Peillon (postcode 06440, pop 1229, ele-vation 456m), 14km east of Nice, is known for its precarious *nid d'aigle* (eagle's nest) location. From the village car park, a foot-path leads to the **Chapelle des Pénitents Blancs**, noteworthy for its set of macabre 15th-century frescoes. Longer trails lead to Peille (two hours on an old Roman road), La Turbie (two hours) and Chapelle St-Martin (1½ hours). North of Peillon, the **Gorges du Peillon** (D21) cut through the Peillon Valley to **L'Escarène** (pop 2138), an important mule stop in the 17th and 18th

centuries for traders working the Route du Sel (salt road) from Nice to Turin.

Places to Stay & Eat
In Peillon, upmarket *Auberge de la Ma-done* (☎ 04 93 79 91 17, fax 04 93 79 99 36, e info@ch-demeure.com) touts three-star doubles costing 470FF to 1600FF, depend-ing on season, room size and view. Its restaurant, specialising in local Peillonnais cuisine, opens Thursday to Tuesday. Both rooms and tables need booking in advance.

GORBIO & STE-AGNÈS
The flowery hill-top village of **Gorbio** (post-code 06920, pop 1162, elevation 360m), 10km north-west of Menton and 2km west of Ste-Agnès as the crow flies, is best known for its annual Fête Dieu in June. On this feast day, during a traditional Proces-sion aux Limaces, villagers light up Gor-bio's medieval cobble streets with snail shells set in pots of sand and filled with burning olive oil.

A trail leads from Gorbio to neighbouring **Ste-Agnès** (pop 1104), which commands a bird's-eye view from its 780m perch and claims to be Europe's highest seaside vil-lage. Steps lead from Montée du Souvenir to the scanty 12th-century chateau ruins that crown the village. Beneath, is **Fort Ste-Agnès**, a 2500 sq metre underground fort, built between 1931 and 1938 as part of a ser-ies of fortifications intended to defend Nice and its coastline. Close to the drawbridge, the reinforced concrete bunkers of one of four artillery blocks are clearly visible. The fort can be visited by guided tour (☎ 04 93 35 87 35 at the tourist office) between 3 and 6 pm, July to September; and 2.30 to 5.30 pm weekends, the rest of the year. Admission costs 20FF (children aged under 16, 10FF).

Menton & Around

MENTON
postcode 06500 • pop 29,266
Menton (Mentan in Provençal) is reputed to be the warmest spot on the Côte d'Azur (par-ticularly in winter). Only a few kilometres

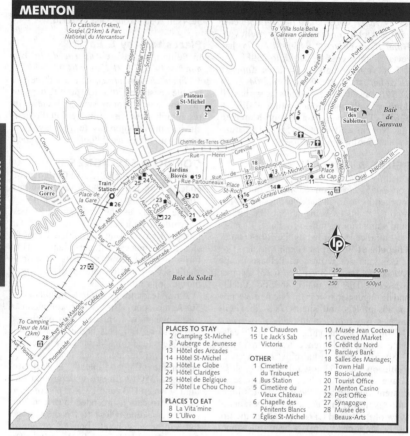

MENTON

PLACES TO STAY
2 Camping St-Michel
3 Auberge de Jeunesse
13 Hôtel des Arcades
14 Hôtel St-Michel
23 Hôtel Le Globe
24 Hôtel Claridges
25 Hôtel de Belgique
26 Hôtel Le Chou Chou

PLACES TO EAT
8 La Vita'mine
9 L'Ulivo

12 Le Chaudron
15 Le Jack's Sab
    Victoria

OTHER
1 Cimetière
    du Trabuquet
4 Bus Station
5 Cimetière du
    Vieux Château
6 Chapelle des
    Pénitents Blancs
7 Église St-Michel

10 Musée Jean Cocteau
11 Covered Market
16 Crédit du Nord
17 Barclays Bank
18 Salles des Mariages;
    Town Hall
19 Bosio-Lalone
20 Tourist Office
21 Menton Casino
22 Post Office
27 Synagogue
28 Musée des
    Beaux-Arts

from the Italian border, it is popular with older holiday-makers, whose way of life have made the town's after-dark life tranquil compared with other coastal hot spots.

Gustave Flaubert, Guy de Maupassant, Katherine Mansfield, and Robert Louis Stevenson all found solace in Menton in the past. Today, the town mainly draws Italians from across the border and retains a magnetic charm free of the airs, graces and pretensions so prevalent elsewhere on the coast.

Historically Menton, along with neighbouring Cap Martin-Roquebrune, found itself under Grimaldi rule until 1848, when its people rebelled and declared a new independent republic under the protection of Sardinia. In 1861, the two towns voted to become part of France, forcing Charles III of Monaco to sell Menton to Napoleon III for four million FF.

Above all, Menton is famed for its cultivation of lemons. Giant, larger-than-life sculptures made from lemons, lemons and more lemons (about 130 tonnes) take over the town for two weeks during Menton's fabulous Fête des Citrons (Lemon Festival) in February. The festival kicks off around the ornamental Jardins Biovès on Mardi Gras.

Orientation & Information

The old town and port are wedged between Baie de Garavan (east) and Baie du Soleil, which stretches 3km westwards to Cap Martin-Roquebrune. Promenade du Soleil and its continuations quai Général Leclerc and quai de Monléon skirt the length of Menton's shingle beach. There are more beaches directly north-east of the old port and east of Port de Garavan, Menton's main pleasure-boat harbour.

Menton tourist office (☎ 04 92 41 76 76, fax 04 92 41 76 78, **e** ot@villedementon .com), 8 ave Boyer, doles out free maps and has information on thematic tours (Menton's *belle epoque*, artists, gardens and so on). It opens 9 am to 7 pm Monday to Saturday, and 9 am to 1 pm Sunday, May to September; and 8.30 am to 12.30 pm and 1.30 to 6 pm weekdays, and 9 am to noon and 2 to 6 pm Saturday, the rest of the year. Its Web site is at www.villedementon.com.

Banks abound on rue Partouneaux. Barclays Bank, 39 ave Félix Faure, has a 24-hour exchange machine outside, as does Crédit du Nord, place St-Roch. The post office is on cours George V.

Walking Tour

Down by the port, a small 17th-century fort crowns the tip of land wedged between Menton's two bays, behind which the old town sprawls. It was built in 1636 to defend Menton and later used as a salt cellar, prison and lighthouse. Today, the seafront bastion houses the **Musée Jean Cocteau** (☎ 04 93 57 72 30), square Jean Cocteau, in which drawings, tapestries and ceramics by the French artist are displayed. Cocteau restored and refurbished the building himself, decorating the outer walls with pebble mosaics. His gravestone, tucked in the shade of the bastion walls and looking out to sea, reads *Je reste avec vous* (I stay with you). In 1957 he was invited to decorate Menton's **Salles des Mariages** inside the town hall on place Ardoïno. The Jean Cocteau Museum opens 10 am to noon and 2 to 6 pm

Wednesday to Monday. Admission costs 20FF (students 15FF). Hours at the Marriage Hall (5FF) are 8 am to noon and 2 to 5 pm weekdays.

From the bastion, walk westwards along quai de Monléon then cut across place du Marché, an outdoor marketplace adjoining **Les Halles**, Menton's bustling indoor market. Walk under the arches at the eastern end of the square and cross cafe-filled **place aux Herbes** to get to rue St-Michel, the main pedestrian street in the **old town**.

From place du Cap a ramp leads up to the Italianate **Église St-Michel**, considered the grandest Baroque church in southern France. Its creamy facade is flanked by a 35m-tall clock tower and a 53m-high steeple, constructed between 1701 and 1703 and topped with a campanile typical of most Provençal churches. The square in front of the church is paved with a grey-and-white pebble mosaic featuring the Grimaldi coat of arms. Perched above St-Michael's Church on place de la Conception is the ornate, apricot **Chapelle des Pénitents Blancs** (1689).

Farther uphill via montée du Souvenir is the cypress-shaded **Cimetière du Vieux Château**, open 7 am to between 6 and 8 pm. The graves of English, Irish, Americans, New Zealanders and other foreigners who died here during the 19th century – including the inventor of rugby, the Reverend William Webb Ellis (1805–72) – can be seen in the cemetery's south-western corner. The view alone is worth the climb.

Continue northwards along steep chemin du Trabuquet to the **Cimetière du Trabuquet**, a much larger, multilevel and landscaped cemetery with stunning panoramic views over Menton and the sea and into Italy. The sign reading 'Commonwealth War Graves' seems a tad imprecise; you soon ascend into clearly marked sections set aside for those who 'died for France' *(mort pour la France)* in campaigns in both Asia and Africa. Even in the 'Commonwealth' section there's something for everyone, with tombstones dating from the late-19th to the mid-20th century in English, French, Flemish and even Russian.

NICE TO MENTON

Blvd de Garavan, which runs northwards parallel with chemin du Trabuquet, leads to the upmarket neighbourhood of **Garavan**, best known for its luxurious villas and imaginative public gardens. Between 1920 and 1921, the sick novelist Katherine Mansfield (1888–1923) stayed at the **Villa Isola Bella**, ave Katherine Mansfield, to try to ease her worsening tuberculosis. Her short story, *The Doves' Nest*, published the year she died, is about a group of lonely women living in a villa on the French Riviera.

Gardens

Garavan gardens include the **Jardin Fontana Rosa**, ave Blasco Ibañez, a garden created by Spanish novelist Blasco Ibañez in the 1920s and featuring fanciful benches, pergolas, pools and columns made from ceramic. Opposite, the **Jardin Exotique**, ave St-Jacques, was laid out for Lord Radcliffe in 1905. In France's most temperate garden, the **Jardin de Maria Serena**, 21 promenade Reine-Astrid, the temperature never falls below 5°C; the Villa Maria Serena was built by Charles Garnier in 1866 and is a venue for musical recitals in summer. The **Jardins des Colombières**, route des Colombières Garavan, was designed by Ferdinand Bac (1859–1952), comic writer and the illegitimate son of Napoleon III, between 1918 and 1927. Visits to all these gardens (30FF each) can be arranged through the tourist office.

At the far south-western end of promenade du Soleil, overlooking the Baie du Soleil, is the early 18th-century **Palais Carnolès**, a former summer residence of Monaco's royal family, which nowadays houses Menton's **Musée des Beaux-Arts** (☎ 04 93 35 49 71), 3 ave de la Madone. Its surrounding **Jardin de Sculptures** features sculptures set amid a lemon and orange grove. The palace opens 10 am to noon and 2 to 6 pm Wednesday to Monday.

Places to Stay

Camping Two-star *Camping St-Michel* (☎ 04 93 35 81 23, route des Ciappes de Castellar), open April to mid-October, is 1km north-east of the train station up plateau St-Michel.

Hostels The 80-bed *Auberge de Jeunesse* (☎ 04 93 35 93 14, fax 04 93 35 93 07, plateau St-Michel), open year round, is a sweaty walk uphill from the train station, with lots of steps. A bed for the night costs 68FF and you have to be in by the midnight curfew.

Hotels Next door to the train station, *Hôtel Le Chou Chou* (☎/fax 04 93 57 69 87, place de la Gare) has nine rooms above the bar costing 180/250FF. Heading into town, *Hôtel de Belgique* (☎ 04 93 35 72 66, fax 04 93 41 44 77, e hoel.de.belqique@ wanadoo.fr, 1 ave de la Gare) has singles with washbasin and bidet for 200FF and doubles with shower and toilet for 280FF.

Near the sea, two-star *Hôtel Claridges* (☎ 04 93 35 72 53, fax 04 93 35 42 90, e hotelclaridges@wanadoo.fr, 39 ave de Verdun) has rooms from 240/300FF. Air-conditioning costs an extra 20FF. At *Hôtel Le Globe* (☎ 04 92 10 59 70, fax 04 92 10 59 71, 21 ave de Verdun), part of the Logis de France chain, you pay 350FF to 400FF for a comfortable double warranting no complaints.

In town, *Hôtel des Arcades* (☎ 04 93 35 70 62, fax 04 93 35 35 97, 41 ave Félix Faures), under the arches, is one of Menton's most picturesque options. Basic washbasin-equipped rooms cost 200/220FF 260/300FF with shower and toilet).

Great sea views can be enjoyed at a price that won't break the bank at *Hôtel St-Michel* (☎ 04 93 57 46 33, fax 04 93 57 71 19, 1684 promenade du Soleil). Doubles with sea/street views start at 450/360FF.

Places to Eat

There are places to eat galore – at any time of day – along ave Félix Faure and its pedestrianised continuation, rue St-Michel. Place Clémenceau and place aux Herbes in the Vieille Ville are equally table-packed. Several spots on place du Cap dish up great Italian-inspired *bruschetta* (toasted bread lavishly piled high with a variety of savoury toppings) for 32FF per meal-sized slice. Pricier places to eat with terraces fanned by cool breezes line promenade du Soleil.

Notable places worth a munch include *La Vita'mine*, a snack bar at the easternmost end of rue St-Michel. Here, you can build your own takeaway 80/100/130g sandwich (8/10/12FF) or micro-/mega-/giga-fruit cocktail (18/27/45FF). *Le Jack's Sab Victoria* (☎ 04 93 57 91 22, promenade du Soleil) is an upbeat spot with beachfront terrace and trendy crowd who come here to lunch.

Sit-down *Le Chaudron* (☎ 04 93 35 90 25, 28 rue St-Michel) serves filling salads for 30FF to 68FF, while challenging bowls of mussels are the mainstay of *L'Ulivo* (☎ 04 93 35 45 65, place du Cap), an Italian-run place that has pasta dishes (starting at 54FF) and pizza (50FF) too.

The *covered food market* on quai de Monléon opens 5 am to 1 pm Tuesday to Sunday.

Shopping
Chocolate chess pieces and a game of draughts made from almond-flavoured Aixois *calissons* are sold at *Bosio-Lalone* (☎ 04 93 35 70 95, 19 rue Partouneaux), a chocolatier/pâtissier.

Getting There & Away
Bus The bus station (☎ 04 93 28 43 27), is next to 12 promenade Maréchal Leclerc, the northern continuation of ave Boyer. The information office opens 8 am to 12.30 pm and 2.15 to 6 pm weekdays, and 9 to 11 am Saturday.

There are buses to Monaco (12.50FF return, 30 minutes), Nice (28FF return, 1¼ hours), Ste-Agnès (43FF return, 45 min-utes), Sospel (60FF return, 45 minutes) and Ventimiglia, in Italy (14FF, 30 minutes).

Rapides Côte d'Azur (☎ 04 97 00 07 00) operates daily buses to/from Nice-Côte d'Azur airport (95/160FF one-way/return, 1¼ hours) via Monaco. Buses coincide with flight times.

Train The left-luggage counter at the train station opens 9 am to noon and 3 to 6.45 pm. Trains to Ventimiglia across the border cost 12FF and take 10 minutes. For more information on Côte d'Azur train services see earlier Getting There & Away sections.

AROUND MENTON
A string of mountain villages peer down on Menton from the **Col de Castillon** (707m), a hair-raising pass (D2566) that wends its way up the Vallée du Carei from the coast to **Sospel** (pop 2937), 21km north of Menton and gateway to the Parc National du Mercantour (see the Haute-Provence chapter). The road cuts through the **Fôret de Menton**, a thick forest traversed with walking trails, following which you pass the **Viaduc du Caramel**, a viaduct formerly used by the old Menton–Sospel tramway, which trundled its way through the valley in former times.

Castillon (pop 283), just south of the top of the pass, is considered a model of modern rural planning; the village was destroyed by an earthquake in 1887 then heavily bombed in 1944. The village was built anew in 1951, perched on the mountain slopes in true Provençal fashion. The Sospel–Menton bus stops in Castillon.

Cannes Area

Cannes is famous for its cultural activities, the most renowned being the 10-day International Film Festival in mid-May, which sees the city's population quadruple overnight. Cannes has just one museum and, since its speciality is ethnography, the only art you're likely to come across is in the many rather chichi galleries scattered around town or on the promenade where henna tattooists draw elaborate patterns on suntanned skins. The town's adopted slogan may well be 'life is a festival', but the main tourist season only runs from May to October.

Offshore from Cannes lie the two Lérins islands. Continuing north-eastwards along the coast, you arrive at Antibes and its singing cape, Vallauris and Golfe-Juan (Picasso territory). Then there's a cluster of arty, inland villages crowned with Matisse's Vence, Chagall's St-Paul de Vence and Renoir's Cagnes-sur-Mer. Farther inland is smelly Grasse.

The most stunning natural feature of the entire Côte d'Azur – apart from the sky blue sea, of course – is the lump of red porphyritic rock known as the Massif de l'Estérel. At its foot is St-Raphaël, a beachside resort town a couple of kilometres south-east of Roman Fréjus.

Cannes & North-East

CANNES
postcode 06400 • pop 68,214
It's the money of the affluent, readily spent with fashionable nonchalance, that keeps Cannes' expensive hotels, restaurants and exorbitant boutiques in business and ocean-liner-sized yachts afloat. But the harbour, the bay, the old quarter of Le Suquet, the beachside promenade, the beaches and the sunworshippers laid out on them, provide more than enough natural beauty to make at least a day trip here well worth the effort.

Highlights

- Stroll the length of La Croisette, the Riviera's classiest promenade, then head up to le Suquet, Cannes' old quarter

- Sail to the Lérins islands to see where the jailed 'Man in the Iron Mask' rotted in hell

- View Picassos in Antibes and Vallauris, Renoirs in Cagnes, and works by Matisse in Vence

- Gape at palatial seaside villas, mansions and fabulous gardens on Cap d'Antibes

- Take a long walk in red-rocked Massif de l'Estérel

- Create a designer perfume you can call your own in smelly Grasse

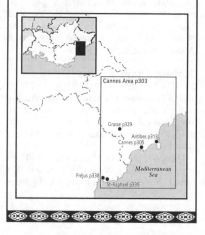

From Cannes (pronounced 'Can' in French; Cano in Provençal), route Napoléon winds northwards, passing Grasse and Castellane on its way to Digne-les-Bains and beyond.

Orientation
Don't expect to be struck down by glitz 'n' glamour the minute you step foot in Cannes. Seedy sex shops and peep shows abound

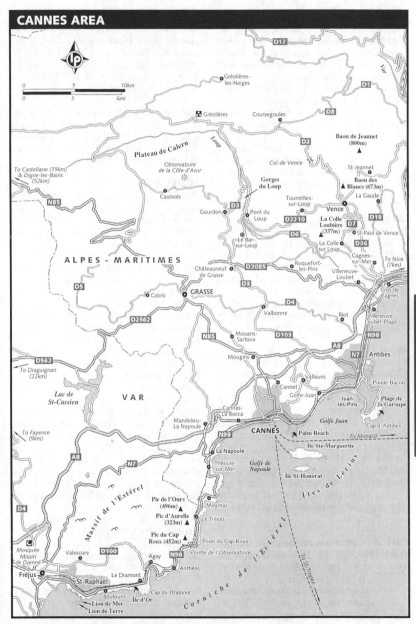

CANNES AREA

around the train station and bus stop on rue Jean Jaurès. Things glam up along rue d'Antibes, the main shop-til-you-drop street a couple of blocks south. Several blocks south again is Palais des Festivals, east of the Vieux Port (old port).

Cannes' famous promenade, the magnificent blvd de la Croisette, begins at Palais des Festivals and continues eastwards along Baie de Cannes to Pointe de la Croisette. Place Bernard Cornut Gentille, home to the main bus station, fills the north-western corner of the Vieux Port. Perched on a hill west of the Vieux Port is the less crowded, pedestrianised quarter of Le Suquet.

Information
Tourist Offices Cannes tourist office (☎ 04 93 39 24 53, 04 93 39 01 01, fax 04 92 99 84 23, e semoftou@palais-festivals-cannes .fr), on the ground floor of Palais des Festivals, opens 9 am to 7 pm weekdays, and 10 am to 6 pm weekends.

The tourist office annexe (☎ 04 93 99 19 77), next to the train station, opens 9 am to noon and 2 to 6 pm weekdays.

Money Banque de France, 8 blvd de la Croisette, exchanges currency 8.30 am to noon weekdays. Commercial banks dot rue d'Antibes and rue Félix Faure.

American Express (Amex; ☎ 04 93 38 15 87), 8 rue des Belges, opens 9 am to 6 pm weekdays, 9 am to noon Saturday; it exchanges all types of travellers cheques. The Thomas Cook bureau, 8 rue d'Antibes, opens 9 am to 10 pm. Office Provençal, inside Maison de la Chance on corner of rue Maréchal Foch and rue Jean Jaurès, opens 8 am to 8 pm. There is a 24-hour banknote exchange machine behind the port building on La Pantiero.

Post & Communications The central post office, 22 rue Bivouac Napoléon, opens 8 am to 7 pm weekdays, 8 am to noon Saturday. It has Cyberposte.

There is an Internet terminal inside the tourist office where you can surf for an initial 9FF, plus 1.10FF per minute. The terminal only accepts payment by credit card. Near the Auberge de Jeunesse (see Hostels under Places to Stay later in this section), Cyber Zone (☎ 04 93 99 14 77, e rochotey@hotmail.com), inside the Institut Riviera Langues at 26 rue de Mimont, charges 35FF per hour.

Bookshops English-language novels and guides are sold at Cannes English Bookshop (☎ 04 93 99 40 08), 11 rue Bivouac Napoléon. It opens 9.30 am to 1 pm and 2 to 7 pm Monday to Saturday.

Walking Tour
Since people-watching is the main reason to come to Cannes, and since people are best watched while strolling, and strolling is one of the few activities in Cannes that doesn't cost anything, taking a leisurely walk is highly recommended. You can even stop and pay to get your shoes polished by hand afterwards or invest in a henna tattoo courtesy of a street artist.

The best spots to walk (and be seen) are not far from the water. The pine- and palm-shaded walkway along **blvd de la Croisette**, known locally as La Croisette, is the Riviera's classiest promenade. **La Malmaison** (1863) at No 47, tucked between the Grand Hôtel and flashy Noga Hilton, hosts occasional art exhibitions. Continuing eastwards is **John Taylor & Son** (☎ 04 93 38 00 66, e jgil@john-taylor.fr), 55 blvd de la Croisette. The sparkling windows of this real-estate agent – founded in 1864 and an agent for Christie's auction house – are ideal for window-shopping, although the photographs of the fabulous properties displayed are likely to be the closest glimpse you'll get of the domiciles of the rich and famous.

When it all gets too much, pop into the **Carlton Inter-Continental**, 58 blvd de la Croisette, for tea on the terrace; this is what stars (who want to be seen) do. The hotel's twin cupolas, erected in 1912, were modelled on the breasts of La Belle Otéro, infamous for the string of lovers – including Spain's Alphonso XIII, Tsar Nicholas II and Leopold II of Belgium – she picked up

(see Hostels under Places to Stay later in this section)

CANNES

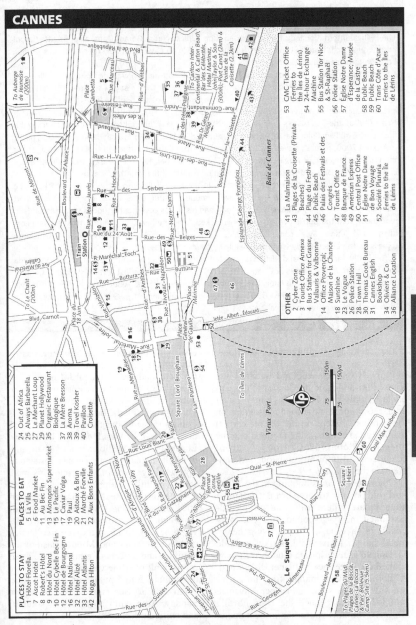

PLACES TO STAY
1 Hôtel Florella
7 Ascot Hotel
8 Robert's Hotel
9 Hôtel du Nord
10 Hôtel Cybelle Bec Fin
12 Hôtel de Bourgogne
16 Hôtel National
32 Hôtel Alizé
33 Hôtel Atlantis
42 Noga Hilton

PLACES TO EAT
5 La Villa
6 Food Market
11 Au Bec Fin
13 Monoprix Supermarket
15 Le Pacific
19 Caviar Volga
19 Paul
20 Astoux & Brun
21 Marché Forville
22 Aux Bons Enfants
24 Out of Africa
25 Always Barbarella
27 Le Mechant Loup
29 Planet Hollywood
35 Organic Restaurant
    Biologique
37 La Mère Bresson
38 Aroma
39 Tovel Kosher
40 Pavillon
    Croisette

OTHER
2 Cyber Zone
3 Tourist Office Annexe
4 Bus Station for Grasse,
    Vallauris & Valbonne
14 Office Provencal;
    Maison de la Chance
18 Sunshine
23 Le Vogue
26 Police Station
28 Town Hall
30 Thomas Cook Bureau
31 Cannes English
    Bookshop
34 Oliviers & Co
36 Alliance Location
41 La Malmaison
43 Plages de la Croisette (Private
    Beaches)
44 Plage du Festival
45 Public Beach
46 Palais des Festivals et des
    Congrès
47 Tourist Office
48 American Express
49 Banque de France
50 Central Post Office
51 Eglise Notre Dame
    de Bon Voyage
52 Société Planaria
    Ferries to the Île
    de Lérins
53 CMC Ticket Office
    (Ferries to
    the Îles de Lérins)
54 24-hour Exchange
    Machine
55 Bus Station Tor Nice
    & St-Raphaël
56 Police Station
57 Eglise Notre Dame
    d'Esperance; Musée
    de la Castre
58 Public Beach
59 Public Beach
60 Trans Côte d'Azur
    Ferries to the Îles
    de Lérins

euro currency converter €1 = 6.56FF

Starring at Cannes

The Festival International du Film is a closed shop. Unless you're Gérard Depardieu, Brigitte Bardot or otherwise rich, beautiful and worth a tabloid splash, you have absolutely no chance of scoring a ticket to the legendary Cannes film festival.

The 10-day festival revolves around the ugly, 60,000-sq-metre Palais des Festivals, called 'the bunker' by local Cannois. At the centre of the competition is the prestigious Palme d'Or, awarded by the jury and its president to the winning film – generally not a box office hit. Notable exceptions include Coppola's *Apocalypse Now* (1979), *Sex, Lies & Video Tape* (1989), David Lynch's *Wild at Heart* (1990) and Tarentino's *Pulp Fiction* (1994). An equally integral part of the annual festival is the Marché du Film (Film Market) where an estimated US$200 million worth of business takes place.

Around 7000 'names', trailed by 3000 journalists, attend the star-studded spectacle. Most stay at the Carlton, Majestic or Noga Hilton hotels. They eat at Eden Roc on the Cap, Alain Ducasse's Le Louis XV in Monaco and Roger Vergé's Moulin de Mougins, 8km north of Cannes.

Starlets have always stripped off at Cannes. In the early days dropping your top shocked. The 1954 festival, for example, saw the unknown Simone Sylva drop her top in front of actor Robert Mitchum who, being a gentleman and all that, had his hands covering her boobs within seconds to hide them from the public eye. The cameras clicked, it hit the headlines, Mitchum's wife was mortified – and Simone Sylva committed suicide six months later. The line of glamour girls who pose topless on the beach today (snapped mainly by tourists) is passé.

The Festival International du Film was created in 1939 to counter Mussolini's fascist propaganda film festival in Venice. It was not until after WWII however that the first festival starred at Cannes. Tickets (to be pitched for no later than 31 March) are issued by the Association France du Festival International du Film (☎ 01 45 61 66 00, [e] festival@festival-cannes.fr), 99 blvd Malesherbes, 75008 Paris. Visit online at www.festival-cannes.fr.

at the legendary gambling tables of Monte Carlo.

Plonked on the headland between the Vieux Port and Baie de Cannes is the legendary **Palais des Festivals** (Festival Palace). Most tourists pose for a photograph on the familiar 22 steps (minus the red carpet) leading up to entrance, then totter along the **allée des Étoiles du Cinèma**, a path of celebrity hand imprints, embedded in concrete on the pavement.

Opposite the boats bobbing in the **Vieux Port** (old port) is **square Lord Brougham**, a huge square where kids ride on an old-fashioned merry-go-round, old men play *pétanque* (a type of bowls using heavy metal balls), teens drink shakes outside McDonald's, and aspiring models wait to be spotted on the terrace of Planet Hollywood. A morning **flower market** fills the northern side of the square. Prosper Mérimée (1803–70), who penned the 1845 novella *Carmen*, which Bizet turned into an opera, died in a house on place Mérimée, east of the square on the corner of blvd de la Croisette and rue Maréchal Joffre.

Just west of the Vieux Port, hilly **Le Suquet** affords spectacular views of Cannes. Lord Brougham, the first foreigner to live in Cannes (after whom the square is named), built himself the **Villa Eleanore** (1862) here. Locals thought the former lord chancellor of England totally nutty when he insisted on laying a large green lawn around his mansion. The hill is topped by the majestic, 12th-century **Église Notre Dame d'Esperance** and adjoining **Chapelle de Ste-Anne** which houses the **Musée de la Castre** (☎ 04 93 38 55 26). Inside is a diverse collection of Mediterranean and Middle Eastern antiquities, and objects of ethnographic interest from all over the world. It opens 10 am to noon and 2 to 5 pm (6 pm April to June, 7 pm July to September) Wednesday to Sunday. Admission costs 10FF (students and children, free).

euro currency converter 10FF = €1.52

Beaches & Boat Excursions

Unlike Nice, Cannes is endowed with sandy beaches. Unfortunately most of the sand lining blvd de la Croisette is sectioned off for guests of the Croisette's fancy hotels. Here, sunworshippers pay for a cushioned sun-lounger – from 70FF per day on **Plage du Festival** to an astonishing 265FF on **Carlton Beach** – and lap up the beachside equivalent of room service (lunch delivered to your deck chair, strips of carpet leading to the water's edge and so on). This arrangement leaves only a relatively small strip of sand near the Palais des Festivals for the bathing pleasure of the picnicking hoi polloi. However, free public beaches, **Plages du Midi** and **Plages de la Bocca**, stretch for several kilometres westwards from the Vieux Port along blvd Jean Hibert and blvd du Midi.

Numerous Cannes-based companies, spread around the Vieux Port, run day trips by boat from Cannes to the Îles de Lérins (see that section later), St-Tropez, Monaco, Île de Port-Cros, Île de Porquerolles and San Remo (in Italy).

Places to Stay

Don't even consider staying in Cannes during the May festival unless you have booked months in advance. Many upmarket places only accept 12-day bookings during this period.

Places to Stay – Budget

Camping In Cannes-La Bocca, lying about 5.5km west of Cannes centre, *Parc Belle-vue* (☎ 04 93 47 28 97, fax 04 93 48 66 25, 67 ave Maurice Chevalier) opens April to October. It charges 102FF for two people with a tent and car. Bus No 9 from the bus station on place Bernard Cornut Gentille stops 400m from the site.

Hostels Cannes' modern *Auberge de Jeunesse* (☎/fax 04 93 99 26 79, e centre .sejour.youth.hostel.cannes@wanadoo.fr, 35 ave de Vallauris) is about 400m north-east of the train station. A bed in a four- or six-person dorm costs 80FF, including one free breakfast. If you don't have a Hostelling

International (HI) card, buy a 19FF one-night stamp. Each floor has a kitchen and there's a laundry room. Reception opens 8 am to 12.30 pm and 2.30 to 10.30 pm weekdays, and 3 to 10 pm weekends. Curfew is at midnight (2 am weekends).

Pleasant private hostel *Le Chalit* (☎ 04 93 99 22 11, e le_chalit@libertysurf.fr, 27 ave du Maréchal Galliéni), is about 300m north-west of the station. It charges 85FF for a bed in rooms for four to eight people. Sheets cost extra and it has two kitchens that guests can use.

Hotels Several budget hotels are clustered around the train station, including friendly *Hôtel Cybelle Bec Fin* (☎ 04 93 38 31 33, fax 04 93 38 43 47, 14 rue du 24 Août), which has basic doubles for 140FF (160FF with shower and toilet), starting at 230FF with shower and toilet). Bathroom-equipped triples cost 280FF. Its adjoining restaurant, Au Bec Fin, has filling 69FF *menus*.

At No 11 on the same street, *Hôtel de Bourgogne* (☎ 04 93 38 36 73, fax 04 92 99 28 41) touts singles/doubles with washbasin costing 190/220FF and doubles/triples with shower for 280/360FF.

Opposite the train station, uninspiring but cheap *Hôtel du Nord* (☎ 04 93 38 48 79, fax 04 92 99 28 20, 6 rue Jean Jaurès) sports basic one-star rooms for 190/230FF (250/300FF with shower and toilet). Around the corner, less busy *Ascot Hotel* (☎ 04 93 99 18 24, fax 04 93 99 12 26, 27 rue des Serbes) is bright and airy; it charges upwards of 150FF for a shower-equipped double (200FF with toilet too).

Heading towards the Auberge de Jeunesse, you pass the excellent-value but little-known *Hôtel Florella* (☎/fax 04 93 38 48 11, 55 blvd République). Its 12 rooms with washbasin cost 130/170FF; doubles with shower, TV and toilet cost 270FF.

One-star *Hôtel National* (☎ 04 93 39 91 92, fax 04 92 98 44 06, 8 rue Maréchal Joffre) has rooms with washbasin, bidet and TV costing 150/240FF (230/300FF with shower). Shower-equipped triples cost 350FF.

As with many hotels on the coast, rooms

CANNES AREA

at *Hôtel Atlantis* (☎ 04 93 39 18 72, fax 04 93 68 37 65, 4 rue du 24 Août) are not nearly as modern as its renovated reception suggests. Costing 220FF per double (240FF with shower and toilet), they are quite adequate for a night's sleep however.

Places to Stay – Mid-Range

Opposite the central post office, *Hôtel Alizé* (☎ 04 93 39 62 17, fax 04 93 39 64 32, e hotelalizecannes@compuserve.com, 29 rue Bivouac Napoléon) has singles/doubles with all mod cons costing upwards of 290/320FF.

Opposite the train station, *Robert's Hôtel* (☎ 04 93 38 05 07, 16 rue Jean Jaurès) has comfortable air-conditioned rooms costing 250/280FF.

Places to Stay – Top End

During the film festival, Cannes' horribly expensive hotels buzz with the frantic comings and goings of journalists, paparazzi and stars. Fortunately for their fans – who can only dream of staying in such places during Cannes' precious days of May – all of the top-end hotels are along blvd de la Croisette. These include *Carlton Inter-Continental* (☎ 04 93 06 40 06, e cannes@interconti.com) at No 58; Art Deco *Hôtel Martinez* (☎ 04 92 98 73 00, e matinez@concorde-hotels.com) at No 73, which hosts elegant musical soirees (80FF) at 11 am on Sunday September to July; *Noga Hilton* (☎ 04 92 99 70 00, e sales-cannes@hilton.com) at No 50; and *Hôtel Majestic* (☎ 04 92 98 77 00, fax 04 93 38 97 90) at No 14 (see the boxed text 'Starring at Cannes' earlier in this chapter). Guests pay at least 1600/3100FF per night for a double with town/sea view in low season (2200/4000FF in high season).

Places to Eat

Restaurants There are a few inexpensive restaurants around rue du Marché Forville and lots of little – though not necessarily cheap – restaurants along pedestrian rue St-Antoine, rue du Suquet and rue Meynadier. Up in Le Suquet, try the beautifully furnished, African-inspired *Out of Africa*

(☎ 04 93 68 98 06, 6–8 rue St-Dizier); or less-tame *Always Barbarella* (☎ 04 92 99 17 33, 16 rue St-Dizier), a house-music restaurant with guest DJs and an 85FF *menu* (served 7 to 9 pm).

Near the train station, *Au Bec Fin* (☎ 04 93 38 35 86, 12 rue du 24 Août) is a backpackers' favourite. It specialises in straightforward *cuisine familiale* (home cooking). *Menus* start at 69FF and mains cost 40FF to 115FF; the *daube de bœuf* (beef stew) a la Provençale and *sauté d'agneau au curry* (curried lamb) come heartily recommended.

Close by is atmospheric *La Villa* (☎ 04 93 38 79 73, 7 rue Marceau), inside a fine 19th-century villa framed with a flowery garden. Mains hover at 100FF and it hosts live music most evenings. The terrace, tucked beneath rambling plants in the shade of deep ochre walls, is enchanting.

Pavillon Croisette (42 blvd de la Croisette) serves a 42FF breakfast, oyster platters and a 98FF express *menu*. *Planet Hollywood* (☎ 04 93 06 78 27, 1 allée de la Liberté), which offers a 59FF Sunday brunch, has happy hour from 5 to 8 pm and provides a refuge for the odd celebrity playing truant from some official function.

For something fishy dine at *Astoux & Brun* (☎ 04 93 39 21 87, 27 rue Félix Faure). Every type and size of oyster is available by the dozen (95FF to 196FF), as well as elaborate fish platters (190/355FF for one/two people). In summer, chefs draw a crowd by preparing shellfish on the pavement outside.

In the centre, *Le Pacific* (☎ 04 93 39 46 71, 14 rue Vénizélos) is a favourite with local Cannois for its generous three-course 65FF *menu*. A 10-meal carnet costs 580FF.

Another hot choice is *Aux Bons Enfants* (80 rue Meynadier), which serves regional dishes such as aïoli garni, *mesclun* (a salad of dandelion greens and other roughage) and a 95FF *menu* in a convivial atmosphere. Other small restaurants dot this end of rue Meynadier.

Le Méchant Loup (☎ 04 93 68 32 67, 17 rue St-Antoine), also in Cannes' old-town maze, serves a refreshing cold cucumber soup and tempting salmon kebabs with

CANNES AREA

peach and orange butter. The Naughty Wolf, as it's translated, has *menus* starting at 125FF and – unusually for these parts – a 145FF vegetarian *menu*.

La Mère Bresson (☎ 04 93 39 59 24, 13 rue des Frères Pradignac) is another Provençal favourite with a pleasing outside terrace and *menus* costing upwards of 100FF.

Tovel Kosher (☎ 04 93 39 24 53, 3 rue du Docteur Gérard Monod) is a kosher spot with kosher *menus* (80FF to 120FF). *Organic Restaurant Biologique* (☎ 04 93 39 49 40, 6 rue Florian) specialises in just that: organic food to eat in or takeaway.

Aroma (22 rue Commandant André) is a classy bagel cafe which serves giant-sized bagels crammed with delectable goodies (such as cheese, cream and basil) to eat in (34FF) or takeaway (25FF).

Self-Catering A *food market* fills place Gambetta every morning (Tuesday to Sunday only in winter). *Marché Forville*, a covered fruit and vegetable market on rue du Marché Forville, two blocks north of place Bernard Cornut Gentille, opens Tuesday to Sunday.

Shops worth an extra-long browse include wine and liqueur specialist *Sunshine* and neighbouring *Caviar Volga* (5 rue Maréchal Joffre), a caviar emporium. *Paul* (10 rue Meynadier), the boulangerie, bakes honey, olive oil and other types of fougasse and an array of filled sesame-seed baguettes. *Oliviers & Co* (☎ 04 93 39 00 38, 4 rue Macé) offers olive oil *dégustation* (tasting).

Monoprix supermarket has entrances on rue Jean Jaurès, rue Maréchal Foch and rue Buttura, and opens 8.30 am to 8 pm Monday to Saturday.

Special Events

Cannes' Festival International du Film (International Film Festival) is held for 10 days in May. In mid-July, during the 10-day Nuits Musicales du Suquet, concerts and plays are held in the square in front of Église Notre Dame d'Ésperance.

Entertainment

Ask the tourist office for a copy of the monthly *Le Mois à Cannes* which lists

what's on where. Nondubbed films are occasionally screened at the cinemas on rue Félix Faure, rue d'Antibes and at the *Olympia (rue de la Pompe)*.

Tickets for the wide variety of spectacles staged in the Palais des Festivals are sold at its box office (☎ 04 92 98 62 77), open noon to 6 pm weekdays.

Hot spots guaranteed to draw a crowd (and stars when they roll into town) include *Pavillon Croisette*, *Planet Hollywood* (see the previous Places to Eat section) and *Le Bar des Célébrités*, inside the Carlton, named after the people sufficiently rich to afford its 2000FF-plus bottles of champagne. *Le Vogue (20 rue du Suquet)* is another in-vogue spot that lures a young and trendy, but more down-to-earth, crowd.

In late 2000, French pop star Johnny Hallyday was rumoured to be opening a nightclub costing 23 million FF in the old club house at Port Canto.

Getting There & Away

Bus Buses leave from the bus station (marked 'Hôtel de Ville' on bus timetables) on place Bernard Cornut Gentille to Nice (32FF, 1¼ hours, 15 daily) and Nice airport (75FF, 50 minutes, every 30 minutes from 7 or 8 am to 7 or 8 pm). The Rapides Côte d'Azur information office (☎ 04 93 39 11 39) at the bus station opens 7 am to 7 pm weekdays, 8.30 am to 6.30 pm Saturday. Buses along the coast to St-Raphaël are operated by Société Varoise d'Autocars BELTRAME (see Getting There & Away under St-Raphaël later in this chapter).

Buses to Grasse (line No 600, 20.50FF, 45 minutes) via Mougins and Mouans-Sartoux, Vallauris (line No 6V, 30 minutes), and Valbonne (line No 5VB or 3VB, 20.50FF, 45 minutes) all depart from Cannes' second bus station, next to the train station on rue Jean Jaurès. The information desk (☎ 04 93 39 11 39) opens 1.45 to 6 pm Monday, Thursday and Friday; 9 am to noon and 1.30 to 6 pm Saturday.

Train At Cannes train station, rue Jean Jaurès, tickets for same-day departures are sold on the ground floor. Advance tickets and reservations are handled on the 1st floor. The left-luggage desk opens 8.55 am to 1 pm and 3 to 5.30 pm (20FF per bag per 24 hours).

Destinations within easy reach include: St-Raphaël (34FF, 25 minutes, two per hour) from where you can get buses to St-Tropez and Toulon; and Marseilles (153FF, two hours). Most trains to and from Nice (32FF, 40 minutes) stop in Antibes (28FF, 15 minutes).

Getting Around

Bus Cannes and destinations up to 7km from town are served by Bus Azur. Its office (☎ 04 93 39 18 71), place Bernard Cornut Gentille, at the bus station, opens 7 am to 7 pm weekdays, and 8.30 am to 6.30 pm Saturday.

A ticket/10-ticket carnet costs 7.70/51FF. A weekly Carte Palm'Hebdo/monthly Carte Croisette costs 57/195FF. Bus No 8 runs along the coast from place Bernard Cornut Gentille to the port and Palm Beach Casino on Pointe de la Croisette; bus Nos 2 and 9 run from the train station, via the bus station, to/from the beaches in Cannes La Bocca; line 620 follows the same route but continues farther south-west along the coast to Théoule-sur-Mer. All routes are listed on the *Plan du Réseau* (free at the ticket office).

Car & Motorcycle Avis (☎ 04 93 94 15 86) has an office next to Hôtel Martinez at 69 blvd de la Croisette and a small annexe (☎ 04 93 39 26 38) in front of the train station on rue Jean Jaurès. On rue d'Antibes, Budget (☎ 04 93 99 44 04) and National Citer (☎ 04 93 94 64 41) are at No 160 and Hertz (☎ 04 93 99 04 20) is at No 147. Excellence (☎ 04 93 94 67 67, ⓔ sales@excellence.fr), 66 blvd de la Croisette, rents Ferraris, Bentleys and other dream cars.

Alliance Location (☎ 04 93 38 62 62, ⓔ alliance.location@wanadoo.fr), 19 rue des Frères Pradignac, rents scooters/motorcycles starting at 250/300FF per day, as well as mobile phones (110FF/day, plus calls), bicycles (80FF/day) and rollerblades (50FF/day). The shop opens 9 am to 7 pm,

April to October. Holiday Bikes (☎ 04 97 06 30 30), 16 rue du 14 Juillet, is another outlet.

Parking in Cannes on the street costs 10FF/hour (maximum stay two hours). Multistorey car parks (12/90FF per hour/24 hours) include Noga Croisette (entrance by the side of La Malmaison on blvd de la Croisette); and Forville, north of the old city across ave des Anciens Combattants d'Afrique du Nord. Motorists staying in Cannes four days or more can buy a parking card *(forfait courte durée)* for up to 30 days (320/460FF for five/10 days) from the Uniparc desk (☎ 04 92 99 84 97), inside tourist office.

Bicycle Alliance Location rents mountain bikes for 80FF per day and Holiday Bikes rents mountain/road bikes for 90/70FF per day (for both see Car & Motorcycle earlier).

ÎLES DE LÉRINS

The two islands of Lérins – Île Ste-Marguerite and Île St-Honorat – lie within a 20-minute boat ride of Cannes. Known as Lero and Lerina in ancient times, these tiny, traffic-free oases of peace and tranquillity remain a world away from the glitz, glamour and hanky-panky of cocky Cannes.

Wild camping, cycling and smoking are forbidden on both islands (well, theoretically, anyway – visitors still light up). There are no hotels or camp sites on either island and St-Honorat, the smaller of the two, has nowhere to eat either. Take a picnic and good supply of drinking water with you.

Neither island has a wildly fantastic beach. Pretty coves can be found on the southern side of Ste-Marguerite (a 45-minute walk from the harbour). On the northern side, sunworshippers lie on rocks and mounds of dried seaweed.

Île Ste-Marguerite

Eucalyptus- and pine-covered Île Ste-Marguerite is 1km from the mainland. The island is famed as the place where the enigmatic Man in the Iron Mask – immortalised by Alexandre Dumas (1802–70) in

The Man in the Iron Mask

More than 68 names have been suggested for this prisoner whose name no one knows, whose face no one has seen: a living mystery, shadow, enigma, problem.

Victor Hugo

The man in the iron mask was imprisoned by Louis XIV (1661–1715) in the fortress on Île Ste-Marguerite from around 1660 until 1690, when he was transferred to the Bastille in Paris. Only the king knew the identity of the man behind the mask, prompting a rich pageant of myth and legend to be woven around the mysterious, ill-fated inmate.

Political and social satirist Voltaire (1694–1778) claimed the prisoner was the king's brother – a twin or an illegitimate older brother. In 1751 he published *Le Siècle de Louis XIV* which attested that Louis XIV's usurped brother, face shrouded in iron, arrived on the island in 1661, was personally escorted to the Bastille by its new governor in 1690, and died in 1703 aged around 60. His featureless mask was lined with silk and fitted with a spring mechanism at the chin to allow him to eat. Prison guards had orders to kill anyone who dared remove his iron face.

JANE SMITH

Countless other identities were showered on the masked prisoner, among them the Duke of Monmouth (actually beheaded under James II), the Comte de Vermandois (son of Louis XIV said to have died from smallpox in 1683), the Duc de Beaufort (killed by the Turks in 1669) and Molière. Some theorists claimed the man in the iron mask was actually a woman.

The storming of the Bastille in 1789 fuelled yet more stories. Revolutionaries claimed to have discovered a skeleton, the skull of which was locked in an iron mask, when plundering the prison, while others focused on a supposed entry found in the prison register which read *détenu 64389000: l'homme au masque de fer* (prisoner 64389000: the man in the iron mask). To the contrary, others provoked a storm with their allegations that there was *no* iron mask entry in the prison register – just a missing page. In 1855, an iron mask was found in a scrap heap in Langres, north of Dijon, consequently displayed in the town museum as the ill-fated mask.

Voltaire's tragic tale of an usurped heir sentenced to a life behind iron inspired a flurry of theatrical tragedies. With the 1850 publication of Alexandre Dumas' novel *Le Vicomte de Bragelonne*, the last of his musketeers trilogy, the royal crime became written in stone: in 1638 Anne of Austria, wife of Louis XIII (1617–43) and mother of Louis XIV, gives birth to twins; one is taken away from her, leaving her to bear the secret alone until an old friend uncovers the terrible truth. The rest is history.

Dozens of iron mask films have been made this century, starring Richard Chamberlain as the masked prince/evil king in 1976 and Leonardo DiCaprio in 1998.

his novel *Le Viscomte de Bragelonne* (1847) – was held in the late 17th century (see 'The Man in the Iron Mask' boxed text).

The island, home to some 20 families, is crisscrossed by walking trails and paths. Its centrepiece is 17th-century **Fort Royal**, built by Richelieu to defend the islands from the Spanish (who still managed to occupy the fort from 1635 to 1637), with later additions by Vauban.

The oldest part of the fort houses the **Musée de la Mer** (☎ 04 93 43 18 17), a museum with interesting exhibits on the fort's history and shipwrecks. A door to the left in the reception hall of the museum leads to the **state prisons** built under Louis XIV. In 1685 six Huguenot pastors who refused to renounce their Protestant faith following the revocation of the Edit of Nantes were kept here. The steamboat inventor, Claude

CANNES AREA

François Dorothée, allegedly came up with his idea while watching slaves row to the island during his imprisonment here between 1773 and 1774.

The story of the prison's most famous inmate, the Man in the Iron Mask, unfolds in the *cellule du masque de fer* (Man in the Iron Mask's cell), open 10.30 am to 12.15 pm and 2 to 5.40 pm (6.30 pm July to September) Wednesday to Monday. Admission costs 10FF.

Île St-Honorat

Forested St-Honorat, 1.5km by 400m, is the smallest and most southern of the two Lérins islands. It was the site of a powerful monastery in the 5th century. Today it is home to Cistercian monks who own the island but welcome people to visit their monastery and the seven small chapels dotted around, which have drawn pilgrims since the Middle Ages.

The Byzantine-inspired **Chapelle de la Trinité**, built between the 5th and 11th centuries on the island's eastern tip, can be visited by guided tour between 10.30 am and 12.30 pm and 2.30 and 4.45 pm Monday to Saturday, and 2.30 to 4.45 pm Sunday, July to September. Admission is free.

The small **fortified monastery** which guards the island's southern shores is all that remains of the original monastery. The donjon was built in 1073 to protect monks from pirate attacks; the entrance stood 4m above ground level and was accessible only by ladder (later replaced by the stone staircase evident today). The elegant arches of the vaulted **cloître de la prière** (cloister of prayer) on the 1st floor date from the 15th century. A magnificent panorama of the Côte d'Azur from the Estérel to Cap d'Antibes can be enjoyed from the terrace. The donjon can be visited from 10.30 am to 4 pm, October to June; and by guided tour only from 10.30 am to 12.30 pm and 2.30 to 4.45 pm Monday to Saturday, and 2.30 to 4.45 pm Sunday, July to September. Admission costs 15FF.

In front of the donjon is the walled, 19th-century **Abbaye Notre Dame de Lérins** (☎ 04 92 99 54 00, @ info@abbayedelerins

.com), today inhabited by 30 monks. Mass is celebrated in the 19th-century church here at 11.25 am weekdays and 9.50 am Sunday. In the souvenir shop you can buy the 50% alcohol *Lérina* liqueur manufactured by the monks. The pea-green liqueur, concocted from 44 different herbs, is the local version of the Chartreuse made by Carthusian monks in the Alps.

Getting There & Away

From Cannes, a handful of companies run daily boats to both islands: Compagnie Maritime Cannoise (CMC; ☎ 04 93 38 66 33, @ cmcrgm@aol.com) runs daily ferries to Île St-Honorat (20 minutes) and Île Ste-Marguerite (15 minutes) year round; to St-Tropez on Saturday in May, and Tuesday to Saturday from June to August; and to Monaco on Monday and Wednesday from June to August. A return ticket for St-Honorat/Ste-Marguerite/St-Tropez/Monaco costs 40/50/150/150FF (children aged five to 10, 20/25/75/75FF).

Société Planaria (☎/fax 04 92 98 71 38, @ info@abbayedelerins.com) is the abbey's boat service and runs hourly boats from 8 am to 6 pm to/from Île St-Honorat. A return fare costs 50FF (children aged five to 10, 25FF). Both companies sell tickets from kiosks on jetée Albert Édouard in Cannes. Boats sail/dock here too.

Based the opposite end of the port, Trans Côte d'Azur (☎ 04 92 98 71 30) charges 55/55/85FF for the return voyage to St-Honorat/Ste-Marguerite/both islands (children aged four to 10, 35/35/50FF). Its office is opposite Hôtel Sofitel on quai St-Pierre; its boats sail from quai Max Laubeuf.

There are also seasonal boats from Juan-les-Pins (see the next Beaches & Boats section in this chapter) and Golfe-Juan (see Boat Excursions under Vallauris later in this chapter).

ANTIBES

postcodes 06600 (Greater Antibes) & 06160 (Cap d'Antibes) • pop 73,383

Antibes (Antibou in Provençal), the next coastal hot spot north-east of Cannes and across the Baie des Anges from Nice, has as many attractions as its larger neighbours but is not as crowded. It has sandy beaches, 16th-century ramparts along the shore, an attractive pleasure-boat harbour (Port Vauban) and an old city with narrow streets and flower-bedecked houses. Picasso, Max Ernst and Nicolas de Staël all found an appealing charm in Antibes. Between 1966 and 1990, acclaimed globetrotter and writer Graham Greene chose Antibes as his base.

Greater Antibes embraces the modern beach resort of Juan-les-Pins and Cap d'Antibes, the exclusive green cape on which Antibes and Juan-les-Pins sit.

Juan-les-Pins sprung up west of Antibes in the 1880s. It is known for its beautiful 2km-long sandy beach backed by pine trees, and outrageous nightlife – a legacy of the 1920s when Americans swung into town with their jazz music and oh-so-brief swimsuits. Party madness peaks in late July when the resort hosts Jazz à Juan, a week-long jazz festival attracting musicians and music lovers worldwide.

Cheap accommodation here is particularly scarce; try the hostel on Cap d'Antibes or a camp site in Biot (see that section later in this chapter).

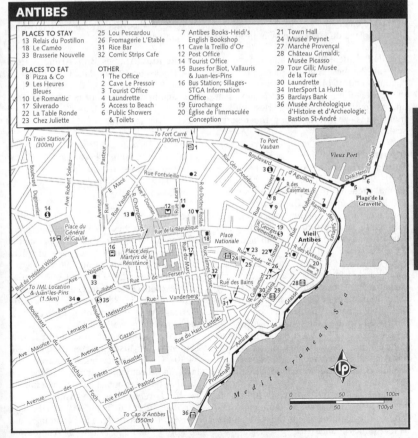

ANTIBES

PLACES TO STAY
13 Relais du Postillon
18 Le Caméo
33 Brasserie Nouvelle

PLACES TO EAT
8 Pizza & Co
9 Les Heures Bleues
10 Le Romantic
17 Silverado
22 La Table Ronde
23 Chez Juliette
25 Lou Pescadou
26 Fromagerie L'Etable
31 Rice Bar
32 Comic Strips Cafe

OTHER
1 The Office
2 Cave Le Pressoir
3 Tourist Office
4 Laundrette
5 Access to Beach
6 Public Showers & Toilets
7 Antibes Books-Heidi's English Bookshop
11 Cave la Treillo d'Or
12 Post Office
14 Tourist Office
15 Buses for Biot, Vallauris & Juan-les-Pins
16 Bus Station; Sillages-STGA Information Office
19 Eurochange
20 Église de l'Immaculée Conception
21 Town Hall
24 Musée Peynet
27 Marché Provençal
28 Château Grimaldi; Musée Picasso
29 Tour Gilli; Musée de la Tour
30 Laundrette
34 InterSport La Hutte
35 Barclays Bank
36 Musée Archéologique d'Histoire et d'Archeologie; Bastion St-André

CANNES AREA

Orientation

Antibes is made up of three parts: the commercial centre around place du Général de Gaulle; Vieil Antibes (old Antibes) south of Port Vauban and the Vieux Port (old port); and, to the south-west, Cap d'Antibes and the contiguous community of Juan-les-Pins.

The principal streets in Antibes centre are blvd Albert 1er and rue de la République, which leads eastwards from place du Général de Gaulle to place des Martyrs de la Résistance (touting a kiddies playground) and tree-lined place Nationale. Ave Robert Soleau links Antibes train station with place du Général de Gaulle. Narrow promenade Amiral de Grasse hugs the waterfront east of the old city.

From place du Général de Gaulle, Juan-les-Pins is a straight 1.5km walk along blvd du Président Wilson which runs southwest off Antibes' central square. From the southern end of blvd du Président Wilson in Juan-les-Pins, ave Guy de Maupassant and its continuation, blvd Charles Guillaumont, runs westwards along the resort's seafront.

Information

Tourist Offices The Antibes tourist office (☎ 04 92 90 53 00, fax 04 92 90 53 01, [e] mdt.accueil@antibes-juanlespins.com), 11 place du Général de Gaulle, opens from 8.45 am to 7.30 pm on weekdays, and 9.30 am to 12.30 pm Saturday, in July and August; and 9 am to 12.30 pm and 2 to 7 pm weekdays, and 9 am to noon and 2 to 7 pm Saturday, the rest of the year. Tickets for cultural events are sold at the *billetterie* (ticket office) inside the tourist office; it shuts 30 minutes before the latter. Visit online at www.antibesjuanlespins.com.

In Vieil Antibes, the tourist office (☎ 04 93 34 65 65), 32 blvd d'Aguillon, inside Porte Marine, opens 10 am to 10 pm in July and August; and 9 am to noon and 2 to 6 pm weekdays, and 9 am to noon Saturday, the rest of the year.

Juan-les-Pins tourist office (☎ 04 92 90 53 05), 51 blvd Charles Guillaumont, overlooking the seafront, keeps the same hours as its Antibes counterpart.

Money In Antibes centre, Eurochange, 4 rue Georges Clémenceau, opens 9 am to 7 pm weekdays, and 10 am to 1 pm Saturday. Barclays Bank is at 11 blvd Albert 1er; commercial banks bespeckle ave Robert Soleau.

Post & Communications The post office in Antibes centre, place des Martyrs de la Résistance (entrance on ave Doumer), opens 8 am to 7 pm weekdays, and 8 am to noon Saturday. Juan-les-Pins' post office, opposite the train station on square Pablo Picasso, opens 8 am to noon and 2 or 2.30 to 6 pm weekdays, and 8 am to noon Saturday. It has Cyberposte.

Surf the Net at The Office (☎ 04 93 34 09 96, [e] theoffice@wanadoo.fr), 8 blvd d'Agiullon.

Bookshops Antibes Books-Heidi's English Bookshop (☎/fax 04 93 34 74 11) at 24 rue Aubernon, stocks the Riviera's biggest and best selection of new and secondhand English-language books. Heidi's opens from 10 am to 7 pm.

Laundry Laverie du Port, 14 rue Thuret, opens 7 am to 9 pm. There is another laundrette at the western end of rue des Bains; it opens 9 am to noon and 2.30 to 7 pm Monday to Saturday.

Vieil Antibes

Because of Antibes' position on the border of France and Savoy, it was fortified in the 17th and 18th centuries, but these fortifications were ripped down in 1896 to give the city room to expand. From the tourist office on place du Général de Gaulle, bear east along rue de la République to **Porte de France**, one of the few remaining parts of the original city walls.

On the southern side of cafe-filled place Nationale is **Musée Peynet** (☎ 04 92 90 54 30). Over 300 pictures, cartoons, sculptures and theatrical costumes designed by Antibes-born cartoonist Peynet, best known for his *Lovers* series, are displayed here. It opens 10 am to 6 pm (10 pm Friday) Tuesday to Sunday, June to September; and 10 am to noon and 2 to 6 pm Tuesday to

Sunday, the rest of the year. Admission costs 20FF (students 10FF).

A splendid morning **Marché Provençal** (Provençal market) sprawls the length of cours Masséna, Tuesday to Sunday, September to May. At the southern end of cours Masséna, 19th-century **Tour Gilli**, 2 rue de l'Orme, houses the **Musée de la Tour** (☎ 04 93 34 50 91), a small arts and traditions museum, open 4 to 7 pm (3 to 5 pm in winter) Wednesday, Thursday and Saturday. Admission costs 10FF.

East of cours Masséna on rue St-Esprit (entrance on montée de la Souchère), is Antibes' **Église de L'Immaculée Conception**, built on the site of an ancient Greek temple with an ochre neoclassical facade. Its tall, square Romanesque bell tower dates from the 12th century.

Five hundred metres south-west of the cathedral on promenade Amiral de Grasse is the **Musée Archéologique d'Histoire et d'Archéologie** (☎ 04 92 90 54 35), inside the Vauban-built **Bastion St-André**. Its displays are devoted to Antibes' Greek history. It opens 10 am to noon and 2 to 6 pm Tuesday to Sunday. Admission costs 20FF (those aged 18 to 26, 10FF, those aged under 18, free).

Musée Picasso

From the cathedral, steps lead to **Château Grimaldi**, set on a spectacular site overlooking the sea. This 12th-century castle served as Picasso's studio from July to December 1946. Today it houses the Picasso Museum, boasting an excellent collection of Picasso's paintings, lithographs, drawings and ceramics as well as interesting displays about his life. A collection of contemporary art by other artists graces the sculpture-lined terrace facing the Mediterranean.

Particularly poignant is Picasso's *La Joie de Vivre* (The Joy of Life), one in a series of 25 paintings which form *The Antipolis Suite*. The young flower girl, happily surrounded by flute-playing fauns and mountain goats, symbolises Françoise Gilot, the 23-year-old love of Picasso (1881–1973) whom he lived with at the time in neighbouring Golfe-Juan. The entire series, along with its preparatory drawings and sketches, are displayed. Some of the ceramic pieces he created in Vallauris (see that section later in this chapter) in 1947–9 can be seen on the 1st and 2nd floors.

The Musée Picasso (☎ 04 92 90 54 20) opens 10 am to 6 pm Tuesday to Sunday, June to September; and 10 am to noon and 2 to 6 pm Tuesday to Sunday, the rest of the year. Admission costs 30FF (children aged under seven, 15FF). Anglophones can hire an English-language audioguide (20FF).

Fort Carré & Port Vauban

The impregnable 16th-century Fort Carré, enlarged by Vauban in the 17th century, dominates the approach to Antibes from Nice. Port Vauban, one of the first pleasure ports to be established on the Mediterranean, is between the fort and Antibes old town.

Inside the fortress, which can be visited by guided tour, a pedestrian walkway takes visitors around the stadium hidden within the star-shaped walls. Guided tours depart every 30 minutes between 10.15 am and 4 pm Tuesday to Sunday, October to May; and 10.15 am to 5.30 pm Tuesday to Sunday, June to September. The surrounding park opens 10 am to 7 pm.

Cap d'Antibes

Nowhere do you feel more like a shrunken Alice in Wonderland than on this select peninsula where larger-than-life villas and pine trees loom above you at every turn. The sense of wonder at the sheer luxury is further exacerbated by the constant buzz of cicadas (see the boxed text 'Love Song' on the following page) whose frenzied chants reach a shrilling crescendo in the midday sun.

The south-western tip of the cape is crowned by the legendary **Hôtel du Cap Eden Roc**, Côte d'Azur's most exclusive hotel, dating from 1870 (see Places to Stay later in this section). It made a name for itself in 1923 when its Italian owner, Antoine Sella, kept his doors open in July and August, heralding the start of a summer season on the coast. Hôtel du Cap Eden Roc was consequently immortalised in F Scott

CANNES AREA

Fitzgerald's novel *Tender is the Night* (1934) under the guise of the fictional Hôtel des Étrangers. By 1925 the luxury complex, sporting the first open-air swimming pool on the Riviera (built in 1914 for WWI servicemen), was known as Eden Roc. Other notable names on Cap d'Antibes' guestbook include Cole Porter, who rented **Château de la Garoupe** in 1922; and novelist Jules Verne (1828–1905), who lived at Les Chênes Verts, 152 blvd John F Kennedy.

Immediately north-west of the hotel is the **Musée Naval et Napoléonien** (☎ 04 93 61 45 32), inside the Tour Sella off blvd John F Kennedy. The museum documents Napoleon's return from exile in 1815. It opens 9.30 am to noon and 2.15 to 6 pm weekdays, and 9.30 am to noon on Sunday, November to September. Admission costs 20FF (students 10FF).

The centre of the cape is dominated by beautiful **Jardin Botanique de la Villa Thuret** (☎ 04 93 67 88 00), 41 blvd du Cap. The botanical gardens dating from 1857 open 8.30 am to 6 pm (5.30 pm in winter) weekdays. Admission is free. The 11-hectare landscaped park surrounding **Villa Eilenroc** (☎ 04 93 67 74 33), ave de Beaumont, right on the tip of Cap d'Antibes, can be visited by free guided tour 9 am to 5 pm Tuesday and Wednesday, September to June (closed in July and August). Eilenroc was designed by Garnier for a Dutchman who scrambled the name of his wife Cornélie to come up with the villa's name.

Sweeping views of the coastline, from St-Tropez to Italy, can be enjoyed from **Chapelle de la Garoupe**, atop a hillock off route du Phare. The neighbouring lighthouse can't be visited. From here, steps lead downhill to ave Aimé Bourreau; bear right, then turn left along ave Guide to get to sandy **Plage de la Garoupe**, first raked clear of seaweed in 1922 by Cole Porter and American artist Gerald Murphy. A coastal path snakes from here to **Cap Gros**, the cape's south-easternmost tip.

Beaches & Boats

Antibes has a small beach, sandy **Plage de la Gravette**, accessible from quai Henri

---

Love Song

The frenzied buzz that serenades sunny days in Provence's hot south is, in fact, *cigales* (cicadas) on the pull.

Cicadas (Family Cicadidae) are transparent-winged insects, most common in tropical or temperate climes. The male cicada courts when the temperatures is above 25°C in the shade. Its shrill love song is produced with tymbals, vibrating music-making plates attached to the abdomen. Female cicadas do not sing.

The life span of a cicada is three to 17 years, all but four to six weeks of which is spent underground. Upon emerging from the soil to embark on its adult life, the cicada attaches itself to a tree where it immediately begins its mating rituals. It dies just weeks later.

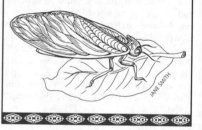

Rambaud at the Vieux Port. The long sandy beaches fronting Juan-les-Pins buzz with business from sunrise to sunset. You can water-ski (150FF for 15 minutes), sail (350FF for 30 minutes), parasail (250/400/550FF for one/two/three jumps) and ride rubber rings from the back of a motorboat (100FF for 15 minutes), play table tennis or go karting. Rollerblading fans can hire a set of blades for 40/80FF per half-day/day from InterSport La Hutte (☎ 04 93 34 20 14), 10 ave Guillabert, in Antibes centre, open 9 am to 12.15 and 2.30 to 7.15 pm Monday to Saturday.

From Juan-les-Pins eight daily ferries (☎ 04 92 93 02 36, @ cmcrgm@aol.com) sail, May and October, to the Îles de Lérins (see that section earlier) from the Ponton Courbet opposite the tourist office on blvd Charles Guillaumont. A return ticket to Ste-Marguerite/St-Honorat/both islands costs 80/60/80FF (children aged four to seven, 40/30/40FF). The same company runs weekly boat trips to St-Tropez (120FF), the **Corniche d'Or** (100FF) and Monaco (150FF) in July and August.

Special Events

Antibes' premier occasion is Jazz à Juan, also known as the Festival de Jazz d'Antibes Juan-les-Pins, which kicks off the third week in July. Juan-les-Pins' Eden Casino (☎ 04 92 93 71 71), blvd Édouard Baudoin, and the gardens fronting the beach on square Gould, are leading venues. Festival programmes and tickets are available from FNAC in Nice or from the Antibes or Juan-les-Pins tourist offices.

Places to Stay

Antibes Try *Brasserie Nouvelle* (☎ 04 93 34 10 07, 1 ave Niquet), a quintessential French cafe that also has five double rooms costing 190FF (230FF with shower). Reception is the ground-floor bar.

Large *Le Caméo* (☎ 04 93 34 24 17, fax 04 93 34 35 80, 62 rue de la République) has 200/250FF singles/doubles (230/280FF with shower, 280/330FF with shower and toilet). Shower-equipped triples cost 330F.

A notch up, but well priced for the comforts offered, is 15-room *Relais du Postillon* (☎ 04 93 34 29 77, fax 04 93 34 61 24, 8 rue Championnet). Cosy rooms for one or two, all named after beautiful cities, islands or villages (Florence, Malta, Vallauris and so on) to reflect their worth, cost upwards of 338/368FF in low/high season.

Juan-les-Pins Juan-les-Pins' two best-value hotels are five minutes' walk from Juan-les-Pins train station. One-star *Hôtel Trianon* (☎ 04 93 61 18 11, 14 ave de l'Éstérel) has rooms for one or two with washbasin/shower for 200/300FF. Neighbouring *Hôtel Parisiana* (☎ 04 93 61 27 03) at No 16 has singles/doubles with shower costing 175/251FF.

F Scott and Zelda Fitzgerald stayed at Villa St-Louis when they rolled into town –

then an untouched spot of paradise – in 1926. Three years later, their humble abode reopened as *Hôtel Belles Rives* (☎ 04 93 61 02 79, fax 04 93 67 43 51, ⓔ belles.rives@atsat.com, 33 blvd Édouard Baudoin), today a four-star oasis of luxury with a private jetty, beach and swimming pool. Guests pay upwards of 700/1150FF per single/double to languish at this 1930s seashore palace.

Cap d'Antibes The cheapest choice is *Relais International de la Jeunesse* (☎ 04 93 61 34 40, fax 04 90 83 65 33, 60 blvd de la Garoupe), south of the centre. B&B costs 75FF and sheets cost 10FF. Campers can pitch their tent here for 50FF per person, including breakfast. Reception opens 8 to 11 am and 5.30 to 11 pm and guests have to evacuate their rooms from 10 am to 5.30 pm. From Antibes' bus station, take bus No 2A (direction Eden Roc) to L'Antiquité stop. The hostel opens March to October.

Expensive but exquisite *Hôtel du Cap Eden Roc* (☎ 04 93 61 39 01, fax 04 93 67 76 04, ⓔ edenroc-hotel@wanadoo.fr, blvd Kennedy) charges 2500FF to 3000FF per double.

Places to Eat

Restaurants The catch of the day can be eaten at Vieil Antibes' *Lou Pescardou* (☎ 04 93 34 59 11, 13 rue Sade). Highlights on its *poisson frais* (fresh fish) menu include bouillabaisse (210FF) and a *royale* (royal) option (330FF) which includes half a crayfish. Fishy *menus* swim in at 99FF, 150FF and 210FF.

Chez Juliette (☎ 04 93 34 67 37, 18 rue Sade) is popular for its wide choice of moderately priced, guaranteed-to-fill dishes, including fresh pasta (from 45FF), salads (40FF) and meat dishes (from 60FF). Juliette serves a 80FF *menu*. Reservations are recommended.

Slavic specialities are the mainstay of *Silverado* (☎ 04 93 34 99 34, 18 rue du Marc). *Menus* costing 85FF are accompanied by home-made cumin and potato bread.

La Table Rotunde (☎ 04 93 34 31 61,

CANNES AREA

5 rue Frédéric Isnard), markets itself as a typically Provençal place, despite touting bison, ostrich and kangaroo steaks on its lengthy, trilingual menus. Meaty *menus* cost upwards of 88FF.

The inventive, vegetarian-friendly **Rice Bar** (☎ 04 93 34 12 84, 1 rue des Bains) serves numerous rice-based dishes on a pretty terrace in an old-town backstreet. *Menus* cost 60FF to 95FF and it has a 35FF kids *menu*.

Romance is a good enough reason to dine at **Le Romantic** (☎ 04 93 34 59 39, 5 rue Rostan), which flaunts a beautiful, timbered ceiling and tempting *menus* for 140FF and 200FF. Dishes take at least 20 minutes to prepare.

Le Seventy (☎ 04 93 67 07 82, 17 rue Dautheville) is a hip 1970s-style joint serving Provençal cuisine.

Cafes In Antibes town centre cafe hot spots include place Nationale, the fountain-bedecked corner of rue Thuret and rue Georges Clémenceau, and most old town streets.

Les Heures Bleues (☎ 04 93 34 50 61, 2 rue des Casemates) is a lively cafe-theatre. Stroll home afterwards munching a slice of fire-baked pizza from **Pizza & Co** opposite.

Equally playful is young and fun **Comic Strips Cafe** (☎ 04 93 34 91 40, 4 rue James Close). Smiling punters are free to flick through the childhood greats, ranging from Tintin and Astérix to the more sophisticated Sempé.

Self-Catering Fresh fish is sold at the *poissonnerie* adjoining Lou Pescardou (see Restaurants on the previous page). Wine, starting at 10FF per litre, is sold at the **Cave le Pressoir** (rue Fontvieille) or from **Cave la Treillo d'Or** (☎ 04 93 34 33 87, 12 rue Lacan), which also makes home/boat deliveries. **Fromagerie L'Etable**, on the corner of rue Sade and rue Guillaumont, is the place for cheese.

Getting There & Away

Bus Antibes bus station (☎ 04 93 34 37 60) is just off rue de la République, a short dis-

tance south-east of place du Général de Gaulle. The Sillages-STGA (Syndicat des Transports Grasse–Antibes) information office (☎ 04 93 64 88 84 in Vallauris) opens 8 am to 12.30 pm and 2 to 6.30 pm weekdays, and 9 am to 12.30 pm and 2 to 5 pm Saturday. Visit the Web site at www.stga-transport.fr.

From the main bus station, Sillages-STGA bus No 200 runs every 20 minutes or so between 6 am and 8 pm, linking Antibes with Nice (24.50FF, 50 minutes), Nice airport (45.50FF, 40 minutes), Cagnes-sur-Mer (12FF, 20 minutes), Golfe-Juan (8FF, 15 minutes) and Cannes (20FF, 30 minutes). From place du Général de Gaulle there are buses to/from Biot (line 10A, 7.50FF, 20 minutes, 7 to 11 buses daily) and Vallauris (line No 5V, 15FF, 30 minutes, hourly between 7 am and 6 pm).

Train Antibes train station, place Pierre Semard, is north of place du Général de Gaulle at the end of ave Robert Soleau, close to Port Vauban. There are frequent trains to/from Nice (22FF, 25 minutes) and Cannes (14FF, 15 minutes).

Unlike Antibes where many TGVs stop, Juan-les-Pins train station on ave de l'Estérel is only served by local trains.

Getting Around

Bus In summer a minibus shuttles travellers between Antibes centre and Vieil Antibes. The Centre Ville line (shaded blue on the route maps displayed at bus stops) links the train station with place du Général de Gaulle and the bus station. The Vieil Antibes line (shaded red) links the train station with Fort Carré. The bus stop is immediately on the right as you exit the train station on ave Robert Soleau. Free minibuses run every 10 minutes between 7.30 am and 7.30 pm Monday to Saturday.

A ticket/10-ticket carnet for other city buses costs 7.50/65FF. One-/three-/eight-daypasses are also available (20/60/180FF). Bus Nos 1A, 3A and 8A link Antibes bus station and place du Général de Gaulle with square du Lys in Juan-les-Pins. Buses run every 10 to 20 minutes.

Bus No 2A to Eden Roc on Cap d'Antibes departs every 30 minutes from Antibes bus station. Between 15 June and 15 September, bus No 2A bis circles the Cap, continuing along the coast from Eden Roc to Juan-les-Pins before returning to Antibes.

Bicycle JML Location (☎ 04 92 93 05 06), at 93 blvd du Président Wilson, rents bikes/scooters/125cc motorcycles for 75/210/330FF per day.

VALLAURIS & GOLFE-JUAN
postcode 06220 • pop 25,931
The traditional potters' town of Vallauris is as closely associated with Picasso as Antibes, 7km east. The town itself has little charm beyond three memorable museums, one of which is dedicated to the eccentric artist who lived in Vallauris with Françoise Gilot from 1948 until 1955.

Clay pots have been churned out in Vallauris since Roman times. A declining trade in the 16th century was boosted by a group of Genoese potters who moved their studios to Vallauris in order to exploit its clay-rich soil. An artistic revival in the 1940s, spearheaded by Picasso, ensured the trade's survival. Today, it is tourism that potters rely on, as visitors flock to Vallauris to visit the museums and buy a signature *marmite* (giant pot, only glazed on the inside and used for cooking Provençal stew).

Vallauris' satellite resort of Golfe-Juan (Goulfe-Jouan in Provençal), 2km south on the coast, is unmonumental beyond its historic claim to fame as the spot where Napoleon landed following his return from exile in 1815. From here, boats sail to the Îles des Lérins in summer.

Orientation & Information
Vallauris bus station adjoins place de la Libération, the central square in the northern part of town. From here, ave George Clémenceau, the main street, leads south to the tourist office (☎ 04 93 63 82 58, fax 04 93 63 95 01, ✉ tourisme.vgj@wanadoo.fr) on square du 8 Mai, nestled in the car park off the D135.

The closest train station is in Golfe-Juan.

From Vallauris tourist office continue south along the D135 to Golfe-Juan's central square Nabonnand. Golfe-Juan tourist office (☎ 04 93 63 73 12), 84 ave de la Liberté, overlooks this square.

Château Musée de Vaullaris
The Castle Museum of Vallauris (☎ 04 93 64 16 05, 04 93 64 98 05), place de la Libération, houses three museums: the **Musée National Picasso** (National Picasso Museum), based around the Picasso-decorated Chapelle La Guerre et La Paix (War and Peace Chapel); the **Musée Magnelli**, devoted to the works of Italian artist Albert Magnelli (1899–1971); and a **Musée de la Céramique** (Ceramic Museum), in which the history of Vallauris' age-old craft is unravelled.

Picasso (1881–1973) was 71 years old when he started work on what he dubbed his *temple de la paix* (temple of peace), a 12th-century chapel built on the site of an abbey dating from the Middle Ages. He painted his dramatic murals on plywood panels secured to the church's stone walls.

The tiny vaulted chapel and its sister museums open 10 am to noon and 2 to 6 pm Wednesday to Monday, October to May; and 10 am to 6.30 pm Wednesday to Monday, the rest of the year. Admission costs 17FF (students 8.50FF). The museum is next to Vaullaris bus station; steps lead from the station to place de la Libération.

Galerie Madoura
A handful of licensed copies of ceramics cast by Picasso while in Vallauris are on sale at Galerie Madoura (☎ 04 93 64 66 39, ✉ info@madoura.com), the pottery where, in 1946, Picasso first dabbled in the clay medium under the guidance of local potters Georges and Suzanne Ramié. He consequently granted the Ramiés the exclusive right to reproduce his work, resulting in a limited edition – between 25 and 500 in number – of 633 different Picasso pieces being cast between 1947 and 1971. These much sought after ceramic *œuvres* (works of art) today can fetch up to 50,000FF today; some pieces can be viewed on the gallery Web site at www.madoura.com.

CANNES AREA

Galerie Madoura on ave Suzanne Ramié, off ave des Anciens Combattants d'Afrique du Nord, opens 10 am to 12.30 pm and 2.30 to 6 pm weekdays. From the bus station, walk south along ave George Clémenceau, then head west (right) along ave des Anciens Combattants d'Afrique du Nord.

The ungainly statue of *L'Homme au Mouton* – a bronze stick figure clutching a sheep by its hind legs – on place Paul Isnard (the tree-filled square adjoining place de la Libération) was a gift from Picasso to Vallauris.

Chapelle de la Miséricorde

This tiny chapel, painted candy pink, on place Jules Isnard, is a contemporary arts centre which plays hosts to temporary exhibitions. It opens 10 am to 6.30 pm Wednesday to Sunday, July and August; and 10 am to noon and 2 to 6 pm Wednesday to Sunday, the rest of the year. Admission costs 10FF.

From place de la Libération, cross place Paul Isnard and continue west along rue Clement Bel to place Jules Isnard.

Maison de la Pétanque

Everything from its invention to its contemporary champions can be discovered in this quaint museum, dedicated to the region's most popular sport. Amateurs can have a spin on the pétanque pitch here, and enthusiasts can get their own set of boules made to measure. See Spectator Sports in the Facts for the Visitor chapter.

The House of Pétanque (☎ 04 93 64 11 36), 1193 chemin de St-Bernard, opens 9 am to noon and 2 to 6.30 pm Monday to Saturday, April to September; and 9 am to noon and 2 to 6.30 pm weekdays, the rest of the year. The museum is 2km north of Vallauris bus station. From the station, head north along ave de Grasse and at the roundabout bear east (right) along chemin St-Bernard.

Boat Excursions

In summer, ferries (☎ 04 93 63 45 94, ✉ cmcrgm@aol.com) sail daily from quai St-Pierre at the Vieux Port in Golfe-Juan to the Îles des Lérins (see that section earlier

in this chapter). From May to October, there are four crossings daily. A return ticket to Ste-Marguerite/St-Honorat/both islands costs 80/60/80FF (children aged four to seven, 40/30/40FF). In July and August, there are a couple of weekly boat trips to St-Tropez (160FF), the Corniche d'Or (100FF) and Monaco (150FF).

To get to the port from Golfe-Juan train station, turn right (east) along ave de Belgique, then turn right (south) onto ave de la Gare, which cuts underneath the railway track towards the sea. At the end of the street, bear south onto blvd des Frères Roustan, the promenade fronting the Vieux Port.

Places to Stay & Eat

In Vallauris centre, cheap nine-room *Hôtel du Stade* (☎ 04 93 64 91 27, 48 ave Georges Clémenceau) is above a local bar. Simple rooms for one or two cost 150FF per night. Shared showers and toilet are in the corridor. *Le Provence* (☎ 04 93 63 86 69, 15–17 ave de la Gare), close to Golfe-Juan train station, is another cheapie, where no-frill singles/doubles cost about 200/250FF.

A staggering assortment of breads and fougasses are baked before your eyes at *Maison Lascasse* (☎ 04 93 63 14 14, 62 ave Georges Clémenceau), a master bakers that usually has 35 of the 55 bread types in stock. It opens 6.30 am to 8 pm Tuesday to Sunday.

Getting There & Away

Golfe-Juan train station, from where there are trains in both directions along the coast, is 3km south of Vallauris town, making bus the most convenient way of getting to/from Vallauris.

From the bus station (☎ 04 93 39 11 39), corner of ave de la Grasse and ave Aimé Berger, bus No 6V goes to Cannes train station (about every 30 minutes between 7.15 am and 7 pm). Bus No 5V serves Antibes bus station (14FF, hourly from about 7 am to 6 pm). Buses are less frequent on Sunday.

Getting Around

There is a regular Sillages-STGA bus (No 4V) between Vallauris bus station and

CANNES AREA

For a quick glimpse of the stars dine at the Carlton Inter-Continental Hotel in Cannes.

La Croisette beachfront in Cannes – if the beach is bare it's probably private.

Indulge yourself at Cannes' glitzy Carlton.

Lose the paparazzi: hide under a beach umbrella.

No less than 36 art galleries line cobbled Rue Grande in St-Paul de Vence.

Golfe-Juan train station (every 15 minutes between 6 am and 7.40 pm). Journey time is 15 minutes.

MOUGINS
postcode 06250 • pop 16,287
• elevation 260m

Elite and elegant Mougins, 9km north-west of Vallauris and 7km from Cannes, prides itself on two things: art and gastronomy. Picasso, who discovered the spot in 1935 with lover Dora Marr and surrealist photographer Man Ray (1890–1976), lived in Mougins with his final love, Jacqueline Roque, from 1961 until his death.

Today the village is known for the culinary wonders cooked up by French chef Roger Vergé and for its innovative photography museum. Bugatti, Rolls-Royce and Ferrari race into gear 5km south in the **Musée de l'Automobiliste** (Automobile Museum, ☎ 04 93 69 27 80, e museauto@club-internet.fr), 772 chemin de Font de Currault, just off the D3. It opens 10 am to 6 or 7 pm and admission costs 40FF (those aged 12 to 18, 25FF).

Between May and October, art exhibitions (free admission) are held in the 19th-century **lavoir** (public washhouse), adjoining Mougins tourist office (☎ 04 93 75 87 67, fax 04 92 92 04 03, e tourisme@pcse.fr) at 15 ave Jean-Charles Mallet. Visit online at www.mougins-coteazur.org. A breathtaking **panorama** of the Mercantour mountains unfolds from the bench-filled terrace opposite.

Musée de la Photographie

Celebrated Riviera photographer Jacques Henri Lartigue (1894–1986) is among the wealth of known photographers represented in the Photography Museum (☎ 04 93 75 85 67), inside Mougin's medieval Porte Sarrazine, behind the church bell tower. The museum was set up in 1989 by André Villers, best known for photographing Picasso, to whom the 3rd floor is dedicated. A collection of antique cameras and a series of aerial photographs of Mougins in the early 1900s are displayed on the 2nd floor, and temporary photographic exhibitions fill the ground floor. The museum opens 2 to 11 pm July to September; and 2 to 6 pm Wednesday to Sunday, the rest of the year (closed November). Admission costs 5FF.

Places to Stay & Eat

The nearest camp site, *L'Eau Vive* (☎ 04 93 75 36 35, 713 chemin des Cabrières), is 1.5km south of Mougins off ave Maréchal Foch (N85). It charges 92FF for two people with a tent and car.

Beyond that, the cheapest places to stay are elsewhere: four-star hotels easily outnumber lesser-starred places in Mougins.

Roger Vergé's illustrious **Moulin de Mougins** (☎ 04 93 75 78 24, fax 04 93 90 18 55, e mougins@relaischateaux.fr, ave Notre Dame de Vie) is in a 16th-century oil mill, crammed with original works by César, Picasso and so on. *Menus* cost upwards of 550F and feature Provençal delights like courgette flowers with black truffles. Hotel rooms cost 850FF to 1800FF. The mill is 2.5km south-east of Mougins off the D3. Visit the Web site at www.moulin-mougins.com.

In the village centre, Vergé runs the more affordable **L'Amandier**; see the Food & Wine section earlier in the book for details. After dining, shop for wine in his wine cellar and for stylish tablecloths and other household nonessentials in Madame Verge's upmarket boutique.

Getting There & Away

Mougins is on the Cannes–Grasse bus route (line No 600) run by Rapides Côte d'Azur (☎ 04 93 39 11 39 in Cannes).

From the bus station next to Cannes train station, buses depart every half-hour between 6.30 am and 7.30 pm to Mougins (9FF, 17 minutes). The service is hourly between 8.30 am and 7.30 pm on Sunday. Grasse is a 20-minute bus ride from Mougins.

MOUANS-SARTOUX
postcode 06370 • pop 9031
• elevation 120m

The main draw of neighbouring Mouans-Sartoux, 4km farther north off route Napoléon (N85), is its **Espace de l'Art Concret**

CANNES AREA

(Centre of Concrete Art; ☎ 04 93 75 71 50, ⒺＭＡＩＬ espace.art.concret@wanadoo.fr). Bold, gigantic geometric shapes, the use of industrial materials, and mischievous tampering with natural light and space create a grandiose juxtaposition with the art museum's unfabricated setting – 16th-century **Château de Mouans** (1504–10).

Concrete art, which focuses on the intellectual aspect of art (as opposed to emotional or aesthetic), was coined by Theo van Doesburg in the 1930s. The chateau-museum, next to the church on place Suzanne de Villeneuve, opens 11 am to 6 pm Wedsnesday to Sunday (to 7 pm June to September). Admission costs 15FF (those aged 12 to 18, 7.50FF).

The art of table decoration a la Alain Ducasse can be discovered at La Soupente (☎ 04 93 75 51 10), a lovely place to browse or buy, on the corner of rue Fréderic Mistral and ave de Cannes (the main street that runs through Mouans).

Places to Stay & Eat

Mouans-Sartoux tourist office (☎ 04 93 75 75 16, ⒺＭＡＩＬ mouans-sartoux@atsat.com), 258 ave de Cannes, has information on accommodation in the region.

In the village centre *Hôtel de la Paix* (☎ 04 92 92 42 80, fax 04 92 92 42 99, 45 rue de Cannes) has basic singles/doubles costing 180/200FF (240/280FF with shower and toilet).

Restaurant du Château (☎ 04 93 75 54 50, 1 place Suzanne de Villeneuve) serves an excellent 55FF *plat du jour* (dish of the day) and a 78FF *menu du jour*; both include a 25cL jug of house wine. Its shaded terrace overlooks Château de Mouans.

Getting There & Away

Mouans-Sartoux is on the same Cannes –Grasse bus route as Mougins (see that section earlier in this chapter).

BIOT

postcode 06410 • pop 7849
• elevation 80m

This charming hill-top village was once an important pottery-manufacturing centre spe-

cialising in large earthenware oil and wine containers. Metal containers brought an end to this industry, but Biot is still active in handicraft production. Its streets are pleasant to stroll around; get there early to beat the hordes. On tiny rue des Bachettes, **Galerie Momiron** (☎ 04 93 65 08 83), a jewellery boutique, and the neighbouring out-of-the-norm art gallery are worth a browse. **Place des Arcades** dates from the 13th century.

The history of the old Templar village comes to life in the **Musée d'Histoire et de Céramique Biotoise** (☎ 04 93 65 54 54), 9 rue St-Sébastien. Opposite, watch a glass-blower at work in the **Verrerie d'Art**. The **Verrerie de Biot** (☎ 04 93 65 03 00, ⒺＭＡＩＬ verrie@verreriebiot.com), at the foot of the village on chemin des Combes, has workshops, a glass ecomuseum and modern glass-art galleries. A complete list of glass-blowing workshops *(verreries)* can be obtained from the tourist office (☎ 04 93 65 78 00, fax 04 93 65 78 04), 46 rue St-Sébastian. Its Web site is at www.biotcoteazur.com (French only).

Musée National Fernand Léger

This museum (☎ 04 92 91 50 30), 2km from Biot centre on chemin du Val de Pôme, dedicated to the artist Fernand Léger (1881–1955) contains some 350 of his works, including paintings, mosaics, ceramics and stained-glass windows. The museum was built by Léger's wife following his death. Léger had bought the land one month earlier to build himself a studio. The foundation stone was laid by Braques, Chagall and Picasso in 1957.

Colourful Léger mosaics decorate the museum facade. The predominant mosaic above the entrance was intended for a sports stadium. Several Léger sculptures bespeckle the surrounding park. Both open 11 am to 6 pm Wednesday to Monday, July to September; and 10 am to 12.30 pm and 2 to 5.30 pm Wednesday to Monday, the rest of the year. Admission costs 38FF.

Bonsaï Arboretum

This Japanese garden (☎ 04 93 65 63 99), created from the private collection of the

Okonek family, displays a wealthy array of Bonsaï trees. Its centrepiece is a Europe's largest Bonsaï forest, 6m in length. In addition to strolling the sculpted gardens, green-fingered visitors can buy their own Bonsaï tree. The gardens, neighbouring the Leger museum at 299 chemin du Val de Pôme, open 10 am to noon and 2 or 3 to 5.30 or 6.30 pm Wednesday to Monday. Admission costs 25FF (students 10FF).

Marineland
Well distanced from the hill-top village is the Disneyland-style **Parc de la Mer** (Sea Park; ☎ 04 93 33 49 49), a giant amusement complex offering a mind-boggling spectacle of games, shows, and activities to amuse kids and adults alike. Waterworld **Marineland**, open 10 am to midnight in July and August (8 pm the rest of the year), is the park's main draw. Acrobatic killer-whale/dolphin shows are held several times daily in summer. Sharks can be viewed through a transparent, underwater tunnel. Admission costs 147FF (children aged three to 12, 98FF).

To get to Marineland take bus No 10A from Antibes bus station to the Marineland stop. By train, turn right out of Biot train station, walk 50m along route de Nice (N7), then turn right along the D4 signposted 'Marineland & Biot'.

Places to Stay
Camping Biot's abundant camp sites seem to attract backpackers like bees to a honey pot. The following sites are within easy walking distance of Biot train station.

Les Embruns (☎ 04 93 33 33 35, fax 04 93 74 46 70, 63 route de Biot), charges 90FF for two people with a tent and car. The site opens June to October. Close by is *Logis de la Brayne* (☎ 04 93 33 54 72, 1221 route de Nice), opposite Biot train station. On the way towards the Fernand Léger museum is pool-equipped *Camping L'Eden* (☎ 04 93 65 63 70, fax 04 93 65 54 22, 63 chemin du Val de Pôme). Both charge similar rates to Les Embruns.

Bus No 10A linking Antibes with Biot village stops outside *Camping du Pylone* (☎ 04 93 33 52 86, fax 04 93 33 30 54, ave

du Pylone). It charges from 25/35/25FF per tent/person/car.

Hotels In Biot village, rambling one-star *Hôtel des Arcades* (☎ 04 93 65 01 04, fax 04 93 65 01 05, 16 place des Arcades) has 12 double rooms with shower or bath and toilet, costing 300FF to 500FF.

Getting There & Away
Biot village is a good 4km from Biot train station. From Antibes, take bus No 10A from the bus station or place du Général de Gaulle to Biot village (7.50FF, 20 minutes, 11 buses daily).

CAGNES-SUR-MER
postcode 06800 • pop 44,207
Cagnes-sur-Mer comprises **Haut de Cagnes**, the old hill-top town; **Le Cros de Cagnes**, the former fishing village by the beach; and **Cagnes Ville**, a fast-growing modern quarter. The old city, with its ramparts, is dominated by the 14th-century Château Grimaldi.

Near Cagnes Ville, the Musée Renoir is dedicated to the artist who spent his last 12 years in Cagnes-sur-Mer. The magnificent olive and orange groves around the Provençal *mas* (farmhouse; today the boutique) and bourgeois house are as much a draw as the museum itself.

Cagnes-sur-Mer tourist office (☎ 04 93 20 61 64, fax 04 93 20 52 63, 🄴 cagnes06 @aol.com, tourisme@cagnes.fr), 6 blvd Maréchal Juin, in Cagnes Ville, is just off the A8. Visit online at www.tourisme.fr /cagnes.

Château Grimaldi
Home to the Grimaldi family until the French Revolution, Château Grimaldi (☎ 04 93 20 85 57), 9 place Grimaldi, at the top of the village, houses a **Musée de l'Olivier** (Olive Tree Museum) featuring paintings of olive groves as well as the predictable ethnographic collection; and a **Musée d'Art Méditerranéen Moderne** (Museum of Modern Mediterranean Art) dedicated to the host of 20th-century artists inspired by the Côte d'Azur. Between June and September, the

CANNES AREA

permanent art collection is replaced by exhibits of the Festival International de la Peinture.

The castle was restored in the early 1900s. Its grandiose banquet hall is dominated by a 17th-century ceiling fresco depicting the Greek mythological fall of Phaeton. The marquise of Grimaldi's old boudoir is filled with a bizarre collection of portraits featuring **Suzy Solidor** (1900–85), a cabaret singer who spent the last 25 years of her life living in Cagnes-sur-Mer. When not starring in Parisian cabarets, sexy Suzy starred on the canvases of Europe's leading artists. Among the 40 portraits she donated to the chateau-museum before her death (out of the 224 she possessed) are pieces by Brayer, Cocteau, Dufy, Kisling and Van Dongen.

Château Grimaldi (signposted 'Château-Musée' from the foot of the village) opens 10 am to noon and 2 to 6 pm Wednesday to Monday, May and September; and 10 am to noon and 2 to 5 pm Wednesday to Monday, the rest of the year. Admission costs 20FF (those aged under 18, 10FF).

Musée Renoir

La Domaine des Collettes, today the Renoir Museum (☎ 04 93 20 61 07), chemin des Collettes, served as home and studio to an arthritis-crippled Renoir (1841–1919), who lived here with his wife and three sons from 1907 until his death.

It has retained its original decor. The wheelchair-bound artist painted, with a brush bandaged to his fingers, in the north-facing, 2nd-floor studios. The chicken wire covering the window protected Renoir from his children's mis-hit tennis balls.

Several of the artist's works are on display, including *Les Grandes Baigneuses* (The Women Bathers; 1892), a reworking of the 1887 original. Photographs documenting his life are dotted around the house, as well as some of Renoir's sculptures, notably *Vénus Victorieuse* (Venus Victorious), a Renoir statue of a fashionably rounded, nude Venus cast in bronze.

The Renoir museum opens 10 am to noon and 2 to 6 pm Wednesday to Monday, May

to September; and 10 am to noon and 2 to 5 pm Wednesday to Monday, the rest of the year. Admission costs 20FF (students and children aged under 12, 10FF). Guided tours in English (1½ hours, 20FF) depart at 10.30 am and 3.30 pm on Thursday in July and August. To get to the museum from Cagnes bus station on place du Général de Gaulle, walk east along ave Renoir and its continuation, ave des Tuilières, then turn left (north) onto chemin des Collettes. From here, the museum is 500m uphill.

Getting There & Away

Cagnes-sur-Mer is served by two train stations, Gare Cagnes-sur-Mer, and Gare Le Cros de Cagnes. Most Cannes–Ventimiglia trains stop at both (two to three minutes apart by train).

Buses from Cannes to Nice (every 20 minutes) stop outside Cagnes-sur-Mer (52 minutes) and Le Cros de Cagnes train stations (one hour), and at Cagnes' central bus station on place du Général de Gaulle. The Grasse–Nice bus (No 500) only stops outside Cagnes-sur-Mer train station (35 minutes, about 10 daily).

From Vence, bus No 400 departs every 30 minutes to Cagnes-sur-Mer (20 minutes) via St-Paul de Vence. Cheap day passes are available on this route (see St-Paul de Vence below).

ST-PAUL DE VENCE
postcode 06570 • pop 2900
• elevation 125m

This picturesque and touristy medieval hill-top village, 10km north of Cagnes-sur-Mer, has been a haven to a great many artists and writers over the centuries and is a must for any art lover following in the footsteps of the 20th-century's great masters. Some of their works are exhibited at the extraordinary Fondation Maeght and, for those into fine dining, at La Colombe d'Or.

St-Paul de Vence was home to Russian artist Marc Chagall (1887–1985) who is buried in the village cemetery. The African-American novelist James Baldwin (1924–85) also spent the last years of his life in St-Paul. Yves Montand (1921–91) was a

CANNES AREA

frequent visitor here for many years. The French singer/actor was best known for his roles in the 1986 film adaptations of Pagnol's novels *Jean de Florette* and *Manon des Sources* (and in 1998 for the controversial exhumation of his corpse for DNA testing as part of a 10-year paternity suit filed against him). He met his wife, the actress Simone Signoret, for the first time in St-Paul in 1949. They threw their wedding reception at La Colombe d'Or.

The tourist office (☎ 04 93 32 86 95, fax 04 93 32 60 27, e artdevivre@wanadoo .fr), 2 rue Grande, is on your right as you enter the old village through its northern gate. It opens 10 am to 7 pm June to September; and 10 am to noon, the rest of the year. It organises one-hour guided tours of the old village between 10 am and 5.30 pm (50FF); on request tours can include a visit to a local artist's studio.

The Village

Strolling the narrow streets packaged within **15th-century ramparts** is how most visitors while away a trip to St-Paul. No less than 36 of its 64 **art galleries** are on rue Grande; the tourist office has a list. Steps from rue Grande lead eastwards to St-Paul's crowning glory, the **Église Collégiale** and adjoining **Chapelle des Pénitents**, place de l'Église. Free organ recitals are held here in July and August.

Marc Chagall and his wife, Vava, are buried in the **cemetery** at end of village's southern end. Beach pebbles are scattered on top of their plain tombs. From the main cemetery entrance, turn right, then left; the Chagall graves are the third on the left.

Fernand Léger's mosaic mural, *Les Femmes au Perroquet* (Women with a Parrot) is among a handful of pieces of modern art that can be viewed at **La Colombe d'Or** (see Places to Stay & Eat later in this section) on place des Ormeaux. This upmarket restaurant is where Braque, Chagall, Dufy, Picasso and other then-impoverished artists dined in the post WWI years in exchange for one of their humble creations – which today form one of France's largest private art collections. Viewing is strictly for

diners; book well in advance. It is closed in November.

Yves Montand was among the handful of celebrities captured on black-and-white film while playing **pétanque** on the village court in front of La Colombe d'Or and Café de la Place. The tourist office hires balls (20FF per set). It can also arrange a training session (200/400FF per hour on weekdays/ weekends) with a local pétanque champ.

Fondation Maeght

The Maeght Foundation – a futuristic building set on a hill in beautiful countryside amid gardens embellished with sculptures and fountains – is one of France's foremost centres for contemporary art. It hosts an exceptional permanent collection of 20th-century works featuring Braque, Bonnard, Chagall, Matisse, Miró and Léger. Its temporary exhibitions are equally extraordinary.

In the gardens behind the museum, visitors can stroll through the **Miró Labyrinth**, a terraced area laid out by Catalan architect José Luis Sert, a pupil of Le Corbusier. The route is studded with gigantic sculptures and mosaics – some spouting water – by Spanish surrealist Joan Miró (1893–1983), who frequently visited the Côte d'Azur to see Picasso and other artists living on the coast. Some of Miró's works are for sale in the gallery's boutique (starting at 70,000FF).

Fondation Maeght (☎ 04 93 32 81 63, e contact@fondation-maeght.com) opens 10 am to 7 pm July to September; and 10 am to 12.30 pm and 2.30 to 6 pm, the rest of the year. Admission costs 50FF (students 40FF) and there's a 15FF camera fee. Dogs and smoking in the grounds are forbidden. The centre, signposted from rond point St-Claire, is 800m from the bus stop. A steep driveway leads up to the Fondation. Approaching St-Paul by car, turn left off the D7 from La-Colle-sur-Loup.

Galerie Guy Pieters

This modern art gallery (☎ 04 93 32 06 46, e info@guypietersgallery.com), chemin des Trious, at the foot of the driveway leading to Fondation Maeght, is a must for big spenders. Stunning (and often monumental) pieces of contemporary work are displayed here; many are for sale. In the gallery's permanent collection (not for sale), star pieces include Andy Warhol's *La Grande Passion* (1984), Tom Wesselmann's *Smoker* (1998) and Arman's 2.8m-tall *Music Power*, which the Nice-born artist created from a dozen violins in 1985. Galerie Guy Pieters opens 10 am to 7 pm Wednesday to Monday. Visit online at www.modern-art-foundation.com.

Places to Stay & Eat
St-Paul de Vence is strictly for the rich and well-to-do. The tourist office stocks a list of hotels: *Hostellerie Les Remparts (☎ 04 93 32 09 88, fax 04 93 32 06 91, 72 rue Grande)* is among the cheapest, with doubles costing 250FF to 520FF.

Le St-Paul (☎ 04 93 32 65 25, ℮ stpaul@ relaischateaux.fr, 86 rue Grande) is one of the Riviera's most exclusive hotels. Four-star rooms cost upwards of 850/1250FF (with a village/valley view).

Pricier still is *La Colombe d'Or* (The Golden Dove; ☎ 04 93 32 80 02, fax 04 93 32 77 78), where rooms for one or two rock in at 1500FF or 1750FF. Tables in its legendary restaurant must be booked at least eight days (months in July and August) in advance. To wine and dine your sweetheart will set you back at least 600FF per head (excluding wine). Visit online at www.la-colombe-dor.com (French only).

Getting There & Away
St-Paul de Vence, listed as St-Paul on bus timetables and road signs, is served by the Nice–Vence bus service (bus No 400). A one-way fare from Nice to St-Paul de Vence (one hour) is 20FF. If you intend stopping at Cagnes-sur-Mer en route or continuing to Vence, buy a one-day Billet Circulaire (35FF), which allows one stop in Nice, Cagnes-sur-Mer, St-Paul and Vence.

VENCE
postcode 06140 • pop 17,184
• elevation 325m
Vence (Venço in Provençal) is a pleasant but touristy inland town, 4km north of

St-Paul de Vence. The area is typically built up with holiday homes and villas, but the medieval centre is perfect for strolling past art galleries and through street markets.

The exceptional Chapelle du Rosaire, designed and decorated by Matisse, is tended today by the community of Dominican nuns for whom the 77-year-old Matisse created the chapel between 1947 and 1951. Matisse lived in Vence for six years, accomplishing works such as *Lemons and Mimosas Against a Black Background* (1943), *Yellow and Blue Interior* (1946) and *Still Life with Pomegranates* (1947) while he was here. His home and studio, called Le Rêve (The Dream) was a villa 200m from the Chapelle du Rosaire, opposite 320 ave Henri Matisse.

Music fills the streets of Vence during its music festival, Nuits du Sud, which occupies place du Grand Jardin during the last two weeks of July and the first week of August. At other times, a morning fruit and vegetable market splashes the central square with colour, Tuesday to Sunday.

Orientation
Large place du Grand Jardin is Vence's central square. To get to the old city, turn left onto ave Marcellin Maurel, which skirts the medieval city's southern wall. Port du Peyra, the main city entrance, is at the western end of ave Marcellin Maurel. Place Clémenceau lies at the heart of the medieval city.

Information
Vence tourist office (☎ 04 93 58 06 38, fax 04 93 58 91 81, ℮ tourisme@ville-vence.fr), place du Grand Jardin, opens 9 am to 1 pm and 2 to 7 pm Monday to Saturday, July and August; and 9 am to 12.30 am and 2 to 6 pm Monday to Saturday, the rest of the year. It issues free maps enabling visitors to take themselves on a 45-minute self-guided tour, with the aid of 25 numbered, bilingual signs in English and French displayed at pertinent points in the old city. The tourist office Web site is at www.ville-vence.fr.

The post office, place Clémenceau, opens 9 am to noon and 2 to 5 pm weekdays, and

9 to 11 am Saturday. Banks line place du Grand Jardin.

Medieval Vence

Porte du Peyra The main gate of the 13th-century wall that encircles the old city leads to place du Peyra and its **fountain** (1578). Gate and square are named after the execution block that once adorned place du Peyra. The western edge of the square is dominated by the imposing **Château de Villeneuve**, 2 place du Frêne, and adjoining 12th-century **watchtower**. The castle houses the **Fondation Émile Hughes** (☎ 04 93 24 24 23), a cultural centre with 20th-century art exhibitions. It opens 10 am to 12.30 pm and 2 to 6 pm Tuesday to Sunday (no break in July and August). A 400-year-old ash tree stands in front of the castle.

From place du Peyra, narrow **rue du Marché** – dotted with delectable food shops selling fresh pasta, fish, fruit and so on – leads east. Cut along rue Alsace-Lorraine to reach **place Clémenceau**, the central square and market place. The **Romanesque cathedral** on the eastern side of the square was built in the 11th century on the site of an old Roman temple.

The best panorama of medieval Vence can be had from Matisse's Chapelle du Rosaire (see that section below). The watchtower provides a ready landmark.

Matisse's Chapelle du Rosaire

Matisse moved from war-torn Nice to Vence in June 1943. Upon his arrival he was reunited with Monique Bourgeois, his former nurse and model who had since become a Dominican nun under the name Sœur Jacques-Marie. She persuaded the artist to design a chapel for her community, the result being the striking **Chapelle du Rosaire** (Chapel of the Rosary; ☎ 04 93 58 03 26), 468 ave Henri Matisse. Matisse was 81 when he completed the project in 1951.

The chapel is still used by the Dominican nuns of the Rosary today. Blue-and-white ceramic tiles coat the low roof, which is topped by a 13m-tall wrought-iron cross and bell tower. Inside, stark white walls provide a dramatic contrast to the stained-glass windows, through which the sun's rays glow. A line image of the Virgin Mary and child is painted on white ceramic tiles on the northern interior wall. The western wall is dominated by the bolder *Chemin de Croix* (Stations of the Cross), numbered in Matisse's frenzied handwriting. St-Dominic overlooks the altar.

Matisse also designed the chapel's stone altar, candlesticks, cross, and the colourful priests' vestments displayed in an adjoining hall. Many of his preparatory sketches and models for the four-year project are here too, as is a photograph of the artist with Sister Jacques-Marie, arms linked in friendly companionship.

The chapel is about 800m north of Vence on route de St-Jeannet (the D2210). From place du Grand Jardin, head east along ave de la Résistance then turn right (north) along ave Tuby. At the next junction, bear right (north-east) along ave de Provence then left (north) onto ave Henri Matisse. It opens 10 to 11.30 am and 2 to 5.30 pm Tuesday and Thursday, and 2 to 5.30 pm Monday, Wednesday and Saturday. During French school holidays, it also opens 2 to 5.30 pm Friday. Sunday Mass (open to everyone) is celebrated at 10 am, followed by a guided tour at 10.45 am. Admission costs 15FF (children aged six to 16, 5FF).

Places to Stay & Eat

The Dominican nuns offer beds for the night in the *Maison Lacordaire* (☎ 04 93 58 03 26, fax 04 93 58 21 10, 466 ave Henri Matisse), adjoining the Chapelle du Rosaire. A night's accommodation costs 220FF per person for full board (160FF half-board). Rooms *must* be reserved at least three to eight days in advance.

The mundane *Hôtel La Lubane* (☎ 04 93 58 01 10, fax 04 93 58 84 44), midway between place du Grand Jardin and Matisse's chapel at 10 ave Joffre, has singles/doubles with washbasin and fine views of the Col de Vence for 180/215FF. Rooms with shower cost 274FF. *Hôtel La Victoire* (☎ 04 93 58 61 30, fax 04 93 58 74 68, place du Grand Jardin) is above a busy bar. Rooms for one or two with shower/bath cost 184/210FF.

CANNES AREA

Le P'tit Provençal (☎ 04 93 58 50 64, 4 place Clémenceau), tucked beside the town hall, serves local cuisine on a pavement terrace. It has a lunchtime 75FF *menu* (which usually includes a fresh fish dish), a 60FF children's dish and adult-sized evening dishes for 105FF and 155FF. Its roasted tuna with baked Provençal vegetables and its fruity soups are notable highlights.

A guitarist delights diners with a soulful repetoire at *Le Passe Muraille (☎ 04 93 58 10 21, 2 rue du Peyra)*, a restaurant in a 13th-century vaulted celler.

Getting There & Away
Bus No 400 to/from Nice (20FF, one hour), Cagnes-sur-Mer (20 minutes) and St-Paul de Vence (10 minutes) use the unmarked stop on place du Grand Jardin, in front of No 14 (a few doors down from the tourist office).

Getting Around
Vence Vélo (☎ 04 93 58 56 00), 7 ave des Poilus, rents bicycles.

AROUND VENCE
Varied **walking, cycling & driving** terrain surrounds Vence. The northbound D2 from Vence leads to the **Col de Vence** (963m), a mountain pass 10km north offering good views of the *baous* (rocky promontories), typical to this region. At the foot of the pass is the **Baou des Blancs** (673m), crowned by the stony remains of the **Bastide St-Laurent**, inhabited by the Templars in the 13th century. Destination Nature (☎/fax 04 93 32 06 93, [e] denature@aol.com), 257 traverse de St-Jeanne, in Châteauneuf de Grasse, organises full- and half-day walks and mountain-bike trips around the col, some of which follow part of the GR51. Details are posted on its Web site at www.riviera-explorer.com/destination-nature.

Coursegoules (pop 323, elevation 1020m), 6km farther north along the D2, is a typical Provençal hill-top village with 11th-century castle ruins and fortifications. From here, head west along the D2 to **Gréolieres** (pop 455), yet another fabulous hill-top village. From here, walkers can follow the GR4

north to **Gréolieres-les-Neiges** (elevation 1450m), a small ski station equipped with 14 lifts (and eight snow canons!), on the northern face of Montagne Cheiron; the GR4 scales Cheiron's 1778m-high peak.

Several hairpin bends and 7km south of Gréolieres along the D603, you hook up with the dramatic **Gorges du Loup**. Destination Nature organises **canyoning** and **rafting** expeditions along the Loup, mid-June and mid-September. The road along the western side of the gorges (the D3) crescendoes with the village of **Gourdon** (pop 384), from where keen stargazers like make a detour 15km or so west to the **Observatoire de la Côte d'Azur** (1270m; ☎ 04 93 40 54 54) atop the Plateau de Calern near Caussols. The road along the eastern ridge (D6) leads to **Pont du Loup**, from where you can follow the eastbound D2210 to Tourrettes-sur-Loup. Some 5km before the village is Ferme des Courmettes (☎ 04 93 59 31 93), a 600-hectare **goat farm** where cheese is made. Guided tours and dégustation sessions are available; Vence tourist office has details. **Tourrettes-sur-Loup** (pop 3921), dubbed the 'city of violets' after its production of the purple flower, is a picturesque, 15th-century hill-top village crammed with art galleries and craft shops.

Six kilometres north-east of Vence, at the foot of **Baou de Jeannet** (800m), is the village of **St-Jeannet** (pop 3647) – the setting for Peter Mayle's fictional *Chasing Cézanne*. A 45-minute marked trail leads from central place Ste-Barbe to the summit of the promontory. Top off the trip with a visit to **La Gaude** (pop 6217), a less touristy hill-top village 1.5km south of St-Jeannet.

GRASSE
postcode 06130 • pop 44,790
• elevation 250m
If it weren't for the scents around Grasse (Grasso in Provençal), 17km north of the Mediterranean and Cannes, you may detect a sea breeze. For centuries Grasse, with its distinct red- and orange-tiled roofs rising up pre-Alpine slopes, has been one of France's leading centres of perfume production.

GRASSE

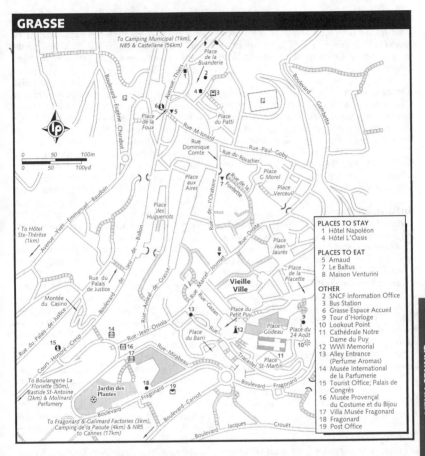

PLACES TO STAY
1 Hôtel Napoléon
4 Hôtel L'Oasis

PLACES TO EAT
5 Arnaud
7 Le Baltus
8 Maison Venturini

OTHER
2 SNCF Information Office
3 Bus Station
6 Grasse Espace Accueil
9 Tour d'Horloge
10 Lookout Point
11 Cathédrale Notre Dame du Puy
12 WWI Memorial
13 Alley Entrance (Perfume Aromas)
14 Musée International de la Parfumerie
15 Tourist Office; Palais de Congrès
16 Musée Provençal du Costume et du Bijou
17 Villa Musée Fragonard
18 Fragonard
19 Post Office

CANNES AREA

These days there are five famous master perfumers – or *nez* (noses), as they're called – in the world. Combining their natural gift with seven years of study, they can identify, from no more than a whiff, about 6000 scents. Somewhere between 200 and 500 of these fragrances are used to make just one perfume. Compelling reading associated with Grasse is *Perfume*, a novel by Patrick Süskind about the fantastic life and amazing nose of Jean-Baptiste Grenouille.

Founded by the Romans, Grasse had become a small republic by the early Middle Ages, exporting tanned hides and oil (from which it may have earned its name since *gras* or *matière grasse* means 'fat' in French). With the advent of perfumed gloves in the 1500s, Grasse discovered a new wealth; glove-makers quickly split from the tanners and set up a separate industry, leading to the eventual creation of perfumeries. In the 18th century, with perfume suddenly becoming all the rage, these blossomed.

Grasse and its surrounds also produce some of France's most highly prized flowers, including lavender (which you'll see growing in profusion in the countryside), jasmine, centifolia roses, mimosa, orange blossom and violets. Cut flowers are sold at the *marché Provençal* (Provençal market) that brings a splash of colour to cours Honoré Cresp on the first and third Saturdays of the month.

Orientation

The small old city of Grasse is densely packed into the hillside. Its steep stairways and roads are best explored on foot. The N85 (the route Napoléon), which leads north to Castellane and Digne-les-Bains and south to Cannes, runs into Grasse, where it becomes the town's main (and often congested) thoroughfare, blvd du Jeu de Ballon.

Information

Grasse Espace Accueil (☎ 04 93 36 21 07), an information bureau two minutes' walk from the bus station at 3 place de la Foux, and the tourist office (☎ 04 93 36 66 66, fax 04 93 36 86 36, e tourisme.grasse@wanadoo.fr), inside Palais de Congrès at 22 cours Honoré Cresp, open 9 am to 7 pm Monday to Saturday, and 9 am to 12.30 pm and 1.30 to 6 pm Sunday, July to mid-September; and 9 am to 12.30 pm and 1.30 to 6 pm Monday to Saturday, the rest of the year. The latter organises medieval city tours on foot (2½ hours, 20FF). Online, try www.ville-grasse.fr.

Commercial banks dot blvd du Jeu de Ballon. The post office is on blvd Fragonard.

Perfumeries

Follow your nose along rue Jean Ossola to the archway at the start of rue Tracastel, where several perfumeries have been conjuring up new scents for years. The air around the alley entrance is saturated with aromas.

Just three of Grasse's 40 *parfumeries* (perfumeries) – all relatively unknown given they sell their essence to factories or by mail order – can be visited. Guided tours take you through every stage of perfume production, from extraction and distillation to the work of the 'noses'. The difference between perfume (which contains 20% pure essence) and its weaker partners, eau de toilette and eau de Cologne (which contain 2% to 6% concentrate), is explained. At the end you'll be squirted with a few of the house scents, invited to purchase as many as you'd like, and leave reeking.

Fragonard (☎ 04 93 36 44 65), 20 blvd Fragonard, online at www.fragonard.com (French only), is the most convenient perfumery for those on foot. Datingto 1926, the perfumery is named after one of the town's original perfume-making families and is in a 16th-century tannery. It's more a tourist showcase than a working factory: the real production factory (open for free visits; ☎ 04 93 77 94 30), route de Cannes, is out of town on the N85. The Fragonard perfumery opens 9 am to 12.30 pm and 2 to 6 pm, October to May; and 9 am to 6.30 pm, the rest of the year.

In a turreted, Provençal-style villa surrounded by immaculate lawns and a blaze of flowers, **Molinard** (☎ 04 93 36 01 62, e molinard.parfum@wanadoo.fr), 60 blvd Victor Hugo, is a ritzier affair than Fragonard. This perfume house dates from 1849 and can be visited 9 am to 12.30 pm and 2 to 6 pm Monday to Saturday, October to May; and 9 am to 6.30 pm, the rest of the year. Molinard offers 'create your own perfume' sessions (1½ hours, 250FF) and various other packages such as perfume creation followed by lunch at Bastide St-Antoine, a cookery session at Vergé's Moulin de Mougins or a furniture painting lesson. Details are on its Web site at www.molinard-parfums.com.

Situated 3km from town, towards Mouans-Sartoux (not far from Fragonard's factory), is the **Galimard** (☎ 04 93 09 20 00) perfume factory, 73 route de Cannes. It receives visitors from 9 am to 6 pm in summer; 9 am to noon and 2 to 5.30 pm, the rest of the year. At its nearby **Studio des Fragrances** (☎ as above) on route de Pégomas you can likewise create your own fragrance from 126 different scents under the guidance of a professional 'nose' (two hours, 220FF). The Galimard perfumery has a second outlet in Èze (see Corniche Inférieure in the Nice to Menton chapter earlier in the book) and a Web site at www.galimard.com.

Museums

Villa Musée Fragonard Named after the artist Jean-Honoré Fragonard, who was born in Grasse in 1732, the villa where the artist lived for a year in 1790 has been turned into a house-museum (☎ 04 93 3 01 61), 23 blvd Fragonard. His paintings, famous for their licentious scenes, are displayed. It opens 10 am to 1 pm and 2 to 7 pm, June to September; and 10 am to noon and 2 to 5 pm Wednesday to Sunday, the rest of the year. Admission is free.

Musée Provençal du Costume et du Bijou Visiting Grasse's colourful costume and jewellery museum comes as a breath of fresh air after touring the town's perfumeries. The museum (☎ 04 93 36 44 65), 2 rue Jean Ossola, is inside stately Hôtel de Clapiers Cabris, the private mansion of the sister of revolutionary Mirabeau, the marquise de Cabris, who lived in Grasse from 1769. It opens 10 am to 1 pm and 2 to 6 pm. Admission is free.

Musée International de la Parfumerie The International Perfume Museum (☎ 04 93 36 80 20), 8 place du Cours Honoré Cresp, examines every detail of perfume production – from extraction techniques to sales and publicity – and traces its 400 years of history in Grasse. One of the most appealing parts of the museum is the rooftop conservatory, where lavender, mint, thyme and jasmine are grown in a heady mix of aromatic scents. It opens 10 am to 7 pm, June to September; and 10 am to noon and 2 to 5 pm Wednesday to Sunday, the rest of the year. Admission costs 25FF (students and those aged under 16, 12.50FF).

Cathédrale Notre Dame du Puy

Although rather uninteresting in itself, the cathedral, built in Provençal Romanesque style in the 12th and 13th centuries and reworked in the 18th century, contains a painting by Fragonard entitled *Washing of the Feet*, and several early paintings by Rubens, including *The Crown of Thorns* and *Christ Crucified*. Summer concerts are occasionally held here.

Special Events

Grasse's two main events – related to flowers and scents *naturellement* – are Exporose in May and La Jasminade, held during the first weekend in August.

Places to Stay

Two-star *Camping Municipal* (☎ 04 93 36 28 69, fax 04 93 36 90 54, 27 blvd Alice de Rothschild), 1km north-east of the bus station, opens year round. It charges 81FF for two people with a tent and car. Bus No 8 marked 'Piscine' leaves from the bus station and stops in front of the site. *Camping de la Paoute* (☎ 04 93 09 11 42, fax 04 93 40 06 40, 160 route de Cannes) is 4km south of Grasse signposted off the N567 towards Cannes.

The cheapest option in town is one-star *Hôtel Napoléon* (☎ 04 93 36 05 87, fax 04 93 36 41 09, 6 ave Thiers). Basic singles/doubles cost 130/160FF and it has a handful of triples/quads. Opposite, small and rather run-down *Hôtel L'Oasis* (☎ 04 93 36 02 72, fax 04 93 36 03 16, place de la Buanderie) has washbasin-equipped doubles for 190FF (240FF with shower).

From *Hôtel Ste-Thérèse* (☎ 04 93 36 10 29, fax 04 93 36 11 73, 39 ave Yves Emmanuel Baudoin), just over 1km uphill from the tourist office, there's a panoramic view of the valley and dusty, orange-roofed town. Rooms start at 160/210FF.

Places to Eat

Charming *Le Baltus* (☎ 04 93 36 32 90, 15 rue de la Fontette) dishes up traditional Provençal cuisine and fare from the sea. *Menus* start at 90FF and bouillabaisse costs 280FF per person. Bistro-style *Arnaud* (☎ 04 93 36 44 88, 10 place de la Foux) is another recommended spot where homemade gnocchi and ravioli are served beneath a vaulted ceiling.

Michelin twin-starred *Bastide St-Antoine* (☎ 04 93 70 94 94, ℮ info@jacques-chibois .com, 48 ave Henri Dunant) is Grasse's gastronomic choice. Inside an 18th-century country house amid a vast olive grove, delicious lunchtime/evening *menus* (starting at 250/550FF) are crammed with regional

CANNES AREA

treats (including truffles) by well-known French chef Jacques Chibois. Bastide St-Antoine has 11 lavish hotel rooms costing about 1000FF.

Fougassettes (sweet brioches delicately perfumed with orange or another sensual flavour) are the speciality of **Maison Venturini** (☎ *04 93 36 20 47, 1 rue Marcel Journet)*, open Tuesday to Saturday. Fans of other French breads should head for **Boulangerie La Floriette** (☎ *04 93 36 68 30, 40 bis blvd Victor Hugo)*, a bakery known for its *pain chaud toute la journée* (hot bread all day), fougasses and different *michettes* (tomato, goat cheese, Roquefort etc), open Friday to Wednesday.

Getting There & Away
Bus The ticket office at the bus station (☎ 04 93 36 08 43), place de la Buanderie, closes at 5.15 pm. Several companies operate from here. Rapides Côte d'Azur (☎ 04 92 96 88 88 in Vallauris, ☎ 04 93 39 11 39 in Cannes) operates bus No 500 to Nice (37FF, 1¼ hours, eight to 10 buses daily) via Cannes (20.50FF, 45 minutes). In addition, buses No 600 or 605 link Grasse with Cannes, stopping at Mouans-Sartoux and Mougins (see those sections earlier for details) en route.

Sillages-STGA (☎ 04 93 36 37 37) operates buses from Grasse to Valbonne and Mouans-Sartoux.

VFD has a morning bus to Grenoble (six hours) which stops in Castellane (near the Gorges du Verdon) and Digne-les-Bains.

Train The train line does not reach Grasse but SNCF has an information office (☎ 04 93 36 06 13) near the bus station. It opens 8.30 am to 5.30 pm Monday to Saturday.

Massif de l'Estérel

Covered by pine, oak and eucalyptus trees until the devastating fires of 1985 and 1986 and now beginning to return to life, this spectacular range sprawls immediately south-west of Cannes. It is roughly marked by Mandelieu-La Napoule to the north and St-Raphaël to the south. The latter, together with its Roman neighbour, Fréjus, serves as the main gateway to the Massif de l'Estérel and St-Tropez. Its inland boundary is hugged by noisy La Provençale (the A8 motorway), immediately north of which spills Lac de St-Cassien, where you can swim, sail and windsurf.

There are all sorts of walks to enjoy in the Massif de l'Estérel, but for the more difficult trails you will need to come equipped with a good map, such as IGN's *Série Bleue* (1:25,000) No 3544ET, which costs 45FF. Those not keen to go it alone can link up with an organised walk; the tourist office in St-Raphaël has details.

CORNICHE DE L'ESTÉREL
The coastal road that runs along the base of the massif is called the Corniche de l'Estérel (also known as the Corniche d'Or and the N98). A drive or walk along this winding road is not to be missed as the views are spectacular. Small summer resorts and inlets (good for swimming) are dotted the length of the 40km-odd coastal stretch, all of which is easily accessible by bus or train (see Getting There & Away later in this section).

If the snail-paced traffic amid the searing heat gets too much in summer, opt for the inland N7. This quieter road runs through the hills and transports you into an entirely different world.

La Napoule
'Once upon a time' is an apt label for the turreted, 14th-century **Château de la Napoule** (☎ 04 93 49 95 05), ave Henry Clews, that dominates this small seaside village. The fanciful castle was the creation of Henry and Marie Clews, an American couple who arrived on the coast in 1918 and spent 17 years rebuilding the sea-facing Saracen tower. Above the main entrance to the chateau, considered a folly by many, are carved the words 'once upon a time'.

The interior and the gardens, overlooking sandy **Plage du Château**, are adorned with fantastical sculptures created by Henry Clews (1876–1937). The monumental statue,

The God of Humormystics, which stands in the courtyard, was the sculptor's wedding present to his wife. Château de la Napoule was occupied during WWII (forcing the widowed Marie to move into the gate-house). In 1951, Marie Clews established the **Fondation d'Art de la Napoule** in commemoration of her husband's eccentric art. His gravestone in the castle grounds reads 'Poet, Sculptor, Actor, Grand Knight of La Mancha, Supreme Master Humormystic, Castelan of Once upon a time, Chevalier de Marie'.

The chateau, which remains privately owned, can be visited with a guided tour, departing from the main entrance at 3 and 4 pm (5 pm in July and August), March to 30 October. Admission costs 25FF (students and children aged under 10, 20FF).

The neighbouring village of **Théoule-sur-Mer** (pop 1304), 2.5km south along the coast, is dominated by **Château de la Théoule**, another privately owned folly built in the same architectural style as its better-known sister. In the 18th century it was a soap factory. Théoule-sur-Mer tourist office (☎ 04 93 49 28 28, fax 04 93 49 00 04) is at 1 Cornichee d'Or.

Le Trayas
Seven kilometres south of Théoule-sur-Mer is Le Trayas, the highest point of the corniche, from where the road gets more dramatic as it twists and turns its way past the **Fôret Domaine de l'Estérel** along the jagged coastline. Needles of red rock strike out amid the splashing sea, hugging small sheltered *anses* (coves). There is a largish beach at **Anse de la Figueirette**, at the northern end of Le Trayas.

There are several parking areas along this stretch of the corniche where you can stop to picnic and take snaps of the red rocks. There are good views of the spectacular **Rocher de St-Barthélemy** (St-Bartholomew's Rock) and Cap Roux from the **Pointe de l'Observatoire**, 2km south of Le Trayas.

Agay
The village resort of Agay, 10km or so south of Le Trayas, is celebrated for its fine views of the **Rade d'Agay**, a perfect horseshoe-shaped bay embraced by sandy beaches and abundant pine trees. Numerous water sports and boat excursions are on offer at busy central Plage d'Agay. Agay tourist office (☎ 04 94 82 01 85), opposite the beach at 577 blvd de la Plage, has details. From Agay, route de Valescure leads inland into the massif, from where various walking trails are signposted, including up to **Pic de l'Ours** (496m), **Pic du Cap Roux** (452m) and **Pic d'Aurelle** (323m). All three *pics* (peaks) offer stunning panoramas of the Massif de l'Estérel.

Le Dramont
Cap du Dramont, also called Cap Estérel, is crowned by a military semaphore and sits at the southern end of the Rade d'Agay. From the semaphore there are unbeatable views of the Golfe de Fréjus flanked by the **Lion de Terre** and the **Lion de Mer** – two red porphyry rocks jutting out of the sea – to the west. Trails lead to the semaphore from Plage du Débarquement in Le Dramont on the western side of the cape. In Agay, a path starts from the car park near Plage du Camp Long, at the eastern foot of the cape. Both beaches are accessible from the N98.

From **Plage du Débarquement** you can sail (15 minutes) to **Île d'Or** (Golden Island), a pinprick island, uninhabited bar a small stone fort that is someone's summer house. You can hire catamarans (about 200/900FF for one/five hours) and sailboards (70/300FF for one/five hours) from the Accueil Base Nautique (☎ 04 94 82 76 57, 06 14 02 44 18), a wooden hut on the beach.

Overlooking Plage du Débarquement, 1km west of Boulouris on the Corniche de l'Estérel (N98), is a large **memorial park**, blvd de la 36ème DI du Texas, which commemorates the landing of the 36th US Infantry Division on the beach here on 15 August 1944. A monumental landing craft faces out to sea. Steps lead from here down to the beach.

Places to Stay
Camping Camp sites are most plentiful around Agay. In Agay centre is *Camping Agay Soleil* (☎ *04 94 82 00 79, 1152 blvd*

CANNES AREA

de la Plage), close to the tourist office and overlooking the bay. The nightly rate is 97FF for a tent, two people and car. The site opens mid-March to mid-November.

Royal Camping (☎ 04 94 82 00 20, fax 04 94 82 00 20), two minutes' walk from Plage du Camp Long on the N98, charges 92FF for a tent, two people and car. It opens February to October.

Equally handy is ***Camping Le Draumont*** (☎ 04 94 82 07 68, fax 04 94 82 75 30, ⓔ contact@campeoples.fr), a pretty site next to Plage du Débarquement on the western side of Cap du Dramont. The site opens mid-March to mid-October and charges 95/145/170FF for two people with a tent and car in low/mid-/high season. It also has caravans to let (minimum three nights) for 1400FF to 2800FF per week for up to five people.

Hostels In Le Trayas, the coastal ***Villa Solange*** (☎ 04 93 75 40 23, fax 04 93 75 43 45, 9 ave de la Véronèse) is a youth hostel on an idyllic site overlooking Anse de la Figueirette. The hostel is 1.5km up the hill from the Auberge Blanche bus stop. The hostel is closed from 10 am and 5 pm. A bed costs 49FF (breakfast costs 19FF and an additional 19FF per night is charged for non HI-card holders) and sheets can be hired for 17FF. Telephone reservations are not accepted. You can camp for 29FF. It opens mid-February to the end of December.

Hotels In La Napoule, two-star ***Hôtel La Calanque*** (☎ 04 93 49 95 11, fax 04 93 49 67 44, ave Henry Clews), opposite Château de la Napoule, is among the cheapest places to stay. It has singles/doubles for about 200/350FF.

At the southern end of Le Trayas on the N98, ***Le Relais des Calanques*** (☎ 04 94 44 14 06, fax 04 94 44 10 93, route des Escalles) offers striking views of the red-rocked sea. The hotel has a pool and private beach, and doubles from 250FF to 400FF (400FF to 600FF in high season).

Agay has numerous hotels to choose from. In Le Dramont near the Plage du Débarquement, zero-starred ***Hôtel du Débarquement***

(☎ 04 94 82 02 51, 04 94 82 84 92) has doubles with shower and toilet for 250FF to 320FF. It is one of the few places along the Corniche de l'Estérel to open year round.

Getting There & Away

Bus Société Varoise d'Autocars BELTRAME (☎ 04 94 83 87 63 in St-Raphaël) runs frequent daily buses along the Corniche d'Estérel to/from Cannes to St-Raphaël (eight between 8 am and 7 pm Monday to Saturday, five on Sunday; plus seven additional buses daily from Le Trayas and/or Agay to St-Raphaël).

From Cannes, buses on this route (labelled 'Ligne de la Corniche d'Or' on timetables) stop at La Napoule, Théole-sur-Mer, Le Trayas, Agay, Cap du Dramont, Le Dramont and Boulouris.

Train There is a train station at Mandelieu-la-Napoule, 4km north of La Napoule, and at Théoule-sur-Mer, Le Trayas, Agay, Le Dramont and Boulouris. These stations are served by the Nice–St-Raphaël–Fréjus–Les Arcs–Draguignan coastal rail route (nine to 11 trains between 8.15 am and 8.45 pm Monday to Saturday; less frequently on Sunday and in winter). There are plenty more trains from Cannes to St-Raphaël (see Getting There & Away under Cannes earlier in this chapter) from where there are regular buses.

ST-RAPHAËL
postcode 83700 • pop 31,196

The old port here was where Napoleon landed in 1799 upon his return from Egypt, and from where he set sail for exile in Elba in 1814. During WWII, it was one of the main landing bases of US and French troops in August 1944.

Created by Félix Martin (1842–99), mayor of the then-small fishing commune, St-Raphaël resort (Sant Rafèu in Provençal) is 2km south-east of Fréjus. A fabulous place to be seen in the 1920s, the suburbs of contemporary St-Raphaël are so intertwined with those of its Roman neighbour Fréjus that the two places almost form a single town. From St-Raphaël, it is a pleasant

10-minute walk westwards along blvd de la Libération to Fréjus beach.

Orientation

The new centre of St-Raphaël is neatly packed between rue Waldeck Rousseau and the promenade de Lattre de Tassigny, which leads west to the Vieux Port (old port); the old town is immediately north of rue Waldeck Rousseau off rue de la Liberté. St-Raphaël's beach activities sprawl as far east as Port Santa Lucia, a modern pleasure port 2km south-east along the coast from the centre.

Information

The tourist office (☎ 04 94 19 52 52, fax 04 94 83 85 40, e touroff@ clubinternet.fr), opposite the train station on rue Waldeck Rousseau, opens 9 am to 7 pm July and August; and 8.15 am to noon and 1.30 to 6 pm Monday to Saturday, the rest of the year. It runs an accommodation service

(☎ 04 94 19 10 60, fax 04 94 19 10 67, e saint-raphael.reservation@wanadoo) and organises two-hour guided tours (15FF) of St-Raphaël, departing at 10 am on Wednesday. Visit online at www.saint-raphael.com.

The post office is east of the tourist office on ave Victor Hugo. Online access is available at the Cyber Bureau (☎ 04 94 95 20 36, e cyberbureau@pacwan.com), next to the train station at 123 rue Waldeck Rousseau.

Beaches & Boat Excursions

St-Raphaël has excellent sandy beaches including **Plage du Veillat**, the main beach. Eastwards, **Plage Beaurivage** is covered in small pebbles. You can parachute behind a speedboat and ride the waves in a rubber tyre from most beaches along this stretch of coastline.

Port Santa Lucia, farther east, is a watersports hub. Club Nautique St-Raphaël (☎ 04 94 95 11 66, e cnsr@comx.fr), blvd Général de Gaulle, offers sailing, surfing and

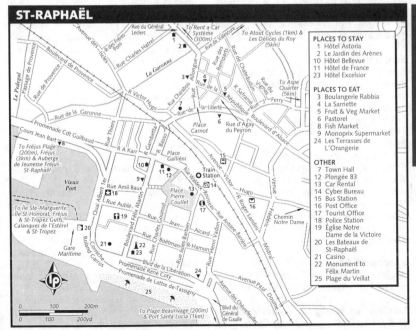

ST-RAPHAËL

PLACES TO STAY
1 Hôtel Astoria
2 Le Jardin des Arènes
10 Hôtel Bellevue
11 Hôtel de France
23 Hôtel Excelsior

PLACES TO EAT
3 Boulangerie Rabbia
4 La Sarriette
5 Fruit & Veg Market
8 Pastorel
8 Fish Market
9 Monoprix Supermarket
24 Les Terrasses de L'Orangerie

OTHER
7 Town Hall
12 Plongée 83
13 Car Rental
14 Cyber Bureau
15 Bus Station
16 Post Office
17 Tourist Office
18 Police Station
19 Église Notre Dame de la Victoire
20 Les Bateaux de St-Raphaël
21 Casino
22 Monument to Félix Martin
25 Plage du Veillat

kayaking lessons. In July and August, the club rents surfboards/catamarans for 360/80FF per five hours.

St-Raphaël is a leading **diving** centre, thanks in part to the **WWII shipwrecks** off the coast. Most diving clubs in town organise dives to the wrecks, which range from a 42m-long US minesweeper to a landing craft destroyed by a rocket in 1944 during the Allied landings. Plongée 83 (☎ 04 94 95 27 18), the diving shop at 29 rue Waldeck Rousseau (also called ave de la Gare), organises night, day and baptism dives (220FF including equipment hire). It has flippers, masks and snorkels to rent at 30/50FF per half-/full day.

Les Bateaux de St-Raphaël (☎ 04 94 95 17 46, 04 94 83 88 55), based at the Gare Maritime at the Vieux Port, runs daily **boat excursions** in summer from St-Raphaël to the Île Ste-Marguerite (90/50FF return adults/children aged two to nine), the Fréjus and St-Tropez gulfs (70/40FF), the Calanques de l'Estérel (60/40FF) and Massif de l'Estérel (70/40FF). It also runs daily boats to/from St-Tropez (see the St-Tropez to Toulon chapter later).

Special Events

St-Raphaël's strong fishing community honours its patron saint, St-Peter, every August with a two-day Fête de la St-Pierre des Pêcheurs. Local fishermen, dressed in traditional costume, joust Provençal-style from flat-bottomed boats moored in the harbour.

Each year, St-Raphaël hosts numerous Provençal jousting competitions; in summer watch out for the Société des Joutes Raphaëloises (Raphaëloises Jousting Society; ☎ 04 94 82 39 74, 06 09 77 89 67) practising in boats around the Vieux Port, usually from 7 pm Tuesday, Wednesday and Thursday.

Places to Stay

Accommodation is not cheap. The Fréjus section later in this chapter lists camp sites.

Hostels The *Auberge de Jeunesse Fréjus-St-Raphaël (☎ 04 94 53 18 75, fax 04 94 53*

25 86, chemin du Couillier), near Fréjus Ville, is set in a seven-hectare park. Dorm beds cost 49/68FF without/with breakfast; sheets cost an extra 17FF and an evening meal is available for 49FF. Camp here for 32FF per night (19FF extra for breakfast). Hostelling cards (114FF) are obligatory; non card-holders pay 19FF per night (free hostelling card after six nights). Guests are evacuated and the hostel closed from 10 am to 6 pm; check in between 7.30 and 10 am or 6 and 9 pm. From St-Raphaël bus station, bus No 7 departs at 8.30 am and 6 pm (6 pm only Sunday) to Les Chênes stop, from where it is a 1km walk uphill along chemin du Couillier. From Fréjus' train or bus station, bus No 3 is the best option.

Hotels The cheapest joint in town is *Le Jardin des Arènes (☎ 04 94 95 06 34, fax 04 94 83 18 97, 31 ave du Général Leclerc)*. Basic rooms for one or two cost 155FF (195FF with shower) and singles/doubles with shower, TV and toilet clock in at 205/255FF. Ranking second is *Hôtel Astoria (☎ 04 94 95 42 79)* at No 77 on the same street, which has grotty rooms with shower, toilet and TV costing 184/234FF.

Two-star *Hôtel Bellevue (☎ 04 94 19 90 10, fax 04 94 19 90 11, 24 blvd Félix Martin)* has good-value singles/doubles/triples starting at 150/200/270FF and rooms for three to five people too. Close by *Hôtel de France (☎ 04 94 95 19 20, fax 04 94 95 61 84, 25 place Galliéni)* has singles/doubles/triples with shower and toilet for 199/249/299FF.

By the seashore, *Hôtel Excelsior (☎ 04 94 95 02 42, fax 04 94 95 33 82, [e] info@excelsior-hotel.com, promenade René Coty)* is an elegant old pile, next to the casino and graced with a beautiful tea terrace overlooking the azure sea. Doubles cost upwards of 630FF.

Places to Eat

Tucked in the shade of a plane tree in the old-town heart is sweet *La Sarriette (☎ 04 94 19 28 13, 45 rue de la République)*. Its 69FF and 88FF *menus* are well doused with Provençal herbs and spices.

Tempting cooking smells waft from *Pastorel* (☎ 04 94 95 02 36, 54 rue de la Liberté), a traditional place dating from 1922 with a 160FF *menu du marché*, ~~well worth~~ every centime.

Les Terrasses de l'Orangerie (☎ 04 94 83 10 50, promenade René Coty) – a lovely brasserie that has peered out to sea since the *belle epoque* days of F Scott Fitzgerald et al – is among St-Raphaël's best-known places to dine. Evening *menus* cost 95FF and 135FF *menus* and it serves a good-value 80FF lunchtime equivalent.

Self-Catering A *fruit and vegetable market* fills place de la République and place Victor Hugo. Fishmongers sell the catch of the day each morning at the Vieux Port *fish market* (cours Jean Bart).

Stock up on a *tarte Tropézienne* (a creamy, sponge cake sandwich which is topped with sugar and almonds), *farinette Niçois* (Niçois bread), *pain blanc bio* (organic white bread) or a choice of olive, bacon bits, anchovy or goat cheese fougasse at splendid *Boulangerie Rabbia* (☎ 04 94 95 07 82, 29 rue Allongue), a family bakery dating to 1885. *Monoprix* supermarket *(58 blvd Félix Martin)* opens 9 am to 8 pm Monday to Saturday.

Les Délices du Roy (47 blvd de l'Aspe), some 5km from the town centre in the Aspe quarter, sells *confiture* (jam) crammed with 55% fruit. Ginger and lemon, orange and Russian vodka, banana and blackcurrant, or chestnut and Provençal *marc* (a fiery spirit similar to Italian grappa) are among the imaginative varieties available.

Getting There & Away
Bus St-Raphaël bus station (☎ 04 94 95 16 71), behind the train station on ave Victor Hugo (accessible via the escalators on the station platforms), doubles as Fréjus' main bus station too. For information on buses to/from Fréjus see Getting There & Away in the Fréjus section later in this chapter.

From St-Raphaël, Estérel Cars operates buses to/from Draguignan (33FF, 1¼ hours, hourly) via Fréjus (8FF). Société Varoise

d'Autocars BELTRAME (☎ 04 94 83 87 63) runs buses along the Corniche de l'Estérel (see that section earlier in the chapter) to Cannes. SODETRAV (☎ 04 94 97 88 51 in St-Tropez) runs buses to St-Tropez (51FF, 1¼ hours, eight to 10 daily) via Port Grimaud or Grimaud (45FF, 55 minutes) and Ste-Maxime (32FF, 35 minutes). Services are less frequent in winter.

Buses (☎ 04 94 83 87 63 for information) run to/from Nice airport (103FF, 1¼ hours, four daily) stopping on place Paul Vernet in Fréjus en route.

Train There is a very frequent service from Nice to Gare de St-Raphaël-Valescure (every 30 minutes), on rue Waldeck Rousseau. The information office here opens 9.15 am to 1 pm and 2.30 to 6 pm. Some trains stop at the small, village train stations along the Corniche d'Estérel (see that section earlier in this chapter for details).

Getting Around
Car & Motorcycle Major car rental agencies are clustered opposite the train station on place Pierre Coullet. Agence Azur Location (☎ 04 94 83 71 08) at No 54 on the square and Rent a Car Système (☎ 04 94 17 07 79), 251 ave du Général Leclerc, both offer competitive rates.

Bicycle Atout Cycles (☎ 04 94 95 56 91), 104 chemin de la Lauve, rents mountain bikes; prices start at 90FF per day.

FRÉJUS
postcode 83600 • pop 47,897
• elevation 250m
Fréjus, first settled by Massiliots (the Greek colonists from Marseilles) and then colonised by Julius Caesar around 49 BC as Forum Julii, is known for its Roman ruins. Once an important port, the town was sacked by various invaders from the 10th century onwards. Much of the town's commercial activity ceased after its harbour silted up in the 16th century.

Fréjus' golden-sand beach, called Fréjus Plage, is lined with buildings from the 1950s. Its chic, ultramodern port – full of

CANNES AREA

expensive places to eat offering every shell-fish imaginable at unimaginable prices – was built in the 1980s.

Place Paul Albert Février, in the old heart of Fréjus Ville, hosts various markets: flowers on Wednesday, Saturday and Sunday morning; fruit and veg every morning, Tuesday to Sunday, June to September; and a Provençal market featuring a bit of everything on Wednesday and Saturday morning, year round. You will find a *marché nocturnal* (night market) spilling across the sand at Fréjus Plage most evenings from June to September.

Orientation

Fréjus comprises hillside Fréjus Ville, 3km from the seafront, and Fréjus Plage, on the Gulf of Fréjus. Fréjus' modern port is at the western end of blvd de la Libération and its continuation, blvd d'Alger. The Roman remains are almost all in Fréjus Ville.

Information

Fréjus tourist office (☎ 04 94 51 83 83, fax 04 91 51 00 26, e frejus.tourisme@ wanadoo.fr), 325 rue Jean Jaurès, opens 9 am to noon and 2 to 6 pm (7 pm in summer) Monday to Saturday, and 10 am to

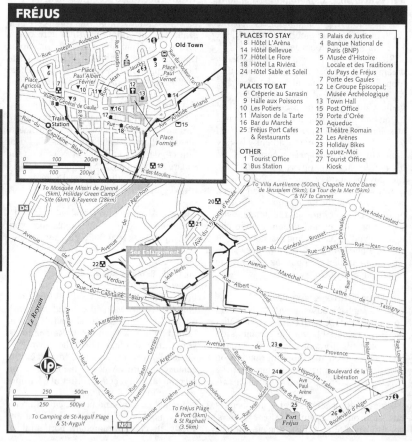

FRÉJUS

PLACES TO STAY
8   Hôtel L'Arèna
14 Hôtel Bellevue
17 Hôtel Le Flore
18 Hôtel La Riviéra
24 Hôtel Sable et Soleil

PLACES TO EAT
6   Crêperie au Sarrasin
9   Halle aux Poissons
10 Les Potiers
11 Maison de la Tarte
16 Bar du Marché
25 Fréjus Port Cafes
    & Restaurants

OTHER
1   Tourist Office
2   Bus Station
3   Palais de Justice
4   Banque National de
    Paris (BNP)
5   Musée d'Histoire
    Locale et des Traditions
    du Pays de Fréjus
7   Porte des Gaules
12 Le Groupe Épiscopal;
    Musée Archéologique
13 Town Hall
15 Post Office
19 Porte d'Orée
20 Aqueduc
21 Théâtre Romain
22 Les Arènes
23 Holiday Bikes
26 Louez-Moi
27 Tourist Office
    Kiosk

noon and 3 to 5.30 pm (6 pm in summer) on Sunday. On the beach, the tourist office kiosk (☎ 04 94 51 48 42), opposite 11 blvd de la Libération, opens 10 am to noon and 3 to 6 pm, June to mid-September. Staff distribute maps locating Fréjus' archaeological treasures and a series of free (French-only) brochures entitled *Les Chemins de Traverse* that detail thematic walks (olives & vineyards, *calanques* (rocky inlets), scents & perfumes, flowers & gardens and so on). The tourist office has a Web site at www.ville-frejus.fr.

Banque National de Paris (BNP), 232 rue Jean Jaurès, opens 8.30 am to noon and 1.45 to 5 pm weekdays. The post office, ave Aristide Briand, opens 8.30 am to 6.30 pm weekdays, and 8.30 am to noon Saturday. It has Cyberposte.

Roman Ruins
West of Fréjus' old city on rue Henri Vadon, past the ancient **Porte des Gaules**, is the mostly rebuilt 1st- and 2nd-century **Les Arènes** (amphitheatre; ☎ 04 94 51 34 31). It once sat an audience of 10,000 and is used for rock concerts and bullfights today. It opens 9 am to noon and 2 to 4.30 pm (6 pm April to November) Wednesday to Monday.

At the south-eastern edge of the old city is the 3rd-century **Porte d'Orée**, rue des Moulins, the only arcade of the monumental Roman thermal baths still standing. North of the old town on rue du Théâtre Romain are the remains of a **théâtre Romain** (Roman theatre). It opens 10 am to 1 pm and 2.30 to 6.30 pm Wednesday to Monday, April to November; and 10 am to noon or 12.30 pm and 1.30 to 5.30 pm Wednesday to Monday, the rest of the year. Part of the stage and the outer walls are all that can be seen today.

North-east, on ave du 15 Corps d'Armée towards La Tour de Mare, you pass a remaining section of a 40km-long **aqueduc** (aqueduct) which once carried water to Roman Fréjus. Continuing 500m farther north along ave du 15 Corps d'Armée, across the roundabout, onto ave du General Calliès, you reach **Villa Aurèlienne**, a 19th-century villa built in 1880 that today hosts temporary photography exhibitions. In its 22-hectare park there's another section of the aqueduct, complete with five arches.

Le Groupe Épiscopal
In the centre of town on place Formigé, occupying the site of a Roman temple, is an episcopal ensemble (☎ 04 94 51 26 30) comprising an 11th- and 12th-century **cathedral**, 58 rue de Fleury, that's one of the first Gothic buildings in the region (though it retains certain Roman features). The carved wooden doors at the main entrance were added during the Renaissance. The occasional concerts held here are well worth the 100FF ticket price (children aged under 14, 75FF).

To the left of the cathedral is the octagonal 5th-century **baptistry**, with a Roman column at each of its eight corners. Stairs from the narthex lead up to the stunning 11th- and 13th-century **cloister**, whose features include some of the columns of the Roman temple and painted wooden ceilings from the 14th and 15th centuries. It looks onto a beautiful courtyard with a well-tended garden and a well. The ensemble opens 9 am to 7 pm April to September; and 9 am to noon and 2 to 5 pm Tuesday to Sunday, the rest of the year. Admission costs 25FF (students 15FF).

Museums
Adjoining Fréjus' episcopal treasures on place Calvini is the **Musée Archéologique**, where a marble statue of Hermes, a head of Jupiter and a magnificent 3rd-century mosaic depicting a leopard are displayed. The museum opens 10 am to noon and 1.30 to 5.30 pm Monday and Wednesday to Saturday, November to April; and 10 am to 1 pm and 2.30 to 6.30 pm Monday and Wednesday to Saturday, the rest of the year. Admission is free.

The town's history is illustrated in the **Musée d'Histoire Locale et des Traditions du Pays de Fréjus** (Local History & Fréjus Traditions Museum; ☎ 04 94 51 64 01), 153 rue Jean Jaurès. It opens 9 am to noon and 3 to 7 pm (2 to 6 pm November to April) Tuesday to Saturday. Admission is free.

CANNES AREA

Chapelle Notre Dame de Jérusalem

This small chapel was one of the last pieces of work embarked upon by Jean Cocteau (1889–1963). Cocteau, best known for the fishermen's Chapelle de St-Pierre he decorated farther up the coast in Villefranche-sur-Mer (see the Nice to Menton chapter), started work on the chapel in 1961. The Chapelle Notre Dame in Fréjus was not completed until 1988 when Cocteau's legal heir, Édouard Dermit, completed his former companion's work. The altar is made from a millstone.

The chapel, ave François Nicolaï, is about 5km north-east of the old city in the quarter of La Tour de Mare (served by bus No 13 – see Getting Around on the following page), on the N7 towards Cannes. It can be visited between 1.30 to 5.30 pm Monday and Wednesday to Friday, and 9.30 am to 12.30 pm and 1.30 to 5.30 pm Saturday, November to April; and 2.30 to 6.30 pm Monday and Wednesday to Friday, and 10 am to 1 pm and 2.30 to 8.30 pm Saturday, the rest of the year.

Mosquée Missiri de Djenné

Along route de Bagnols-en-Forêt (the D4 towards Fayence), 5km north of Fréjus, is the Mosquée Missiri de Djenné, rue des Combattants d'Afrique du Nord. The mosque was built in 1930 for Sudanese troops stationed at a marine base in Fréjus and is a replica of a mosque in Djenné, Mali.

Places to Stay

Hostellers note: it is equally feasible to stay in the hostel in St-Raphaël (see Hostels under St-Raphaël earlier in this chapter).

Camping Fréjus has more than a dozen camp sites, one of the best being four-star *Holiday Green* (☎ 04 94 19 88 30, fax 04 94 19 88 31, rue des Combattants d'Afrique du Nord), on the D4 towards Fayence, which opens April to mid-October. It's 7km from the beach but has its own large pool. Nightly rates start at 109FF for two people with a car and tent.

Practically on the beach is *Camping de*

St-Aygulf Plage (☎ 04 94 17 62 49, fax 04 94 81 03 16, 270 ave Salvarelli) in St-Aygulf, south of Fréjus. This huge camp site, with space for 1100 tents, opens April to the end of October and charges similar rates.

Hotels In Fréjus Ville, one-star *Hôtel La Riviéra* (☎ 04 94 51 31 46, fax 04 94 17 18 34, 90 rue Grisolle) has doubles with shower from 170FF, rooms for three or four people for 250FF and a ground-floor restaurant which serves a hearty 50FF plat du jour (including 25cL of wine) and a 69FF *menu*.

Zero-star, 11-room *Hôtel Bellevue* (☎ 04 94 17 16 10, place Paul Vernet), overlooks a large car park. It touts doubles/triples with washbasin for 149/180FF and shower-equipped doubles without/with a window for 220/250FF. Reception is the adjoining bar, which serves a cheap 69FF *menu*.

Hôtel Le Flore (☎ 04 94 51 38 35, fax 04 94 52 28 20, 35 rue Grisolle) has 290FF doubles. Napoleon stayed at *Hôtel L'Aréna* (☎ 04 94 17 09 40, fax 04 94 52 01 52, 📧 info@arena-hotel.com, 145 rue du Général de Gaulle), then called Auberge du Chapeau Rouge, when passing through town in October 1799. The three-star, Logis de France inn has charming singles/doubles /triples starting at 350/420/550FF in low season and 400/480/750FF in high season.

Near the beach, *Hôtel Sable et Soleil* (Sand & Sun; ☎ 04 94 51 08 70, fax 04 94 53 49 12, 158 ave Paul Arène) has comfortable doubles costing from 250/350FF in low/high season.

Places to Eat

For a handful of top cafes and restaurants, with a view of bobbing boats moored in port, try Port Fréjus.

In Fréjus Ville, *Bar du Marché* has a busy terrace on place de la Liberté and serves giant pizzas from 40FF and bowlfuls of *moules frites* (mussels and fries) for 45FF. *Crêperie au Sarrasin* (☎ 04 94 53 36 92, place Agricola), with its 64FF *menu* and dozens of different sweet/savoury crepes (from 8/21FF), is another cheap lunchtime choice.

Tucked down a quiet narrow backstreet,

quaint *Les Potiers* (☎ *04 94 51 33 74, 135 rue Potiers)* has a 125FF *menu* and desserts such as a spiced wine and strawberry soup with old-fashioned rice pudding, or creme brulee flavoured with a choice of lavender, orange, rosemary or chocolate. It opens Wednesday evening to Monday.

Well-filled baguettes, bread rolls (20FF) and a succulent array of sweet tarts (strawberry, pear, pine kernel and so on) are sold by the slice (13FF) to take away at *Maison de la Tarte* (☎ *04 94 51 17 34, 33 rue Jean Jaurès)*, a top-quality boulangerie-cum-tarterie. Self-caterers can buy fresh fish at *Halle aux Poissons* (*122 rue du Général de Gaulle)* and more mundane groceries at the *Casino* supermarket, south of the centre on rond point de la Mougrano.

Getting There & Away

Bus Fréjus bus station (☎ 04 94 53 78 46), place Paul Vernet, is only served by buses to/from Draguignan (32FF, one hour, hourly) and buses to/from St-Raphaël (8FF, 20 or 27 minutes). Estérel Bus No 5 links the bus station with St-Raphaël's bus station and Fréjus' train station. Buses Nos 6 and 7 link place Paul Vernet and St-Raphaël – No 6 via the coastal road and No 7 via ave de Provence.

Train Fréjus train station, rue du Capitaine Blazy, is on the Nice–Marseilles rail route, although few trains stop here beyond services to/from St-Raphaël.

Getting Around

Bus Bus No 6 links the beaches of Fréjus-Plage with place Paul Vernet in Fréjus-Ville. Bus No 13 runs between Fréjus train station, bus station and Cocteau's Chapelle Notre Dame de Jérusalem.

Car & Motorcycle Near the beach, Louez-Moi (☎ 04 94 52 10 00), just off blvd d'Alger at 808 rue Hippolyte Fabre, rents ultra-trendy, roofless road buggies for 350/490FF per half-/full day, including unlimited kilometres.

Midway between Fréjus Ville and Plage, Holiday Bikes (☎ 04 94 52 30 65), 943 ave de Provence (corner of rue de Triberg) rents cars from around 200FF per day and 50cc scooters/125cc motorcycles for 170/320FF per day. It opens 9 am to noon and 2.30 to 7 pm.

Bicycle Holiday Bikes (see under Car & Motorcycle above) rents bicycles for 70FF per day.

CANNES AREA

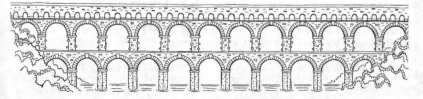

St-Tropez to Toulon

In 1956 St-Tropez was the setting for the film *Et Dieu Créa la Femme* (And God Created Woman), starring Brigitte Bardot. Its stunning success brought about St-Tropez's rise to stardom – or destruction – depending on your viewpoint. But one thing is clear: the peaceful little fishing village of St-Tropez, somewhat isolated from the rest of the Côte d'Azur at the end of its own peninsula, suddenly became the favourite of the jet set. The Tropeziens – with their cats on leads, dogs in handbags and prima donnas dusting sand from between their toes with shaving brushes – have thrived on their sexy image ever since.

Inland from St-Tropez, medieval Les Arcs-sur-Argens is equidistant (31km) between the coastal towns of St-Raphaël and Ste-Maxime. Ten kilometres north is Pays Dracénois (literally 'country of Draguignan people'), with Draguignan at its heart, which embraces some of the region's least-spoilt villages.

West from St-Tropez sprawls a wild, remote and heavily forested massif, smothered with fine pine, chestnut and cork oak trees. Its vegetation makes it appear almost black and gives rise to the name Massif des Maures, which is derived from the Provençal word *mauro* (dark pine wood). The arc-shaped massif stretches from Fréjus in the north-east to pretty palm-tree lined Hyères – a launch pad for day trips to the golden Île d'Hyères – in the south-west.

Toulon, 20km west along the coast, is a base for the French navy's Mediterranean fleet and as such is France's most important naval port. As a result of heavy bombing in WWII, the city's run-down centre is pretty grim – some would say downright ugly – compared to Nice, Cannes or even Marseilles. Farther west still, the islands off Toulon's shores, dubbed the Îles du Fun (Islands of Fun), were acquired by French industrialist Paul Ricard in the 1950s and rapidly transformed into concrete playgrounds.

Highlights

- View works by the world's great pointillists, the Nabis, Fauvists and cubists at St-Tropez's Musée de l'Annonciade
- Go island hopping around the golden Îles d'Hyères
- Walk around the Chartreuse de la Verne monastery in the Massif des Maures
- Window-shop in St-Tropez and sip pastis at its Vieux Port
- Explore the drowsy hill-top villages and abbeys of the northern Var; shop for black truffles in Aups, wine in La Celle and terracotta tiles in Salernes
- Sample a dozen different Côtes de Provence wines in Les Arcs-sur-Argens, then lunch at the Domaine de la Maurette

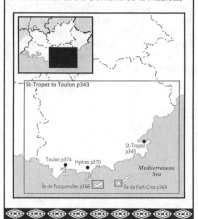

St-Tropez & Around

ST-TROPEZ
postcode 83990 • pop 5542

Attempts to keep St-Tropez (Sant Troupez in Provençal) small and exclusive have created

ST-TROPEZ TO TOULON

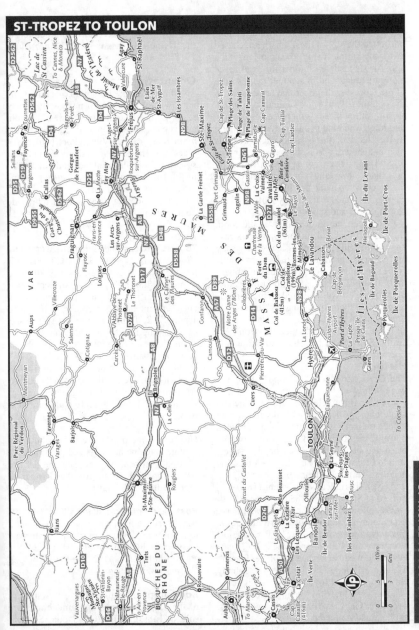

euro currency converter €1 = 6.56FF

at least one tangible result: huge traffic queues into town. Yachts, way out of proportion to the size of the old harbour, chased away the simple fishing boats a long time ago. Artists jostle each other for easel space along the quay, and in summer there's little of the intimate village air that artists such as the pointillist Paul Signac found so alluring.

Still, sitting in a cafe on place des Lices in late May, watching people playing pétanque in the shade of the age-old plane trees, is pleasant enough – as is that seductive image of St-Tropez from out at sea. Arriving by boat, the yellow- and orange-painted church tower crowned with a typically Provençal campanile stands majestically aloft amid the sloping roofs and sprawling citadel.

Once seen, never forgotten is the food, flower, clothing and antique market extravaganza that fills place des Lices on Tuesday and Saturday morning. Equally memorable is the spectacle of rich people dining aboard their floating palaces, within spitting distance of the crowds gathered on the portside to gawk at them manipulating their silver knives and forks.

Tropeziens call St-Tropez 'St-Trop' (literally 'St-Too Much'). Beautifully apt.

History

The Greeks founded Athenopolis here and were followed by the Romans in 31 BC who called it Heraclea. St-Tropez gained its contemporary name in AD 68 when a boat landed on its shores bearing the decapitated body of the Roman officer, Torpes, whom Nero had beheaded in Pisa for his conversion to Christianity. The village adopted the headless Torpes as their saint.

A syphilis-ridden Maupassant (1850–93) arrived in St-Tropez in 1887. Signac (1863–1935) followed in his boat *L'Olympia* five years later, exclaiming upon arrival, '*Je ne fais pas escale. Je me fixe*' ('I'm not just stopping here. I'm staying'). Sexy St-Tropez has not looked back since – Colette, Pagnol, Matisse, Marlène Dietrich, Bardot, Johnny Hallyday, Pink Floyd ('As I reach for a peach/Slide a line down behind a sofa in San Tropez') George Michael, Joan Collins, Mohammad Al-Fayed...

And it's not only glitzy, but explosive too: torpedoes have been manufactured at the Usine de Gassin in St-Tropez since 1912.

Orientation

St-Tropez lies at the southern end of the narrow Golfe de St-Tropez, within easy reach of the Massif des Maures. The old city is packed between quai Jean Jaurès, the main quay of the Vieux Port (old port); place des Lices, a vast shady rectangular square a few blocks inland; and what's left of the 16th-century citadel overlooking the town from the north-east.

Visiting floating palaces moor alongside quai Suffren.

Information

Tourist Offices The tourist office (☎ 04 94 97 45 21, fax 04 94 97 82 66 ℮ tourisme@ nova.fr), quai Jean Jaurès, opens 9.30 am to 1 pm and 2.30 to 9 pm, July to September; 9.30 am to 1 pm and 2 to 7 pm, April, June, and September to November; 9.30 am to 1 pm and 2.30 to 7 pm the last two weeks of December; and 9 am to noon and 2 to 6 pm, the rest of the year. It has a Web site at www.nova.fr/saint-tropez.

City tours on foot depart from in front of the tourist office at 10.30 am on Thursday, April to October. It also organises tours of Gassin and Ramatuelle (by appointment only).

Money At the port, there is a 24-hour exchange machine outside Crédit Lyonnais at 21 quai Suffren. Master Change, 18 rue Allard, opens 8.30 am to 10 pm (to midnight in July and August).

Post & Communications The post office, place Celli, opens 9 am to noon and 2 to 5 pm weekdays, 9 am to noon Saturday. Cybercafe FCDCI (☎ 04 94 54 84 81, ℮ infos@fcdci.com), 2 ave Paul Roussel, charges 60FF per hour.

Bookshop English-language newspapers of the day, magazines and guidebooks are sold at Librairie du Port, 5 quai Suffren,

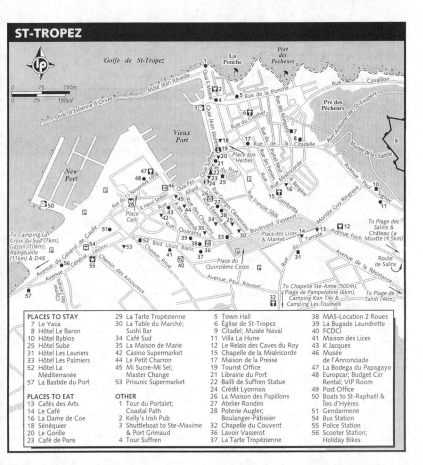

ST-TROPEZ

PLACES TO STAY	
7	Le Yaca
8	Hôtel Le Baron
10	Hôtel Byblos
25	Hôtel Sube
31	Hôtel Les Lauriers
33	Hôtel Les Palmiers
52	Hôtel La Méditerranée
57	La Bastide du Port

PLACES TO EAT	
13	Cafés des Arts
14	Le Café
16	La Dame de Coe
18	Sénéquier
20	Le Gorille
23	Café de Paris

29	La Tarte Tropézienne
30	La Table du Marché; Sushi Bar
34	Café Sud
35	La Maison de Marie
42	Casino Supermarket
44	Le Petit Charron
45	Mi Sucre-Mi Sel; Master Change
53	Prisunic Supermarket

OTHER	
1	Tour du Portalet; Coastal Path
2	Kelly's Irish Pub
3	Shuttleboat to Ste-Maxime & Port Grimaud
4	Tour Suffren

5	Town Hall
6	Église de St-Tropez
9	Citadel; Musée Naval
11	Villa La Hune
12	Le Relais des Caves du Roy
15	Chapelle de la Miséricorde
17	Maison de la Presse
19	Tourist Office
21	Librairie du Port
22	Bailli de Suffren Statue
24	Crédit Lyonnais
26	La Maison des Papillons
27	Atelier Rondini
28	Poterie Augier; Boulanger-Pâtissier
32	Chapelle du Couvent
36	Lavoir Vasserot
37	La Tarte Tropézienne

38	MAS-Location 2 Roues
39	La Bugade Laundrette
40	FCDCI
41	Maison des Lices
43	K Jacques
46	Musée de l'Annonciade
47	La Bodega du Papagayo
48	Europcar; Budget Car Rental; VIP Room
49	Post Office
50	Boats to St-Raphaël & Îles d'Hyères
51	Gendarmerie
54	Bus Station
55	Police Station
56	Scooter Station; Holiday Bikes

and the Maison de la Presse on the corner of rue Gambetta and rue de la Citadelle.

Laundry La Bugade, 5 rue Quaranta, opens 7 am to 10 pm.

Walking Tour

The **Vieux Port** – the heart of Tropezien life – is as good a place as any to take a stroll and watch the antics of the rich and not-so-famous. On quai Suffren, a **statue of the Bailli de Suffren** cast from a 19th-century cannon peers out to sea. The bailiff of Suffren (1729–88) was a sailor who fought

with a Tropezien crew against Britain and Prussia during the Seven Years' War. The western side of the port is dominated by the Musée de l'Annonciade (see that section on the following page).

In a backstreet one block south-west of quai Péri is **La Maison des Papillons** (House of Butterflies; ☎ 04 94 97 63 45), 9 rue Étienne Berny. Some 4500 of the winged creatures are pinned to the wall. The 1st-floor collection of European species is that of Dany Lartigue, son of Riviera photographer, Jacques Henri Lartigue (1894–1986). The cottage-museum was the Lartigue home

ST-TROPEZ TO TOULON

until 1993 when Dany gave it to the town. Family photos taken by his father line the staircase. The museum opens 10 am to noon and 3 to 7 pm Wednesday to Monday, May to October; and 10 am to noon and 2 to 6 pm Wednesday to Monday, the rest of the year. Admission costs 20FF.

The old fishing quarter of **La Ponche** is north-east of the Vieux Port. To get to the fishing harbour (where Signac and company docked) from quai Suffren, walk to the northern end of its continuations, quai Jean Jaurès and quai Frédéric Mistral. At the 15th-century **Tour du Portalet**, turn right (east) to the sandy fishing cove. From here a coastal path snakes its way around the St-Tropez peninsula (see Coastal Walks later in this section).

From the southern end of quai Frédéric Mistral, place Garrezio sprawls east from the 10th-century **Tour Suffren** to place de l'Hôtel de Ville. From here, rue Guichard leads south-east to the 18th-century **Église de St-Tropez**, built in 1785 in an Italian Baroque style on place de l'Ormeau. Inside, in one of the chapels is the bust of St-Tropez, which is honoured during Les Bravades (see Special Events later in this section).

A 16th-century **citadel** dominates the hillside overlooking St-Tropez to the east. Steps lead from the eastern end of rue de la Citadelle, up montée de la Citadelle, to the citadel. Good photographs of St-Tropez can be taken from its grounds. Ave Paul Signac, the road that runs along the southern edge of here, is named after the painter who lived in **Villa La Hune** on the street from 1897. The citadel's former dungeons house a **Musée Naval** (☎ 04 94 97 59 43) dedicated to the town's maritime history and the Allied landings in August 1944. It opens 11 am to 5.30 pm Wednesday to Monday in summer; and 10 am to noon and 1 to 4 pm, the rest of the year, except November. Admission costs 25FF (students 15FF).

South of rue de la Citadelle on rue Miséricorde is 17th-century **Chapelle de la Miséricorde** (1645) with its pretty bell tower and dome, decorated with coloured ceramic tiles. One block farther south is

> **Tourist Warning!**
>
> If you want to visit museums in St-Tropez don't bother visiting on Tuesday or in November – they will all be closed.

place des Lices, whose 200m length is lined with plane trees and pétanque players. **Chapelle du Couvent** (1757) and **Chapelle Ste-Anne** (1618) lie south of here along ave Augustin Grangeon. Inside Chapelle Ste-Anne, there is an impressive collection of ex-votive paintings and centuries-old miniature boats given by Tropezien fishermen. They can be viewed once a year – on 26 July, the feast day of St-Anne.

Musée de l'Annonciade

The graceful Musée de l'Annonciade (☎ 04 94 97 04 01), in an early 16th-century chapel on place Grammont at the Vieux Port, contains an impressive collection of modern art, with works by Matisse, Bonnard, Dufy, Derain, Rouault and Signac.

The pointillist collection in the first room on the 2nd floor includes Signac's *St-Tropez, L'Orage* (1895), *St-Tropez, Le Quai* (1899) and *St-Tropez, Le Sentier Côtier* (1901). The second room is dedicated to the self-named Nabis group ('nabhi' means 'prophet' in Hebrew) and displays works by painters such as Vuillard, Bonnard, Maurice Denis and Valloton. The third room features the Fauvists: Matisse's *La Gitane* (The Gypsy; 1905–6) is here. Matisse spent the summer of 1904 in St-Tropez, starting preliminary studies for *Luxe, Calme et Volupté*. Cubists, such as George Braque and Picasso, are also represented.

The museum opens 10 am to noon and 3 to 7 pm Wednesday to Monday, June to September; and 10 am to noon and 2 to 6 pm Wednesday to Monday, the rest of the year, except November. Admission costs 30FF (students 15FF).

Art exhibitions are held in summer in the 19th-century **Lavoir Vasserot**, the former public washhouse on rue Quaranta, open 11 am to 12.30 pm and 4.30 to 8 pm.

ST-TROPEZ TO TOULON

BB

Brigitte Bardot epitomised sex appeal in the 1950s and 1960s. An icon of sexual liberation, the Paris-born model-turned-actress sprang to stardom in 1956 as a young woman, baring more than most, in Vadim's *Et Dieu Créa la Femme* (And God Created Woman). She moved to St-Tropez in 1958.

A year later she met French singer Serge Gainsbourg with whom she went on to record several tracks, including in 1967 the breathlessly erotic *Je t'aime...moi non plus*, which she refused to release (the BBC and Vatican promptly banned the re-recorded version with Jane Birkin), and the raunchy *Harley Davidson*, which saw the starlet clad in leather coquetting a motorbike. Serge Gainsbourg's subsequent hit called *Initials BB* (1968) – a melodious tribute to the Bardot myth – became a legend in its own time.

JANE SMITH

Animals became Bardot's passion after she retired from screen. She founded the Fondation Brigitte Bardot in 1986, consequently donating her celebrated 1960s St-Tropez home – Villa La Madrague overlooking Baie des Cannebiers – to the animal activist campaign group. From her Pointe du Capon seaside villa, where she lives with a menagerie of furry friends, Bardot continues to campaign tirelessly for the foundation (☎ 01 45 05 14 60, fax 01 45 05 14 80), at 45 rue Vineuse, 75116 Paris.

The 1990s saw the actress – now in her sixties – in court. In 1998, Bardot was found guilty of inciting racial hatred during a public criticism of the Muslim ritual involving slaughter of sheep and was fined 20,000FF. The previous year, her ex-husband (one of three) and son successfully sued her for libellous comments made in the first of her two-volume autobiography. The media pounced on Bardot's fourth marriage to National Front politician Bernard d'Ormale in 1992 as ultimate proof that the 1960s icon leans very heavily (politically speaking) towards the extreme right.

Beaches

About 4km south-east of the town is the start of the magnificent sandy **Plage de Tahiti**, and its continuation, **Plage de Pampelonne**, which overlooks Baie de Pampelonne. The beach runs for about 9km between Cap du Pinet and the rocky Cap Camarat, which is dominated by France's second-tallest **lighthouse** (130m), dating from the 19th century. To get to the beach on foot, head out of town along ave de la Résistance (south of place des Lices) to route de la Belle Isnarde and then route de Tahiti. Otherwise, the bus to Ramatuelle, a village south of St-Tropez, stops at points along a road that runs about 1km inland from the beach.

On the southern side of Cap Camarat is the secluded nudist beach, **Plage de l'Escalet**. Several streams also attract bathers in the buff. To get there take the bus to Ramatuelle, but you'll have to walk or, if you are lucky, hitch the next 4km south-east to the beach.

Closer to St-Tropez is **Plage des Salins**, a long, wide sandy beach 4.5km east of town at the southern foot of Cap des Salins. To get here, follow route des Salins to its end. En route you pass **La Treille Muscate** (The Wine Trellis), a rambling villa framed with red-ochre columns wrapped in honeysuckle. In 1927 Colette wrote *La Naissance du Jour*, which evokes a 1920s unspoilt St-Tropez, here. After she left the town in 1938, two further villas, named after her novels, were built on the grounds.

At the northern end of Plage des Salins, on a rock jutting out to sea, is the **tomb** of **Émile Olivier** (1825–1913), who served as first minister to Napoleon III until his exile in 1870. Olivier's 17-volume *L'Empire Libéral* is preserved in the library of **Château La Moutte**, his former home on Cap des Salins. Musical soirees are held in summer in the chateau. Its unmarked entrance is on chemin de la Moutte, the road running parallel (to the north) with route des Salins. A sandy track leads from the car

ST-TROPEZ TO TOULON

park at the end of chemin de la Moutte to the beach.

Olivier's sea-facing tomb looks out towards **La Tête de Chien** (The Dog's Head), a rocky islet named after the legendary dog who was flung in the boat, along with a cock, to eat the decapitated remains of St-Torpes. Thankfully for the Tropeziens, neither did.

Farther south, **Pointe du Capon** is a beautiful cape crisscrossed with walking trails. BB – Brigitte Bardot – lives here.

Coastal Walks

A picturesque coastal path leads 35km south from St-Tropez to the beach at Cavalaire-sur-Mer, and around the St-Tropez peninsula as far west as Le Lavandou (60km), passing rocky outcrops and hidden bays en route.

In St-Tropez the path, flagged with a yellow marker, starts at **La Ponche**, immediately east of Tour du Portalet at the northern end of quai Frédéric Mistral. From here, trails lead to Baie des Cannebiers (2.7km, 50 minutes), La Moutte (7.4km, two hours), Plage des Salins (8.5km, 2½ hours) and Plage de Tahiti (12km, 3½ hours). Alternatively, drive to the end of route des Salins, from where it is a shorter walk along the coastal path to Plage de Tahiti (2.7km, 45 minutes) and the nudist Plage de la Moutte (1.7km, 30 minutes) on Cap des Salins.

Cap Lardier, the peninsula's southernmost cape, is protected by the Parc National de Port-Cros (see that section later in this chapter). Motorised vehicles are forbidden on the rocky headland, which is frequented by large colonies of birds and smaller schools of dolphins.

Boat Excursions

The boats that sail from St-Tropez to St-Raphaël, Ste-Maxime, Port Grimaud, Les Issambres and around the Baie des Cannebiers make for a jolly day out. See Getting There & Away later in this section.

Special Events

Guns blaze and flags flutter in St-Tropez on 15 June during the Bravades des Espagnols,

a festival held to mark St-Tropez's victory over 21 Spanish galleons that attacked the port on 15 June 1637. The militaristic street processions are led by a nominated *capitaine de ville* (town captain) who, between 1481 and 1672, when St-Tropez enjoyed a special autonomy, served as captain of the town.

The most important *bravades* (Provençal for 'bravery') fall on 16, 17 (St Torpes' day) and 18 May. These have been celebrated since 1558 and see Tropeziens process through the streets wearing traditional costume. During this festival the town captain, followed by an army of 140 musket-firing *bravadeurs*, moves through the street bearing a bust of the saint.

Places to Stay – Budget & Mid-Range

St-Tropez touts no cheap hotel, let alone a hostel, and camping on the beach is illegal. Contact the tourist office for details on *rooms* to rent (starting at 200/300FF per night in low/high season), two-person *apartments* (1400/2200FF plus per week in low/high season) and four- to 14-person *villas* to rent for a week or more.

Camping There are several multistarred sites along Plage de Pampelonne. *Camping Kon Tiki* (☎ 04 94 79 80 84, e 100776 .3460@compuserve.com, route des Tamaris) starts at the northern end of the beach and charges about 120FF per night for two people with tent and car. It opens mid-March to October.

Rates at four-star *Camping Les Tournels* (☎ 04 94 55 90 90, fax 04 94 55 90 99, route de Camarat), on Cap Camarat, start at 112FF for a two-person tent and car space. The site opens mid-February to December. *Camping La Croix du Sud* (☎ 04 94 79 80 84, route des Plages), 7km south of St-Tropez on the D93 to Ramatuelle, charges similar rates. It opens April to mid-October.

Hotels Cheapest is 13-room *Hôtel La Méditerranée* (☎ 04 94 97 00 44, 21 blvd Louis Blanc). Doubles, above a tatty bar, start at 200/300FF in low/high season.

ST-TROPEZ TO TOULON

Well worth it is unpretentious *Hôtel Le Baron* (☎ 04 94 97 06 57, fax 04 94 97 58 72, e hotellebaron@wanadoo.fr, 23 rue de l'Aïoli). Its 10 comfortable doubles at the foot of the citadel cost upwards of 300/350/450FF in low/mid-/high season.

Two-star *Hôtel Les Lauriers* (☎ 04 94 97 04 88, fax 04 94 97 21 87, rue du Temple) has comfortable doubles costing upward of 485FF and opens March to November.

Hôtel Les Palmiers (☎ 04 94 97 01 61, fax 04 94 97 10 02, 24–26 blvd Vasserot) offers a prime view of place des Lices' pétanque players from its square-facing rooms. Fully equipped doubles cost 480FF to 700FF (suites 1090FF).

Places to Stay – Top End

At the Vieux Port, behind the Bailli de Suffren statue, *Hôtel Sube* (☎ 04 94 97 30 04, fax 04 94 54 89 08, e sube@nova.fr, quai Suffren) has rooms with garden view costing 390/590FF in low/high season and plusher port-view equivalents from 990/1500FF.

Overlooking Port Pilon at St-Tropez's western entrance is *La Bastide du Port* (☎ 04 94 97 87 95, fax 04 94 97 91 00, ave du 15 Août 1944), a spacious and airy villa with terracotta-tiled floors and contemporary Provençal furnishings. Three-star doubles average 750FF. It opens March to December

The decor at four-star *Le Yaca* (☎ 04 94 55 81 00, fax 04 94 97 58 50, e hotel-le-yaca@wanadoo.fr, 1 blvd d'Aumale) combines old world with new. Rates reflect window view and room size. Suites with sea view cost 4800/5400FF in low/high season. Le Yaca opens March to early January.

Equally worthy of a postcard to home is four-star *Hôtel Byblos* (☎ 04 94 56 68 00, fax 04 94 56 68 01, e saint-tropez@byblos.com, ave Paul Signac), open mid-April to mid-October. Painted in a rainbow of pastels from terracotta to lavender-blue, its luxurious rooms warrant no complaints at 1580FF to 3800FF a throw. Byblos is one of the Riviera's choicest spots.

Places to Eat

Don't leave St-Tropez without sampling a sweet and creamy *tarte Tropézienne*, a sponge-cake sandwich filled with custard-cream and topped with sugar and almonds.

Restaurants Quai Jean Jaurès is lined with restaurants – most have 150FF *menus* and a strategic view of the silverware and crystal of those dining on the decks of their yachts. In the old town at northern end of rue des Ramparts, there is a lesser-known cluster of places overlooking Port des Pêcheurs at La Ponche.

La Table du Marché (☎ 04 94 97 85 20, 38 rue Georges Clémenceau) is an informal bistro cooking traditional Provençal dishes from market produce. The Market Table's 99FF *menu* is cheap by St-Tropez's standards. The same team runs snazzy *Sushi Bar* (same ☎) next door. *La Dame de Cœur* (☎ 04 94 97 23 16, 2 rue de la Miséricorde) likewise caters to a more budget-orientated crowd. No name is signposted outside; look for the Queen of Hearts playing card.

Tasteful *Café Sud* (☎ 04 94 97 42 52, 12 rue Étienne Berny) is tucked down a pedestrian street off places des Lices. It has a 140FF *menu* and tables are in a star-topped courtyard. Specialities include crayfish fritters with apple and mango julienne, a variety of grilled fish, and sautéed king prawns with ginger. Café Sud's other outlet, *La Plage des Jumeaux* (☎ 04 94 79 84 21, e moreu@nova.fr, route de l'Épi), is on Plage Pampelonne. Its stuffed *petits farcis Provençaux* (Provençal filled vegetables), especially the stuffed courgette (zucchini) flowers, are delicious.

Back in town, *La Maison de Marie* (☎ 04 94 97 09 99, 26 rue des Charrons), entrance at 2 rue Quaranta, is an oasis of calm. Light and sunny dishes, such as melon and asparagus salad or salmon with sage, are served in its intimate walled garden. Great value two-/three-course lunchtime *menus* cost 90/110FF (200FF in the evening).

Le Petit Charron (☎ 04 94 97 73 78, 5 rue Charrons) is another inviting bet with enticing *menus* for 165FF and 190FF. Don't miss the lavender-scented creme brulee.

Cafes & Fast Food St-Tropez's most famous cafe is Café des Arts, next to the

ST-TROPEZ TO TOULON

cinema on place des Lices, where artists and intellectuals have been meeting for years. Today the historic cafe is called *Le Café* (☎ 04 94 97 44 69, e rayond@lecafe.fr). Don't confuse it with the newer, red-canopied *Café des Arts* on the corner of place des Lices and ave du Mai Foch which (despite its copycat name) has no connection with the former haunt of BB and her glam friends and foes.

Another people-watching spot, also boasting a large terrace filled with red tables and chairs, is buzzing *Sénéquier* (☎ 04 94 97 00 90, quai Jean Jaurès) where Sartre wrote parts of *Les Chemins de la Liberté*. It serves breakfast from 7.30 or 8 am. *Le Gorille*, on the same quay, opens 24 hours and is another hot spot for a pastis at dusk or breakfast at sunrise.

Café de Paris (☎ 04 94 97 00 56, 15 quai Suffren) is a sushi bar with a terrace opposite the pleasure palaces moored at the port. Sushi costs upwards of 46FF per portion, a 15-piece sushi and tekkamaki platter costs 200FF, and a (presumably non-sushi) 48FF breakfast is served from 7 am.

Portside *Mi Sucre-Mi Sel* (☎ 04 94 97 18 76, 20 rue Allard) sells well-filled sandwiches and bread rolls (18FF to 30FF) and salads (starting at 25FF) to eat on the move.

Self-Catering A morning *fresh fish market* fills place aux Herbes daily (Tuesday to Sunday only in winter); walk under the archway directly behind the tourist office on rue de la Citadelle. Place aux Herbes is also home to an excellent *fromagerie*. On Tuesday and Saturday morning, a huge *market* fills place des Lices.

La Tarte Tropézienne (36 rue Georges Clémenceau) sells tartes Tropéziennes, cooked up by boulanger Micka in Cogolin in 1955. Its larger outlet at 9 blvd Louis Blanc sells freshly baked bread; arrive at 6.30, 9, 10.30 am, noon or 5.30 pm for warm loaves straight from the oven. Some 22 different types of breads, including *fougasse* (flat bread stuffed with bits of bacon or other savoury fillings), are baked at the *Boulanger-Pâtissier* (22 rue Georges

Clémenceau). It opens at 6 am if you're up and about early.

There's a *Prisunic* supermarket at 9 ave du Général Leclerc (open until 10 pm June to August) and a *Casino* at 39 rue Allard.

Entertainment

Among the hot spots to dance the night away or rub shoulders with a star is *Le Relais des Caves du Roy* (☎ 04 94 56 68 20, e saint-tropez@byblos.com, ave Foch), a bistro-style place with an Italian-inspired menu and flood-lit terrace. *VIP Room* (☎ 04 94 97 14 70, Résidences du Port) is St-Tropez's other nightclub, open midnight to 6 am in summer (weekends only out of season).

At the Vieux Port, ultra-trendy *La Bodega du Papagayo* (☎ 04 94 97 76 70, Rési-

---

Beach Legends

If you really want to spot a star, hang out at **La Voile Rouge** (The Red Sail; ☎ 04 94 79 84 34) or **Le Club 55** (☎ 04 94 79 80 14), St-Tropez's two most legendary bars on Plage de Pampelonne. Both jet-set joints, bang-slap on the sand, have played decadent host to celebrities since the 1950s.

Vadim shot parts of Bardot in *And God Created Woman* at La Voile Rouge (little more than a beach hut at the time) in 1955, while his film crew haggled for drinks at Le Club 55 (hence its name, so the story goes). Boobs and bums were flashed here first, with the advent of topless bathers at La Voile Rouge in 1970 (prompting founder and current owner Paul Tomaselli to be taken to court for allowing such indecent exposure) and, a decade or so on, the g-string bikini.

The antics of the filthy rich and famous remain as hedonistic as ever. Attempts by the Ramatuelle's socialist mayor to shut down La Voile Rouge in summer 2000 backfired after Tomaselli appealed against the court decision to close his famous bar – and won.

Count on paying at least 500FF per head to lunch at either place. Both open April to the end of September. Advance reservations are essential.

ST-TROPEZ TO TOULON

dences du Port, on quai Bouchard) is a restaurant, nightclub and terrace all in one.

Kelly's Irish Pub (☎ 04 94 54 89 11, quai Frédéric Mistral) is as un-Irish as any other Irish pub along the coast. Still, it serves Guinness until 1 am (3 am in high season).

Shopping St-Tropez is loaded with expensive boutiques, gourmet food shops and galleries overflowing with bad art. The covered Grand passage, which links rue Allard with rue Georges Clémenceau, is crammed with designer fashion shops.

Traditional sandals, said to have been inspired by a simple leather pair brought by Colette from Greece to show her local cobbler, are all part of the St-Tropez myth. Buy a pair costing upwards of 500FF from Atelier Rondini (☎ 04 94 97 19 55, e nova @nova.fr), 16 rue Georges Clémenceau, where the strappy footwear has been crafted since 1927; or from K Jacques, 25 rue Allard, whose family has cobbled since 1933.

Poterie Augler, 22 rue Georges Clémenceau, is a pottery with plenty of giant-sized urns to lug home. Oliviers & Co at No 11 sells olive oil from Provence and the Mediterranean. Wine can be tasted at Le Cave de St-Tropez, ave Paul Roussel. Tropézienne brides-to-be place their wedding lists at Maison des Lices, 18 blvd Louis Blanc, a St-Tropez institution which sells crisp white table linen and other luxurious equivalents of housekeeping essentials.

Getting There & Away

Bus St-Tropez bus station, ave du Général de Gaulle, is on the main road out of town on the south-western edge. The information office (☎ 04 94 97 88 51) opens 9 to 11.30 am and 1.45 pm and 4 pm weekdays.

Buses to Ramatuelle (17.50FF, 40 minutes, five daily) and Gassin (17.50FF, 50 minutes, three daily), two villages in the middle of the peninsula, run parallel to the coast about 1km inland.

SODETRAV (☎ 04 94 97 88 51) also runs buses to/from St-Raphaël (51FF, 1¼ hours, eight to 10 daily) via Grimaud or Port Grimaud (19FF, 20 minutes); to/from Ste-Maxime (25.50FF, 40 minutes) and

Fréjus (48FF, one hour). Buses to/from Toulon (97FF, 2¼ hours, seven daily) go inland before joining the coast at Cavalaire-sur-Mer; they also stop at Le Lavandou (56FF, one hour) and Hyères (82FF, 1¼ hours). Services are less frequent in winter.

There are daily buses to Hyères-Toulon airport (106FF, one hour).

Boat Les Bateaux de St-Raphaël (☎ 04 94 95 17 46) runs two daily boats from St-Tropez to St-Raphaël (110FF return, 50 minutes) between April and July. Boats depart from the new port, from the jetty off ave du 8 Mai 1945 opposite the bus station.

MMG (☎ 04 94 96 51 00), online at www.nova.fr/mmg, runs daily boat trips around Baie des Cannebiers (50/25FF for adults/children aged four to 12) and runs a *navette* (shuttleboat) service between St-Tropez and Ste-Maxime from April to November (32/16FF one-way, 30 minutes, at least hourly). It runs an additional shuttle to/from Port Grimaud between June and mid-September (30/15FF, 20 minutes, nine to 11 daily) and to/from Les Issambres in July and August (34FF, 20 minutes, eight or nine daily). Shuttleboats depart from the pier off quai Jean Jaurès at the Vieux Port. Tickets are sold five minutes before departure from the portside kiosk. A weekly pass covering unlimited travel on these routes costs 180FF.

Les Bateaux Verts (see Getting There & Away under Ste-Maxime later in this chapter) also runs shuttleboats between St-Tropez and Ste-Maxime. It operates two boats per week to Port-Cros (1¼ hours) and Porquerolles (1¾ hours), two of the three Îles d'Hyères, from June to September. Boats depart from St-Tropez at 8.40 am on Thursday and Sunday. A return trip to Port-Cros/Porquerolles costs 160/185FF (children aged four to 12, 102/117FF). Island boats depart from the new harbour.

Getting Around

Bus In July and August a free minibus shuttles lazy tourists from the car park opposite the bus station to/from ave du Général Leclerc, ave Gambetta (place des Lices) and quai Suffren (Vieux Port).

ST-TROPEZ TO TOULON

The Ramatuelle bus (see the previous Getting There & Away section) stops at Plage de Pampelonne.

Taxi There is a taxi rank (☎ 04 94 97 05 27) in front of the Musée de l'Annonciade at the Vieux Port.

Car & Motorcycle Europcar (☎ 04 94 97 15 41) and Budget (☎ 04 94 54 86 54) have an office in the Résidences du Port on blvd 11 Novembre 1918. Avis (☎ 04 94 97 03 10) is on ave du 8 Mai.

Scooter rental outlets are at the western end of ave du Général de Gaulle: Scooter Station (☎ 04 94 97 40), 12 ave du Général Leclerc (entrance on ave du Général de Gaulle too), rents 50/125cc scooters for 149/199FF per day or 199/249FF per 24 hours, including helmet and unlimited kilometres. It opens 9 am to 1 pm and 2 to 8 pm. Holiday Bikes (☎ 04 94 97 09 39, ave du Général de Gaulle) next door has 50cc scooters/600cc motorcycles/cars to rent costing from 150/620/300FF per day.

Bicycle Holiday Bikes (see Car & Motorcycle above) rents bicycles for 90/450FF per day/week, plus 1500FF deposit. In town, MAS-Location 2 Roues (☎/fax 04 94 97 00 60), 3–5 rue Joseph Quaranta, rents road/mountain bikes for 50/80FF per day and 250/450FF per week. It opens 9 am to 7 pm (3 pm Sunday).

Boat To order a boat taxi call Le Royale (☎ 06 09 53 15 47), open 9 am to midnight, Easter to October.

GASSIN & RAMATUELLE
The sparsely populated interior of the **Presqu'île de St-Tropez** (St-Tropez peninsula) is crossed by sprawling vineyards and a handful of roads that link the villages of Gassin and Ramatuelle to the coast.

In medieval **Gassin** (postcode 83580, pop 2752, elevation 200m), 11km south-west of St-Tropez, narrow streets wend uphill to the 16th-century **church** (1558), which tops the rocky promontory on which the village is built.

From Gassin, route des Moulins de Paillas snakes 3km south-east, past the ruins of ancient **windmills**, to **Ramatuelle** (postcode 83350, pop 2174, elevation 136m), 10km from St-Tropez via the D61. The fruits of the peninsula's lush vineyards – Côtes de Provence wines – can be tested at various chateaux along the D61, including the Domaine de la Rouillère (☎ 04 94 55 72 60). The two-week Festival de Ramatuelle brings live jazz and theatre to the streets in early August.

Ramatuelle tourist office (☎ 04 94 79 26 04, fax 04 94 79 12 66), place de l'Ormeau, organise guided tours of both villages.

GOLFE DE ST-TROPEZ
The Gulf of St-Tropez, north-west of St-Tropez, is dominated by the brash resort of **Ste-Maxime** at the northern end of the bay, and the more pleasing, architectural wonder of **Port Grimaud**, 8km south-west. In summer, boats plough their way back and forth across the gulf between St-Tropez and the two resorts.

Accommodation can be booked through the Golfe de St-Tropez tourist office (☎ 04 94 55 22 02, fax 04 94 55 22 03, ℮ semgst@ franceplus.com), which overlooks the busy roundabout in Carrefour de la Foux, 2km south of Port Grimaud, on the N98. The centre opens 9 am to 8 pm weekdays, and 10 am to 7 pm weekends, July and August; and 9 am to 7 pm weekdays, and 10 am to 6 pm Saturday, the rest of the year. It posts information on its Web site at www .franceplus.com (French only).

Ste-Maxime
postcode 83120 • pop 11,978
Sandy-beached Ste-Maxime (Santo Massimo in Provençal), 24km south of St-Raphaël and 14km north-west of St-Tropez, is a crowded, modern, ugly resort with few thrills greater than those offered at the countless water-sports clubs that line the beachfront.

Ste-Maxime's old town, centred around rue Gambetta, is crammed with touristy cafes, craft stalls and souvenir shops. Giant pans of paella, fruit stalls and pastry shops

Sun-dried flags in the backstreets of St-Tropez

Art for all palettes...

DAN HERRICK

NICOLA WILLIAMS

Cruise around St-Tropez or relax with a pleasant stroll down to the harbour.

MANFRED GOTTSCHALK

Monaco, with its palatial yachts, grand apartments and soaring skyline, is the 'Hong Kong of Europe'.

Take a chance at the world-famous Monte Carlo casino, Monaco – you just may win!

line rue Courbet, a cobbled street that leads to the town's main market square, place du Marché. Flowers, fish, olives, oil, wine, tartes Tropéziennes and other culinary delights are sold in the *covered market (4 rue Fernard Bessy)*.

The tourist office (☎ 04 94 96 19 24, fax 04 94 49 17 97), promenade Simon Lorière, has information on water sports and other seafaring activities. Deep-sea fishers can contact Les Bateaux Verts (see Getting There & Away below), which organises weekly fishing trips (3½ hours, 160FF).

Getting There & Away There are regular buses between St-Tropez and Ste-Maxime (see Getting There & Away under St-Tropez earlier in this chapter).

The shuttleboats to/from St-Tropez depart from quai Léon Condroyer at the port. From here, Les Bateaux Verts (☎ 04 94 49 29 30, e bateaux.verts@wanadoo.fr) run regular boat excursions around Baie des Cannebiers (also known as Baie des Stars); three-hour trips to the Calanque de l'Estérel 95/57FF for adults/children aged four to 12); to Cap Camarat, Cap Taillat and Cap Lardier (95/57FF, two hours); and twice-weekly day trips to Port-Cros (160/102FF) and Porquerolles (185/117FF) Boats to the Îles de Lérins depart on Monday only (160/102FF).

Port Grimaud

Pretty little Port Grimaud was built in the 1960s on top of a 100 hectare-large swamp. Within the high-wall barricading the floating village in, Provençal cottages – painted all colours – stand gracefully alongside yacht-laden waterways. On Thursday and Sunday morning a market fills place du Marché, from where a wooden bridge leads to Port Grimaud's modernist church. Inside, sunbeams sparkle through a stained-glass window designed by Vasarely. A panorama of sloping red rooftops fans out from the top of the bell tower (admission 5FF).

Alsatian architect Francis Spoerry, who conceived the entire project, fought for four years (1962–6) to get the authorities to agree to his water-world proposal. Pictures of prehistoric lagoon towns displayed in Zürich's Landesmuseum were apparently Spoerry's inspiration. He went on to design Port Liberty in New York.

Cars are forbidden to enter this Venice of Provence. Bronzed residents either walk (rare) or cruise around in speedboats. Port Grimaud is endowed with 12km of quays, 7km of 4m-deep canals and mooring space for 3000 luxury yachts – gaped at by 400,000 visitors a year. *Tenue correcte* (correct dress) is insisted upon, except on the wide sandy beach which can be accessed on foot from Grand rue. In summer, a small tourist office (☎ 04 94 56 28 87, 04 94 43 26 98) operates on the roadside (N98) in St-Pons Les Mûres, opposite Porche Poterne, the main pedestrian entrance into Port Grimaud.

Places to Stay & Eat There are a couple of camp sites immediately north of Port Grimaud on the N98. Three-star *Camping des Mûres (☎ 04 94 56 16 97, fax 04 94 56 37 91)* charges 106FF for two people with tent and car and opens mid-March to September. Next door, *Camping de la Plage (☎ 04 94 56 31 15, fax 04 94 56 49 61)* charges 114FF and opens mid-March to mid-October. Buses from St-Raphaël and Ste-Maxime stop in front of both sites. About 500m farther south along the N98, overlooking the busy roundabout in St-Pons les Mûres, is *Camping Les Prairies de la Mer (☎ 04 94 79 09 09, fax 04 94 56 34 23)*, which touts similar rates.

Port Grimaud has one hotel. Four-star *Hôtel Giraglia (☎ 04 94 56 31 33, fax 04 94 56 33 77, e legiraglia@aol.com, place du 14 Juin)* has doubles that ooze romance and cost upwards of 890/1200FF in low/high season. *Menus* (270FF) in its poolside *L'Amphitrite* restaurant are served with a flourish by waiters dressed in dinner jackets.

Getting There & Away There are buses between Port Grimaud and Grimaud (9FF, 10 minutes, five daily) and St-Tropez (19FF, 20 minutes, eight to 10 daily).

Between April and mid-October, a tourist train (☎ 06 81 35 77 90) shunts visitors between Port Grimaud and Grimaud. From Port

ST-TROPEZ TO TOULON

Grimaud, there are five daily trains between 10.15 am and 6.25 pm, with extra evening trains until 10.05 pm from mid-June to August. A one-way/return ticket costs 17/32FF (children aged four to 12, 12/17FF). In Port Grimaud, the stop is opposite Porche Poterne, the pedestrian entrance to the marine village; in Grimaud it's on central place Neuve.

From June to mid-September MMG (☎ 04 94 96 51 00) runs regular shuttleboats between Port Grimaud and St-Tropez (nine to 11 daily). Boats dock at the jetty next to the beach, accessible on foot via Grand rue and place du 14 Juin. A one-way/return ticket costs 30/55FF (children aged four to 12, 15/30FF). Shuttleboats to/from Ste-Maxime (see Getting There & Away in that section earlier) are operated by Les Bateaux Verts.

A combined ticket covering a return ride on the Port-Grimaud–Grimaud train and the MMG shuttleboat departing from St-Tropez/Ste-Maxime costs 70/100FF (children aged four to 12, 45/50FF).

Getting Around Les Coches d'Eau (☎ 04 94 56 21 13), 12 place du Marché, runs boat tours (20 minutes) of Port Grimaud, departing from place du Marché every 10 minutes between 9 am and 10 pm, mid-June to mid-September; and 10 am to noon and 2 to 6 pm, the rest of the year. Tickets cost 18FF (children aged three to 12, 9FF).

Across the bridge on place de l'Église you can hire an electric boat *(barque électrique)*, costing 100/180FF per 30/60 minutes for up to four people, between Easter and mid-November.

Inside Porche Poterne, Nautic Location (☎ 04 94 43 47 27), 22 place du Sud, rents speedboats. A 40/60cv for six/five people without a permit costs from 150/200FF per hour or 400/650FF per day; a 2500FF deposit is required. The same company rents jet skis (400FF for 30 minutes) and bicycles (20FF per hour).

Grimaud
postcode 83310 • pop 3847
• elevation 105m
Port Grimaud's popular medieval sibling is 3km inland. The typically Provençal hill-

top village is most notable for the ruins of its **Château du Grimaud**, originally built in the 11th century and fortified four centuries later. In summer, look out for posters advertising musical concerts here.

The tourist office (☎ 04 94 43 26 98, fax 04 94 43 32 40, [e] bureau.du.tourisme .grimaud@wanadoo.fr), 1 blvd des Aliziers, has accommodation details. Visit online at www.nova.fr/grimaud.

There are eight to 10 direct daily buses from St-Tropez to Grimaud or Port Grimaud (19FF, 20 minutes) and a few to/from St-Raphaël (45FF, one hour).

Northern Var

The northern half of the Var department – generally understood to be everything north of the dusty, noisy A8 autoroute – is a vastly different kettle of fish to its coastal counterpart. Here, in this surprisingly rural hinterland, hill-top villages drowse in peace beneath the midday sun to create a happy illusion of an unspoilt Provence from a bygone era.

The largest town in this lovely neck of the woods is dull Draguignan, home to the French army whose military base occupies the vast Plateau de Canjuers. This plateau sprawls for some 30km north to the foot of the Gorges du Verdon (see the Haute-Provence chapter). The greener area east of Draguignan, known as Pays Dracénois, is pierced by the hill-top village of Fayence. Black truffles, terracotta tiles and ceramics are the mainstay industries of the rural populace west of Draguignan. Regional wines can be tried and tasted in and around medieval Les Arcs-sur-Argens.

DRAGUIGNAN
postcode 83300 • pop 34,814
• elevation 187m
A sign at the entrance to Draguignan, 40km north of St-Tropez, welcomes visitors to France's 'Capital d'Artillerie' (artillery capital), where an artillery school has been based since 1976. The **Musée de l'Artillerie** (☎ 04 98 10 83 85), in the school, can be

visited 8.30 am to noon and 2.30 to 5 or 6 pm weekdays. Admission is free. In Draguignan's American cemetery, a monument pays homage to the heavy combat that occurred around Draguignan during WWII – 9000 American and British soldiers were dropped here by parachute on 15 August 1944.

Traditional Provençal costumes, musical instruments and other ethnographic finds are displayed in the **Musée des Traditions Provençales** (☎ 04 94 47 05 72), 15 rue Roumanille. In the tiny last patch of Draguignan's old town, the 18m-tall **tour d'horloge** (clock tower), topped with an ornate, wrought-iron campanile, is worth a visit.

The tourist office (☎ 04 98 10 51 05, [e] officedetourisme@ville-draguignan.fr), 2 blvd Lazare Carnot, has details on accommodation in and around town; the best places to stay are in Pays Dracénois (see Around Draguignan below), accessible by car or bicycle. The tourist office rents bikes for 80/150/210FF for one/two/three days. In town, *Hôtel Touring (☎/fax 04 94 68 15 46, place Claude Gay)* has cheap singles/doubles costing 110/140FF (130/160FF with shower). Other places to stay are listed on the tourist office Web site at www.ville-draguignan.fr (French only).

Getting There & Away
Estérel Cars (☎ 04 94 52 00 50 in Fréjus) runs 16 daily buses to St-Raphaël (32/250FF for one ticket/carnet of 10). There are less frequent services to Grasse, Marseilles and Toulon (58FF, 1¼ hours).

Draguignan is served by regular daily buses to/from Les Arcs-sur-Argens, where the closest train station is. Advance train tickets are sold at the SNCF office (open 9 am to 5.30 pm Monday to Saturday) at Draguignan bus station on blvd des Martyrs de la Résistance.

AROUND DRAGUIGNAN
Pays Dracénois
From Draguignan head eastwards along the D562, then follow the D225 and D25 north to **Callas** (pop 1400). A stunning panorama of the red-rock Massif de l'Ésterel unfolds as the road climbs up to the village. *Hôtel de France (☎ 04 94 76 61 02, [e] francois garcia@free.fr, place Georges Clémenceau)* is a typical Provençal village hotel, with a melon-flesh coloured facade and basic doubles costing 170FF. Stock up on oil from Moulin de Callas (☎ 04 94 76 68 05, [e] moulin.callas@libertysurf.fr), a mill dating to 1928 at the southern end of the village.

Six kilometres north is **Bargemon** (pop 1228; ☎/fax 04 94 47 81 73 for the tourist office), where charming rooms at the *Auberge des Arcades (☎ 04 94 76 60 36, ave Pasteur)* cost 250FF with shower. Its terrace restaurant has *menus* starting at 98FF and serves several truffle-inspired dishes.

Big spenders and honeymooners should head straight for *Hostellerie Les Gorges de Pennafort (☎ 04 94 76 66 51, fax 04 94 76 67 23)*, 8km south of Callas on the vineyard-lined D25. The grand old hostellerie, in the middle of nowhere, has its own lake and overlooks the stunning **Gorges de Pennafort** – ideal for gentle hand-in-hand strolls. Doubles fit for queens cost from 750/850FF in low/high season.

Medieval **Fayence** (postcode 83440, pop 3502, elevation 350m), in the hills about 25km east of Draguignan, makes a pretty stepping stone between Pays Dracénois and Cannes country (see the Cannes Area chapter). *Hôtel Le Sousto (☎ 04 94 76 02 16, [e] guy.corteccia@wanadoo.fr, 4 rue du Paty)*, in the pedestrian heart of the old town, offers fantastic-value rooms with kitchenette and bathroom costing 270/360FF for two/four people.

Fayence tourist office (☎ 04 94 76 20 08), place Léon Roux, has details on other accommodation options. Its most idyllic choice is *Moulin de la Camandoule (☎ 04 94 76 00 84, fax 04 94 76 10 40, [e] moulin .camandoule@wanadoo.fr, chemin Notre Dame des Cyprès)*, a 19th-century mill with 11 bedrooms (starting at 475/515FF in low/high season), 1.5km west off the D19 to Seillans.

Haut-Var
West of Draguignan rises Haut-Var (literally 'high Var'), the northernmost part of

ST-TROPEZ TO TOULON

the Var department, best known for the black truffles that are snouted out of its rich earth, November to March.

In season, an abundance of these deceptively ugly nuggets of black fungus can be viewed in all their unattractiveness at the Thursday morning **truffle market**, held on the central square in **Aups** (pop 1796). Truffle hunts and demonstrations of pig-snouting techniques lure a crowd, to the otherwise unremarkable village, on the fourth Sunday in January when Aups throws its Journée de la Truffe (Day of the Truffle). Truffles are dished up in various tantalising forms at *Le St-Marc* (☎ *04 94 70 06 08, fax 04 94 70 13 65, rue de l'Église)*, an oil mill dating to 1833, since converted into a hotel-restaurant. Doubles/triples cost 200/270FF (250/320FF with shower and toilet) and *menus* start at 95FF.

Some 9km south of Aups along the wiggly D31 is **Salernes** (pop 3343) where handmade terracotta tiles, known as *terres cuites* (literally 'baked earth'), have been manufactured since the 18th century. Ask at the tourist office (☎ *04 94 70 69 02*), place Gabriel Péri, for a copy of the free *Guide des Artisans Terres de Salernes*, which includes a list of 16 Salernais potters and tilemakers who open their workshop doors to visitors; many close in August.

Cotignac (pop 2040), 11km south-west of Salernes, and hill-top **Entrecasteaux** (pop 868), with its 17th-century chateau 9km east, are other pretty Varois villages worth a mooch. **Château de Bernes** (☎ *04 94 60 43 53*), a vineyard 2km north of Lorgues, offers wine tasting and jazz picnics (130FF).

Le Thoronet & La Celle

From Cotignac, the picturesque D13 snakes though Carcès and around **Lac de Carcès**. At the lake's southern end, continue 4km eastwards to the Romanesque **Abbaye de Thoronet**, the third in a trio of great abbeys built by the Cistercian order in Provence in the 12th and 13th centuries.

Thoronet Abbey (☎ *04 94 60 43 90*) was built between 1160 and 1190, housing some 20 monks and several dozen lay brothers by the early 13th century. By 1790 just a handful of elderly monks remained. The church, the monks' cells and cloisters were all built with dry stone. The chapter house, where the monks met each morning to discuss any community problems, is noticeably more ornate than the rest of the austere abbey. This was because it was the only secular room, where prayers were never held. Early Gothic influences are evident in the pointed arches, which rest on two columns.

The abbey opens 9 am to 7 pm Monday to Saturday, and 9 am to noon and 2 to 7 pm Sunday, April to September; and 10 am to 1 pm and 2 to 5 pm, the rest of the year. Admission costs 35FF (those aged 18 to 25, 23FF, those aged under 18, free). Musical soirees are held here in summer.

About 15km south-west of Thoronet is **Abbaye de la Celle** (☎ *04 94 59 10 05*), a 12th-century Benedictine abbey in the tiny village of La Celle, 2km south of Brignoles. It was a women's convent from 1225 until its eventual closure in 1657. The **church** continues to serve the village community today and the **abbey cloister** can be visited 9.30 am to 12.10 pm and 2 to 5.30 pm (2.30 to 5.45 pm on weekends). Admission costs 20FF (those aged over 60 and students, 15FF).

The adjoining **convent** hosts the **Maison des Vins Coteaux Varois** (☎ *04 94 69 33 18*, e cotvarois@aol.com), where you can taste and buy Coteaux Varois AOC wines.

Hostellerie de l'Abbaye de la Celle (☎ 04 98 05 14 14, fax 04 98 05 14 15, e contact @abbaye-celle.com) is a fabulous four-star hotel and restaurant run by Alain Ducasse (see the special Food & Wine section for more details). Count on paying upwards of 1300FF for one of its 11 country-style rooms; the bathroom in the Cedar Tree room has a bathtub with legs and Salernes tiles on its walls.

LES ARCS-SUR-ARGENS
postcode 83460 • pop 5515

The two draws to Les Arcs, 11km south of Draguignan and 28km from the coast, are its perfectly restored old town perched on a hillock and its House of Wines, where you can buy, taste and learn about Côtes de Provence wines.

The tourist office (☎/fax 04 94 73 37 30), 21 blvd Gambetta, overlooking place de Général de Gaulle, sits at the foot of the medieval village. The 11th-century castle that crowns it shelters the elegant *Logis du Guetteur* (☎ 04 94 73 30 82, fax 04 94 73 39 95, place du Château), a luxury hotel with doubles costing 600FF and *menus* starting at 150FF.

The *Auberge du Vieux Moulin* (☎ 04 94 70 87 59), midway between Les Arcs and Draguignan in Trans en Provence, is worth a nibble for its unusual interior – a cave partly filled with stalactites. Gourmet *menus* in the former oil mill start at 115FF.

Wine Tasting

The Centre de Dégustation inside the **Maison des Vins Côtes de Provence** (☎ 04 94 99 50 20), 2.5km south of the village on the westbound N7, is the obvious place to start. Twelve different Côtes de Provence wines are available for tasting each week and some 620 different wines are for sale. Bottles are sold at producers' prices and cost 15.20FF to 156FF. The Tasting Centre opens 10 am to 1 pm and 1.30 to 6, 7 or 8 pm.

Beautifully placed among sprawling vineyards is **Château Ste-Roseline** (☎ 04 94 99 50 30, e contact@chateau-ste-roseline.com), 4.5km east of Les Arcs-sur-Argens on the D91 towards La Motte. Its prestigious *cru classé* wine, produced here since the 14th century, can be sampled 9 am and noon and 2 to 7 pm weekdays, and 10 am to noon and 2 to 6 pm Saturday. A 1975 mosaic by Marc Chagall illuminates the 13th-century Romanesque **Chapelle de Ste-Roseline**, which has housed the corpse of St-Roseline since 1329. Piano recitals and other musical concerts are held here in the **Espace d'Art** in July and August; tickets cost 150FF (280FF including supper).

A farther 3km east along the D91 (across the N555) is **La Motte**, the first village in Provence to be liberated after the August 1944 Allied landings. For the ultimate Provençal feast, head eastwards out of La Motte along the D47 to **Domaine de la Maurette** (☎ 04 94 45 92 82) on the intersection of the D47 and the D25. On this wine estate, you can taste and buy wine, and dine in its *ferme auberge*, open for lunch and dinner (summer only). There is a choice of two menus (105FF or 150FF) and the atmosphere of chattering people dining on good, wholesome, home-made food is electric. The place is packed by 1 pm.

Getting There & Away

Les Arcs-sur-Argens train station is 2km south of the tourist office off ave Jean Jaurès. Exit the train station, turn left, then turn right (north) at the end of the street onto ave Jean Jaurès, from where it is a straight 2km walk to place de Général de Gaulle.

Les Arcs is on the rail line between St-Raphaël and Toulon and is well served by coastal trains to Nice (93FF, 1½ hours), Toulon (79FF, 45 minutes) and Marseilles (121FF, 1½ hours).

Les Arcs also serves as the train station for Draguignan. Les Rapides Varois (☎ 04 94 47 05 05 in Draguignan) operates buses every 30 minutes between 6.30 am and 8.30 pm between Les Arcs train station and Draguignan.

Massif des Maures

Much of the heavily forested Massif des Maures ('maouro' in Provençal meaning 'dark') is inaccessible by car, but there are five roads you can take through the hills. The lowest, straightest, southernmost road (N98) cuts eastwards, through vineyards and cork oak tree plantations, from St-Tropez to **Bormes-les-Mimosas** (pop 6399) and onto Hyères. The parallel D14 runs through **Collobrières**, the largest town in the massif, known for its chestnut produce. This road is particularly popular with cyclists and is graced with good panoramas.

The mountainous, hairpin-laced D39, which leads north from the D14 just east of Collobrières, snakes between **La Sauvette** (779m) and **Notre Dame des Anges** (780m), the massif's highest peaks. The Massif des Maures, not surprisingly, offers superb walking and cycling opportunities too. The GR9 penetrates the massif at its northern

ST-TROPEZ TO TOULON

edge, near **Carnoules** (pop 2622), and wends its way past Notre Dame des Anges (topped by a small chapel) and La Sauvette to the unspoilt village of **La Garde Freinet**, a perfect getaway spot. From here it runs south to Port Grimaud on the coast. From Collobrières, the southbound GR90 – which cuts straight through the village – loops 12km east to the isolated monastery, **La Chartreuse de la Verne**. Northbound, it hooks up with the GR9 at Notre Dame des Anges.

Collobrières tourist office publishes an English-language guide (10FF) outlining five short village walks (two to 6km).

COLLOBRIÈRES
postcode 83610 • pop 1710
If you like chestnuts, then Collobrières (Couloubriero in Provençal) – a village renowned for its chestnut puree and *marrons glacés* (candied chestnuts) – is for you. It lies 24km west of Grimaud and is the 'capital' of the Maures. In summer, slabs of cork and home-made chestnut puree are sold on the square in front of the tourist office. Market day is Thursday (July and August) and Sunday (year round).

Across the 12th-century bridge, the **Confiserie Azuréenne** (☎ 04 94 48 07 20) sells a nutty array of products. Sample *glaces aux marrons glacés* (sweet chestnut ice cream), *crème de marrons* (chestnut cream), *marrons au sirop* (chestnuts in syrup), or a shot of *liqueur de châtaignes* (chestnut liqueur). Opposite the shop is a small **Musée de la Fabrique** that explains the art of making *marrons glacés* (glacé chestnuts). Both open 9.30 am to 1 pm and 2 to 7 or 8 pm. Admission is free.

Collobrières marks its annual Grande Fête des Fontaines in August by cooking up a monstrous-sized aïoli. It celebrates a Fête de la Châtaigne (Chestnut Festival) on the last three Sundays in October, and its Fête de la Transhumance in April.

Almost 12,000 hectares of protected forest surround the town.

Information
The tourist office (☎ 04 94 48 08 00, fax 04 94 48 04 10, ⒺＥ collotour@compuserve.com),

on blvd Charles Caminat at the eastern end of the village, opens 10 am to 12.30 pm and from 3 to 6.30 pm Monday to Saturday, July and August; and 2 to 6 pm Tuesday to Saturday, the rest of the year. It takes accommodation bookings and has details on joining in the October chestnut harvest and participating in guided forest walks (45FF) organised by the Office National des Fôrets (ONF). Three short walking trails – including a 200m-trail to a *châtaigneraie* (chestnut grove) – are mapped out on the noticeboard in front of the tourist office. Visit online at www.collotour.com (French only).

Places to Stay & Eat
Collobrières offers reasonably priced accommodation and a rash of farmhouses that turn home-grown produce into memorable *tables d'hôtes*.

Camping Signposted off place Général de Gaulle, 200m from the village, *Camping St-Roch* (☎ 04 94 48 08 00, Ⓔ *marie-de-collobrieres@wanadoo.fr*) charges 17.50FF per night for a car and tent or caravan, plus 8.50/5.50FF per adult/child aged under eight. Reception opens 8 am to noon and 5 to 10 pm; the site opens June to September.

Gîtes d'Étape & Chambres d'Hôtes Twelve kilometres east of Collobrières on the D14, *La Ferme de Capelude* (☎ 04 94 56 80 35, Ⓔ *capelude@club-internet.fr*) is a restored 16th-century farm that has beds in an eight- or 10-person dorm for 90FF per night, including breakfast. Half-board costs 200FF per person. It also has rooms with private bathroom for two/four people costing 250/400FF. While you're here, stock up on home-made chestnut honey, lavender honey and fruity jams from the farm shop.

Some 6km north of Collobrières along the relentlessly winding D39 is *La Bastide de la Cabrière* (☎ 04 94 48 04 31, Ⓔ *loic .de.saleneuve@libertysurf.fr*), a chambre d'hôte with doubles costing 390/490FF in low/high season and delicious home-grown meals costing 190FF.

Continuing 1km farther north along the D39, then 2.5km along a gravel track sign-

ST-TROPEZ TO TOULON

posted 'Piste des Condamines' brings you to *L'Aurier (☎ 04 94 48 09 47)*, another farm offering dorm and B&B accommodation starting at 210FF per person (half-board). Farther north still, 1km east of the Tortoise Village (see the boxed text 'Le Village des Tortues') on the D75, is *Château Rose d'Or (☎ 04 94 60 00 56,* ⓔ *realdon@free .fr)*, a vineyard where you can taste wine and sleep (500FF for two people, including breakfast). About 500m farther along the D75, *Domaine de la Fouguelle (☎ 04 94 60 00 69)* is another estate that produces Côtes de Provence wine and offers B&B.

Approaching Collobrières from the south (D41), consider a stop for a hearty lunchtime munch at *Chèvrerie du Peigros' (☎ 04 94 48 03 83)*, a goat farm 1.8km along a gravel track, signposted from the top of Col de Babaou (414m). See the special Food & Wine section for details.

In the centre of Collobrières, cosy 10-room *Hôtel-Restaurant des Maures (☎ 04 94 48 07 10, fax 04 94 48 02 73)*, above a bar at 19 blvd Lazare Carnot, has basic rooms for one or two costing 120FF. Its restaurant is on a terrace above the river.

LA CHARTREUSE DE LA VERNE

The majestic, 12th- to 13th-century monastery of La Chartreuse de la Verne (420m) is in a forest, 12km south-east of Collobrières. It was founded in 1190 by the bishop of Toulon for the Carthusian monks who settled here from 1170. Huguenots destroyed most of the original charterhouse in 1577.

The solitary complex, under restoration since the 1960s, is home to 15 Carthusian nuns today. One of the old monks' cells has been fully restored, complete with the small garden and covered corridor, where the monk would pray as he paced its length. A 70m-long cloister, bakery and mill can be visited. Various **walking trails** lead from the monastery into its forested surroundings.

The monastery (Monastère de la Verne; ☎ 04 94 43 45 51) opens 11 am to 6 pm (5 pm in winter) Wednesday to Monday, February to December. Admission costs 30FF (children aged eight to 14, 20FF).

Le Village des Tortues

About 20km north of Collobrières on the northern tip of the massif is a Tortoise Village, where one of France's rarest and most endangered species can be viewed in close quarters. The Hermann tortoise *(Testudo hermanni)*, once common along the Mediterranean coastal strip, is today found only in the Massif des Maures and Corsica. Forest fires in 1990 destroyed 250,000 hectares of forest in the massif, reducing the tortoise population further still.

The Station d'Observation et de Protection des Tortues des Maures (SOPTOM; Maures Tortoise Observation and Protection Station) was set up in 1985 by French writer and filmmaker Bernaud Devaux and an English biologist to ensure the Hermann's survival. Since 1988 some 8000 tortoises have been returned to the wild.

A well-documented trail (captions in English) leads visitors around the centre, from the quarantine quarter and reproduction enclosures to the tropical conservatory, egg hatcheries (home to pregnant females from mid-May to end of June), and nurseries, where the young tortoises (a delicacy for preying magpies, rats, foxes and wild boars) spend the first three of their 60 to 100 years. The tortoise mating season runs from March to May and August to September. From November through to early March, they hibernate. In the tortoise clinic, wounded tortoises – usually wild ones kept as domestic pets – are treated. Dog bites and lawnmower injuries are the most common wounds. Following their rehabilitation in the centre, most are repatriated into the Maures forest.

The Village des Tortues (☎ 04 94 78 26 41, ⓔ soptom@compuserve.com) opens 9 am to 7 pm, March to November. Admission costs 40FF (those aged six to 16, 30FF). It costs 100FF to sponsor a tortoise. The village, about 6km east of Gonfaron, is only accessible by private transport; follow the signs from Gonfaron.

Smoking and revealing clothes are forbidden. From Collobrières, follow route de Grimaud (D14) eastwards for 6km, then turn right (south) onto the narrow D214. Follow this road for a farther 6km to the monastery; the final section of the single-track road is unpaved.

LA GARDE FREINET
postcode 83310 • pop 1658
• elevation 380m

This village is a delight to explore in late summer when its streets are quiet. A fantastic panorama of red rooftops can be viewed from the **ruins** of **Fort Freinet** (450m). The fort was built in the 13th century but abandoned 200 years later when the villagers moved down to the plateau. Below the ruins is a large stone cross where pilgrims pay their respects on May 1 each year. The cross and fort are a 20-minute uphill walk from the village centre (signposted from place Neuve).

La Garde Freinet celebrates its traditional Fête de la Transhumance, marking the seasonal moving of the flocks in mid-June, and hosts a Fête de la Châtaigne (Chestnut Fair) in mid-October. Markets fill the old town squares on Wednesday and Sunday morning. Village traditions and customs unfold in the adjoining **Conservatoire du Patrimoine et du Traditions du Freinet** (☎ 04 94 43 67 41), 1 place Neuve, open 10 am to noon and 3 to 6 pm Tuesday to Saturday. Admission costs 10FF (children aged under 12, free). Next door, the tourist office (☎ 04 94 43 67 41, fax 04 94 43 08 69), 1 place Neuve, has details on walking, wine tasting and chambres d'hôtes in the massif.

Hôtel La Claire Fontaine (☎ 04 94 43 63 76, fax 04 94 43 60 36, place Vieille) has rooms for 190FF (210FF with shower). Rustic *Auberge La Sarrazine* (☎ 04 94 43 65 98, route Nationale) is a lovely place to sample Provençal fare in front of an open fire (winter) or on a flowery patio (summer). Its *menu Provençal* costs 99FF (lunch *formule* 79FF).

COGOLIN & LA MÔLE
Industrious **Cogolin** (pop 9181; Cougoulin in Provençal), 15km south of La Garde

Freinet, is known for its wooden pipes, cork products and carpets, the latter being woven in the village since the 1920s when Armenian refugees settled here. St-Tropez's sweet and creamy tarte Tropézienne was created in 1955 at the Micka patisserie **La Tarte Tropézienne** (☎ 04 94 54 42 59, 2 rue Beausoleil), online at www.tarte-tropezienne.com. The tourist office (☎ 04 94 55 01 50), place de la République, has a list of artisans to visit and arranges of the old town and its pipe makers. Cogolin's sandy beach and pleasure port is 5km north-east.

Equally inviting to the tastebuds is neighbouring **La Môle** (pop 803), 9km south-west along the vineyard-laden N98. The village is known for the olive bread produced in its bakery and for the culinary delights served with a Provençal flourish at blue-canopied *Auberge de La Môle* (☎ 04 94 49 57 01), a former petrol station on place de l'Église. Lunch/dinner *menus* cost 150/310FF (credit cards not accepted). Sample local wine here or at one of the many **chateaux** along the westbound N98.

From La Môle, narrow route du Canadel (D27) leads perilously to the coast. The one blemish in an otherwise mesmerising landscape is the *Village de Plein Air Pachacaid* (☎ 04 94 55 70 80, ⓔ pacha@pachacaid.com), a huge site where you can rent a mobile home (1500FF plus per week) or splash out on an afternoon at the **Niagara Parc Nautique**. The Niagra water park, with its giant water slides, opens 10.30 am to 7 pm, June to September. Admission costs 82FF (children aged five to 12, 66FF).

Private jets and commercial flights take to the skies from St-Tropez-La Môle airport (Aéroport International St-Tropez-La Môle; ☎ 04 94 49 57 29, fax 04 94 49 58 08), 1km east of La Môle on the N98. See the Getting There & Away chapter for details.

FÔRET DU DOM & BORMES-LES-MIMOSAS
Vineyards melt into a rich patchwork of cork oak, pine and chestnut trees as the N98 continues its path westwards into the **Fôret du Dom**, 12km west of La Môle.

From the top of the (199m), the steep D41

ST-TROPEZ TO TOULON

climbs northwards over the **Col de Babaou** (415m) towards Collobrières. This road is a popular cycling route. Southbound, the D41 wiggles its way across the **Col de Caguo-Ven** (237m), from where there are good views of **Bormes-les-Mimosas** (pop 6399, elevation 180m). The attractive 12th-century village is famous for its great diversity of flora and draws lots of artists and crafts people, many of whom you will see at work as you wander through the tiny streets. The tourist office (☎ 04 94 71 15 17) is at 1 place Gambetta.

CORNICHE DES MAURES

From La Môle, the breathtaking 267m **Col de Canadel** (D27) plummets to the Corniche des Maures, a 26km coastal road (D559) that stretches south-west from La Croix-Valmer to Le Lavandou. The mountain pass offers unbeatable views of the Massif des Maures, the coastline and its offshore islands. The heart-stopping descent brings motorists to a coastal road, trimmed with sandy beaches ideal for swimming, sunbathing and windsurfing. Resorts it passes include **Cavalaire-sur-Mer** and **Le Rayol**.

From Le Rayol, a narrow road leads south to **Domaine du Rayol** (☎ 04 94 05 32 50), ave des Belges. The fabulous 20-hectare garden dates to 1910, when a Parisian banker built himself a seaside villa here. In July and August, you can dive in the underwater **Jardin Marin** (Marine Garden). Admission costs 80FF (those aged 8 to 16, 60FF); bookings are required. The Domaine du Rayol opens 9.30 am to 12.30 pm and 4.30 to 8 pm, July and August; and 9.30 am to 12.30 pm and 2.30 to 6.30 pm, February to June and September to November. Admission to the gardens costs 40FF (those aged 8 to 16, 20FF). In July and August, the estate hosts open-air musical soirees (130FF) at 9 pm. Advance reservations (☎ 04 94 05 32 50) are essential.

LE LAVANDOU

postcode 83980 • pop 5508

Once a fishing village, Le Lavandou (from the Provençal 'Lou Lavandou', meaning 'washhouse') is 5km east of Bormes-les-Mimosas. It is a popular resort, thanks to its 12km sandy beach, good value accommodation, and its proximity to the idyllic Îles d'Hyères, just a boat-ride away from here.

The south-western end of the resort is dominated by concrete blocks and should be avoided. The Vieille Ville (old town) at its north-eastern end, however, is beautifully intact. Here, the pétanque pitch beneath trees on quai Gabriel Péri buzzes with activity; while an age-old *lavoir* (communal washhouse) sits serenely on square des Héros, at the eastern end of ave du Général de Gaulle. Dramatist Bertolt Brecht and composer Kurt Weill wrote parts of *The Threepenny Opera* while holidaying here in 1928.

Le Lavandou sits north-east of **Cap de Brégançon**, a rocky cape embraced by a beautiful sandy beach in **Cabasson**, on its western side, and crowned with the 16th- to 18th-century Fort de Brégançon. Since 1968 the heavily guarded fortress (good views from Cabasson beach) has served as the president of France's summer residence.

Orientation & Information

Quai Gabriel Péri and its continuation, quai Baptistin Pins, runs north-east along the beach front. The port (Gare Maritime), quai des Îles d'Or, sits at its easternmost end, opposite the old town. Public showers (12FF) and toilets (2FF) at the port open 8.15 to 11 am and 5 to 7 pm.

The bus station is nothing more than a shelter either side of the D559. From the station, walk one block south then turn left (east) onto ave des Martyrs de la Résistance to get to the centre. Its continuation, ave du Général de Gaulle, traverses the old town.

The tourist office (☎ 04 94 00 40 50, fax 04 94 00 40 59, ⓔ info@lelavandou .com) is opposite the port on quai Gabriel Péri. It has an informative Web site at www.lelavandou.com.

Boat Excursions

Compagnie de Transports Maritimes Vedettes Îles d'Or (☎ 04 94 71 01 02), 15 quai Gabriel Péri and at the port, operates boats to the Îles d'Hyères. It has a Web site at www.vedettesilesdor.fr.

ST-TROPEZ TO TOULON

Boats sail to **Île du Levant** (127/84FF return for adult/child, 30 minutes, two to seven daily) and **Port-Cros** (130/86FF, 40 minutes), except in November when boats only sail on Thursday, Saturday and Sunday (twice daily). If you are visiting both islands, buy a combined ticket costing 155/111FF.

Boats to **Porquerolles**, the last of the Îles d'Hyères trio, sail daily in July and August (149/109FF, 55 minutes, one daily). In April, May and September, the boat runs on Monday, Wednesday and Saturday. Boats occasionally run in October, depending on the weather.

The Compagnie de Transports Maritimes' boat trips to **St-Tropez** are also seasonal. A boat departs every Saturday from Le Lavandou to St-Tropez in July and August (169/106FF). There is one weekly boat on Tuesday during the second half of June and the first half of September.

Excursions along the coast in a **glass-bottomed boat** (71/47FF) depart every 40 minutes from the port between 9 am and 7 pm all summer.

All boats depart from the port (☎ 04 94 71 13 09) on quai des Îles d'Or. Tickets are sold at the ticket office, open 30 minutes before departure (except in July and August when never-ending queues ensure it remains open all day).

Places to Stay

Camping The tourist office has a list of camp sites nearby; some are clustered along route Benat, some 2km south in the suburb of La Favière. Heading towards Cap de Brégançon, *Camping La Griotte* (☎ 04 94 15 20 72, 2168 route de Cabasson) opens May to October.

Hotels Overlooking the port on quai Baptistin Pins is delightful *Hôtel Le Rabelais* (☎ 04 94 71 00 56, fax 04 94 71 82 55, e hotel.lerabelais@wanadoo.fr, 2 rue Rabelais), a rambling building offering good-value rooms for 310/360FF without/with a sea view. All rooms have shower, toilet and TV. It opens from January to mid-November.

Hôtel Côte d'Azur (☎ 04 94 71 01 79, fax 04 94 15 13 07, 17 ave des Martyrs de la Résistance) has singles/doubles costing upwards of 150/180FF (180/210FF with shower and toilet). Reception is on the 1st floor. The hotel opens April to November.

Another charming place is two-star *La Ramade* (☎ 04 94 71 20 40, 16 rue Patron Ravello), which has rooms for two people with kitchenette starting at 300/350FF in low/high season. Opposite, on the same busy pedestrian street, is good value, one-star *Auberge Provençale* (☎ 04 94 71 00 44, fax 04 94 15 02 25, e provencale .auberge@wanadoo.fr, 11 rue Patron Ravello). Rooms for one or two cost 170FF (220FF with shower).

Places to Eat

The old town overflows with terrace restaurants. *Chez Mimi* (☎ 04 94 71 00 85), overlooking the pétanque pitch from its portside perch on blvd de Lattre de Tassigny, is an ideal spot to breakfast in the early morning sun from 7 am (6.30 am in July and August) or sip an aperitif in the early evening shade.

One spot guaranteed to please is *La Pignato* (☎ 04 94 71 13 02, rue de L'Église), which specialises in *cuisine Provençale*. As part of its 88FF *menu*, start off with grilled sardines or a Roquefort and nut salad, followed by battered squid laced with spices.

Slightly more expensive but equally satisfying is *La Fanouille* (☎ 04 94 71 34 29), occupying a small square on the corner of ave Patron Ravello and Abbé Helin. Service is impeccable. Note the sloping tables!

Nearby, *La Ramade* (see Places to Stay earlier) serves huge bowls of *moules* (mussels) for 65FF and a giant *aïoli Provençal complet*.

Shopi Supermarché (14 ave des Martyrs de la Résistance) opens from 8.30 am to 12.30 pm and 3.15 to 7.30 pm Monday to Saturday, 8.30 am to 12.30 pm Sunday.

Getting There & Away

Le Lavandou is on the main SODETRAV (☎ 04 94 12 55 00 in Hyères) bus route between St-Tropez (70FF, one hour) and

Toulon (58FF, 1¼ hours). Buses follow the coastal road, stopping en route in Le Rayol, Le Lavandou, Bormes-les-Mimosas, La Londe and Hyères. In summer, there are seven St-Tropez–Toulon buses daily (less in winter). Between July and September, additional buses between Le Lavandou to Toulon stop en route in Hyères.

Getting Around

Hire a set of wheels from Holiday Bikes (☎ 04 94 15 19 99), ave Vincent Auriol. Daily rates for a pair of rollerblades/ mountain bike/50cc scooter/650cc motorcycle start at 50/70/140/460FF. It opens 9 am to 12.30 pm and 3 to 7 pm.

Bleu Marin (☎ 04 94 71 42 48), quai Baptistin Pins, hires rollerblades for 45/ 60FF for a half-day/day. Next door, Star Bike (☎ 04 94 01 03 82) rents mountain bikes and scooters/motorcycles.

The Islands

The alluring Îles d'Hyères are also known as the Îles d'Or (Islands of Gold; Lis Isclo d'Or in Provençal). According to legend, the islands in this archipelago were created from beautiful princesses who, upon being chased by pirates while swimming, were turned by the gods into golden islands.

Porquerolles, 7km long and 3km wide, is the westernmost and largest. Port-Cros – the middle island – is a national park; while its eastern sister, Île du Levant, is a nudist colony. Wild camping is forbidden throughout the archipelago.

Rather less magical are the Îles du Fun, the overdeveloped islands of Bendor and Embiez, farther west off Toulon's shores.

ÎLE DE PORT-CROS
postcode 83400 • pop 54

Created in 1963 to protect at least one small part of the Côte d'Azur's natural beauty from overdevelopment, **Parc National de Port-Cros** is France's smallest national park. It encompasses the 675 hectares of the island of Port-Cros (4km long and 2.5km wide) and an 1800-hectare zone of water around it. Until the end of the 19th century, the islanders' vineyards and olive groves ensured their self-sufficiency. Today, tourism is their sustenance.

The island can be visited all year, but walkers – of which 220,000 descend on Port-Cros annually – must stick to the marked paths. Fishing, fires, camping, dogs, motorised vehicles and bicycles are not allowed. Smoking is forbidden outside the portside village.

Port-Cros, the smallest of the Îles d'Hyères, is primarily a marine reserve but is also known for its rich variety of insects, butterflies and birds. Keeping the water around it clean (compared with the rest of the coast) is one of the national reserve's big problems.

An **underwater trail** (sentier sous-marin), marked off the island's northern shore, allows snorkellers to discover some of the park's marine flora and fauna, which include 500 algae species and 180 types of fish. Miniscule **Îlot de la Gabinière**, an islet off Port-Cros' southern shore, is popular with experienced divers. Lavandou Plongée (☎/fax 04 94 71 83 65) in Le Lavandou, arranges dives here. Inscriptions at its office, at the easternmost end of the port, take place 8.15 to 8.45 am (7.45 to 8.15 am Wednesday to Friday) and 2.15 to 2.45 pm.

Parc National de Port-Cros also manages neighbouring **Île de Bagaud** (40 hectares), the fourth of the Îles d'Hyères due west of Port-Cros. The densely vegetated island is used for scientific research and is off-limits for tourists.

Orientation & Information

Boats dock at the port in the village on the island's north-western shores.

The Maison du Parc (☎ 04 94 01 40 72) at the port sells maps of the island (25FF) and stocks the *Guide de Sentier Sous-Marin* (30FF), a plastic card used underwater by snorkellers to identify species. The office has information on walking and diving too. It opens 10 am to noon and 2 to 6 pm, May to October; and for 30 minutes after boats dock the rest of the year. The park's headquarters are in Hyères.

ST-TROPEZ TO TOULON

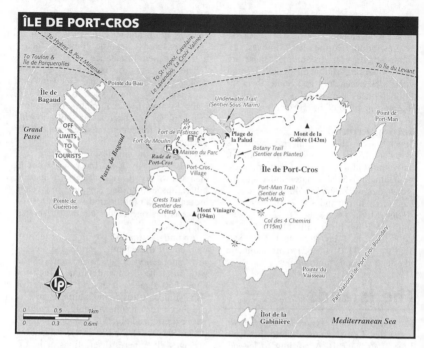

ÎLE DE PORT-CROS

(map labels)

To Hyères & Port Miramar
To Toulon & Île de Porquerolles
To St-Tropez, Cavalaire, Le Lavandou, La Croix Valmer
To Île du Levant
Pointe du Bau
Île de Bagaud
OFF LIMITS TO TOURISTS
Grand Passe
Passe de Bagaud
Pointe de Guérétion
Underwater Trail (Sentier Sous-Marin)
Fort de l'Estissac
Fort du Moulin
Maison du Parc
Rade de Port-Cros
Port-Cros Village
Plage de la Palud
Mont de la Galère (143m)
Point de Port-Man
Botany Trail (Sentier des Plantes)
Île de Port-Cros
Port-Man Trail (Sentier de Port-Man)
Crests Trail (Sentier des Crêtes)
Mont Viniagre (194m)
Col des 4 Chemins (115m)
Parc National de Port-Cros Boundary
Pointe du Vaisseau
Îlot de la Gabinière
Mediterranean Sea
0 0.5 1km
0 0.3 0.6mi

Things to See & Do

At the port, between April and October, you can gaze into Port-Cros' fishy waters from the subterranean depths of **Aquascope** (☎ 04 94 05 92 22), a glass-bottomed vessel. The 30-minute trip, which departs about every 40 minutes, costs 70FF (children aged four to 10, 40FF).

From the portside post office, a track leads inland, from where 30km of marked footpaths crisscross the island. Fifteenth-century **Fort du Moulin** is the starting point for a circular, 1½-hour **botany trail** (sentier des plantes), which leads to Plage de la Palud and returns along an inland route. The beach itself, on the island's northern shores, is a 30-minute walk from the fort. Between mid-June and mid-September, snorkellers can follow a 30-minute **underwater trail**, open 10 am to 4.30 pm. At the port, Sun Plongée inside Sun Bistrot (☎ 04 94 05 90 16) and the nameless souvenir shop (☎ 04 94 05 91 08) next door rent snorkelling gear.

The afore-mentioned botany trail also takes in imposing, 16th-century **Fort de L'Estissac**, which hosts exhibitions in summer. Climb the tower for a panoramic view of Port-Cros and its neighbouring islands. The fort opens 10 am to noon and 2 to 4.30 pm, June and September; and 10 am to 12.30 pm and 2 to 5.30 pm, July and August. Admission is free.

The more demanding, three-hour **crests trail** (sentier des crêtes) explores the southwestern corner of the island, while the slightly easier **Port-Man trail** (sentier de Port-Man) is four hours and takes walkers to Port-Cros' north-eastern tip.

Places to Stay & Eat

Accommodation is limited and needs to be booked well in advance.

Next door to the Maison du Parc *Maison du Port* (☎ 04 94 05 92 72) has quaint, self-catering studios (one-week minimum stay) and a couple of rooms (two-day minimum stay) to rent. Four-person apartments cost 800/1000FF per day in low/high season, and two-person apartments cost 450/550FF per day. Double rooms start at 250/350FF in low/high season. High season is 15 June to 30 September.

On the opposite side of the port, *Hostellerie Provençale* (☎ 04 94 05 90 43, fax 04 94 05 92 90) has five comfortable doubles with shower and toilet, costing 395FF per person for half-board, April to June, September and October; and 435FF per person in July and August.

The exclusive option is 23-room *Le Manoir* (☎ 04 94 05 90 52, fax 04 94 05 90 89), an atmospheric manor with singles /doubles costing upwards of 1020/1560FF in low season and 1560/1760FF in high season. Le Manoir opens April to October.

Five restaurants – offering sea-inspired cuisine – surround the port. Self-caterers can shop at the *épicerie*, tucked beside Hostellerie Provençale.

Getting There & Away

Le Lavandou (see the previous Boat Excursions section) is the main stepping stone to Port-Cros. There are also frequent boats year round from Hyères.

There are seasonal boats – several times a week – from Toulon and St-Tropez (June to September); and Port Miramar, La Croix-Valmer and Cavalaire-sur-Mer (July and August).

ÎLE DU LEVANT
postcode 83400 • pop 186
Nowhere is the quest for natural beauty more explicit than on oddball Île du Levant, a narrow 8km strip of an island, of which 90% is a military camp and strictly off-limits. The remaining pocket of **Héliopolis**, on the island's north-eastern tip, has been a nudist colony since the 1930s. Its tiny population increases ten-fold in summer when the village is overrun with bathers baring all.

Boats arrive/depart from **Port de L'Ayguade**. A small tourist information hut (☎ 04 94 05 93 52 or 04 94 05 91 65 at the town hall) operates here in summer. The central square, place du Village, is a 1km-

walk uphill along route de L'Ayguade, the street running along Héliopolis' southern boundary. The post office, cafes and hotels are clustered around this square. The island's only camp site, *Le Colombéro* (☎ 04 94 05 90 29, route de l'Ayguade), is 150m from the port and opens Easter to the end of September. It charges 40FF per person.

The eastern part of the colony is covered by the **Domaine des Arbousiers**, a nature reservation with rare island plants such as the eryngium tricuspidatum (a type of thistle). A nature trail leads from place du Village, east into the protected area. Contact the tourist office for information on guided tours.

Baring all is not obligatory – except on sandy **Plage Les Grottes**, the main nudist beach east of Port de L'Ayguade. From the port, walk in the direction of Plage de Sable Levant along **sentier Georges Rousseau**, a rocky coastal path. Bold signs reading *'Nudisme Intégral Obligatoire'* mark the moment you are obliged to strip.

Getting There & Away
Île du Levant is 10 minutes by boat from Port-Cros. There are regular boats year round from Le Lavandou and Hyères (see those sections), and in July and August from Port Miramar (La Londe), La Croix-Valmer and Cavalaire-sur-Mer.

ÎLE DE PORQUEROLLES
postcode 83400 • pop 341
Despite being the most developed of the Îles d'Hyères, Porquerolles is home to a wide variety of indigenous and tropical flora, including the requien larkspur, which grows nowhere else in the world. In winter, blossoming mimosas bring a splash of colour to the green island. April and May are the best months to spot some of its 114 bird species. The monk seal, which used to be a regular visitor to Porquerolles, is rarely seen around its shores today.

Most of the island is protected by the Parc National de Port-Cros, which manages 1000 of its 1254 richly vegetated hectares. Exploring by foot or by bike is as good a reason as any to visit. Avoid July and August

ST-TROPEZ TO TOULON

when the happy owners of Porquerolles' numerous *résidences secondaires* return to the island, increasing the population six-fold. Smoking is forbidden outside the village.

Orientation & Information

Boats dock at the port on the island's northern coast. Walk to the tourist office at the end of the jetty, then bear right along rue de la Ferme to place d'Armes, the central village square.

The tourist office (☎ 04 94 58 33 76, fax 04 94 58 36 39, e bip.porquerolles@wanadoo.fr) opens 9 am to 5.30 pm, April to November; and 9 am to 1 pm Friday to Wednesday, the rest of the year. It sells island maps (10FF) showing the *pistes cyclables* (cycling paths) and *sentiers pédestres* (footpaths), and the plastic *Guide Sous-Marin des Espèces Méditerranéenes*, designed to help snorkellers identify underwater flora (70FF). The tourist office Web site is at www.porquerolles.com.

Société Marseillaise de Crédit, 3 rue de la Ferme, has an ATM and currency exchange, open 9.30 am to 12.30 pm and 2 to 4 pm weekdays in summer; and 9.30 am to 12.30 pm and 2 to 4 pm Monday, the rest of

the year. The post office, next to Église Ste-Anne on the southern side of place d'Armes, opens 9 am to noon and 1 to 3 pm weekdays, and 9 am to noon Saturday.

There is laundrette on rue de la Douane. The showers (10FF/five minutes) and free toilets behind the tourist office open from 8 am to 7 pm.

Things to See & Do

Central **place d'Armes** is dominated by a giant, tree-shaded pétanque pitch. In summer, music concerts are held in **Église Ste-Anne**, on the southern side of the square. Festivities fill both the church and the square on 25 July, when islanders celebrate their patron saint's day.

From place d'Armes, head southwards along chemin Ste-Agathe to 16th-century **Fort Ste-Agathe** (☎ 04 94 12 30 40), built in 1518 and the only one of Porquerolles' fortifications open to visitors. Much of the edifice dates from between 1812 and 1814 when Napoleon had the fort rebuilt following its plundering and destruction by the British in 1739. The fort hosts summer exhibitions. An awesome island panorama is visible from the tower. It opens 10 am to

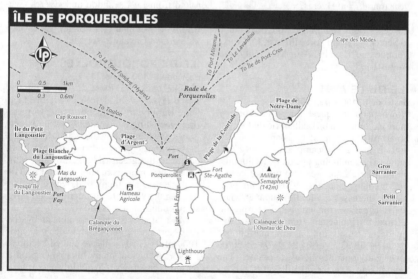

ÎLE DE PORQUEROLLES

noon and 2 to 5.30 pm, May to September. Admission costs 25FF (those aged 12 to 18, 15FF; children aged five to 12, 10FF). For a guided tour, call ☎ 04 94 12 30 40.

From place d'Armes, walk or cycle southwards along rue de la Ferme and turn right at the crossroads. The **Hameau Agricole**, home to the Conservatoire Botanique National Méditerranéen (☎ 04 94 12 30 32, e cbn@www.see.it) is 700m along this trail. Inside the laboratories a well-documented history of the island flora is presented. A botanical trail leads visitors through gardens featuring plants typical to the island: 20 types of almond trees, 150 fig types, 83 lauriers rose types, and numerous olive trees. The centre opens 9.30 am to 12.30 pm and 1.30 to 5 pm, May to September. Admission is free.

The island's 82m-tall **lighthouse**, built in 1837 to tip the island's southernmost cape, is 2km farther along rue de la Ferme. In summer the keeper allows visitors to climb to the top of his tower, which offers a stunning panorama on clear days. A military semaphore (142m) north-east of here marks the highest point of the island; it cannot be visited.

Porquerolles' **vineyards**, covering 110 hectares on the western part of the island, are tended by three wine producers. Each offers *dégustation* (wine tasting) sessions of their predominantly rosé wines; the tourist office has a list.

Beaches
The island's northern coast is laced with white sandy beaches, including **Plage de la Courtade** signposted 800m east from the port (follow the track uphill behind the tourist office). **Plage de Notre-Dame**, Porquerolles' largest and most beautiful beach, is 2.5km farther east along the same track. **Plage d'Argent**, 2km west of the village, is popular with families because of its beachside café-restaurant and lifeguards in summer; walk along rue de la Ferme, then turn right and follow the signs to get here.

More secluded is the **Plage Blanche du Langoustier**, a former lobster farm 4.5km from the village on the northern shores of the Presqu'île du Langoustier. It is called 'white' beach in contrast to the black sand that darkens the peninsula's southern shores around Port Fay – the legacy of a 19th-century soda processing plant which produced potash and soda from sulphuric acid and sea salt between 1828 and 1876.

Cliffs line the island's more dangerous southern coast where swimming and diving is restricted to **Calanque du Brégançonnet** to the east and **Calanque de l'Oustaou de Dieu** (literally 'House of God') to the west. Both are accessible by bicycle or foot. Porquerolles Plongée (☎ 04 98 04 72 22, e info@porquerolles-plongee.com), at the port, organises **diving** courses and expeditions here.

Places to Stay & Eat
Porquerolles is expensive. It has no camp site and wild camping is forbidden. You can rent a *self-catering apartment* on a weekly basis through Agence Porquerolles Vacances Immobilier (☎ 04 94 14 00 05, ☎/fax 04 94 58 31 36, e porquerolles .vacances@wanadoo.fr), 1 rue de la Douane. Hotels mainly only accept guests on a half-board basis in July and August.

The island's cheapest hotel is cranky but cool *Relais de la Poste* (☎ 04 94 58 30 26, fax 04 94 58 33 57, e relaispost@aol.com, place d'Armes). Doubles with shower and toilet cost 450FF.

Hôtel-Résidence Les Mèdes (☎ 04 94 12 41 24, fax 04 94 58 32 49, e hotel-les-medes@wanadoo.fr, rue de la Douane) has modern rooms costing from 250/315/380FF per person in low/mid-/high season, and self-catering studios from 200/265/375FF per person/night (minimum two nights).

Reception staff at two-star *Hôtel Ste-Anne* (☎ 04 94 58 30 04, fax 04 94 58 32 92, e steanne.porquerolles@wanadoo.fr, place d'Armes) lend boules to guests keen to have a spin on the pétanque pitch; as do staff at *L'Oustaou de Porquerolles* (☎ 04 94 58 30 13, fax 04 94 58 34 93), on the opposite side of the square. Doubles at Ste-Anne start at 490/1010FF in low/high season, rates at L'Oustaou are slightly lower.

ST-TROPEZ TO TOULON

Charming *Auberge des Glycines* (☎ 04 94 58 30 36, fax 04 94 58 35 22, @ auberge .glycines@wanadoo.fr, place d'Armes) has comfortable doubles costing 490FF in low season (October to March) or starting at 590/790FF per person for half-board in mid-/high season. Its restaurant specialises in tasty *cuisine Porquerollaise* – lots of fish dishes.

Four-star *Mas du Langoustier* (☎ 04 94 58 30 09, fax 04 94 58 36 02, @ lagoustier@ compuserve.com) offers stunning views from its seaside perch on the island's south-western tip. Decadent doubles kick off at 1015/1083FF per person (half-board) in low/high season. Its restaurant is simply divine, darling.

Place d'Armes is armed with fruit stalls, a boucherie, charcuterie and boulangerie, enabling you to build that perfect picnic. *Cocci* supermarket at the port opens 8 am to 1 pm and 3.30 to 7 or 7.30 pm.

Getting There & Away

Le Pélican (☎ 04 94 58 31 19), based at the port, operates a morning and evening boat between Porquerolles and Port-Cros on Tuesday and Thursday in July and August.

Regular boats operated by TLV link La Tour Fondue near Hyères (see Boat Excursions under Hyères later in this chapter) with Porquerolles year round. From June to September, there is one boat daily to/from Toulon; three boats a week to/from St-Tropez; and to/from Le Lavandou (see Boat Excursions in those sections).

Boats operated by Vedettes Îles d'Or (☎ 04 94 00 45 76) sail from Port Miramar at La Londe, a small port town between Le Lavandou and Hyères Monday to Saturday in July and August. The same company operates boats from La Croix-Valmer and Cavalaire-sur-Mer in July and August too.

Getting Around

Two options: feet or wheels (motorised tourist vehicles forbidden). There are no less than nine bicycle rental outlets in the village, including La Meduse (☎ 04 94 58 34 27) and Chez Nanard (☎ 04 94 58 34 89) at the port. Both open 7 am to 6 or 7 pm,

March to September, and charge 75/60FF per day for an adult/child's bike. Energetic parents can hire covered buggies *(remorques)* to pedal the kids around the island for 75FF per day. In the village, Le Cycle Porquerollais (☎ 04 94 58 30 32), 1 rue de la Ferme, has all types of two-wheel contraptions, including tandems that cost 120/180FF per half-day/day.

Boat Locamarine 75 (☎ 04 94 58 35 84), opposite the tourist office at the port, rents speedboats (6cv without a licence) for 390/490FF per half-day/day for up to five people.

Le Pélican (☎ 04 94 58 31 19, 06 09 52 31 19) operates a 24-hour boat taxi service.

ÎLE DE BENDOR

The pinprick island of Bendor lies 300m off the shore from Bandol, 19km east of Toulon. The rocky islet – seven hectares large – was uninhabited until 1951 when Paul Ricard, best known for his pastis production, bought the isle and dramatically transformed it into one big leisure centre. The rock served as a place of exile during the 17th century.

Ricard's larger-than-life creations dominating the island include the **Espace Culturel Paul Ricard** (☎ 04 94 29 44 34), where art exhibitions are held; a **Palais des Congrès** (Congress Centre); and the **Exposition Universelle des Vins et Spiritueux**, in which the history and production of wine and spirits is unravelled. More than 8000 bottles from 52 countries are represented in the exhibition contained within the wildly painted, frescoed walls. Opening hours are 10 am to noon and 2 to 6 pm, Tuesday to Sunday. Admission is free.

Getting There & Away

Boats to Île de Bendor (☎ 04 94 29 44 34) depart from Bandol (see the Toulon section later) every half-hour between 7 and 2 am year round. Return boats from Île de Bendor leave every 30 minutes between 6.45 am and 1.45 am. A return ticket costs 28FF (children aged under 12, 18FF). Journey time is seven minutes. Services are reduced in winter.

ÎLES DES EMBIEZ

Bendor's big sister, the Embiez archipelago, sits less than a kilometre off the Presqu'île du Cap Sicié, between Sanary-sur-Mer and Toulon.

The largest of the islet cluster, officially Île de la Tour Fondue but better known as Île des Embiez, is also home to a Ricard creation: the **Institut Océanographique Paul Ricard** (☎ 04 94 34 02 49), in an old fort. Here over 100 Mediterranean species can be viewed close up in its 27 sea-water aquariums and marine museum. It opens 10 am to 12.30 pm and 1.30 to 5.30 pm (6.30 pm July and August); closed Saturday morning, September to April. Admission costs 25FF (children aged four to 11, 12FF).

The rest of Ricard's 95 hectare island, purchased in 1958, is occupied by a vast **pleasure port**, patches of pine forest and maquis scrub, apartment blocks, and a couple of expensive hotels.

Getting There & Away

Boats to the island leave year round from the quay at **Le Brusc**, a small beach resort adjoining Six-Fours-les-Plages, 5km south of Sanary-sur-Mer. In summer boats run about every 40 minutes between 6.40 am and midnight. From mid-November until mid-March, boats only run after 9.30 pm on Friday, Saturday and Sunday. From mid-March to mid-June and from mid-September to mid-November, daily boats stop running at 11.30 pm. A return fare costs 37FF (children aged three to 12, 27FF). Journey time is 12 minutes.

Between June and September, there are also boats to the island from the port at **Sanary-sur-Mer**. See Sanary-sur-Mer later in this chapter for details.

Toulon & Around

HYÈRES

postcode 83400 • pop 53,258

Relatively unspoilt coastline becomes increasingly urban as you head westwards to Toulon and Marseilles. The exception is Hyères (Iero in Provençal), which, with its age-old palm trees, retains a charm of its own.

Hyères was settled by Greeks from Marseilles in 350 BC, who named their colony Olbia (later renamed Pomponiana by the Romans). Tolstoy in the 1860s was followed by Robert Louis Stevenson in the 1880s, who lived in Hyères from 1883 and started work on *Kidnapped* (1886) in the town.

La Capte, 4km south of Hyères centre, comprises two narrow sand bars supporting salt pans (Les Salins des Presquiers) and a lake (Étang des Presquiers). Pink flamingos add a splash of colour to the otherwise barren landscape in mid-September. The spectacular, western sand bar – the route du Sel (Salt Road) – is only accessible in summer. Buses use the eastern bar road (D42), the northern section of which is lined with a silky smooth, two-lane cycling track that runs for 2km from the beach resort of **L'Ayguade** to the roundabout in front of Toulon-Hyères airport.

At the foot of La Capte sits beach-lined **Presqu'île de Giens**. French poet and 1960 Nobel Literature prize winner, St-John Perse (1887–1975) is buried in the tiny cemetery off route Madrague, on the Presqu'île's north-western shores.

Orientation

Hyères' medieval Vieille Ville (old town) is perched on a hillside north of the new town. The nearest beach is 4km south on La Capte. The pleasure port, Port d'Hyères, from where boats to Le Levant and Port-Cros depart, is on La Capte's eastern shore. Boats to Porquerolles depart from La Tour Fondue – the port on the south-eastern corner of Presqu'île de Giens.

Hyères train station, place de l'Europe, is 1.5km south of the old town centre. On foot, walk north-east from the station along ave Edith Cavelland to place du 11 Novembre, then head northwards along palm tree-lined ave Gambetta, the main street in the new town. Buses to the centre depart from rue de la Gare, opposite the train station. Buses to Port d'Hyères and La Tour Fondue leave from the place de l'Europe stop, immediately in front of the station.

ST-TROPEZ TO TOULON

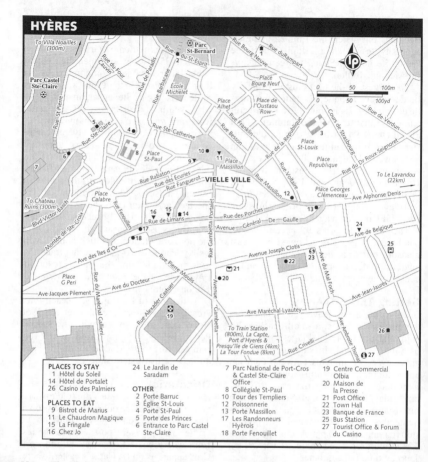

HYÈRES

PLACES TO STAY	24 Le Jardin de	7 Parc National de Port-Cros	19 Centre Commercial
1 Hôtel du Soleil	Saradam	& Castel Ste-Claire	Olbia
14 Hôtel de Portalet		Office	20 Maison de
26 Casino des Palmiers	**OTHER**	8 Collégiale St-Paul	la Presse
	2 Porte Barruc	10 Tour des Templiers	21 Post Office
PLACES TO EAT	3 Église St-Louis	12 Poissonnerie	22 Town Hall
9 Bistrot de Marius	4 Porte St-Paul	13 Porte Massillon	23 Banque de France
11 Le Chaudron Magique	5 Porte des Princes	17 Les Randonneurs	25 Bus Station
15 La Fringale	6 Entrance to Parc Castel	Hyèrois	27 Tourist Office & Forum
16 Chez Jo	Ste-Claire	18 Porte Fenouillet	du Casino

Maps The Maison de la Presse, 5 ave Gambetta, stocks an excellent range of maps and guides, many in English.

Information

Tourist Office Hyères tourist office (☎ 04 94 01 84 50, fax 04 94 01 84 51, e tourisme @provence-azur.com), 3 ave Ambroise Thomas, is inside Forum du Casino. It runs an accommodation reservation service (☎ 04 94 01 84 30, fax 04 94 01 84 31, e reservation @provence-azur.com) for the Hyères region and arranges guided tours. It opens 9 am to noon and 2 to 5.45 pm Monday to Saturday,

and has Web sites at www.ville-hyeres.fr and www.provence-azur.com.

Les Randonneurs Hyèrois (☎ 04 94 35 67 05, 04 94 41 66 18) is a local walking club with a small office on rue de Limans, open 3 to 6 pm Monday, and 10 am to noon Friday.

National Park Office The administration (☎ 04 94 12 82 30, fax 04 94 12 82 31, e port-cros@espaces-naturels.fr) of the Parc National de Port-Cros and Castel Ste-Claire, 50 rue Ste-Claire, opens 10 am to noon and 2 to 6 pm weekdays. Information can be found on the Web at www.parcs-nationaux.org.

Money Exchange hours at Banque de France, ave Joseph Clotis, are 8.30 to noon weekdays.

Post & Communications The post office, next to the town hall on ave Joseph Clotis, opens 8.30 am to 5.55 pm (4.55 pm on Wednesday) weekdays, and 8.30 to 11.55 am Saturday. It has Cyberposte.

Walking Tour

A Saturday morning market fills **place Georges Clémenceau** with a colourful jumble of second-hand furniture, floor tiles, shoes, handbags, marmalade spiced with lavender and the like. The 13th-century **Porte Massillon**, on the western side of the square, is the main entrance to the Vieille Ville. Walk westwards along cobbled rue Massillon to the beautifully arcaded **rue des Porches**.

North of the market square is 13th-century **Église St-Louis**, a fine example of sober, Romanesque-style architecture. Weave your way uphill to rue Bourg Neuf, then walk westwards along its continuation, rue St-Esprit, to the limestone arch of **Porte Barruc**. From here, steps pass an iron gate to the rambling hillside grove of the **Parc St-Bernard**. Remnants of the 12th-century defensive city wall and **Château St-Bernard** are visible.

Below the walls stands the imposing **Villa Noailles**, designed by Robert Mallet-Stevens in 1923 for Vicomte Charles de Noailles, a devoted patron of modern art. The architect's mission: to build a winter residence 'interesting to inhabit'. The result: a cubist maze of concrete and glass, set within a Mediterranean park designed by Noailles and featuring a cubist garden designed by Gabriel Guevrekian in 1925. Contemporary design exhibitions are held here in summer (free).

Heading back downhill along rue Barbacane, you come to the 12th-century **Porte St-Paul**, the first city gate to be built. It frames the **Collégiale St-Paul**, comprising

two churches dating from the 12th and 14th centuries joined together perpendicularly. The Gothic part houses a vast collection of predominantly 18th-century, ex-votive paintings. The oldest painting dates from 1613, the newest from 1997. From the terrace in front of the church, a marvellous panorama of old and new Hyères unfolds.

West of Porte St-Paul, rue St-Paul and rue Ste-Claire lead to the **Parc Castel Ste-Claire**, a 17th-century convent converted into a private residence. The American writer Edith Wharton lived here from 1927. Its grounds can be strolled through freely.

Boat Excursions

Boats, operated by Transport Littoral Varois (TLV) sail from Hyères to the three Îles d'Hyères year round. Visit online at www.tlv-tvm.com.

TLV boats to Porquerolles depart from the Gare Maritime de La Tour Fondue (☎ 04 94 58 21 81) on the Presqu'île de Giens. There are 13 to 21 boats daily from May to September (every 30 minutes between 7.30 am and 7 pm in July and August); and six to 10 daily boats the rest of the year. Sailing time is 20 minutes. A one-way/return ticket costs 48/83FF (children aged under four, free). Transporting an adult/child's bicycle costs 45/65FF. It is also possible to sail from La Tour Fondue to Porquerolles in a glass-bottomed catamaran (☎ 04 94 58 95 14) from April to September; there are two to four sailings daily and a return ticket costs 98FF (children aged four to 12, 64FF).

Three-island tours, kicking off in La Tour Fondue, are available between July and September. A three-island ticket, enabling you to visit Port-Cros and Le Levant from Porquerolles, costs 145FF (children aged four to 12, 85FF). Motorists have to pay 30FF per day to park at La Tour Fondue.

Boats to Île du Levant and Port-Cros leave Hyères from Port d'Hyères (also called Port de la Gavine; ☎ 04 94 57 44 07) on La Capte. There are two return sailings daily from Port d' Hyères to Île du Levant (1½ hours) between mid-March and June, and in September and October, stopping at

Port-Cros (one hour) en route. In July and August, five boats sail daily. One boat only sails on Monday, Wednesday, Friday and Saturday between January and mid-March (extra Sunday service in March). A return ticket to one of the two islands costs 120FF (children aged four to 12, 80FF); a combined ticket allowing passage to Le Levant and Port-Cros costs 140FF (children aged four to 12, 88FF).

Places to Stay

Camping There are no less than nine sites on Presqu'île de Giens. In Giens, *Camping Le Clair de Lune* (☎ 04 94 58 20 19, 27 ave du Clair de Lune) charges from 71FF for two people with car and tent; the site opens February to mid-November. *Camping La Bergerie* (☎ 04 94 58 91 75, fax 04 94 58 14 28, 4231 route de Giens) opens mid-February to January and charges 80FF for two people with a tent and car; buses to La Tour Fondue stop almost directly outside. Both sites are 300m from the sand.

Hotels Medieval Hyères' best hotel is two-star *Hôtel du Soleil* (☎ 04 94 65 16 26, fax 04 94 35 46 00, @ soleil@hotel-du-soleil.fr), an ivy-clad building at the top of very steep (read: not for the unfit) rue du Rampart. Singles/doubles/triples cost 190/220/370FF. Comfortably snug at the bottom of the hill is *Hôtel de Portalet* (☎ 04 94 65 39 40, fax 04 94 35 86 33, 4 rue de Limans). Large airy rooms with appealing age-old furnishings cost 160/170FF for a single/double (200/210FF with shower and toilet). Bathroom-equipped triples go for 320FF.

Top-notch in style is plush, glass-topped, 15-room *Casino des Palmiers* (☎ 04 94 12 80 80, fax 04 94 12 80 94, 1 rue Ambroise Thomas). Four-star doubles cost 490FF to 1090FF.

Places to Eat

Rue de Limans, rue Portalet and rue Massillon in the lower part of the Vieille Ville are lined with touristy places to eat. Particularly tasty is *Chez Jo* (☎ 04 94 65 31 13, 22 rue de Limans), a rustic place where you can eat well for around 80FF. Another stand-out eatery is *La Fringale* (☎ 04 94 35 42 52, 12 rue de Limans), a small bistro sporting a blue ceiling, modern paintings on its walls and fresh pasta/pizza dishes for no more than 50FF a shot.

Place Massillon is one big restaurant in summer. *Bistrot de Marius* (☎ 04 94 35 88 38), at No 1 on the square, specialises in fish dishes and has *menus* from 92FF. For a hearty plate of *aïoli Provençal complet* (a boiled egg, boiled potatoes, a mound of boiled vegetables, shellfish and a bowl of garlicky aïoli) lunch at *Le Chaudron Magique* (☎ 04 94 35 38 45) at No 8.

Opposite the bus station, *Le Jardin de Saradam* (☎ 04 94 65 97 53, 35 ave de Belgique) dishes up Mediterranean and oriental cuisine in a beautiful, flowerpot-filled garden. Its tajines (around 80FF) and couscous – eight varieties, costing 50FF to 150FF – are reputed to be the best in town.

A *fruit and veg market* fills the northern end of ave Gambetta on Saturday morning. In the old town, there is a *poissonnerie* (fishmonger) on rue Massillon.

Getting There & Away

Air Toulon-Hyères airport (☎ 04 94 00 83 83) is 3km south of Hyères centre towards La Capte, and 25km east of Toulon.

Bus From the bus station on place du Mal Joffre, SODETRAV (☎ 04 94 12 55 00) operates at least seven buses daily buses to/from Toulon (36FF, 40 minutes), Le Lavandou (25FF, 30 minutes) and St-Tropez (82FF, 1¼ hours).

Train From Hyères train station, place de l'Europe, there are numerous local trains to/from Toulon (78FF, 17 minutes). The Marseilles–Hyères train (72FF, 1¼ hours, four daily) stops at Cassis, La Ciotat, Bandol, Ollioules-Sanary and Toulon.

Getting Around

To/From the Airport SODETRAV operates a regular shuttle bus from Toulon-Hyères airport to Hyères bus station (25.50FF, 10 minutes). There are also regular daily services in summer along the coast to Toulon and St-Tropez via Le Lavandou. Buses coincide with flight arrivals/departures.

Bus Every 30 minutes, a bus links Hyères bus station with the train station (five minutes), Port d'Hyères (15 minutes), La Capte (20 minutes), Giens (30 minutes) and La Tour Fondue (35 minutes). A one-way ticket costs 10.50FF. Buses run 6.25 am to 10 pm.

For Port d'Hyères (boats to Îles du Levant and Port-Cros), get off at Le Port stop, ave de la Meditérranée. For Tour Fondue (boats to Porquerolles), get off at the Tour Fondue stop.

Bicycle Holiday Bikes (☎ 04 94 38 79 45), in the Centre Commercial Nautique at Port d'Hyères, rents mountain bikes/scooters from 70/200FF per day and rollerblades/scooters for 50/140FF per day. It opens 9 am to 12.30 pm and 3 to 7 pm.

TOULON
postcode 83000 • pop 166,442

Originally a Roman colony, Toulon (Touloun in Provençal) only became part of France in 1481; the city grew in importance after Henri IV established an arsenal here. In the 17th century the port was enlarged by Vauban. The young Napoleon Bonaparte first made a name for himself in 1793 during a siege in which the English, who had taken over Toulon, were expelled.

As in any large port, there's a lively quarter, close to the water, with heaps of bars, where locals and sailors spill out of every door. Women travelling on their own should avoid some of the old city streets at night, particularly around rue Chevalier Paul and the western end of rue Pierre Sémard.

A flea market fills place du Théâtre every Friday.

All in all, it's a city like no other on the Côte d'Azur, though it's unclear why anyone would want to spend much time here when pulsating Marseilles, fine beaches and the tranquil Îles d'Hyères are so close.

Orientation
Toulon is built around a *rade*, a sheltered bay lined with quays. Westwards is the

naval base and eastwards the ferry terminal, where boats set sail for Corsica. The city is at its liveliest along quai de la Sinse and quai Constradt – from where ferries depart for the Îles d'Hyères – and in the old city. Northwest of the old city is the train station.

Separating the old city from the northern section is a multilane, multinamed thoroughfare (known as ave du Maréchal Leclerc and blvd de Strasbourg as it runs through the centre), which teems with traffic. It continues westwards to Marseilles and eastwards to the French Riviera. Immediately north-west of here, off rue Chalucet, is a pleasant city park. Toulon's central square is enormous place de la Liberté.

Raimu, the great Provençal actor (see the Facts about Provence chapter), was born in a house at 6 rue Anatole France, off place d'Armes, just north of the arsenal building.

Information
Tourist Offices The tourist office (☎ 04 94 18 53 00, fax 04 94 18 53 09, 🖻 tourisme@wanadoo.fr), place Raimu, opens 9 am to 6 pm Monday to Saturday, and 10 am to noon Sunday. It arranges guided city tours on Saturday and Wednesday costing 20FF (those aged 12 to 18, 10FF), which should be booked in advance. Its Web site is at www.toulon.com (French only).

The Maison de l'Étudiant (☎ 04 94 93 14 21), rue de la Glacière, and the Bureau d'Information Jeunesse (☎ 04 94 09 09 79, 🖻 bijtoulon@wanadoo.fr), place Raimu, are handy information sources.

Money Banque de France, ave Vauban, opens 8.30 am to noon and 1.30 to 5.30 pm weekdays. Commercial banks line blvd de Strasbourg.

Post & Communications The post office, rue Dr Jean Bertholet, opens 8 am to 7 pm (6 pm on Tuesday) weekdays, and 8 am to noon Saturday. It has Cyberposte.

The Bureau d'Information Jeunesse (see Information above) charges 20FF per hour to access the Internet. Alternatively, surf at Computer Net Cybercafe (☎ 04 94 92 40 30, 🖻 computernet@free.fr), 4 rue Corneille,

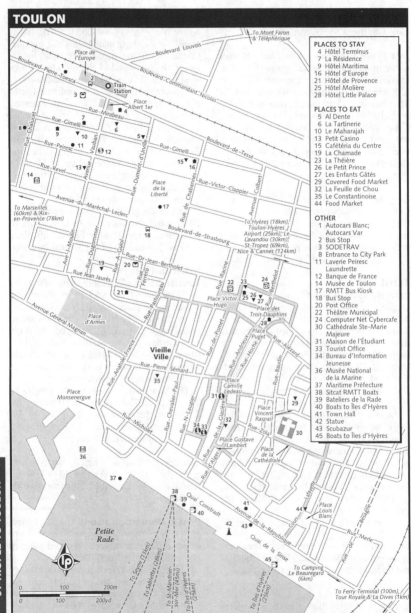

TOULON

PLACES TO STAY
4 Hôtel Terminus
7 La Résidence
9 Hôtel Maritima
16 Hôtel d'Europe
21 Hôtel de Provence
25 Hôtel Molière
28 Hôtel Little Palace

PLACES TO EAT
5 Al Dente
6 La Tartinerie
10 Le Maharajah
13 Petit Casino
15 Cafétéria du Centre
19 La Chamade
23 La Théière
26 Le Petit Prince
27 Les Enfants Gâtés
29 Covered Food Market
32 La Feuille de Chou
35 Le Constantinoise
44 Food Market

OTHER
1 Autocars Blanc;
   Autocars Var
2 Bus Stop
3 SODETRAV
8 Entrance to City Park
11 Laverie Peiresc
   Laundrette
12 Banque de France
14 Musée de Toulon
17 RMTT Bus Kiosk
18 Bus Stop
20 Post Office
22 Théâtre Municipal
24 Computer Net Cybercafe
30 Cathédrale Ste-Marie
   Majeure
31 Maison de l'Étudiant
33 Tourist Office
34 Bureau d'Information
   Jeunesse
36 Musée National
   de la Marine
37 Maritime Préfecture
38 Sitcat RMTT Boats
39 Bateliers de la Rade
40 Boats to Îles d'Hyères
41 Town Hall
42 Statue
43 Scubazur
45 Boats to Îles d'Hyères

ST-TROPEZ TO TOULON

euro currency converter 10FF = €1.52

open 10 am to noon and 2 to 7.30 pm Monday to Saturday (45FF per hour).

Travel Agencies Voyages Wasteels (☎ 08 03 88 70 28) has an office at 3 blvd Pierre Tosca.

Laundry Toulon has several laundrettes. Laverie Peiresc, 16 rue Peiresc, opens 7 am to 8.30 pm.

Musée de Toulon

Toulon Museum (☎ 04 94 36 81 00), 113 ave du Maréchal Leclerc, houses an unexceptional **Musée d'Art**, open 1 to 6 pm; and a moth-eaten **Musée d'Histoire Naturelle** in a Renaissance-style building, open 9.30 am to noon and 2 to 6 pm weekdays, and 1 to 6 pm weekends. Admission is free.

Musée National de la Marine

The National Marine Museum (☎ 04 94 02 02 01), in the lovely old arsenal building on place Monsenergue, opens 10 am to 6.30 pm, April to September; and 10 am to noon and 2 to 6 pm Wednesday to Monday, the rest of the year. Admission costs 29FF (students aged up to 25 and those aged eight to 18, 19FF).

Tour Royale & La Dives

The sturdy **Tour Royale** (Royal Tower) on the Pointe de la Mître in the suburb of Le Mourillon, just south of Toulon centre and the ferry terminal, was constructed under Louis XII at the start of the 16th century. A prison in the past, it is a small naval museum (☎ 04 94 02 17 99) today. It opens 10 am to 6.30 pm April to September; and 1.30 to 6 pm, school holidays only, the rest of the year. Admission is free. Views of the rade, Toulon and Mont Faron, from the top of the tower are quite breathtaking.

Next to the tower, the cumbersome **La Dives** (☎ 04 94 02 06 96), a 102m landing craft, in service between 1961 and 1986, can be visited by guided tour.

Mont Faron

Overlooking the old city from the north is Mont Faron (580m), from which you can see Toulon's port in its true magnificence. Near the hill's summit rises the **Mémorial du Débarquement** (☎ 04 94 88 08 09), which commemorates the Allied landings that took place along the coast here in August 1944. It can be visited between 9.45 and 11.45 am and 2 to 4.30 pm Tuesday to Sunday. Admission costs 25FF (those aged five to 16, 10FF).

A cable car (☎ 04 94 92 68 25) climbs the mountain from blvd Amiral Vence. It runs 9 am to noon and 2 to 5.30 pm Tuesday to Sunday. A return ticket costs 38FF (children aged four to 12, 26FF). If you intend visiting the **zoo** (☎ 04 94 88 07 89) here, buy a combination ticket costing 6FF (children 35FF). The zoo opens 10 am to 6 pm (closed on rainy days).

To get to the cable car, take bus No 40 from place de la Liberté to the téléphérique stop. It does not operate on windy days.

Boat Excursions

Excursions around the rade, with a commentary (French only) on the events that took place here during WWII, leave from quai Cronstadt or its continuation, quai de la Sinse. One-hour trips cost 50FF.

Between June and September, Bateliers de la Rade (☎ 04 94 46 24 65), quai de la Sinse, runs a daily boat to Îles d'Hyères (100FF return to Porquerolles; 150FF to Port-Cros; 160FF to Porquerolles, Port-Cros and Le Levant). The trip to Porquerolles takes one hour. It's another 40 minutes to Port-Cros, from where it is only a 20-minute hop to Île du Levant.

Between May and September, Compagnie de Navigation SNRTM (☎ 04 94 62 41 14), 1247 route du Faron and at the port, operates a boat to the three Îles d'Hyères on Wednesday (170FF return) and a boat to the Îles des Embiez and the Calanques near Marseilles on Tuesday (160FF return).

Sitcat boats (☎ 04 94 46 35 46) run by RMTT, the local transport company, link quai Cronstadt with the towns on the peninsula across the harbour, including La Seyne (line 8M), St-Mandrier-sur-Mer (line 28M) and Sablettes (line 18M). The 20-minute ride costs 8FF (10FF if you buy your ticket

ST-TROPEZ TO TOULON

aboard). The ticket office at the port opens 8 am to 12.15 pm and 2 to 5.15 pm weekdays. Boats run from around 6 am to 8 pm.

Scubazur, 334 ave de la République, is a first-class diving shop with information on diving clubs and schools on the Côte d'Azur.

Special Events

For nearly 50 years, Toulon has held an International Festival of Music (mainly classical) in various locations around town, including the Théâtre Municipal on place Victor Hugo, from June to early July.

Places to Stay

There are plenty of cheap options in the old city, though some (particularly those at the western end of rue Jean Jaurès) are said to double as brothels.

Opposite the train station is cheap and unsmiling *Hôtel Terminus* (☎ 04 94 89 23 54, 7 blvd de Tessé), which has singles with washbasin for 115FF and doubles with shower from 185FF. It flogs 59FF *menus* in its adjoining restaurant.

Another one, again close to the stations, is *La Résidence* (☎ 04 94 92 92 81, 18 rue Gimelli), a two-star pad with an impressive lobby, complete with its enormous gilt mirror and worn Oriental carpets. Rooms are not so grand, but still a steal at 120/130FF for singles/doubles (200FF with shower).

Hôtel Maritima (☎ 04 94 92 39 33, 9 rue Gimelli) has equally simple singles/doubles for 125/140FF (180/220FF for doubles with shower/shower and toilet).

Pleasant *Hôtel Little Palace* (☎ 04 94 92 26 62, fax 04 94 89 13 77, 6 rue Berthelot) has basic rooms for two, in the hub of things, costing 100/130/150/180FF with washbasin/shower/shower and TV/shower, TV and toilet.

Next to the opera, one-star *Hôtel Molière* (☎ 04 94 92 78 35, fax 04 94 62 85 82, 12 rue Molière) has no-frills singles/doubles costing 85/110FF (125/150FF with shower, 180/230FF with shower and toilet).

Dirt-cheap *Hôtel de Provence* (☎ 04 94 93 19 00, 53 rue Jean Jaurès) is often full,

despite its somewhat shady location near several sex shops. Rock-bottom singles/doubles with shared bathroom cost 135/145FF (155/165FF with shower, 180/120FF with shower and toilet). Triples/quads with shared facilities go for 205/240FF, while the lone traveller can plump for a bed in a room with strangers for 110FF.

East of the train station, *Hôtel d'Europe* (☎ 04 94 92 37 44, fax 04 94 62 37 50, 7 rue de Chabannes) has rooms for one or two, with shower and toilet, starting at 230FF. Photographs of each room are displayed in reception.

Places to Eat

Pricey restaurants, terraces and bars with occasional live music are abundant along the quays; count on paying at least 15.50FF for a soft drink or 80FF to 100FF for a tiny bouillabaisse or aïoli garni. Another lively area is place Victor Hugo and neighbouring place Puget. Cheaper fare can be found in the dilapidated streets around rue Chevalier Paul.

Restaurants A simple but absolutely charming bistro is *La Feuille de Chou* (☎ 04 94 62 09 26, 15 rue de la Glacière), complete with a peaceful terrace on olive tree-bespeckled place Eugene Baboulene. It serves an imaginative 55FF plat du jour and good-value three-course *formules*. Don't miss the framed beer mat collection adorning the interior walls.

Another contemporary spot is *Les Enfants Gâtés* (☎ 04 94 09 14 67, 7 rue Corneille). The Spoilt Children, as it's translated, is run by a young crowd and is a pleasant place to dine without breaking the bank. *Le Petit Prince* (10 rue de l'Humilité) is named after Antoine de St-Exupéry's children's book.

A more upmarket option is one-star *La Chamade* (☎ 04 94 92 28 58, 25 rue Comédie). Its handwritten 195FF *menu* features temptations such as foie gras, pan-fried in three types of vinegar, or chocolate soup with caramelised fruits and hot pistachio gateau. Reservations are required.

At the other extreme, male travellers can

euro currency converter 10FF = €1.52

share a hearty meal with menfolk at the humble Algerian restaurant *Le Constantinoise (rue Pierre Sémard)*, frequented exclusively by local men although friendly (male) outsiders are apparently welcomed. Couscous with salad costs goes for as little as 40FF.

La Théière, at the western end of rue Corneille, is a sparkling tea room and ice-cream parlour serving tasty salads (60FF) as well as sweet treats.

The train station area is loaded with tummy-filling options, including *Al Dente (☎ 04 94 93 02 50, 15 rue Gimelli)*, a cool and elegant Italian place serving 11 types of fresh pasta for 50FF a throw, various salads and 60/106FF lunch/evening *menus*. Nearby, *Le Maharajah (☎ 04 94 91 93 46, 15 rue Gimelli)* is an Indian eatery with a spicy plat/menu du jour for 49/60FF and a 129FF *menu*.

Cafétéria du Centre (☎ 04 94 92 68 57, 27–29 rue Gimelli and 4–8 rue de Chabannes) serves cheap three-course *menus* (39.50FF) from 11 am to 2.30 pm and 6.30 to 10 pm Monday to Saturday.

Self-Catering The southern half of cours Lafayette is one long *food market* held, in typical Provençal style, under the plane trees. There's a covered *food market* on place Vincent Raspail. Both open Tuesday to Sunday.

Near the station, *La Tartinerie (21 rue Mirabeau)* serves sandwiches, salads and 25FF coffee-and-cake deal. There's a *Petit Casino* supermarket at 7 ave Vauban.

Getting There & Away

Air Toulon-Hyères airport (Aéroport de Toulon-Hyères; ☎ 04 94 00 83 83) is 25km east of Toulon.

Bus Intercity buses leave from the bus terminal on place de l'Europe, to the right as you exit the train station. SODETRAV (☎ 04 94 28 93 40), 4 blvd Pierre Toesca, operates buses along the coast; while Autocars Blanc and Autocars Var (☎ 04 94 09 15 49) – in a kiosk a little farther west along blvd Pierre Toesca – run buses inland. Both

open 8 am to noon and 2 to 6 pm weekdays. Buy tickets here or on the bus.

Bus No 103 to Hyères (36FF, 40 minutes, seven daily) continues eastwards along the coast, stopping at Le Lavandou (62FF, 1¼ hours) and other towns, before arriving in St-Tropez (97FF, 2¼ hours). AutoCars Blanc (☎ 04 94 69 08 28 in Brignoles) operates six buses daily to/from Brignoles (48FF, 1½ hours) and St-Maximin (48.50FF, 1¾ hours). Services to Draguignan (58FF, 1¼ hours) are handled by Autocars Vars.

Francelignes (☎ 04 91 61 83 27 in Marseilles) runs four daily buses (two on Sunday in July and August) to Aix-en-Provence (88/134FF one-way/return, one hour). Phocéens Cars (☎ 04 93 85 66 61 in Nice) operates two buses daily to/from Nice (132FF, 2½ hours) via Hyères and Cannes.

Train The train station, place de l'Europe, fronts blvd Pierre Toesca. The information office opens 6.34 am to 7 pm Monday to Thursday and Saturday, 6.34 am to 8.45 pm Friday, and 6.34 am to 8.15 pm on Sunday.

There are frequent connections to numerous coastal cities, including Marseilles (78FF, 40 minutes), St-Raphaël (96FF, 50 minutes, hourly), Cannes, Antibes, Nice (134FF, 1½ hours, hourly), Monaco and Menton; as well as inland trains to/from Avignon, Nîmes and Arles.

Boat Ferries to Corsica and Sardinia are run by the SNCM (☎ 04 94 16 66 66), which has an office at 49 ave de l'Infanterie de Marine (opposite the ferry terminal). For more information see the Getting There & Away chapter.

For information on boats to the Îles d'Hyères see Boat Excursions earlier in this chapter.

Getting Around

To/From the Airport SODETRAV (☎ 04 94 12 55 00 in Hyères) operates shuttle buses from Toulon-Hyères airport to Toulon train station (58FF, 35 minutes), via Hyères (25.50FF, 10 minutes). Buses coincide with flight arrivals/departures. Tickets are sold on the bus.

ST-TROPEZ TO TOULON

Bus Local buses are run by RMTT (☎ 04 94 03 87 03), which has an information kiosk at the main local bus hub on place de la Liberté. It opens 7.30 am to noon and 1.30 to 6.30 pm weekdays. A single ticket/10-ticket carnet costs 8/54FF and a one-day/week pass, allowing unlimited travel, costs 20/55FF. Buses run until around 8 pm. Sunday service is limited.

TOWARDS MARSEILLES

Heading towards Marseilles from Toulon, there are a couple of spots worth a stop. Sanary-sur-Mer is as serene as its name suggests; Bandol is best known for its wines; while inland, the Circuit du Castellet is strictly for wannabe boy racers.

Sanary-sur-Mer
postcode 83110 • pop 17,177
This quiet seaside resort, 15km east of Toulon, was home to novelist Aldous Huxley (1894–1963) in the early 1930s, his biographer Sybille Bedford in the late 1930s, and to a host of German refugees very soon after. Thomas Mann and his brother, Heinrich, both sought refuge here, as did the German painter Feuchtwanger.

Its sandy beaches are packed in summer. Sanary-sur-Mer (Sanari in Provençal) is 6km north of La Brusc, from where boats depart to the Îles des Embiez (see that section earlier in this chapter). SMS (☎ 04 94 07 69 89) operates boats from Sanary to Île des Embiez between June and September; a return costs 45FF (children aged under 10, 25FF; 15 minutes; four boats daily in summer, two boats daily, Friday to Sunday, in winter). The tourist office in Sanary (☎ 04 94 74 01 04), Jardin de la Ville, has details.

Bandol
postcode 83150 • pop 7975
In the 1900s, Bandol (Bandòu in Provençal), 8km west of Sanary-sur-Mer (postcode 83110, pop 17,117) was a refuge for ailing foreigners such as novelists DH Lawrence and Katherine Mansfield. Today it is better known for its viticulture, an industry that is far from ailing. The terraced vineyards stretching for about 15km inland from the coast (as far north as St-Anne du Castellet) are managed by 50 wine producers who have sold their wine under their own coveted AOC since 1941.

The Association Les Vins de Bandol (☎ 04 94 90 29 59), Espace Mistral, 2 ave St-Louis, in Le Beausset, 10km north of Bandol, has a complete list of all the producers. Most allow you to visit their wine cellars to taste their wine. Alternatively, contact Bandol tourist office (☎ 04 94 29 41 35, @ otbandol@bandol.org), opposite the port on allées Vivien and online at www.bandol.org; or its counterpart 17km west along the coast in Les Lecques (☎ 04 94 26 73 73), place de l'Appel du 18 Juin. The latter takes bookings for a **Wine Train** that takes passengers on day trips through AOC Bandol vineyards, stopping en route at wineries to taste and buy. The train departs from Port des Lecques at 9 am on Tuesday and Saturday (returning at 6 pm); tickets cost 220FF per person.

From Bandol port, boats run year round to Île de Bendor.

Circuit du Castellet
The calm and tranquillity that caresses the northern realms of the Bandol vineyards around the perched village of **Le Castellet** (pop 3839, elevation 252m) is smashed with racy aplomb at the **Circuit du Castellet**, a motorsports race track built by industrialist Paul Ricard in 1970 and sold to Formula One racing magnate Bernie Ecclestone in mid-1999. The 5.8km circuit hosts the Grand Prix de France Moto in July, the Bol d'Or in mid-September (see Spectator Sports in the Facts for the Visitor chapter) and could well see the French Grand Prix scream round its track in 2002.

Monaco

postcode 98000 • pop 30,000

The tiny Principality of Monaco has been under the rule of the Grimaldi family for most of the period since 1297. It is a sovereign state, whose territory, surrounded by France, covers just 1.95 sq km.

Since 1949 Monaco has been ruled by Prince Rainier III, whose sweeping constitutional powers make him much more then a mere figurehead. For decades, the family has been featured on the front pages of tabloids, though since the death of the much-loved Princess Grace (best remembered from her Hollywood days as the actress Grace Kelly) in 1982, the media has concentrated on the far-from-fairytale love lives of the couple's two daughters, Caroline and Stephanie, and their ageing bachelor son, Albert.

Glamorous Monte Carlo – Monaco's capital – is famed for its casino and its role as host to the annual Formula One (F1) Monaco Grand Prix, which sees drivers tear round a track that winds through the town and around the port. Unsurpassable views of the race, the principality and its legendary skyscraper skyline – the 'Hong Kong' of Europe – can be enjoyed from Monaco's Musée Océanographique's terrace restaurant and the Trophée d'Auguste' in La Turbie, France (see the Nice to Menton chapter).

Citizens of Monaco (known as Monégasques), of whom there are only about 5000, do not pay any taxes. They have their own flag (red and white), national anthem and national holiday (19 November), country telephone code (377) and traditional dialect, Monégasque – broadly speaking a mixture of French and Italian – which is taught in schools alongside French, Monaco's official language. Many of the street signs are bilingual. The official religion is Roman Catholicism. There are no border formalities upon entering Monaco from France. The principality was admitted to the UN as a full member in 1993.

Highlights

- See the changing of the guard at Monaco palace
- Gape at the glamorous yachts moored in the port
- Discover the underwater world at the Musée Océanographique
- Window-shop or shop till you drop in Monte Carlo
- Indulge in a night at the opera or a flutter at Monte Carlo Casino
- Dine a la Ducasse at Bar & Bœuf, then go dancing at Jimmy'z

ITALY

Monaco p380-1

Mediterranean Sea

By law, it is forbidden to walk around town barechested, barefooted or bikini-clad.

HISTORY

Monoïkos (Monaco) was settled by the Greeks in the 4th century and later by the Romans. In 1297, François Grimaldi entered Monaco disguised as a monk and seized the fortress, marking the start of Grimaldi rule. In 1346 the family purchased Menton and Roquebrune to add to their territory.

MONACO

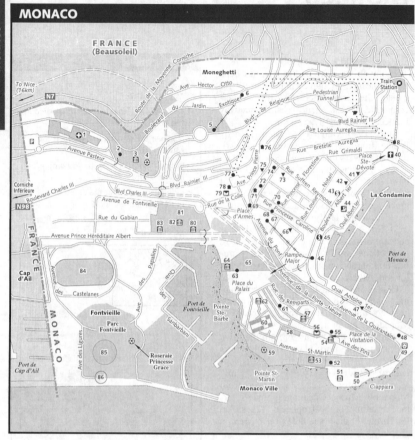

Monégasque independence was first recognised in 1489 by Charles VIII, king of France. Monaco fell under Spanish protectorship from 1525 until 1641, when the French drove out the Spanish and established their own alliance with the principality instead. During the French Revolution, Monaco was seized by France and the Monégasque royal family were arrested. Their palace was turned into a warehouse and their land renamed Fort Hercule.

Under the 1814 Treaty of Paris the Grimaldi family was restored to the throne. In 1860 Monégasque independence was recognised for a second time by France and consolidated a year later when Monaco relinquished all claims over its former territories of Menton and Roquebrune which it had lost in 1848. A customs and monetary union agreement was signed with France in 1865, sealing future cooperation between the two countries.

Monaco's absolute monarchy was replaced in 1911 by a constitution, reformed by Rainier III in 1962. The ruling prince is assisted by a national council comprising 18 democratically elected members. Only Monégasques aged 21 or over can vote in

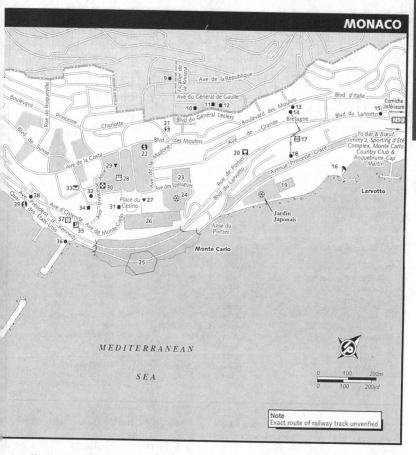

council elections, held every five years; Monégasque nationality is only granted to people born in Monaco or of Monégasque parentage.

ORIENTATION

Monaco consists of five principal areas: Monaco Ville (also known as the old city or Le Rocher), a 60m-high outcrop of rock 800m long on the southern side of the Port de Monaco where the Palais du Prince (Prince's Palace) is; Monte Carlo, famous for its casino and annual Grand Prix, which is north of the port; La Condamine, the flat

area south-west of the port; Fontvieille, the industrial area south of Monaco Ville; and Larvotto, the beach area east of Monte Carlo. The French town of Beausoleil is three streets up the hill from Monte Carlo.

INFORMATION
Tourist Offices

The national tourist office (☎ 377-92 16 61 16, fax 377-92 16 60 00, e dtc@monaco-congres.com), 2a blvd des Moulins, opens 9 am to 7 pm Monday to Saturday, and 10 am to noon on Sunday. From mid-June to mid-September, it operates a tourist information

MONACO

MONACO

PLACES TO STAY
10 Hôtel Diana
11 Hôtel Olympia
12 Hôtel Cosmopolite
31 Hôtel de Paris; Le Louis XV
34 Hôtel Hermitage
69 Hôtel Le Versailles
71 Hôtel Cosmopolite; Hôtel de France; Hall de la Presse
76 Centre de la Jeunesse Princesse Stéphanie
78 Hôtel Terminus

PLACES TO EAT
27 Café de Paris
29 Haagen-Däz
41 Caves & Gourmandises
42 Casino Supermarket
47 Stars 'n' Bars
66 La Cigale
73 Le Texan
75 Restaurant de Trende

OTHER
1 Centre Hospitalier Princess Grace
2 Public Lift
3 Musée d'Anthropologie Préhistorique
4 Jardin Exotique
5 Public Lift
6 Public Lift
7 Public Lift
8 Public Lift
9 Laundrette
13 Divina & Co

14 Public Lift
15 Public Lift
16 Plage du Larvotto
17 Musée National
18 Public Lift
19 Grimaldi Forum
20 McCarthy's Irish Pub
21 American Express
22 National Tourist Office
23 Centre Commercial Le Métropole
24 Jardins du Casino
25 Centre de Congrès Auditorium
26 Monte Carlo Casino; Salle Garnier
28 Cinéma Le Sporting
30 Entrance to Galerie du Sporting
32 Square Beaumarchais
33 Post Office
35 Les Thermes Marins
36 Les Bateaux de la French Riviera
37 Théâtre Princesse Grace
38 CAM Office
39 Tourist Office Kiosk
40 Église Ste-Dévote
43 Barclays Bank
44 Stade Nautique Rainier III
45 Tourist Office Kiosk
46 Public Lift
48 Yacht Club de Monaco
49 Théâtre du Fort Antoine
50 Parking des Pêcheurs
51 Monte Carlo Story

52 Escalator to Monte Carlo Story
53 Musée Océanographique
54 Musée de la Chapelle de la Visitation
55 Ministère d'Etat
56 Post Office
57 Musée de Cires
58 Town Hall
59 Jardins St-Martin
60 Cathédrale De Monaco
61 Princess Grace Irish Library
62 Musée de Vieux Monaco
63 State Apartments
64 Musée des Souvenirs Napoléoniens
65 Palais du Prince
67 Public Lift
68 MBK-Auto Moto Garage
70 Scruples
72 Galerie Riccadonna
74 Boutique Formule 1
77 Entrance to Train Station
79 Post Office
80 Musée des Timbres et des Monnaies
81 Centre Commercial de Fontvieille
82 Collection de Voitures Anciennes
83 Musée Naval
84 Stade Louis II
85 Espace Fontvieille
86 Monaco Heliport

kiosk at the train station, next to the Jardin Exotique, on blvd Albert 1er and on quai des États-Unis overlooking the port.

The tourist office has a Web site at www.monaco-congres.com. Monaco Online at www.monaco.mc is another useful site.

Money

Monaco uses the French franc. Both French and Monégasque franc coins are in circulation, but the latter are hard to find inside the principality and not accepted outside of it. Monaco will trade in its Monégasque franc for the euro from 2002 onwards (see the boxed text 'Euroland' in the Facts for the Visitor chapter).

In Monte Carlo there are numerous banks in the vicinity of the casino. American Express (☎ 377-97 70 77 59), 35 blvd Princesse Charlotte, opens 9 am to noon and 2 to 6 pm Monday to Saturday. Barclays Bank has several branches dotted around the principality: the branch at 17 Blvd Albert 1er has a 24-hour currency exchange outside.

Post

Monégasque stamps are only valid for letters sent within Monaco. Postal rates are the same as those in France. Contrary to France's yellow post boxes, Monaco's are red.

The main post office is in Monte Carlo,

inside Palais de la Scala at 1 ave Henri Dunant. It opens 8 am to 7 pm on weekdays, and 8 am to noon on Saturday. The branch office next to the train station (tucked down the steps to the side of Hôtel Terminus) opens the same hours.

Telephone

Telephone numbers in Monaco only have eight digits. Calls between Monaco and the rest of France are treated as international calls. Dial ☎ 00 followed by Monaco's country code, 377, when calling Monaco from the rest of France or abroad. To call France from Monaco, dial ☎ 00 and France's country code, 33. This applies even if you are only making a call from the eastern side of blvd de France (in Monaco) to its western side (in France)!

Monaco's public telephones accept Monégasque or French phonecards.

Email & Internet Access

The cybercorner inside Stars 'n' Bars (e info@starsnbars.com), 6 quai Antoine 1er, opens 10 am to midnight. Online access costs 40FF for 30 minutes.

Radio

French- and Italian-language Radio Monte Carlo (RMC) transmits from antennas on the Plateau de Fontbonne and the Col de la Madone and attracts a nationwide audience (0.9 million listeners). It can be picked up in Monaco on 98.8MHz FM.

Monte Carlo-based Riviera Radio can be reached in Monaco on 106.3MHz FM.

Bookshops

Scruples (☎ 93 50 43 52), 9 rue Princesse Caroline, is an English-language bookshop open 9 am to 12.30 pm and 2.30 to 7 pm Monday to Saturday.

An unsurpassable choice of English- and other foreign-language newspapers are sold at Hall de la Presse (☎ 93 30 16 71), 1 bis rue Grimaldi, open 6 am to 7.30 pm.

Libraries

The Princess Grace Irish Library (☎ 93 50 12 25, e pglib@monaco.mc), 9 rue Princesse

Marie de Lorraine, opens 9 am to 4 pm on weekdays. Grace Kelly's grandparents hailed from Drimurla in county Mayo, Ireland, a remote spot visited by Kelly and Rainier in 1961.

The English Library, 22 ave Grande Bretagne, opens 10 am to noon and 4 to 6 pm Wednesday.

Laundry

In Beausoleil, the laundrette at 1 Escalier de la Riviéra opens 7 am to 9 pm.

MONACO VILLE

Poetically named Le Rocher (The Rock) to reflect its geographical location, Monaco Ville is home to the state's most alluring sights.

Musée Océanographique

The world-renowned Musée Océanographique de Monaco (☎ 93 15 36 00, e rela@ oceano.org), ave St-Martin, has to be seen to be believed. It was founded in 1910 by Prince Albert I (1848–1922) who had set up an oceanographic institute for marine science here in 1906. An exhibition hall was added to display his collection of oceanographic finds acquired during his seafaring career. Today, it houses 90 tanks and 4500 fish (450 different species) in an underground aquarium through which 250,000 litres of fresh sea water are pumped daily, a zoological hall dominated by a 20m-long whale skeleton, and various exhibits on ocean exploration. Since November 2000 visitors have been able to view a coral reef at close quarters – from either side, or on top of, the 7.5m long and 5.9m tall glass tank that the spectacular reef is ensnared.

Its ornate interior, which features fanciful seabird-shaped chandeliers, monumental staircases, mosaic floors, and oak door frames carved into marine-inspired shapes such as the effigy of Neptune, is like no other. Beautiful views of Monaco and the French and Italian Rivieras are on offer from the terrace restaurant.

The museum opens 9 am to 7 pm, April to September; and 10 am to 6 pm, the rest of the year. Admission costs 70FF (students and children aged six to 12, 35FF). Detailed explanatory captions in the museum are in English; audioguides to the aquarium cost 20FF to hire.

Bus Nos 1 and 2 from place d'Armes are the alternatives to a relatively long walk up the hill. The train stop for the Azur Express tourist train is opposite the museum entrance. Tickets for the 35-minute city tour cost 37FF (children aged under five, free).

Monte Carlo Story

The horribly tacky Monte Carlo Story (☎ 93 25 32 33, ⓔ mcstory@cyber-monaco.mc) is underground and can be reached by an escalator opposite the Musée Océanographique. The soap-opera-style 30-minute film, screened in six languages, recalls the history of the Grimaldi dynasty. Admission, which includes entrance to a display of cinematic posters featuring Monte Carlo through the ages, costs 38FF (students 30FF; children aged six to 14, 20FF). The museum opens 11 am to 5 or 6 pm, March to October; and 2 to 5 pm the rest of the year.

Reclining gracefully next to both museums are the coastal **Jardins St-Martin**. The statue-studded gardens are open from

---

The Grimaldi Dynasty

The House of Grimaldi has ruled 'The Rock' with a golden fist since 1297 when François Grimaldi, disguised as a monk, sneaked through the city gates and claimed it as his own. The dynasty almost died in 1731 when Antoine I failed to produce a male heir. His daughter stepped in as queen, retaining her Grimaldi name to ensure the dynasty's survival.

Two centuries on, pioneering Prince Charles III (1818–89) gave the poverty-stricken state independence, followed in 1865 by the casino and its accompanying million-dollar fortune. His successor, seafaring Prince Albert I (1848–1922), preferred marine biology to money-making playgrounds and devoted his life to oceanographic research. In 1873 he sailed around the Mediterranean and the Atlantic to the Azores in a 200-tonne sailing boat.

Reigning monarch, Rainier III (1923) succeeded his grandfather Prince Louis II to the throne in 1949. Monaco's longest ruling monarch won the heart of a nation with his fairytale marriage to Grace Kelly in 1956. The legendary Philadelphia-born actress had made 11 films in the 1950s, including Hitchcock's *Dial M for Murder* (1954), *Rear Window* (1954), and *To Catch a Thief* (1955) in which she starred as the quintessential cool blonde on the coast. The movie took Kelly to Cannes, then to the Monégasque palace to attend a *Paris Match* photo shoot with Rainier. One year later Monaco's prince charming wed Hollywood's movie queen. The princess made no more films. She died in a car crash in 1982.

The love lives of the couple's three children – Caroline, Albert and Stephanie, born 1957, 1958 and 1965 respectively – take centre stage today. Princess Caroline was widowed in 1990 when her second husband (her marriage to the first was annulled), and father of her three children, was killed in a speedboat accident. On her 42nd birthday, she wed Prince Ernst of Hanover, a cousin to Britain's Queen Elizabeth. Eight lone guests attended the civil ceremony, which took place secretly.

In 1995 Princess Stephanie wed her bodyguard and divorced him a year later after photographs of him frolicking by a pool with a Belgian stripper were published in Italian magazines. In July 1998, she gave birth to baby Camille Grimaldi, her third child (father unnamed). During the 1980s and early 1990s the entrepreneurial princess launched her own swimwear label – ironically called Pool Position – and released three albums and a flurry of pop singles, including *Ouragan* (Hurricane), *How can it be?* and *I am waiting for you*.

The *Bal de la Rose* (Rose Ball in May), the *Bal de l'Été* (Summer Ball) organised for Europe's jet-setting uppercrust, fundraising *Gala de la Croix Rouge* (Red Cross Ball) and the Gala Ball, hosted by the charitable Princess Grace Foundation, are Monaco's key society events. They afford a rare glimpse of the House of Grimaldi in a fairytale spotlight. Tickets cost around US$1000 per head.

MONACO

7 am to 6 pm (to 8 pm from April to September).

Palais du Prince

The **changing of the guard** at the Prince's Palace takes place daily, on place du Palais at the southern end of rue des Remparts, at precisely 11.55 am. The guards of the Compagnie des Carabiniers du Prince, who carry out their state duties in smart dress uniform (white in summer, black in winter), appear resigned to the comic-opera nature of their duties. Even more comic are the acrobatic antics among the huge crowd that gathers to watch the whole affair. If the Grimaldi standard is flying from the top of the palace tower, it means Prince Rainier is at home.

The palace (☎ 93 25 18 31), with its Renaissance facade , was built on the site of a 13th-century Genoese fortress, later fortified by Vauban. A tour of the **state apartments** allows visitors a glimpse of its interior grandeur, including the 16th- and 17th-century frescoes depicting mythological scenes in the Galerie d'Hercule. You can visit the **palace apartments** between 9.30 am and 6.30 pm, June to September; 10 am to 5 pm in October; and 10.30 am to 12.30 pm and 2 to 5 pm, the rest of the year. Obligatory guided tours (35 to 40 minutes) in English leave every 15 or 20 minutes; be prepared to queue for up to 45 minutes in July and August just to get in. Admission costs 30FF (children aged eight to 14, 15FF).

The palace's southern wing houses the **Musée des Souvenirs Napoléoniens et Archives Historiques du Palais** (Museum of Napoleonic Souvenirs & Historical Palace Archives). Its displays include some of Napoleon's personal effects (handkerchiefs, a sock etc) and a fascinating collection of the type of bric-a-brac (medals, coins, uniforms swords,), collected by princely dynasties over the centuries. It opens the same hours as Palais du Prince. Admission costs 20FF (children aged eight to 14, 10FF). A ticket for both sights costs 40FF (reduced 20FF).

Cathédrale de Monaco

The unspectacular Romanesque-Byzantine cathedral (1875), 4 rue Colonel, has one draw: the grave of legendary Hollywood star Grace Patricia Kelly (1929–82). Her plain, modest tombstone lies on the western side of the cathedral choir. It is inscribed with the Latin words *Gratia Patricia Principis Rainerii III* and is heavily adorned with flowers. The remains of other members of the royal family, buried in the church crypt since 1885, today rest behind Princess Grace's grave.

Between September and June, Sunday Mass in the cathedral (☎ 93 30 87 70) is celebrated at 10 am. Mass is sung by Les Petits Chanteurs de Monaco – Monaco's boys choir. Between July and October free evening organ recitals are occasionally held here.

Other Museums

Life-sized wax figures capture 24 snapshots from the history of the Grimaldi dynasty in the **Musée de Cires** (Wax Museum; ☎ 93 30 39 05), 27 rue Basse, open 9.30 am to 6 pm, February to September; and 10 am to 4 pm the rest of the year. Admission costs 22FF (children aged six to 12, 12FF).

The private art collection of Piasecka Johnson is showcased in a 17th-century Baroque chapel at the enchanting **Musée de la Chapelle de la Visitation** (☎ 93 50 07 00), place de la Visitation, open 10 am to 4 pm Tuesday to Sunday. Admission costs 20FF (students, seniors aged over 65 and children aged six to 14, 10FF).

Monte Carlo

In the 1850s, Monaco was the poorest state in Europe. Its luck changed with the opening of **Monte Carlo Casino** – Europe's first – in 1865. The rather dull-sounding Plateau des Sélugues on which it stood was renamed Monte Carlo (the Liguan translation of 'Mont Charles' after Charles III) in 1866 and within months it ranked as one of Europe's most glamorous playgrounds.

Monte Carlo's alluring face is captured in a series of black-and-white photographs, posted behind glass on information boards in the floral gardens on place du Casino. The series, entitled *Monte Carlo Célébrissime*, features shots of Monte Carlo's celebrated guests from 1900 through to 1999: Puccino

Loser Risks All

The beautiful *belle epoque* decor of Monte Carlo Casino – Europe's oldest – is as extravagant as those who play in it. It went up in several phases, the earliest being the **Salon de l'Europe**, built in 1865 and splendidly lit with eight bohemian crystal chandeliers from 1898. Each weighs 150kg. The second phase saw French architect Charles Garnier, who'd just completed Paris' opera house, move to Monte Carlo to create the luxurious fresco-adorned **Salle Garnier** in 1878. The **atrium** – the main entrance hall with its 28 marble columns and flurry of gamblers and voyeurs – opened the same year. The third part, the **Salle Empire**, was completed in 1910.

Monte Carlo Casino remains in the hands of its founding owners, the Société des Bains de Mer (SBM; Sea Bathing Society) established by French entrepreneur François Blanc in 1863. Original shareholders included Monaco's Prince Charles III who held a 10% stake. Indeed, the state remains the leading shareholder today. In 1875, when the Prince and Princess of Wales visited, around 150,000 players per day were frequenting the casino. Shotgun suicides hot on the heels of a heavy loss at the gaming tables were common well into the 1920s. When Charles Deville Wells broke the bank in 1891 – the first and last to do so – gaming tables were draped in black for three days.

Despite an initial drop in revenue in 1933 following the legalisation of the roulette wheel in neighbouring France, Monte Carlo Casino continues to rake it in. The SBM is Monaco's largest corporation, owning all the principality's upmarket hotels and restaurants. Annual sales in 1997 totalled 1.78 billion FF. Income from gambling accounts for 4.31% of Monaco's total state revenue, although it used to account for most of the government's budget.

(1903), Anna Pavlova (1909), Frank Sinatra and Roger Moore (1980), Michael Jackson (1996), Laetitia Casta (1999)...

The colourful geometrical mosaic entitled *Hexa Grace* (1975), which adorns the roof of the Centre de Congrès Auditorium, is a Vasarely creation – best viewed from the skies. From Monte Carlo a **coastal path** (two to three hours) leads to Roquebrune-Cap Martin.

Casino

The drama of watching people risk all (or, at the very least, shedloads of money) in Monte Carlo's spectacularly ornate casino (☎ 92 96 20 00) makes visiting the gaming rooms almost worth the stiff admission fees. These are 50/120/250/350FF for a day/week/month/year pass into the Salon Ordinaire, which has European roulette and trente et quarante, and 100FF for the Salons Privés, which offer baccarat, chemin de fer, craps, English roulette and so on. Flutterers accustomed to different rules should ask for a copy of the English-language brochure entitled *European Games*.

To enter the casino, you must be aged at least 21 (you have to show a piece of ID irrespective of age). Short shorts (but not short skirts) are forbidden in the Salon Ordinaire (opens noon). For the Salons Privés (opens 4 pm), men must wear a jacket and tie. The *appareils automatiques* (one-armed bandits and other cheap-thrill devices; opens 2 pm), tucked to the right as you enter the main reception, do not command an entrance fee or dress code.

Jardin Japonais & Grimaldi Forum

Sandwiched between the built-up quarters of Monte Carlo, Larvotto and the Mediterranean, this Japanese garden is intended as an enchanting piece of paradise. It was blessed by a Shinto high priest; quiet contemplation and meditation is encouraged in the peaceful Zen garden, accessible from ave Princesse Grace and open 9 am to dusk.

Exit the garden through its eastern gate to get to the **Grimaldi Forum** (☎ 99 99 20 00, **e** gf@grimaldiforum.cm), 10 ave Princesse Grace, Monaco's congress and conference centre that hosts occasional contemporary art exhibitions – always eclectic and well worth seeing. All the more astonishing is the gigantic glass edifice itself, two-thirds of which is submerged below sea level. It opened in July 2000.

Musée National

In a sumptuous Garnier-designed villa, Monaco's National Museum (☎ 93 30 91 26), 17 ave Princesse Grace, contains a fascinating collection of 18th- and 19th-century *poupées* (dolls) and mechanical toys made in Paris. Around 250 figurines nestle in the 18th-century *crèche* (crib scene), originating from Naples.

The museum opens 10 am to 6.30 pm, Easter to September; and 10 am to 12.15 pm and 2.30 to 6.30 pm, the rest of the year. Admission costs 30FF (students and children aged six to 14, 20FF).

FONTVIEILLE

Adjoining Cap d'Ail in neighbouring France, Fontvieille covers the westernmost part of Monaco. From here a 3.5km **coastal path** leads west to Cap d'Ail. The lush gardens of **Parc Fontvieille** are equally pleasant for a summer stroll; over 4000 rose bushes adorn the **Roseraie Princesse Grace** (Princess Grace Rose Garden), planted in her memory in 1984. Swans swim on the small lake. Contemporary sculptures – including *Le Poing* (The Fist) by César and *Cavalleria Eroica* by Arman – stud the length of the park's **Chemin des Sculptures**. Museum-wise, Fontvieille is Monaco's 'collector's corner'.

Collection de Voitures Anciennes

Over 100 vehicles are on display in this vintage car museum housing the private collection of Rainier III. Highlights include the Rolls Royce Silver Cloud that was given by local shop keepers to Prince Rainier to mark his marriage to Grace Kelly in 1956, and a black London cab (Austin 1952) fitted out especially for the Hollywood actress. The first F1 racing car to win the Monaco Grand Prix – the Bugatti 1929 – can be seen in the *salon d'honneur* (room of honour), as can a helmet belonging to the late Brazilian racing driver Ayrton Senna (1960–94).

Monaco's Vintage Cars Collection (☎ 92 05 28 56), inside the Centre Commercial de Fontvieille on esplanade Rainier III, opens 10 am to 6 pm. Admission costs 30FF (children aged eight to 14, 15FF).

Musée Naval

An impressive collection of model ships constructed by Grimaldi princes are displayed in Monaco's Naval Museum (☎ 92 05 28 48), inside the Centre Commercial de Fontvieille. The oldest ship in the 200-odd piece collection was stuck together by Albert I in 1874. Other pieces include: an imperial gondola built in 15 days for Napoleon to admire; the *Fiorentino Emigrato* sailing ship built in the 17th century; a miniature of the *Missouri*, where the armistice with Japan was signed in 1945; and a 5m-long model of the US aircraft carrier *Nimitz*. The museum opens 10 am to 6 pm. Admission costs 25FF (children aged eight to 14, 15FF).

Musée des Timbres et des Monnaies

Prince Rainier also has a stamp and coin collection – displayed in the Stamp and Money Museum (☎ 93 15 41 50) in the Centre Commercial de Fontvieille, open 10 am to 5 or 6 pm. Monégasque stamps dating from 1885 and numismatic wonders dating from 1640 are exhibited. Admission costs 20FF (seniors, students and children aged 12 to 14, 10FF) and includes a free Monégasque stamp.

MONEGHETTI

The steep slopes of the Moneghetti district, immediately north of Fontvieille, are home to the wonderful **Jardin Exotique** (☎ 93 15 29 80, ✉ jardin-exotique@monte-carlo.mc), 62 blvd du Jardin Exotique. The exotic garden boasts some 7000 varieties of cacti and succulents from all over the world – including a 100-year-old South American cacti and 10m-tall African candelabras. The spectacular view alone is worth at least half the 40FF admission fee (students and those aged six to 18, 19FF), which also gets you into the on-site **Musée d'Anthropologie**

The Formula One Grand Prix

The Grand Prix Automobile de Monaco – which dates to 1911 – is the world's most glamorous race. It screams round the streets each year in May, lapping a 3.328km circuit highly revered in the racing world for its narrow, unrelenting *virages* (bends) and awkward chicances.

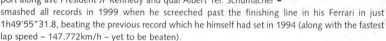

Few succeed in completing the required 78 laps of the course which takes drivers from the port, through a right-hand bend, and uphill along ave d'Ostende to place du Casino where the track bombs downhill around a hairpin and two sharp rights into the tunnel and back to the port along ave Président JF Kennedy and quai Albert 1er. Schumacher

JANE SMITH

smashed all records in 1999 when he screeched past the finishing line in his Ferrari in just 1h49'55"31.8, beating the previous record which he himself had set in 1994 (along with the fastest lap speed – 147.772km/h – yet to be beaten).

The race is watched by 150,000 spectators from stands around the port and on place du Casino. The cheapest spot is ave de la Porte Neuve. The wealthy survey the spectacle from Hôtel Hermitage or from a yacht deck in the harbour. The Grimaldis watch the start and finish from the royal box at the port, retiring in between for a champagne brunch at an undisclosed address overlooking the circuit. Mechanics, girlfriends, driver support teams and so on hobnob at Stars 'n' Bars near the paddock area on quai Antoine 1er.

Time trials and various races including the Grand Prix de Monaco 3000 take place during the three days leading up to the Formula One Grand Prix, which is always held on Sunday afternoon. Tickets for all races, including the Grand Prix, are available from the Automobile Club de Monaco (☎ 93 15 26 00, fax 92 25 80 08, e f1@monaco.mc), 23 blvd Albert 1er, BP 464, 98012 Monaco. Grand Prix tickets in 2000 cost 220FF on ave de la Porte Neuve and 800FF to 2200FF on place du Casino and around the port. Tickets go on sale in January and are snapped up in hours. Archive images can be viewed on the official Web site at www.monaco.mc/monaco/gprix.

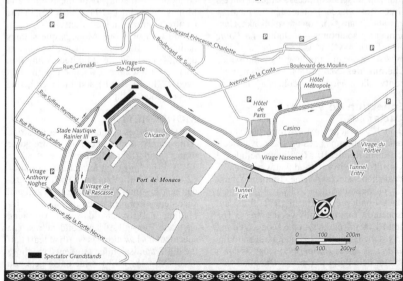

Préhistorique (Museum of Prehistoric Anthropology; ☎ 93 15 80 06) and includes a guided tour (30 minutes) of the **Grottes de l'Observatoire**. The prehistoric Observatory Caves comprise a fantastical network of stalactite and stalagmite caves 279 steps down the hillside. Prehistoric rock scratchings found here are among the oldest of their kind in the world.

The Jardin Exotique opens 9 am to 7 pm, mid-May to mid-September; and 9 am to 6 pm or dusk, the rest of the year. From the tourist office, take bus No 2 to the Jardin Exotique terminus.

BEACHES & BOAT EXCURSIONS

Boats and water dominate the central quarter of La Condamine, namely the **Port de Monaco** where palatial pleasure crafts of all (exceedingly large) shapes and sizes languish. At the eastern end of quai Antoine 1er is the exclusive members-only **Yacht Club de Monaco** (☎ 93 10 63 00, fax 93 50 80 88, @ ycm@yacht-club-monaco.mc), 16 quai Antoine 1er. Visit online at www .yacht-club-monaco.mc.

Lesser mortals can sail the waters in a glass-bottomed boat operated by Les Bateaux de la French Riviera (☎ 92 16 15 15, @ cntm@atlantis.mc), at the eastern end of quai des États-Unis. **Boat excursions** (55 minutes) depart several times daily, April to October. Tickets costs 70FF (students and those aged three to 18, 50FF).

The nearest **beaches**, Plage du Larvotto and Plage de Monte Carlo, are a couple of kilometres east of Monte Carlo in the easternmost **Larvotto quarter**. Both fine shingle beaches have private, paying sections where you can hire cushioned sun-loungers and parasols (50FF to 70FF). Take bus No 4 from the train station or bus No 6 from the port to, Le Sporting, stop.

POOLS & BATHS

The pool to swim in and be seen is the **Stade Nautique Rainier III** (☎ 93 30 64 83), the Olympic-sized outdoor pool overlooking the boats bobbing in the port on quai Albert I. It opens 9 am to 8 pm, May to June, September and October; and 9 am to 8 pm in July

and August. Admission costs 24FF (those aged over 60, 15FF, children aged three to 11, 14FF) and cheaper 10-/20-ticket carnets are also available. You can hire a nice comfortable mattress and parasol, each for 22FF per day, and swimming lessons (sexy instructor not guaranteed) cost 77FF per hour.

Prestigious **Les Thermes Marins** (☎ 92 16 49 46, @ thermes@sbm.mc), 2 ave de Monte Carlo, has a heated sea-water pool (29°C), solarium and offers a variety of spa treatments.

SPECIAL EVENTS

The Fête de la Ste-Dévote on 27 January celebrates the feast day of Monaco's patron saint, Dévote, whose corpse was flung in a boat and left to drift at sea following her death at the hands of a Roman general in Corsica. Thanks to a dove who blew the boat in the right direction, Dévote's corpse landed on the shores of Monaco in AD 312. Each year, a traditional Mass is celebrated in Monégasque is the Église Ste-Dévote ☎ 93 50 52 60), place Ste-Dévote. In the evening a torchlit procession, blessing and symbolic burning of a boat take place in front of the church.

Dancers in traditional Monégasque folk costume dance around a big bonfire on place du Palais on 23 June, the eve of St John's Day. The beginning of August brings a glittering International Fireworks Festival to the port area, while a carnival spirit fills the streets with the Fête Nationale Monégasque – Monaco's National Holiday – on 19 November.

PLACES TO STAY

Cheap accommodation is pretty much nonexistent in Monaco; some 75% of the principality's hotel rooms sport four stars. Fortunately, Nice is not too far away.

PLACES TO STAY – BUDGET & MID-RANGE
Hostels

The *Centre de la Jeunesse Princesse Stéphanie* (☎ 93 50 83 20, fax 93 25 29 82, @ info@youthhostel.asso.mc, 24 ave Prince Pierre), 200m up the hill from the train station, only accepts travellers aged 16 to 31. A bed in an eight- to 10-bed dorm costs 80FF, including a breakfast, shower and sheets. Between September and June, hostel accommodation is in rooms with four beds. The hostel opens 7 to 1 am (usually full by 3 pm). Reception is in the block behind the pink building visible on ave Prince Pierre; continue uphill past the pink facade then bear right down the steps.

Hotels

In La Condamine, clean and pleasant, one-star *Hôtel Cosmopolite* (☎ 93 30 16 95, fax 93 30 2 05, 4 rue de la Turbie) has basic singles/doubles for 217/258FF and shower-equipped equivalents for 298/338FF. A cut above the latter is *Hôtel de France* (☎ 93 30 24 64, fax 92 16 13 34, ℮ hotel-france@ monte-carlo.com, 6 rue de la Turbie) a renovated pad with comfortable singles/doubles/triples with bathroom costing 390/490/610FF, including breakfast.

Hôtel Le Versailles (☎ 93 50 79 34, fax 93 25 53 64, ℮ hotelversailles@monte-carlo.mc, 4 ave Prince Pierre) offers good-value singles/doubles starting at 350/450FF. Nearby *Hôtel Terminus* (☎ 92 05 63 00, fax 92 05 20 10, 9 ave Prince Pierre), is part of the Tulips Inn international hotel chain and has elegant singles/doubles/triples/quads costing 540/760/910/1060FF in low season and 600/830/990/1150FF in high season.

Blvd du Général Leclerc is the street to head for in Beausoleil (France): At No 17, *Hôtel Diana* (☎ 04 93 78 47 58, fax 04 93 41 88 94) has basic rooms for one or two costing 180FF (200FF with shower). Singles/doubles/triples with shower and toilet clock in at 265/290/390FF. At No 19, *Hôtel Cosmopolite* (☎ 04 93 78 36 00, fax 04 93 41 84 22), unrelated to the hotel of the same name in La Condamine, has singles with shower, TV and telephone for 220FF and air-conditioned singles/doubles/triples, complete with hair dryer in the bathroom, for 330/350/420FF. Sandwiched in between at No 17 bis is 32-room *Hôtel Olympia* (☎ 04 93 78 12 70, fax 04 93 41 85 04), home to toilet- and shower-equipped

singles/doubles/triples costing 324/360/480FF. Don't forget to call the country code for France when dialling these numbers from Monaco (eg, from the train station). The even-numbered side of blvd du Général Leclerc is in Monaco and is called blvd de France. The nearest bus stop is the 'Crémaillère' stop, served by bus Nos 2 and 4.

PLACES TO STAY – TOP END

Monaco's world-famous pad is magnificent *Hôtel de Paris* (☎ 92 16 30 00, fax 92 16 38 50, ℮ hp@sbm.mc, place du Casino), where writer Colette spent the last years of her life. The hotel – Monte Carlo's first – was built between 1859 and 1864 and hosts a gastronomic temple (see Places to Eat below). Singles/doubles cost upwards of 3090/3710FF per person per night.

Four-star *Hôtel Hermitage* (☎ 92 16 40 00, fax 93 16 38 52, ℮ hh@sbm.mc, square Beaumarchais) has a Italian-inspired facade and a pink-marbled restaurant. Prices reflect the luxurious *belle epoque* ambience of both hotels. Expect to pay a minimum of 2100FF for a double room fit for a queen.

PLACES TO EAT

In Monte Carlo, the place to people-watch is from the legendary – and today sprawling – terrace of *Café de Paris (place du Casino)* which dates to 1882.

Restaurants

Near the Larvotto and Monte Carlo beaches on ave Princesse Grace, Sporting d'Été houses the ultimate in designer dining: *Bar & Bœuf* (☎ 92 16 60 60) overlooks the ocean, is home to a minimalist wood and glass interior designed by Philippe Starck and a chic crowd of exquisitely dressed beautiful people. The most recent venture of top French chef, Alain Ducasse, Bar & Bœuf specialises in just that – sea-perch *(bar)* and beef *(bœuf)*. Count at least 400FF to 700FF per head (open evenings only).

Decadent diners seeking a more traditional setting should head west to Monte Carlo's three-star *Louis XV* (☎ 92 16 30 01), also run by Ducasse inside Hôtel de Paris (see Places to Stay above); some say it's the best restaurant on the Riviera. *Menus* start at 860FF and the wine list offers the pick of some 250,000 bottles of wine (many priceless) stashed in a cellar carved from rock.

Flashy **Stars 'n' Bars** (☎ 97 97 95 95, *6 quai Antoine 1er*) is a blues bar and restaurant that sports one of Monaco's sexiest terraces overlooking the port. Dishes of American-sized portions and excellent-quality (also huge) salads are served in the restaurant from 11 am to midnight; it has a nightclub on its 1st floor (see Entertainment below). The same Texan businessman runs **Le Texan** (☎ 93 30 34 54, *4 rue Suffren Reymond*), a meaty joint specialising in steaks.

Traditional, cosy and far from flashy is humble **Restaurant de Trende** (☎ 93 30 37 72, *19 rue de la Turbie*). The decor is completely 1930s and the food, absolutely Provençal.

Italianate **La Cigale** (☎ 93 30 16 14, *18 rue de Millo*) is another of those rare down-to-earth places, dishing up delicious plates of authentic pasta, pizza and meats at prices that won't break the bank. It has a 65FF *plat du jour* and its *menus* cost 98FF and 135FF.

There are plenty of snack-attack places around the port. **Haagen-Däz** has a great little ice-cream outlet and *salon de thé* in the pavilion in the public gardens in front of the casino, and another inside the Galerie du Sporting on place du Casino.

Self-Catering

A *food market* fills place d'Armes in La Condamine every morning. **Caves & Gourmandises** (☎ 97 70 54 94, *35 blvd Albert 1er*) is an upmarket épicerie crammed with delicious delights to eat and drink.

The **Casino** supermarket (*17 blvd Albert 1er*) has a well-stocked boulangerie that sells hot slices of pizza, crepes and other snacks. It opens 8.30 am to 8 pm Monday to Saturday.

ENTERTAINMENT

In addition to the box offices mentioned below, tickets for most cultural events are sold at FNAC (☎ 93 10 81 81), inside the Centre Commercial Le Métropole at 17 ave Spélugues.

Bars & Nightclubs

On Thursday, **McCarthy's Irish Pub** (☎ 93 25 87 67, *7 rue du Portier*) hosts a DJ and it has live bands on Friday and Saturday. It rocks from 6 pm to dawn. **The Living Room** (☎ 93 50 80 31, *7 ave des Spélugues*) is a hybrid piano bar-disco that swings from 11 pm to dawn.

Monaco's best-known nightclub is **Jimmy'z** (☎ 92 16 22 77, 92 16 36 36, *26 ave Princesse Grace*), open 11.30 pm to dawn in the Sporting d'Eté complex near the beaches. Other star-studded spots include **L'X Club** (☎ 93 30 70 55, *13 ave des Spélugues*), **Tiffany's** (☎ 93 50 53 13, *3 ave des Spélugues*) and **Stars 'n' Bars** (☎ 97 97 95 95, *6 quai Antoine 1er*), a port-side club that opens 11.30 pm to 3 or 4 am and commands a 150FF admission fee.

Cinemas

Cinéma Le Sporting (☎ 93 25 36 81, 08 36 68 00 72, *place du Casino*) shows films in their original language (usually English) daily at 5, 6 or 9 pm. Tickets cost 55FF (seniors over 60 and those aged under 18, 36FF). Check out its Web site at www .cinemasporting.com (French only) to see what's on.

Theatre

A charming spot to while away a summer evening is the **Théâtre du Fort Antoine** (☎ 93 25 66 12, *ave de la Quarantaine*), a marvellous open-air theatre in a fortress built between 1709 and 1713. Plays and musical concerts are staged here at 9 or 9.30 pm on Monday in July and August; tickets costing 60FF or 80FF (students 30FF) are sold at the theatre 45 minutes before performances start.

The interior decor of the **Théâtre Princesse Grace** (☎ 93 25 32 27, *12 ave d'Ostende*) was designed by Princess Grace.

Ballet, Opera & Classical Music

The **Salle Garnier** (1892) adjoining Monte Carlo Casino on place du Casino is home to the Opéra de Monte Carlo and ballet company. Ticket bookings can be made at the **Atrium du Casino** (☎ 92 16 22 99), inside

Shopping Spree

To window-shop or shop till you drop, hit Monte Carlo.

Kick-start your shopping spree on the western side of place du Casino, where you can swirl through **Cartier, Chanel, Céline** and **Sonia Rykiel** in one fell swoop. Duck through Galerie du Sporting – a covered shopping arcade linking place du Casino with ave Princesse Alice – if you're seeking wine, antiques or antique wine. **Sotherby's** (☎ 93 30 88 80) auction house is here, as is a clutch of antique galleries and **L'Œnothèque** (☎ 93 25 82 66), a lavish wine and champagne cellar which any oenophilist will adore.

Yves St-Laurent, Christian-Dior, luxury-leather designer **Louis Vuitton** and Swiss watch-maker **Piaget** stand in temptation's way along ave des Beaux-Arts, the street skirting the southern side of Galerie du Sporting. Back on place du Casino, whirl past Hôtel de Paris and downhill along ave de Monte Carlo, a short but chic street laden with **Gucci, Valentino, Hermès Lalique** and **Prada**. Kenzo brings a splash of colour to the **Centre Commercial Le Métropole,** an indoor shopping centre opposite the Jardins du Casino.

Having exhausted Monte Carlo, serious window-shoppers and shoppers with serious amounts of money still to spend can try their luck on rue Grimaldi in La Condamine. **Galerie Riccadonna** at No 7 sells fabulously funky, one-off pieces of designer furniture. **Boutique Formule 1** at No 15 – a shop dedicated to the glamorous side of motor racing – stocks watches, cigarette lighters etc, by **Porsche Design** and **Ferrari**.

In Larvotto, socialites flutter along blvd des Moulins and ave Princesse Grace. **Divina & Co** (36 blvd des Moulins) sells rings as big as gobstoppers, see-through handbags and a fantastic array of other fantasy gems, costume jewels and accessories. **Hugo Boss** struts his stuff at No 39 on the same street, and *haute-couture* **Loris Azzaro** stands tall at No 19. **DKNY, Adonis** – a boutique crammed with **Klein, Joseph, Gaultier** and **Galliano** labels and British designer **Karen Millen** – all gaze out to sea at 39 ave Princesse Grace. Adonis also sells traditional national costumes.

Essential reading for committed shoppers and fashion aficionados is the 155-page *Monaco Shopping* guide, published annually and available for free at the tourist office.

the casino, between 10 am to 5.30 pm Tuesday to Sunday.

Performances by the Monte Carlo Philharmonic Orchestra (1863) are held in the *Auditorium Rainier III* inside the Centre de Congrès Auditorium (☎ 93 10 84 00, blvd Louis II). In July and August its venue shifts to the beautiful, star-topped *Cour d'Honneur* (Courtyard of Honour) at the Palais du Prince. Predictably, tickets (also available from the Atrium du Casino) are like gold dust.

SPECTATOR SPORTS

The sporting calendar kicks off with the legendary Rallye Automobile Monte Carlo (Monte Carlo Rally) in January. The four-day event is a series of timed stages, with the rally starting and finishing at the Monégasque port, and ripping through Haute-

Provence in between. The traditional night stage and the concentration run where drivers set off from various European cities to meet in Monte Carlo – such as Disney's Herbie (the VW Beetle) did on screen in the 1970s – were both scrapped in 1997. Lots more details are on the Web at www .acm.mc.

The Monte Carlo International Tennis Championships, held at the Monte Carlo Country Club (☎ 04 93 41 30 15), ave Princesse Grace, opens the hard-court season in April.

Soccer team AS Monaco can be seen in action on their home ground, the Stade Louis II (☎ 92 05 40 11), 7 ave des Castelans, Fontvieille. Guided tours in English (45 minutes) of the stadium depart at 2.15 and 3.45 pm on Monday, Tuesday, Thursday and Friday; they cost 20FF (seniors aged over 65 and children aged under 12, 12.50FF). The AS Monaco boutique, ASM Football Pro (☎ 97 77 74 74, [e] info@ asm-footpro.mc), 16 rue Grimaldi, sells all the red-and-white gear, from shorts and shirts to ash trays and champagne flutes.

GETTING THERE & AWAY
Air
Héli Air Monaco (☎ 92 05 00 50), Héli Inter Riviera (☎ 97 77 84 84) and MonacAir (☎ 97 97 39 00), all based at Monaco heliport on ave des Ligures, can twirl you anywhere along the coast your heart desires, for a not-so-small fee, including to/from Nice airport (see the introductory Getting Around chapter).

Bus
Rapides Côte d'Azur (☎ 04 97 00 07 00) operates daily buses from Monaco to Nice-Côte d'Azur airport (80/140FF one-way/ return, 45 minutes). In Monaco, buses use the stop in front of the national tourist office. Bus times coincide with flight arrivals and departures.

Train
Monaco train station – gleaming new with polished marble floors and moving walkways – is at the eastern end of blvd Rainier III; enter the station on ave Prince Pierre or via the public lift linking place Ste-Dévote with blvd de Bélgique.

Trains to/from Monaco are run by France's SNCF and taking the train along this coast is highly recommended – the sea and the mountains provide a magnificent sight. There are frequent trains eastwards to Menton (12FF, 10 minutes) and the first town across the border in Italy, Ventimiglia (Vintimille in French; 19FF, 25 minutes). For trains to Nice (20FF, 25 minutes) and onward connections to other towns, see under Getting There & Away in the Nice to Menton chapter.

Car & Motorcycle
If you are driving out of Monaco, either eastwards towards Italy or westwards to Nice, and you want to go via the A8, you need to join the Corniche Moyenne (N7). For Italy, look for signs indicating Gênes (Genoa in English; Genova in Italian). Blvd du Jardin Exotique leads to the N7 in the direction of Nice.

GETTING AROUND
Some 15 *ascenseurs publics* (public lifts) run up and down the hillside, all marked on the free map distributed by the tourist office. Most operate 24 hours; some run 6 am to midnight or 1 am.

Bus
Monaco's urban bus system has six lines. Line No 2 links Monaco Ville with Monte Carlo and then loops back to the Jardin Exotique. Line No 4 links the train station with the tourist office, the casino and Larvotto beach. A one-way ticket/one-day pass costs 8.50FF/21FF. Alternatively, buy four-/eight-ride magnetic cards (21/33FF) from the bus driver or from vending machines at most bus stops. Buses run 7 or 7.30 am to 9 pm.

Local bus company, Compagnie des Autobus de Monaco (CAM; ☎ 93 50 62 41, 3 ave du Président John F Kennedy, on the port's northern side, opens 8.30 am to noon and 2 to 6 pm Monday to Thursday, and 8.30 am to noon and 2 to 5 pm on Friday.

Taxi
Dial ☎ 93 15 01 01 to order a taxi.

Bicycle
MBK-Auto Moto Garage (☎ 93 50 10 80, fax 93 50 10 82), 7 rue de Millo, has road/mountain bikes to rent for 50/80FF per day, as well as 50/80cc scooters that cost 170/280FF to hire for 24 hours. The shop opens 8 am to noon and 2 to 7 pm weekdays, and 8 am to noon on Saturday.

Language

Standard French is taught and spoken in Provence. However, travellers accustomed to schoolbook French, or the unaccented, strait-laced French spoken in cities and larger towns, will find the lyrical, flamboyant French spoken in Provence's rural heart (and by most in Marseille) absolutely incomprehensible. Here, words caressed by the heavy southern accent end with a flourish: vowels are sung; the traditional rolling 'r' is turned into a mighty long trill. So *douze* (the number 12) becomes 'douz-eh' with an emphasised 'e', and *pain* (bread) becomes 'peng'. Take time to tune in and you'll quickly pick up the beat

PROVENÇAL

Despite the bilingual signs that greet tourists when they enter most towns and villages, the region's mother tongue – Provençal – is scarcely heard on the street or in the home. Just a handful of older people in rural Provence (Prouvènço) keep alive the rich lyrics and poetic language of their ancestors.

Provençal (*prouvençau* in Provençal) is a dialect of *langue d'oc* (Occitan), the traditional language of southern France. Its grammar is closer to Catalan and Spanish than to French. In the grand age of courtly love between the 12th and 14th centuries, Provençal was the literary language of France and northern Spain and even used as far afield as Italy. Medieval troubadours and poets created melodies and elegant poems motivated by the ideal of courtly love, and Provençal blossomed.

The 19th century witnessed a revival of Provençal after its rapid displacement by *langue d'oïl*, the language of northern France that originated from the vernacular Latin spoken by the Gallo-Romans and which gave birth to modern French (*francés* in Provençal). The revival was spearheaded by Frédéric Mistral (1830–1914), a poet from Vaucluse, whose works in Provençal landed him the Nobel Prize for Literature in 1904.

Mistral was the backbone of Félibrige, a literary society created in 1854 to safeguard Provençal literature, culture and identity. A wealth of literature in Provençal was published by Félibrige, which, from its contemporary base at Aix-Marseille University (☎ 04 42 26 23 41, fax 04 42 27 52 89, ℮ info@felibrige.com), Parc Jourdan, 8bis ave Jules Ferry, 13100 Aix-en-Provence, remains as vocal today as it was in years past. It has a Web site at www.felibrige.com.

FRENCH

While the French rightly or wrongly have a reputation for assuming that all human beings should speak French – until WWI it was the international language of culture and diplomacy – you'll find that any attempt to communicate in French will be much appreciateded. Your best bet is always to approach people politely in French, even if the only sentence you know is *Pardon, madame/monsieur/mademoiselle, parlez-vous anglais?* (Excuse me, madam/sir/miss, do you speak English?).

Some basic French words and phrases are listed below. For a more comprehensive guide to the French language, get hold of Lonely Planet's French phrasebook.

Grammar

An important distinction is made in French between *tu* and *vous*, which both mean 'you'. *Tu* is only used when addressing people you know well, children or animals. When addressing an adult who is not a personal friend, *vous* should be used unless the person invites you to use *tu*. In general, younger people insist less on this distinction, and you may find that they use *tu* from the beginning of an acquaintance.

All nouns in French are either masculine or feminine and adjectives reflect the gender of the noun they modify. The feminine form of many nouns and adjectives is indicated by a silent 'e' added to the masculine form, as in *étudiant* and *étudiante*, the masculine and feminine for 'student'. In the following phrases we have indicated both masculine and feminine forms where necessary; the masculine form comes first, separated from the feminine by a slash. The gender of a noun is also often indicated by a preceding article: *le/un/du* (m), *la/une/de la* (f) (the/a/some); or a possessive adjective, *mon/ton/son* (m), *ma/ta/sa* (f) (my/your/his/her). With French, unlike English, the possessive adjective agrees in number and gender with the thing possessed: *sa mère* (his/her mother).

Pronunciation

Most letters in French are pronounced more or less the same as their English equivalents. A few that may cause confusion are:

j   as the 's' in 'leisure', eg *jour* (day)
c   before **e** and **i**, as the 's' in 'sit'; before **a**, **o** and **u** it's pronounced as English 'k'. When underscored with a 'cedilla' (**ç**) it's always pronounced as the 's' in 'sit'.

French has a number of sounds that are difficult for Anglophones to produce. These include:

- The distinction between the 'u' sound (as in *tu*) and 'oo' sound (as in *tout*). For both sounds, the lips are rounded and projected forward, but for the 'u' the tongue is towards the front of the mouth, its tip against the lower front teeth, whereas for the 'oo' the tongue is towards the back of the mouth, its tip behind the gums of the lower front teeth.

- The nasal vowels. With nasal vowels the breath escapes partly through the nose and partly through the mouth. There are no nasal vowels in English; in French there are three, as in *bon vin blanc*, (good white wine). These sounds occur where a syllable ends in a single **n** or **m**; the **n** or **m** is silent but indicates the nasalisation of the preceding vowel.

- The **r**. The standard **r** of Parisian French is produced by moving the bulk of the tongue backwards to constrict the air flow in the pharynx while the tip of the tongue rests behind the lower front teeth. It's similar to the noise made by some people before spitting, but with much less friction.

USEFUL WORDS
Basics

Yes.	*Oui.*
No.	*Non.*
Maybe.	*Peut-être.*
Please.	*S'il vous plaît.*
Thank you.	*Merci.*
You're welcome.	*Je vous en prie.*
Excuse me.	*Excusez-moi.*
Sorry/Forgive me.	*Pardon.*

Greetings & Civilities

Hello/Good day.	*Bonjour.*
Hello. (informal)	*Salut.*
Good evening.	*Bonsoir.*
Good night.	*Bonne nuit.*
Goodbye.	*Au revoir.*
How are you?	*Comment allez-vous?* (polite) *Comment vas-tu?/ Comment ça va?* (informal)
Fine, thanks.	*Bien, merci.*
What's your name?	*Comment vous appelez-vous?*

Signs

Entrée	Entrance
Sortie	Exit
Ouvert	Open
Fermé	Closed
Chambres Libres	Rooms Available
Complet	No Vacancies
Renseignements	Information
Interdit	Prohibited
(Commissariat de) Police	Police (Station)
Toilettes, WC	Toilets
Hommes	Men
Femmes	Women

My name is ...	Je m'appelle ...
I'm pleased to meet you.	Enchanté (m)/ Enchantée (f).
How old are you?	Quel âge avez-vous?
I'm ... years old.	J'ai ... ans.
Do you like ...?	Aimez-vous ...?
Where are you from?	De quel pays êtes-vous?

I'm from ...	Je viens ...
Australia	d'Australie
Canada	du Canada
England	d'Angleterre
Germany	d'Allemagne
Ireland	d'Irlande
New Zealand	de Nouvelle Zélande
Scotland	d'Écosse
the USA	des États-Unis
Wales	du Pays de Galle

Language Difficulties

I understand.	Je comprends.
I don't understand.	Je ne comprends pas.
Do you speak English?	Parlez-vous anglais?
Could you please write it down?	Est-ce que vous pouvez l'écrire?

Getting Around

I want to go to ...	Je voudrais aller à ...
I'd like to book a seat to ...	Je voudrais réserver une place pour ...

What time does the ... leave/arrive?	À quelle heure part/arrive ...?
aeroplane	l'avion
bus (city)	l'autobus
bus (intercity)	l'autocar
ferry	le ferry(-boat)
train	le train
tram	le tramway

Where is (the) ...?	Où est ...?
bus stop?	l'arrêt d'autobus
metro station	la station de métro
train station	la gare
tram stop	l'arrêt de tramway
ticket office	le guichet

I'd like a ... ticket.	Je voudrais un billet ...
one-way	aller-simple
return	aller-retour
1st-class	de première classe
2nd-class	de deuxième classe
How long does the trip take?	Combien de temps dure le trajet?

The train is ...	Le train est ...
delayed	en retard
on time	à l'heure
early	en avance

Do I need to ...?	Est-ce que je dois ...?
change trains	changer de train
change platform	changer de quai

left-luggage locker	consigne automatique
platform	quai
timetable	horaire

I'd like to hire ...	Je voudrais louer ...
a bicycle	un vélo
a car	une voiture
a guide	un guide

Around Town

I'm looking for ...	Je cherche ...
a bank/ exchange office	une banque/ un bureau de change
the city centre	le centre-ville
the ... embassy	l'ambassade de ...
the hospital	l'hôpital
my hotel	mon hôtel
the market	le marché
the police	la police
the post office	le bureau de poste/ la poste
a public phone	une cabine téléphonique
a public toilet	les toilettes
the tourist office	l'office de tourisme/ le syndicat d'initiative

Where is ...?	Où est ...?
the beach	la plage
the bridge	le pont

the castle/mansion	*le château*
the cathedral	*la cathédrale*
the church	*l'église*
the island	*l'île*
the lake	*le lac*
the main square	*la place centrale*
the mosque	*la mosquée*
the old city/town	*la vieille ville*
the palace	*le palais*
the quay/bank	*le quai/la rive*
the ruins	*les ruines*
the sea	*la mer*
the square	*la place*
the tower	*la tour*

What time does it open/close?	*Quelle est l'heure d'ouverture/ de fermeture?*
I'd like to make a telephone call.	*Je voudrais téléphoner.*

I'd like to change ...	*Je voudrais changer ...*
some money	*de l'argent*
travellers cheques	*chèques de voyage*

Directions

How do I get to ...?	*Comment dois-je faire pour arriver à ...?*
Is it near/far?	*Est-ce près/loin?*
Can you show me on the map/ city map?	*Est-ce que vous pouvez me le montrer sur la carte/le plan?*
Go straight ahead.	*Continuez tout droit.*
Turn left.	*Tournez à gauche.*
Turn right.	*Tournez à droite.*

at the traffic lights	*aux feux*
at the next corner	*au prochain coin*
behind	*derrière*
in front of	*devant*
opposite	*en face de*
north	*nord*
south	*sud*
east	*est*
west	*ouest*

Accommodation

I'm looking for ...	*Je cherche ...*
the youth hostel	*l'auberge de jeunesse*

the camp site	*le camping*
a hotel	*un hôtel*

Where can I find a cheap hotel?	*Où est-ce que je peux trouver un hôtel bon marché?*
What's the address?	*Quelle est l'adresse?*
Could you write it down, please?	*Est-ce vous pourriez l'écrire, s'il vous plaît?*
Do you have any rooms available?	*Est-ce que vous avez des chambres libres?*

I'd like to book ...	*Je voudrais réserver ...*
a bed	*un lit*
a single room	*une chambre pour une personne*
a double room	*une chambre double*
a room with a shower and toilet	*une chambre avec douche et WC*

I'd like to stay in a dormitory.	*Je voudrais coucher dans un dortoir.*

How much is it ...?	*Quel est le prix ...?*
per night	*par nuit*
per person	*par personne*

Is breakfast included?	*Est-ce que le petit dé-jeuner est compris?*
Can I see the room?	*Est-ce que je peux voir la chambre?*

Where is ...?	*Où est ...?*
the bathroom	*la salle de bains*
the shower	*la douche*

Where is the toilet?	*Où sont les toilettes?*

I'm going to stay ...	*Je resterai ...*
one day	*un jour*
a week	*une semaine*

Health

I'm sick.	*Je suis malade.*
I need a doctor.	*Il me faut un médecin.*
Where is the hospital?	*Où est l'hôpital?*
I have diarrhoea.	*J'ai la diarrhée.*
I'm pregnant.	*Je suis enceinte.*

Emergencies

Help!	Au secours!
Call a doctor!	Appelez un médecin!
Call the police!	Appelez la police!
Leave me alone!	Fichez-moi la paix!
I've been robbed.	On m'a volé.
I've been raped.	On m'a violée.
I'm lost.	Je me suis égaré/ égarée. (m/f)

I'm ...	Je suis ...
diabetic	diabétique
epileptic	épileptique
asthmatic	asthmatique
anaemic	anémique
I'm allergic ...	Je suis allergique ...
to antibiotics	aux antibiotiques
to penicillin	à la pénicilline

antiseptic	l'antiseptique
aspirin	l'aspirine
condoms	les préservatifs
contraceptive	un contraceptif
medicine	le médicament
nausea	la nausée
painkillers	des analgésiques
sunblock cream	la crème solaire haute protection
tampons	les tampons hygiéniques

Time & Dates

What time is it?	Quelle heure est-il?
It's (two) o'clock.	Il est (deux) heures.
When?	Quand?
today	aujourd'hui
tonight	ce soir
tomorrow	demain
day after tomorrow	après-demain
yesterday	hier
all day	toute la journée
in the morning	du matin
in the afternoon	de l'après-midi
in the evening	du soir

Monday	lundi
Tuesday	mardi
Wednesday	mercredi
Thursday	jeudi
Friday	vendredi
Saturday	samedi
Sunday	dimanche
January	janvier
February	février
March	mars
April	avril
May	mai
June	juin
July	juillet
August	août
September	septembre
October	octobre
November	novembre
December	décembre

Numbers

1	un
2	deux
3	trois
4	quatre
5	cinq
6	six
7	sept
8	huit
9	neuf
10	dix
11	onze
12	douze
13	treize
14	quatorze
15	quinze
16	seize
17	dix-sept
18	dix-huit
19	dix-neuf
20	vingt
21	vingt-et-un
22	vingt-deux
23	vingt trois
30	trente
40	quarante
50	cinquante
60	soixante
70	soixante-dix
80	quatre-vingts
90	quatre-vingts-dix

100	*cent*
1000	*mille*
2000	*deux mille*
one million	*un million*

FOOD GLOSSARY
Appetisers

anchoïade – anchovy puree laced with garlic and olive oil

assiette Anglaise – plate of cold mixed meats and sausages

assiette de crudités – plate of raw vegetables with dressings

banon à la Feuille – goat's cheese dipped in eau-de-vie and wrapped in a chestnut leaf

brandade de morue – mix of crushed salted cod, olive oil and garlic

brebis – sheep's milk dairy product

fromage de chèvre – goat's cheese (also called *brousse*)

pissala – Niçois paste mixed from pureed anchovies

pissaladière – anchovy, onion and black olive 'pizza' from Nice

tapenade – sharp, black olive-based dip

tomme Arlesienne – moulded goat's cheese from Arles

Soups

bourride – fish stew; often eaten as a main course

bouillon – broth or stock

croûtons – fried or roasted bread cubes, sprinkled on top of soups

potage – thick soup made with pureed vegetables

soupe au pistou – vegetable soup made with basil and garlic

soupe de poisson – fish soup

Meat, Chicken & Poultry

agneau – lamb

aiguillette – thin slice of duck fillet

alouettes sans têtes – meat slices wrapped around a stuffing; literally, 'headless larks'

bœuf – beef

bœuf haché – minced beef

brochette – kebab

canard – duck

cervelle – brains

chapon – capon

charcuterie – cooked or prepared meats

cheval – horse meat

chèvre – goat

chevreau – kid (baby goat)

chevreuil – venison

cuisses de grenouilles – frogs' legs

entrecôte – rib steak

daube de bœuf à la Provençale – beef stew

épaule d'agneau – shoulder of lamb

escargot – snail

estouffade de bœuf – Carmargais beef stew with tomatoes and olive

faisan – pheasant

faux-filet – sirloin steak

filet – tenderloin

foie – liver

foie gras de canard – duck liver paté

gibier – game

gigot d'agneau – leg of lamb

jambon – ham

lapin – rabbit

lard – bacon

lardon – pieces of chopped bacon

lièvre – hare

mouton – mutton

pieds de porc – pig trotters

pieds et paquets – sheep tripe; literally 'feet and packages'

pigeon aux gousses d'ail – pigeon cooked with garlic cloves

pigeonneau – squab (young pigeon)

pintade – guinea fowl

poulet – chicken

rognons – kidneys

sanglier – wild boar

saucisson – large sausage

saucisson d'Arles – sausage made from pork, beef, wine and spice

saucisson fumé – smoked sausage

taureau de Camargue – Camargais beef

tournedos – thick slices of fillet steak

tripes – tripe

veau – veal

viande – meat

volaille – poultry

Fish & Seafood

aïoli Provençale complet – shellfish, vegetables, boiled egg and aïoli
anchois – anchovy
anguille – eel
brème – bream
brochet – pike
cabillaud – fresh cod
calmar – squid
carrelet – plaice
chaudrée – fish stew
colin – hake
coquillage – shellfish
coquille St-Jacques – scallop
crabe – crab
crevette grise – shrimp
crevette rose – prawn
écrevisse – small, freshwater crayfish
fruits de mer – seafood
gambas – king prawns
goujon – gudgeon (small freshwater fish)
hareng – herring
homard – lobster
huître – oyster
langouste – crayfish
langoustine – very small salt-water 'lobster'
lotte – monkfish
loup – sea bass
maquereau – mackerel
merlan – whiting
morue – dried, salted cod
morue pochée – poached cod
moules – mussels
oursin – sea urchin
paella – rice dish with saffron, vegetables and shellfish
palourde – clam
poisson – fish
poulpe – octopus
raie – ray
rascasse – spiny scorpion fish
rouget – red mullet
St-Pierre – a flat fish used in bouillabaisse
saumon – salmon
seiche – cuttlefish
sole – sole
stockfish (*estocaficada* in Niçois) – dried salt fish soaked in water for four to five days, stewed for two hours with onion, tomato and white wine, then laced with anchovies and black olives.
thon – tuna
truite – trout

Vegetables, Herbs & Spices

ail – garlic
aneth – dill
anis – aniseed
artichaut – artichoke
asperge – asparagus
avocat – avocado
barbouillade – stuffed or stewed aubergine
basilic – basil
betterave – beetroot
blette de Nice – white beet
cannelle – cinnamon
carotte – carrot
céleri – celery
cèpe – cepe (boletus mushroom)
champignon – mushroom
chou – cabbage
citrouille – pumpkin
concombre – cucumber
cornichon – gherkin (pickle)
courgette – courgette (zucchini)
échalotte – shallot
endive frisée – chicory
épice – spice
épinards – spinach
estragon – tarragon
fenouil – fennel
fève – broad bean
fleur de courgette – courgette flower
genièvre – juniper
gingembre – ginger
haricots – beans
haricots blancs – white beans
haricots rouge – kidney beans
haricots verts – French (string) beans
herbe – herb
laitue – lettuce
légume – vegetable
légumes farcis – stuffed vegetables
lentilles – lentils
maïs – sweetcorn
marjolaine – sweet marjoram
menthe – mint
mesclun – Niçois mix of lettuce

aubergine – aubergine (eggplant)

navet – turnip
oignon – onion
origan – oregano
oseille – sorrel
panais – parsnip
persil – parsley
petit pois – pea
poireau – leek
poivron – green pepper
pomme de terre – potato
ratatouille – casserole of aubergines, tomatoes, peppers and garlic
riz – rice
riz de Camargue – Camargais rice
romarin – rosemary
salade Niçoise – green salad featuring tuna, egg and anchovy
sarrasin – buckwheat
sarriette – savory
seigle – rye
thym – thyme
tian – vegetable and rice gratin served in a dish called a 'tian'
tomate – tomato
tourta de bléa – Niçois white beetroot and pine kernel pie
truffe – black truffle

Sauces & Accompaniments

aïoli – garlicky sauce to accompany bouillabaisse
béchamel – basic white sauce
huile d'olive – olive oil
mornay – cheese sauce
moutarde – mustard
pistou – pesto (pounded mix of basil, hard cheese, olive oil and garlic)
Provençale – tomato, garlic, herb and olive oil dressing or sauce
rouille – aïoli-based sauce spiced with chilli pepper; served with bourride
tartare – mayonnaise with herbs
vinaigrette – salad dressing made with oil, vinegar, mustard and garlic

Fruit & Nuts

abricot – apricot
agrumes – citrus fruits
amande – almond
ananas – pineapple
banane – banana
blonde de Nice – variety of orange
cassis – blackcurrant
cerise – cherry
citron – lemon
datte – date
figue – fig
fraise – strawberry
framboise – raspberry
fruits confits – candied fruits
fruits glazée – glazed fruits
grenade – pomegranate
groseille – redcurrant or gooseberry
mangu – mango
marron – chestnut
melon – melon
melon canteloup – type of Cavaillon melon
mirabelle – type of plum
myrtille – bilberry (blueberry)
noisette – hazelnut
noix de cajou – cashew
pamplemousse – grapefruit
pastèque – watermelon
pêche – peach
pignon – pine kernel
pistache – pistachio
poire – pear
pomme – apple
prune – plum
pruneau – prune
raisin – grape

Desserts & Sweets

bergamotes – orange-flavoured confectionary
berlingots – hard caramel originating in Carpentras
calisson – almond-based sweet from Aix-en-Provence
crème caramel – caramel custard
crêpe – thin pancake
crêpes suzettes – orange-flavoured crepes flambéed in liqueur
dragée – sugared almond
éclair – pastry filled with cream
flan – egg-custard dessert
gâteau – cake
gelée – jelly
glace – ice cream

île flottante – cooked egg white, floating on a creamy sauce; literally 'floating island'
macarons – macaroons (sweet biscuit made of ground almonds, sugar and egg whites)
tarte – tart (pie)
tarte aux pommes – apple tart
tarte Tropézienne – cream sandwich cake from St-Tropez
yaourt – yoghurt

Breads & Biscuits

brioche – sweet soft bread
chichi freggi – sugar-coated donuts from around Marseilles
fougasse – elongated Niçois bread stuffed with olives, chopped bacon *(lardons)* or anchovies *(anchois)*
fougassette – brioche perfumed with orange flower
galette – wholemeal or buckwheat pancake; also a type of biscuit
gâteaux secs aux amandes – crisp almond biscuits
michettes – Niçois bread stuffed with cheese, olives, anchovies and onions
navettes – canoe-shaped, orange-blossom-flavoured biscuits from Marseilles
pain à l'ail – garlic bread
pain au son – bran bread
pain aux noix – walnut bread
pain aux oignons – onion bread
pain aux olives – olive bread

pain aux raisins – sultana bread
pain aux roquefort – blue-cheese bread
pain complet – wholemeal bread
pain de mie – sandwich loaf
pain des Alpes – white crusty bread sold by weight (kg) rather than in loaves
pain de seigle – rye bread
pain de seigle aux raisins – rye bread with sultanas
pan bagnat – Niçois bread soaked in olive oil and filled with anchovy, olives, green pepper
panisses – chickpea flour patties from in and around Marseilles
sablé – shortbread biscuit
socca – Niçois chickpea flour & olive oil pancake

Basics

beurre – butter
chocolat – chocolate
confiture – jam
crème fraîche – unsweetened cream
farine – flour
lait – milk
miel – honey
œufs – eggs
poivre – pepper
sel – salt
sucre – sugar
vinaigre – vinegar

Glossary

Word gender is indicated as (m) masculine, (f) feminine.

accueil (m) – reception
aire naturelle (f) – farm camp site
aire naturiste (f) – nudist camp
anse (f) – cove
alimentation (f) – grocery shop
aller-retour – round trip (return)
aller or **aller-simple** – one way (single)
appellation d'origine contrôlée (AOC) – wines which have met stringent government regulations governing where, how and under what conditions the grapes and wines are grown, fermented and bottled
arène (f) – amphitheatre
arrière-pays (m) – hinterland
atelier (m) – artisan's workshop
auberge (f) – inn
auberge de jeunesse (f) – youth hostel

baie (f) – bay
barrage (m) – dam
bastide (f) – country house
belvédère (m) – view point
billetterie (f) – ticket office or counter
boulangerie (f) – bread shop
bravade (f) – Tropézian festival with cannons and gun fire; literally 'act of bravado'

calanque (f) – rocky inlet
cap (m) – cape
cave (f) – wine or cheese cellar
centre (de) hospitalier (m) – hospital
chambre d'hôte (f) – bed and breakfast accommodation, usually in a private home
charcuterie (f) – pork butcher's shop and delicatessen
château (m) – castle or stately home
chèvre (m) – goat
cime (f) – mountain summit or peak
cluse (f) – transverse valley
col (m) – mountain pass
commune (f) – district, parish
corniche (f) – coastal or cliff road
corso (nautique) (m) – procession of floral floats (boats)

cour (f) – courtyard
cour d'honneur (f) – courtyard of honour
climatisation (f) – air conditioning
crèche vivante (f) – nativity scene with real people; literally 'living crib'
crémerie (f) – dairy
cuvée (f) – a limited wine vintage

défilé (m) – procession or cortege
dégustation (f) – the fine art of tasting wine, cheese, olive oil or sea food
défense forestière contre l'incendie (DFCI) – fire road (public access forbidden)
département (m) – administrative area (department)
député (m) – member of Parliament
digue (f) – dike or sea wall
domaine (m) – a wine-producing estate
douane (f) – customs

eau potable (f) – drinking water
écluse (f) – lock
embarcadère (m) – pier or jetty
épicerie (f) – small grocery shop
escalier (m) – stairs or staircase
étang (m) – lagoon, pond or lake

faïence (f) – earthenware
féria (f) – bullfighting festival
ferme auberge (f) – family-run inn attached to a farm or chateau
fête (f) – party or festival
formule (f) – fixed main course plus starter or dessert
fromagerie (f) – cheese shop

gardian (m) – Camargue horseman
gare routière (m) – bus station; sometimes called **gare d'autobus**
garrigue (f) – cover of aromatic plants
gîte d'étape (m) – hiker's accommodation, usually in a village
gîte rural (m) – country cottage
golfe (m) – gulf
goût (m) – taste
grand cru (m) – wine of recognised superior quality; literally 'great growth'

hôtel de ville (m) – town hall
hôtel particulier (m) – private mansion

jardin (botanique) (m) – (botanic) garden
jetée (f) – pier
joute Provençale (f) – nautical jousting tournament

lacet (m) – hairpin bend
laiterie (f) – dairy
lait de vache (m) – cow's milk
lait cru (m) – unpasteurised milk
levée (f) – embankment

mairie (f) – town hall
manadier (m) – herdsman
marais (m) – marsh or swamp
marais salant (m) – salt pan
marché aux puces (m) – flea market
marché couvert (m) – covered market
marché Provençal (m) – open air market
mas (m) – farmhouse
méduse (f) – jellyfish
menu (m) – meal at a fixed price with two or more courses
millésime (m) – an exceptional wine from a year of optimum climatic conditions
mistral (m) – incessant north wind
moulin (m) – mill
moulin à huile/à vent (m) – oil/windmill

négociant (m) – a wine merchant

œuvre (f) – work of art or literature
orangeaie (f) – orange grove
orangerie (f) – orangery

papeterie (f) – stationery shop
parapente (f) – paragliding
parc (m) – park
pâtisserie (f) – cake & pastry shop
pavillon (m) – pavilion or lodge
pétanque (f) – a game not unlike lawn bowls
phare (m) – lighthouse
pic (m) – mountain peak
pied noir (m) – Algerian-born citizen
place (f) – square
plage (f) – beach
planche à voile (f) – surfboard
plat du jour (m) – dish of the day

plongée (f) – diving
plongée baptême (f) – baptism dive
pont (m) – bridge
pourboire (m) – tip
port de plaisance (m) – marina or harbour for pleasure boats
porte (f) – gate or door, old-town entrance
presqu'île (f) – peninsula
prieuré (m) – priory
producteur (f) – a wine producer or grower, also known as a **vigneron**
produits du terroir (m) – local food products

rade (f) – gulf or harbour
ravin (m) – gully or ravine
refuge (m) – hikers' shelter (mountain hut)
région (m) – administrative region
rive droite (f) – right bank of river
rive gauche (f) – left bank of river
robe (f) – a wine's colour
route forestière – forest road

salin (m) – salt marsh
saut à l'élastique (m) – bungee jump
savonnerie (f) – soap factory
savon (f) – soap
sentier (m) – trail, footpath
sentier sous-marin (m) – underwater trail
site d'escalade (m) – climbing site
son et lumière (m) – sound-and-light show
spectacle (m) – show, performance
sur rendez-vous (SRV) – by appointment only

tabac (m) – tobacconist (also selling newspapers, bus tickets, *télécartes* etc)
table d'orientation (f) – viewpoint sign
télécabine – (m) cable car or gondola
téléférique – (m) cableway
télésiège/téléski – (m) chair lift/drag lift

vendange (f) – grape harvest
vieux port (m) – old port
vieille ville (f) – old town
vin de garde (m) – a wine best drunk after several years in storage
vin de pays (m) – literally 'country wine'
VTT (m) – *vélo tout terrain*; mountain bike

LONELY PLANET

You already know that Lonely Planet produces more than this one guidebook, but you might not be aware of the other products we have on this region. Here is a selection of titles that you may want to check out as well:

Corsica
ISBN 0 86442 792 1
US$15.95 • UK£9.99

Cycling France
ISBN 1 86450 036 0
US$19.99 • UK£12.99

France
ISBN 0 86450 151 0
US$24.99 • UK£14.99

French phrasebook
ISBN 0 86442 450 7
US$5.95 • UK£3.99

The Loire
ISBN 1 86450 358 0
US$17.99 • UK£11.99

Out to Eat Paris
ISBN 1 86450 107 3
US$14.99 • UK£7.99

Paris
ISBN 1 86450 125 1
US$15.99 • UK£9.99

Paris City Map
ISBN 1 86450 011 5
US$5.95 • UK£3.99

Paris condensed
ISBN 1 86450 044 1
US$9.95 • UK£5.99

Southwest France
ISBN 1 86450 382 3
US$17.99 • UK£11.99

Walking in France
ISBN 0 86442 601 1
US$19.99 • UK£12.99

Available wherever books are sold

Lonely Planet Guides by Region

Lonely Planet is known worldwide for publishing practical, reliable and no-nonsense travel information in our guides and on our Web site. The Lonely Planet list covers just about every accessible part of the world. Currently there are 16 series: Travel guides, Shoestring guides, Condensed guides, Phrasebooks, Read This First, Healthy Travel, Walking guides, Cycling guides, Watching Wildlife guides, Pisces Diving & Snorkeling guides, City Maps, Road Atlases, Out to Eat, World Food, Journeys travel literature and Pictorials.

AFRICA Africa on a shoestring • Botswana • Cairo • Cairo City Map • Cape Town • Cape Town City Map • East Africa • Egypt • Egyptian Arabic phrasebook • Ethiopia, Eritrea & Djibouti • Ethiopian Amharic phrasebook • The Gambia & Senegal • Healthy Travel Africa • Kenya • Malawi • Morocco • Moroccan Arabic phrasebook • Mozambique • Namibia • Read This First: Africa • South Africa, Lesotho & Swaziland • Southern Africa • Southern Africa Road Atlas • Swahili phrasebook • Tanzania, Zanzibar & Pemba • Trekking in East Africa • Tunisia • Watching Wildlife East Africa • Watching Wildlife Southern Africa • West Africa • World Food Morocco • Zambia • Zimbabwe, Botswana & Namibia
Travel Literature: Mali Blues: Traveling to an African Beat • The Rainbird: A Central African Journey • Songs to an African Sunset: A Zimbabwean Story

AUSTRALIA & THE PACIFIC Aboriginal Australia & the Torres Strait Islands •Auckland • Australia • Australian phrasebook • Australia Road Atlas • Cycling Australia • Cycling New Zealand • Fiji • Fijian phrasebook • Healthy Travel Australia, NZ & the Pacific • Islands of Australia's Great Barrier Reef • Melbourne • Melbourne City Map • Micronesia • New Caledonia • New South Wales • New Zealand • Northern Territory • Outback Australia • Out to Eat – Melbourne • Out to Eat – Sydney • Papua New Guinea • Pidgin phrasebook • Queensland • Rarotonga & the Cook Islands • Samoa • Solomon Islands • South Australia • South Pacific • South Pacific phrasebook • Sydney • Sydney City Map • Sydney Condensed • Tahiti & French Polynesia • Tasmania • Tonga • Tramping in New Zealand • Vanuatu • Victoria • Walking in Australia • Watching Wildlife Australia • Western Australia
Travel Literature: Islands in the Clouds: Travels in the Highlands of New Guinea • Kiwi Tracks: A New Zealand Journey • Sean & David's Long Drive

CENTRAL AMERICA & THE CARIBBEAN Bahamas, Turks & Caicos • Baja California • Belize, Guatemala & Yucatán • Bermuda • Central America on a shoestring • Costa Rica • Costa Rica Spanish phrasebook • Cuba • Cycling Cuba • Dominican Republic & Haiti • Eastern Caribbean • Guatemala • Havana • Healthy Travel Central & South America • Jamaica • Mexico • Mexico City • Panama • Puerto Rico • Read This First: Central & South America • Virgin Islands • World Food Caribbean • World Food Mexico • Yucatán
Travel Literature: Green Dreams: Travels in Central America

EUROPE Amsterdam • Amsterdam City Map • Amsterdam Condensed • Andalucía • Athens • Austria • Baltic States phrasebook • Barcelona • Barcelona City Map • Belgium & Luxembourg • Berlin • Berlin City Map • Britain • British phrasebook • Brussels, Bruges & Antwerp • Brussels City Map • Budapest • Budapest City Map • Canary Islands • Catalunya & the Costa Brava • Central Europe • Central Europe phrasebook • Copenhagen • Corfu & the Ionians • Corsica • Crete • Crete Condensed • Croatia • Cycling Britain • Cycling France • Cyprus • Czech & Slovak Republics • Czech phrasebook • Denmark • Dublin • Dublin City Map • Dublin Condensed • Eastern Europe • Eastern Europe phrasebook • Edinburgh • Edinburgh City Map • England • Estonia, Latvia & Lithuania • Europe on a shoestring • Europe phrasebook • Finland • Florence • Florence City Map • France • Frankfurt City Map • Frankfurt Condensed • French phrasebook • Georgia, Armenia & Azerbaijan • Germany • German phrasebook • Greece • Greek Islands • Greek phrasebook • Hungary • Iceland, Greenland & the Faroe Islands • Ireland • Italian phrasebook • Italy • Kraków • Lisbon • The Loire • London • London City Map • London Condensed • Madrid • Madrid City Map • Malta • Mediterranean Europe • Milan, Turin & Genoa • Moscow • Munich • Netherlands • Normandy • Norway • Out to Eat – London • Out to Eat – Paris • Paris • Paris City Map • Paris Condensed • Poland • Polish phrasebook • Portugal • Portuguese phrasebook • Prague • Prague City Map • Provence & the Côte d'Azur • Read This First: Europe • Rhodes & the Dodecanese • Romania & Moldova • Rome • Rome City Map • Rome Condensed • Russia, Ukraine & Belarus • Russian phrasebook • Scandinavian & Baltic Europe • Scandinavian phrasebook • Scotland • Sicily • Slovenia • South-West France • Spain • Spanish phrasebook • Stockholm • St Petersburg • St Petersburg City Map • Sweden • Switzerland • Tuscany • Ukrainian phrasebook • Venice • Vienna • Wales • Walking in Britain • Walking in France • Walking in Ireland • Walking in Italy • Walking in Scotland • Walking in Spain • Walking in Switzerland • Western Europe • World Food France • World Food Greece • World Food Ireland • World Food Italy • World Food Spain **Travel Literature:** After Yugoslavia • Love and War in the Apennines • The Olive Grove: Travels in Greece • On the Shores of the Mediterranean • Round Ireland in Low Gear • A Small Place in Italy

Lonely Planet Mail Order

Lonely Planet products are distributed worldwide. They are also available by mail order from Lonely Planet, so if you have difficulty finding a title please write to us. North and South American residents should write to 150 Linden St, Oakland, CA 94607, USA; European and African residents should write to 10a Spring Place, London NW5 3BH, UK; and residents of other countries to Locked Bag 1, Footscray, Victoria 3011, Australia.

INDIAN SUBCONTINENT & THE INDIAN OCEAN Bangladesh • Bengali phrasebook • Bhutan • Delhi • Goa • Healthy Travel Asia & India • Hindi & Urdu phrasebook • India • India & Bangladesh City Map • Indian Himalaya • Karakoram Highway • Kathmandu City Map • Kerala • Madagascar • Maldives • Mauritius, Réunion & Seychelles • Mumbai (Bombay) • Nepal • Nepali phrasebook • North India • Pakistan • Rajasthan • Read This First: Asia & India • South India • Sri Lanka • Sri Lanka phrasebook • Tibet • Tibetan phrasebook • Trekking in the Indian Himalaya • Trekking in the Karakoram & Hindukush • Trekking in the Nepal Himalaya • World Food India **Travel Literature:** The Age of Kali: Indian Travels and Encounters • Hello Goodnight: A Life of Goa • In Rajasthan • Maverick in Madagascar • A Season in Heaven: True Tales from the Road to Kathmandu • Shopping for Buddhas • A Short Walk in the Hindu Kush • Slowly Down the Ganges

MIDDLE EAST & CENTRAL ASIA Bahrain, Kuwait & Qatar • Central Asia • Central Asia phrasebook • Dubai • Farsi (Persian) phrasebook • Hebrew phrasebook • Iran • Israel & the Palestinian Territories • Istanbul • Istanbul City Map • Istanbul to Cairo • Istanbul to Kathmandu • Jerusalem • Jerusalem City Map • Jordan • Lebanon • Middle East • Oman & the United Arab Emirates • Syria • Turkey • Turkish phrasebook • World Food Turkey • Yemen **Travel Literature:** Black on Black: Iran Revisited • Breaking Ranks: Turbulent Travels in the Promised Land • The Gates of Damascus • Kingdom of the Film Stars: Journey into Jordan

NORTH AMERICA Alaska • Boston • Boston City Map • Boston Condensed • British Columbia • California & Nevada • California Condensed • Canada • Chicago • Chicago City Map • Chicago Condensed • Florida • Georgia & the Carolinas • Great Lakes • Hawaii • Hiking in Alaska • Hiking in the USA • Honolulu & Oahu City Map • Las Vegas • Los Angeles • Los Angeles City Map • Louisiana & the Deep South • Miami • Miami City Map • Montreal • New England • New Orleans • New Orleans City Map • New York City • New York City City Map • New York City Condensed • New York, New Jersey & Pennsylvania • Oahu • Out to Eat – San Francisco • Pacific Northwest • Rocky Mountains • San Diego & Tijuana • San Francisco • San Francisco City Map • Seattle • Seattle City Map • Southwest • Texas • Toronto • USA • USA phrasebook • Vancouver • Vancouver City Map • Virginia & the Capital Region • Washington, DC • Washington, DC City Map • World Food New Orleans **Travel Literature**: Caught Inside: A Surfer's Year on the California Coast • Drive Thru America

NORTH-EAST ASIA Beijing • Beijing City Map • Cantonese phrasebook • China • Hiking in Japan • Hong Kong & Macau • Hong Kong City Map • Hong Kong Condensed • Japan • Japanese phrasebook • Korea • Korean phrasebook • Kyoto • Mandarin phrasebook • Mongolia • Mongolian phrasebook • Seoul • Shanghai • South-West China • Taiwan • Tokyo • Tokyo Condensed • World Food Hong Kong • World Food Japan **Travel Literature:** In Xanadu: A Quest • Lost Japan

SOUTH AMERICA Argentina, Uruguay & Paraguay • Bolivia • Brazil • Brazilian phrasebook • Buenos Aires • Buenos Aires City Map • Chile & Easter Island • Colombia • Ecuador & the Galapagos Islands • Healthy Travel Central & South America • Latin American Spanish phrasebook • Peru • Quechua phrasebook • Read This First: Central & South America • Rio de Janeiro • Rio de Janeiro City Map • Santiago de Chile • South America on a shoestring • Trekking in the Patagonian Andes • Venezuela **Travel Literature**: Full Circle: A South American Journey

SOUTH-EAST ASIA Bali & Lombok • Bangkok • Bangkok City Map • Burmese phrasebook • Cambodia • Cycling Vietnam, Laos & Cambodia • East Timor phrasebook • Hanoi • Healthy Travel Asia & India • Hill Tribes phrasebook • Ho Chi Minh City (Saigon) • Indonesia • Indonesian phrasebook • Indonesia's Eastern Islands • Java • Lao phrasebook • Laos • Malay phrasebook • Malaysia, Singapore & Brunei • Myanmar (Burma) • Philippines • Pilipino (Tagalog) phrasebook • Read This First: Asia & India • Singapore • Singapore City Map • South-East Asia on a shoestring • South-East Asia phrasebook • Thailand • Thailand's Islands & Beaches • Thailand, Vietnam, Laos & Cambodia Road Atlas • Thai phrasebook • Vietnam • Vietnamese phrasebook • World Food Indonesia • World Food Thailand • World Food Vietnam

ALSO AVAILABLE: Antarctica • The Arctic • The Blue Man: Tales of Travel, Love and Coffee • Brief Encounters: Stories of Love, Sex & Travel • Buddhist Stupas in Asia: The Shape of Perfection • Chasing Rickshaws • The Last Grain Race • Lonely Planet ... On the Edge: Adventurous Escapades from Around the World • Lonely Planet Unpacked • Lonely Planet Unpacked Again • Not the Only Planet: Science Fiction Travel Stories • Ports of Call: A Journey by Sea • Sacred India • Travel Photography: A Guide to Taking Better Pictures • Travel with Children • Tuvalu: Portrait of an Island Nation

Index

Text

Bold indicates maps.

Bold indicates maps.

Boxed Text

Bold indicates maps.

MAP LEGEND

BOUNDARIES

	International
	Regional
	Suburb

HYDROGRAPHY

	Coastline
	River, Creek
	Lake
	Canal

✿	Park, Gardens
	Urban Area

✿ PARIS	Capital City
● Fréjus	City or Large Town
○ La Napoule	Town
○ Anthéor	Village

●	Point of Interest
▲	Place to Stay
⬛	Camp Site
⬛	Caravan Park
⬛	Chalet or Hut
▼	Place to Eat
⬛	Pub or Bar
⬛	Airport
	Ancient or City Wall

ROUTES & TRANSPORT

	Autoroute
	Primary Road
	Secondary Road
	Tertiary Road
	Unsealed Road
	City Autoroute
	City Primary Road
	City Road
	City Street, Lane

AREA FEATURES

	Building
	Market

MAP SYMBOLS

⊖	Bank
⊼	Beach
⬛ ⬛	Bus Stop, Station
⬛	Castle or Fort
⬛ ⬛	Cathedral or Church
⬛ ⬛	Theatre, Cinema
	Cliff or Escarpment
⬛	Embassy
⬛	Fountain
⬛	Hospital
⬛	Internet Cafe
※ ⬛	Lookout
⬛	Monument
▲ ⌒⌒	Mountain, Range

	Pedestrian Area
⊃⊂	Tunnel
⊢⊢⊙⊢	Train Route & Station
⬛	Metro & Station
⬛	Tramway
⊬⊬⊬⊬	Cable Car or Chairlift
	Walking Track
	Walking Tour
⬛	Ferry Route & Terminal

	Beach
//////////	Key Area Hatch

⬛	Museum
→	One Way Street
⬛	Parking
)(	Pass
⬛	Police Station
⬛	Post Office
⬛	Ruins
⬛	Shopping Centre
⬛	Ski Field
⬛	Stately Home or Palace
⬛	Swimming Pool
⬛	Telephone
⬛	Tourist Information
⬛	Transport
⬛	Vineyard

Note: not all symbols displayed above appear in this book

LONELY PLANET OFFICES

Australia
Locked Bag 1, Footscray, Victoria 3011
☎ 03 9689 4666 fax 03 9689 6833
email: talk2us@lonelyplanet.com.au

USA
150 Linden St, Oakland, CA 94607
☎ 510 893 8555 TOLL FREE: 800 275 8555
fax 510 893 8572
email: info@lonelyplanet.com

UK
10a Spring Place, London NW5 3BH
☎ 020 7428 4800 fax 020 7428 4828
email: go@lonelyplanet.co.uk

France
1 rue du Dahomey, 75011 Paris
☎ 01 55 25 33 00 fax 01 55 25 33 01
email: bip@lonelyplanet.fr
www.lonelyplanet.fr

World Wide Web: www.lonelyplanet.com or **AOL keyword: lp**
Lonely Planet Images: lpi@lonelyplanet.com.au